Praise for *The Resident's Guide to Ambulatory Care*

"I have used the *Resident's Guide* since medical school and still use it daily in my outpatient clinic. The efficient organization makes it ideal for assisting with clinical decisions during a busy clinic day. It is the one resource that will not leave my bookshelf any time soon."

David D. Stone, M.D.
Chief Resident
Fairview Hospital/Cleveland Clin   y Program

"Please count me as an avid fan of the   accustomed of speaking highly."

John M. Stang, M.D.
Powelson Professor of Medicine (Division of Internal Medicine)
Assistant Dean for Student Counseling and Tutoring
The Ohio State University College of Medicine and Public Health

"Concise, easy access to data."
"Easy to read quickly, medications in bold print so easy to find, well organized."

Comments by reviewers for
The Society of Teachers of Family Medicine

"The document is excellent."
Care of Patients with HIV/AIDS Section in prior editions

John Bartlett, M.D.
Chief, Division of Infectious Diseases
The Johns Hopkins University School of Medicine and
The Johns Hopkins Hospital

"As a Certified Physician Assistant who has been practicing for 9 years, I have used multiple resources to keep myself current on patient care. The *Resident's Guide* has been, by far, an outstanding resource. This book provides quick, pertinent information, at your fingertips, in a matter of seconds. I would not hesitate to recommend this book."

S. Lamport PA-C

"Thorough and well organized, this handbook is unsurpassed as a quick and easy reference for family medicine residents."

Ellen Hight, M.D.
Former Chief Resident
Brown University
Family Medicine Program

"The *Resident's Guide* has proven itself to be an extremely useful resource to the resident physicians in our Family Residency Program. The residents have found the *Guide* to be a concise, practical reference that encompasses the broad scope of clinical problems that they frequently encounter in our office practice. The authors have utilized a format that allows for quick, easy reference during a busy office session."

Susan E. Mercer, M.D.
Program Director
Family Practice Residency of Aultman Hospital

THE

RESIDENT'S GUIDE

TO

AMBULATORY CARE

Frequently Encountered and *Commonly Confused* Clinical Conditions

FIFTH EDITION

2004–2005

Michael B. Weinstock, MD
Daniel M. Neides, MD

Anadem
Publishing

 **Anadem**
Publishing
3620 North High Street
Columbus, Ohio 43214
Tel: 1 (800) 633-0055

THE RESIDENT'S GUIDE TO AMBULATORY CARE:
Frequently Encountered and *Commonly Confused* Clinical Conditions: Fifth Edition
Michael B. Weinstock
Daniel M. Neides

Second Printing 2004
Third Printing 2004

PRINTED IN THE UNITED STATES OF AMERICA

ISBN 1-890018-48-1

USING THIS BOOK
Publisher's Notes

The Guide is based upon information from sources believed to be reliable. In developing *The Guide* the publisher, authors, contributors, reviewers, and editors have made substantial efforts to make sure that the regimens, drugs, and treatments are correct and are in accordance with currently accepted standards. Readers are cautioned to use their own judgment in making clinical decisions and, when appropriate, consult and compare information from other resources since ongoing research and clinical experience yield new information and since there is the possibility of human error in developing such a comprehensive resource as this. Attention should be paid to checking the product information supplied by drug manufacturers when prescribing or administering drugs, particularly if the prescriber is not familiar with the drug or does not regularly use it.

Readers should be aware that there are legitimate differences of opinion among physicians on both clinical and ethical/moral issues in treating patients. With this in mind, readers are urged to use individual judgment in making treatment decisions, recognizing the best interests of the patient and his/her own knowledge and understanding of these issues. The publisher, authors, reviewers, contributors, and editors disclaim any liability, loss or damage as a result, directly or indirectly, from using or applying any of the contents of *The Guide*.

FOREWORD TO FIRST EDITION

Each year the scope of clinical problems encountered in Family Practice expands, especially as health care shifts to the ambulatory setting. Recognizing this, the authors have written *The Resident's Guide to Ambulatory Care.* An impressive list of outstanding physicians has also contributed to this book. It is a notable achievement, being written by residents for residents. *The Guide* is a collection of strategies, tips and practical information drawn from the authors' and contributors' observations and experience in the day-to-day management of outpatient problems. The authors are two highly committed, conscientious and hard working residents who have justifiably earned my support in their efforts. They have written this book in an easy to read and quick to reference style.

A manual of this type would be extremely valuable not only for any resident practicing ambulatory medicine, but for medical students and physicians alike. *The Resident's Guide to Ambulatory Care* belongs in the library of every person learning to provide ambulatory care.

Bill G. Gegas, M.D.
Associate Program Director
Family Practice Residency
Riverside Methodist Hospitals

Michael B. Weinstock, MD

Michael Weinstock finished Family Practice residency at Riverside Methodist Hospital in Columbus, Ohio in 1995. He is currently a Clinical Assistant Professor at The Ohio State University in the HIV clinic and an emergency department attending at Mount Carmel St. Ann's Hospital in Columbus. Michael obtained his bachelor's degree with a major in economics from Northwestern University and his medical degree from The Ohio State University College of Medicine. He has practiced medicine on both a local and global scale, including volunteer medical work in Papua New Guinea, Nepal, and the West Indies. In addition to medicine, other passions include skiing, backpacking, traveling and writing. He is a folk and blues acoustic singer-songwriter and recently completed a compact disc. Michael married a family physician, Beth Weinstock, in 1997 and they have a growing family including an energetic, inquisitive 4 year old girl named Olivia, a sweet 2 year old boy named Eli whose favorite word is "why" and a terrier named Daisy.

Daniel M. Neides, MD

Daniel Neides, MD is the Section Head of Family Medicine at The Cleveland Clinic Foundation–Solon Family Health Center in Cleveland, Ohio. He attended The Ohio State University in Columbus, Ohio earning both undergraduate and medical degrees. Dr Neides completed his residency training in Family Medicine at Riverside Methodist Hospitals in Columbus, Ohio. He is the Predoctoral Director of Ambulatory Medicine at The Cleveland Clinic Foundation and on many committees coordinating the curriculum development of the Cleveland Clinic Lerner College of Medicine of Case Western Reserve University. Dr. Neides was awarded the 1999-2000 Distinguished Educator of the Year from The Cleveland Clinic Foundation and The Ohio State University. In 2003, The Ohio State University College of Medicine inducted him into AOA and the Division of Regional Medical Practice at CCF granted him The Outstanding Educator award for his dedication to medical student education. When he is not practicing medicine, Dr. Neides enjoys spending time with his wife Karen, their children Melissa and David, and their dog, Bailey.

PREFACE TO FIFTH EDITION

This update, after exhaustive literature review over a period of almost 1 ½ years, is finally ready for release! The new edition includes comprehensive new charts and tables, algorithms, and current national guidelines for evaluation and management of many ambulatory conditions. We have added 4 new chapters including management of concussions, pediatric asthma, the postpartum visit and UTI's in children. We have eliminated some chapters which were not commonly used (e.g., encopresis) to keep the book a manageable size. The references have been updated and some chapters have web links to "living documents."

As in past editions, each chapter reflects the insight of its resident author and the specific material presented. We have provided a guide to evaluation and management of commonly encountered clinical situations, and left the "zebras" for other sources. We continue to provide "clinical pearls" at the end of each chapter, algorithms in selected chapters, and many charts and tables. Medications listed in the chapters have the doses included, and appear in bold print for rapid reference. Blank pages are provided for important pager and phone numbers.

All of the chapters were physician-reviewed as well as reviewed by a pharmacologist and several editors. In addition to contributions from virtually every subspecialty, contributors also included physician assistants, nurses, medical students and medical educators. Chapters were reviewed for medical accuracy as well as ease of use and the ability to quickly access the information that is being sought.

The first edition was published just as Danny and I were finishing our residency (we thought that residency was not time consuming enough!) Our original mission had been to provide a reference used specifically by residents in the ambulatory care setting; this mission has expanded to include attendings from primary care specialties as well as those that infrequently encounter certain conditions and need further guidance (e.g., the orthopedist treating sinusitis or the OB/GYN answering a question about chest pain).

Each year the number of physicians using The Guide has grown. Our total circulation increased by 13% in 2001, and by 27% in 2002, mostly by word-of-mouth. This is a testament not only to the comprehensive and easy-to-understand nature of the book, but to each of its devoted authors, reviewers and readers. We thank you for your continued support!

Michael B. Weinstock
Daniel M. Neides
August 2003

P R E F A C E   T O   F I R S T   E D I T I O N

Our goal in writing *The Resident's Guide to Ambulatory Care* is to provide a *framework* for the rapid diagnosis and management of ambulatory conditions commonly encountered by residents treating patients in the ambulatory setting. Whereas other ambulatory books attempt to incorporate everything that could possibly be encountered in the ambulatory setting, our goal is to provide more detailed chapters on some of the most *frequently seen* diagnoses. For example, this manual provides well organized, easily accessed, and detailed information on contraception, ambulatory management of HIV/AIDS, and hypertension, and leaves the management of less frequently encountered conditions (Waldenstrom's macroglobulinemia) to other references. It will neither provide a comprehensive didactic summary nor behave as a textbook for in-depth study.

This pocket manual incorporates essential topics covered by handbooks of internal medicine, family practice, pediatrics and obstetrics into one *easy to access* source. It is a "pocket companion / ancillary brain" for the resident who must be familiar with an extraordinary amount of medical knowledge, including:

1) *Office based care* (Diagnosis and management of frequently encountered clinical conditions)
2) *Preventive medicine* (Immunization schedules, cancer screening, cholesterol management)
3) *Surgery* (Pre-op evaluation, pain management, evaluation of abdominal pain, suturing)
4) *Geriatric medicine* (Drug-drug interactions, side effects more prevalent in the elderly, addressing code status, "pronouncing" a patient, incontinence, falls)
5) *Care of the pregnant woman* (Prenatal care, sample admission and delivery notes, answers to questions expecting parents commonly ask)
6) *Ambulatory management of HIV/AIDS* (Schedule of visits, prophylactic medications, algorithms for work-up of cough, diarrhea, headache, FUO, etc.)

The manual emphasizes the diagnostic importance of the history and physical exam, and the importance of preventive medicine in ambulatory care. We feel that these issues are important in an era of health care reform where cost effective ambulatory care is essential.

We have tried to enhance the readability of this reference by including "clinical pearls" at the end of each chapter, including algorithms in selected chapters, and providing charts and tables for quick comparisons. Blank pages are provided for important pager and phone numbers. Most chapters follow a consistent format, but some deviate due to the creative insight of the authors and in the interests of space.

Contributors include a broad spectrum of physicians from the specialties of family medicine, internal medicine, pediatrics, cardiology, dermatology, psychiatry, pulmonology, ophthalmology, urology, neurology, physical medicine and rehabilitation, and obstetrics and gynecology. Other contributors include medical students and medical educators. We hope *The Resident's Guide to Ambulatory Care* will serve as a helpful resource for residents, medical students, and clinicians in practice and that it will serve to improve ambulatory patient care and medical education. We welcome feedback for future editions.

Michael B. Weinstock
Daniel M. Neides
June 1995

CONTRIBUTORS

Michael B. Weinstock, M.D.
Clinical Assistant Professor, HIV Clinic
The Ohio State University College of Medicine
Attending, Emergency Department
Mt. Carmel St. Ann's Hospital
Columbus, Ohio

Daniel M. Neides, M.D.
Section Head, Family Medicine
The Cleveland Clinic Foundation
Solon, Ohio
Assistant Professor
Department of Family Medicine
The Ohio State University College of Medicine
Columbus, Ohio

Rugen Alda, M.D.
Family Practice Resident
Riverside Methodist Hospitals
Columbus, Ohio

Jim Alexander, M.D.
Family Practice Resident
Riverside Methodist Hospitals
Columbus, OH

Thomas Archer, M.D.
Columbus Cardiology
Columbus, Ohio

Ann M. Aring, M.D.
Assistant Director
Family Practice Residency Program
Riverside Methodist Hospitals
Clinical Instructor
The Ohio State University College of Medicine
Columbus, Ohio

Thomas D. Armsey, Jr., M.D.
Assistant Professor
Director of Sports Medicine
Department of Family Practice
University of Kentucky Medical Center
Lexington, Kentucky

Kate Baltrushot, M.D.
Family Practice Resident
Riverside Methodist Hospitals
Columbus, Ohio

John G. Bartlett, M.D.
Chief, Division of Infectious Diseases
The Johns Hopkins University School of
　Medicine & The Johns Hopkins Hospital
Baltimore, Maryland

Eric Bates, P.A.
St. Ann's Emergency Department
Immediate Health Associates
Columbus, Ohio

Julie Beard, M.D.
3rd year Family Practice Resident
Riverside Methodist Hospitals
Columbus, Ohio

Jonathan M. Bertman, M.D.
Family Practice Resident
Brown University Department of Family Medicine
Assistant Clinical Instructor
Brown University Medical School
Memorial Hospital of Rhode Island
Pawtucket, Rhode Island

Tom Boes, M.D.
Attending, Pulmonology
Riverside Pulmonary Associates, Inc.
Riverside Methodist Hospitals
Columbus, Ohio

Edward T. Bope, M.D.
Past President
American Board of Family Practice
Director
Riverside Methodist Hospital Family Practice
Clinical Instructor
The Ohio State University College of Medicine
Columbus, Ohio

Ed Boudreau, D.O.
Attending, St. Ann's Emergency Department
Immediate Health Associates
Columbus, Ohio

Ryan Bowman, P.A.-C.
Immediate Health Associates
Columbus, Ohio

Pamela Jelly Boyers, Ph.D.
Director, Medical Education
Riverside Methodist Hospitals
Columbus, Ohio

Cari Brackett, Pharm. D., B.C.P.S.
Columbus, Ohio

Chad Braun, M.D.
Family Practice Resident
Riverside Methodist Hospitals
Columbus, Ohio

Darrin Bright, M.D.
Family Practice Resident
Riverside Methodist Hospitals
Columbus, Ohio

Steve Brook, M.D.
Chief Resident
Department of Family Practice
University of Kentucky Medical Center
Lexington, Kentucky

David Hugh Brown, M.D.
Columbus Urology, Inc.
Clinical Faculty
The Ohio State University
Columbus, Ohio

David Buck, M.D.
Family Practice Resident
Riverside Methodist Hospitals
Columbus, OH

Brent Cale, M.D.
Family Practice Resident
Riverside Methodist Hospitals
Columbus, Ohio

John Carlin, P.A.-C.
Department of Orthopedics
Southern California Permanente Medical Group
Bellflower, California

James Cassady Jr., M.D.
Assistant Program Director
Riverside Family Practice Residency Program
Riverside Geriatrics Fellowship
Riverside Methodist Hospitals
Columbus, Ohio

Miriam Chan, Pharm. D.
Director Pharmacy Education
Family Practice Residency Program
Riverside Methodist Hospitals
Columbus, OH

Christine Costanzo, M.D.
Attending, Psychiatry
Madison, Wisconsin

Rob Crane, M.D.
Assistant Professor
Family Practice
The Ohio State University
Columbus, Ohio

Kathryn A. Crea, Pharm. D., B.C.P.S.
Westerville, Ohio

Laurie Dangler, M.D.
Family Practice Resident
Riverside Methodist Hospitals
Columbus, Ohio

Joseph DeRosa, M.D.
Family Practice Resident
Riverside Methodist Hospitals
Columbus, Ohio

Jason Diehl, M.D.
Family Practice Resident
Riverside Methodist Hospitals
Columbus, OH

Doug DiOrio, M.D.
Family Practice Resident
Riverside Methodist Hospitals
Columbus, Ohio

Mary DiOrio, M.D.
Family Practice Resident
Riverside Methodist Hospitals
Columbus, Ohio

Marc Duerden, M.D.
Clinical Assistant Professor
Department of Physical Medicine & Rehabilitation
Indiana University College of Medicine
Bloomington, Indiana

Geoffrey Eubank, M.D.
Attending, Neurology
Neurological Associates
Columbus, Ohio

Barry Fagan, M.D.
Attending, Pulmonary Critical Care
Mt. Carmel St. Ann's Hospital
Columbus, Ohio

Philip Favia, M.D.
Family Practice Resident
Riverside Methodist Hospitals
Columbus, OH

Budd Ferrante, Ed.D., A.B.P.P.
Psychologist, Private Practice
Hilliard, Ohio

Deb Frankowski, M.D.
Family Practice Resident
Riverside Methodist Hospitals
Columbus, Ohio

Bill Gegas, M.D.
Associate Director, Riverside Family Practice
Riverside Methodist Hospitals
Clinical Instructor
The Ohio State University College of Medicine
Columbus, Ohio

Curt Gingrich, M.D.
Associate Director, Riverside Family Practice
Riverside Methodist Hospitals
Columbus, OH

Joe Ginty, M.D.
Family Practice, Private Practice
Lancaster, Ohio

Tim Graham, M.D.
Family Practice Resident
Riverside Methodist Hospitals
Columbus, OH

Carol Greco, M.D.
Attending, Obstetrics and Gynecology
Kingsdale Gynecologic Associates
Riverside Methodist Hospitals
Columbus, Ohio

Cathy Greiwe, M.D.
Family Practice Resident
Riverside Methodist Hospitals
Columbus, Ohio

Ken Griffiths, M.D.
Family Practice Resident
Riverside Methodist Hospitals
Columbus, Ohio

Brian Grischow, D.O.
Attending, General Surgery
Columbus, Ohio

Eric Hansen, M.D.
Family Practice Resident
Riverside Methodist Hospitals
Columbus, Ohio

Ryan Hanson, M.D.
Family Practice Resident
Riverside Methodist Hospitals
Columbus, Ohio

Melissa Harris, M.D.
Family Practice Resident
Riverside Methodist Hospitals
Columbus, Ohio

Karen Hazelton, P.A.-C.
Immediate Health Care Associates
Columbus, Ohio

Mike Hemsworth, M.D.
Family Practice Resident
Riverside Methodist Hospitals
Columbus, Ohio

Adam J. Houg, M.D.
Family Practice Resident
Riverside Methodist Hospitals
Columbus, Ohio

Jonathan Jaffrey, M.D.
Internal Medicine Resident
University of Vermont
Burlington, Vermont

Susanne Johnson, M.D.
Family Practice Resident
Riverside Methodist Hospitals
Columbus, Ohio

Wendy Johnson, M.D.
Resident
Albuquerque Health Sciences
Albuquerque, New Mexico

Douglas Knutson, M.D.
Family Practice Resident
Riverside Methodist Hospitals
Clinical Instructor
The Ohio State University College of Medicine
Columbus, Ohio

Mary Kay Kuzma, M.D.
Associate Professor of Pediatrics
Columbus Children's Hospital
The Ohio State University College of Medicine
Columbus, Ohio

T. R. Lange, M.D.
Family Practice Resident
Riverside Methodist Hospitals
Columbus, OH

Loren Leidheiser, D.O.
Attending, St. Ann's Emergency Department
Immediate Health Associates
Columbus, Ohio

Charles E. Levy, M.D.
Clinical Assistant Professor
Department of Physical Medicine & Rehabilitation
The Ohio State University Hospitals
The Ohio State University College of Medicine
Columbus, Ohio

Steve Markovich, M.D.
Assistant Director
Riverside Family Practice Residency Program
Riverside Methodist Hospitals
Columbus, Ohio

Kim Martin, P.A.
St. Ann's Emergency Department
Immediate Health Associates
Columbus, Ohio

Michael Martin, M.D.
Family Practice Resident
Riverside Methodist Hospitals
Columbus, Ohio

Dawn Mattern, M.D.
Attending, Family Practice
Columbus, Ohio

Susan May, M.D.
Attending, Pediatrics
Columbus Children's Hospital
The Ohio State University College of Medicine
Columbus, Ohio

Matt McHugh, M.D.
Preceptor, Riverside Methodist Hospitals
Family Practice Residency Program
Columbus, Ohio

Joyce Miller, P.A.-C.
Immediate Health Associates
Columbus, Ohio

Diane Minasian, M.D.
Assistant Clinical Professor
Department of Family Medicine
Brown University
Pawtucket, Rhode Island

Douglas L. Moore, M.D.
Family Practice Resident
Riverside Methodist Hospitals
Columbus, Ohio

Tina Nelson, M.D.
Family Practice Resident
Riverside Methodist Hospitals
Columbus, Ohio

Dana Nottingham, M.D.
Assistant Director, Riverside Family Practice
Riverside Methodist Hospitals
Columbus, Ohio

William Oley, M.D.
Family Practice Resident
Riverside Methodist Hospitals
Columbus, OH

Michael Para, M.D.
Professor, Infectious Disease
The Ohio State University College of Medicine
Columbus, Ohio

Kathleen Provanzana, M.D.
Family Practice Resident
Riverside Methodist Hospitals
Columbus, Ohio

Mark Reeder, M.D.
Attending, Family Practice
Columbus, Ohio

Shonna Reidlinger, P.A.-C.
Immediate Health Associates
Columbus, Ohio

John Rockwood, P.A.-C.
Immediate Health Associates
Columbus, Ohio

Sarita Salzberg, M.D.
Assistant Medical Director, WorkHealth
Columbus, Ohio

Tim Scanlon, P.A.
St. Ann's Emergency Department
Immediate Health Associates
Columbus, Ohio

Anita Schwandt, M.D.
Family Practice Resident
Riverside Methodist Hospitals
Columbus, Ohio

Mrunal Shah, M.D.
Assistant Director, Riverside Family Practice
Riverside Methodist Hospitals
Columbus, Ohio

David Sharkis, M.D.
Chief Resident
Eastern Virginia School of Medicine
De Paul Hospital
Norfolk, VA

James Simon, M.D.
Attending, Urology
Columbus Urology, Inc.
Riverside Methodist Hospitals
Columbus, Ohio

Michael Stiff, M.D.
Attending, Gastroenterology
Mt. Carmel St. Ann's Hospital
Columbus, Ohio

Linda Stone, M.D.
Attending, Family Practice
U.S. Health Corporation
Riverside Methodist Hospitals
Columbus, Ohio

Lynn Stratton, R.N.C.
Perinatal Nurse
Riverside Methodist Hospitals
Columbus, Ohio

Marti Y. Taba, M.D.
Family Practice Resident
Riverside Methodist Hospitals
Columbus, Ohio

Michael Taxier, M.D.
Attending, Gastroenterology
Mid-Ohio Gastroenterology Associates
Riverside Methodist Hospitals
Columbus, Ohio

Timothy Timko, M.D.
Attending, Cardiology
Clinical Cardiology Specialists, Inc.
Riverside Methodist Hospitals
Columbus, Ohio

John A. Vaughn, M.D.
Family Practice Resident
Riverside Methodist Hospitals
Columbus, Ohio

Elizabeth Walz, M.D.
Clinical Assistant Professor
Department of Neurology
The Ohio State University Hospitals
The Ohio State University College of Medicine
Columbus, Ohio

Beth Weinstock, M.D.
Family Practice Resident
Riverside Methodist Hospitals
Columbus, Ohio
Attending, Family Practice
Private Practice
Columbus, Ohio

Frank J. Weinstock, M.D.
Professor, Department of Ophthalmology
Northeastern Ohio University College
of Medicine
Canton, Ohio

Cindy Williams, M.D.
Attending, Endocrinologist
City of Hope
Los Angeles, California

Ivan Wolfson, M.D.
Director, Traveler's Aid Society of Rhode Island
Pawtucket, Rhode Island

Frank Wright, M.D.
Attending, Obstetrics and Gynecology
Wright, Goff, Krantz, Stockwell, Harmon, &
Jones, M.D.s, Inc.
Riverside Methodist Hospitals
Columbus, Ohio

Steve Yakubov, M.D.
Attending, Cardiology
Mid-Ohio Cardiology Consultants, Inc.
Riverside Methodist Hospitals
Columbus, Ohio

Peter P. Zafrides, M.D.
2nd year Psychiatry Resident
The Ohio State University Hospitals
Clinical Instructor, The Ohio State University
College of Medicine
Columbus, Ohio

Note: Contributors are listed by their academic/professional status at the time of their contribution.

Authors' Note: We would like to thank David C.F. Davisson, Nancy A. Eikenberry, Karla G. Gale, Cynthia McNaughton, and Roman G. Shabashevich of Anadem Publishing, Inc. for all of their hard work and dedication in the preparation of this text. Thanks also to David R. Schumick of Cleveland, Ohio for the front cover art and many of the charts. Thanks to Miriam Chan, Pharm. D. for her support and hard work in reviewing all the medications in the book.

TABLE OF CONTENTS

I. Care of Children

1. The Newborn Exam 3
2. The Developing Child & Normal Pediatric Vital Signs 5
3. Childhood Immunization Schedule & Health Care 6
4. Infant Formula & Breast-feeding 10
5. Neonatal Jaundice 13
6. Fever Without a Source in Infants 0-36 Months of Age:
   Evaluation of the Febrile Infant & Toddler 15
7. Asthma in Children 18
8. Otitis Media 22
9. Pharyngitis 25
10. Croup (Acute Laryngotracheitis) 28
11. Bronchiolitis 29
12. Diarrhea in Children 31
13. Constipation in Children 35
14. Urinary Tract Infections in Children 38
15. Enuresis 40
16. Rashes in Children 42
17. Attention Deficit Hyperactivity Disorder (ADHD) 45

(Ocular Disorders & Screening – See Chapter 66)
(Seizure Disorders – See Chapter 57)

II. Care of the Pregnant Patient & Breast-feeding

18. Prenatal Care 51
19. Medications During Pregnancy & Lactation 55
20. Questions Expecting Parents Commonly Ask/Radiation
    in Pregnancy 61
21. OB Admission Note 64
22. OB Delivery Note 65
23. Postpartum Discharge Instructions 65
24. Postpartum Checkup 66

(Infant Formula & Breast-feeding – See Chapter 4)
(Radiation exposure in pregnancy – See Chapter 20)

III. Women's Health

25. Contraception 69
26. Pap Smears: Indications & Interpretation 75
27. Abnormal Uterine Bleeding 79
28. Amenorrhea 82

29. Menopause & Hormone Replacement Therapy 84
30. The Premenstrual Syndrome & Dysmenorrhea 88
31. Evaluation of Breast Mass, Breast Pain & Nipple Discharge 90
32. Vaginitis & Sexually Transmitted Diseases (STDs) 92
33. Pelvic Inflammatory Disease (PID) 95

IV. Preventive Medicine

34. Cancer Statistics, Screening & Periodic Health Exams 99
35. Smoking Cessation 102
36. Endocarditis Prophylaxis 104
37. Tuberculosis Screening 108

V. Cardiology & Pulmonary Disorders

38. Evaluation of Chest Pain 113
39. ECG Interpretation 117
40. Hyperlipidemia 122
41. Hypertension 128
42. Coronary Artery Disease 136
43. Heart Failure 140
44. Atrial Fibrillation 145
45. Ambulatory Post-MI Management 150
46. Cardiac Stress Testing 152
47. Shortness of Breath 154
48. Community-Acquired Pneumonia (CAP) 158
49. Asthma in Adults 162
50. Chronic Obstructive Pulmonary Disease (COPD) 166
51. Acute Bronchitis 169

VI. Management of Common Ambulatory Conditions

52. Diabetes Mellitus 173
53. Thyroid Disease & Testing 182
54. Headache: Diagnosis & Management 189
55. Evaluation & Management of Dizziness 192
56. Prevention & Management of CVAs 195
57. Seizure Disorders 199
58. Concussion Evaluation 202
59. Liver Function Tests 205
60. Diagnosis & Management of Hepatitis B 208
61. GERD & PUD 211
62. Evaluation of Diarrhea in Adults 216
63. Constipation in Adults 219
64. Hemorrhoids 220
65. Anemia 222
66. Ocular Disorders & Screening 225
67. Allergic Rhinitis/Seasonal Allergies 229
68. Acute Sinusitis 232
69. Differential Diagnosis of Arthritis 235
70. Osteoarthritis 238
71. Rheumatoid Arthritis 239
72. Gouty Arthritis 243
73. Osteoporosis 246

74. Urinary Tract Infections 249
75. Hematuria 252
76. Proteinuria... 255
77. Benign Prostatic Hyperplasia.. 257
78. Calcium Disorders... 260
79. Potassium Metabolism 263
80. Adverse Drug Interactions & Prescribing Errors 266
81. Medication Adherence 270

(Otitis Media – See Chapter 8)
(Pharyngitis – See Chapter 9)

VII. Musculoskeletal/Sports Medicine

82. Common Fractures/Describing Fractures 275
83. Ankle Injuries 277
84. Knee Injuries 281
85. Shoulder Injuries.. 285
86. Elbow Injuries 288
87. Carpal Tunnel Syndrome 291
88. Low Back Pain 292
89. Corticosteroid Injection of Joints 296

VIII. Dermatology

90. Describing Dermatologic Lesions 301
91. Contact Dermatitis 303
92. Acne & Rosacea 305
93. Skin Biopsies 309
94. Topical Steroids 312
95. Warts, Scabies, Lice & Superficial Tinea Infection Management 313
96. Hair Changes & Balding 315

IX. Surgery

97. Evaluation of Abdominal Pain 319
98. Diverticulosis & Diverticulitis 323
99. Management of Wounds 325
100. Pain Management in Adults & Children............................. 329
101. Preoperative Evaluation 332

X. Care of Patients with Psychiatric Disorders

102. Anxiety Disorders... 339
103. Depression & Dysthymia 342
104. Sexual Dysfunction 347
105. Alcohol and Other Drugs of Abuse 352

XI. Care of the Geriatric Patient

106. Periodic Health Screening in the Elderly 357
107. Drugs to be Cautious of in the Elderly 358
108. Falls in the Elderly 362
109. Compression Fractures 364
110. Urinary Incontinence in the Elderly 365

111. Evaluation of Mental Status Changes 368
112. Addressing Code Status 372

XII. HIV & AIDS

113. Ambulatory HIV/AIDS Management 375
114. AIDS-Defining Conditions 383
115. CD4 Cell Counts & Associated Clinical Manifestations 384
116. Work-up in Patients with HIV/AIDS 385
117. Post-exposure Prophylaxis of HIV 390

XIII. Appendix

118. Formulas 395
119. Symptomatic Medications: Colds & Flu, Sinusitis, Bronchitis, Etc. 396
120. Adult Advanced Cardiac Life Support (ACLS) Protocols 398
121. Common Adult Emergency Drug Dosage 407
122. Preparation of Infusion for Adult Emergency Drugs 408

Index 409

I. Care of Children

1. The Newborn Exam 3

2. The Developing Child & Normal Pediatric Vital Signs 5

3. Childhood Immunization Schedule & Health Care 6

4. Infant Formula & Breast-feeding 10

5. Neonatal Jaundice 13

6. Fever Without a Source in Infants 0-36 Months of Age: Evaluation of the Febrile Infant & Toddler 15

7. Asthma in Children 18

8. Otitis Media 22

9. Pharyngitis 25

10. Croup (Acute Laryngotracheitis) 28

11. Bronchiolitis 29

12. Diarrhea in Children 31

13. Constipation in Children 35

14. Urinary Tract Infections in Children 38

15. Enuresis 40

16. Rashes in Children 42

17. Attention Deficit Hyperactivity Disorder (ADHD) 45

Related subjects:

Ocular Disorders & Screening .... *see Chapter 66*

Seizure Disorders .... *see Chapter 57*

Daniel M. Neides, MD
Julie Beard, MD
Beth Weinstock, MD

1. The Newborn Exam

I. HISTORY

Obtain perinatal, pregnancy, and family histories; inquire about feeding, stooling, voiding, and Apgar scores at birth. Inquire about parents/siblings health, smokers in house

II. THE PHYSICAL EXAM

  A. General: Neonate should be completely undressed prior to the exam. Observe for normal muscle tone (flexion of upper and lower extremities), movement of all extremities, and respiratory pattern. Evaluate size for SGA (weight < 10th percentile) or LGA (weight > 90th percentile)

  B. Respiratory

    1. Color: Central and peripheral (Peripheral cyanosis is normal for several hours after birth)

    2. Breathing: Normal respiratory rate is 40–60/minute; grunting and nasal flaring are not normal—if detected, further work-up is necessary. Expiratory grunting and decreased air entry are observed in hyaline membrane disease

    3. Auscultation: Perform prior to any manipulation of the infant (holding the infant or providing a finger to suck on may quiet a crying infant). Listen for equal and bilateral breath sounds

  C. Cardiovascular

    1. Rate is normally between 120–160 BPM

    2. An irregularly irregular heart rate, caused by premature atrial contractions, is common and benign in the first few days of life

    3. Murmurs

      a. Not necessarily an important finding on the newborn exam; infants with major cardiac anomalies may not have a murmur while an infant with a closing ductus arteriosis may; it is important to take into account other factors: *color, perfusion, blood pressure, feeding ability*

      b. If further work-up is warranted, start with a chest x-ray, ECG, and blood pressure in all 4 extremities

    4. Pulses: Palpate femoral pulses (if absent, may indicate coarctation of the aorta)

  D. Gastrointestinal: Because of relatively weak abdominal musculature, palpation of internal organs is possible

    1. The liver should be palpable and often extends below the costal margin

    2. The spleen usually is not palpable

    3. Palpate for renal/abdominal masses (Wilms' tumor, neuroblastoma)

  E. Genitourinary

    1. Males

      a. Palpate testicles (testicles may need to be guided down from above scrotum into scrotum). Hydroceles are common and will usually resolve within the first 6 months. Transilluminate to confirm a hydrocele

      b. Check the penis for hypospadias or epispadias—if present, consult a urologist and do *not* circumcise the infant

    2. Females

      a. The labia majora may appear large because of maternal hormones

      b. Spread the labia, and observe for vaginal wall cysts or imperforate hymen

      c. A white discharge may be seen as well as pseudomenses (due to maternal hormones)

    3. Rectal inspection: Check for position and patency (monitor for bowel movement). A fistula can be mistaken for a normal anus; however, position of a fistula is usually anterior or posterior to the location of a normal anus

  F. Extremities

    1. Hip clicks: 2 maneuvers are performed

a. **Barlow test:** Adduction and posterior pressure may produce a "clunk" of subluxation or dislocation of femur

b. **Ortolani test:** Abduct and lift femur back into place

2. Assess for club feet (plantar flexion of foot, inversion deformity of heel, and forefoot varus), polydactyly or syndactyly, and forefoot adduction
3. Examine for crepitus or discoloration over the clavicles and decreased movement of affected arm (most commonly fractured bones in infants)
4. Examine the back for pilonidal sinus tracts or sacral dimple. If a pilonidal sinus tract is detected and the base cannot be seen, spine films may be indicated (meningocele)

G. Head, eyes, and mouth

1. Head:
   a. Examine the skull for caput succedaneum (tissue swelling that crosses suture lines—no therapy needed), or cephalohematomas (well-demarcated swelling that does not cross suture lines, which may be associated with skull fracture)
   b. Mobility of the suture lines (craniosynostosis)
   c. Fontanelles: If head circumference is normal (32–36cm) and suture lines are mobile, size of fontanelles are not important; anterior fontanelle should be palpated, but the posterior fontanelle may not be palpable
2. Eyes: Examine for bilateral red reflex with ophthalmoscope at a distance of 1–2 feet. If there is difficulty opening neonate's eyes, try sitting infant up or holding upside down and rapidly bringing to an upright position (infant gets disoriented and instinctively opens eyes). Subconjunctival hemorrhages are common after vaginal delivery
3. Mouth: Palpate and visualize for cleft palate. Small white cysts (Epstein's pearls) may be noted on the hard palate and are a normal finding. Natal teeth usually require removal and may be associated with congenital anomalies

H. Neurologic: Most of the neurologic exam is done while performing the rest of the neonatal physical exam. Important aspects of the neurologic exam include watching the baby's movements, evaluating body tone when handled, and observing appropriate crying during the exam. Check for facial nerve paralysis due to trauma during delivery

1. **Moro (startle) reflex:** Grasp the neonate's hands and carefully pull the baby up—as you bring the head back down toward the crib, let go and the Moro reflex should occur. (Abduction of arms and legs, extension of elbow and knees followed by flexion)
2. **Sucking and rooting reflex:**
   a. Rooting occurs when the baby's lips are stroked laterally and the head turns toward the ipsilateral side
   b. Assess the suck reflex by placing a finger in the infant's mouth
3. **Stepping reflex:** Hold the infant upright and lean him/her forward. This should cause the baby to instinctively produce a stepping action (this reflex does not always occur)
4. **Head control:** Assess head lag while holding the infant's hands and pulling him/her upright. Head should lag, come to the midline briefly, then fall forward

I. Skin: Common normal findings include:

1. **Milia:** Small white cysts on the baby's nose, cheeks, or forehead
2. **Nevi or Mongolian spots:** Brown/blue patches on the torso that typically disappear within months
3. **Macular hemangiomas:** "Angel kiss" or "stork bites" on the face or neck
4. **Erythema toxicum neonatorum:** Fleeting erythematous papules and pustules
5. **Sucking blister:** On upper or lower lip
6. **Dry skin:** With cracking and peeling in post-dates infants
7. **Miliaria:** Blocked sweat glands ducts appear as papules and/or pustules

III. FOLLOW-UP INSTRUCTIONS

1. Hepatitis B vaccine: See Chapter 3, Childhood Immunization Schedule
2. If infant is discharged in less than 48hrs, a repeat state screen should be done at the initial exam
3. Follow-up at 2–4 weeks of age for routine exam (1–2 weeks if breast-feeding, see Chapter 4, Infant Formula & Breast-feeding)

4. Discuss with the parents signs/symptoms of neonatal sepsis (*lethargy, poor feeding habits, crying and inconsolable, rectal temperature > 100.4° F*). Instruct parents to contact family physician if these problems arise

References

French LM, Dietz FR. Screening for developmental dysplasia of the hip. Am Fam Phys 1999;60:177–88.

Alexander M, Kuo KN. Musculoskeletal assessment of the newborn. Orthop Nurs (US), Jan–Feb 1997;16:21–31.

Pressler JL, Hepworth JT. Newborn neurologic screening using NBAS reflexes. Neonatal Netw (US), Sep 1997;16(6):33–46.

Daniel M. Neides, MD

2. THE DEVELOPING CHILD & NORMAL PEDIATRIC VITAL SIGNS

I. CHILD DEVELOPMENTAL STAGE

AGE of child	LANGUAGE	GROSS MOTOR	FINE MOTOR	SOCIAL
NEWBORN	crying	lacks control of muscle groups	no skill	fixes on objects; startles easily
1 MONTH	cooing; single vowel sounds	lifts chin briefly	no skill	indefinite stare at surroundings
2 MONTHS	cooing; single vowel sounds	lifts head up 45 degrees	hand to mouth	**social smile**
4 MONTHS	laughs; squeals	**rolls over**; head up 90 degrees (prone)	two hand reach and grasp	follows 180 degrees; recognizes bottle
6 MONTHS	monosyllable babbling	**sits alone without support**	reaches for dropped toy; palmar grasp	talks to mirror image and plays peek-a-boo
9 MONTHS	single syllables; responds to NO	crawls-pulls to stand; "cruises"	**thumb-finger (pincer) grasp**	stranger anxiety; shout for attention
12 MONTHS	**First word**; uses "mama", "dada" correctly	**walks alone**; pivots to pick up objects	fine pincer grasp; learns to use cup	takes toys off table to play on floor
15 MONTHS	4–6 words	stands without support	builds tower of two blocks	points to and vocalizes wants
18 MONTHS	**Two words together**; knows 6–10 words	walks up steps; kicks ball	turns pages two at a time; scribbles	performs simple tasks; hugs doll
2 YEARS	50 words; **2–3 word sentences**	walks down steps; overhand throw	copy vertical line; turns door knob	"MINE"; dry at night
3 YEARS	knows full name; 4 word sentences	jumps from bottom step; rides tricycle	zips and unzips; copy circle	**toilet trained; dresses with help**
4 YEARS	5 word sentences; sings songs	hops on one foot; running jump	laces shoes; buttons clothes	separates from parents; bathes self
5 YEARS	counts to 10; asks "why"	skips; balances on one foot	may tie shoe laces	dresses / undresses without help

The chart items in **bold** are important milestones and easy ones to remember

NORMAL PEDIATRIC VITAL SIGNS

Age	Pulse	Resp	Blood Pressure
NB	120–160	30–60	systolic = 60–70
< 1 yr	120–140	30–50	
1–2 yrs	100–140	30–40	systolic = 70 + (2 × age)
3–5 yrs	100–120	20–30	diastolic = 2/3 systolic
6–10 yrs	80–100	16–20	

CLINICAL PEARLS
- It is reassuring to inform parents what they can expect developmentally before the next well-baby visit
- If a child falls significantly behind developmentally, complete developmental testing (e.g., Denver Development Screening Test) should be performed

Reference
Vaughn VC. Assessment of growth and development during infancy and early childhood. Pediatrics in Rev 1992;13:88–96.

Daniel M. Neides, MD

3. CHILDHOOD IMMUNIZATION SCHEDULE & HEALTH CARE

I. CHILDHOOD IMMUNIZATION SCHEDULE

RECOMMENDED CHILDHOOD AND ADOLESCENT IMMUNIZATION SCHEDULE • UNITED STATES • JANUARY–JUNE 2004

This schedule indicates the recommended ages for routine administration of currently licensed childhood vaccines, as of December 1, 2003, for children through age 18 years. Any dose not given at the recommended age should be given at any subsequent visit when indicated and feasible. ▨ indicates age groups that warrant special effort to administer those vaccines not previously given. Additional vaccines may be licensed and recommended during the year. Licensed combination vaccines may be used whenever any components of the combination are indicated and the vaccine's other components are not contraindicated. Providers should consult the manufacturers' package inserts for detailed recommendations. Clinically significant adverse events that follow immunization should be reported to the Vaccine Adverse Event Reporting System (VAERS). Guidance about how to obtain and complete a VAERS form can be found on the Internet: www.vaers.org or by calling 800-822-7967.

Footnotes—Recommended Childhood and Adolescent Immunization Schedule—United States, January–June 2004

1. **Hepatitis B vaccine (HepB).** All infants should receive the first dose of hepatitis B vaccine soon after birth and before hospital discharge; the first dose may also be given by age 2 months if the infant's mother is HBsAg-negative. Only monovalent HepB can be used for the birth dose. Monovalent or combination vaccine containing HepB may be used to complete the series. Four doses of vaccine may be administered when a birth dose is given. The second dose should be given at least 4 weeks after the first dose, except for combination vaccines which cannot be administered before age 6 weeks. The third dose should be given at least 16 weeks after the first dose and at least 8 weeks after the second dose. The last dose in the vaccination series (third or fourth dose) should not be administered before age 24 weeks.

   <u>Infants born to HBsAg-positive mothers</u> should receive HepB and 0.5 mL Hepatitis B Immune Globulin (HBIG) within 12 hours of birth at separate sites. The second dose is recommended at age 1–2 months. The last dose in the immunization series should not be administered before age 24 weeks. These infants should be tested for HBsAg and anti-HBs at age 9–15 months.

   <u>Infants born to mothers whose HBsAg status is unknown</u> should receive the first dose of the HepB series within 12 hours of birth. Maternal blood should be drawn as soon as possible to determine the mother's HBsAg status; if the HBsAg test is positive, the infant should receive HBIG as soon as possible (no later than age 1 week). The second dose is recommended at age 1–2 months. The last dose in the immunization series should not be administered before age 24 weeks.

2. **Diphtheria and tetanus toxoids and acellular pertussis vaccine (DTaP).** The fourth dose of DTaP may be administered as early as age 12 months, provided 6 months have elapsed since the third dose and the child is unlikely to return at age 15–18 months. The final dose in the series should be given at age ≥ 4 years. **Tetanus and diphtheria toxoids (Td)** is recommended at age 11–12 years if at least 5 years have elapsed since the last dose of tetanus and diphtheria toxoid-containing vaccine. Subsequent routine Td boosters are recommended every 10 years.

3. *Haemophilus influenzae* **type b (Hib) conjugate vaccine.** Three Hib conjugate vaccines are licensed for infant use. If PRP-OMP (PedvaxHIB or ComVax [Merck]) is administered at ages 2 and 4 months, a dose at age 6 months is not required. DTaP/Hib combination products should not be used for primary immunization in infants at ages 2, 4 or 6 months, but can be used as boosters following any Hib vaccine. The final dose in the series should be given at age ≥ 12 months.

4. **Measles, mumps, and rubella vaccine (MMR).** The second dose of MMR is recommended routinely at age 4–6 years but may be administered during any visit, provided at least 4 weeks have elapsed since the first dose and that both doses are administered beginning at or after age 12 months. Those who have not previously received the second dose should complete the schedule by the 11–12 year old visit.

5. **Varicella vaccine.** Varicella vaccine is recommended at any visit at or after age 12 months for susceptible children (i.e., those who lack a reliable history of chickenpox). Susceptible persons aged ≥ 13 years should receive 2 doses, given at least 4 weeks apart.

6. **Pneumococcal vaccine.** The heptavalent **pneumococcal conjugate vaccine (PCV)** is recommended for all children age 2–23 months. It is also recommended for certain children age 24–59 months. The final dose in the series should be given at age ≥ 12 months. **Pneumococcal polysaccharide vaccine (PPV)** is recommended in addition to PCV for certain high-risk groups. See *MMWR* 2000;49(RR-9):1-38.

7. **Hepatitis A vaccine.** Hepatitis A vaccine is recommended for children and adolescents in selected states and regions, and for certain high-risk groups; consult your local public health authority. Children and adolescents in these states, regions, and high risk groups who have not been immunized against hepatitis A can begin the hepatitis A immunization series during any visit. The 2 doses in the series should be administered at least 6 months apart. See *MMWR* 1999;48(RR-12):1-37.

8. **Influenza vaccine.** Influenza vaccine is recommended annually for children age ≥ 6 months with certain risk factors (including but not limited to asthma, cardiac disease, sickle cell disease, HIV, and diabetes; and household members of persons in high-risk groups; see *MMWR* 2003;52(RR-8):1-36) and can be administered to all others wishing to obtain immunity. In addition, healthy children age 6–23 months are encouraged to receive influenza vaccine if feasible, because children in this age group are at substantially increased risk for influenza-related hospitalizations. For healthy persons age 5–49 years, the intranasally administered live-attenuated inluenza vaccine (LAIV) is an acceptable alternative to the intramuscular trivalent inactivated influenza vaccine (TIV). See *MMWR* 2003;52(RR-13):1-8.

Children receiving TIV should be administered a dosage appropriate for their age (0.25 mL if age 6–35 months or 0.5 mL if age ≥ 3 years). Children age ≤ 8 years who are receiving influenza vaccine for the first time should receive 2 doses (separated by at least 4 weeks for TIV and at least 6 weeks for LAIV).

For additional information about vaccines, including precautions and contraindications for immunization and vaccine shortages, please visit the National Immunization Program Website: www.cdc.gov/nip or call the National Immunization Information Hotline: 800-232-2522 (English) or 800-232-0233 (Spanish).

Approved by the Centers for Disease Control and Prevention (www.cdc.gov/nip, the American Academy of Pediatrics (www.aap.org), and the American Academy of Family Physicians (www.aafp.org)

Source: Centers for Disease Control and Prevention. www.cdc.gov/nip/recs/child-schedule.htm#Printable (Catch-up Schedule also available at same website)

II. PREVENTIVE PEDIATRIC HEALTH CARE RECOMMENDATION

Recommendations for Preventive Pediatric Health Care (A)

AGE	NB	2-4d.	1mo	2mo	4mo	6mo	9mo	12mo	15mo	18mo	24mo
History		*	*	*	*	*	*	*	*	*	*
Measurements											
Height and Weight	*	*	*	*	*	*	*	*	*	*	*
Head Circumference	*	*	*	*	*	*	*	*	*	*	*
Sensory Screening											
Vision	*	*	*	*	*	*	*	*	*	*	*
Hearing	OBJ[1]	*	*	*	*	*	*	*	*	*	*
Developmental/ Behavioral	*	*	*	*	*	*	*	*	*	*	*
Procedures–General											
Metabolic Screening	*	*									
Immunization	*		*	*	*	*	*	*	*	*	*
Hematocrit							*———▶	*	HR[2]	HR	HR
Procedures–High Risk											
Lead Screening							HR				HR
Tuberculin Test								HR	HR	HR	HR
Cholesterol Screening											HR
Anticipatory Guidance											
Injury Prevention	*	*	*	*	*	*	*	*	*	*	*
Violence Prevention	*	*	*	*	*	*	*				
Sleep Positioning	*	*	*	*	*	*					
Nutrition Counseling	*	*	*	*	*	*	*	*	*	*	*
Dental Referral											

KEY: * indicates the exam/test should be done at time of visit.
  1. OBJ – Objective test should be performed at this time. All other visits a subjective assessment of hearing and vision should be done during the exam.
  2. HR – High risk

Recommendations for Preventive Pediatric Health Care (B)

AGE	3y	4y	5y	6y	8y	10y	11y	12y	13y	14y
History	*	*	*	*	*	*	*	*	*	*
Measurements										
Height and Weight	*	*	*	*	*	*	*	*	*	*
Blood Pressure	*	*	*	*	*	*	*	*	*	*
Sensory Screening										
Vision	OBJ	OBJ	OBJ	OBJ	OBJ	OBJ	*	OBJ	*	*
Hearing	*	OBJ	OBJ	OBJ	OBJ	OBJ	*	OBJ	*	*
Developmental/ Behavioral	*	*	*	*	*	*	*	*	*	*
Procedures–General										
Immunization	*	*	*	*	*	*	*	*	*	
Hematocrit	HR	HR	HR					◀———		F[3]
Urinalysis			*							
Procedures–High Risk										
Lead Screening										
Tuberculin Test	HR	HR	HR	HR	HR	HR	HR	HR	HR	HR
Cholesterol Screening	HR	HR	HR	HR	HR	HR	HR	HR	HR	HR
STD Screening								HR	HR	HR
Pelvic Exam								HR	HR	HR
Anticipatory Guidance										
Injury Prevention	*	*	*	*	*	*	*	*	*	*
Violence Prevention	*	*	*	*	*	*	*	*	*	*
Nutrition Counseling	*	*	*	*	*	*	*	*	*	*
Dental Referral	*									

KEY: * indicates the exam/test should be done at time of visit.
  3. F – all menstruating adolescents should be screened annually for iron-deficiency anemia.

Adapted from: American Academy of Pediatrics Committee on Practice and Ambulatory Medicine. Recommendations for preventive pediatric health care (RE 9939). © 2000 by the American Academy of Pediatrics. Used with permission. Pediatrics 2000;105(3):645. www.aap.org/policy/re9939.html

III. FLUORIDE RECOMMENDATIONS

A. Currently about 100 million Americans do not benefit from fluoridated drinking water. These populations are at risk for greater incidences of tooth decay

B. Monitor intake of fluoride in children younger than 6 years of age because overuse can result in enamel fluorosis. Use pea-size amount of fluoride toothpaste in children < 6 years. Brushing with fluoride toothpaste should be limited to twice a day, and should be supervised to limit swallowing. Supplements are appropriate for children at high-risk for tooth decay (limited parental education, abuse or neglect victims, those not receiving regular dental care, consumption of high quantities of sugars, use of orthodontic appliances)

IV. LEAD-SCREENING RECOMMENDATIONS

A. Strong association exists between blood lead levels and intellectual function in children

B. Primary prevention: Anticipatory guidance for parents regarding minimizing exposure to lead-based paint chips, dust, soil. Discuss importance of dietary iron to prevent absorption of environmental lead

C. Secondary prevention: Begin at 9–12 months, consider again at 24 months

1. Targeted screening for at-risk communities and through risk-assessment questionnaires:
   - Does your child live in or regularly visit a house or child-care facility built before 1950?
   - Does your child live in or visit a house or child-care facility built before 1978 that is being or has recently been renovated or remodeled?
   - Does your child have a sibling or playmate who has or did have lead poisoning?

2. Other populations in which to consider screening: Immigrants from countries with high levels of lead poisoning, iron-deficiency anemia, developmental delay +/- pica, abuse or neglect victims, parental exposure to lead at work, low-income families receiving government assistance

3. Screening: Venous samples preferable, but finger stick okay if collected correctly

4. Elevated Blood Lead Levels (BLL): Always obtain confirmatory sample!
   a. BLL 10–14 mcg/dL: General education on reducing environmental lead exposure, repeat BLL in 3 months
   b. BLL 15–19 mcg/dL: Careful environmental history, optimal nutrition including iron and calcium supplementation, frequent small meals to decrease absorption of lead, repeat BLL within 2 months
   c. BLL > 20 mcg/dL: Obtain confirmatory test within 1 week, thorough environmental/nutritional assessment, probable referral to local health department, referral to specialist in lead toxicity therapy/chelation therapy
   d. BLL > 70 mcg/dL: Hospitalize patient, chelation therapy

CLINICAL PEARLS

- Recommendation for Pneumococcal Conjugated Vaccine from ACIP and AAFP (released 2/00):

1. Heptavalent pneumococcal conjugate vaccine (**Prevnar**) should be given to all infants less than 2 years old and high risk children between 2–5 years of age (e.g., sickle cell, HIV, asplenia, chronic illness, immunocompromising conditions, Alaskan-Native, and American Indians)

2. The dosing schedule of **Prevnar**
   a. For children < 6 months of age, 0.5mL given inter muscular at 2 months, 4 months, 6 months, and 12–15 months
   b. For children > 7 months

Age of first dose	Total no. of doses	Dosing
7–11 months	3	2 doses at least 4 weeks apart 3rd dose after 12 months of age and at least 2 months after the 2nd dose
12–23 months	2	At least 4 weeks apart
>24 months–9 yr	1	

- A child with a minor illness (e.g., URI) but afebrile (<101°F) may still receive scheduled immunizations
- Children with chronic diseases who are susceptible to pneumococcus (sickle cell, asplenia, renal disease, HIV and other immunodeficiency states) should receive the **Pneumovax** (given once) after age 2 years
- Children susceptible to influenza (severe asthma, cystic fibrosis (CF), bronchopulmonary dysplasia (BPD), cardiac disease, HIV and other immunodeficiency states) should receive the influenza vaccine yearly after age 6 months

References

Recommendations for using fluoride to prevent and control dental caries in the United States. MMWR Aug 17, 2001;50:No. RR-14.

American Academy of Pediatrics Policy Statement. Screening for elevated blood lead levels. June 1998;101(6):1072–8.

Daniel M. Neides, MD
Mary DiOrio, MD
T. R. Lange, MD

4. Infant Formula & Breast-Feeding

I. BREAST MILK: Gold standard of infant nutrition; can nurse up to 4–6 months without supplementing solids

   A. Goals: Healthy People 2010 has a goal of having 75% of all mothers initiate breast-feeding and 50% continue breast-feeding at 6 months and 25% breast-feeding at 1 year

   B. Benefits of breast-feeding

     1. There is no better nutrition for the baby than breast milk. The caloric and nutritional content of the breast milk naturally changes as the baby ages, providing the optimal nutrition for the infant at any age. The nutrients in breast milk are easier to assimilate than those in formula because breast milk is easier to digest

     2. Mothers who breast-feed reduce their risks of getting ovarian and breast cancer

     3. Breast-feeding utilizes calories (~200 kcal/day) and may help the mother regain her pre-pregnancy weight. A higher caloric intake is required for lactation

     4. Breast-feeding is convenient and saves money

     5. Enhanced maternal-infant bonding

     6. The early breast milk, colostrum, provides antibodies to the infant, decreasing the infant's incidence of upper respiratory infections, diarrheal illnesses, otitis media (etc.) in the first year of the child's life

     7. Exclusively breast-feeding the infant for at least 3 months reduces the chance that the child will develop Type 1 Diabetes Mellitus

     8. Breast-fed infants are less likely to develop food allergies, because the breast-milk antibodies prevent the absorption of allergy-provoking proteins

     9. Colostrum has a laxative effect assisting with the early evacuation of meconium

     10. Exclusive breast-feeding may be an effective birth control method for several months after delivery, although this should not be relied upon

     11. The breast-fed baby's stools are relatively odor-free

   C. Common breast-feeding problems

     1. Breast engorgement

       a. Often occurs for the first time when the milk comes in, usually the second or third postpartum day. Can occur at any time when the mother has not breast-fed or pumped her breasts

       b. To decrease engorgement, the mother should pump or express her breasts to release some of the excess milk build-up. Warm compresses or a hot shower can help the milk let-down. Frequent nursing during this stage is important

     2. Mastitis

       a. Initially women *may* experience flu-like symptoms with myalgias, fevers, and chills. One of the breasts then becomes erythematous, tender, and edematous in

a particular area
  b. Management
    i. Frequent breast-feedings (with both breasts being utilized), rest, plenty of fluids, acetaminophen
    ii. Warm compresses to the affected breast for pain relief
    iii. ATBs: For the most common mastitis-causing organisms, staphylococcus and streptococcus, use **Cephalexin (Keflex)** 500mg PO QD. **Erythromycin** or **Clindamycin** can be used for penicillin-allergic patients. Duration of treatment is 10–14 days
  c. Bilateral mastitis: Rare and may be a sign of a Group B Streptococcal infection which has been transmitted to the mother from the infant. (This is a serious infection and would require immediate treatment of the infant and the mother)
3. Yeast infections: If the infant develops thrush, it may transmit the infection to the mother and she may develop "thrush nipples"
  a. The symptoms of "thrush nipples" are erythematous, edematous, cracked, painful nipples. Both the infant and the mother need to be treated
  b. The infant is given **Nystatin Oral Suspension** (100,000 u/mL) 1mL PO QID for 2 weeks given after nursing
  c. The mother should apply an anti-fungal ointment after nursing (see Chapter 95, Warts, Scabies, Lice & Superficial Tinea Infection Management)
4. Breast abscess
  a. Rare complication of mastitis
  b. Treatment: Surgical drainage
5. Cracked or bleeding nipples
  a. Can occur at any time during the nursing process. Prevention is important
  b. Infant needs to be properly positioned on the breast
  c. Daily shower or bath with warm water is sufficient to keep the breasts clean. Soaps and detergents should not be used on the breasts since they are drying to the skin. Breast creams are unnecessary and may actually cause sore nipples
  d. Breast milk that is left on the breast after nursing may be gently rubbed on the nipples
  e. Plastic-lined breast pads and wet breast shields should be avoided
  f. The mother should invest in several good cotton nursing bras that provide support but are not constricting. Bras that are too tight may lead to blocked ducts
6. Galactocele: Blocked lactiferous duct
  a. Round, well circumscribed, easily mobile cystic mass
  b. Treatment: Initially warm compresses and frequent feedings or pumping to open and drain blocked duct. Often needs needle aspiration. Thick milky secretion confirms diagnosis

D. Nursing frequency
1. Initially the infant should breast-feed frequently, usually 8–15 feedings in a 24hr period
2. The infant can be kept on the first breast until interest lost in feeding (usually 10–20 minutes). Then remove from that breast, burp, and place on the second breast. May not feed as long on the second breast. Because of this, should start at this breast at the next breast-feeding session.
3. Breast-feeding works on a supply-and-demand basis. The more an infant feeds, the more milk the breasts will produce. It is important the infant nurse frequently and for as long as desired so that an adequate milk supply will be produced
4. Supplementation is not necessary and may hinder the establishment of a good breast-feeding relationship

E. Vitamin supplementation
1. Vitamin D: If still exclusively breast fed, then consider supplementing with 400 IU of Vitamin D per day starting at 6 months of age, especially for those infants with darkly pigmented skin or those infants that do not receive enough sunlight exposure (i.e., those born in late fall or winter)
2. Iron
  a. There is debate about when iron supplementation should be done
  b. The term newborn has about a 4 month store of iron accumulated during gestation. At 4

months of age the physician needs to decide if the infant needs iron supplementation or if the infant is eating enough iron-fortified cereal to meet iron needs

  c. The preterm infant should receive supplementation starting at birth

3. Fluoride: If still exclusively breast fed, then consider supplementation with 0.25mg per day starting at 6 months

F. **Medications and lactation:** See Chapter 19, Medications During Pregnancy & Lactation

II. STANDARD MILK-BASED FORMULA: *First line formula*

Nutrient profile resembles human milk, heat-treated for easier digesting and to lower allergic potential. Begin with formula containing iron

A. **Carbohydrate:** Lactose

B. **Protein:** Whey, casein

C. **Fat:** Soy, corn, coconut, safflower, or palm olein oils

Formula Available: Advance, Carnation, Gerber, Good Start, Enfamil, Similac, SMA

III. SOY FORMULAS: *Second line formula*

For infants with cow milk protein allergies or lactose intolerant. Begin with formula containing iron

A. **Carbohydrate:** Sucrose or corn syrup

B. **Protein:** Soy, L-methionine, L-carnitine, taurine

C. **Fat:** Soy, corn, coconut, oleo, or safflower oils

Formula available: Isomil, Isomil SF (sucrose-free), Nursoy, ProSobee (sucrose-free)

IV. SPECIAL NUTRITIONAL NEEDS

A. **Alimentum:** For infants with problems with digestion or absorption; hypoallergenic

B. **Nutramigen:** Lactose and sucrose free; hypoallergenic

C. **Portagen:** For infants who have difficulty digesting fats

D. **Pregestimil:** For infants with malabsorption problems, allergies, intractable diarrhea, short-gut syndrome, or cystic fibrosis

V. FEEDING SCHEDULES

Formula-fed infants should eat 5–6 ounces of formula/kg/day (*see chart*). Solid foods (cereals) can safely be started at 4–6 months

Recommended Bottle Feedings for a Normal Infant by Age

AGE	Number	Volume per feeding
Birth – 1 week	6 – 10	1 – 3 oz
1 week – 1 month	7 – 8	2 – 4 oz
1 month – 3 months	5 – 7	4 – 6 oz
3 months – 6 months	4 – 5	6 – 7 oz
6 months – 9 months	3 – 4	7 – 8 oz
10 months – 12 months	3	7 – 8 oz

CLINICAL PEARLS

- Infants should not receive cow's milk prior to 1 year of age secondary to increase risk of occult GI bleeding and subsequent anemia
- Roughly 50% of all mothers initiate breast-feeding. 25% quit within first month and only 25% continue until 5 months or more

References

Mortensen EL, et al. The association between duration of breastfeeding and adult intelligence. JAMA 2002;287:2365–71.

American Academy of Pediatrics. Breast-feeding and the use of human milk (RE9729). Pediatrics 1997;100:1035–9. Available online at: http://www.aap.org/policy/re9729.html

Wright KcS, et al. Infant acceptance of breast milk after maternal exercise. Pediatrics 2002;109:585–9.

Brent N, et al. Sore nipples in breast-feeding women. A clinical trial of wound dressings vs conventional care. Arch Pediatr Adolesc Med Nov 1998;152:1077–82.

Sheard NF. Breast-feeding protects against otitis media. Nutrition Reviews 1993;51(9):275–7.

Daniel M. Neides, MD
Michael B. Weinstock, MD

5. NEONATAL JAUNDICE

DEFINITION: An abnormality of bilirubin production, metabolism, or excretion which results in bilirubin levels high enough to discolor sclera or skin

I. HISTORY

Distinguish between physiologic and non-physiologic jaundice. The following cause/increase the risk of non-physiologic jaundice:

A. Family history of jaundice or anemia: Hereditary hemolytic anemia (spherocytosis), ABO incompatibility, breast milk jaundice, G6PD deficiency

B. Maternal illness during pregnancy: Congenital infections (toxoplasmosis, rubella, cytomegalovirus, herpes simplex virus)

C. Maternal drugs: Sulfonamides, Nitrofurantoin, or antimalarial drugs (in a G6PD deficient infant)

D. Labor and delivery history: Trauma, asphyxia, delayed cord clamping or prematurity

II. CLINICAL SIGNS AND SYMPTOMS

Jaundice (apparent with bilirubin levels > 5mg/dL), lethargy, poor feeding, vomiting, poor Moro reflex, high-pitched cry, and constipation

III. PHYSIOLOGIC JAUNDICE

A transient increase of *unconjugated bilirubin* in the full-term infant apparent on the 3rd day of life that resolves by the 10th day of life

A. Laboratory: Total bilirubin < 12mg/dL and direct bilirubin < 1.5mg/dL

B. Etiology

1. Increased bilirubin load secondary to polycythemia, birth trauma, decreased survival of fetal RBCs, increased enterohepatic circulation
2. Decreased hepatic uptake of bilirubin
3. Poor conjugation secondary to decreased glucuronyl transferase activity and decreased hepatic blood flow
4. Decreased excretion of bilirubin

IV. NON-PHYSIOLOGIC JAUNDICE

A. Laboratory: "The Rule of Toos"

1. Bilirubin rises *too early*: Jaundice apparent in the first 24hrs of life
2. Bilirubin rises *too fast*: Bilirubin increases more than 5mg/dL/day
3. Bilirubin rises *too long*: Jaundice apparent > 10 days in a full-term infant—*or*— > 2 weeks in a pre-term infant
4. Bilirubin rises *too high*: Total bilirubin > 12mg/dL in full-term infant—*or*— > 15mg/dL in a pre-term infant
5. Bilirubin is *too direct*: Direct bilirubin > 1.5mg/dL

B. Etiology

1. Abnormal (excess) bilirubin production: ABO incompatibility, red cell membrane defects (spherocytosis), infection, drugs, hemoglobinopathies, disseminated intravascular coagulation (DIC), pyloric stenosis (increased enterohepatic circulation of bilirubin), dehydration, and polycythemia
2. Abnormal bilirubin metabolism: Crigler-Najjar syndrome, Gilbert's disease, Dubin-Johnson syndrome, Rotor syndrome, galactosemia, hypothyroidism, and infants of diabetic mothers

V. BREAST MILK JAUNDICE

A. Etiology: Inhibitor of conjugation present in breast milk and decreased excretion of bilirubin in stool

B. Late-onset jaundice occurs in 1% of breast-fed infants

C. Bilirubin increases after the 3rd day of life, can reach 30mg/dL by age 2 weeks, and normalizes by 4–12 weeks

D. Cessation of breast-feeding is only recommended for diagnostic purposes, but is not necessary. Once stopped, bilirubin should decrease in 48hrs and rise only 2–4mg/dL when breast-feeding is restarted

E. 70% recurrence rate in subsequent pregnancies

VI. ALGORITHM APPROACH TO "CLINICALLY SIGNIFICANT" JAUNDICE

(Term newborns > 24hrs and < 2 weeks of age without signs of serious underlying illness—lethargy, apnea, tachypnea, temperature instability, behavior changes, HSM, persistent vomiting or feeding problems)

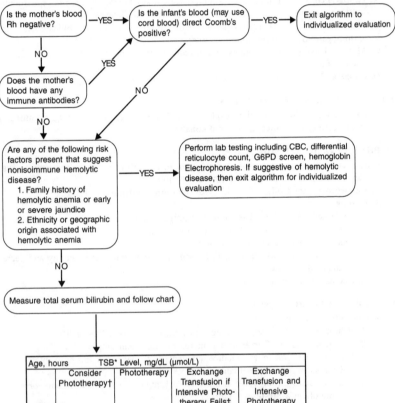

Age, hours	TSB* Level, mg/dL (µmol/L)			
	Consider Phototherapy†	Phototherapy	Exchange Transfusion if Intensive Phototherapy Fails‡	Exchange Transfusion and Intensive Phototherapy
≤24§	...	...	...	...
25-48	> 12 (210)	≥ 15 (260)	≥ 20 (340)	≥ 25 (430)
49-72	≥ 15 (260)	≥ 18 (310)	≥ 25 (430)	≥ 30 (510)
>72	≥ 17 (290)	≥ 20 (340)	≥ 25 (430)	≥ 30 (510)

*TSB medicates total serum bilirubin.
†Phototherapy at these TSB levels is a clinical option, meaning that the intervention is available and may be used on the basis of individual clinical judgment.
‡Intensive phototherapy should produce a decline of TSB of 1 to 2 mg/dL within 4 to 6 hours and the TSB levels should continue to fall and remain below the threshold level of exchange transfusion. If this does not occur, it is considered a failure of phototherapy.
§Term infants who are clinically jaundiced at ≤24 hours old are not considered healthy and require further evaluation.

Adapted from Practice Parameter: The management of hyperbilirubinemia in the healthy term newborn. Pediatrics 1994;94:560. © 1994 by the American Academy of Pediatrics. Table used with permission. www.aap.org/policy/hyperb.htm

VII. TREATMENT

A. Goal is to prevent kernicterus which occurs when free, unconjugated bilirubin accumulates in the central nervous system (see following chart)

B. In otherwise healthy, full-term infants, kernicterus is unlikely with bilirubin < 20–25mg/dL if the bilirubin is increasing slowly and the jaundice was not apparent before 24hrs of age

C. Infants who are preterm (< 37 weeks gestation), ill, or who have hemolytic disease have a higher risk of kernicterus with lower bilirubin levels

D. In all infants with hyperbilirubinemia:

1. Ensure adequate hydration with early Q2hrs feedings to help decrease enterohepatic circulation of bilirubin

   a. Monitor feeding behavior, stool output, and urine output

   b. Breast fed infants may need temporary supplements with formula—do not supplement with bottled water as it decreases hepatic function and stooling

2. Correct factors that decrease albumin's ability to bind bilirubin: hypoalbuminemia, sepsis, acidosis, hypoglycemia, increased free fatty acids, or sulfonamides

3. Correct factors that can disrupt the blood-brain barrier: Anoxia, ischemia, prematurity, hypothermia, and hypotension

CLINICAL PEARLS

- Jaundice occurs in all infants as they transition from intra- to extra-uterine life
- Jaundice is usually a benign, self-limited condition that can be managed with close observation and reassurance
- Levels of bilirubin considered safe in healthy full-term infants may be pathologic in the sick or premature infant
- It is not necessary to stop breast-feeding in physiologic or breast milk jaundice
- Use the "Rule of Toos" to guide your investigation and treatment of the jaundiced infant

References

Practice Parameter: the management of hyperbilirubinemia in the healthy term newborn. Pediatrics 1994;94:560.

Gourley GR, et al. Neonatal jaundice and diet. Arch Pediatr Adolesc Med 1999;153:184–8.

Gartner LM. Neonatal jaundice. Pediatrics in Review 1994; 15:422–32.

Daniel M. Neides, MD
Beth Weinstock, MD
Julie Beard, MD

6. FEVER WITHOUT A SOURCE IN INFANTS 0–36 MONTHS OF AGE (Febrile Infant & Toddler)

DEFINITION: An acute febrile illness in which the etiology of the fever is not apparent after a careful history and physical exam

- Fever is defined as rectal temperature ≥ 100.4° F (38.0° C)—axillary, oral, and tympanic temperature not as reliable
- Concern for the possibility of occult bacteremia or underlying sepsis occurs in infants 0–90 days old with temperature > 100.4° F and in infants 3–36 months old with a temperature > 102.2° F (39.0° C)
- See Chapter 2, The Developing Child for a table of normal values for pulse, respiratory rate and blood pressure
- A finding of otitis media on exam should not be considered a cause of fever in this age group; the incidence of bacteremia does not differ significantly in febrile infants and young children with or without otitis media

I. IDENTIFICATION OF HIGH-RISK PATIENTS

A. Degree of fever: A temperature greater than 39.0° C is a predictor for occult bacteremia. (In infants 0–90 days old, using a cut-point of T > 38.0° C is standard-of-care)

    B. Level of irritability (Yale Observation Scale)—quality of cry, reaction to parents, color, hydration, response to social overtures

    C. Peripheral WBC > 15,000/mm³ increases risk for occult bacteremia

    D. Known chronic illness (leukemia, sickle cell, HIV, congenital heart anomalies) place the infant in high-risk category and require more aggressive therapy—see III. B.)

    E. Recent ATB therapy may alter manifestation of serious bacterial infection, e.g., meningitis

    F. Day-care attendance may place infant at increased risk for invasive pneumococcal infection—always inquire if infant has received the pneumococcal vaccine

II. FEVER WITHOUT A SOURCE < 28 DAYS OLD

Temperature > 100.4° F (Approximately 10% will harbor a serious bacterial infection)

    A. Risk factors: Prematurity, premature rupture of membranes (>18hrs), chorioamnionitis, maternal fever, maternal UTI, twin pregnancy, meconium aspiration

    B. Signs and symptoms of bacteremia or focal serious infection: Temperature instability, respiratory distress, lethargy, feeding intolerance, jaundice, diarrhea, tachycardia, seizures, skin rash

    C. Diagnosis
        1. CBC with differential, electrolytes, serum glucose, CSF Gram stain and cell count
        2. Cultures from blood, CSF, and urine (catheter specimen)
        3. Group B strep antigen from urine and CSF
        4. Chest x-ray

    D. Management: Requires hospital admission and empiric parenteral ATBs

III. FEVER WITHOUT A SOURCE 28–90 DAYS OLD

Temperature > 100.4° F: Obtain CBC with differential, urinalysis (send for culture)

    A. Low risk infants (No past medical history, level of irritability low)
        1. If WBC > 15,000/mm³:
            a. Obtain blood cultures and consider cerebrospinal fluid (CSF) for Gram stain and culture, cell count, glucose, and protein
            b. If abnormal CSF analysis, admit patient and begin parenteral ATBs
            c. If negative CSF analysis and negative urine culture:
                i. **Ceftriaxone** 50mg/kg IM (maximum dose is 1g)
                ii. Patient should return for re-evaluation within 24hrs
        2. If positive urine culture:
            a. If patient is still febrile or unable to take PO, admit for parenteral ATBs
            b. If afebrile and able to take PO, patient may receive oral ATBs as outpatient
            c. Patient should return for re-evaluation within 24hrs
        3. If infant meets all low-risk clinical criteria and laboratory data are negative (WBC < 15,000/mm³ and urinalysis and CSF Gram stain are negative) and the parents seem reliable and close follow-up is ensured, the infant can be managed expectantly as an outpatient. Patient should return for re-evaluation or parent should call physician's office with an update on child's condition within 24hrs

    B. High risk infants: Admit to hospital and begin parenteral ATBs

IV. FEVER WITHOUT A SOURCE 3–36 MONTHS OLD

    *_Streptococcal pneumoniae_ most common cause of serious bacterial infection in this age group

    A. Low Risk Infants
        1. If child appears well and fever is < 102.2° F, no diagnostic tests or ATBs are necessary; **Tylenol** (15mg/kg) and/or **Ibuprofen** (10mg/kg) may be given PRN fever; parents should be instructed to return if fever persists > 48hrs or patient's condition worsens
        2. If temperature ≥ 102.2° F (39.0° C): Obtain **CBC with differential** and:
            a. **Urine culture** in all infants and children < 2 years old who are treated with empiric ATBs
            b. **Stool culture** if blood or mucus in stool or ≥ 5 WBCs/hpf in stool
            c. **Chest x-ray** if dyspnea, tachypnea, rales, or decreased breath sounds are present; consider also, if asymptomatic and WBC ≥ 20,000/mm³

    d. **Blood cultures** if both fever ≥ 102.2° F and WBC ≥15,000/mm³

    e. **CSF cultures** are indicated when diagnosis of sepsis or meningitis is suspected based on history, observation, or physical exam

3. Empiric ATB therapy (parenteral **Ceftriaxone:** 50mg/kg IM (maximum dose of 1g) should be given if temperature ≥ 102.2° F (39.0° C) *and* WBC ≥ 15,000/mm³· May also treat with oral therapy: **Amoxicillin** (50mg/kg/d) or **Augmentin** (50mg/kg/d). Oral ATBs will be effective for occult bacteremia, even penicillin-resistant, because there is no deep-seeded focus of infection

4. Follow-up in 24–48hrs

    a. If blood culture **positive**:

        i. Re-evaluate child within 24hrs and if child is still febrile or unable to take PO, admit for parenteral ATBs

        ii. If child is afebrile and taking PO, patient may receive oral ATBs as an outpatient (individualize therapy)

    b. If urine culture **positive:**

        i. If patient is toxic appearing or unable to take PO, admit for parenteral ATBs

        ii. If afebrile and able to take PO, patient may receive oral ATBs as an outpatient

B. High risk infants—Evaluate in emergency department

Remember: A careful history and physical exam are an essential part in determining treatment. Pneumococcal conjugate vaccine (**Prevnar**) will most likely change our management of fever without a source in infants in the next few years—the risk of invasive pneumococcal disease will be dramatically decreased

CLINICAL PEARLS

- Children < 90 days old may not exhibit meningeal signs, despite having meningitis
- Observation is a key component of the physical exam—a child who is smiling and/or playful is rarely septic
- Risk of bacteremia rises as temperature rises. A temperature of 105.6° F (40.9° C) is about 3 times more likely to harbor bacteremia than a temperature of 102.2° F (39° C)
- 10% of infants and young children with fever and streptococcus pneumoniae bacteremia progress to serious bacterial focal infection (meningitis, osteomyelitis, septic joint, etc.)

References

Baraff LJ. Management of fever without source in infants and children. Ann Emerg Med 2000;36:602–14.

Rothrock SG, et al. Do oral antibiotics prevent meningitis and serious bacterial infections in children with streptococcus pneumoniae occult bacteremia? A meta-analysis. Pediatrics 1997;99:438–44.

Luszczak M. Evaluation and management of infants and young children with fever. Am Fam Phys 2001;64:1219–26.

Finkelstein JA, et al. Fever in pediatric primary care: occurrence, management, and outcomes. Pediatrics 2000;105:260–6.

Kramer MS, Shapiro ED. Management of the young febrile child: a commentary on recent practice guidelines. Pediatrics 1997;100:128–34.

Beth Weinstock, MD

7. ASTHMA IN CHILDREN

I. DEFINITION: Chronic inflammatory disease causing airway hyper-responsiveness, airflow limitation and persistent respiratory symptoms which are usually reversible, either spontaneously or with therapy

II. EPIDEMIOLOGY AND EFFECTS OF ASTHMA ON CHILDREN
  A. Approximately $1/3$ of asthmatics are children; affects nearly 5 million children in US
  B. Prevalence is 5–10% in children; results in more severe disability and more frequent hospitalizations in black children than in white children
  C. 29% increase in prevalence, 43% increase in hospitalization rate, and 46% increase in death rate over last decade
  D. About 50% of children with asthma miss school because of the disease
  E. Uncontrolled childhood asthma can produce permanent damage to the child's respiratory system

III. HISTORY
  A. Symptoms: Episodic or chronic cough, shortness of breath, wheeze or cough with exertion. Symptoms are often worse during the evening or early morning hours
  B. Other: Allergies, family history of asthma or allergy, perinatal exposure to tobacco smoke, viral URI history, low birth weight

IV. PHYSICAL EXAM: Enlarged turbinates, rhinitis, nasal polyps, wheezing, increased respiratory effort, use of accessory muscles, eczema/atopic dermatitis. Note: Children with a clear lung exam in the office can still be symptomatic at night or with exertion

V. DIFFERENTIAL DIAGNOSIS
  A. Obstruction of large airways—foreign body, congenital
  B. Obstruction of large and small airways—infection (bronchiolitis and chlamydia), cystic fibrosis, bronchopulmonary dysplasia

VI. EVALUATION (Individualized)
  A. CXR: May show hyperinflation
  B. Pulmonary function tests: Pre- and post-bronchodilator spirometry. Post-bronchodilator assessment should be done 15–20 minutes after inhalation of a short-acting bronchodilator. Results consistent with asthma include variable airflow obstruction (20% or more) with serial spirometry or peak-flow measurements, and an increase in forced expiratory volume in 1 second (FEV_1) of 12% or more after bronchodilator therapy
  C. Peak expiratory flow meter: Highest of 3 peak flow measurements is recorded (patient must exhale as hard and fast as possible). Measurements can be compared to norms for height and weight, and compared to patient's baseline when asymptomatic. Peak flow meters serve to increase patient and caregiver awareness of disease status

VII. MANAGEMENT OF CHRONIC ASTHMA—TABLE 1

Stepwise Approach for Managing Infants and Young Children (5 Years of Age and Younger) With Acute or Chronic Asthma – (see Chapter 49, Asthma, for treating asthma in children > 5 years of age)		
Classify Severity: Clinical Features Before Treatment or Adequate Control		Medications Required to Maintain Long-Term Control
	Symptoms/Day **Symptoms/Night**	**Daily Medications**

Step 4
 Severe Persistent
	Continual
	 Frequent
		• Preferred treatment:
		 – High-dose inhaled corticosteroids
		   AND
		 – Long-acting inhaled beta$_2$-agonists
		   AND, if needed,
		 – Corticosteroid tablets or syrup long term (2 mg/kg/day, generally do not exceed 60 mg per day). (Make repeat attempts to reduce systemic corticosteroids and maintain control with high-dose inhaled corticosteroids)

Step 3 Moderate Persistent	Daily > 1 night/week	• Preferred treatments: – Low-dose inhaled corticosteroids and long-acting inhaled beta$_2$-agonists OR – Medium-dose inhaled corticosteroids • Alternative treatment: – Low-dose inhaled corticosteroids and either leukotriene receptor antagonist or theophylline If needed (particularly in patients with recurring severe exacerbations): • Preferred treatment: – Medium-dose inhaled corticosteroids and long-acting beta$_2$-agonists • Alternative treatment: – Medium-dose inhaled corticosteroids and either leukotriene receptor antagonist or theophylline
Step 2 Mild Persistent	> 2/week but < 1x/day > 2 nights/month	• Preferred treatment: – Low-dose inhaled corticosteroid (with nebulizer or MDI with holding chamber with or without face mask or DPI). • Alternative treatment (listed alphabetically): – Cromolyn (nebulizer is preferred or MDI with holding chamber) OR leukotriene receptor antagonist
Step 1 Mild Intermittent	≤ 2 days/week ≤ 2 nights/month	• No daily medication needed

Quick Relief
 All Patients
	• Bronchodilator as needed for symptoms. Intensity of treatment will depend upon severity of exacerbation
	   – Preferred treatment: Short-acting inhaled beta$_2$-agonists by nebulizer or face mask and space/holding chamber
	   – Alternative treatment: Oral beta$_2$-agonist
	 • With viral respiratory infection
	   – Bronchodilator Q 4-6 hours up to 24 hours (longer with physician consult); in general, repeat no more than once every 6 weeks
	   – Consider systemic corticosteroid if exacerbation is severe or patient has history of previous severe exacerbations
	 • Use of short-acting beta$_2$-agonists > 2 times a week in intermittent asthma (daily, or increasing use in persistent asthma) may indicate the need to initiate (increase) long-term control therapy

Step down Review treatment every 1 to 6 months; a gradual stepwise reduction in treatment may be possible **Step up** If control is not maintained, consider step up. First, review patient medication technique, adherence, and environmental control	**Note** • The stepwise approach is intended to assist, not replace, the clinical decision making required to meet individual patient needs • Classify severity: assign patient to most severe step in which any feature occurs • There are very few studies on asthma therapy for infants • Gain control as quickly as possible (a course of short systemic corticosteroids may be required); then step down to the least medication necessary to maintain control • Provide parent education on asthma management and controlling environmental factors that make asthma worse (e.g., allergies and irritants) • Consultation with an asthma specialist is recommended for patients with moderate or severe persistent asthma. Consider consultation for patients with mild persistent asthma

Goals of Therapy: Asthma Control	
• Minimal or no chronic symptoms day or night • Minimal or no exacerbations • No limitations on activities; no school/parent's work missed	• Minimal use of short-acting inhaled beta$_2$-agonist (< 1x per day, < 1 canister/month) • Minimal or no adverse effects from medications

Source: NAEPP expert panel report. Guidelines for the diagnosis and management of asthma—updated topics 2002. Bethesda, MD: National Institutes of Health, National Health, Lung & Blood Institute, 2002:NIH publication no. 02–5075. http://www.nhlbi.nih.gov/guidelines/asthma/execsumm.pdf

TABLE 2: MEDICATION FOR LONG-TERM TREATMENT

Usual Dosages for Long-Term-Control Medications		
Medication	**Dosage Form**	**Child Dose***
Inhaled Corticosteroids *(See Estimated Comparative Daily Dosages for Inhaled Corticosteroids)*		
Systemic Corticosteroids		*(Applies to all three corticosteroids)*
Methylprednisolone	2, 4, 8, 16, 32 mg tablets	• 0.25-2 mg/kg daily in single dose in a.m. or QOD as needed for control
Prednisolone	5 mg tablets, 5 mg/5 cc, 15 mg/5 cc	
Prednisone	1, 2.5, 5, 10, 20, 50 mg tablets; 5 mg/cc, 5 mg/5 cc	• Short-course "burst": 1–2 mg/kg/day, maximum 60 mg/day for 3–10 days
Long-Acting Inhaled Beta₂-Agonists (Should not be used for symptom relief or for exacerbations. Use with inhaled corticosteroids)		
Salmeterol	MDI 21 mcg/puff	1–2 puffs Q 12 hours
	DPI 50 mcg/blister	1 blister Q 12 hours
Formoterol	DPI 12 mcg/single-use capsule	1 capsule Q 12 hours
Combined Medication		
Fluticasone/Salmeterol	DPI 100, 250, or 500 mcg/50 mcg	1 inhalation BID; dose depends on severity of asthma
Cromolyn and Nedocromil		
Cromolyn	MDI 1 mg/puff	1–2 puffs TID-QID
	Nebulizer 20 mg/ampule	1 ampule TID-QID
Leukotriene Modifiers		
Montelukast	4 or 5 mg chewable tablet	4 mg QHS (2-5 yrs) 5 mg QHS (6-14 yrs) 10 mg QHS (> 14 yrs)
	10 mg tablet	
Zafirlukast	10 or 20 mg tablet	20 mg daily (7-11 yrs) (10 mg tablet BID)
Methylxanthines *(Serum monitoring is important [serum concentration of 5–15 mcg/mL at steady state])*		
Theophylline	Liquids, sustained-release tablets, and capsules	Starting dose 10 mg/kg/day; usual max: • < 1 year of age: 0.2 (age in weeks) + 5 = mg/kg/day • ≥ 1 year of age: 16 mg/kg/day

*Children ≤ 12 years of age

Adapted from: NAEPP expert panel report. Guidelines for the diagnosis and management of asthma—updated topics 2002. Bethesda, MD: National Institutes of Health, National Health, Lung & Blood Institute, 2002:NIH publication no. 02–5075. http://www.nhlbi.nih.gov/guidelines/asthma/execsumm.pdf

TABLE 3: ESTIMATED COMPARATIVE DAILY DOSAGES

Estimated Comparative Daily Dosage for Inhaled Corticosteroids			
Drug	**Low Daily Dose Child***	**Medium Daily Dose Child***	**High Daily Dose Child***
Beclomethasone CFC 42 or 84 mcg/puff	84–336 mcg	336–672 mcg	> 672 mcg
Beclomethasone HFA 40 or 80 mcg/puff	80–160 mcg	160–320 mcg	> 320 mcg
Budesonide DPI 200 mcg/inhalation	200–400 mcg	400–800 mcg	> 800 mcg
Inhalation suspension for nebulization (child dose)	0.5 mg	1.0 mg	2.0 mg
Flunisolide 250 mcg/puff	500–750 mcg	1,000–1,250 mcg	> 1,250 mcg
Fluticasone MDI: 44, 110, or 220 mcg/puff	88–176 mcg	176–440 mcg	> 440 mcg
DPI: 50, 100, or 250 mcg/inhalation	100–200 mcg	200-400 mcg	> 400 mcg
Triamcinolone acetonide 100 mcg/puff	400–800 mcg	800–1,200 mcg	> 1,200 mcg

*Children ≤ 12 years of age

Adapted from: NAEPP expert panel report. Guidelines for the diagnosis and management of asthma—updated topics 2002. Bethesda, MD: National Institutes of Health, National Health, Lung & Blood Institute, 2002:NIH publication no. 02–5075. http://www.nhlbi.nih.gov/guidelines/asthma/execsumm.pdf

VIII. ADJUVANT THERAPY

A. Education of family is essential—recognition of change in disease status allows early intervention. Daily self-management plans and emergency action plans are important for parents, and templates can be obtained from the National Asthma Education and Prevention Program of the National Heart, Lung, and Blood Institute (www.nhlbisupport.com)

B. Avoidance of allergens and triggers: Aspirin and NSAIDs, tobacco smoke, remove pets from house (or at least from bedroom), limit outdoor activities when pollen counts are high or if air is cold, dust mite precautions (encasing mattresses, removing carpet and stuffed animals, washing all bedding every 1 to 2 weeks in hot water). Some irritants include fireplace smoke, perfumes, cleaning agents. Stress and GERD can also contribute

C. Ask about nocturnal symptoms and number of inhalers used per year. Children should not use more than 2 or 3 **Albuterol** inhalers per year—if so, the patient needs better chronic control of the disease. Spacers make MDIs easier to use and are essential in children < 5 years; dry powder inhalers are okay for children if they can master the technique

IX. MANAGEMENT OF ACUTE EPISODES

A. Assessment of signs and symptoms, home PEFR, office PEFR, office pulse oximetry

B. To determine need for hospitalization: Respiratory rate, accessory muscle use, color, lung exam (inaudible breath sounds are sign of severe exacerbation), speech pattern, alertness

C. Medication: See "Quick Relief" on Table 1, in this chapter

CLINICAL PEARLS

- Long-term data show that children who use inhaled steroids over a period of years grow to their expected height, comparable with peers and family
- Goals of treatment: Child should sleep though the night, should have no restrictions on activity or attendance at school, normal PFTs, few to no side effects from meds

References

NAEPP expert panel report. Guidelines for the diagnosis and management of asthma—updated topics 2002. Bethesda, MD: National Institutes of Health, National Health, Lung & Blood Institute, 2002:NIH publication no. 02–5075. http://www.nhlbi.nih.gov/guidelines/asthma/execsumm.pdf

Suissa S, et al. Low-dose inhaled corticosteroids and the prevention of death from asthma. N Engl J Med 2000;343,332–336.

Evans R, 3rd. Asthma among minority children. Chest 1992;101 (6 Suppl):368S–71S.

Daniel M. Neides, MD
Eric Hansen, MD
Timothy Graham, MD

8. OTITIS MEDIA

I. INTRODUCTION

    A. Otitis media (OM) is the most common medical diagnosis made in children under age 15

    B. 85% of children have 1 episode of acute otitis media by age 3

    C. Environmental risk factors: Exposure to second-hand smoke, bottle feeding, and enrollment in day care

    D. An article published in the journal Pediatrics in August 2001 reviewed 74 randomized, controlled trials or cohort studies published between 1966 and 1999 found the following (see reference Takata, et al):

        1. Approximately 80% of cases of OM achieve clinical resolution without ATB therapy within 7 days

        2. Number needed to treat (NNT) with **Amoxicillin** to avoid 1 clinical failure at 2–7 days is 8

        3. Rate of mastoiditis in untreated patients is approximately 1/1,000

        4. Studies addressing the use of specific ATBs, high- or low-dose regimen, and duration of ATB treatment fail to demonstrate superiority of any 1 regimen over another

    E. ATB recommended for initial treatment is **Amoxicillin**

II. ETIOLOGY

    A. Bacterial: *S. pneumoniæ, H. influenzæ (nontypeable), M. catarrhalis, S. aureus,* Group A Strep (a rare cause of otitis media, but is associated with a higher rate of acute perforation and more rapid destruction of the tympanic membrane). In chronic serous otitis media, the most common bacterial agents include *P. aeruginosa, S. aureus, S. epidermidis, S. viridans,* and *S. pneumonia*

    B. Viral: Parainfluenza, RSV, Influenza, Adenovirus, Enterovirus

III. DIAGNOSIS

    A. Signs/Symptoms (percentage of children affected in parentheses):

        1. Ear pain (47–83%)

        2. Fever (22–69%)

        3. Associated respiratory symptoms including cough and/or rhinitis (94%)

        4. Irritability (56%)

        5. Pulling at ear (12%)

        6. Drainage from ear (if tympanic membrane is ruptured)

    B. Physical exam, predictive value in parentheses

        1. Erythematous tympanic membrane (65%)

        2. Bulging tympanic membrane (89%)—occurs first in the postero-superior area

        3. Cloudy tympanic membrane (80%)

        4. Impaired mobility of tympanic membrane (78%)

        5. Note: Slightly impaired mobility of tympanic membrane (33%)

        6. Note: Slightly erythematous tympanic membrane (16%)

IV. TREATMENT: Since the causative agent of OM is usually unknown, initiate a 10 day course of empiric ATB therapy (see table below, Drugs Commonly Used with Otitis Media)

    A. General

        1. Patients should be re-evaluated in 2 weeks to see if the treatment was successful. If there is presence of a middle ear effusion, consider:

           a. Re-evaluate in 6 weeks

           b. Re-treat with different ATB

2. Antipyretics/Analgesics (oral)
   a. **Acetaminophen** 15mg/kg Q 4–6hrs (drops 0.8mL=80mg, susp. 160mg/5cc)
   b. **Ibuprofen** 10mg/kg Q 8hrs (drops 1.25mL=50mg, susp. 100mg/5cc)
3. Analgesic (topical): **Auralgan otic suspension** 2–4 drops in affected ear QID (do not use with perforated TM)

B. Acute Otitis Media (AOM): See table below, Drugs Commonly Used with Otitis Media

C. Persistent OM: Occurs after initial course of ATBs in up to 25% of patients
1. Definition: Persistence of AOM within 6 days of beginning ATBs or recurrence of AOM within a few days of completion of a 10 day course of ATBs
2. Consider other diagnosis
   a. Mastoiditis
   b. Meningitis
   c. Other infections
3. Management: Change ATBs to one that covers β-lactamase producing organisms

D. Recurrent OM
1. Definition: 3 episodes of OM in 6 months or 4 episodes in 12 months
2. Consider other diagnosis
   a. Sinusitis
   b. Allergies
   c. Immune deficiencies (C3 and C5 deficiency)
   d. Submucous cleft palate
   e. Tumor of the nasopharynx
3. Prevention
   a. ATB prophylaxis
      i. **Amoxicillin** 20mg/kg PO QHS
      ii. **TMP/SMX** 4/20mg/kg PO QHS
      iii. **Erythromycin-Sulfisoxazole** 20mg/kg/day (if > 2 years old)
   b. Myringotomy with tympanostomy tube insertion

E. Ruptured TM
1. Treat with **Cortisporin Otic Suspension** 2 drops QID for 3–5 days in addition to oral ATBs per above recommendations
2. **Fluoroquinolone otic solutions** have been recently approved for use in children and are not known to be ototoxic
3. Continued otorrhea despite oral ATBs may necessitate a culture of the drainage from the perforation site
4. Careful otologic examination is required for otorrrhea lasting longer than 2 weeks despite ATB use
5. Chronic otorrhea (lasting 6 or more weeks) is most commonly caused by chronic serous otitis media but may be caused by a myriad of different processes including cholesteatoma, foreign body, granuloma, immunodeficiency and neoplasm

F. Serous OM
1. Persistent middle ear effusion without infection
2. Check hearing at 3 months. If decreased, refer to ENT
3. No role for steroids or decongestants. Oral ATB usually not necessary

V. PREVENTION

A. Pneumococcal conjugate vaccine appears to be only minimally efficacious in reducing the incidence of acute OM because it only works for the serotypes included in the vaccine. Estimated overall reduction is approximately 6%. Prevnar has recently been FDA approved for prevention of otitis media, although only 25% of OM are caused by 1 of the 7 serotypes. Thus, the protection against OM is expected to be much lower than protection against invasive disease

Drugs Commonly Used with Otitis Media			
Drug	Dose	Availability	Common side effects
Amoxicillin	40-45mg/kg/day in 2 divided doses High dose therapy is 80-90mg/kg/day in 2 divided doses	Suspension: 125mg/5cc, 200mg/5cc, 250mg/5cc, 400mg/5cc Chewable: 125, 200, 250, 400mg Tabs or capsules: 250, 500, 875mg	GI, urticaria, hyperactivity
TMP/SMX (Bactrim/Septra)	Children over 2 months: SMX 40mg/kg/day (TMP 8mg/kg/day) in 2 divided doses Adults: 1 DS tab BID	Suspension: SMX 200mg/5mL TMP 40mg/5mL Tabs: SS: SMX 400mg and TMP 80mg DS: SMX 800mg and TMP 160mg	GI, photosensitivity, neutropenia, thrombo-cytopenia. Use a different antibiotic if G6PD deficiency
Erythromycin Sulfisoxazole (Pediazole)	Children over 2 months: Erythro 50mg/kg/day (Sulf 150mg/kg/day) in 3 divided doses	Suspension: Erythro 200mg/Sulfisoxazole 600mg/5mL	GI, rash
Amoxicillin-Clavulanate (Augmentin)	30–40mg/kg/day in 3 divided doses In treatment failure: 90mg/kg/day of Augmentin ES–600	Suspension: 125mg/5mL, 200mg/5mL, 250mg/5mL, 400mg/5mL, 600mg/5mL Chewable: 125, 200, 250, 400mg Tabs: 250, 500, 875mg	Diarrhea, rash, urticaria
Loracarbef (Lorabid)	30mg/kg/day in 2 divided doses	Suspension: 100mg/5mL, 200mg/5mL Tabs: 200, 400mg * Empty stomach	GI, rash
Cefixime (Suprax)	8mg/kg/day in 1 dose per day (under 6 months — not recommended)	Suspension: 100mg/5mL Tabs: 200, 400mg	GI, rash, photosensitivity
Cefdinir (Omnicef)	7mg/kg/Q12hr or 14mg/kg/Q24hr	Suspension: 125mg/5mL Capsule: 300mg	GI, Drug interaction with antacids and iron supplements
Azithromycin (Zithromax)	Day 1: 10mg/kg 1 dose Days 2–5: 5mg/kg 1 dose, or 30mg/kg 1 dose	Suspension: 100mg/5mL, 200mg/5mL Caps: 250mg	GI
Clarithromycin (Biaxin)	15mg/kg divided BID	Suspension: 125mg/5mL, 250mg/5mL Tabs: 250, 500mg	GI, bad taste, HA
Ceftriaxone	50mg/kg x 1 IM max 1gm for severe infection can be given up to 3 shots	250mg, 500mg, 1000mg vials	Painful injection
Cefuroxime (Ceftin)	30mg/kg/day in 2 divided doses	125mg/5mL 250mg/5mL, 125, 250, 500mg tab	GI

CLINICAL PEARLS

- Decongestants, antihistamines, and glucocorticoids have not been shown to be helpful with AOM
- **Auralgan** drops (2 drops Q2hrs PRN) may decrease the symptom of ear pain
- A crying child may have an erythematous TM because of crying
- Recurrent OM may result in hearing loss. Be alert for behavioral changes or learning difficulties
- Up to 10% of patients may develop tympanosclerosis with permanent hearing loss after tympanotomy

References

Jacobs MR. Prevention of otitis media: role of pneumococcal conjugate vaccines in reducing incidence and antibiotic resistance. J Pediatr August 2002;141:287–93.

Takata GS, et al. Evidence assessment of management of acute otitis media: I. The role of antibiotics in the treatment of uncomplicated acute otitis media. Pediatrics 2001;108(2):239.

Eskola J, et al. Efficacy of a pneumococcal conjugate vaccine against acute otitis media. N Engl J Med 2001;344:403–9.

Sabella C. Management of otorrhea in infants and children. Pediatr Infect Dis J 2000:19;1007-8.

Paradise JL, et al. Effect of early or delayed tympanostomy tubes for persistent otitis media on developmental outcomes at the age of three years. N Engl J Med 2001;344:1179–87.

McCormick DP, et al. Definition and diagnostic criteria for acute otitis media. Pediatrics 2002; 109:717–8.

Cohen R, et al. One dose ceftriaxone vs. 10 days of amoxicillin-clavulanate therapy for acute otitis media: clinical efficacy and change in nasopharyngeal flora. Pediatr Infect Dis J May 1999;18:403–9.

Michael B. Weinstock, MD
Daniel M. Neides, MD
Timothy P. Graham, MD

9. PHARYNGITIS

I. DEFINITION: An inflammatory process involving the mucous membranes and underlying structures of the oropharynx

II. PRESENTATION
   A. History
      1. Chief complaint and associated symptoms (see below)
      2. Immunization history
      3. Sexual history (when indicated)
   B. Signs and symptoms
      1. Sore throat
      2. Enlarged tonsils
      3. Fever, chills, headache, malaise, and anorexia
      4. Oropharyngeal erythema and/or exudate
      5. Rash
      6. Cervical adenopathy
      7. Rhinitis
   C. Symptomatic tetrad of streptococcal pharyngitis (Centor criteria)
      1. Fever > 102.2° F
      2. Anterior cervical lymphadenopathy
      3. Exudative tonsillitis
      4. Absence of cough

III. ETIOLOGY
   A. Bacterial: Group A beta-hemolytic streptococcus (causal agent in 10% of cases of adult pharyngitis), *Mycoplasma pneumoniæ, Hæmophilus influenzæ, Corynebacterium diphtheria, Neisseria gonorrhoeæ*
   B. Viral: Adenovirus, Influenzæ viruses (A&B), Parainfluenza viruses, Epstein-Barr virus, Herpes simplex virus

IV. EVALUATION
   A. Laboratory
      1. Rapid strep test (RSS)—up to 96% sensitive
      2. Many clinicians recommend stopping the evaluation with a negative RSS. Primary reason for treating strep throat is to prevent rheumatic fever. There is an exceedingly low chance that there would be a false negative RSS and that the undetected strep would cause the patient to develop clinically significant rheumatic fever
      3. Strep culture
         a. Obtain based on clinical judgment if there is reason to suspect the RSS would give a false negative, to look for other etiologies than GABHS, etc.
         b. Is not routinely recommended, even with a negative RSS
         c. Has low test to test agreement; does not always correlate with antistreptolysin

titers; produce varied results depending on technique, sample site, culture medium, incubation conditions, and whether the results were checked at 24 or 48hrs; and fails to distinguish acute infection from the carrier state

4. Decision to screen adults should be based on the presence or absence of the four Centor criteria (see I. C.)
   a. If none or 1 of the criteria are present—consider not screening
      i. There is a negative predictive value of 80% with the absence of 3 or 4 of the Centor criteria. If none of the criteria are present, < 5% chance of strep
      ii. If recently exposed to strep, use clinical judgment
   b. If 2 or more criteria are present
      i. The patient should be screened, but only treated with ATB if the screen is positive—or—
      ii. Diagnostic tests may be deferred in patients with four criteria, and they may be empirically treated with ATBs. If 3–4 of the Centor criteria are present, the positive predictive value of a positive test is 40–60%
5. Use appropriate culture medium if other bacteria (e.g., *Neisseria* or *Corynebacterium*) suspected

V. TREATMENT

A. **From the CDC as published in 2001 in the Annals of Internal Medicine:** "The preferred antimicrobial agent for treatment of acute pharyngitis is penicillin, or erythromycin for penicillin-allergic patients. There is no evidence of group A beta-hemolytic streptococcus resistance to or tolerance of penicillin, and erythromycin resistance rates are low in the United States"

B. The goal of initiating therapy is to decrease the chance of secondary complications (including rheumatic fever). This therapy can safely be initiated up to 9 days after onset of symptoms and still be effective

C. The classic triad of fever, pharyngeal exudate and anterior cervical lymphadenopathy are present in only 15% of cases of strep pharyngitis

D. Medical personnel are correct in only 50–75% of cases where diagnosis is made based on clinical criteria alone

E. Compliance with ATBs is a major problem with 71% of children discontinuing ATBs by day 6

F. **Group A streptococcus**
   1. Oral penicillin
      a. Children: **Pen Vee K** 250mg PO BID–QID × 10 days
      b. Adolescents and adults: **Pen Vee K** 500mg PO BID–TID
   2. Intramuscular penicillin
      a. **Benzathine penicillin (Bicillin LA):** Long acting PCN
         i. If greater than 1 month and < 27kg: 600,000 U
         ii. Children > 27kg and adults: 1.2 million U
      b. **Benzathine penicillin/Procaine penicillin (Bicillin C-R)**
         i. Injection may be less painful
         ii. There are different amounts of penicillin in the different preparations of Bicillin C-R. Use the above recommendations for the amount of Benzathine penicillin per injection
   3. Penicillin-Allergic
      a. **Erythromycin**
         Children: 30–50mg/kg/day divided TID–QID × 10 days
         Adults: 250mg PO QID × 10 days—*or*—
      b. **Cephalexin (Keflex)**
         Children: 25–50mg/kg/day divided BID–QID × 10 days
         Adults: 250mg PO QID × 10 days—*or*—
      c. **Azithromycin (Zithromax)** powder for oral suspension 12mg/kg once daily for 5 days, not to exceed 500mg/day. To be given at least 1hr before or 2hrs after a meal. Should **not** be taken with food. No refrigeration necessary
   4. Treatment failures: Patients with streptococcal pharyngitis remaining symptomatic after

treatment are considered treatment failures and should be retreated with an ATB that is not degraded by penicillinase-producing organisms such as **Amoxicillin-Clavulanate Potassium:**
   a. Children: 40 mg/kg/day divided BID–TID × 10 days
   b. Adults: 500–875 mg BID × 10 days

G. Viral
   1. Symptomatic relief
      a. Gargle with warm salt water TID
      b. **Chloraseptic** spray or lozenges PRN sore throat
      c. **Acetaminophen** or **Ibuprofen** for pain, fever

VI. COMPLICATIONS
   A. Rheumatic fever (secondary to Group A Strep)
      1. Carditis is the most serious complication associated with acute rheumatic fever (seen in 50 to 91% of cases of pediatric rheumatic fever and 33% of adult rheumatic fever)
      2. Can lead to permanent valvular dysfunction
      3. Rheumatic fever is rare in adults
   B. Post-strep glomerulonephritis
      1. Rare
      2. No evidence that ATB treatment of pharyngitis decreases the incidence of this complication
   C. Peritonsillar abscess/Retropharyngeal abscess
   D. Scarlet fever
   E. Cervical lymphadenitis
   F. Sinusitis
   G. Mastoiditis
   H. Otitis Media
   I. Meningitis
   J. Bacteremia
   K. Pneumonia

CLINICAL PEARLS
   • Untreated, streptococcal pharyngitis will resolve. ATB therapy is necessary, however, to prevent complications including acute rheumatic fever
   • School-aged children who develop strep pharyngitis can return to school 24hrs after therapy is initiated
   • Patients complaining of an associated rhinitis most likely have a viral etiology of their pharyngitis
   • A Mono-spot test is a quick way to determine EBV (mononucleosis) infection; associated findings may include posterior cervical adenopathy, prolonged course of symptoms, or splenomegaly

References
Snow V, et al. Principles of appropriate antibiotic use for acute pharyngitis in adults. Ann Intern Med. 2001;134:506–8. (Clinical Practice Guideline, Part 1).
Cooper RJ, et al. Principles of appropriate antibiotic use for acute pharyngitis in adults: Background. Ann Intern Med 2001;134:507–17. (Clinical Practice Guideline, Part 2).
Ebell MH, et al. Does this patient have strep throat? JAMA 2000;284:2912–8.
Bisno AL, et al. Diagnosis and management of group A streptococcal pharyngitis: a practice guideline. Infectious Diseases Society of America. Clin Infect Dis 1997;25:574–83.
Hayes CS, Williams H Jr. Management of group A beta-hemolytic streptococcal pharyngitis. Am Fam Phys 2001;63:1557–64.

Daniel M. Neides, MD

10. Croup (Acute Laryngotracheitis)

DEFINITION: A viral illness characterized by a "barky" cough, inspiratory stridor, and fever

I. PRESENTATION
Affects children ages 3 months–3 years. Most frequently occurs in autumn
   A. Signs and symptoms: Gradual onset
   1. Barking, spasmodic cough, inspiratory stridor, hoarseness, and low-grade fever
   2. Upper respiratory infection (coryza) prodrome for 1–7 days
   3. Tachypnea, intercostal retractions, nasal flaring, dyspnea, and fatigue
   4. Cyanosis
   B. Westley croup score: Commonly used assessment of severity of croup—5 clinical parameters
   1. Conscious level
   2. Cyanosis
   3. Stridor
   4. Air entry
   5. Chest wall retractions
   C. Differential diagnosis
   1. Epiglottitis
   2. Foreign body aspiration
   3. Bacterial tracheitis
   4. Subglottic stenosis

II. ETIOLOGY
   A. Viral
   1. Parainfluenza viruses (most common), Influenza viruses, RSV and Adenovirus
   2. Enteroviruses (coxsackievirus A & B and echovirus) are common causes of "summertime croup"
   3. Measles virus (endemic areas)
   B. Bacterial: *Mycoplasma pneumoniæ*

III. Evaluation: The diagnosis is usually a clinical diagnosis. More severe cases may warrant further work-up
   A. PA and lateral neck x-rays (obtain only if unsure of diagnosis)
   1. "Steeple Sign": Common x-ray finding secondary to subglottic narrowing
   2. Will help rule out epiglottitis ("thumb" sign on x-ray) as an etiology
   B. Laboratory: Usually only entails a pulse oximetry reading
   1. WBC usually $< 10,000/mm^3$ with a predominately lymphocytic differential
   2. O_2 saturation

IV. MANAGEMENT: Mild cases can be effectively managed at home
   A. Dexamethasone: 0.6mg/kg IM or PO as a 1 time dose—Benefit to children with mild, moderate, and severe croup. Results in decreased rates of hospitalization and endotracheal intubation. Also results in improved clinical course—children begin to feel better sooner
   B. For moderate to severe cases: **Racemic Epinephrine.** May be rebound so the patient does need to be observed for 2–4hrs after treatment. Hospitalize if more than 1 nebulization is required
   C. Inhalation of humidified air (vaporizer): Commonly used in clinical practice but has not been demonstrated effective in clinical trials
   D. Increase fluid intake, decrease agitation, observe carefully, follow-up closely
   E. Indications for admission:
   1. Stridor at rest
   2. Low oxygen saturation
   3. Tachypnea/retractions

4. Ill appearance, poor color, decreased level of consciousness
5. Questionable diagnosis (possible epiglottis, foreign body, etc.)

CLINICAL PEARLS
- Croup is usually preceded by a viral prodrome or URI symptoms
- Annual incidence of croup in the US is 18/1000 which peaks at 60/1000 in children 1–2 years of age
- Nebulized **Racemic Epinephrine** has an onset of action of 10–30 mins

References

Rittichier KK, Ledwith CA. Outpatient treatment of moderate croup with dexamethasone: intramuscular vs oral dosing. Pediatrics 2000;106:1344–8.

Luria, JW, et al. Effectiveness of oral or nebulized dexamethasone for children with mild croup. Arch Pediatr & Adol Med 2001;155:1340.

Johnson DW, et al. A comparison of nebulized budesonide, intramuscular dexamethasone, and placebo for moderately severe croup. N Engl J Med 1998;339:498–503.

Jaffe DM. The treatment of croup with glucocorticoids. N Engl J Med 1998;339:553–5.

Klassen TP, Rowe PC. Outpatient management of croup. Cur Opin Pediatr 1996;8:449.

Daniel M. Neides, MD

11. BRONCHIOLITIS

DEFINITION: An inflammatory process involving the bronchi and bronchioles

I. PRESENTATION
Occurs mostly in winter and spring
A. Criteria for diagnosis
1. First episode of acute wheezing
2. Age < 24 months
3. Symptoms associated with viral infection (cough, fever, coryza)
4. Pneumonia is ruled out as a cause of the wheezing
5. No family history of atopy or asthma
B. Signs and symptoms
1. Expiratory wheezing and inspiratory rales
2. Temperature usually < 101° F
3. Grunting, intercostal retractions, dyspnea, tachypnea, prolonged expiratory phase
4. Sore throat, cough, and coryza
5. May have associated otitis media
C. Differential diagnosis
1. Asthma
2. Allergies (IgE-mediated hypersensitivity)
3. Foreign body aspiration
4. Pneumonia
5. Gastroesophageal reflux disease (GERD)
6. Congestive heart failure (CHF)
7. Cystic fibrosis

II. ETIOLOGY
A. Viral: Respiratory syncytial virus (RSV), parainfluenza, adenovirus, rhinovirus, influenza virus
B. Bacterial: *Mycoplasma pneumoniae, Chlamydia pneumoniae*

III. EVALUATION
A. Chest x-ray (CXR)
1. Obtain on all "first-time wheezers" to rule out foreign body aspiration, pneumonia or CHF, and those patients requiring inpatient management

2. Common radiologic findings associated with bronchiolitis
   a. Increased A-P diameter
   b. Atelectasis
   c. Flattening of the diaphragms
   B. **Laboratory:** Only necessary for severe cases (see criteria for inpatient management below)
   1. Arterial blood gas: monitor for hypoxemia, acidosis, and hypercarbia
   2. Nasopharyngeal (viral) cultures: for detection of RSV

IV. MANAGEMENT
A. Home management
1. Most patients can and should be treated at home
2. Symptomatic relief
   a. Anti-pyretics (**Tylenol, Ibuprofen**)
   b. Anti-tussives (**Dextromethorphan, Codeine**-based syrup)
3. Bronchodilator therapy
   a. In patients with mild and moderately severe symptoms, studies suggest that bronchodilators improve clinical scores in the short term
   b. Studies suggest that bronchodilators do not improve oxygen saturation or reduce admission rates
   c. May cause tachycardia, increased BP, decreased oxygen saturation, flushing, hyperactivity, prolonged cough and tremors
4. Adequate hydration
5. Avoid exposure to other children (incubation period of RSV is 4–6 days)
6. No smoking around child
7. Parents should be instructed to call the physician for worsening symptoms (respiratory distress, lethargic behavior, poor feeding, signs of dehydration)
8. **Note:** Steroids have *not* been shown to be beneficial in altering disease course
B. Criteria for inpatient management of bronchiolitis
1. Tachypnea, marked intercostal retractions, increasing respiratory distress, cyanosis, hypoxemia, or dehydration
2. Immunocompromised patients
3. Patients with a history of cardiopulmonary disease

CLINICAL PEARLS
- 1 child in 50 will require hospitalization secondary to RSV bronchiolitis. Of these, 3–7% develop respiratory failure and 1% will die
- The mortality rate from nosocomial RSV in ill infants is as high as 20%
- ATBs should be withheld unless a bacterial etiology is suspected

References
Kellner JD, et al. Bronchodilators for bronchiolitis. In: The Cochran Library, Issue 4, 2000. Oxford: Update Software.
Flores G, Horwitz RI. Efficacy of beta 2-agonists in bronchiolitis: a reappraisal and meta-analysis. Pediatrics 1997;100:233–9.
Bulow SM, et al. Prednisolone treatment for respiratory syncytial virus infection: a randomized controlled trial of 147 infants. Pediatrics 1999;104:77.
Berger I, et al. Efficacy of corticosteroids in acute bronchiolitis: short-term and long-term follow-up. Pediatr Pulmonol 1998;26:162–6.
Goebel J, et al. Prednisolone plus albuterol versus albuterol alone in mild to moderate bronchiolitis. Clin Pediatr 2000;39:213-20.

Chad Braun, MD
Daniel M. Neides, MD
Michael B. Weinstock, MD

12. DIARRHEA IN CHILDREN

I. GENERAL
  A. Definition: An increase in the frequency, fluidity or volume of bowel movements as compared to the normal habit of the individual. Diarrhea may be acute (< than 2 weeks) or chronic
  B. Diarrhea worldwide is responsible for 4–5 million deaths/year in children < age 5. In US, acute gastroenteritis (AGE) historically accounts for 10% of hospital admissions of children < age 5

II. ETIOLOGY: Viruses are responsible for 60% of cases; bacteria, 20%; parasites, 5%; parenteral illnesses, 10%; and only 5% are in an unknown category
  A. Viral: Rotavirus (35% of hospitalizations for acute diarrhea), Adenovirus, Norwalk virus, Enterovirus
  B. Bacterial: *Aeromonas* species, *Vibrio cholerae, E. coli, Yersinia enterocolitica, Salmonella, Shigella, Clostridium difficile, Campylobacter jejuni*
  C. Parasitic: *Cryptosporidium, Entamoeba histolytica, Giardia lamblia*
  D. Other: Formula intolerance, protein intolerance, carbohydrate intolerance, lactose intolerance, post-infectious diarrhea secondary to lactose intolerance, overfeeding, inflammatory bowel disease (IBD), chronic nonspecific diarrhea of infancy, excessive fluid intake, celiac disease, pancreatic disease, constipation with overflow diarrhea, functional tumors, intestinal obstruction, irritable bowel syndrome (IBS), laxative abuse
  E. Non-GI causes: Otitis media, sepsis, toxic ingestion, immunodeficiency, hyperthyroidism
  F. Etiologies of acute diarrhea by age
    1. Infant: Gastroenteritis (viral), systemic infection, ATB use, primary disaccharidase deficiency and Hirschsprung toxic colitis
    2. Child: Gastroenteritis, food poisoning, systemic infection, ATB use, toxic ingestion, hyperthyroidism
  G. Etiologies of chronic diarrhea by age
    1. Infant: Postinfectious secondary lactase deficiency, cow's milk intolerance, soy milk intolerance, celiac disease, cystic fibrosis, secretory tumors, familial villous atrophy, and primary immune defects
    2. Child: IBS, IBD, celiac disease, lactose intolerance, giardiasis, laxative abuse (adolescents), AIDS enteropathy, immune defects, secretory tumors, pseudo-obstruction, and factitious diarrhea

III. HISTORY
  A. Chief complaint and associated symptoms (vomiting, tenesmus, malaise/lethargy, fever, weight loss, abdominal pain)
  B. Frequency and character of stool (blood, pus, watery, foamy)
  C. Onset and duration of illness
  D. Dietary history (e.g., poorly cooked meat), well water vs. city water
  E. Hydration status: Urine output, tears with cry, ability to take PO fluids/food
  F. Travel history and exposures (day care center, sibling with diarrhea, etc.)
  G. Developmental history
  H. Medications, past medical history, family history (IBD, IBS, etc.)

IV. PHYSICAL EXAM
  A. General: Fever, irritability, height, weight, growth charts, mental status
  B. Hydration status: Tears with cry, capillary refill, dry mucous membranes
  C. GI/GU: Blood or pus in stool, vomiting, urine output
  D. Skin: Rash, skin turgor

Assessment of Dehydration			
Variable	Mild, 3% - 5%	Moderate, 6% - 9%	Severe, ≥ 10%
Blood pressure	Normal	Normal	Normal to reduced
Quality of pulses	Normal	Normal or slightly decreased	Moderately decreased
Heart rate	Normal	Increased	Increased†
Skin turgor	Normal	Decreased	Decreased
Fontanelle	Normal	Sunken	Sunken
Mucous membranes	Slightly dry	Dry	Dry
Eyes	Normal	Sunken orbits	Deeply sunken orbits
Extremities	Warm, normal capillary refill	Delayed capillary refill	Cool, mottled
Mental status	Normal	Normal to listless	Normal to lethargic or comatose
Urine output	Slightly decreased	<1 mL/kg/h	<1 mL/kg/h
Thirst	Slightly increased	Moderately increased	Very thirsty or too lethargic to indicate

†Bradycardia may appear in severe cases.

Source: American Academy of Pediatrics, Provisional Committee on Quality Improvement Subcommittee on Acute Gastro-enteritis. The management of acute gastroenteritis in young children. Pediatrics 1996;97(3):424–35. Adapted from Duggan C, et al. The management of acute diarrhea in children; oral rehydration, maintenance, and nutritional therapy. MMWR 1992;41(RR-16). © 1996 by the American Academy of Pediatrics. Used with permission.

V. EVALUATION: Not usually indicated with acute diarrhea and minimal or moderate dehydration

  A. Stool studies

    1. Reducing substances: Seen with lactose intolerance

    2. Occult blood, fecal leukocytes

    3. Stool cultures (e.g., *E. coli* 0157:H7): Consider if high likelihood of bacterial etiology (i.e. blood in stool, toxic appearance, high fever)

    4. Ova and parasite exam (O&P) or stool antigen for Giardia. Diarrhea usually occurs > 10 days

    5. *Salmonella, Shigella, Campylobacter, Yersinia (S,S,Y,C), Clostridiium difficile toxin (C. diff)*

    6. Rotazyme, pH

  B. Laboratory studies: Obtain in moderately dehydrated patients with inconsistent history and in all severely dehydrated patients

    1. Electrolytes: Consider measuring with severe dehydration

    2. CBC with differential

    3. Total protein, albumin, liver function tests if clinically indicated

VI. MANAGEMENT: See algorithm below

  A. Estimate degree of dehydration (see table in IV.)

  B. Rehydration

    1. Minimal or mild dehydration: Rehydration can usually be accomplished with oral rehydration therapy (ORT), e.g., **WHO-ORS, Pedialyte**, etc. Calculate fluid deficit and replace

    2. Moderate dehydration: May attempt to give PO replacement with ORT (above), and if unsuccessful, then proceed to IV fluid replacement

    3. Severe dehydration: IV fluid replacement with normal saline (NS) or **Ringer's Lactate (LR)**—10–20mL/kg bolus every hr until circulatory status is restored, then oral rehydration solution (ORT)

    4. If the patient is vomiting, then attempt to give small quantities frequently (5cc every 2–3 minutes) and if unsuccessful, consider antiemetics (Phenergan or Tigan rectal suppositories)

    5. If serum sodium is > 150, then replace the deficit over 12hrs to prevent seizures

CALCULATION OF MAINTENANCE FLUID REQUIREMENTS	
Body weight (kilograms)	Milliliters water/kilogram
3-10	100
11-20	50
> 20	20

C. Dietary management
1. Continue breast-feeding
2. Early re-feeding (within 4hrs of rehydration) with milk or food. This may reduce the duration of diarrhea by about half a day and is recommended by the AAP to restore nutritional balance. It does not prolong diarrhea

D. Symptomatic medications:
Usually symptomatic meds are not indicated since rehydration is the most important therapy. AAP practice guidelines for acute gastroenteritis recommend against antiemetics or antidiarrheal agents

E. Prevention:
Good hygiene is the most effective intervention

MANAGEMENT OF ACUTE GASTROENTERITIS IN YOUNG CHILDREN
Rehydration and Refeeding Algorithm

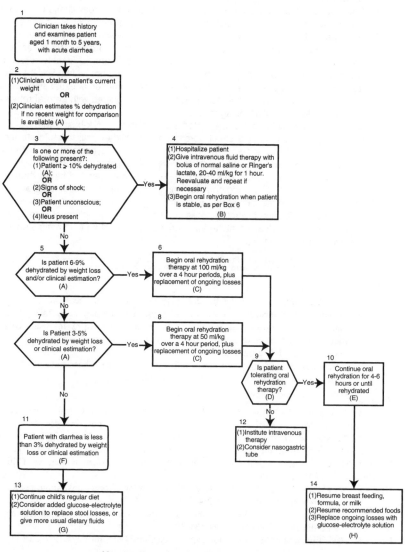

(Annotations for algorithm on next page)

A. See Table, Assessment of Dehydration, Section IV. above

B. Restoration of cardiovascular stability is critical and is accomplished by giving bolus IV therapy with normal saline or Ringer's lactate solution (see text). In the patient who does not respond, consider the possibility of an underlying disorder, such as myocarditis, myocardiopathy, pericarditis, septic shock, or toxic shock syndrome. When the patient is in stable condition and has achieved satisfactory mental status, ORT can be used according to the ORT guidelines

C. Solutions containing 45 to 90mmol/L sodium should be given in a volume of 100mL/kg for moderate dehydration and 50mL/kg for mild dehydration. Giving the child these volumes requires patience and persistence, and progress must be monitored frequently.

D. Intractable, severe vomiting, unconsciousness, and ileus are contraindications to ORT. Persistent refusal to drink may require a trial of IV therapy.

E. The rehydration phrase usually can be completed in 4hrs; reevaluation should occur every 1 to 2hrs. See text for guidance to decide when rehydration has been achieved.

F. The type and intensity of therapy will vary with the individual clinical situation.

G. Often, a child has diarrhea but remains adequately hydrated. The parent can be reassured but should be taught to assess hydration and to identify a worsening condition. If the stool output remains modest, ORT might not be required if early, age-appropriate feeding is instituted and increased consumption of usual dietary fluids is encouraged. More significant stool looses can be replaced with an oral rehydrating solution at the rate of 10mL/kg for each stool.

H. Breastfeeding should be resumed. Nonlactose formula, milk-based formula, or milk may be given, although a small percentage of children will not tolerate lactose-containing fluids. Lactose-containing solutions seem to be tolerated better when combined with complex carbohydrates in weaned children. Children who are eating foods may resume eating, although certain foods are tolerated better than others. Recommended foods include complex carbohydrates (rice, wheat, potatoes, bread, and cereals), lean meats, yogurt, fruits, and vegetables. Avoid fatty foods and foods high in simple sugars (including juices and soft drinks). Supplement feeding with an oral electrolyte solution, 10mL/kg for each diarrheal stool and the estimated amount vomited for each emesis.

Source: American Academy of Pediatrics. Practice parameter: The management of acute gastroenteritis in young children. Pediatrics 1996;97:424–35. Used with permission. www.aap.org/policy/gastro.htm

CLINICAL PEARLS

- In the US, children < 5 have 1.3–2.3 episodes of acute diarrhea/year
- Rotavirus has an incubation period of 1–3 days. Vomiting may occur for up to 3 days, and watery diarrhea for up to 8 days. May be accompanied by fever and URI signs
- Adenovirus causes more prolonged diarrhea than rotavirus. Norwalk virus usually occurs in epidemic outbreaks
- Children who are dehydrated rarely refuse ORT, whereas those not dehydrated will often refuse secondary to the salty taste of ORT

References

American Academy of Pediatrics. Practice Guideline: The management of acute gastroenteritis in young children. Pediatrics 1996;97:424–35, www.aap.org/policy/gastro.htm

Burkhart DM. Management of acute gastroenteritis in children. Am Fam Phys 1999;60:2555–66.

Leung A, et al. Evaluating the child with chronic diarrhea. Am Fam Prac 1996;53:611.

Guerrant RL, et al. Practice guidelines for the management of infectious diarrhea. Clin Infect Dis Feb 1, 2001;32:33–48.

Duggan C, et al. The management of acute diarrhea in children: oral rehydration, maintenance, and nutritional therapy. MMWR 1992;4 (RR-16):1–20.

Duggan C, Nurko S. "Feeding the gut": the scientific basis for continued enteral nutrition during acute diarrhea. J Pediatr 1997;131:801–8.

Leung A, et al. Evaluating the child with chronic diarrhea. Am Fam Phys 1996;53:611.

13. CONSTIPATION IN CHILDREN

I. INTRODUCTION

A. Definition: Delay or difficulty in defecation present for > 2 weeks which causes distress to patient

B. Normal number of stools in infants is 5/week to 40/week (3/day in breast fed and 2/day in bottle fed) and in children > 3yrs is 3–14/week

C. Approximately 3% of pediatric visits are related to defecation disorder complaints

D. In children the most common cause is functional (idiopathic/functional fecal retention/withholding) constipation

II. HISTORY

A. What family means by constipation (frequency, consistency, size, painful BM), duration of symptoms, toilet training, encopresis, fecal soiling

B. Time after birth of first BM

C. Blood on toilet paper or in stool

D. Abdominal pain

E. Fever, nausea, vomiting, anorexia, weight loss (or poor weight gain)

F. Medications (current meds plus any meds used for constipation in the past)

G. Psychosocial (family dynamics, use of school bathrooms)

H. Other: Coarse hair, dry skin, or other symptoms of thyroid disease, cystic fibrosis, celiac disease

I. Family history of Hirschsprung disease, constipation

III. PHYSICAL EXAM

A. General appearance of infant/child, growth parameters

B. Abdomen: Distention, mass, hepatosplenomegaly

C. GU

    1. External exam of perineum and perianal area for perianal wink, sensation, fissures, dermatitis, abscess, fistula

    2. If indicated, perform digital rectal exam for anal tone, blood in stool, rectal size, fecal impaction

D. Back/spine: Dimple, tuft of hair

E. Neuro: Tone, strength, cremasteric reflex, DTRs

IV. EVALUATION AND MANAGEMENT OF INFANTS < 1 YEAR

A. Those with a normal history and physical exam and no red flags (fever, vomiting, bloody diarrhea, failure to thrive, anal stenosis, tight empty rectum, impaction or distention, delayed passage of meconium) may be managed for functional constipation with dietary modification or meds (lactulose or sorbitol, malt extract, corn syrup or occasional glycerine suppositories). If any red flags are present, then obtain consultation with pediatric gastroenterologist

    1. Malt Soup Extract (**Maltsupex**)

        a. Breast-fed infant: 1–2 tsp in 2–4 oz of water or juice BID

        b. Bottle-fed infant: 1–2 tsp with every other feeding × 3–4 days, then 1–2 tsp QD

    2. Dioctyl Sodium Sulfosuccinate (**Colace**): ½ tsp PO BID

V. EVALUATION AND MANAGEMENT OF INFANTS > 1 YEAR

A. General

1. Treat impaction if present with oral meds (mineral oil, polyethylene glycol electrolyte solutions), or rectal disimpaction (phosphate soda, saline, or mineral oil enemas). May also try glycerine suppositories in infants and bisacodyl suppositories in children
2. Dietary modification (increase fluids, fruit juices, balanced diet)
3. Oral maintenance med including mineral oil, magnesium hydroxide, lactulose or sorbitol or combination of 2. Wean after having regular BMs for several months
4. Parental education and behavioral modification including regular toileting. May keep stool diary with reward system

Management of children >1yr. with constipation

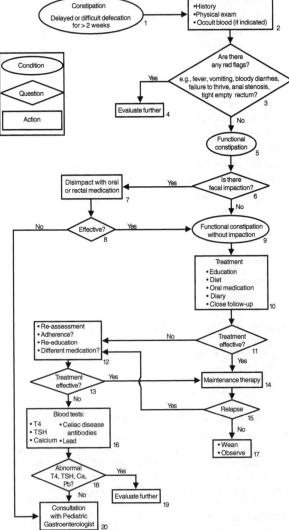

Source: North American Society for Pediatric Gastroenterology and Nutrition Position Statement. Constipation in infants and children: Evaluation and treatment. J Pediatric Gastroenterol Nutr 1999;29:612. © 1999 Lippincott-Raven Publishers. Used with permission.

B. Medications

Medications for Use in Treatment of Constipation			
Laxatives		**Dosage**	**Side Effects**
Osmotic	Lactulose or Sorbitol	1-3 mL/kg/day in divided doses	Abdomen cramps, flatulence
	Barley malt extract*	2-10 mL/240 mL of milk or juice	Bloating, flatulence
	Magnesium hydroxide*	> 1 year of age: 1-3 mL/kg/day of 400 mg/5 mL 2-5 years – 5-15 mL/d 6-14 years – 15-30 mL/d Available as liquid, 400 mg/5 mL, 800 mg/5 mL and tablets	Magnesium toxicity, dehydration, abdominal cramps
	Magnesium citrate*	1-6 years – 1-3 mL/kg/day as QD 6-12 years – 100-150 mL/day > 12 years – 150-300 mL/day Single or divided doses	Magnesium toxicity, dehydration, abdominal cramps
Osmotic Enema	Phosphate enemas	≥ 2 years old: 6 mL/kg up to 135 mL	Abdominal distention, vomiting
Lubricant	Mineral oil*	< 1 year old: not recommended Disimpaction: 15-30 mL/year of age, up to 240 mL daily Maintenance: 1-3 mL/kg/day	Foreign body reaction in intestinal mucosa
Stimulants	Senna	2-6 years old: 2.5-7.5 mL/day 6-12 years old: 5-15 mL/day	N/V, abdominal cramps
	Bisacodyl	≥ 2 years old: 0.5-1 suppository, 1-2 tablets per dose Available in 5 mg tablets and 10 mg suppositories	Rectal irritation, abdominal pain, bloating
	Glycerin suppositories	< 6 years – 1 infant supp > 6 years – 1 adult supp	Rectal irritation, abdominal pain, bloating

*Adjust dose to induce a daily bowel movement for 1-2 months

Source: North American Society for Pediatric Gastroenterology and Nutrition Position Statement. Constipation in infants and children: Evaluation and treatment. J Pediatric Gastroenterol Nutr 1999;29:612–626. © 1999 Lippincott-Raven Publishers. Used with permission. www. naspghan.org/PDF/constipation.pdf

VI. HIRSCHSPRUNG DISEASE

A. Lack of ganglion cells in distal colon which results in sustained contraction and dilation of bowel in segment proximal to aganglionic segment (due to distal obstruction)

B. Occurs in 1/5,000 births, often associated with trisomy 21

C. Mean age of diagnosis is 2½ months, but 8–20% are diagnosed after age 3

D. Symptoms may include bilious vomiting, abdominal distension, and refusal to feed

E. Approximately 90% of normal infants pass meconium in the first 24hrs of life compared to less than 10% of patients with Hirschsprung disease

F. May present later in childhood with "short segment" Hirschsprung disease

G. Enterocolitis is most serious complication with a mortality of 20% and symptoms including sudden onset of fever, abdominal distension, and bloody diarrhea (which may be explosive)

H. Diagnosis through rectal manometry and rectal biopsy

CLINICAL PEARLS

- Soapsuds, tap water, and magnesium enemas are not recommended for rectal disimpaction
- In children with constipation refractory to treatment, consider Hirschsprung disease
- Risk factors for developing chronic constipation: acute constipation, painful defecation, or harsh or too early toilet training

References

North American Society for Pediatric Gastroenterology and Nutrition Position Statement. Constipation in infants and children: evaluation and treatment. J Pediatric Gastro Nutrition 1999;29:612.

Hyams JS, et al. Effect of infant formula on stool characteristics of young infants. Pediatrics 1995;95:50–4.

Partin PE, et al. Painful defecation and fecal soiling in children. Pediatrics 1992;89:1007–9.

14. Urinary Tract Infections In Children

I. TWO MONTHS TO TWO YEARS OF AGE (For evaluation of infants younger than 2 months with fever, see Chapter 6, Fever without a Source in Infants. For children older than 2yrs, see II. below)

A. Prevalence of UTI
  1. Approximately 5%
  2. Prevalence in girls is more than twice that in boys
  3. Rate in uncircumcised boys may be between 5–20 times higher than in circumcised boys

B. Risk of Undiagnosed UTI
  1. Incidence of vesicoureteral reflux (VUR) is much higher in age group < 2yrs; thus, this group is at much higher risk for incurring renal injury. Severity of VUR is greater in infants. Severe form (intrarenal reflux) is limited to infants
  2. Initial UTI may bring to attention obstructive congenital anomalies also
  3. Delay in instituting treatment for UTI, especially acute pyelonephritis, increases the risk of kidney damage
  4. Risk of renal damage increases with the number of UTI recurrences

C. Etiology
  1. Gram-negative rods, especially *E. coli*
  2. *Lactobacillus* species, coag.-negative staphylococci, and *Corynebacterium* species are not considered clinically relevant in the otherwise healthy infant/child. If the child has recurrent UTIs or has had instrumentation recently, consider coag.-neg. staph or enterococcus

D. History
  1. Clinical symptoms (dysuria, frequency) may be absent, but may include a history of fever, crying on urination, foul-smelling urine, or an altered voiding pattern
  2. Ask about nonspecific findings of increased irritability, vomiting, diarrhea or constipation

E. Physical exam
  1. Vital signs including rectal temperature
  2. Degree of toxicity and dehydration
  3. Irritability

F. Lab/evaluation
  1. Determining a diagnosis of UTI in children is similar to that in adults and relies mostly on an evaluation of the urine. The most reliable specimen is a transurethral cath specimen, but if time allows, a bag specimen may be attempted first and if normal then a UTI is excluded (see below)
  2. A culture should be done on children with a temp > 102.2° F in all boys < 6 months and girls < 2yrs old and for patients who are toxic appearing. Culture should also be done on children with recurrent UTIs, children who have recently been treated, or those with treatment failure
  3. A colony count on a cath specimen > 10^3 of any bacteria is likely to be true infection. A count > 10^5 on a mid stream collection is likely to be a true infection. Contaminant is suggested by multiple organisms
  4. If the patient is assessed as being sufficiently ill (dehydrated, unable to maintain oral intake, toxic-appearing) to warrant ATB therapy +/- hospitalization, then a urine specimen should be obtained by *transurethral* catheterization

Sensitivity and Specificity of Components of the Urinalysis, Alone and in Combination		
Test	**Sensitivity % (Range)**	**Specificity % (Range)**
Leukocyte esterase	83 (67–94)	78 (64–92)
Nitrite	53 (15–82)	98 (90–100)
Leukocyte esterase *or* nitrite positive	93 (90–100)	72 (58–91)
Microscopy: WBCs	73 (32–100)	81 (45–98)
Microscopy: bacteria	81 (16–99)	83 (11–100)
Leukocyte esterase *or* nitrite *or* microscopy positive	99.8 (99–100)	70 (60–92)

From: American Academy of Pediatrics, Practice Guideline. The diagnosis, treatment, and evaluation of the initial urinary tract infection in febrile infants and young children (AC9830). Pediatrics 1999:103; 843–52. With permission from Elsevier.

G. Treatment
1. If the patient is assessed as toxic/dehydrated/unable to maintain PO intake, initial therapy should be parenteral and the patient should be hospitalized
2. In the non-toxic child with a positive urinalysis or urine culture:
   a. **TMP/SMX (Bactrim):** 8mg TMP, 40 mg SMX/kg/day divided BID
   b. **Cephalexin (Keflex):** 50–100mg/kg/day divided QID
   c. **Sulfisoxazole:** 120–150 mg/kg/day divided QID
   d. **Cefixime (Suprax):** 8 mg/kg/day in divided BID
   e. **Cefpodoxime (Vantin):** 10 mg/kg/day divided BID
   f. **Loracarbef (Lorabid):** 15–30 mg/kg/day in divided BID
3. If the expected response does not occur in 2 days, the child should be re-evaluated and another urine specimen should be cultured
4. Data show that a 7–14 day course is adequate to eliminate UTI (less than 7 days of therapy in children has been shown to be inadequate)

H. Prophylaxis:
After a 7–14 day course of ATB, infants and young children with UTI should receive prophylactic ATBs until imaging studies are complete (to minimize risk of renal scarring due to recurrence—this risk is highest during the first months after UTI)
1. **TMP/SMX (Bactrim)**: 2mg TMP, 10mg SMX/kg as single bedtime dose or 5mg TMP, 25mg SMX/kg twice/week
2. **Nitrofurantoin (Macrobid)**: 1–2mg/kg as single daily dose
3. **Sulfisoxazole**: 10–20mg/kg divided BID
4. **Nalidixic Acid**: 30mg/kg divided BID

I. Evaluation
1. UTIs in infants and young children serve as markers for abnormalities of the urinary tract. Imaging of the urinary tract is recommended in every febrile infant and young child with a first UTI
2. Ultrasound of kidneys and bladder
   a. Should be done promptly in patients who do not respond within 2 days of ATB therapy. Can be delayed in children responding to treatment
   b. A normal ultrasound does not exclude VUR
3. Voiding cystourethrography (VCUG)
   a. Will detect vesicoureteral reflux. Grades of severity are recognized (I–V)
   b. Child should be free of infection at time of this study to avoid bladder irritability (see H. Prophylaxis section above)

II. GREATER THAN 2YRS OF AGE
A. Diagnosis may be simpler as the child may be able to localize symptoms to the urinary tract as well as provide a clean-catch specimen
B. Children in this age group are much less likely to have factors predisposing them to renal damage and are at lower risk of developing renal damage

C. In all patients < 5yrs and in boys > 5yrs diagnostic imaging with ultrasound and voiding cystourethrogram should be considered. Further management is dictated by findings on diagnostic imaging and clinical course

D. In girls > 5yrs with no systemic signs, diagnostic imaging is not necessary with the first UTI, but may be indicated in cases of recurrent UTI

CLINICAL PEARLS

- Between 1–2yrs, the prevalence of UTIs in febrile girls is 8.1% and in boys is 1.9%
- Treatment of asymptomatic bacteriuria is controversial, but some studies have indicated that the risk of renal scarring is low and that treatment does not decrease the risk of UTI recurrence
- Recurrent UTI is 2 UTIs over a 6 month period. It is important to determine if a subsequent UTI is a recurrence or an inadequately treated initial UTI

References

Bulloch B, et al. Can urine clarity exclude the diagnosis of urinary tract infection? Pediatrics 2000; 106(5):e60.

American Academy of Pediatrics, Practice Guideline. The diagnosis, treatment, and evaluation of the initial urinary tract infection in febrile infants and young children (AC9830). Pediatrics 1999:103; 843–52.

Ahmed SM, Swedlund S. Evaluation and treatment of urinary tract infections in children. Am Fam Phys 1998;57:1573.

Kramer MS, et al. Urine testing in young febrile children: a risk-benefit analysis. J Pediatr 1994;125:6–13.

Michael Martin, MD
Michael B. Weinstock, MD

15. ENURESIS

I. DEFINITIONS

A. Involuntary or intentional loss of urine into bedclothes or undergarments after age 5, without medical or medication causes

B. Primary enuresis refers to a failure to ever achieve bladder control. Primary nocturnal enuresis accounts for 90% of all causes of enuresis and is 3 times as common in boys

C. Secondary enuresis refers to a return to incontinence after bladder control was previously achieved and is usually associated with psychological stressors (after birth of a sibling, significant loss or family discord), anxiety, or psychiatric disorders

II. ETIOLOGY: Probably multi-factorial; maturational delay of sleep and arousal mechanisms, delay in development of increased bladder capacity, and heredity (see clinical pearls)

III. HISTORY

A. **Type and severity:** Determine if the episodes of enuresis are nocturnal (nighttime), diurnal (daytime), mixed (day and night) and primary or secondary. Determine number of enuretic nights per week, the number of episodes per night, and the amount voided with each episode

B. **Voiding history:** Weak urinary stream, urgency, infrequent voiding, previous UTI, encopresis, constipation

C. Evaluation for other conditions which may cause enuresis including diabetes, constipation, seizure disorders, neurologic disorders, UTIs

D. **Family history:** Enuresis or urinary tract abnormalities

IV. PHYSICAL

A. Neurologic: Complete neurological exam

B. Spinal cord pathology: Inspect back for evidence of sacral dimpling or cutaneous abnormalities suggesting spinal pathology

C. Abdominal and genital exam

V. LABORATORY EVALUATION

A. Urinalysis and urine culture to exclude renal, metabolic, and infectious pathology

B. If indicated, consider a renal sonogram, a voiding cystourethrogram, and spine films (if spinal pathology is suspected on history and physical)

VI. TREATMENT FOR PRIMARY NOCTURNAL ENURESIS

A. Reassurance: Family education and motivation are important to resolution. Inform parents and child that enuresis is a developmental lag and not indicative of an emotional problem and will be outgrown even without treatment. Enuresis is no one's fault and the child should not be punished for bed wetting

B. Combinations of treatment options are most effective

C. Options include:

1. Alarm System: Often used as first line in combination with **Imipramine** or **Desmopressin**. Fairly inexpensive ($50–70) with a success rate of 70% and a relapse rate of 30%

2. **Imipramine:** 1–2.5mg/kg orally at bedtime. There is a high relapse rate, therefore, consider use when a short period of dryness is important (overnight visits or camp). ECG monitoring at baseline and during chronic therapy has been recommended

3. **Desmopressin (DDAVP):** 20–40 mcg (1–2 puffs) intranasally or 0.2–0.6mg (1–3 tabs) orally at bed time. Effective for short term control in 50% as long as treatment is continued

4. **Oxybutynin (Ditropan):** Rarely beneficial

5. Bladder stretching: Child is instructed to withhold voiding for increasing amounts of time each day after an oral fluid load. Limited evidence to support use

6. Charting: Child keeps a chart of wet and dry nights and is given rewards for dry nights

7. Treat constipation

8. Evening fluid restriction: Limited evidence to support use

CLINICAL PEARLS

- Incidence of primary nocturnal enuresis at ages 5, 10, and 14 is 15%, 3–5%, and 1% respectively
- Primary nocturnal enuresis accounts for approximately 80% of all cases of enuresis
- Spontaneous remission occurs at about 15% per year
- 70% of children in whom both parents were enuretic will also be enuretic

References

Evans JH. Nocturnal enuresis. West J Med Aug 2001;175:108–11.

Cendron M. Primary nocturnal enuresis: current concepts. Am Fam Phys 1999;56:1205.

Ullol-Minnich MR. Diagnosis and management of nocturnal enuresis. Am Fam Phys 1996;54:2259.

Robson WLM, Leung AKC. Advising parents on toilet training. Am Fam Phys 1991;44:1263.

Daniel M. Neides, MD
Steve Markovich, MD
Beth Weinstock, MD

16. RASHES IN CHILDREN

I. MACULOPAPULAR EXANTHEMS

A. Measles (Rubeola) Low incidence due to immunization

1. Incubation: 10–14 days
2. Prodrome: Cough, coryza, conjunctivitis, 3 days high fever; child appears toxic
3. Exanthem: Fever peaks when rash appears: Erythematous macules and papules appear on upper neck and face, then begin to progress down to extremities and become confluent. Petechial eruption may appear on the soft palate 1–2 days before rash followed by Koplik's spots (blue-white macules with surrounding erythema found on the buccal mucosa adjacent to the second molars). Rash co-exists with fever and leukopenia and lasts 7–10 days
4. Lab: Measles IgM antibody at least 3 days after onset of rash
5. Complications: Pneumonia, encephalitis, (1 in 2000), otitis media, thrombocytopenia, hemorrhagic measles, pneumothorax, hepatitis
6. Management: Supportive

B. Rubella

1. Incubation: 14–21 days
2. Prodrome: Nonspecific respiratory symptoms and lymphadenopathy (postauricular, suboccipital)
3. Exanthem: Pink, begins on face and progresses downward, lasts 2–3 days, and fades in reverse direction
4. Complications: Arthritis common in women after 2–3 days of illness (knee, wrist, finger), encephalitis, thrombocytopenia
5. Virus can be isolated from throat or urine up to 2 weeks after onset of rash
6. Management: Supportive—isolate patient from pregnant women (virus is highly teratogenic if exposure occurs in first trimester)

C. Erythema infectiosum (*fifth disease*—Parvovirus B19)

1. Incubation: 7–14 days, occurs in winter-spring epidemics in school-age children
2. Prodrome: None
3. Exanthem:
   Stage I. Red-flushed cheeks with circumoral pallor (slapped cheek)
   Stage II. Maculopapular eruption on proximal extensor surfaces of extremities spreads distally and often to trunk, neck and buttocks. Palms and soles are spared (lacelike)
4. Complications: Arthritis, aplastic crisis
5. Management: Supportive

D. Roseola (Human herpes virus—Type 6): Occurs in children age 6 months to 3 years

1. Incubation: 10–14 days
2. Prodrome: 3–4 days of high fever which precedes rash; child looks great despite fever
3. Exanthem: Macules with secondary erythema which appear when fever breaks. Initially seen on chest, it spreads to involve face and extremities. Lymphadenopathy may be present (suboccipitally)
4. Complications: Febrile seizures
5. Management: Supportive

E. Scarlet fever (Group A B-hemolytic streptococci)

1. Incubation: 2–4 days. Follows pharyngitis or skin infection
2. Prodrome: 1–2 days of fever, vomiting, sore throat; toxic appearing
3. Exanthem: Erythematous, sandpaper texture; starts on neck, axillae, inguinal areas and then spreads to rest of body. Petechiae in antecubital and axillary skin folds (Pastia's Lines) are helpful in making diagnosis. Lasts 7 days and then desquamates. Can also see red strawberry tongue

4. Complications: Rheumatic fever, acute glomerulonephritis
5. Management: Penicillin—see Chapter 9, Pharyngitis, for dosage information

F. Hand, foot and mouth disease (enteroviruses: Coxsackie virus a16, a5, and a10)
  1. Incubation: 4–6 days (exposure through enteric route; oral-oral or fecal-oral)
  2. Prodrome: Low-grade temperature, sore throat, malaise, lymphadenopathy
  3. Exanthem: Aphthae-like lesions anywhere in the mouth followed by 3–7mm red macules on palms and soles. These develop into cloudy vesicles with red halos. Can also see mild peri-orbital edema
  4. Complications: None
  5. Management: Supportive including viscous **Lidocaine** and **Diphenhydramine elixir** —both swish and spit

G. Kawasaki's disease (Mucocutaneous lymph node syndrome)
  1. Incubation: Unknown
  2. Prodrome: Abrupt, high spiking fever (101–104°F), unresponsive to antipyretics. Occasionally diarrhea, cough or abdominal pain
  3. Exanthem: Within 3 days of fever
     a. Bilateral bulbar conjunctival congestion
     b. Erythematous mouth and pharynx with strawberry tongue and red, cracked lips
     c. Edema of the hands and feet with erythema of the palms and soles
     c. Cervical lymphadenopathy
     d. Generalized rash that can be morbilliform, maculopapular, scarlatiniform or may resemble erythema multiform
  4. Complications: Arthritis, meningitis, coronary, aneurysm (20–25%)
  5. Management: Supportive care, detection of coronary disease and anti-inflammatories (IVIG and Aspirin). Hospital admission

H. Lyme disease
  1. Etiology: Vector-borne illness caused by spirochete *Borrelia burgdorferi*, transmitted by bite of *Ixodes scapularis* tick (deer tick)—size of pin head
  2. Prodrome: Erythema migraines develop in about 80% of patients with disease and appear 2–20 days after bite. May be accompanied by fever, chills, myalgia, headaches, arthralgia
  3. Exanthem: Appears at site of inoculation as enlarging erythematous macular rash with central clearing
  4. Complications: Secondary and tertiary illness may involve facial palsy, chronic arthritis, myocarditis, axonal polyneuropathy, and encephalopathy
  5. Management: ATBs are only recommended with infection and include Doxycycline (not recommended for children < 8yr), Amoxicillin, and Cefuroxime. One recent study did show benefit with preventive treatment for Lyme disease, but only after the patient presented for treatment after removing Ixodes tick from body within previous 72hrs

II. VESICULAR EXANTHEM

A. Chickenpox (varicella zoster virus)
  1. Incubation: 10–20 days
  2. Prodrome: Malaise; low grade fever
  3. Exanthem: Develops over 3–6 day period usually starting along hairline of face; each lesion begins as a macule that progresses to a papule and vesicle and finally a crusted vesicle; rash emerges in crops over the trunk and finally the extremities; lesions in different stages are present throughout the first week
  4. Complications: Bacterial infection of vesicular lesions, pneumonia, hepatitis, arthritis, glomerulonephritis, CNS disease
  5. Management
     a. Cut patient's fingernails short to prevent scratching and secondary infection
     b. Wash lesions BID with soap and water
     c. **Benadryl,** cold washcloth or oatmeal baths (Aveeno bath) will help decrease itching
     d. **Acyclovir (Zovirax)** can be used for high risk patients (immunocompromised)
     e. **Varicella zoster immune globulin (VZIG)** is available for patients at risk for developing progressive chickenpox (immunocompromised patients)

B. Rhus dermatitis (poison ivy)—See Chapter 91, Contact Dermatitis

III. PETECHIAL RASH

A. Meningococcemia

1. Etiology: Meningococci are gram-negative organisms which contain endotoxins in their cell walls
2. Prodrome: Cough, headache, sore throat, nausea, vomiting (all may be of very short duration prior to rash appearing). Patient usually appears toxic
3. Rash: May be maculopapular in early stages. Purpura and petechiae are seen over the extremities and trunk
4. Complications: Acute purulent meningitis, DIC, septic arthritis, pericarditis
5. Differential: H. flu, pneumococcus, enterovirus, rickettsial disease, Henoch-Schonlein purpura, and blood dyscrasias can all cause a similar petechial rash
6. All children who are ill-appearing and febrile with a petechial rash should be hospitalized until meningococcemia is ruled-out

B. Rocky Mountain Spotted Fever

1. Incubation: 3–12 days after tick bite
2. Etiology: Tick-borne illness caused by Rickettsia rickettsii. Dogs and rodents are reservoirs. Transmission requires tick attachment for greater than 6hrs; occurs most commonly along eastern seaboard, Oklahoma, Arkansas, Texas
3. Prodrome: High fever, severe headache, myalgia, shaking rigor, photophobia, nausea
4. Exanthem: Typically develops around fourth day of illness. Begins as pink macules on wrists, forearms, ankles, palms, and soles, and then spreads centrally within 6–18hrs to arms, thighs, trunk, and face. Within 2–4 days, lesions become petechial
5. Complications: Splenomegaly, conjunctivitis, edema, irritability, and confusion. Mortality rate is 5–7% due to severe vasculitis
6. Treatment: **Chloramphenicol** (> 8yrs) or **Doxycycline** (preferable for older children) is mainstay of treatment

CLINICAL PEARLS

- VZV vaccine if used within 3–5 days postexposure of household or hospital contact may abort infection and reduce symptoms
- The management of most rashes in children is supportive—rule out the "life threatening" causes of rashes with a thorough history and physical exam
- Most petechial rashes are caused by viruses
- Risk of Lyme disease transmission is small with ticks attached < 48hrs, and significantly increases with attachment > 72hrs

References

Nadelman RB, et al. Prophylaxis with single-dose doxycycline for the prevention of Lyme Disease after an *Ixodes Scapularis* tick bite. N Engl J Med 2001;345(2):79–84.

McKinnon HD, Howard T. Evaluating the febrile patient with a rash. Am Fam Phys 2000;62:804–16.

Centers for Disease Control and Prevention. Measles, mumps, and rubella—vaccine use and strategies for elimination of measles, rubella, and congenital rubella syndrome and control of mumps. MMWR 1998;47(RR-8):24.

Nelson, DG, et al. Evaluation of febrile children with petechial rashes: is there consensus among pediatricians? Ped Infect Dis J 1998;17:1135.

American Academy of Pediatrics. 1997 Red book: Report of the Committee on Infectious Diseases. 24th ed. Elk Grove Village, IL: Am Acad Ped 1997.

Daniel M. Neides, MD
Christina Costanzo, MD

17. ATTENTION DEFICIT HYPERACTIVITY DISORDER (ADHD)

DEFINITION: A behavior problem characterized by inattention, hyperactivity, and impulsivity. **Note:** *Recommendations apply to patients 6–12yrs*

I. INTRODUCTION
   A. Prevalence 8–10% of school-aged children
   B. Male to female ratio is 3:1
   C. Onset usually before age 4
   D. Etiology unknown but there is strong genetic component
   E. Increased risk for ADHD with fetal alcohol syndrome, fetal exposure to drugs of abuse, past brain injury, and AIDS
   F. ADHD occurs with developmental disorders, learning disabilities, speech and language delays, and with oppositional defiant disorder, conduct disorder, depression, and anxiety disorder
   G. Children may experience school difficulties, academic underachievement, troublesome interpersonal relationships with family members and peers, and low self-esteem which may continue into adolescence or adult life

II. HISTORY AND PHYSICAL EXAM
   A. History
   1. Specific description of behaviors with focus on inattention, hyperactivity, and impulsivity
   2. Emotional history: Irritability, temper tantrums, sleep problems
   3. Developmental milestones, hearing or visual problems
   4. History of abuse or neglect
   5. Parents' response to child's behavior
   6. Parent and teacher input may differ significantly. Seek input from other adults who supervise the child (child care, after school activities, etc.)
   7. Connors' Parent Rating Scale and Comprehensive Teacher Rating Scale will assess for conduct problems, learning problems, psychosomatic problems, hyperactivity, and anxiety
   8. Screening questions for other psychiatric conditions including oppositional defiant disorder (coexist in about 35%), conduct disorder (coexist in about 25%), mood disorders/depression (coexist in about 18%), anxiety (coexist about 25%), and learning disabilities (coexist 12–60%)
   B. Physical: Thorough physical exam including neurologic exam
   C. Lab: Generally lab studies are *not indicated* unless directed by the history or physical exam

III. DIAGNOSIS
   A. The AAP practice guideline for ADHD emphasizes these points for diagnosis
   1. Initiate evaluation in children 6–12yrs who present with inattention, hyperactivity, impulsivity, academic underachievement, or behavior problems
   2. Diagnose ADHD according to DMS-IV criteria
   3. Obtain evidence from parents or caregivers as well as teachers or other school professionals
   4. Assess for associated coexisting conditions
   5. Diagnostic tests are not routinely indicated but may be used to assess for coexisting conditions
   B. There are numerous rating scales including Connors' Parent and Teacher Rating Scales and Barkley's School Situations Questionnaire

C. DSM-IV criteria for diagnosis. **Note:** There are some limitations of the DSM-IV criteria as most of the development and testing was done in psychiatric settings and not in traditional ambulatory care. Clinicians using these criteria should apply them in the context of their clinical judgment

---

DSM-IV Diagnostic Criteria for ADHD

A. Either 1 or 2
1) Six (or more) of the following symptoms of inattention have persisted for at least 6 months to a degree that is maladaptive and inconsistent with developmental level:

Inattention
   a) Often fails to give close attention to details or makes careless mistakes in schoolwork, work, or other activities
   b) Often has difficulty sustaining attention in tasks or play activities
   c) Often does not seem to listen when spoken to directly
   d) Often does not follow through on instructions and fails to finish schoolwork, chores, or duties in the workplace (not due to oppositional behavior or failure to understand instructions)
   e) Often has difficulty organizing tasks and activities
   f) Often avoids, dislikes, or is reluctant to engage in tasks that require sustained mental effort (such as schoolwork or homework)
   g) Often loses things necessary for tasks or activities (eg, toys, school assignments, pencils, books, or tools)
   h) Is often easily distracted by extraneous stimuli
   i) Is often forgetful in daily activities
2) Six (or more) of the following symptoms of hyperactivity-impulsivity have persisted for at least 6 months to a degree that is maladaptive and inconsistent with developmental level:

Hyperactivity
   a) Often fidgets with hands or feet or squirms in seat
   b) Often leaves seat in classroom or in other situations in which remaining seated is expected
   c) Often runs about or climbs excessively in situations in which it is inappropriate (in adolescents or adults, may be limited to subjective feelings of restlessness)
   d) Often has difficulty playing or engaging in leisure activities quietly
   e) Is often "on the go" or often acts as if "driven by a motor"
   f) Often talks excessively

Impulsivity
   g) Often blurts out answers before questions have been completed
   h) Often has difficulty awaiting turn
   i) Often interrupts or intrudes on others (eg, butts into conversations or games)
B. Some hyperactive-impulsive or inattentive symptoms that caused impairment were present before 7 years of age.
C. Some impairment from the symptoms is present in 2 or more settings (eg, at school [or work] or at home).
D. There must be clear evidence of clinically significant impairment in social, academic, or occupational functioning.
E. The symptoms do not occur exclusively during the course of a pervasive developmental disorder, schizophrenia, or other psychotic disorder and are not better accounted for by another mental disorder (eg, mood disorder, anxiety disorder, dissociative disorder, or personality disorder).

Code based on type:
   314.01 Attention-Deficit/Hyperactivity Disorder, Combined Type: if both criteria A1 and A2 are met for the past 6 months
   314.00 Attention-Deficit/Hyperactivity Disorder, Predominantly Inattentive Type: if criterion A1 is met but criterion A2 is not met for the past 6 months
   314.01 Attention-Deficit/Hyperactivity Disorder, Predominantly Hyperactive, Impulsive Type: if criterion A2 is met but criterion A1 is not met for the past 6 months
   314.9 Attention-Deficit/Hyperactivity Disorder Not Otherwise Specified

---

IV. DIFFERENTIAL DIAGNOSIS OF ADHD

A. Dysfunctional family
   1. Acute family stressors: E.g., Divorce, death
   2. Poor parenting: Lack of limit setting, teen parents, parental depression, mental illness in parents
B. Learning disability: Performance several grade levels below expectations for age
C. Mental retardation or lower IQ
D. Hearing or visual disorder
E. Oppositional defiant disorder
F. Conduct disorder
G. Cognitive impairment from other disorders
   1. Lead Poisoning
   2. Medication reaction (Theophylline, Phenobarbital, antihistamines)
   3. Hypo- or hyper-thyroidism
   4. Seizure disorder
H. Childhood depression, obsessive compulsive disorder, anxiety, PTSD
I. Inappropriate parental expectations for normal developmental maturity
J. Tourette's syndrome

V. TREATMENT
A. Parental interventions
1. Rules and limits: Must be *consistent* and *firm* in enforcing them; consequences should be *predictable*
2. Environmental structure: Routines at home will help the child accept consistency
3. Reinforce positive behavior: One method involves a "token economy system" where the child earns tokens for good behavior, doing homework, finishing tasks, etc. and then trades in tokens for rewards
4. Set aside time each day where all of the attention is on child (reading or playing age appropriate games)
5. Provide a special place for doing homework that is quiet and free of distractions

B. Teacher interventions
1. Seat child in front of classroom
2. Allow child to move around occasionally by having him/her hand out papers or erase chalkboard
3. Keep instructions brief and clear
4. Give student positive reinforcement whenever possible
5. Weekly report will allow parents to monitor behavior

C. Medications
- 80% of ADHD patients who take psychostimulants (**Ritalin**, **Cylert**, and **Dexedrine**) show an improved response
- Adverse effects of the drugs include anorexia, sleep disturbances, irritability, dysphoria, headache, abdominal pain, and growth delay
- "Drug holidays" over weekends or school holidays are not recommended (especially if the child wants to participate in weekend activities). This area is controversial. Therapy should be individualized for child. Some may do fine on a drug holiday during playtime (summer vacation), while others may need continuous therapy.
- Repeat the behavior rating scale 2–4 weeks after initiating therapy to monitor efficacy
- Monitor for side effects at 2 month intervals initially. May decrease frequency of visits if child is stable (e.g., every 6 months)

1. **Methylphenidate (Ritalin):** 0.3–0.5mg/kg/dose
   a. Initially 5mg QD-BID. If started QD the first dose is usually in the morning. If BID, add the second dose at lunch
   b. May titrate in increments of 2.5–5.0mg. Keep on lowest dose to effect appropriate response while monitoring side effects. (Available 5, 10, 20mg scored tablets)
   c. Average dose is 20–30mg/day. Max dose 60mg/day
   d. Onset 20–60 minutes, peak 2hrs, duration of effect 3–6hrs
   e. Some children may need a mid-afternoon dose to concentrate on homework or extracurricular activities. If there is difficulty with sleeping, the last dose should not be taken after 6PM
   f. Side effects weight loss, elevated blood pressure, difficulty with sleep
   g. **Methylphenidate sustained release (Ritalin-SR** 20mg tabs, **Concerta** 18, 36, and 54mg tabs QD). Dose is the same as for immediate release preparation; may be combined with immediate release

2. **Dextroamphetamine Sulfate (Dexedrine, Dextrostat):** 0.15mg/kg/dose
   a. Available 5, 10mg. Dose range 5–40mg/day divided BID
   b. Alternative drug when **Ritalin** is not effective or side effects occur
   c. Usually given in the morning only but may be dosed BID
   d. Onset 20–60 minutes, peak 1–2hrs, duration of effect 4–6hrs
   e. High potential for *abuse*
   f. Side effects: Weight loss, HTN, difficulty with sleep
   g. Extended release **Dexedrine Spansules** 5, 10, 15mg QD-BID and **Adderall** 5, 10, 20, 30mg given QD–BID

3. **Pemoline (Cylert):** 0.5-2.5mg/kg/day (available 18.75, 37.5, 75mg tablets, and 37.5mg chewable tablets)
   a. May be administered in single morning dose usually starting with 18.75mg and may increase to BID. Dose range from 18.75–112.5mg/day

b. Onset 2hrs, steady state in 2–3 days, duration of effect 6–10hrs

c. Must monitor liver function tests

d. Side effects: Weight loss, difficulty with sleep, hepatic dysfunction

4. **Clonidine HCl (Catapres):** 4–5mcg/kg/day

   a. Start with 0.05mg in the evening (because of sedative properties)

   b. Increase by increments of 0.05mg on a weekly basis to a maximum of 0.3–0.4mg/day

   c. Usually dosed QID because of sedative properties

   d. Alternative drug in treating attention deficits (effective against hyperactivity impulsivity, and inattention)

   e. If discontinuing therapy, should be tapered down—never stop abruptly secondary to rebound HTN or cardiac dysfunction

5. **Tricyclic Antidepressants (Imipramine or Desipramine)**

   a. May be a third line of therapy if psychostimulants or **Clonidine** fail or produce undesirable side effects

   b. Both may be dosed 1–4 mg/kg/day usually divided BID (may be given QD)

   c. More appropriate for older adolescents or adults secondary to potential cardiovascular side effects

   d. Consider psychiatry referral

6. **Wellbutrin SR, Effexor SR:** Used at antidepressant doses

7. **Atomoxetine (Strattera):** 0.5–1.2mg/kg/d (available 10, 18, 25, 40, 60mg caps)

   a. Start at 0.5mg/kg/d, increase after a minimum of 3 days to 1.2mg/kg. Maximum 1.4mg/kg or 100mg

   b. Monitor growth, BP and HR

   c. Side effects: Dyspepsia, NIV, fatigue, decreased appetite, dizziness and mood swings

   d. Drug interactions: MAO inhibitors, CYPCD6 inhibitors (e.g., Paroxetine, Fluoxetine, Quinidine)

CLINICAL PEARLS

- Normal attention span is approximately 3–5 minutes per year of age
- Controlled studies have NOT shown that children with ADHD benefit from dietary control of sugar and other additives
- ADHD is a *clinical diagnosis* that requires integration of many factors. Meds should not be started simply to pacify the parents
- Recent studies have shown that untreated hyperactive boys showed a significantly higher rate of adult psychiatric problems including antisocial and drug abuse disorders

References

Clinical practice guideline: diagnosis and evaluation of the child with attention-deficit/hyperactivity disorder. Pediatrics 2000;105:1158–70. Available at: http://www.aap.org/policy/ac0002.html

Smucker WD, Hedayat M. Evaluation and treatment of ADHD. Am Fam Phys 2001;64:817–29,831–2.

Szymanski ML, Zolotor A. Attention-deficit/hyperactivity disorder: management. Am Fam Phys 2001;64:1355–62.

Jadad AR, et al. Treatment of attention-deficit/hyperactivity disorder. Rockville, MD: Agency for Healthcare Research and Quality, 1999; Evidence report/technology assessment No. 11 (prepared by McMaster University under contract 290-97–0017); AHRQ Pub. No. 00E005.

Goldman LS, et al. Diagnosis and treatment of attention-deficit/hyperactivity disorder in children and adolescents. JAMA 1998;279:1100–7.

II. Care of the Pregnant Patient & Breast-feeding

18. Prenatal Care 51

19. Medications During Pregnancy & Lactation 55

20. Questions Expecting Parents Commonly Ask/Radiation in Pregnancy 61

21. OB Admission Note 64

22. OB Delivery Note 65

23. Postpartum Discharge Instructions 65

24. Postpartum Checkup 66

Related subjects:

Infant Formula & Breast-feeding .... see Chapter 4

Radiation Exposure in Pregnancy, Table: Estimated fetal exposure of

various diagnostic imaging methods .... see Chapter 20

Beth Weinstock, MD
Bill Gegas, MD
Curt Gingrich, MD

18. PRENATAL CARE

(See table "Estimated fetal exposure for various diagnostic imaging methods,"
Chapter 20 Questions Expecting Parents Commonly Ask, V.)

I. SCHEDULE OF PRENATAL VISITS: Schedules vary by patient population and practitioner
    A. Pre-conception counseling: Ideally should be first visit. Patient should be given 400mcg **Folic Acid** supplementation to reduce the risk of neural tube defects. Rubella immunity should be checked and consideration of vaccination if not immune (patients should be counseled to not become pregnant for 3 months after receiving immunization)
    B. Every 4 weeks until 28 weeks
    C. Every 2 weeks from 28–36 weeks
    D. Every week from 36 weeks until delivery
    E. Bi-weekly non stress tests if post-term. Consider modified biophysical profile for amniotic fluid index (AFI) depending on risk factors
    F. Consider induction in uncomplicated patient between 41–42 weeks

II. INITIAL ASSESSMENT: Forms may vary by practice
    A. History
        1. Pregnancy: Date of first day of last menstrual period (LMP) and timing and flow (normal or light) of LMP
        2. Birth history: History of preterm labor, PIH/preeclampsia, gestational diabetes, incompetent cervix, gestational age of previous births, birth weights, type of anesthesia used, use of vacuum or forceps, episiotomy
        3. Past medical history: History of diabetes, hypertension, sexually transmitted diseases (STDs), depression or post-partum depression, history of varicella, and immunization history
        4. Past surgical history: Cesarean section (determine classical vs. low transverse and obtain written confirmation if at all possible), prior gynecological or cervical surgeries
        5. Drug sensitivities/allergies
        6. Family history including history of genetic abnormalities
        7. Social history: Alcohol, tobacco and drug use, physical and/or emotional abuse
        8. Family support systems, involvement of "father of the baby"
        9. Diet and exercise, weight gain with past pregnancies
        10. Patient preferences: Anesthesia/analgesia, breast vs. bottle feeding, etc.
    B. Physical: Perform a full physical including thyroid, breast and pelvic exams
    C. Labs and other tests
        1. Routine
            a. Blood group type and Rh factor
            b. Indirect Coombs (antibodies to other blood group antigens)
            c. Hepatitis surface antigen (chronic hepatitis B)
            d. H/H
            e. Blood glucose
            f. Rubella antibody titer
            g. Syphilis serology
            h. HIV: If first test is negative and patient has significant risk factors, then repeat in 3–6 months
            i. Urinalysis and culture
            j. *Gonorrhea, Chlamydia* cultures (DNA probe)
            k. Pap smear
            l. If history of blood transfusions, check titers for Duffy and Kell antibodies. If increased, then patient is a candidate for amniocentesis

OB

    2. Optional
       a. Sickle cell (at-risk populations)
       b. PPD (pregnancy mimics immunocompromised state): Consider in high-risk patients
       c. Ultrasound: Obtain if unsure of LMP or the LMP was abnormal. Not necessary if EDC by dates is reliable
       d. Toxo, CMV, varicella: Varicella zoster antibodies if patient has not been exposed

D. Vaccines
    1. **Influenza vaccine:** Should be given to all pregnant women who will be in second or third trimester during influenza season
    2. **Varicella (Varivax):** *Should not* be given to pregnant women. Women should avoid pregnancy within 1 month of receiving the vaccine

III. INITIAL VISIT—28 WEEKS

A. History
    1. Contractions: Frequency, intensity
    2. Fetal movements (First felt at 18–20 weeks in primip, 16–18 weeks in multip)
    3. Vaginal discharge or bleeding
    4. Symptoms of preeclampsia (after 20 weeks)
       a. Edema (distinguish ankle edema vs. hand/face edema—latter is more significant for preeclampsia, particularly in third trimester)
       b. Headache
       c. Blurred vision
       d. Abdominal pain (round ligament pain begins at approx. 20 weeks)
    5. Alcohol or drug use
    6. Compliance with prenatal vitamins

B. Physical
    1. Blood pressure (should be below 140/90)
    2. Weight gain: Based on body mass index
       a. Underweight women: 28–40 pounds desired
       b. Normal weight women: 25–35 pounds desired (5 lbs in first 20 weeks, then 1 lb/wk through end of pregnancy)
       c. Overweight women: 15–20 pounds desired (need supervision and diet instruction)
    3. Fetal heart tones: Heard by Doppler at 10–12 weeks
    4. Fundal height (FH): Measure with bladder empty and legs extended, from the pubic symphysis to top of uterine mass (full bladder can increase FH 3 cm)
    5. Urine dip (done in office at every visit) : Check for protein, glucose, ketones and leukocytes
       a. Protein: "Trace" or 1+ is WNL. If 2+ or more, then check 24hr urine for protein
       b. Glucose: "Trace" is normal with pregnancy due to increased GFR. If risk factors or more than "trace," then consider one 1hr glucola screen
       c. Asymptomatic bacteriuria (incidence during pregnancy is 2–7%): Major cause of maternal and fetal morbidity. If untreated, 25–30% may develop pyelonephritis
          i. Diagnosis based upon isolation of $> 10^5$ organisms per mL of urine in 2 consecutive clean-catch specimens. *E Coli* is most common offending organism
          ii. Give 3 day course of Nitrofurantoin (Macrobid) or Amoxicillin and screen with Q month cultures
          iii. If greater than 1 UTI or more than 1 incidence of asymptomatic bacteriuria: Need prophylaxis for duration of pregnancy
          iv. Symptomatic bacteriuria (hematuria, dysuria, urgency, fever, flank pain, etc): Give a 7 day course of Amoxicillin or Nitrofurantoin (Fluoroquinolones are contraindicated in pregnancy)

C. Labs: *Optional testing*
    1. **Maternal serum alpha fetal protein (MSAFP)**
       a. Indication: To screen pregnancies for neural tube defects (NTD). Will detect 90% of anencephalic and 80% spina bifida cases
       b. When AFP is combined with HCG and unconjugated estriol (triple analyte screening or AFP[3]), the sensitivity for Down's syndrome increases from 20% to

60–65%. Some clinicians use the "triple test" for women > 35, and others use it for all women.

The classic laboratory results of the "triple test" will be a low AFP, low unconjugated estriol, and high HCG

  c. Perform at 16–18 weeks
  d. If abnormal, then obtain ultrasound to ensure dates are correct (if not already done)
  e. *If AFP is low* then fetus has increased risk of incidence of Down's syndrome. Perform level II ultrasound and amniocentesis (see below)
    i. Statistically 4–5% of all AFPs will be low
    ii. Down's syndrome occurs in 1.3 of 1000 live births
  f. *If AFP is high* then AFP needs to be repeated. If still high, then fetus has increased incidence of neural tube defects. Other causes of elevated AFP include threatened abortion, twins, fetus misdated, and abdominal wall defects. Perform amniocentesis (see below)
    i. Statistically 3–5% of all AFPs will be high. Of 100 high AFPs, 95 will be "unexplained high" AFPs. These patients do not have neural tube defects, but will be at increased risk for problems in pregnancy. These women should have NSTs Q week after 32 weeks
    ii. Neural tube defects occur in 1–2 of 1000 pregnancies. If there is a positive family history, the risk rises to 2%

 2. **Chorionic Villus Sampling**
  a. Indication: To determine karyotype and genetic disorders in women with advanced maternal age (> 35) or high risk for genetic abnormalities. Does *not* evaluate for spina bifida
  b. Perform at 10–12 weeks
  c. Risk of fetal loss is 3–5%

 3. **Amniocentesis:** *Recommended option of choice for age > 35*
  a. To test for chromosomal abnormalities including Down's, Tay-Sachs, Sickle Cell disease
  b. Indications
    i. Advanced maternal age (> 35) or women with high risk of genetic abnormalities
    ii. Follow-up abnormal analyte screen
  c. Perform at 15–20 weeks gestation
  d. The chance of fetal trisomies at maternal age 35 is 1/200; age 45 is 1/20
  e. < 1% risk of fetal loss from amniocentesis if performed with ultrasound guidance

IV. WEEKS 28—36

 A. History: Same as above. Inquire about > 4 contractions/hr, vaginal bleeding, leaking, fluid or UTI symptoms
 B. Physical: Same as above
 C. Other
  1. **1 hr post glucola (1 hr PG):** Done at 26–30 weeks
   a. Consists of 50g glucose load
   b. 15% of population will be abnormal. 1–2% of pregnant mothers are diabetic
   c. Normal is < 140. If > 140 then obtain 3hr GTT
   d. 3hr GTT is abnormal if 2 or more values are abnormal:
     i. Fasting < 105
     ii. 1hr < 190
     iii. 2hrs < 165
     iv. 3hrs < 145
  2. H/H: 28 weeks (get with 1hr PG)
  3. Repeat *GC/chlamydia* and syphilis serology in high risk population. Bacterial vaginosis screen if higher risk of premature labor
  4. If mother is Rh negative: **RhoGAM 300mcg IM** at 28–32 weeks. If "father of baby" is Rh+, check indirect Coombs prior to giving RhoGAM
  5. If desired, sign consent for tubal ligation/tubal referral

OB

6. Discuss premature labor: Assess Group B β-Hemolytic *strep* infection risk (see section below). Guidelines for treating contractions in pregnancy vary. Prophylaxis in labor if positive risk including: prior affected infant, preterm, PROM
7. Counsel patient on fetal movements/give kick graph. (She should feel 10 fetal movements by 6 PM. If not, then she must call and may need to be scheduled for a NST)
8. Discuss birthing classes (Lamaze or patient's preference)

V. WEEK 36—DELIVERY

A. **History:** Same as above
B. **Physical:** Same as above—*plus*—
   1. Weekly cervical exams beginning at 37 weeks
   2. Palpate abdomen for fetal lie and position
C. **Labs:** Group B strep screening per recommendations below
D. **Discuss** anesthesia during labor (Epidural, Nubain), episiotomy, and labor and delivery procedures. Offer patient opportunity to watch labor and delivery videotape if available
E. **Advise** patient to call physician or report to Labor and Delivery if:
   1. She suspects ROM
   2. If contractions are Q 5–6 minutes for 1hr for primip, Q 8–10 minutes for 1hr if multip
   3. Vaginal bleeding
   4. Reduced or absent fetal movement (< 10 kicks/hr)

VI. RECOMMENDATIONS FOR PROPHYLAXIS OF GROUP B *STREPTOCOCCUS* (Centers for Disease Control guidelines)

A. Intrapartum treatment based on risk factors (see table below) vs. universal screening. Vaginal and perirectal culture at 35–37 weeks gestation. All positive cultures should be treated with intrapartum prophylaxis (see below)
B. Summary of Recommendations for Prevention of Neonatal Group B Streptococcus Disease

STRATEGY 1
Give intrapartum chemoprophylaxis to all women who previously had an infant with invasive group B streptococcal disease, who have group B streptococcal bacteriuria in the present pregnancy or who go into labor or have rupture of the membranes before the fetus has reached an estimated gestational age of 37 weeks
Perform prenatal screening when the fetus is at an estimated gestational age of 35 to 37 weeks and offer intrapartum chemoprophylaxis to all maternal carriers of group B streptococci
Give intrapartum chemoprophylaxis to all maternal carriers of group B streptococci who have intrapartum risk factors and to pregnant women without group B streptococcal culture results who have risk factors†

STRATEGY 2
Give intrapartum chemoprophylaxis to all women with intrapartum risk factors‡

* Source of recommendations: Centers for Disease Control and Prevention (1996), American College of Obstetrics and Gynecology (1996) and American Academy of Pediatrics (1997)
† These risk factors include rupture of the membranes for 18 hours or more or an intrapartum fever (temperature: 38°C [100.4°F]) or higher)
‡ These risk factors are a previous infant with invasive group B streptococcal disease, group B streptococcal bacteriuria during this pregnancy, labor or rupture of the membranes when the fetus has an estimated gestational age of less then 37 weeks, rupture of the membranes for 18 hours or more or an intrapartum fever (temperature: 38°C [100.4°F] or higher)

Source: Keenan C. Prevention of neonatal Group B streptococcal infection. Am Fam Phys 1998;57:2713, table 3. Used with permission.

C. Antibiotics

1. **Penicillin G** IV 5 million units initially then 2.5 million units Q 4hrs until delivery—*or*—
2. **Ampicillin** IV 2g, then 1g Q 4hrs until delivery
3. PCN allergic:
   a. **Clindamycin** 900mg IV Q 8hrs until delivery
   b. **Erythromycin** 500mg IV every 6hrs until delivery

OB

CLINICAL PEARLS

- 5–10% of patients will deliver on their due date
- Women should ideally receive folate at 28 days prior to conception through the first 8 weeks of pregnancy to decrease the risk of neural tube defects. If patient has had a previous pregnancy affected by a neural tube defect, then a daily 4mg dose of folate is recommended
- A 20 week uterus will be palpated at the umbilicus
- If patient experiences vaginal bleeding associated with a closed cervix, and a fetus is seen on ultrasound, then miscarriage rate is < 3%
- Antiretroviral use during pregnancy decreases risk of transmission of HIV by at least $^2/_3$ and should be *strongly* recommended (in consultation with an HIV specialist) to every HIV positive woman

References

Graves JC, et al. Maternal serum triple analyte screening in pregnancy. Am Fam Phys 2002;65:915–20.

Report of the National High Blood Pressure Education Program Working Group on High Blood Pressure in Pregnancy. Am J Obstet Gynecol 2000;183(1):S1-S22.

Cram LF, et al. Genitourinary infections and their association with preterm labor. Am Fam Phys 2002;65:241–8.

Alexander JM, et al. Forty weeks and beyond: pregnancy outcomes by week of gestation. Obstet Gynecol Aug 2000;96:291–4.

Toppenberg KS, et al. Safety of radiographic imaging during pregnancy. Am Fam Phys 1999;59:1813.

Werler MM, et al. Achieving a public health recommendation for preventing neural tube defects with folic acid. Am J Public Health Nov 1999; 89:1637–40.

Cnattingius S, et al. Prepregnancy weight and the risk of adverse pregnancy outcomes. New Engl J Med 1998;338:147–52.

Centers for Disease Control and Prevention. Prevention of perinatal group B streptococcal disease: a public health perspective. MMWR 1996;45(RR–7):1–24 [Published erratum appears in MMWR 1996;45(31):679].

Mary DiOrio, MD
Douglas Knutson, MD
Michael B. Weinstock, MD

19. MEDICATIONS DURING PREGNANCY & LACTATION

I. INTRODUCTION: Although most meds with systemic effects in the mother will cross the placenta, many of these meds do not seem to adversely affect the fetus. Still, many effects of meds are not known, and it is important to not prescribe meds during pregnancy unless the benefit will outweigh the risk

II. FDA CLASSIFICATIONS

Schedule A: Controlled studies *in humans* have demonstrated no fetal risks

Schedule B: *Animal studies* have indicated no fetal risk, but there are no human studies to support the data, *OR*, fetal risks have been demonstrated in animals, but *not* in well-controlled human studies

OB

Schedule C: *No adequate studies* in either humans or animals have been done—*or*—adverse effects have been seen in animal studies, but there is no human data available

Schedule D: There is *evidence of fetal risk*, but the benefits of the medication may outweigh the risks to the fetus

Schedule X: There are *proven fetal risks* which clearly outweigh the benefits of using the medication

III. MEDICATIONS USED DURING PREGNANCY FOR VARIOUS CONDITIONS

Note: Antimicrobial drugs of choice include penicillins, cephalosporins and macrolides

Selected Drugs that Can be Used Safely During Pregnancy, According to Condition*			
Condition	**Drugs of Choice**	**Alternative Drugs**	**Comments**
Acne	Topical: erythromycin, clindamycin, benzoyl peroxide	Systemic erythromycin, topical tretinoin (vitamin A acid)	Isotretinoin is contraindicated
Allergic rhinitis	Topical: glucocorticoids, cromolyn, decongestants, xylometazoline, oxymetazoline, naphazoline, phenylephrine; systemic diphenhydramine, dimenhydrinate, tripelennamine, astemizole		
Constipation	Docusate sodium, calcium, glycerin, sorbitol, lactulose, mineral oil, magnesium hydroxide	Bisacodyl, phenolphthalein	
Cough	Diphenhydramine, codeine, dextromethorphan		
Depression	Tricyclic antidepressant drugs, fluoxetine	Lithium	When lithium is used in first trimester, fetal echocardiography and ultrasonography are recommended because of small risk of cardiovascular defects
Diabetes	Insulin (human)	Insulin (beef or pork)	Hypoglycemic drugs should be avoided
Headaches Tension	Acetaminophen	Aspirin and nonsteroidal antiinflammatory drugs, benzodiazepines	Aspirin and nonsteroidal antiinflammatory drugs should be avoided in third trimester
Migraine	Acetaminophen, codeine, dimenhydrinate	ß-adrenergic-receptor antagonists and tricyclic antidepressant drugs (for prophylaxis)	Limited experience with ergotamine has not revealed evidence of teratogenicity, but there is concern about potent vasoconstriction and uterine contraction
Hypertension	Labetalol, methyldopa	ß-adrenergic-receptor antagonists, prazosin, hydralazine	Angiotensin-converting-enzyme inhibitors should be avoided because of risk of severe neonatal renal insufficiency
Hyperthyroidism	Propylthiouracil, methimazole	ß-adrenergic-receptor antagonists (for symptoms)	Surgery may be required; radioactive iodine should be avoided
Mania (and bipolar affective disorder)	Lithium, chlorpromazine, haloperidol	For depressive episodes tricyclic antidepressant drugs, fluoxetine, valproic acid	If lithium is used in first trimester, fetal echocardiography and ultrasonography are recommended because of small risk of cardiac anomalies; valproic acid may be given after neural-tube closure is complete
Nausea, vomiting, motion sickness	Diclectin (doxylamine plus pyridoxine)	Chlorpromazine, metoclopramide (in third trimester), diphenhydramine, dimenhydrinate, meclizine, cyclizine	
Peptic ulcer disease	Antacids, magnesium hydroxide, aluminum hydroxide, calcium carbonate, ranitidine	Sucralfate, bismuth subsalicylate	
Pruritus	Topical: moisturizing creams or lotions, aluminum acetate, zinc oxide cream or ointment, calamine lotion, glucocorticoids; systemic: hydroxyzine, diphenhydramine, glucocorticoids, astemizole	Topical: local anesthetics	
Thrombophlebitis, deep-vein thrombosis	Heparin, antifibrinolytic drugs, streptokinase		Streptokinase is associated with a risk of bleeding; warfarin should be avoided

*Data are from Smith et al

Common Drugs Initially Thought To Be Teratogenic But Subsequently Proved Safe		
DRUG	INITIAL EVIDENCE OF RISK	SUBSEQUENT EVIDENCE OF SAFETY
Diazepam*	Oral clefts	No increase in risk in large cohort and case-control studies
Oral Contraceptives	Birth defects involving the vertebrae, anus, heart, trachea, esophagus, kidney· and limbs; masculinizing effects on female fetuses resulting in pseudohermaphroditism	No association between first-trimester exposure to oral contraceptives and malformations in general or external genital malformations in two meta-analyses
Spermicides	Limb defects, tumors, Down's syndrome, and hypospadias	No increase in risk in a meta-analysis
Salicylates	Cleft palate and congenital heart disease	No increase in risk in large cohort studies
Bendectin (doxylamine plus pyridoxine)	Cardiac and limb defects	No increase in risk in two meta-analyses
*Diazepam taken near term may cause the neonatal withdrawal syndrome or cardiorespiratory instability.		

Drugs With Proven Teratogenic Effects In Humans*	
DRUG	TERATOGENIC EFFECT
Aminopterin†, methotrexate	CNS and limb malformations
Angiotensin-converting—enzyme inhibitors	Prolonged renal failure in neonates, decreased skull ossification, renal tubular dysgenesis
Anticholinergic drugs	Neonatal meconium ileus
Antithyroid drugs (propylthiouracil and methimazole)	Fetal and neonatal goiter and hypothyridism, aplasia cutis (with methimazole)
Carbamazepine	Neural-tube defects
Cyclophosphamide	CNS malformations, secondary cancer
Danazol and other androgenic drugs	Masculinization of female fetuses
Diethylstilbestrol†	Vaginal carcinoma and other genitourinary defects in female and male offspring
Hypoglycemic drugs	Neonatal hypoglycemia
Lithium	Ebstein's anomaly
Misoprostol	Moebius sequence
Nonsteroidal antiinflammatory drugs	Constriction of the ductus arteriosus‡, necrotizing enterocolitis
Paramethadione†	Facial and CNS defects
Phenytoin	Growth retardation, CNS deficits
Psychoactive drugs (e.g., barbiturates, opioids, and benzo diazepines)	Neonatal withdrawal syndrome when drug is taken in late pregnancy
Systemic retinoids (isotretinoin and etretinate)	CNS, craniofacial, cardiovascular, and other defects
Tetracycline	Anomalies of teeth and bone
Thalidomide	Limb-shortening defects, internal-organ defects
Trimethadione†	Facial and CNS defects
Valproic acid	Neural-tube defects
Warfarin	Skeletal and CNS defects, Dandy-Walker syndrome

*Only drugs that are teratogenic when used at clinically recommended doses are listed. The list includes all drugs proved to affect neonatal morphology or brain development and some of the toxic manifestations predicted on the basis of the pharmacologic actions of the drugs. Data are from Briggs et al. CNS denotes central nervous system.

† The drug is not currently in clinical use.

‡ Sulindac probably does not have this effect.

IV. MEDICATIONS USED DURING LACTATION

Drugs of Choice for Breast-Feeding Women*		
Drug Category	**Drugs and Drug Groups of Choice**	**Comments**
Analgesic drugs	Acetaminophen, ibuprofen, flurbiprofen, ketorolac, mefenamic acid, sumatriptan, morphine	Sumatriptan may be given for migraines. For potent analgesia, morphine may be given
Anticoagulant drugs	Warfarin, acenocoumarol, heparin (regular and low-molecular-weight)	Among breast-fed infants whose mothers were taking warfarin, the drug was undetectable in plasma and the bleeding time was not affected
Antidepressant drugs	Sertraline, tricyclic antidepressant drugs	Other drugs such as fluoxetine may be given with caution
Antiepileptic drugs	Carbamazepine, phenytoin, valproic acid	The estimated level of exposure to these drugs in infants is less then 10% of the therapeutic dose standardized by weight
Antihistamines (histamine H_1 blockers)	Loratadine	Other antihistamines may be given, but data on the concentrations of these drugs in breast milk are lacking
Antimicrobial drugs	Penicillins, cephalosporins, aminoglycosides, macrolides	Avoid the use of chloramphenicol and tetracycline
ß-Adrenergic antagonists	Labetalol, propranolol	Angiotensin-converting-enzyme inhibitors and calcium-channel-blocking agents are also considered safe
Endocrine drugs	Propylthiouracil, insulin, levothyroxine	The estimated level of exposure to propylthiouracil in breast-feeding infants is less than 1% of the therapeutic dose standardized by weight; the thyroid function of the infants is not affected
Glucocorticoids	Prednisolone and prednisone	The amount of prednisolone that the infant would ingest in breast milk is less than 0.1% of the therapeutic dose standardized by weight
*This list is not exhaustive. Cases of overdoses of these drugs must be assessed on an individual basis.		

OB

DRUGS AND SUBSTANCES THAT REQUIRE A CAREFUL ASSESSMENT OF RISK BEFORE THEY ARE PRESCRIBED TO BREAST-FEEDING WOMEN		
CATEGORY	SPECIFIC DRUGS OR COMPOUNDS	MANAGEMENT PLAN AND RATIONALE
Analgesic drugs	Meperidine, oxycodone	Use alternatives to meperidine and oxycodone. Breast-fed infants whose mothers were receiving meperidine had a higher risk of neurobehavioral depression than breast-fed infants whose mothers were receiving morphine. In breast-fed infants, the level of exposure to oxycodone may reach 10 percent of the therapeutic dose. For potent analgesia, morphine may be given cautiously. Acetaminophen and nonsteroidal antiinflammatory drugs are safe.
Antiarthritis drugs	Gold salts, methotrexate, high-dose aspirin	Consider alternatives to gold therapy. Although the bioavailability of elemental gold is unknown, a small amount is excreted in breast milk for a prolonged period. Therefore, the total amount of elemental gold that an infant could ingest may be substantial. No toxicity has been reported. Consider alternatives to methotrexate therapy, although low-dose methotrexate therapy for breast-feeding woman with rheumatic diseases has lower risks of adverse effects in their infants than does anticancer chemotherapy. High-dose aspirin should be used with caution, since there is a case report of metabolic acidosis in a breast-fed infant whose mother was receiving high dose therapy. Although the risk seems small, the infant's condition should be monitored clinically if the mother is receiving long-term therapy with high-dose aspirin.
Anticoagulant drugs	Phenindione†	Use alternatives to phenindione. Currently available vitamin K antagonists such as warfarin and acenocoumarol are considered safe, as is heparin.
Antidepressant drugs and lithium	Fluoxetine, doxepin, lithium†	Use fluoxetine, doxepin, and lithium with caution. Although the concentrations of these drugs in breast milk are low, colic (with fluoxetine) and sedation (with doxepin) have been reported in exposed infants. Near-therapeutic plasma concentrations of lithium were reported in an infant exposed to the drug in utero and through breast-feeding. The incidence of these adverse events is unknown.
Antiepileptic drugs	Phenobarbital, ethosuximide, primidone	In breast-fed infants, the level of exposure to phenobarbital, ethosuximide, and primidone may exceed 10 percent of the weight-adjusted therapeutic dose. Consider alternatives such as carbamazepine, phenytoin, and valproic acid.
Antimicrobial drugs	Chloramphenicol, tetracycline	Use alternatives to chloramphenicol and tetracycline. Idiosyncratic aplastic anemia is a possibility among breast-fed infants whose mothers are receiving chloramphenicol. Although tetracycline-induced discoloration of the teeth of breast-fed infants has not been reported, the potential risk of this event needs to be clearly communicated to lactating women. *...continued next page*

OB

DRUGS AND SUBSTANCES THAT REQUIRE A CAREFUL ASSESSMENT OF RISK BEFORE THEY ARE PRESCRIBED TO BREAST-FEEDING WOMEN (continued)		
CATEGORY	**SPECIFIC DRUGS OR COMPOUNDS**	**MANAGEMENT PLAN AND RATIONALE**
Anticancer drugs	All (e.g., cyclophos-phamide†, metho-trexate†, doxorubicin†)	Because of their potent pharmacologic effects, cytotoxic drugs should not be given to breast-feeding women.
Anxiolytic drugs	Diazepam, alprazolam	Avoid long-term use of diazepam and alprazolam in breast-feeding women. Intermittent use poses little risk to their infants, but regular use may result in the accumulation of the drug and its metabolites in the infants. Lethargy and poor weight gain have been reported in an infant exposed to diazepam in breast milk, and the withdrawal syndrome was reported in a breast-fed infant after the mother discontinued alprazolam.
Cardiovascular and anti-hypertensive drugs	Acebutolol, amiodarone, atenolol, nadolol, sotalol	The use of acebutolol, amiodarone, atenolol, nadolol, and sotalol by breast-feeding women may cause relatively high levels of exposure among their infants, and these agents should therefore be used with caution.

Source: Adapted from Koren G. et al. Drugs in pregnancy. N Engl J Med 1998;338:1128. Copyright 1998. Massachusetts Medical Society. All rights reserved.

References

Ito S. Drugs of choice for breast-feeding women. N Engl J Med 2000;343:118.

Koren G, et al. Drugs in pregnancy. N Engl J Med 1998;338:1128–37.

Broussard CN, et al. Treating GERD during pregnancy and lactation: what are the safest therapy options? Drug Safety 1998;19(4):325–37.

American Academy of Pediatrics, Work Group on Breast-feeding. Breastfeeding and the use of human milk. Pediatrics 1997;100:1035–9.

Reed BR. Dermatologic drugs, pregnancy, and lactation. A conservative guide. Arch Dermatology 1997;133(7):894–8.

Lynn Stratton, RN
Michael B. Weinstock, MD

20. Questions Expecting Parents Commonly Ask/Radiation In Pregnancy

Many of these issues should be discussed with your patients before they ask

I. WHAT ACTIVITIES ARE SAFE TO PARTICIPATE IN?

Pregnancy is not an illness and expecting mothers should not be treated as if they were sick. Pregnant women may have sexual intercourse, drive a car, fly in an airplane, go swimming, take tub baths and paint the nursery. Adequate rest, exercise and nutrition are advisable for the best pregnancy outcomes

II. WHAT ACTIVITIES SHOULD BE AVOIDED?

Douching, cleaning the litter-box, dieting to lose weight, high risk activities (skiing, sky diving), new vigorous exercise programs, high impact aerobics, vibrating machines, tanning booths, saunas

III. WHICH DANGER SIGNS SHOULD NOT BE IGNORED?

A. Bleeding (more than a few spots) from the vagina
B. A sudden gush of fluid or a slow leak of fluid
C. Severe abdominal pain
D. Chills and fever
E. Fainting
F. Pain or burning with urination

IV. WHAT CAN BE DONE TO HELP WITH MORNING SICKNESS?

Eat crackers or toast before getting out of bed. Sit on the edge of the bed for several minutes before getting up in the morning. Eat more frequently, but smaller meals (5–6 times per day). Avoid greasy and spicy foods. Drink water freely between meals. Take the prenatal vitamin after eating. Participate in stress relieving activities like walking outside 20–30 minutes 5 times per week or practicing deep breathing, asking others to help with stressful activities, and participating in organized stress relief groups. **Vitamin B$_6$** 50mg PO TID; **Emetrol** 15–30mL PO Q1–2hrs as tolerated

V. ARE X-RAYS SAFE IN PREGNANCY?

There is always a risk vs. benefit in medical testing and therapies. The most sensitive time of central nervous system development is 10–17 weeks and routine testing should be delayed until after this time. Generally an x-ray is safe as there is only a very small amount of radiation exposure to the fetus. It is recommended the unborn children not be exposed to more than 5.0 rads during the pregnancy. As reference point, the amount of radiation in a 2 view chest x-ray is 0.00007 rads

Estimated Fetal Exposure for Various Diagnostic Imaging Methods

Examination type	Estimated fetal dose per examination (rad)*	Number of examinations required for a cumulative 5-rad dose†
Plain films		
Skull	0.004	1,250
Dental	0.0001	50,000
Cervical spine	0.002	2,500
Upper or lower extremity	0.001	5,000
Chest (two views)	0.00007	71,429
Mammogram	0.020	250
Abdominal (multiple views)	0.245	20
Thoracic spine	0.009	555
Lumbosacral spine	0.359	13
Intravenous pyelogram	1.398	3
Pelvis	0.040	125
Hip (single view)	0.213	23
CT scans (slice thickness: 10 mm)		
Head (10 slices)	<0.050	>100
Chest (10 slices)	<0.100	>50
Abdomen (10 slices)	2.600	1
Lumbar spine (5 slices)	3.500	1
Pelvimetry (1 slice with scout film)	0.250	20
Fluoroscopic studies		
Upper GI series	0.056	89
Barium swallow	0.006	833
Barium enema	3.986	1
Nuclear medicine studies		
Most studies using technetium (^{99m}Tc)	<0.500	>10
Hepatobiliary technetium HIDA scan	0.150	33
Ventilation-perfusion scan (total)	0.215	23
• Perfusion portion: technetium	0.175	28
• Ventilation portion: xenon (^{133}Xe)	0.040	125
Iodine (^{131}I), at fetal thyroid tissue	590.000	‡
Environmental sources (for comparison)		
Environmental background radiation (cumulative dose over nine months)	0.100	N/A

CT=computed tomographic; GI=gastrointestinal; HIDA=hepatobiliary iminodiacetic acid; N/A=not applicable.
*--Where the reference provides a range of estimated doses, the highest value of the range is listed here.
†--Authors' calculation from data provided in reference; values rounded to lowest whole number.
‡--Iodine (^{131}I) is contraindicated during pregnancy.

Source: Toppenberg KS, et al. Safety of radiographic imaging during pregnancy. Am Fam Phys 1999:59;1813. Used with permission.

VI. WHAT IF I HAVE HERPES?

The ACOG (American College of Obstetricians and Gynecologists) published a bulletin in 'Obstetrics and Gynecology' October 1999. It recommends treatment of herpes during pregnancy with antiviral drugs such as **Acyclovir, Valacyclovir** and **Famciclovir**. It recommends C-section delivery for patients with HSV and active genital lesions during the delivery

VII. WHAT IF I AM EXPOSED TO A VIRUS?

A. Chicken pox: If you are immune, there is no further therapy warranted. If you are not immune, see your doctor immediately to test for immunity and possibly receive a medication to decrease the severity of your infection
B. Fifth disease (slapped cheek): Fifth disease does not cause birth defects but can cause miscarriage and may cause anemia, so you should see your doctor for further evaluation

OB

C. Influenza: Flu shot is recommended for pregnant women and for women who may get pregnant

VIII. TENDER BREASTS

Wearing a good support bra may help. If not effective, consider wearing it at night. Leaking breasts may be managed with nursing pads or tissues placed in the bra

IX. CONSTIPATION

Increase intake of fresh fruits and vegetables, grains and bran. Increase fluid intake and consider a cup of hot water 3 times per day. Continue to exercise including walking 20–30 minutes 5 × per week. **Psyllium (Metamucil):** 1 tsp in 8 oz water or 1 wafer QD–TID. **Perdiem (Senna-fiber):** Start with 1 tsp PO QD, may increase to 2 tsp PO QID

X. LOW BACK PAIN

Reassure that this is to be expected. Rest frequently during the day. Maintain good posture. Use a footstool while sitting. Wear low heeled shoes and avoid overly soft beds and chairs

XI. PELVIC PAIN (ROUND LIGAMENT PAIN)

As the uterus enlarges the ligaments supporting it will stretch, causing pelvic pain. May use **Tylenol** as needed. Do not make sudden movements. Get out of bed slowly. Massage may be helpful

XII. ARE DENTAL PROCEDURES SAFE DURING PREGNANCY?

Use of local anesthetic agents are generally considered safe in pregnancy. Teeth cleaning/ plaque control is considered safe. Dental radiographs are probably safe with use of a lead apron, but should be obtained only when absolutely necessary

XIII. IS CAFFEINE SAFE DURING PREGNANCY?

Drinking *large amounts* of caffeine has been associated with increased fetal loss, and women should be counseled on decreasing the amount of caffeine from coffee as well as other sources (tea, colas, chocolate, OTC drugs). In addition, *heavy* caffeine use may cause caffeine withdrawal in newborns. Most physicians consider drinking low to moderate amounts of caffeine acceptable during pregnancy

XIV. IS ASPARTAME (NUTRASWEET) SAFE DURING PREGNANCY?

Studies have not shown adverse fetal or maternal effects from aspartame during pregnancy

XV. IS THERE A PROBLEM WITH VIDEO DISPLAY TERMINALS?

No. They are considered safe during pregnancy

XVI. ARE INSECTICIDES SAFE?

Pregnant women should avoid use of insecticides and fumigants in the home or in the yard

XVII. WHAT OTC MEDICATIONS ARE SAFE TO USE?

See Chapter 19, Medications during Pregnancy & Lactation

XVIII. SHOULD SEAT BELTS BE WORN DURING PREGNANCY?

The leading nonobstetric cause of fetal death is maternal trauma. The use of a diagonal shoulder strap and a lap belt is strongly recommended during pregnancy

References

Toppenberg KS, et al. Safety of radiographic imaging during pregnancy. Am Fam Phys 1999:59;1813.

Hueston WJ, et al. Common questions patients ask during pregnancy. Am Fam Phys 1995;52:1465–72.

American College of Obstetricians and Gynecologists. Exercise during pregnancy and the postpartum period. ACOG technical bulletin No. 189. Washington D.C., Feb 1994.

Michael B. Weinstock, MD
Curt Gingrich, MD

OB

21. OB ADMISSION NOTE

HISTORY: Patient is a ___ y/o G__P__AB__ female with a ___ weeks gestation by LMP (and/or) ___ week ultrasound with EDC of __/__/__. She presents to labor and delivery with complaint of **. She (denies/reports) vaginal bleeding or ROM. She reports ____ (positive/decreased/no) fetal movements. Her prenatal course has been complicated by ____ (smoking/alcohol/ drugs/sexually transmitted diseases/multiple gestation/ preterm labor, gestational diabetes/PIH/preeclampsia etc.)

> **Examples:
> 1. Contractions which began at __ o'clock, occurring every __ minutes, lasting ___ seconds
> 2. "My water broke" __ hours ago with ____ (clear, green, bloody, malodorous) fluid
> 3. Induction of labor for ____ (post-dates, preeclampsia, oligohydramnios, IUGR)

PRENATAL LABS: Blood type and Rh status, antibody screen, HbsAg, HIV, gonorrhea and chlamydia testing, RPR/VDRL, rubella status, Group B strep status, Pap results, H/H, sickle prep if increased risk group, Sullivan test results and 3 hr GTT results if done, Triple Screen results if performed. Note if RhoGAM was given and when

PAST MEDICAL HISTORY
1. Past illness
2. Medications (prenatal vitamins/iron)
3. Allergies
4. Past obstetrical history: List each birth by year, gestational age at delivery, weight and sex of infant, route of delivery, and complications
5. Past surgical history

PHYSICAL EXAM
1. Cervix: dilation/effacement/station
2. Fetal lie, presenting part, and position (if possible)
3. Fetal monitor shows heart tones ___ bpm with ____ (good/poor) short and long term variability
4. Status of amniotic membranes (intact/ruptured) with (clear/meconium stained fluid)

ASSESSMENT: __ y/o G__P__ female at ___ weeks who presents to L&D for ____ (induction of labor, ROM, active labor/etc). Other problems include ____

PLAN: Admit to L&D. Monitor (external/internal). Pertinent labs. Anticipate spontaneous vaginal delivery *or* will augment labor with pitocin
If patient presenting for induction, list type of induction to be performed (Prostaglandin gel, Pitocin, Foley, Cytotec, etc.)

Michael B. Weinstock, MD
Curt Gingrich, MD

22. OB Delivery Note

The delivery note should include all of the following information:

1. Type of birth (NSVD, VBAC, Forceps assisted, Vacuum assisted, C-section). The indications for any instrumented delivery or C-section should be listed
2. Surgeon (name of person delivering as well as attending/assistant)
3. Sex of infant
4. Apgar scores of infant at 1 and 5 minutes. Further Apgar scores as clinically indicated and a record of any resuscitative efforts performed. Cord gases should be recorded if available
5. Type of anesthesia (epidural/pudendal block/local)
6. Estimated blood loss. The average for a vaginal delivery is 250–500cc and for C-section is 800–1000cc
7. Method of delivery of placenta (spontaneous/manual) and whether the placenta was intact or if there were retained fragments. Note if the uterus is explored. Note number of umbilical cord vessels
8. Episiotomy including degree (1,2,3,4) and type (midline, mediolateral). Include type of suture used to repair the episiotomy as well as any associated lacerations (periurethral, vaginal wall, cervical)
9. Complications (nuchal cord, retained placenta, uterine atony, meconium, post-partum hemorrhage, etc)
10. Time of first, second, and third stages of labor

Michael B. Weinstock, MD

23. Postpartum Discharge Instructions

These issues should be discussed with all home-going mothers:

1. No heavy lifting (anything heavier than the baby) or driving for 1–2 weeks. This needs to be individualized as the reason not to drive is that episiotomy pain may cause hesitancy while driving
2. No vaginal intercourse, tampons or douching for 6 weeks. This allows the vaginal musculature to tighten and the episiotomy to heal
3. Sitz baths (sitting in a warm bath) may help episiotomy pain
4. Contraception: Ask all mothers what type of birth control they will be using. Breast-feeding alone is a poor contraceptive. **Depo-Provera** can be started on postpartum day 1. Progesterone-only oral contraceptives can be started on day 1 even for mothers who are breast-feeding. An estrogen-containing contraceptive may decrease milk production and contribute to the normal hypercoagulable state of postpartum patients. An estrogen-containing oral contraceptive may safely be started after 3–4 weeks. For undecided patients, encourage using a condom with or without contraceptive foam until first postpartum visit
5. Pain medications: **Tylenol** will usually be all that is needed for vaginal deliveries. Sitz baths may help episiotomy pain. A narcotic after C-section is reasonable. **Vicodin** or **Percocet** are good choices. See Chapter 100, Pain Management in Adults & Children
6. Call office if temperature > 100.5°F or with increased pain
7. Consider a stool softener (**Colace** 100mg PO BID)
8. Vaginal bleeding: Patients can expect some lochia for 3–4 weeks postpartum. Anything heavier than a normal menstrual period should be evaluated
9. Breast-feeding. See Chapter 4, Infant Formula & Breast-feeding
10. Postpartum depression
    a. It may be helpful to discuss postpartum blues and postpartum depression with patients prior to hospital discharge

    b. Postpartum depression includes despondent mood, feelings of inadequacy as a parent, sleep and appetite disturbances, with impaired concentration, and presents in 10–20% of US women within 6 months

    c. Postpartum blues is a transient state of emotional reactivity (cry easily, irritability, emotionally labile)—occurs in about 50% of women after birth and peaks at 3–5 days after delivery

    d. Antidepressant meds commonly prescribed include the serotonin selective reuptake inhibitors (SSRIs) and the tricyclic antidepressants. **Fluoxetine (Prozac)** and **Citalopram (Celexa)** have occasionally been associated with sleep disturbance in nursing infants. See Chapter 19, Medications During Pregnacy & Lactation

    e. Women with previous history of postpartum depression are at increased risk for recurrence with subsequent pregnancies

References

Miller LJ. Postpartum depression. JAMA 2002;287:762.

Gagnon AJ, et al. A randomized trial of a program of early postpartum discharge with nurse visitations. Am J Obstet Gynecol 1997;176:205–11.

Georgiopoulos AM, et al. Routine screening for postpartum depression. J Fam Pract 2001;50:117–22.

Josefsson A, et al. Prevalence of depressive symptoms in late pregnancy and postpartum. Acta Obstet Gynecol Scand 2001;80:251–5.

Curt Gingrich, MD

24. POSTPARTUM CHECKUP

The following information should be included in the postpartum office visit. The postpartum visit is usually performed 6 weeks after delivery

HISTORY

1. Gravid and Parity
2. Type of delivery (Vaginal, Assisted, VBAC, C-section)
3. Number of weeks postpartum
4. Complication of labor and delivery (maternal and newborn)
5. Episiotomy or lacerations
6. Breast or bottle feeding
7. Fevers
8. Bowel, bladder problems, vaginal discharge
9. Symptoms of postpartum depression and discussion of the possibility of developing depressive/dysthymic symptoms
10. Lochia/menses (date if has already occurred)
11. Resumption of intercourse (if yes, then type of contraception used). Type of birth control desired
12. Assessment of support systems

PHYSICAL EXAM

1. Vital signs including BP
2. Thyroid
3. Breast Exam
4. Heart and Lung exam
5. Perineum (episiotomy, laceration repair) and vaginal vault
6. Cervix (obtain Pap if needed)
7. Bimanual exam (assess uterine size and adnexa)

LABORATORY

1. H/H if anemic prior to labor or postpartum hemorrhage
2. FBS if gestational diabetes
3. TSH if indicated by symptoms or exam

III. Women's Health

25. Contraception 69

26. Pap Smears: Indications & Interpretation 75

27. Abnormal Uterine Bleeding 79

28. Amenorrhea 82

29. Menopause & Hormone Replacement Therapy 84

30. The Premenstrual Syndrome & Dysmenorrhea 88

31. Evaluation of Breast Mass, Breast Pain & Nipple Discharge 90

32. Vaginitis & Sexually Transmitted Diseases (STDs) 92

33. Pelvic Inflammatory Disease (PID) 95

Michael B. Weinstock, MD
Beth Weinstock, MD
Kate Baltrushot, MD

25. CONTRACEPTION

I. ORAL CONTRACEPTIVES (OCs)

OCs act by suppression of ovulation and thickening of cervical mucus

A. Advantages

1. Theoretical and actual failure rates of 0.5% and 3% respectively
2. Decreased risk of ovarian and endometrial cancer by 40% and 50%, respectively
3. Decreased risk of ectopic pregnancy and pelvic inflammatory disease (PID)
4. Lighter menstrual flow, relief of dysmenorrhea, decreased ovarian cysts
5. Decreased endometriosis, PMS symptoms and acne
6. Decreased incidence of fibrocystic breast disease and fibroadenoma
7. Fertility returns within 3 months of discontinuing OCs in most patients
8. Decreased perimenopausal symptoms, such as vasomotor instability (low-dose estrogen)

B. Contraindications (to *Estrogen-containing* OCs)

1. Absolute
   a. Pregnancy
   b. Thrombophlebitis or thromboembolic disorders past or present
   c. CVA, CAD, or structural heart disease
   d. Breast cancer or Estrogen-dependent cancer (some feel this is a relative contraindication)
   e. Liver disease
2. Relative
   a. Age > 35 and smoker
   b. Cervical dysplasia
   c. Hypertension (BP > 160/100)
   d. Cardiac, renal, gallbladder disease
   e. Migraines, with focal neurologic symptoms
   f. Postpartum < 21 days or lactation (avoid OCPs until lactation well-established); see I. and J. below
   g. Diabetes, surgery, fracture, severe injury (prolonged bedrest with increased risk of DVT), lactation, significant depression

C. Drug interactions:
Patients taking the following drugs will need to use another form of contraception: Rifampin, Phenobarbital, Phenytoin (Dilantin), Griseofulvin, Primidone (Mysoline), Carbamazepine (Tegretol), St. John's Wort, and ATBs. OCs can also decrease the hepatic metabolism of certain drugs, resulting in increased toxicity (some Benzodiazepines, β-blockers, Theophylline, TCAs). Pioglitazone (Actos) and Ethosuximide can decrease effectiveness

D. Follow-up:
Return 3 months after beginning OCs to have blood pressure checked. Inquire about side effects, spotting, failure to withdrawal bleed (see following tables.) Then follow-up every year. Check blood lipids in same fashion as for non-pill users

E. Beginning OCs:
It is safe to begin all contraceptives on the first Sunday after the onset of menses or on the first day of menses. If menses begin on a Sunday, start that night and no other form of contraception is required. If OC is not started within 5 days of onset of menses, then some clinicians advise using an alternate form of birth control for the first week (e.g., condoms and spermicidal foam). Most physicians will start with any of the OCs except a Progestin-only pill (failure rates ~3%). Modify according to side effects

GYN

F. Age > 35
   1. Smokers: Discontinue OCs or change to progesterone only pill
   2. If patient is a non-smoker and blood pressure, lipids, and fasting blood sugar, are within normal limits, then OCs may be continued until menopause. Use a low dose (20mcg **Ethinyl Estradiol**) OC if patient > age 40, e.g., **Loestrin 1/20**
   3. Women > age 45 on OCs should have FSH checked every year (on 6th day of a 7-day pill-free interval) and be changed to Estrogen replacement therapy (ERT) when FSH > 30

G. Missed pills
   1. 1 missed pill: Take as soon as patient remembers, take next pill on schedule, no back-up required
   2. 2 missed pills: Take 2 pills on each of next 2 days and use a back-up for 7 days
   3. 3 missed pills: Continue to take pills and use back-up until menstruation

H. Amenorrhea while taking OCs:
   1. For 1–2 cycles: Check β-hCG
   2. For 3 cycles: Increase estrogen, decrease progestin, or follow

I. Lactation: Use a Progestin-only pill or Depo-Provera because Estrogen may cause a decrease in production of milk. The failure rate of Progestin-only minipill is extremely low when combined with the contraceptive action of prolactin due to lactation. Estrogen containing pills *are safe* for lactating mothers

J. Postpartum: Use a Progestin-only pill or wait until the first postpartum (≥ 4 weeks) visit due to hyper-coagulable state with Estrogen-containing OCs

K. Postponing menstruation: Often desired for wedding, vacation. Patient should omit the 7 day hormone-free interval. She should start a new pack the day after finishing the 21 active pills

L. Pregnancy occurring while on OCs: Using OCs during early pregnancy does not appear to increase the risk of fetal deformities. The OC should be stopped after pregnancy is diagnosed

M. Types of oral contraceptives
   1. Estrogen-Progestin Combinations:
      a. Two most commonly used Estrogen compounds are Ethinyl Estradiol (EE) or Mestranol. Mestranol is estimated to be 50% less potent than EE
      b. Progestational component in OCs varies in both dose and type of Progestin— leads to differences in pharmacologic effect
      c. Biphasic and triphasic OCs vary dose of Progestin (and often Estrogen) in 2 or 3 phases. These attempt to duplicate the pattern of a normal menstrual cycle. Clinically, very little difference is observed between monophasic and multiphasic OCs
      d. OCs most frequently prescribed contain 30–35mcgs of EE and a Progestin that is less androgenic (Norgestimate or Desogestrel)
      e. Low Estrogen-Progestin combinations are now available (**Alesse, Mircette**)
      f. Use of Spironolactone analogue (3mg **Drospirenone**) instead of Progestin-Yasmin. Has antimineralocorticoid and antiandrogenic effects: no weight gain, improvement in acne
         i. New drug interaction concerns: ACE inhibitors, angiotensin-II receptor antagonists, K+ sparing diuretics, heparin, chronic use of NSAIDs
         ii. Consider checking potassium in first cycle of **Yasmin**
   2. Progestin-only products ("mini-pills")
      a. Contain decreased dose of Progestin relative to combination OCs
      b. Preferred for use during breast-feeding, and for women who have contraindication to estrogens (especially smokers > age 35)
      c. Have a slightly higher failure rate (1–4%) and may lead to more irregular bleeding

ORAL CONTRACEPTIVE SIDE EFFECT ADJUSTMENTS

SYMPTOM	PROBABLE ETIOLOGY	CHANGE REQUIRED
Break through bleeding (BTB) spotting first 10 days	Estrogen deficiency	Increase estrogen*
BTB or spotting second 10 days	Estrogen and/or progestin deficiency	Increase estrogen* or progesterone
Prolonged or heavy menses	Progestin deficiency	Increase progestin
Delayed onset of menses	Progestin deficiency	Increase progestin
Shortened menses	Progestin excess	Decrease progestin
No menses	Progestin excess or estrogen deficiency	Continue one cycle then increase estrogen
Weight gain	Progestin excess	Decrease progestin
Hirsutism, loss of scalp hair, acne	Progestin excess	Decrease progestin or change to progestin with low androgenicity
Cervicitis, candidal vaginitis	Progestin excess	Decrease progestin
Depression, decreased libido, fatigue	Progestin excess	Decrease progestin
Nausea, vomiting	Estrogen excess	Decrease estrogen
Chloasma (skin discoloration)	Estrogen excess	Decrease estrogen
Uterine cramps	Estrogen excess	Decrease estrogen
Edema, bloating, breast tenderness and enlargement, headaches	On pills — Estrogen excess On placebo week — Progestin excess	Decrease offending steroid, diuretics
Migraine, blurring of vision	Estrogen excess	Needs further evaluation, consider stopping pills
Androgenic symptoms	Progestin excess	Change to 3rd generation progestin (desogestrel)
Dyslipidemia	Progestin excess	Change to 3rd generation progestin (desogestrel)

*An easy way to increase the Estrogen without decreasing the Progesterone is to administer Conjugated Estrogen (Premarin) 1.25mg QD x 7 days. This may be attempted no matter where patient is in her cycle

Type	Name	Estrogen	mcg	Progestin	mg
Composition of Combination OCs					
Low Androgenic Activity of Progestin Component					
Monophasic	Modicon Brevicon Necon 0.5/35	EE	35	norethindrone	0.5
	Ovcon 35	EE	35	norethindrone	0.4
	Ortho-Cyclen	EE	35	norgestimate	0.25
	Ortho-Cept Cyclessa Desogen	EE	30	desogestrel	0.15
Biphasic	Mircette	EE	20/0/10	desogestrel	0.15
Triphasic	Ortho Tri-Cyclen	EE	35/35/35	norgestimate	0.18/0.215/0.25
Medium Androgenic Activity of Progestin Component					
Monophasic	Ovcon 50	EE	50	norethindrone	1.0
	Ortho-Novum 1/50 Zovia 1/50 Nelova 1/50 Norinyl 1 + 50	mestranol	50	norethindrone	1.0
	Ortho-Novum 1/35 Norinyl 1 + 35 Necon 1/35	EE	35	norethindrone	1.0
	Alesse	EE	20	levonorgestrel	1.0
	Loestrin 1/20 +/- Fe Microgestin 1/20	EE	20	norethindrone acetate	1.0
Biphasic	Ortho-Novum 10/11 Necon 10/11 Jenest-28	EE	35/35	norethindrone	0.5/1.0
Triphasic	Ortho-Novum 7/7/7	EE	35/35/35	norethindrone	0.5/0.75/1.0
	Tri-Norinyl	EE	35/35/35	norethindrone	0.5/1.0/0.5
	Triphasil Trivora Tri-Levlen	EE	30/40/30	levonorgestrel	0.05/0.075/0.125
	Estrostep	EE	20/30/35	norethlndrone	1.0
High Androgenic Activity of Progestin Component					
Monophasic	Ovral Ogestrel	EE	50	norgestrel	0.5
	Loestrin 1.5/30 +/- Fe	EE	30	norethindrone acetate	1.5
	Lo-Ovral Low-Ogestrel	EE	30	norgestrel	0.3
	Nordette	EE	30	levonorgestrel	0.15
	Levlen	EE	30	levonorgestrel	0.15
Composition of Progestin-Only OCs					
Monophasic	Micronor	None	N/A	norethindrone	0.35
	Nor-QD	None	N/A	norethindrone	0.35
	Ovrette	None	N/A	norgestrel	0.075

- Failure rates with the Progestin-only minipill are higher than other OCs (1–4%). They also do not offer protection against functional ovarian cysts
- Ethynodiol, Desogestrel and Norgestimate have a low amount of androgenicity and may be good first line agents for women with acne and hirsutism
- Some clinicians feel that assessing the relative progesterone potency is not clinically useful

II. PROGESTERONE IMPLANTS AND INJECTIONS

A. Depo-Provera (Medroxyprogesterone Acetate) 150mg IM Q11–13 weeks

1. Failure rate of 0.3% first year; cumulative 5–year 0.9%
2. Check urine pregnancy test before administering first dose. Should also check urine pregnancy before re-administering Depo-Provera if patient > 1 week late for injection
3. If first dose is given during menstruation, contraception begins immediately. If not, then use alternate form of contraception until next menses
4. May give postpartum even if mothers are lactating
5. Side effects: Irregular bleeding, amenorrhea, weight gain (5–10 lbs), headache, increased risk of bone loss with long-term use, breast tenderness, depression, irritability
6. If spotting occurs, patient should be informed that irregular bleeding usually disappears after 1yr. Consider giving **Premarin** 1.25mg QD × 7 days which may be increased to 2.5mg QD × 7 days or 2.5mg QD × 21 days. This therapy should not be continued longer than 1–2 months. If unsuccessful then consider another form of contraception
7. Disadvantage: Delayed return to fertility, average 10 months
8. Useful for patients with seizure disorder, sickle-cell anemia (crises reduced by 70%). Also helpful for dysmenorrhea, endometriosis, and menses-related anemia

B. Norplant: No longer commonly used

III. MALE CONDOM

A. Theoretical and actual failure rates: 2% and 10%, respectively. Patients should be instructed in use as the actual failure rate can fall dramatically with correct use
B. Better protection against STDs (including HIV if condoms with nonoxynol-9 are used)
C. Patients should be instructed not to use with oil-based lubricants, such as Vaseline
D. If used with a spermicidal vaginal foam, contraception failure rates approach OCs

IV. FEMALE CONDOM

A. Failure rate 5–20%
B. Difficult to use
C. Protects against STDs
D. Can use any lubricant

V. DIAPHRAGM

A. Theoretical and actual failure rates: 2% and 20% when used with spermicide
B. Provides protection against pelvic infection and cervical dysplasia. Increased risk of UTIs
C. Must be inserted prior to intercourse, but does not need to be removed and reinserted for subsequent intercourse for next 12hrs (do need to use extra spermicide after 6hrs). Cannot be left in longer than 12–18hrs (increased risk of UTIs)
D. Must wait 4–6 weeks postpartum to fit.

VI. PRENTIF CERVICAL CAP

A. Thimble-shaped device, fitted to cervix with small amount of spermicide
B. Advantage: May be used for multiple episodes of intercourse, up to 48hrs, and requires less contraceptive gel than diaphragm
C. Porous cervix may be difficult to fit
D. Pap smear needed prior to fitting, 3 months later, and annually thereafter

VII. COMBINATION HORMONAL PATCH (Ortho Evra)

A. Pregnancy rates equivalent to OCPs
B. 20cm^2 adhesive patch contains 6mg **Norelgestromin** and 0.75mg **Ethinyl Estradiol**
C. Patch placed on trunk or arm once a week—use for 3 weeks, then off for 1 week
D. Side effects: Device-related problems, headache, emotional lability, weight gain (1%)

VIII. HORMONAL VAGINAL CONTRACEPTIVE

Etonogestrel 120mcg per day/**Ethinyl Estradiol** 15mcg per day (**NuvaRing**)
A. One ring is inserted on or before day 5 of cycle and left in place for 3 weeks then removed for 1 ring-free week

GYN

B. If switching from combination OCP, then insert within 7 days of last active pill

C. Vaginitis, leukorrhea, side effects of estrogen and progesterone

IX. VAGINAL SPERMICIDES

A. Failure rates from 3–20% per year

B. Inserted before intercourse and may be used without replacement for repeated acts of intercourse for 12–18hrs

C. Available OTC

D. 2–4% of couples have allergic reactions

X. INTRAUTERINE DEVICE (NONHORMONAL)—IUD

A. Failure rates 1–2%; spontaneous expulsion rate 5%

B. Copper Paragard T380A

C. Implant during menses, mid-cycle to prevent expulsion, or 12 weeks postpartum. Copper T380A should be changed every 10yrs

D. Especially useful in women who have completed child bearing and have only 1 sexual partner. Risk of PID and ectopic pregnancy are increased

E. Menstrual flow and cramping will most likely increase, may prescribe NSAIDs prophylactically

XI. INTRAUTERINE DEVICE (HORMONAL)—MIRENA

A. Failure rate 0.7% cumulative for 5yrs

B. Releases 20mcg **Levonorgestrel** per day

C. Insert during first 7 days of cycle, approved for 5yrs of use

D. Mechanism—thickens cervical mucus, sperm motility impairment, inhibition of ovulation, inhibition of fertilization

E. Side effects: Mastalgia, headache. No reported weight gain. Contraindicated in women at risk for ectopic pregnancy

F. May decrease incidence of dysmenorrhea, menorrhagia, PMS, endometrial hyperplasia

G. Rapid return to fertility: 79% pregnant by 12 months

XII. COITUS INTERRUPTUS

Failure rates 20–25% per year

XIII. FERTILITY BASED AWARENESS (Basal body temperature, calendar)

Failure rates from 2–20% depending on expertise of user

XIV. STERILIZATION

A. Male

1. Failure rate of only 0.1%
2. Couple needs to be sure that no more children are desired
3. In office procedure with 'scalpel-less' procedure
4. Easy to perform, local anesthesia

B. Female

1. Failure rates depend on procedure used—most effective postpartum
2. Failure rates increase over 10yrs from 0.8% to 4%. Counsel the couple on their certainty of sterilization. Can possibly be reversed, but at a cost of ~$10,000
3. Salpingectomy (part of tube removed and ends tied) is most effective

XV. NO METHOD

Pregnancy rate of 85–90% per year

XVI. POSTCOITAL CONTRACEPTION

A. May be used for unprotected sex, broken condom (mid-cycle), rape

B. First dose must be given within 72hrs with the second dose administered 12hrs later

C. Perform pregnancy test first!

D. Failure rates of ~1.5%. Efficacy improved if taken early

E. Medications
  1. **Plan B**–1 pill as soon as possible, then 1 pill 12hrs later. This is the preferred formulation (highest efficacy, least side effects)
  2. **Preven kit**–2 tabs as soon as possible, then 2 tabs 12hrs later
  3. **Ovral**–2 pills as soon as possible, then 2 pills 12hrs later
F. Include Rx for antiemetic—e.g., **Phenergan** 25mg PO or PR Q 4–6hrs PRN
G. Should experience bleeding in 3–4 weeks. If not, check pregnancy test

CLINICAL PEARLS

- Most cases of condom failure result from inappropriate usage. The number of condoms that break is less than 2 per 100
- The number of women with *chlamydia* and *gonorrhea* who later develop infertility ranges from 10–40%. Correct use of a male (or female) condom can drastically reduce the chance of contracting a sexually transmitted disease
- Nearly half of all pregnancies in US are unintended

References

Audet M, et al. Evaluation of contraceptive efficacy and cycle control of a transdermal contraceptive patch vs an oral contraceptive. A randomized controlled trial. JAMA 2001;285:2347–54.

Vandenbroucke JP, et al. Medical progress: oral contraceptives and the risk of venous thrombosis. N Engl J Med 2001;344:1527–35.

Berenson AB, et al. A prospective, controlled study of the effects of hormonal contraception on bone mineral density. Obstet Gynecol 2001;98:576–82.

Beral V, et al. Mortality associated with oral contraceptive use: 25yr follow up of cohort of 46,000 women from Royal College of General Practitioners' oral contraception study. BMJ Jan 9, 1999;318:96–100.

Cerel-Suhl SL, Yeager BF. Update on oral contraceptive pills. Am Fam Phys 1999;60:2073–84.

International Federation of Fertility Societies. Consensus conference on combination oral contraceptives and cardiovascular disease. Fertil Steril 1999;71(suppl 3):1s–6s.

Michael B. Weinstock, MD

26. PAP SMEARS:
INDICATIONS & INTERPRETATION

I. INTRODUCTION

In 2001 the new Bethesda System terminology was introduced. This chapter is based upon the new terminology. Approximately 90% of the labs in the US use some form of the Bethesda system. Approx. 50 million women have Pap tests each year and 7% will have an abnormality which requires further testing

II. INDICATIONS AND SCHEDULE

A. The American College of Obstetrics and Gynecology (ACOG), American Cancer Society (ACS), National Cancer Institute (NCI), and the American Medical Association (AMA) recommend beginning Pap smears with the onset of sexual activity or by age 18. If a low-risk patient has 3 consecutive negative annual Pap smears, they may be performed at less frequent intervals at physician's discretion (see risk factors below)

B. **Risk factors for cervical cancer**
  1. Early first intercourse
  2. Large number of lifetime sexual partners
  3. History of STDs, especially human papilloma virus (HPV)
  4. High-risk sexual partners
  5. Cigarette smoking
  6. Lack of normal immune response (HIV increases chances of cervical cancer 8–11 times)

7. High parity
8. Low socioeconomic status
9. History of abnormal Pap smear
Note: Smoking and HPV are the only independent risk factors to be consistently shown to have statistical significance in multiple studies

III. RECOMMENDED TECHNIQUE FOR PERFORMING PAP SMEAR

A. Ideally the entire portio should be visualized prior to obtaining smear
B. Vaginal discharge when present in large quantities should be carefully removed so epithelium is not disturbed
C. Portio sample should be obtained first with the spatula and then with the endobrush because of risk of endocervical bleeding interfering with sample collection and drying
D. Sample collection should be uniformly applied and spray fixative applied. Spray fixative should be applied from at least 10 inches away to prevent dispersal and destruction of cells
E. Steps 3 and 4 can be interchanged with using the "broom" which obtains both ecto- and endocervical samples
F. Perform Gonococcus and Chlamydia cultures next (if indicated), then pelvic exam

IV. TECHNIQUES FOR SCREENING

A. **Fluid Based Technology—ThinPrep**
   1. ThinPrep (FDA approved) uses fluid-based technology. Process removes multiple contaminants (mucous, small amounts of blood, protein) and allows for a thin even cell layer on slide
   2. Advantages: Several studies have demonstrated that ThinPrep and other monolayer systems have lower false negative rates than conventional slide preparations. Studies have also shown a decrease in unsatisfactory specimens
   3. HPV typing can be performed from the same ThinPrep container as the Pap smear
   4. Disadvantage: There is a slight increase in cost of monolayer preparations over conventional slides

B. **Neural Network Computer Technology:** AutoPap and PapNet are 2 FDA-approved systems to rescreen 100% of negative Pap smears. Studies have shown a decrease in the false negative rate with the computerized systems versus conventional manual rescreening of 10% of samples. These techniques are not currently being used

V. PATHOLOGY REPORT AND ACTION: A–D below describe the possible descriptive diagnosis with the 2001 Bethesda System of reporting

A. **Negative for intraepithelial lesion or malignancy:** This finding may specify non-neoplastic findings including the following. Action should be taken based on the specific result
   1. Trichomonas vaginalis
   2. Fungal organisms morphologically consistent with *Candida* species
   3. Shift in flora suggestive of bacterial vaginosis
   4. Bacteria morphologically consistent with *Actinomyces* species
   5. Cellular changes consistent with herpes simplex virus
   6. Reactive cellular changes associated with inflammation (includes typical repair)
   7. Radiation
   8. Intrauterine contraceptive device
   9. Glandular cells status posthysterectomy
   10. Atrophy

B. **Atypical squamous cells (ASC)**
   1. This category may be reported as ASC-US (atypical squamous cells of undetermined significance) or ASC-H (atypical squamous cells, cannot exclude high-grade squamous intraepithelial lesion (HSIL))
   2. General: 5–17% of patients with ASC will have biopsy proven HSIL and 0.1– 0.2% will have invasive cancer. Of patients with ASC-H, 24–94% will have HSIL. In patients with ASC, 31–60% will have high-risk types of HPV
   3. All ASC is now considered suggestive of SIL
   4. Action for ASC-US
      a. High risk or non-compliant patient: Perform colposcopy

GYN

b. Low risk patient: Repeat Pap smear in 4–6 months and at 1yr and then Q6 months × 1yr. If any abnormal Pap smear during that time period, perform colposcopy. If 2 consecutive "negative for intraepithelial lesion or malignancy" results, return to routine testing

c. If tested for HPV (HPV DNA test), and if positive, perform colposcopy

d. If post-menopausal, may try intravaginal estrogen and repeat Pap 1wk later. If negative, then repeat in 4–6 months and if still negative, return to routine testing

5. Action for ASC-H: Colposcopy

C. Squamous intraepithelial lesion (SIL)

1. **Low-Grade Squamous Intraepithelial Lesions (LSIL):** LSIL is equivalent to the older classification of HPV, mild dysplasia or CIN 1

a. 15–30% will have HSIL on subsequent Pap

b. Approximately 80%–90% of LGSIL will spontaneously regress and 3–16% will progress

c. Action

i. Colposcopy

ii. Special circumstances: If post menopausal or adolescent, may repeat Pap at 6 and 12 months and perform colposcopy if ASC or higher

2. **High Grade Squamous Intraepithelial Lesions (HSIL):** HSIL is equivalent to the older classification of moderate or severe dysplasia and to CIN II, CIN III, and carcinoma in situ (CIS)

a. 70–75% of patients will have biopsy proven CIN II, III and 1–2% will have invasive cancer

b. Action: Colposcopy

D. Atypical glandular cells

1. May be reported as:

a. Atypical glandular cells, either endocervical, endometrial, or "glandular cells" not otherwise specified (AGC NOS)

b. Atypical glandular cells, either endocervical or "glandular cells" favor neoplasia (AGC "favor neoplasia")

c. Endocervical adenocarcinoma in situ (AIS)

2. Patients with AGUS Pap smears have a much higher risk of dysplastic disease. Between 9–41% of patients with AGC NOS will have biopsy-proven HSIL or cancer compared to 27–96% of patients with AGC "favor neoplasia." Patients must be aggressively evaluated

3. Action: Colposcopy (and endometrial biopsy if postmenopausal)

VI. PREGNANCY AND THE ABNORMAL PAP

A. In pregnancy, the same indications for colposcopy should be followed. However, LGSIL should be referred for colposcopy and not just followed. If colposcopy is satisfactory and negative for any visible lesions, the colposcopy can be repeated postpartum without any further evaluation during the pregnancy. If a lesion is visualized, it should be biopsied. The ECC should NOT be performed during pregnancy. If biopsy negative or LGSIL, then repeat colposcopy can be postponed until postpartum

B. If a patient has HGSIL on Pap with a satisfactory colposcopy or a biopsy consistent with HGSIL, colposcopy should be repeated every 8wks until delivery and then postpartum with ECC

C. Microinvasion on a biopsy will require conization

VII. HIV POSITIVE FEMALES

A. If no history of prior cervical disease, the Pap smear should be obtained twice in the first year after diagnosis. If these are both normal, then yearly Pap smears can be performed

B. Once a patient becomes immunocompromised, colposcopy every 6 months should be considered

VIII. TREATMENT OF SQUAMOUS INTRAEPITHELIAL LESIONS *

A. Indications for surgical excision (Cone)

1. Unsatisfactory colposcopic examination (lesion extends into the cervical canal and is not visualized)

2. Pap and colposcopy do not agree

3. Diagnosis of microinvasive carcinoma based on punch biopsy

B. Cryosurgery

GYN

    C. Laser vaporization techniques
    D. Loop electrosurgical excision procedure (LEEP)/Large Loop excision of transforma-
      tion zone (LLETZ): Removal of lesion with tissue diagnosis
* After the procedure, all patients will need Pap smears Q3 months × 1yr, Q6 months × 1yr, then
  Qyr if follow-up Paps are within normal limits

IX. **HUMAN PAPILLOMA VIRUS (HPV):** HPV is a double stranded DNA virus that has been
    repeatedly shown to be a strong risk factor for the development of cervical dysplasia
    A. Low risk: 6, 11, 40, 42, 43, 44
    B. High Risk: 16, 18, 31, 33, 35, 45, 51, 52, 56
    Currently, HPV typing cannot be recommended as a standard clinical practice or standard of
      care. However, it can be used in determining conservative versus aggressive measures in
      those patients with ASCUS or LGSIL Pap smears

CLINICAL PEARLS
    • In 1998, an estimated 13,700 females in the US were diagnosed with cervical cancer
      and there were approximately 4900 deaths
    • Since the introduction of the Pap smear in the US, the incidence and mortality from cervi-
      cal cancer has declined by more than 40%
    • There were 13,000 cases of cervical cancer and 600,000 cases of CIN in 1991. The inci-
      dence of cervical cancer has decreased about 80% in the last 50 years
    • 15% of CIN I will progress to CIN III. 60% of CIN I will regress spontaneously. CIN I can
      be followed expectantly because so many regress spontaneously
    • The rate of false negative Pap smears is 15–40%
    • There is no "magic formula" to getting repeat Pap smears Q3 months. Important to perform
      frequent Paps to decrease the false negative rate. With 2 Paps the false negative rate falls
      to 2–16%, with 3 Paps it falls to 0.3–6%, and with 4 Paps it falls to 0.05–2.5%

References
Solomon D, et al, for the Forum Group Members and the Bethesda 2001 Workshop. The 2001 Bethesda
    System: terminology for reporting results of cervical cytology. JAMA 2002;287:2114–9.
Wright TC Jr, et al, for the 2001 ASCCP-Sponsored Consensus Conference. 2001 Consensus guide-
    lines for the management of women with cervical cytological abnormalities. JAMA
    2002;287:2120–9.
Janicek, MF, Averette HE. Cervical cancer: prevention, diagnosis, and therapeutics. CA Cancer J Clin
    2001:51;92-114.
Flowers LC, McCall MA. Diagnosis and management of cervical intraepithelial neoplasia. Obstet
    Gynecol Clin North Am Dec 2001;28(4):667–84.
Mandelblatt JS, et al. Benefits and costs of using HPV testing to screen for cervical cancer. JAMA
    2002;287:2372.
Melnikow J, et al. Do follow-up recommendations for abnormal papanicolaou smears influence pa-
    tient adherence? Arch Fam Med 1999;8:510.

Michael B. Weinstock, MD
Beth Weinstock, MD

27. ABNORMAL UTERINE BLEEDING

I. HISTORY

A. Onset of menarche: Initial cycles after menarche are usually anovulatory due to a delay in the maturation of the hypothalamic-pituitary axis

B. Usual menstrual pattern: Frequency, cyclicity, amount (number pads soaked per day), and duration

C. Duration and extent of abnormal bleeding

D. Previous therapy for abnormal bleeding

E. Sexual history: Birth control, recent sexual activity

F. Stress, weight change, exercise, trauma, history of eating disorder

G. Medications: Estrogen replacement therapy, oral contraceptives including progestin-only pills, long acting contraceptives (Depo-Provera, Nuvaring, Mirena IUD)

H. Past medical history: Endometriosis, fibroids, polyps, history of abnormal Pap smears, polycystic ovarian syndrome, systemic diseases (especially thyroid, renal, hepatic, and coagulopathies), radiation therapy

II. TERMINOLOGY

A. Menorrhagia: Prolonged or excessive uterine bleeding occurring at regular intervals

B. Metrorrhagia: Uterine bleeding occurring at irregular, frequent intervals

C. Menometrorrhagia: Prolonged uterine bleeding occurring at irregular intervals

D. Polymenorrhea: Uterine bleeding occurring at regular intervals of less than 21 days

E. Oligomenorrhea: Uterine bleeding in which the interval between bleeding episodes varies from 35 days to 6 months

F. Amenorrhea: No uterine bleeding for at least 6 months

III. PHYSICAL

A. General exam: Weight, surgical scars, signs of thyroid abnormalities, hirsutism

B. Vaginal exam: Lesions, masses, discharge

C. Pelvic exam: Cervical motion tenderness, adnexal mass, uterine enlargement, cervical polyps, cervical dilation

IV. DIAGNOSIS

A. Exclude non-uterine causes of bleeding

1. Lower tract bleeding (vaginal, cervical, urinary bleeding)
2. Pregnancy (intrauterine, ectopic, molar)

B. Differentiate between anatomic (normal cycle) **vs. dysfunctional** (irregular cycle) **uterine bleeding**

1. Anatomic uterine bleeding

   a. Bleeding within normal cycles as a result of a structural abnormality, such as polyps, fibroids, endometriosis, adenomyosis, endometritis, implantation bleeding, cancer, complications of pregnancy (ectopic or spontaneous abortion)

   b. Characteristics of ovulatory cycles: Regular cycle length, presence of premenstrual symptoms, dysmenorrhea, change in cervical mucus, mittelschmerz, biphasic temperature curve

2. Dysfunctional uterine bleeding (DUB)

   a. Excessive, irregular uterine bleeding without demonstrable organic cause. Usually a "hormonal problem" of anovulation and unopposed estrogen due to progesterone deficiency

   b. Note: During the normal cycle, progesterone surge occurs after ovulation which allows for cyclic endometrial sloughing. Results in a proliferative endometrium as there is no ovulation and no progesterone surge

   c. Characteristics of anovulatory cycles: Unpredictable cycle length and bleeding pattern, frequent spotting, monophasic temperature curve

GYN

  d. DUB is a diagnosis of exclusion: If the reproductive-age woman is not pregnant and has a normal physical exam and ultrasound, abnormal uterine bleeding is usually dysfunctional in nature and can be managed with hormonal therapy (see VII. B)

  e. Polycystic ovarian disease (PCO): Another cause of anovulation usually associated with obesity, increased circulating androgens, and insulin resistance. Excess androgens are converted to estrogen in peripheral tissues. Unopposed estrogen state increases risk of endometrial hyperplasia and cancer

  f. Ovulatory dysfunctional bleeding: Less common. Menses occurs regularly, but menorrhagia/midcycle spotting occurs. May signify a structural lesion (fibroids, polyps) or a bleeding disorder. Suspect von Willebrand's disease in adolescents

V. LABORATORY: If indicated

 A. Pregnancy test

 B. CBC, TSH, prolactin

 C. Pap smear: If sexually active or if age 18 or older

 D. Pelvic cultures (if sexually active): *GC, Chlamydia, Trichomonas*

 E. Coagulation studies (PT/PTT, bleeding time)

 F. Consider LH, FSH, DHEA-S, free testosterone if PCO is suspected

VI. ABNORMAL UTERINE BLEEDING IN *ADOLESCENTS*

 A. General

  1. Cycles are often anovulatory and irregular following menarche (up to 80% in first year after menarche)

  2. Hypothalamic-pituitary-ovarian axis is usually mature within 18 months of menarche

 B. Pelvic exam: Not necessary if within 18 months of menarche and not sexually active

 C. Management

  1. If bleeding is not severe: Cycle patients for 3–6 months on oral contraceptive pills

  2. For severe bleeding: Consider further work-up for possible underlying coagulopathy

VII. ABNORMAL UTERINE BLEEDING IN *REPRODUCTIVE AGE* WOMEN

 A. Anatomic uterine bleeding: Hormonal therapy may be attempted (see below, DUB), but patient will probably need definitive therapy (D&C, surgery, etc.)

 B. Dysfunctional uterine bleeding

  1. Endometrial biopsy: Long-term unopposed estrogen stimulation can result in endometrial hyperplasia; consider endometrial biopsy in any women over age 30 with an extended anovulatory period or any women over 20 with prolonged bleeding

  2. Management

   a. Oral contraceptives: Low dose (35mcg) monophasic or triphasic pills can regulate cycles

   b. **Medroxyprogesterone (Provera)** 10mg PO QD × 10 days

VIII. ABNORMAL UTERINE BLEEDING IN *PERIMENOPAUSAL* WOMEN: Age 35 to menopause

 A. Anatomic uterine bleeding: Perform D&C

 B. Dysfunctional uterine bleeding

  1. Perform endometrial (Pipelle) biopsy to exclude malignancy

  2. If normal, then prescribe hormonal therapy as described above. Use of oral contraceptives that contain estrogen are contraindicated if patient is a smoker (see Chapter 25, Contraception)

 C. Diagnosis of DUB vs. menopause (see Chapter 29, Menopause & HRT)

  1. If patient has 3 months of amenorrhea: Determine if patient is in menopause

   a. Obtain FSH level

    i. If FSH is high (> 40mIU/mL), then patient is in menopause

    ii. If FSH is low, then patient has DUB. Perform Pipelle biopsy to exclude malignancy. Cycle with **Provera** 10mg QD × 7 days per month or low-dose oral contraceptives

   b. **Provera:** 10mg QD × 7 days to see if patient has withdrawal bleeding

    i. If no withdrawal bleeding, then repeat in 3 months. If still no withdrawal bleeding, assume she is in menopause

ii. If there is withdrawal bleeding, then patient is not in menopause. Continue workup for sources of abnormal uterine bleeding/amenorrhea

2. If patient has heavy menses (passing clots or social inconvenience) for 3 months, bleeding between menses for 3–4 months, or 3 consecutive months of menses which last longer than 7 days, then perform Pipelle biopsy, consider pelvic ultrasonography to measure the endometrial thickness, or D&C. Manifestations of malignancy (bleeding) must not be dismissed as early menopause

D. Management
1. **Medroxyprogesterone (Provera):** 10mg per day × 10 days, or
2. **Progesterone (Prometrium)** 400mg PO BID × 10 days (available 100mg, 200mg caps)
3. Oral contraceptives: Use 20mcg pills. Note: OCPs are contraindicated in women > 35 who smoke

GYN

IX. ABNORMAL UTERINE BLEEDING IN *POST-MENOPAUSAL* WOMEN

A. Perform endometrial biopsy and consider pelvic ultrasonography to measure endometrial thickness. 5–10% are found to have endometrial cancer
  1. Results of endometrial biopsy
    a. Hyperplastic endometrium: Patient needs D&C/hysteroscopy. Associated with malignancy 15% of the time
    b. Atrophic: Can begin HRT
    c. Cancer: Referral for TAH/BSO
  2. Endometrial biopsy vs. transvaginal ultrasound
    a. Meta-analysis showed that 96% of women with endometrial cancer, and 92% of those with endometrial disease, had endometrial stripe thickness of > 5mm whether or not they used HRT
    b. If endometrial stripe on ultrasound > 5mm, endometrial sampling should be performed
    c. Both tests have comparable costs; biopsy is more uncomfortable and may be difficult in patients with cervical stenosis

B. Patients on HRT
  1. 30% of these patients will have uterine pathology
  2. Women on continuous HRT may experience breakthrough bleeding due to missed pills, medication interactions, or malabsorption. If bleeding occurs in 2 or more cycles, further evaluation is indicated
  3. On continuous HRT, up to 40% have irregular bleeding in first 4–6 months of therapy. Most experts recommend evaluation of abnormal bleeding if it lasts > 6–9 months after initiation of HRT

C. Management for women on HRT
  1. If early withdrawal bleeding occurs, increase the progesterone dose
  2. If intermenstrual bleeding occurs, increase the estrogen dose
  3. If on continuous HRT try cyclic
  4. Try a different type of estrogen

CLINICAL PEARLS
- All post-menopausal bleeding must be worked up as 7% of post-menopausal bleeding is the result of malignancy!
- Consider β-hCG in all pre-menopausal women with abnormal bleeding

References

Oriel KA, Schrager S. Abnormal uterine bleeding. Am Fam Phys 1999;60:1371.

Archer DF, et al. Uterine bleeding in postmenopausal women on continuous therapy with estradiol and norethindrone acetate. Obstet Gynecol Sep 1999;94:323–9.

Smith-Bindman R, et al. Endovaginal ultrasound to exclude endometrial cancer and other endometrial abnormalities. JAMA 1998;280:1510–7.

Langer RD, et al. Transvaginal ultrasonography compared with endometrial biopsy for the detection of endometrial disease. N Engl J Med 1997;337:1792–8

Bayer SR, DeCherney AH. Clinical manifestations and treatment of dysfunctional uterine bleeding. JAMA 1993;269:1823–8.

Cathy Greiwe, MD

28. AMENORRHEA

GYN

I. INTRODUCTION: First exclude the most common cause; pregnancy. A history and physical including detailed gynecological exam will guide the evaluation and subsequent lab studies

II. DEFINITION: Amenorrhea (absence of menses) is divided into the following:

A. Primary: No spontaneous uterine bleeding by age 14 in the absence of the development of secondary sex characteristics or by age 16 in otherwise normal development

B. Secondary (more common): Absence of menses for 6 months in woman with prior regular menses or for 12 months in women with prior oligomenorrhea

III. HISTORY

A. Medical

1. Endocrine or metabolic disorders
2. Galactorrhea (need to exclude pituitary adenoma)
3. Past or present serious illnesses
4. Previous radiation therapy or chemotherapy
5. Recent weight gain or loss/eating disorder
6. Psychological disturbance/depression/stress
7. Athletic training/intense exercise

B. Menstrual

1. Age at menarche
2. Date of last menstrual period
3. Previous menstrual pattern
4. Events surrounding the onset of amenorrhea

C. Reproductive

1. Contraceptive use
2. Gynecologic or obstetric procedures
3. Pregnancies—outcomes, complications
4. Pubertal development

D. Family

1. Age of mother and sister(s) at menarche and menopause
2. Autoimmune disorders
3. Congenital anomalies
4. Endocrinopathies
5. Infertility
6. Menstrual dysfunction
7. Tuberculosis

E. Medications: Associated with amenorrhea

1. Drugs that increase prolactin
   a. Antipsychotics: Phenothiazines, Haloperidol (Haldol), Pimozide (Orap), Clozapine (Clozaril)
   b. Antidepressants: Tricyclic antidepressants, Monoamine oxidase inhibitors
   c. Antihypertensives: Calcium channel blockers, Methyldopa (Aldomet), Reserpine
2. Drugs with estrogenic activity: Digitalis, Marijuana, Flavinoids, Oral contraceptives
3. Drugs with ovarian toxicity: Busulfan (Myleran), Chlorambucil (Leukeran), Cisplatin (Platinol), Cyclophosphamide (Cytoxan, Neosar), Fluorouracil

IV. PHYSICAL

A. General: Body habitus and proportion, obesity, body hair extent and distribution

B. HEENT: Excessive facial hair, acne, funduscopic exam to evaluate for papilledema, visual fields. Assess thyroid for goiter or nodules

C. Breast development and presence of galactorrhea (fat globules visible per microscope exam)

D. Abdomen: Striae in nulliparous women (hypercortisolism)

E. Genitalia: Refer to Tanner Stages

V. LABS

A. Pregnancy test
B. See algorithm below for TSH, Prolactin, FSH, and LH
C. Other labs to consider obtaining to rule out systemic disease include: CBC, Calcium, Phosphorous, Thyroxine, thyroid antibodies, ESR, total Protein, RF, ANA

VI. EVALUATION

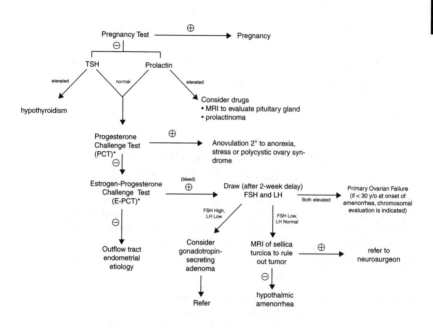

*Refer to text for description of these diagnostic tests

A. Progesterone Challenge Test (PCT)
1. Method: Give **Medroxyprogesterone Acetate (MPA)** 10mg PO QD × 5 days, or **Progesterone (Prometrium)** 400mg PO BID × 5 days
2. Results: The test is positive if there is *any* vaginal bleeding within 2–7 days after the fifth tablet. This confirms a diagnosis of anovulation. There is adequate endogenous estrogen, and the outflow tract is patent

B. Estrogen-Progesterone Challenge Test (E-PCT)
1. Method: Give **Conjugated Estrogen** 1.25mg PO QD × 21 days, add **MPA** 10mg (or **Progesterone (Prometrium)** 400mg PO BID) days 16–21. Repeat cycle if no bleeding by day 28
2. Results: A positive test indicates menstruation is possible if adequate stimulatory estrogen is available. The workup is depicted in diagram. A negative test requires referral to a gynecologist for further studies

VII. MANAGEMENT

A. Anovulation secondary to inadequate Progesterone (i.e., positive PCT) indicates increased risk of endometrial cancer because of hyperplastic effect of unopposed estrogen. In addition, there may also be increased risk for breast cancer
1. To reduce risk of endometrial disease and to provide cycle regularity, give MPA 10mg PO QD (or **Progesterone (Prometrium)** 400mg BID) for first 7–10 days of each month

2. If pregnancy is desired, consider ovulation induction
3. If pregnancy is not desired, then give low dose cyclic oral contraceptives

B. Hypoestrogenic women (i.e. negative PCT and positive E-PCT) should be further evaluated with LH and FSH (see algorithm). Elevated levels are indicative of primary ovarian failure. If onset of amenorrhea is age < 30, chromosomal analysis is indicated

CLINICAL PEARLS
- Normally, the arm span and height measures are similar. If the arm span is 5cm greater than the height, suspect hypogonadal disease
- Prevalence of secondary amenorrhea is higher in certain subgroups such as college students, ballet dancers, and competitive endurance athletes

Reference
Kiningham, RB; Apgar BS, Schwenk TL. Evaluation of amenorrhea. Am Fam Phys 1996;53:1185–94.

Michael B. Weinstock, MD
Tina Nelson, MD
Beth Weinstock, MD

29. MENOPAUSE & HORMONE REPLACEMENT THERAPY

DEFINITION: Menopause is amenorrhea for 12 months in the presence of signs of hypoestrogenemia and a serum follicle-stimulating hormone (FSH) level higher than 40 IU/l. Menopause can also be diagnosed on the basis of subjective symptoms such as hot flashes, or the result of a progesterone withdrawal. (Mean age 51, range ages 40–58)

I. SIGNS: The perimenopause begins with skipped periods, increased or decreased interval between menses, or long or heavy bleeding

II. SYMPTOMS: Vasomotor (hot flashes, sweating), insomnia, nervousness, atrophic vaginitis, urinary atrophy (stress or urge incontinence), skin atrophy (wrinkles), osteoporosis, arteriosclerosis. Symptoms last from several months to several years. Some women may be asymptomatic

III. DIAGNOSIS
  A. If patient has 3 months of amenorrhea: Obtain FSH level or give **Provera** to stimulate withdrawal bleeding
  1. Obtain FSH level: Sequential measurements may be helpful
    a. *If FSH is high* (> 40mIU/mL), then patient is in menopause. The pituitary is trying to stimulate ovulation, but patient is in menopause/ovarian failure. Consider starting hormone replacement therapy (HRT) (see IV below)
    b. *If FSH is low* (< 40mIU/mL), then the patient is not in menopause. May be perimenopausal. Cycle with **Provera 10mg QD (or Prometrium 400mg BID)** × 7 **days per month if patient wants to induce menses**
  2. Withdrawal bleeding: **Provera 10mg QD × 7 days**
    a. If there is no withdrawal bleeding, then repeat in 3 months. If she still has no withdrawal bleeding, assume she is in menopause. Consider starting HRT (see IV below)
    b. If there is withdrawal bleeding, then patient is not in menopause
  B. If patient is having symptoms (hot flashes, etc.) and is not amenorrheic and FSH is elevated (> 20mIU/mL), then she is in the transitional phase and menopause will most likely occur in the next several years
  1. These patients may be placed on low dose oral contraceptives, such as **Loestrin** 1/20, for symptom relief. Patients should be free of the following risk factors: hypertension, hypercholesterolemia, cigarette smoking, previous thromboembolic disorders, cerebrovascular disease or coronary artery disease
  2. Cyclic progestins may be used for women who are not candidates for OCP. One approach is **Provera** 10mg daily (or **Prometrium** 400mg BID) for 10 days each month to

induce withdrawal bleeding and decrease the risk of endometrial hyperplasia
- **C. If the patient is on oral contraceptives,** measure the FSH on the 6th day of the pill-free interval. If FSH > 40 mIU/mL, then change to HRT
- **D. If patient has heavy menses** (passing clots or social inconvenience) for 3 months, bleeding between menses for 3–4 months, or 3 consecutive months of menses which last longer than 7 days, then perform Pipelle biopsy and/or transvaginal ultrasound. Manifestations of malignancy (bleeding) *must not* be dismissed as early menopause

IV. MANAGEMENT OF MENOPAUSE
- **A. Hormone replacement therapy (HRT)**
  1. Advantages of HRT
     - a. Control of vasomotor symptoms
     - b. Avoid or reverse atrophic vaginitis
     - c. Prevention of colon cancer and osteoporotic fractures
     - d. Prevents urinary tract atrophy symptoms such as dysuria, urgency, recurrent urinary tract infections and stress urinary incontinence
     - e. May improve short-term memory and psychological function in postmenopausal women
  2. Disadvantages
     - a. Increased risk of breast cancer
     - b. Double the risk of gallbladder disease
     - c. Increase the risk of thromboembolic diseases and CHD
     - d. Possible small increase in risk of breast cancer
     - e. Growth of uterine myomas
     - f. Endometrial cancer if not taken with progestins
     - g. Cost and inconvenience
  3. Contraindications to HRT
     - a. Breast cancer that is estrogen receptor positive
     - b. Unexplained abnormal uterine bleeding
     - c. History of thrombophlebitis, thromboembolic disorders, or stroke
     - d. Active liver disease
     - e. Known or suspected pregnancy
  4. Controversies: Two recent trials (see references below) suggest that there may be an increase in coronary heart disease events in combination hormone therapy patients who have a history of heart disease
- **B. Dose:** If the patient has had a hysterectomy, progesterone is not necessary
  1. Continuous HRT
     - a. **Premarin** (**Conjugated Estrogen** derived from urine of pregnant mares) 0.3mg, 0.45 mg, 0.625mg, 0.9mg, or 1.25mg—plus—**Provera** 2.5mg or 5mg QD. Can start **Premarin** at standard dose of 0.3 or 0.625mg and can increase dose for several months to 0.9mg or 1.25mg if vasomotor symptoms are persistent. Breakthrough bleeding may be decreased by increasing **Provera** from 2.5mg to 5.0mg
     - b. **Prempro** (**Premarin** 0.625mg/**Provera** 2.5mg or 5mg), 0.45/1.5
     - c. **FemHRT** (**Ethinyl Estradiol** 5mg and **Norethindrone Acetate** 1mg)
     - d. **Ortho-Prefest** (**Estradiol** 1mg alone for 3 days, then **Estradiol** 1mg with **Norgestimate** for 3 days, alternating)
     - e. **Activella** (soy-derived **Ethinyl Estradiol** 1mg and **Norethindrone Acetate** 1mg)
     - f. All of the above products are effective, but seem to have different effects on lipids and breakthrough bleeding. **Prempro** and **Ortho-Prefest** tend to lower LDL and increase HDL. **Activella** and **FemHRT** lower both LDL and HDL cholesterol, but seem to work better to induce amenorrhea (97% of women are amenorrheic at 1yr on **Activella**, 83% on **FemHRT**, and 65% on **Prempro**)
     - g. Side effects: Breast pain, headache, weight gain, back pain, nausea, emotional lability, URI/sinusitis, and breakthrough bleeding
  2. Cyclic HRT:
     - a. **Premarin** 0.625mg, day 1–25 or QD, plus **Provera** (10mg) or **Prometrium**

(200mg) day 1–12 or last 12 days of estrogen administration. Can also use **Micronized Estradiol (Estrace)** for cyclic HRT

    b. **Premphase** combination tablet: 0.625mg **Premarin** day 1–14, then 0.625mg **Premarin** plus 5mg **Provera** (in same tablet) for day 15–28

    c. **Esterified Estrogens (Estratab, Menest)** 0.3, 0.625, 2.5mg. Indicated for cyclic use, 3 weeks on, then 1 week off, with a progesterone as needed

    d. Withdrawal bleeding will continue in 40–60% of women

3. Natural HRT (continuous): The use of hormones that the human body makes rather than synthetic analogs

    a. **Estrace (Micronized Estradiol)** 0.5, 1, or 2mg QD

    b. **Ogen, Ortho-Est (Estropipate)** 0.625, 1.25, or 2.5mg QD

    c. **Prometrium (Micronized Progesterone)**: 100mg QD. Reported not to adversely affect lipids compared to synthetic progesterones. Also produced by special compounding as a topical cream (40–1000mg/day of 1.5 or 3% strength) applied BID to abdomen or inner thighs. Absorption of topical cream may be unpredictable

4. Combination estrogen/testosterone therapy: **Estratest** (esterified estrogens 0.625mg, methyltestosterone 2.5mg) or **Estratest HS** (0.625/1.25mg). Often used to improve sense of well-being and libido. Controversial due to change in lipid profile (decrease in HDL cholesterol)

5. Transdermal HRT

    a. **Estrogen**: **Climara** and **FemPatch** are applied once weekly. **Alora**, **Estraderm**, and **Vivelle** are applied twice weekly. Convenient in women after hysterectomy

    b. **Estrogen/Progesterone patch**: **Combipatch** (0.05mg **Estradiol**/0.14mg **Norethindrone**) is applied twice weekly for women with an intact uterus

6. Soy supplementation

    a. **Isoflavones** found in soy products have weak estrogenic effects and may be an alternative to estrogen for vasomotor symptoms and prevention of osteoporosis

    b. Advantages: Natural product, reported to lower total cholesterol by 10%, improve hot flashes

    c. Disadvantages: Less effective than estrogens, need more than 4 servings of soy food products per day to relieve vasomotor symptoms, benefits disappear after 6 weeks, may stimulate estrogen-sensitive malignancies

C. Hot flashes: May use if patient has contraindications to HRT, for patients with vasomotor intolerance who are not ready for HRT, or concurrently with HRT

1. **Clonidine**: 0.1–0.15mg PO QD or **Clonidine Patch** (0.1mg/week). Side effects minimal at these doses, but may include dry mouth, drowsiness, decreased blood pressure

2. Progestins such as **Medroxyprogesterone** (10–30mg orally/day) or **Megestrol Acetate** (20–40mg orally/day) may be helpful for hot flashes. If either of these results in intolerable side effects, alternative progestins may be given

3. **Venlafaxine (Effexor)** 75–150mg PO QD

4. **Black Cohosh** is an herbal supplement that some women use to treat hot flashes and other menopausal symptoms. Limit use < 6 months

5. Soy products: See previous section

6. Many women have mild hot flashes that may need treated. If they are not taking hormone replacement therapy, they should be told that symptoms subside slowly over 3–5yrs

D. Vaginal atrophy/dyspareunia

1. **Premarin, Estrace, Dienestrol, Ogen vaginal cream** (0.01% mg/gm): 1/8 applicatorful nightly for 7–10 nights, then every other night or twice weekly after restoration of vaginal mucosa

2. **Estring**: Estradiol vaginal ring (2mg/ring) that is inserted into upper 1/3 of vaginal vault and replaced every 3 months

E. Other therapies

1. **Calcium**: 1000–1500mg QD and **Vitamin D$_3$** 400–800 IU QD

2. Exercise and diet
3. Avoidance of smoking, excessive alcohol, and caffeine

F. For management of osteoporosis—See Chapter 73, Osteoporosis
G. Patient monitoring
1. Annual Pap smear
2. Annual mammography
3. Endometrial sampling or vaginal ultrasound in patients with abnormal uterine bleeding
4. Dual-energy x-ray absorptiometry (DEXA) scan to evaluate for osteoporosis if > 65 or with risk factors
5. Monitor lipid profile periodically

GYN

CLINICAL PEARLS

- In a recent study, absolute risk of breast cancer was shown to be increased by an additional 1 to 2 breast cancers per 1000 women on HRT for about 5yrs or longer after the age 50. For those women who take HRT for longer than 10yrs, there will be 6 excess cases of breast cancer
- 85% of women will have hot flashes and night sweats when they go through menopause
- 10% of women stop having their menstrual period by 45–46yrs of age. 1% enter menopause before age 40. Women live $^1/_3$ to ½ of their lives in menopause
- The Framingham Heart Study found that 10-year incidence of CVD in postmenopausal women age 50–59 was 4-fold higher than in premenopausal women of the same age range. Menopause occurring before age 35 has been associated with a 2- to 3-fold increased risk of myocardial infarction. Oophorectomy (before age 35) increases the risk 7-fold
- Late menopause is a risk factor for breast cancer and uterine cancer

References

Rowan T, et al. Influence of estrogen plus progestin on breast cancer and mammography in healthy postmenopausal women: The women's health initiative randomized trial. JAMA 2003;289:3243–53.

Li C, et al. Relationship between long durations and different regimens of hormone therapy and risk of breast cancer. JAMA 2003;289:3254–3263.

Writing Group for the Women's Health Initiative Investigators. Risks and benefits of estrogen plus progestin in healthy postmenopausal women. Principal results from the Women's Health Initiative randomized controlled trial. JAMA 2002;288:321–33.

Zandi PP, et al. Hormone replacement therapy and incidence of Alzheimer disease in older women. JAMA Nov 6, 2002;288:2123–9.

Collaborative Group on Hormonal Factors in Breast Cancer. Breast cancer and hormone replacement therapy: combined reanalysis of data from 51 epidemiological studies involving 52,705 women with breast cancer and 108,411 women without breast cancer. Lancet 1997;350:1047–59.

Hulley S, et al. Radomized trial of estrogen plus progestin for secondary prevention of coronary heart disease in postmenopausal women. Heart and Estrogen/Progestin Replacement Study (HERS) Research Group. JAMA 1998;280:605–13.

Archer DF, et al. A comparative study of transvaginal uterine ultrasound and endometrial biopsy for evaluating the endometrium of postmenopausal women taking hormone replacement therapy. Menopause Fall 1999;6:201–8.

Archer DF, et al. Uterine bleeding in postmenopausal women on continuous therapy with estradiol and norethindrone acetate. Obstet Gynecol Sep 1999;94:323–9.

Bachmann GA. Vasomotor flushes in postmenopausal women. Am J Obstet Gynecol 1999;180:312–6.

de Aloysio D, et al. The effect of menopause on blood lipid and lipoprotein levels. Atherosclerosis 1999;147:147–3.

Mike Hemsworth, MD
Daniel M. Neides, MD

GYN

30. THE PREMENSTRUAL SYNDROME & DYSMENORRHEA

Comparative features between PMS and Primary Dysmenorrhea

Feature	PMS	Primary Dysmenorrhea
Time of Onset:	10–14 days before menses	1 day before or on 1st day of menses
Improvement:	Onset of menses	End of menses
Childbirth:	Worsens	Improves

PART I: THE PREMENSTRUAL SYNDROME (PMS)

DEFINITION: A condition characterized by debilitating affective, behavioral, cognitive, and somatic complaints which interferes with normal functioning. It develops in the 7–14 days before menses and subsides with the onset of menstruation

I. PREVALENCE and statistics
   A. Age of affected women is 25–40
   B. Affects about 33% of premenopausal women
   C. 40–50% of women presenting to the physician with premenstrual complaints will meet criteria for PMS

II. ETIOLOGY: No specific deficiency or abnormality has been identified. Theories include:
   A. Deficiency of progesterone—now mostly disregarded
   B. Alterations in ovarian hormone production/derangements in relative amounts of estrogen and progesterone—no abnormal hormone levels found
   C. Alterations at the hypothalamic or suprahypothalamic level

III. SYMPTOMS AND SIGNS: There are no diagnostic physical signs of PMS
   A. **Affective:** Irritability, emotional lability, anxiety, depression
   B. **Behavioral:** Food cravings, hostility, aggression, altered libido
   C. **Cognitive:** Forgetfulness, poor concentration, confusion
   D. **Somatic:** Bloating, fluid retention, weight gain, headache, mastalgia, fatigue, insomnia

IV. DIAGNOSIS based on the following:
   A. Symptom complex consistent with PMS as above
   B. Symptoms must occur exclusively in the luteal phase
   C. Symptoms must be severe enough to interfere with normal functioning
   D. Prospective symptom report over a period of at least 2 or 3 cycles
   E. Exclusion of other psychological and physical disorders by detailed history and physical exam

V. MANAGEMENT: No one treatment is effective for everyone with PMS. It is important to educate and reassure the patient, and tailor the treatment to the individual. It may take some time to find the best option for each patient
   A. **Lifestyle changes:** Try as an initial approach
      1. Nutrition
         a. Avoid refined sugar, salt, red meat, alcohol, and caffeine
         b. A good PMS diet consists of 60% complex carbohydrates, 20% protein, 20% fat
         c. Rely more on fish, poultry, whole grains, and legumes for protein, and less on red meats and dairy products

        d. Nutritional supplements may be helpful:
            Vitamin B$_6$ 50–500mg QD: Discontinue if no improvement due to risks of
                neurologic symptoms
            Vitamin E 400 IU QD: May reduce mood symptoms and food cravings
            Magnesium 360mg QD
    2. Avoid smoking
    3. Aerobic exercise
    4. Stress management: Identify stressors first, then look for ways to deal with them
    5. Adequate sleep
B. Medications
    1. SSRIs: These are effective for relieving tension, irritability, and dysphoria. **Fluoxetine
        (Prozac)** 20mg QD has been studied most, but all are probably equally effective
    2. Oral contraceptive pills: May also worsen symptoms
    3. Tricyclic antidepressants
    4. GnRH agonists: **Lupron, Depot-Lupron, Buserelin** (investigational drug in US). Cause a
        medical menopause with menopausal side effects. Not recommended for > 6 months
    5. **Danazol:** May reduce premenstrual mastalgia, but has adverse side effects
    6. Diuretics: **Spironolactone** is the only diuretic shown to be effective. May alleviate
        bloating
    7. **Benzodiazepines:** For high anxiety before menes. High addictive potential
C. Surgery: TAH and BSO is last resort. GnRH agonists should be used first to predict
    response to oophorectomy

PART II: PRIMARY DYSMENORRHEA

DEFINITION: Primary dysmenorrhea is painful menstruation without detectable pelvic disease.
    Secondary dysmenorrhea is painful menstruation associated with an anatomic cause
    (endometriosis, adhesions, fibroids, other anomalies)

I. PREVALENCE: Frequency decreases after age 20. Affects 50–75% of women, with 5–6% having
    incapacitating pain

II. ETIOLOGY: Increased endometrial prostaglandin production causing higher uterine tone and
decreased blood flow

III. SIGNS AND SYMPTOMS
    A. Abdominal cramping: May radiate to the back or inner thighs
        1. Onset usually begins many hours prior to menstruation with most severe cramping occurring
            on the first day
        2. Cramping may last anywhere from several hours up to 2–3 days
    B. Dizziness, headache, flushing
    C. Nausea, vomiting, diarrhea
    D. Depression

IV. DIAGNOSIS: Exclude pelvic pathology with thorough history and physical exam. Consider
cultures and other diagnostic studies as indicated

V. MANAGEMENT
    A. Primary dysmenorrhea: NSAIDs are treatment of choice. Begin with onset of bleeding
        and continue for 2–3 days
    B. Secondary dysmenorrhea: Causes often include endometriosis, pelvic inflammatory
        disease, submucous myoma, IUD use, cervical stenosis. Address underlying cause

CLINICAL PEARLS
    • Patients who experience mood swings with PMS can also develop mild to moderate depres-
        sion, which is known as premenstrual dysphoric disorder (PMDD). Selective serotonin
        reuptake inhibitors (SSRIs) have been found to be an effective treatment

- Patients who complain of worsening abdominal cramping with each period or who complain of pain not associated with menstruation may have secondary dysmenorrhea (e.g., endometriosis, fibroids)

References

Wyatt K, et al. Premenstrual syndrome. Clin Evidence 2000;4:1121.

Wilson M, et al. Dysmenorrhea. Clin Evidence 2000;4:1045.

Freeman E, et al. Differential response to antidepressants in women with premenstrual syndrome/premenstrual dysphoric disorder: A randomized controlled trial. Arch Gen Psychiatry Oct 1999;56:932.

Deuster PA, et al. Biological, social, and behavioral factors associated with premenstrual syndrome. Arch Fam Med Mar/Apr 1999;8:122.

American College of Obstetricians and Gynecologists Committee on Gynecologic Practice. ACOG committee opinion: premenstrual syndrome. Int J Gynaecol Obstet 1995;50:80–84.

Michael B. Weinstock, MD
Beth Weinstock, MD

31. EVALUATION OF BREAST MASS, BREAST PAIN & NIPPLE DISCHARGE

I. NIPPLE DISCHARGE: 3–10% of breast complaints. Under age 60, ~ 7% cancer. Over age 60, ~ 32% cancer (usually intraductal carcinoma)
 A. History
  1. Duration of symptoms
  2. Unilateral or bilateral. Color of discharge (clear, serous, milky, bloody, green). Bilateral milky discharge suggests endocrine etiology; pathologic discharges are usually unilateral and confined to 1 duct
  3. Presence of blood (increases chances of malignancy)
  4. Medication use (oral contraceptives, phenothiazines, antihypertensives)
  5. Lactation/breast-feeding history
  6. Spontaneous or with stimulation (spontaneous discharge more common with pathologic discharge)
 B. Physical exam: Asymmetry, mass, express both nipples for discharge, hemocult the discharge
 C. Evaluation
  1. If discharge is *heme-negative and bilateral*, then conservative management with follow-up in 1–2 months. Obtain mammogram if not up to date. Evaluate for endocrine abnormalities if indicated. If the discharge is still present in 1–2 months, then proceed as if it were heme-positive
  2. All patients with spontaneous or unilateral nipple discharge should be referred for surgical evaluation regardless if discharge is bloody or clear. If discharge is *heme-positive*, then consult a surgeon to perform diagnostic mammography followed by possible terminal duct excision
  3. Cytology is generally not useful
  4. Galactorrhea (milky discharge) is evaluated differently than pathologic or clear discharge. Galactorrhea may be secondary to chest wall trauma, nipple stimulation, or meds. Also may be secondary to hypothyroidism, pituitary adenomas, and amenorrhea syndromes. Surgical referral generally not necessary

II. BREAST PAIN (MASTALGIA)
 A. Differential
  1. Fibrocystic breast disease
  2. Cancer: Cyclical mastalgia (7–17% of patients with cancer reported mastalgia in 1 study)

3. Costochondritis
4. Trauma
5. Mastitis (See Chapter 4, Infant Formula & Breast-feeding)
B. Physical exam—as above
C. Evaluation
   1. If mass is present, see next section
   2. If < age 35 and no mass, have patient return for follow up exam in 1–2 months
   3. If > age 35 and no mass, then proceed to breast imaging. If negative, have patient follow up in 1–2 months for a recheck
D. Treatment
   1. **Danazol**: Approved by FDA for treatment of breast pain. 100–400mg/day. 75% response rate, but high incidence of side effects
   2. Alternatives: Evening primrose oil, caffeine avoidance, Vitamin E may be helpful

GYN

III. BREAST MASS
A. History
   1. Age of patients
   2. Duration
   3. Change in size
   4. Fluctuation with menstrual cycle
   5. Previous biopsies or masses
B. Physical exam
   1. Cystic or solid
   2. Regular or irregular borders
   3. Movable or fixed
   4. Enlarged lymph nodes
   5. Skin changes; peau d'orange
C. Evaluation of solitary breast mass: Cystic or solid (determine by exam or ultrasound)
   1. If cystic, then proceed to aspiration (22 gauge needle)
      a. If aspiration is non bloody and mass disappears, follow-up in 4–6 weeks and imaging per American Cancer Society (ACS) guidelines—cytology not necessary
      b. If aspiration is bloody or mass does not disappear, then breast imaging and referral for biopsy
   2. If solid, then breast imaging and referral for biopsy

IV. TESTING
A. Needle aspiration
B. Mammography
C. Ultrasound
D. Biopsy

V. INDICATIONS FOR OPEN BREAST BIOPSY
A. Equivocal cytologic findings on aspiration
B. Bloody cyst fluid on aspiration
C. Failure of mass to disappear completely after fluid aspiration
D. Recurrence of cyst after one or two aspirations
E. Bloody nipple discharge
F. Nipple excoriation (Paget's disease of breast)
G. Skin edema and erythema suggestive of inflammatory breast carcinoma

CLINICAL PEARLS
• Mammography is 75–90% sensitive at differentiating between benign and malignant disease. Sensitivity is very dependent on interpreter's skill
• The differential diagnosis of a breast mass in a lactating woman includes blocked milk ducts and mastitis. A blocked duct may be relieved by massaging the breast during nursing

References

Sox H. Screening mammography for younger women: back to basics [Editorial]. Ann Intern Med Sept 3, 2002;137:361–2.

U.S. Preventive Services Task Force. Screening for breast cancer: recommendations and rationale. Ann Intern Med Sept 3, 2002;67:339–44.

Morrow M. Evaluation of common breast problems. Am Fam Phys 2000;61:2371–8.

Dixon JM, et al. Risk of breast cancer in women with palpable breast cysts: a prospective study. Lancet 1999;353:1742–5.

Duijm LE, et al. Value of breast imaging in women with painful breasts: observational follow-up study. BMJ 1998;317:1492–5.

Greenberg R, et al. Management of breast fibroadenomas. J Gen Intern Med 1998;339:1021–9.

Morrow M, Wong S, Venta L. The evaluation of breast masses in women younger than forty years of age. Surgery 1998;124:634–41.

Elmore JG, et al. Ten-year risk of false positive screening mammograms and clinical breast examinations. N Engl J Med 1998;338:1089–96.

Gulay H, Bora S, Kilicturgay S, et al. Nipple discharge and rate of malignant breast disease. J Am Coll Surg 1994;178:471–4.

Michael B. Weinstock, MD
Ann M. Aring, MD

32. VAGINITIS &
SEXUALLY TRANSMITTED DISEASES (STDs)

DEFINITION: Vaginitis is inflammation of the vagina which results from infection (bacterial, fungal, protozoan), atrophic changes, dermatitis, or mechanical factors

I. GENERAL: An estimated 3% of the population 18 to 35 has untreated chlamydia infection and about 5.3% has untreated gonorrhea infection

II. HISTORY
   A. Vaginal discharge: Color, smell, viscosity, duration, relation to menses
   B. Vaginal and vulvar itching
   C. Sexual history: New sexual partner, unprotected sex, partner with known STD, previous STDs
   D. Predisposing factors: Recent ATB use, hot tubs, swimming pools, diabetes, HIV, immunosuppressed state (predisposition to *Candida* infection)
   E. Contact dermatitis questions (new clothes, pads, soaps, feminine deodorant soap, latex condoms)

III. PHYSICAL
   A. Visually inspect skin, labia, vaginal walls, and cervix for discharge, erythema, lesions, warts
   B. Bi-manual examination for adnexal or cervical motion tenderness (CMT)
   C. Abdominal examination for suprapubic tenderness (UTI) or bilateral lower abdominal tenderness (PID), unilateral lower abdominal tenderness (cyst, ectopic pregnancy, tubo-ovarian abscess, or PID)

IV. LABORATORY
   A. *Gonorrhea* and *Chlamydia* cultures if indicated
   B. Appearance
      1. White, cottage cheese, yeast smell: *Candida*
      2. Green, bubbly, with "strawberry spots" on vaginal walls and cervix: *Trichomonas*
      3. Grey, low viscosity, adherent to vaginal walls: Bacterial vaginosis
   C. Vaginal pH
      1. pH 3.5 to 4.5: *Candida*
      2. pH > 4.5: Bacterial vaginosis (*Gardnerella*); pH <4.5, it is unlikely patient has BV
      3. pH > 6: *Trichomonas*
      4. pH > 7: Atrophic
   D. Wet mount (KOH and saline): Apply 2 samples to 2 areas of slide, then place 1 drop of KOH to the first and normal saline to the other. Cover and examine under microscope

1. Pseudomycelia: *Candida* (there is a significant false negative rate with wet mounts for *Candida*. If the wet mount is negative and *Candida* is suspected, then treat empirically and/or plate specimen on Nickersons agar)
2. Clue cells, positive "whiff" test: Bacterial vaginosis (*Gardnerella*)
   a. Clue cells: Epithelial cells appear stippled due to presence of bacteria
   b. "Whiff test": Bacterial vaginosis infection will give off characteristic fishy odor when saturated with KOH. The presence of *Lactobacillus* or pH < 4.5 excludes the diagnosis of bacterial vaginosis
3. Motile organisms with flagella: *Trichomonas*

GYN

V. MANAGEMENT OF DISEASES CHARACTERIZED BY VAGINAL DISCHARGE

A. Vulvovaginal candidiasis: Evaluate for contributing causes including pregnancy, diabetes, use of ATB, or corticosteroids. Local factors contributing to risk may include heat, moisture, and occlusive clothing
   1. Oral
      a. **Fluconazole (Diflucan):** 150mg PO × 1. Side effect: GI upset. Cost is comparable or less than topical meds
      b. **Nystatin:** 100,000 units PO QD–BID × 2 weeks—refractory cases
   2. Topical/Intravaginal
      a. **Miconazole (Monistat-3)** vaginal suppositories: 1 intravaginally QHS × 3 days or Miconazole vaginal cream QHS × 7 days
      b. **Clotrimazole (Gyne-Lotrimin):** 2–100mg tablets intravaginally or cream QHS × 3 days
      c. **Terconazole (Tetrazol)** vaginal cream 0.4%: 1 applicator intravaginally QHS × 7 days
      d. **Gentian violet:** Paint vaginal walls Q month in office × 3 months

B. Recurrent vulvovaginal candidiasis (RVVC)
   1. Definition: 4 episodes in 1yr or 3 episodes unrelated to ATB use in 1yr
   2. For chronic recurrent RVVC caused by *C. Albicans*, use initial course of therapy (see above) and then follow by a 6 month maintenance regimen:
      a. **Clotrimazole (Gyne-Lotrimin):** Two, 100mg tablets intravaginally twice weekly
      b. **Ketoconazole (Nizoral):** 100mg PO QD
      c. **Fluconazole (Diflucan):** 150mg PO once per month
      d. **Boric acid:** 600mg vaginal suppository QD for 5 days with the onset of menstruation

C. Bacterial vaginosis *(Gardnerella)*: Is not sexually transmitted
   1. **Metronidazole (Flagyl):** 500mg PO BID × 7 days —*or*— 2g PO × 1
   2. **Clindamycin Phosphate cream (Cleocin) 2%*:** 1 applicator 5g intravaginally QHS × 7 days
   3. **Metronidazole gel 0.75% (Metrogel vaginal)*:** 1 applicator 5g intravaginally BID × 5D
   * Topical therapy of BV is slightly less effective than PO

D. *Trichomonas*: Protozoal flagellate which is sexually transmitted
   Metronidazole (Flagyl): 2g PO × 1 *(Treat partner!)*

E. *Chlamydia trachomatis* (urethral, cervical or rectal): Recommend testing for syphilis and HIV. See Chapter 33, Pelvic Inflammatory Disease for treatment of PID. Also treat partner
   1. **Doxycycline (Vibramycin, Doryx):** 100mg PO BID × 7days
   2. **Azithromycin (Zithromax):** 1g PO × 1
   3. **Ofloxacin (Floxin):** 300mg PO BID × 7days

F. *Gonorrhea* (urethral, cervical or rectal), uncomplicated. Consider testing for syphilis and HIV. See Chapter 33, Pelvic Inflammatory Disease for treatment of PID. Also treat partner
   Note: Each of the following is given with **Doxycycline** 100mg PO BID × 7days or **Azithromycin (Zithromax)** 1g PO × 1
   1. **Ceftriaxone (Rocephin):** 125mg IM × 1
   2. **Cefixime (Suprax):** 400mg PO × 1
   3. **Ciprofloxacin (Cipro):** 500mg PO × 1
   4. **Ofloxacin (Floxin):** 400mg PO × 1

G. Atrophic vaginitis
   1. **Estrogen cream (Premarin** 1–2g, **Ogen** 2–4g) intravaginally QHS. Use for 3 weeks/month

2. **Premarin** 0.625mg PO QD: Add **Provera** if patient still has uterus. See Chapter 29, Menopause & Hormone Replacement Therapy

VI. MANAGEMENT OF DISEASES CHARACTERIZED BY GENITAL LESIONS

A. Herpes simplex virus

1. First episode: Obtain viral culture to confirm diagnosis
   a. **Acyclovir (Zovirax):** 400mg PO TID for 7–10 days or 200mg PO 5 × day for 7–10 days
   b. **Famciclovir (Famvir):** 250mg PO TID for 7–10 days
   c. **Valacyclovir (Valtrex):** 1g PO BID for 7–10 days
2. Recurrent episodes
   a. **Acyclovir:** 400mg PO TID for 5 days or 200mg PO 5 × day for 5 days or 800mg PO BID for 5 days
   b. **Famciclovir:** 125mg PO BID for 5 days
   c. **Valacyclovir:** 500mg PO BID for 5 days
3. Daily suppressive therapy
   a. **Acyclovir:** 400mg PO BID
   b. **Famciclovir:** 250mg PO BID
   c. **Valacyclovir**
      i. For patients with < 10 episodes/yr: 500mg PO QD
      ii. For patients with > 10 episodes/yr: 1000mg PO QD
4. Counseling is an important aspect of managing patients who have genital herpes
   a. Discuss natural history of the disease with emphasis on potential for recurrent episodes, asymptomatic viral shedding, and sexual transmission
   b. Abstain from sexual activity when lesions or prodromal symptoms are present and inform their sex partner. Use of condoms during all sexual exposures with new or uninfected sex partners should be encouraged
   c. Sexual transmission of HSV can occur during asymptomatic periods. Asymptomatic viral shedding occurs more frequently in patients who have genital HSV-2 infection than HSV-1 infection and in patients who have had genital herpes for less than 12 months
   d. The risk for neonatal infection should be explained to all patients, including men. Childbearing-aged women who have genital herpes should be advised to inform healthcare providers who care for them during pregnancy

B. Human papilloma virus (HPV) or genital warts

1. **External genital area**
   a. **Podofilox (Condylox):** 0.5% solution BID for 3 days, wait 4 days and repeat as necessary for 4 cycles
   b. **Imiquimod (Aldara):** 5% cream daily at bedtime 3 times a week for up to 16 weeks
   c. **Cryotherapy** with liquid nitrogen by physician. May be repeated every 1 to 2 weeks
   d. **Trichloroacetic Acid** or **Bichloracetic Acid** 80 to 90% applied by physician weekly
   e. **Podophyllum** 10 to 25% applied by physician weekly
2. **Vaginal**
   a. **Cryotherapy** with liquid nitrogen by physician. May be repeated every 1 to 2 weeks
   b. **Trichloroacetic Acid** or **Bichloracetic Acid** 80 to 90% applied by physician weekly
   c. **Podophyllum** 10 to 25% applied by physician weekly

CLINICAL PEARLS

- In women with RVVC who fail to respond to treatment, it is important to reestablish the diagnosis and make sure they are being treated appropriately
- Patients with a STD may initially present with a complaint of dysuria
- Genital ulcerations may be caused by syphilis, herpes, chancroid, or lymphogranuloma venereum. Herpes and chancroid are painful, others are not
- Vulvar pruritus is the most common presentation of vulvar dysplasia. If patient has a negative workup for vaginitis then patient should be worked up for vulvar dysplasia by using toluidine blue stain and biopsy or vulvar colposcopy and biopsy

- Perform the "sniff test" by applying KOH *to the speculum* for better sensitivity for bacterial vaginosis
- An early manifestation of HIV may be recurrent vaginal yeast infections

References

Centers for Disease Control and Prevention: Sexually transmitted disease treatment guidelines—2002. MMWR 2002;51(RR06):1–80. Available at: http://www.cdc.gov/mmwr/pdf/rr/rr5106.pdf

Turner CF, et al. Untreated gonococcal and chlamydia infection in a probability of sample adults. JAMA 2002; 287(6):726–33.

Nyirjesy P. Chronic vulvovaginal candidiasis. Am Fam Phys 2001;63:697–702.

Michael B. Weinstock, MD
Ann M. Aring, MD

GYN

33. Pelvic Inflammatory Disease (PID)

I. GENERAL
  A. One million cases per year in the US
  B. Long term sequelae include infertility, increased risk of ectopic pregnancy, chronic pain

II. RISK FACTORS: Multiple sexual partners, history of STDs, substance abuse, frequent vaginal douching, young age, IUD use

III. HISTORY: Lower abdominal pain, vaginal discharge, vaginal bleeding, dyspareunia, dysuria, fever, nausea/vomiting. Inquire about risk factors listed above

IV. PHYSICAL EXAM: Fever, lower abdominal tenderness (bilateral vs. unilateral), vaginal discharge, cervical motion tenderness, adnexal tenderness

V. CRITERIA FOR DIAGNOSIS OF PID
  A. **Essential for diagnosis** (all must be present)
    1. Lower abdominal pain
    2. Tenderness on lower abdominal examination
    3. Cervical motion tenderness (CMT)
    4. Adnexal tenderness or mass
  B. **Supportive** (One should be present) Each additional finding raises likelihood of PID by 5–10%
    1. Temp > 38° C
    2. CBC > 10,500
    3. Culdocentesis shows WBC and/or bacteria
    4. Ultrasound or pelvic exam reveals pelvic mass
    5. Increased ESR or CRP
    6. Positive cultures/DNA probe

VI. PATHOGENS: *Chlamydia, N. gonorrhoeæ,* Gram negative facultative bacteria (e.g., *E. coli*), anaerobes, *Streptococcus, Mycoplasma, Actinomyces, G. Vaginalis, H. Influenzæ*

VII. INDICATIONS FOR HOSPITALIZATION FOR ACUTE PID
  A. Suspected or confirmed tubo-ovarian abscess
  B. Adolescent patient or patient with fertility issues
  C. High fever or severe vomiting or dehydration
  D. Pregnancy
  E. Patient has failed outpatient therapy or concern for adherence with outpatient therapy
  F. Immunosuppression
  G. IUD in place

VIII. MANAGEMENT
   A. Outpatient (oral) therapy:
      1. **Regimen A**
         Ofloxacin: 400mg orally twice a day for 14 days—*plus*—
         Metronidazole: 500mg orally twice a day for 14 days
      2. **Regimen B**
         Ceftriaxone: 250mg IM once—*or*—
         Cefoxitin: 2g IM plus **Probenecid:** 1g orally in a single dose concurrently once—*or*—
         Other parenteral third-generation Cephalosporin (e.g., Ceftizoxime or Cefotaxime)—
            plus—
         Doxycycline: 100mg orally twice a day for 14 days (Include this regimen with one
            of the above regimens)
   B. **Follow-up within 72hrs:** Patients should demonstrate significant clinical improvement within
      this time. If not, then additional testing or diagnosis needs to be assessed
   C. **Partner needs to be tested and treated:** Test for HIV, syphilis, and counsel on safe
      sexual practices

CLINICAL PEARLS
   • With 1, 2, or 3 incidences of PID, the chance of infertility is 15, 35, and 55%,
     respectively
   • Risk of ectopic pregnancy is increased 7–10 times—inform patients of increased risk
   • A tubo-ovarian abscess will develop in 7–16% of patients who have had PID. 60–80%
     will resolve with ATBs
   • Recurrent infection occurs in 20–25% of patients who have had PID
   •The major contributing factors in the development of PID with IUDs are the number of sex
     partners and exposure to sexually transmitted diseases

References
Centers for Disease Control and Prevention: Sexually transmitted disease treatment guidelines—
   2002. MMWR 2002;51(RR06):1–80, Available at: http://www.edc.gov/mmwr/pdf/rr/rr5106.pdf
Sarma S. Relationship between use of the intrauterine device and pelvic inflammatory disease. Arch
   Fam Med 1999;8:197.
Aral SO, et al. Morbidity associated with pelvic inflammatory disease. JAMA 1991;266:2570.
Augenbraun M, et al. Compliance with doxycycline therapy in sexually transmitted disease clinics.
   Sex Trans Dis 1998;25:1.

IV. Preventive Medicine

34. Cancer Statistics, Screening & Periodic Health Exams 99

35. Smoking Cessation 102

36. Endocarditis Prophylaxis 104

37. Tuberculosis Screening 108

PREV

PREV

Michael B. Weinstock, MD
Daniel M. Neides, MD

34. Cancer Statistics, Screening & Periodic Health Exams

In 2001—1,268,000 new cancers diagnosed and 553,400 Americans died from cancer related deaths

I. LUNG CANCER

In 2001, there were 169,500 cases of lung cancer with 157,400 deaths. The 5-yr survival rate is < 14%. Survival rate is 49% if the disease is still localized but only 15% of lung cancers are found that early

II. COLORECTAL CANCER

In 2001, there were 135,400 cases of colorectal cancer with 56,700 deaths. The 5-yr survival rate is 61%

III. BREAST CANCER

In 2001, there were 193,700 cases of breast cancer with 40,600 deaths. The 5-yr survival is 97% for localized disease, 77% with regional metastases, and 21% with distant metastases

IV. PROSTATE CANCER

In 2001, there were 198,100 cases of prostate cancer with 31,500 deaths. The 10-yr survival is 72% and 15-yr survival is 53%. Mortality in black men is twice as high as rates in white men

V. PANCREATIC CANCER

In 2001, there were 29,200 cases of pancreatic cancer with 28,900 deaths. The 5-yr survival is 4%

VI. OVARIAN CANCER

In 2001 there were 23,400 cases of ovarian cancer with 13,900 deaths. The 5-yr survival is 79% if confined to the ovary, but only 28% if diagnosed with distant metastases

VII. BLADDER CANCER

In 2001, there were 54,300 cases of bladder cancer with 12,400 deaths. The 5-yr survival is 93% for localized disease. For regional and distant metastases, 5-yr survival is 49% and 6%, respectively

VIII. MALIGNANT MELANOMA

In 2001, there were 51,400 cases of malignant melanoma with 7,800 deaths. The 5-yr survival is 88%. For localized melanoma, the 5-yr survival is 96%. For regional metastases the 5-yr survival is 59%. For those with distant metastases, 5-yr survival is 13%

IX. ORAL CANCER

In 2001 there were 30,100 cases of oral cancer with 7,800 deaths. The 5-yr survival is 54% for all stages combined with a 10-yr survival rate of 43%

X. ENDOMETRIAL CANCER

In 2001 there were 38,300 cases of uterine cancer with 6,600 deaths. The 5-yr survival is 96% if diagnosed at an early stage but drops to 64% if diagnosed at a regional stage

XI. CERVICAL CANCER

In 2001, there were 12,900 cases of cervical cancer with 4,400 deaths. The 5-yr survival is 70%

XII. THYROID CANCER

In 2001, there were 19,500 cases of thyroid cancer with 1,300 deaths. The 5-yr survival is 96%

XIII. TESTICULAR CANCER

In 2001, there were 7,200 cases of testicular cancer with 400 deaths. The 5-yr survival is 96%

American Cancer Society Guidelines for the Early Detection of Cancer (2002) – Note: These guidelines are more conservative than other task force recommendations			
Type of cancer	**Age**	**Test/exam**	**Frequency**	**Comments**
Lung	--	Not recommended. Note: If patients request spiral CT, encourage participation in trials. High rate of positives and complex algorithm for evaluating small nodules		
Colorectal[2]	50	Use one of the following: 1. Fecal occult blood test (FOBT)[1] – annually 2. Flexible sigmoidoscopy – every 5 years 3. FOBT[1] annually and flex sig every 5 years 4. Double contrast barium enema (DCBE) – every 5 years 5. Colonoscopy – every 10 years		Combining flex sig and FOBT is more sensitive and is recommended by the ACS as a better choice than either alone. Recommendations updated 2001
Breast	20	Breast self-exam (BSE)	Monthly	No upper age limit for women in good health. Women with positive family history should consider earlier screening. Recommendations updated 1997
	20-39	Clinical breast exam (CBE)	Every 3 years	
	40	Mammogram and CBE	Annual	
Prostate	50[4]	Prostate specific antigen (PSA) and digital rectal exam (DRE)	Annual if life expectancy is > 10 years	Discuss benefits and limitations with patients prior to testing. Patients who ask the doctor to make the decision should be tested. Data from randomized trials are not yet available
Cervical	18 or with onset of sexual activity	PAP	Initially annually. After 3 negative tests, at the discretion of the physician	Recommendations updated 1991 and are to be revised 2003. See chapter 26, PAP smears: Indications and interpretation
Endometrial	Not recommended for patients at average risk. Ask patients at increased risk about vag. bleeding or other CA warning signs. Women at high risk[3] should have screening at age 35. Recommendations updated 2001		

[1]FOBT should be performed by collecting 2 samples from 3 consecutive at home specimens and not as single test in the office (colonic neoplasms bleed intermittently). Positive results should be followed with colonoscopy.
[2]Patients at increased/high risk should have individualized screening (see article):
- People previously diagnosed as having adenomatous polyps.
- A personal history of curative-intent resection of colorectal cancer.
- A family history of either colorectal cancer or colorectal adenomas diagnosed in a first-degree relative before age 60.
- Inflammatory bowel disease of significant duration.
- Individuals with one of two hereditary syndromes that place them at very high risk for colorectal cancer).
[3] Women at high risk include those known to carry HNPCC-associated genetic mutations, women who have a substantial likelihood of being a mutation carrier (i.e., a mutation is known to be present in the family), and women without genetic testing results, but who are from families with suspected autosomal dominant predisposition to colon cancer.
[4]Men at high risk (African descent, men with a first-degree relative diagnosed at a younger age) should begin testing at age 45. Men at very high risk (multiple first-degree relatives diagnosed with prostate cancer at an early age) could begin testing at age 40. If PSA is less than 1.0 ng/ml, no additional testing is needed until age 45. If PSA is 1 - 2.5, annual testing is recommended. If > 2.5, consider biopsy.

Adapted from: Smith, RA, et al. American Cancer Society guidelines for the early detection of cancer. CA Cancer of J Clin 2002,52(1):8–22.

XIV. PERIODIC HEALTH EXAMINATIONS AND PREVENTIVE CARE

Expert Recommendations for Preventive Care for Asymptomatic, Low-Risk Adults								
	United States Preventive Services Task Force			American College of Physicians			Canadian Task Force on the Periodic Health Examination		
Preventive Service	Sex	Age	Minimum Frequency[1]	Sex	Age	Minimum Frequency	Sex	Age	Minimum Frequency[1]
Physical Examination									
Blood pressure	MF	18+	Q 2 yrs	MF	18+	Q 2 yrs	MF	25-64	Q 5 yrs
Clinical breast examination	F	50-69[2]	Q 1-2 yrs[3]	F	40+	Annually	MF / MF / F	65+ / 50-69	Q 2 yrs / Annually
Laboratory tests									
Papanicolaou smear	F	18[4]-65	Q 3 yrs	F	20[4]-65[5]	Q 3 yrs	F	18[4]-69	Q 3 yrs[6]
Stool for occult blood	MF	50+	Annually	MF	50-70/80	Annually[7]	NR	NR	NR
Sigmoidoscopy	MF	50+	Q ? yrs	MF	50-70	Q 10 yrs	NR	NR	NR
Mammography	F	50-69[2]	Q 1-2 yrs	F	50-75	Q 2 yrs	F	50-69	Annually
Cholesterol	M / F	35-65 / 45-65	Q ? yrs	M / F	35-65 / 45-65	Once	M	30-59	Q ? yrs
Immunizations									
Tetanus- diphtheria booster	MF	18+	Q 15-30 yrs	MF	18+	Q 10 yrs or once at age 50	MF	18+	Q 10 yrs
Influenza vaccination	MF	65+	Annually	MF	65+	Annually	MF	65+	Annually
Pneumococcal vaccination	MF	65+	Once[8]	MF	65+	Once[8]	NR	NR	NR
Counseling[9]	MF	18+	At routine visits	MF	18+	At routine visits	MF	18+	At routine visits

NR = no recommendations; ? = "periodic"
[1]Where question marks appear, the appropriate interval is left to clinical discretion because of lack of evidence.
[2]There is insufficient evidence to recommend for or against routine mammography or clinical breast examination for women age 40-49 or age ≥ 70, though recommendations for high-risk women in these age groups may be made on other grounds.
[3]Combined with mammography. There is insufficient evidence to recommend for or against clinical breast examination alone.
[4]Or following onset of sexual activity.
[5]There is insufficient evidence to recommend for or against an upper age limit for Papanicolaou testing after age 65 in women with regular previous normal smears.
[6]After two normal annual smears.
[7]For persons who decline screening sigmoidoscopy, barium enema, or colonoscopy.
[8]Reimmunize at age 65 those high-risk individuals who are 6 years or more after primary dose.
[9]Regarding tobacco use, nutrition, exercise, sexual behavior, substance abuse, injury prevention, and dental care.

Source: Tierney LM, et al., eds. 2002 Current medical diagnosis and treatment. Lange/McGraw-Hill. New York. 41st ed. Used with permission.

CLINICAL PEARLS

- Screening for cancer also includes counseling patients on ways to decrease risks of developing cancer
- Inform patients about using sunscreen
- Cancer screening highlights the importance of obtaining thorough family and social histories
- Encourage patients to perform monthly *self exams* (breast, testicular, skin)

References
Smith RA, et al. American Cancer Society guidelines for the early detection of cancer 2002. CA Cancer J Clin 2002;52:8–22. Available at: http://www.cancer.org/docroot/PUB/content/PUB_3_8X_american_cancer_society_guidelines_for_the_early_detection_of_cancer.asp
Cancer facts and figures 2001 (American Cancer Society) Available at: http://www.cancer.org/docroot/stt/stt 0.asp (this site is updated yearly).

Michael B. Weinstock, MD
David P. Buck, MD
Mark Reeder, MD

35. SMOKING CESSATION

I. RELEVANCE

  A. Cigarette smoking is a leading cause of death in the world today accounting for more than 40% of preventable deaths in the US. Smoking is estimated to cause over 430,000 deaths annually in the US. Approximately 3,000 children and adolescents become regular users of tobacco every day in the US

  B. There is a link between cigarette smoking and cancer, atherosclerotic vascular disease, COPD, gastritis, skin, and connective tissue diseases

  C. Smoking cessation benefits all age groups and extends to those individuals already afflicted with smoking-related diagnoses

  D. Evidence suggests that smoking cessation is more likely when physician actively identifies a smoker and encourages cessation

  E. Effective smoking cessation encompasses both the physiologic and the psychologic addictions

II. PHARMACOLOGIC INTERVENTIONS

Currently there are 5 first-line and 2 second-line pharmacotherapies available for smoking cessation. Each has been found to be effective when used alone or in combination with behavioral modifications

  A. First-line agents

   1. **Bupropion Hydrochloride (Zyban), sustained release**
      a. Atypical antidepressant that has both dopaminergic and adrenergic actions
      b. Begin treatment 1 week prior to anticipated stop date
      c. Dosage: 150mg PO QD for 3 days then 150mg PO BID
      d. Duration: 7–12 weeks; maintenance up to 6 months
      e. Adverse effects: Insomnia, dry mouth, and lowers seizure threshold
      f. Precautions/Contraindications: History of seizure disorder, anorexia, head trauma or excessive alcohol use

   2. **Nicotine gum (Nicorette, Nicorette DS), OTC**
      a. Single (2mg) and double strength (4mg) dosages
      b. Use single strength dose for those who smoke < 25 cigarettes/day. Use double strength dose for those who smoke > 25 cigarettes/day
      c. Dosage: 1 piece Q1–2hrs then repeat PRN. Daily maximum is 30 pieces of single strength and 24 pieces of double strength
      d. Duration: Daily for 6 weeks, then taper for 6 weeks
      e. Adverse effects: Dyspepsia and mouth soreness
      f. Precautions/Contraindications: None

   3. **Nicotine inhaler (Nicotrol)**
      a. Inhaler is a plastic rod with a nicotine plug that provides a nicotine vapor when puffed on. Acts as a substitute for some of the behavior features of smoking
      b. Delivers nicotine buccally
      c. Dosage: 6–16 cartridges/day
      d. Duration: 12 weeks; maintenance up to 6 months.
      e. Adverse effects: Local irritation of mouth and throat
      f. Precautions/Contraindications: None

   4. **Nicotine nasal spray (Nicotrol NS)**
      a. Delivers nicotine more rapidly than gum, inhaler, or patch, but less than cigarettes
      b. Peak levels occur within 10 minutes
      c. Dosage: 1–2 sprays each nostril Q1hr. Minimum dose: 8/days, Maximum dose: 40/days
      d. Duration: 3–6 months

      e. Adverse effects: Nasal irritation, throat irritation, rhinitis, sneezing, coughing, and watering eyes. Tolerance occurs in the first week

      f. Precautions/Contraindications: None

   5. **Nicotine patch (Nicoderm, Nicoderm CQ, Habitrol, Nicotrol)** Note: OTC patches are also effective

      a. Apply patch daily to a different site. Wear for 16hrs/day

      b. Ensure smoking cessation to avoid nicotine toxicity

      c. Dosage: Nicoderm CQ 21mg patch daily for 6 weeks, then 14mg patch daily for 2 weeks, and then 7mg patch daily for 2 weeks

      d. Duration: 8 weeks; maintenance unknown

      e. Adverse effects: Local skin reaction and insomnia

      f. Precautions/Contraindications: None

B. Second line agents

   1. **Clonidine**

      a. Dosage: 0.15–0.75mg/day

      b. Duration: 3–10 weeks

      c. Adverse effects: Dry mouth, sedation, drowsiness, and dizziness

      d. Precautions/Contraindications: Rebound hypertension

   2. **Nortriptyline (Pamelor)**

      a. Dosage: 75–100mg/day

      b. Duration: 12 weeks

      c. Adverse effects: Dry mouth and sedation

      d. Precautions/Contraindications: Risk of arrhythmias

III. BEHAVIORAL MODIFICATION

Should be used in conjunction with appropriate pharmacotherapies to be maximally effective. Modifications should be individualized. There are several strategies that may be effective. One example of a simple 4-step plan follows

A. Assist the patient with a quit plan

   1. Set a quit date. Ideally the date should be within 2 weeks

   2. Tell family and friends about quitting. Ask for accountability, support, and understanding

   3. Keep a smoking journal. Record times and situations that trigger smoking, then avoid these situations if possible

   4. Remove tobacco products from the environment

B. Provide practical counseling and skills training

   1. Total abstinence is essential

   2. Anticipate triggers or upcoming challenges

   3. Limit or abstain from alcohol

   4. Identify alternative behaviors in place of smoking. Examples are chewing gum, cinnamon sticks, or carrots, woodworking (activities with hands), etc.

C. Assist the patient with extratreatment support

   1. Provide and show videotapes that model support skills

   2. Encourage patient to establish a smoke-free home

   3. Inform patients of community resources (hotlines, helplines, etc.)

   4. Request social support from family, friends and coworkers

D. Arrange follow-up contact

   1. Should occur soon after the scheduled quit date, ideally, within the first week

   2. Second follow-up contact should occur within the first month

   3. Can be either in person or via telephone

   4. Congratulate success

CLINICAL PEARLS

- Most patients will attempt smoking cessation several times before they are successful
- Most patients initially attempt smoking cessation on their own without any intervention
- Only about 7% of smokers achieve long-term success when trying to quit on their

own. Success rates increase to 15–30% by using appropriate therapies
- Even brief physician interactions of 3 minutes or less results in about a 10% quit rate. Physician's advice to quit smoking is an important motivator cited by many smokers
- For every 4–5 patients encouraged to quit smoking, 1 life will be saved
- Nearly 43% of children 2 months to 11yrs live in homes with at least 1 smoker. Evidence suggests that smoke exposure during childhood is associated with increased illnesses including: upper and lower respiratory diseases, middle ear infections with effusion, asthma, and sudden infant death syndrome

References

Fiore MC, et al. Treating tobacco use and dependence. Clinical practice guideline. Washington, DC: U.S. Dept. of Health and Human Services, Public Health Service. 2000. AHRQ Pub. No. 000032. Available at: http://www.surgeongeneral.gov/tobacco/

Tobacco Use and Dependence Clinical Practice Guideline Panel, Staff, and Consortium Representatives. A clinical practice guideline for treating tobacco use and dependence. A U.S. Public Health Service report. JAMA 2000;283:3244–54.

Jaén CR, et al. Making time for tobacco cessation counseling. J Fam Pract 1998;46:425–8.

Siqueira LM, et al. Smoking cessation in adolescents. The role of nicotine dependence, stress, and coping methods. Arch Pediatr Adolesc Med 2001;155:489–95.

Hughes JR, et al. Recent advances in the pharmacotherapy of smoking. JAMA 1999;281:72–6.

Silagy C, et al. Nicotine replacement therapy for smoking cessation. Cochrane Database Syst Rev 2000;(2):CD000146. www.cochrane.org

36. ENDOCARDITIS PROPHYLAXIS— 1997 AHA RECOMMENDATIONS

The following are guidelines based on recommendations from the American Heart Association published in 1997. Available on the web at: http://www.americanheart.org/scientific/statements/1997/079701.hml. An excellent review of infectious endocarditis was published in the New England Journal of Medicine in November 2001. See references below

I. CARDIAC CONDITIONS

A. Endocarditis prophylaxis recommended:

1. High-risk category
   a. Prosthetic cardiac valves, including bioprosthetic and homograft valves
   b. Previous bacterial endocarditis
   c. Complex cyanotic congenital heart disease (e.g., single ventricle states, transposition of the great arteries, tetralogy of Fallot)
   d. Surgically constructed systemic pulmonary shunts or conduits
2. Moderate-risk category
   a. Most other congenital cardiac malformations (other than above and below)
   b. Acquired valvular dysfunction (e.g., rheumatic heart disease)
   c. Hypertrophic cardiomyopathy
   d. Mitral valve prolapse with valvular regurgitation and/or thickened leaflets

B. Endocarditis prophylaxis not recommended:

1. Negligible-risk category
   a. Isolated secundum atrial septal defect
   b. Surgical repair of atrial septal defect, ventricular septal defect, or patent ductus arteriosus (without residua beyond 6 months)
   c. Previous coronary artery bypass graft surgery
   d. Mitral valve prolapse without valvular regurgitation
   e. Physiologic, functional, or innocent heart murmurs
   f. Previous Kawasaki disease without valvular dysfunction

   g. Previous rheumatic fever without valvular dysfunction
   h. Cardiac pacemakers (intravascular and epicardial) and implanted defibrillators
C. Cardiac risk: Patients at high risk are at much greater risk for developing severe endocardial infection

Source: Dajani AS, Taubert KA, et al. Prevention of bacterial endocarditis. Recommendations by the American Heart Association. JAMA 1997;22:1795. Copyright 1997, American Medical Association. Used with permission.

II. PROCEDURES—DENTAL OR SURGICAL

A. Endocarditis prophylaxis recommended (Prophylaxis is recommended for patients with high- and moderate-risk cardiac conditions):
   1. Dental extractions
   2. Periodontal procedures including surgery, scaling and root planing, probing, and recall maintenance
   3. Dental implant placement and reimplantation of avulsed teeth
   4. Endodontic (root canal) instrumentation or surgery only beyond the apex
   5. Subgingival placement of ATB fibers or strips
   6. Initial placement of orthodontic bands but not brackets
   7. Intraligamentary local anesthetic injections
   8. Prophylactic cleaning of teeth or implants where bleeding is anticipated

B. Endocarditis prophylaxis not recommended:
   1. Restorative dentistry (operative and prosthodontic) with or without retraction cord. This includes restoration of decayed teeth (filling cavities) and replacement of missing teeth. Clinical judgment may indicate ATB use in selected circumstances that may create significant bleeding
   2. Local anesthetic injections (nonintraligamentary)
   3. Intracanal endodontic treatment; post placement and buildup
   4. Placement of rubber dams
   5. Postoperative suture removal
   6. Placement of removable prosthodontic or orthodontic appliances
   7. Taking of oral impressions
   8. Fluoride treatments
   9. Taking of oral radiographs
   10. Orthodontic appliance adjustment
   11. Shedding of primary teeth

Source: Dajani AS, Taubert KA, et al. Prevention of bacterial endocarditis. Recommendations by the American Heart Association. JAMA 1997;22:1797. Copyright 1997, American Medical Association. Used with permission.

III. PROCEDURES—OTHER

A. Endocarditis prophylaxis recommended:
   1. Respiratory tract
      a. Tonsillectomy and/or adenoidectomy
      b. Surgical operations that involve respiratory mucosa
      c. Bronchoscopy with a rigid bronchoscope
   2. Gastrointestinal tract (Prophylaxis is recommended for high-risk patients; optional for medium-risk patients)
      a. Sclerotherapy for esophageal varices
      b. Esophageal stricture dilation
      c. Endoscopic retrograde cholangiography with biliary obstruction
      d. Biliary tract surgery
      e. Surgical operations that involve intestinal mucosa
   3. Genitourinary tract

          a. Prostatic surgery
          b. Cystoscopy
          c. Urethral dilation
  B. Endocarditis prophylaxis not recommended († indicates prophylaxis is optional
  for high-risk patients):
     1. Respiratory tract
          a. Endotracheal intubation
          b. Bronchoscopy with a flexible bronchoscope, with or without biopsy†
          c. Tympanostomy tube insertion
     2. Gastrointestinal tract
          a. Transesophageal echocardiography†
          b. Endoscopy with or without gastrointestinal biopsy†
     3. Genitourinary tract
          a. Vaginal hysterectomy†
          b. Vaginal delivery†
          c. Cesarean section
          d. In uninfected tissue:
              i. Urethral catheterization
             ii. Uterine dilation and curettage
            iii. Therapeutic abortion
             iv. Sterilization procedures
              v. Insertion or removal of intrauterine devices
     4. Other
          a. Cardiac catheterization, including balloon angioplasty
          b. Implanted cardiac pacemakers, implanted defibrillators, and coronary stents
          c. Incision or biopsy of surgically scrubbed skin
          d. Circumcision

IV. PROPHYLACTIC REGIMENS FOR DENTAL, ORAL, RESPIRATORY TRACT, OR ESOPHAGEAL PROCEDURES

SITUATION	AGENT	REGIMEN*
Standard general prophylaxis	Amoxicillin	Adults: 2.0 g; children: 50 mg/kg orally 1 h before procedure
Unable to take oral medications	Ampicillin	Adults: 2.0 g intramuscularly (IM) or intravenously (IV); children: 50 mg/kg IM or IV within 30 min before procedure
Allergic to penicillin	Clindamycin *or*	Adults: 600 mg; children: 20 mg/kg orally 1 h before procedure
	Cephalexin† or cefadroxil† *or*	Adults: 2.0 g; children:50 mg/kg orally 1 h before procedure
	Azithromycin or clarithromycin	Adults: 500 mg; children: 15 mg/kg orally 1 h before procedure
Allergic to penicillin and unable to take oral medications	Clindamycin *or*	Adults: 600 mg; children: 20 mg/kg IV within 30 min before procedure
	Cefazolin†	Adults: 1.0 g; children: 25 mg/kg IM or IV within 30 min before procedure

  * Total children's dose should not exceed adult dose
  † Cephalosporins should not be used in individuals with immediate-type hypersensitivity reaction
    (urticaria, angioedema, or anaphylaxis) to penicillins

V. CLINICAL APPROACH TO DETERMINATION OF THE NEED FOR PROPHYLAXIS IN PATIENTS WITH SUSPECTED MITRAL VALVE PROLAPSE

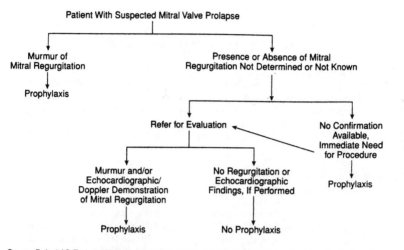

Source: Dajani AS, Taubert KA, et al. Prevention of bacterial endocarditis. Recommendations by the American Heart Association. JAMA 1997;22:1796. Copyright 1997. American Medical Association. Used with permission.

References

Dajani AS, et al. Prevention of bacterial endocarditis: Recommendations by the American Heart Association. Circulation 1997;96:358–66.

Mylonakis E, Calderwood SB. Infective endocarditis in adults. N Engl J Med 2001;345:1318–30.

Seto TB, et al. Physicians' recommendations to patients for use of antibiotic prophylaxis to prevent endocarditis. JAMA 2000;284:68.

Diane Minasian, MD
Ivan Wolfson, MD
William Oley, MD

37. TUBERCULOSIS SCREENING

I. TRANSMISSION

A. TB is spread primarily through respiratory droplets. Respiratory droplets may remain airborne within a room for hours after a cough or sneeze. In 6–12 weeks most people infected with TB develop cell-mediated immunity which halts the spread of infection. The PPD (purified protein derivative of TB) test becomes positive by 12 weeks. Approximately 10% of those infected with TB will develop active TB infection at some time in their life

II. HIGH RISK POPULATIONS

A. Contacts of people with infectious TB

B. IV drug users

C. Medical Risk Factors/Immunosuppressed: HIV/AIDS, DM, chronic steroid use, immunosuppressive therapies, CRF, malignancy, silicosis, weight > 10% below ideal body weight, gastrectomy, jejunoileal bypass, CXR with fibrotic lesions consistent with old TB

D. Residents and employees of high risk congregate settings: Prisons, nursing homes, health care facilities, homeless shelters, residential settings for HIV+ persons

E. Immigrants from high prevalence countries (most countries in Africa, Asia, Latin America)

F. Low income/medically underserved

G. Health care workers

III. SCREENING

A. All high risk individuals should be screened annually

B. All pregnant women at high risk should be screened

C. Exceptions to routine screening include:
  1. Documented skin test positive in past
  2. Prior course of treatment for positive skin test

IV. SKIN TESTING

A. **Mantoux test**
  1. The Mantoux test is the standard of care. The TINE TEST should not be used in screening
  2. Should be read 48–72hrs after injection, preferably by a health care worker
  3. The measurement is based on the *induration*, not the erythema
  4. The measurement should be 1 number (e.g., 8mm) which should be measured in the transverse plane. Recording "positive" or "negative" is not sufficient

B. **Negative skin test:** Does *not* exclude TB infection. A reaction may not occur in patients who are immunocompromised, severe febrile illness, virus vaccinations (MMR, OPV), malnutrition, old age, overwhelming TB infections and HIV disease

C. **Booster phenomenon**
  1. Explanation: Repeated testing of uninfected individuals does *not* sensitize them to tuberculin. However, delayed sensitivity to tuberculin (a positive test) may wane over time. Certain individuals who were exposed to TB early in their life may have no reaction many years later (false negative). In these individuals, it is necessary to do 2 tests, 1 week apart. If the second test (performed 1–2 weeks later) is positive, this represents a booster phenomenon (remote infection) and *not* a recent conversion
  2. Indications: Indicated for the *initial screening* of residents and employees of long-term care facilities and others who will be receiving yearly skin testing. It is done to avoid misinterpreting a boosted reaction as a recent infection

V. CRITERIA FOR A POSITIVE TEST

Positivity is based on patient's risk and the fact that the larger the reaction, the greater the likelihood of infection

A. Greater than 5mm induration is considered positive for the following patients:
1. Persons with recent close contact with persons who have active TB
2. Persons who are HIV+ or risk factors for HIV with unknown HIV status
3. Persons with fibrotic CXR changes consistent with healed TB
4. Persons with organ transplant and/or other immunosuppressed conditions

B. Greater than 10mm induration is considered positive in all patients who do not meet above criteria, but belong to one or more of the following high risk groups (also see section II)
1. IV drug abusers known to be HIV negative
2. Children < 4yrs, or infants, children, adolescents exposed to adults in high risk categories
3. Any person with social/medical conditions listed in, but not limited to, section II.

C. Greater than 15mm induration is positive in all other patients

VI. PRIOR BCG VACCINATION

A. History of BCG (Bacille bilie' de Calmette-Guérin) vaccination does not alter guidelines for interpreting skin test results
B. Effectiveness of BCG varies from 0–76% in major trials

VII. INDICATIONS FOR PREVENTIVE THERAPY

Patients with inactive disease, (positive skin test and negative CXR), and a positive test based on the criteria listed in V. above, should be considered for prophylactic therapy. Decision to treat is based upon the risk of medication toxicity, (primarily Isoniazid induced hepatitis), versus the risk of developing active TB

A. Age < 35
1. All patients with positive skin test and negative CXR
2. Recent convertors: > 10mm increase in induration within 2yr period

B. Age > 35 with positive skin test and negative CXR
1. HIV positive
2. Close contacts of persons with active TB
3. Recent convertor (> 10mm increase in induration within 2yr period)
4. IV drug abusers
5. Previously treated or inadequately treated with abnormal CXR—consider referral to infectious disease specialist
6. Persons with medical conditions which increase risk of developing active TB

C. Cases of known TB exposure: Persons who are close contacts of infectious TB cases, especially children, should be given preventive therapy regardless of skin test reaction. After 3 months of therapy, those who were skin test negative should have the test repeated. If test remains negative, and close contact with active TB is broken, treatment may be stopped

D. Pregnant women: If positive skin test, then obtain CXR after 20 weeks gestation
1. If CXR negative, then begin preventive therapy 3 months postpartum. Breast-feeding is not a contraindication to **Isoniazid** therapy, although the breastfed infant should receive **Pyridoxine** supplementation
2. High risk women (likely to have been recently infected) should begin therapy after the first trimester. Use **Pyridoxine** with **Isoniazid** during pregnancy to decrease the chance of developing peripheral neuropathy associated with **Isoniazid**

E. Newborns of skin test positive mothers: Congenital transmission is very rare. Most newborns who develop TB do so after birth
1. All household contacts of the skin test positive mother should be skin tested *prior to delivery* to identify any active cases
2. CDC recommendation is to test newborns between 3 and 4 months old

VIII. PREVENTIVE THERAPY TO TREAT INACTIVE DISEASE

Isoniazid (10mg/kg/day, up to 300 mg/day) dosed QD for 9–12 months

- **A. Efficacy**: Shown to reduce incidence of clinical TB by 54–88% when taken for 12 months
- **B. Contraindications**: Acute or active chronic liver disease of any etiology or a history of previous completion of an entire course of **Isoniazid** preventive therapy
- **C. Warning**: Persons with conditions in which neuropathy may be a common feature (pregnant women, breast-feeding children, patients with seizure disorders) should take **Pyridoxine** (50mg/day)
- **D. Labs**: 10–20% chance of mild **Isoniazid** induced liver function test changes. Some clinicians only check labs if patient is symptomatic
    1. Age < 20: No baseline or periodic labs necessary unless symptomatic
    2. Age 20–35: Baseline AST and repeat at 2 months
    3. Age > 35 and Daily EtOH users: Baseline AST and then Q month for 3–4 months. If SGOT elevated 3–5 × upper limit of normal, discontinue **Isoniazid**
- **E. Monitoring**: Monthly follow-up to assess compliance, signs of neuropathy, or signs of liver toxicity

References

Targeted tuberculin testing and treatment of latent tuberculosis infection, official statement of the American Thoracic Society. Am J Respir Crit Care Med 2000;161:S221-47.

Core curriculum on tuberculosis. 4th ed. U.S. Dept. of Health and Human Services, Public Health Service, Center for Disease Control, 2002.

Ozuah PO, et al. Evaluation of a risk assessment questionnaire used to target tuberculin skin testing in children. JAMA 2001;285:451-3.

Slovis BS, et al. The case against anergy testing as a routine adjunct to tuberculin skin testing. JAMA 2000;283:2003.

V. Cardiology & Pulmonary Disorders

38. Evaluation of Chest Pain 113

39. ECG Interpretation 117

40. Hyperlipidemia 122

41. Hypertension 128

42. Coronary Artery Disease 136

43. Heart Failure 140

44. Atrial Fibrillation 145

45. Ambulatory Post-MI Management 150

46. Cardiac Stress Testing 152

47. Shortness of Breath 154

48   Community-Acquired Pneumonia (CAP) 158

49. Asthma in Adults 162

50. Chronic Obstructive Pulmonary Disease (COPD) 166

51. Acute Bronchitis 169

CARD

Daniel M. Neides, MD
Michael B. Weinstock, MD
David Sharkis, MD

38. EVALUATION OF CHEST PAIN

I. INTRODUCTION

A. One of the most common complaints evaluated in ER, on wards, and in office setting

B. Tables and charts listed below will help to stratify patients into high or low risk groups, and then the decision on how to further evaluate these patients can be made according to the pre-test likelihood of cardiac or other etiology. See Chapter 42, Coronary Artery Disease and Chapter 46, Cardiac Stress Testing for more specific information on evaluation

II. DIFFERENTIAL DIAGNOSIS OF CHEST PAIN

A. Cardiovascular: Ischemic, valvular disease, hypertrophic cardiomyopathy, aortic dissection, hypertensive crisis, pulmonary hypertension

B. Pulmonary: Pulmonary embolus (PE), pneumothorax/tension pneumothorax, pneumonia, asthma, pleurisy

C. Gastrointestinal:
1. Esophageal: Esophageal rupture (Boerhaave's syndrome), esophageal reflux or spasm, esophageal foreign body, esophagitis (chronic reflux, Barrett's esophagus, candida, etc.)
2. Peptic ulcer disease/gastritis
3. Mallory-Weiss tear
4. Pancreatitis
5. Cholecystitis/symptomatic cholelithiasis
6. Hepatitis

D. Musculoskeletal: Costochondritis/musculoskeletal chest wall strain, thoracic outlet syndrome, cervical disk disease

E. Psychogenic: Anxiety/panic disorder, depression

F. Other: Herpes zoster, breast disease, post-nasal drip

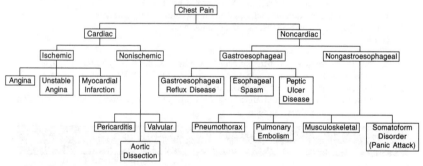

Source: Panju AA. Is this patient having a myocardial infarction? JAMA 1998;280:1256–63. Copyright©1998. Used with permission.

III. HISTORY: See tables listed below

A. Character/radiation of discomfort (It may be more helpful to ask patients about "chest discomfort" instead of asking them about "chest pain")
1. Dull pressure, squeezing, burning: Consider CAD or esophageal pain (GERD)
2. Radiation of pain to neck/shoulder/jaw: Consider CAD
3. Radiation of pain to the back: Consider aortic dissection, pancreatitis, or perforated peptic ulcer
4. Radiation to the epigastrium: Consider GI etiology, pancreatitis, inferior wall MI, AAA
5. Sharp, stabbing pain: Consider muscular chest wall pain/costochondritis, pleurisy, pericardial pain, or PE

B. Onset
1. Sudden onset: Consider PE, pneumothorax, or aortic dissection
2. Slow onset (building over 2–5 minutes): Consider CAD

C. Activity at onset
1. Exertion
2. Lifting/moving the body

3. Arguing
4. Eating
5. Coughing

D. Exacerbation/Relief
1. Exacerbated by exercise or stress and relieved by rest: Consider CAD
2. Relieved by **Nitroglycerin**: Consider CAD or esophageal spasm
3. Exacerbated by movement of body (positional) or deep inspiration: Consider muscu-loskeletal, pericardial, pleuritic disease, or PE
4. Worse when supine and better with upright position: Consider pericarditis

E. Other symptoms associated with CAD: See tables below
1. Dyspnea
2. Diaphoresis
3. Palpitations
4. Light-headedness
5. Nausea/vomiting
6. Radiation to neck arm or jaw
7. Syncope
8. CHF-related symptoms: Orthopnea, paroxysmal nocturnal dyspnea (PND), peripheral/dependent edema

F. Past medical history
1. Determine risk factors for CAD: Known coronary artery disease or vascular disease, family history, smoking, diabetes, hypertension, dyslipidemia, male > 45, female > 55, obesity, sedentary lifestyle
2. Complete past history including childhood illnesses (rheumatic fever)
3. Obtain results of stress tests, cardiac catheterizations, ECHOs, PTCA/STENT, and CABG
4. Current meds including nitrates, anti-hypertensives, β-blockers, and aspirin

IV. PHYSICAL EXAM
A. Vital Signs: Check heart rate and BP, consider BP in both arms and legs (to evaluate for coarctation, dissection, AAA
B. Neck: Assess for midline trachea, JVD, carotid bruits
C. Lungs: Listen for bilateral and equal breath sounds, rales, wheezes
D. Chest: Palpate for subcutaneous air or tenderness
E. Heart
1. Inspect (for presence of surgical scars)
2. Palpate for parasternal lift, increased LV impulse, point of maximal impulse
3. Auscultate for friction rub, gallops, murmurs, clicks (MVP), distant heart sounds
F. Abdomen: Pulsatile abdominal mass, bruits
G. Extremities: Assess for unilateral leg swelling (DVT), cyanosis, clubbing, or edema; palpate femoral pulses (dissection)

Clinical Features That Increase the Probability of a Myocardial Infarction in Patients Presenting with Acute Chest Pain	
Clinical Feature	**Likelihood Ratio (95% Confidence Interval)**
Pain in chest or left arm	2.7*
Chest pain radiation	
Right shoulder	2.9 (1.4 - 6.0)
Left arm	2.3 (1.7 - 3.1)
Both left and right arm	7.1 (3.6 - 14.2)
Chest pain most important symptom	2.0*
History of myocardial infarction	1.5 - 3.0†
Nausea or vomiting	1.9 (1.7 - 2.3)
Diaphoresis	2.0 (1.9 - 2.2)
Third heart sound on auscultation	3.2 (1.6 - 6.5)
Hypotension (systolic blood pressure ≤80 mm Hg)	3.1 (1.8 - 5.2)
Pulmonary crackles on auscultation	2.1 (1.4 - 3.1)

*Data not available to calculate confidence intervals.
†In heterogeneous studies the likelihood ratios are reported as ranges.

Source: Panju AA. Is this patient having a myocardial infarction? JAMA 1998;280:1256–63. Copyright©1998. Used with permission.

Clinical Features That Decrease the Probability of a Myocardial Infarction in Patients Presenting with Acute Chest Pain	
Clinical Feature	**Likelihood Ratio (95% Confidence Interval)**
Pleuritic chest pain	0.2 (0.2 - 0.3)
Chest pain sharp or stabbing	0.3 (0.2 - 0.5)
Positional chest pain	0.3 (0.2 - 0.4)
Chest pain reproduced by palpation	0.2 - 0.4*

*In heterogeneous studies the likelihood ratios are reported as ranges.

Source: Panju AA. Is this patient having a myocardial infarction? JAMA 1998;280:1256–63. Copyright©1998. Used with permission.

CARD

V. FIVE LIFE THREATENING CAUSES OF CHEST PAIN

Five Life Threatening Causes of Chest Pain: Presentation and Diagnosis						
Condition	Location of Pain	Quality of Pain	Duration of Pain	Aggravating or Relieving Factors	Signs or Symptoms	Diagnosing the Condition
Myocardial Infarction/ Unstable Angina	Substernal, may radiate to jaw, neck or shoulder/arm(s)	Pressure, heaviness, squeezing, burning	Builds over several minutes to hours	Worse with exertion and relieved with rest	SOB, diaphoresis, N/V, lightheadedness	EKG, cardiac enzymes, stress testing, cardiac cath
Pneumothorax	Unilateral	Sharp, pleuritic	Sudden onset	Worse with inspiration	Dyspnea, decreased breath sounds, tracheal deviation, tachypnea	Chest x-ray and physical exam
Pericarditis (and Tamponade)	Retrosternal and left precordial	Sharp, stabbing, pleuritic	Hours to days	Worse with deep breaths or supine position, better with upright and forward position	Friction rub, pulsus paradoxus, tamponade	EKG, CXR, ECHO to eval. for tamponade
Pulmonary Embolus	Substernal	Pleuritic	Sudden onset	Worse with breathing	Dyspnea, tachypnea, tachycardia rales, hemoptysis peripheral edema	ABG, ventilation/ perfusion (V/Q) scan, helical CT, pulmonary angiogram
Aortic Dissection	Anterior chest with radiation to back	Severe pain, tearing sensation	Sudden onset	Unable to relieve	Lower BP in one arm, decreased femoral pulses, AR murmur, pulsus paradoxus	Chest x-ray, CT, Angiography, TEE, MRI

VI. EVALUATING CHEST PAIN

A. There are many clinical prediction rules, but they are user dependent and there is a question if they are better than history and physical exam. Percentage of patients sent home from emergency departments with acute MI has decreased and is now approximately 2%. Any clinical prediction rule (for emergency departments) would have to have a sensitivity of greater than 98%

B. Probably most important aspect of assessment is determination of pretest probability of pain being ischemic in origin. If it is determined that there is a likelihood of pain being ischemic, then subsequent tests (after the ECG and CXR) usually include a stress test and/or cardiac catheterization. See Chapter 42, Coronary Artery Disease and Chapter 46, Cardiac Stress Testing

C. EKG: Important for diagnosing myocardial ischemia or infarction as well as pericardial disease. May rarely show findings consistent with PE ($S_1 Q_3 T_3$). See table below and also see Chapter 39, ECG Interpretation

D. Chest x-ray: Will aid in diagnosing pneumothorax, assessing cardiac silhouette, and determining a widened mediastinum vs. non cardiac etiologies such as infiltrate, effusion, or rib fracture

E. Laboratory: Initial labs in an emergency department setting include CPK with isoenzymes (CPK-MB peaks at 8–12hrs), troponin I (same peak as CPK-MB but remains elevated for 2–3 days), CBC, chemistry, oxygen saturation, and possibly arterial blood gas

F. Echocardiography: Looking for segmental wall motion abnormalities, pericardial effusion, root size, aortic insufficiency, mitral regurgitation or papillary muscle dysfunction

CARD

Features of the Electrocardiogram That Increase the Probability of a Myocardial Infarction in Patients Presenting With Acute Chest Pain	
Feature of the Electrocardiogram	**Likelihood Ratio (95% Confidence Interval)**
New ST-segment elevation ≥ 1 mm	5.7 - 53.9*
New Q wave	5.3 - 24.8*
Any ST-segment elevation	11.2 (7.1 - 17.8)
New conduction defect	6.3 (2.5 - 15.7)
New ST-segment depression	3.0 - 5.2*
Any Q wave	3.9 (2.7 - 5.7)
Any ST-segment depression	3.2 (2.5 - 4.1)
T-wave peaking and/or inversion ≥ 1 mm	3.1†
New T-wave inversion	2.4 - 2.8*
Any conduction defect	2.7 (1.4 - 5.4)

*Data not available to calculate confidence intervals.
†In heterogeneous studies the likelihood ratios are reported as ranges.

Source: Panju AA. Is this patient having a myocardial infarction? JAMA 1998;280:1256–63. Copyright©1998. Used with permission.

CLINICAL PEARLS

- 10% of acute MI patients state that chest pain is relieved by antacids. No published data supports use of antacids + viscous Lidocaine to "rule out" an MI
- 10–20% of patients who have MI will have either normal EKG or "nonspecific" changes. Patient with good history for myocardial ischemia in light of "normal" EKG still needs to be admitted for cardiac evaluation
- Chewing 1 aspirin in patient suspected of having acute MI is fast, cheap, and benign way to initiate therapy

References

Panju AA, et al. Is this patient having a myocardial infarction? JAMA 1998;280:1256–63.

Canto JG, et al. Prevalence, clinical characteristics, and mortality among patients with myocardial infarction presenting without chest pain. JAMA 2000;283.

Lee TH, Goldman L. Evaluation of the patient with acute chest pain. N Engl J Med 2000; 342(16):1187–95.

Douglas PS, Ginsburg GS. The evaluation of chest pain in women. N Engl J Med 1996; 334(20):1311–5.

Grundy SM, et al. AHA/ACC scientific statement: Assessment of cardiovascular risk by use of multiple-risk-factor assessment equations: a statement for healthcare professionals from the American Heart Association and the American College of Cardiology. J Am Coll Cardiol 1999;34:1348.

39. ECG INTERPRETATION

Note: All criteria listed below are not required for diagnosis

I. SEQUENCE TO READ ECG

A. Rate: Rate < 60 = bradycardia, rate > 100 = tachycardia

B. Rhythm: Sinus, junctional, ventricular

C. Axis: Normal axis is -30° to 100°

D. Hypertrophy and heart block: Atrial or ventricular hypertrophy (check P, QRS), heart block (check PR interval, P before each QRS, etc.) and bundle branch block (RBBB, LBBB, LAHB, LPHB)

E. Ischemia/infarction: Check each lead for Q waves, ST elevation or depression, hyperacute or inverted T waves

F. Electrolyte or Digoxin disturbances: Check QT, U waves

II. AXIS

If leads I and II have the largest R waves, or the net of I plus aVF is positive, the axis can be considered normal

Normal axis is -30° to 100°

A. Causes of left axis deviation (LAD) (-30 to -120)
1. Left ventricular hypertrophy (LVH)
2. Left bundle branch block (LBBB)
3. Left anterior fascicular block (LAHB)

B. Causes of right axis deviation (RAD) (100 to 180)
1. Right ventricular hypertrophy (RVH)
2. Right bundle branch block (RBBB)
3. Left posterior fascicular block (LPHB)
4. COPD, pulmonary emboli (PE), cor pulmonale

III. HYPERTROPHY

A. Right atrial enlargement (RAE)
1. ECG diagnosis
   a. Tall P waves in II, III, aVF > 0.12 seconds wide or 3mm tall (P pulmonale)
   b. Large diphasic P wave in V_1 with initial component > 1.5mm
   c. P > 0.11 seconds
2. Differential diagnosis of RAE
   a. Pulmonary HTN (COPD, PE)
   b. Tricuspid or pulmonic valvular dysfunction (TR, TS, PR, PS)
   c. Congenital disorder

B. Left atrial enlargement (LAE)
1. ECG diagnosis
   a. P wave in lead I > 0.12 seconds
   b. Terminal negativity of P wave in V_1 > 1mm with duration > 0.04 seconds
2. Differential diagnosis of LAE
   a. Systemic HTN
   b. Aortic or mitral valvular dysfunction (AR, AS, MR, MS)
   c. Left ventricular failure

C. Right ventricular hypertrophy (RVH)
1. ECG diagnosis
   a. Right axis deviation > 100°
   b. R > S in right precordium (V_{1-2}) and deep S waves over left precordium (V_{5-6})
   c. ST depression and inverted T wave in V_{1-2}
   d. Associated RAE
   e. Normal QRS

2. Differential diagnosis of RVH
   a. Pulmonary HTN (COPD, PE)
   b. Pulmonary stenosis, MS, MR, left to right shunt

D. Left ventricular hypertrophy (LVH)
1. ECG diagnosis: The Estes point system for LVH (95% specific, 50% sensitive)
   a. Amplitude (Any of the following) 3
      i. Largest R or S in limb leads ≥ 20mm
      ii. S in V_1 or V_2 ≥ 25mm
      iii. R in V_5 or V_6 ≥ 25mm
   b. ST segment changes of strain
      i. Without Digitalis 3
      ii. With Digitalis 1
   c. LA abnormality 3
   d. Left axis deviation ≥ -30° 2
   e. QRS duration ≥ 0.09 seconds 1
   f. Intrinsicoid deflection* in V_5 or V_6 > 0.05 seconds 1
      Intrinsicoid deflection is the time to the beginning of the rapid fall from the peak of the R
         Probable LVH = 4 total points
         LVH = 5 total points
2. Differential diagnosis of LVH
   a. Systemic arterial HTN
   b. AS, AR
   c. Hypertrophic cardiomyopathy
   d. Coarctation of the aorta

IV. HEART BLOCK
Normal PR = 0.12–0.2 seconds; QRS = 0.08–0.12 seconds; QT_c = < 0.37 seconds (males),
   < 0.40 seconds (females). QT_c = QT (seconds) / $\sqrt{RR}$ (seconds)
Note: Small blocks are 0.04 seconds; large blocks are 0.2 seconds

A. AV block
1. First degree heart block: PR interval > 0.2 seconds
2. Second degree heart block
   a. Mobitz I (Wenckebach): PR interval gradually increases until the AV node is not conducted and a QRS is dropped
   b. Mobitz II: PR is constant with QRS occasionally dropped
3. Third degree heart block: Complete heart block with no atrial impulses reaching the ventricles. The P waves and the QRS complexes both independently "march out"

B. Bundle branch block
1. Right bundle branch block (RBBB)
   a. Total QRS > 0.12 seconds (QRS = 0.10–0.11 seconds in incomplete RBBB)
   b. RSR' in right precordial leads (V_{1-2})
   c. Terminal broad S in I, V_{5-6}
   d. Right axis deviation (RAD)
2. Left bundle branch block (LBBB)
   a. Total QRS > 0.12 seconds (QRS = 0.10–0.11 seconds in incomplete LBBB)
   b. Broad R wave in I, V_{5-6}
   c. ST depression and T wave inversion in I, aVL, V_{5-6}
   d. Displacement of the ST segment and T wave in a direction opposite to the major QRS deflection
   e. Left axis deviation (LAD)
   f. Absence of Q wave in I, V_{5-6}
   g. Poor R wave progression
3. Left anterior fascicular block (LAHB)
   a. LAD (QRS axis -30° to -90°)
   b. Small R in II, III, aVF
   c. S in V_{5-6}
   d. Small Q in I, aVL
   e. Normal QRS duration

4. Left posterior fascicular block (LPHB)
   a. RAD (QRS axis > 100°)
   b. Small S in II, III, aVF
   c. Small R in I, aVL
   d. Normal QRS duration
   e. Exclude other causes of RAD: RVH, COPD, lateral MI

V. ISCHEMIA/INFARCTION
A. ECG changes
1. Ischemia: Horizontal ST segment depression or downsloping ST segment, T waves upright or inverted
2. Injury: Acute ST segment elevation (convex)
3. Infarction: Q waves (Q waves must be > 25% of succeeding R wave and > 0.04 seconds)

B. ECG changes by ischemic/infarction location
1. Inferior MI: Changes in leads II, III, aVF (right coronary artery or circumflex)
2. Anterior MI: Changes in leads I, V_{3-4} (left anterior descending artery)
3. Posterior MI: R wave in V_{1-2}, upright T in V_1, ST depression V_{1-2} (circumflex artery or RCA)
4. Lateral MI: Changes in leads I, aVL, V_{5-6}
5. Anterolateral MI: Changes in leads V_{3-6}, aVL
6. Anteroseptal MI: Changes in leads V_{1-4}
7. Right ventricular MI: ST elevation in lead V4R seen on a *right sided ECG*

C. For an excellent table on the features of the electrocardiogram which increase the probability of MI, see Chapter 38, Evaluation of Chest Pain, Section VI. F.

VI. DIFFERENTIAL DIAGNOSIS OF SPECIFIC ABNORMALITIES (ST, QT, ETC.)
A. Increased PR interval
1. AV block
2. Hyperthyroidism
3. Digitalis effect
4. Hypothermia

B. Shortened PR interval
1. Wolff-Parkinson-White (WPW)
2. AV junctional rhythm with retrograde P wave conduction
3. Lown-Ganong-Levine (accessory pathway)
4. HTN

C. Increased QRS interval
1. Hyperkalemia
2. Bundle branch block
3. Hypothermia
4. Quinidine
5. Procainamide
6. Tricyclic overdose

D. ST segment elevation
1. Q wave MI
2. Pericarditis (diffuse ST segment elevation)
3. Ventricular aneurysm (ST segment elevation persists > 2 weeks)
4. Early repolarization: Seen best in V_{1-2}, no other ECG abnormalities present, cannot be distinguished from MI. If patient is > age 30, may need to be admitted to exclude MI. Check old ECGs
5. Prinzmetal's angina
6. Nonspecific

E. ST segment depression
1. Ischemia
2. Non Q wave MI

    3. Ventricular hypertrophy (typically downsloping)

    4. Interventricular Conduction Defect (IVCD)

    5. Digoxin effect, Quinidine effect

    6. Hypokalemia

    7. "Reciprocal" changes in MI

F. Prolonged QT$_c$: measured from the beginning of the Q to the end of the T wave (> 0.37 seconds in men and > 0.40 seconds in women — due to delayed repolarization of the ventricular myocardium). QT$_c$ = QT (seconds) / $\sqrt{RR}$ (seconds)

    1. Ischemia, CHF

    2. Drugs: Quinidine, Procaine, Norpace, Phenothiazines, Tricyclics, Terfenadine, Cisapride

    3. Hypocalcemia, hypokalemia, hypomagnesemia

    4. Hypothermia

    5. Mitral valve prolapse (MVP)

    6. Ventricular hypertrophy

    7. Intracranial hemorrhage

G. Shortened QT$_c$

    1. Hypercalcemia

    2. Digoxin

H. Inverted T waves

    1. Ischemia

    2. Non Q wave MI

    3. Chronic pericarditis

    4. Ventricular hypertrophy

    5. Intraventricular conduction defect (IVCD)

    6. Intracranial hemorrhage

    7. Hypokalemia

    8. Pulmonary embolism (PE)

I. Tall/peaked T waves

    1. Hyperkalemia

    2. Acute MI

    3. Intracranial hemorrhage

    4. Normal variant

J. Tall R wave in V$_1$

    1. Posterior MI

    2. RVH

    3. Incomplete RBBB

    4. Duchenne's muscular dystrophy

    5. WPW

    6. Normal variant (counterclockwise rotation of the heart)

K. RSR' in V$_1$

    1. Complete or incomplete RBBB

    2. RVH

    3. WPW

    4. Pectus or straight back deformities

    5. Normal variant—occurs in 5% of young people

L. U waves: Considered abnormal when amplitude is > 1.5mm in any lead; best seen in V$_3$

    1. Bradycardia

    2. Electrolyte imbalance (hypokalemia, hypercalcemia or hypomagnesemia)

    3. Drugs (Digitalis, Quinidine, Procainamide, Phenothiazines, Epinephrine)

    4. CNS disease

    5. LVH

    6. Hyperthyroidism

    7. Mitral valve prolapse (MVP)

    8. Intracranial hemorrhage

    9. Negative U waves are suggestive of severe triple vessel disease

CARD

M. **Poor R wave progression (precordial leads)**
1. COPD
2. LV dilation
3. LAHB
4. Anterior MI

VII. DRUG EFFECTS

A. **Digitalis**
1. Digitalis *effect*: Seen in most patients on Digitalis. Digitalis is often stopped several days before exercise stress testing so that Digitalis effect (ST depression, T wave changes) will not be confused with ischemia
   a. Increased PR interval
   b. ST segment depression (downsloping ST segment)
   c. Flattening of T waves, diphasic T, inverted T
   d. Shortening of QT interval
   e. Increase of U wave amplitude
2. Digitalis *toxicity*: This is a clinical and not an ECG diagnosis
   a. Evidence of increased automaticity and impaired conduction
   b. Examples: Bradyarrhythmia, junctional rhythm, AV block, PAT with 2:1 AV block, PVCs, bi-/trigeminy, atrial fib, V. Tach, V. Fib.

B. **Quinidine**
1. Quinidine *effect*: Changes seen on ECG
   a. Wide, notched P
   b. Wide QRS (> 0.12 seconds)
   c. ST depression
   d. Prolonged QT_c
   e. U wave
2. Quinidine *toxicity*: This is a clinical and not an ECG diagnosis
   a. Widening of QRS (> 0.12 seconds)
   b. AV block, sinus bradycardia, sinus arrest
   c. Ventricular arrhythmias, syncope, sudden death
   d. Torsade de pointes

VIII. ELECTROLYTE ABNORMALITIES

A. **Hyperkalemia**
1. Tall, narrow, peaked T waves (hyperacute T waves)
2. Widening of QRS > 0.10 seconds
3. Wide, flat P waves
4. Bradyarrhythmias, tachyarrhythmias, AV block, ventricular fibrillation, cardiac arrest

B. **Hypokalemia**
1. Flattening and inversion of T wave
2. Prominent U wave
3. ST depression
4. Ventricular ectopy and AV block

C. **Hypercalcemia:** Decreased QT interval, U waves

D. **Hypocalcemia (hypomagnesemia):** Increased QT interval

IX. ECG CHANGES ASSOCIATED WITH VARIOUS CONDITIONS

A. **Pulmonary embolism (PE):** Sinus tachycardia, S in lead I, Q in lead III, inverted T in lead III, RAD, ST segment decreased in lead II, transient RBBB, T wave inversion in right precordial leads, right atrial enlargement. Note: the most common is a normal ECG

B. **Chronic lung disease:** RAD, RVH, right atrial enlargement, low voltage, multifocal atrial tachycardia (MAT), right atrial enlargement

C. **Pericardial effusion:** Sinus tachycardia, electrical alternans, low voltage (< 5mm), ST segment elevation

D. LV strain: Depressed and wavy ST segment in V_5

E. RV strain: Depressed and wavy ST segment in V_2

F. Wolff-Parkinson-White syndrome (WPW): PR < 0.12, QRS > 0.11, delta wave, ST/T changes, associated with paroxysmal tachycardia

G. Ventricular aneurysm: Persistent ST elevation (> 2 weeks) after MI (usually anterior MI)

H. Early repolarization/normal variant: QRS slurs into ST with high J point and concave up ST segment, most common in lateral and inferior leads

I. Pericarditis: Diffuse ST segment elevation (concave) present in all leads except aVR and V_1, PR segment depression, QRS changes are absent

J. Hypothermia: Prolonged PR, prolonged QT_c, sinus bradycardia syndrome

K. Sick sinus syndrome: Severe sinus bradycardia, sinus arrest, bradycardia alternating with tachycardia, chronic atrial fibrillation, AV junctional escape rhythm

CLINICAL PEARLS
- Reciprocal changes for inferior infarctions may involve I, aVL. Reciprocal changes for a lateral MI may involve II, III, aVF
- Approximately 15% of normal individuals may have a Q wave and/or T wave inversion in lead III
- Q waves may be normal in lead III, V_1 and sometimes V_2

References
Panju AA, et al. Is this patient having a myocardial infarction? JAMA 1998;280:1256–63.
Phibbs BP. Advanced ECG: Boards and beyond. 1st ed. Boston: Little, Brown, 1997.
Seelig CB. Simplified EKG analysis. Philadelphia: Hanley & Belfus, 1992.
Marriott HJL. Practical electrocardiography. 8th ed. Baltimore: Williams & Wilkins, 1988.

Beth Weinstock, MD
Michael B. Weinstock, MD
Miriam Chan, PharmD
Matt McHugh, MD

40. HYPERLIPIDEMIA

I. SIGNIFICANCE
- **A.** A major modifiable risk factor for coronary heart disease, which is the leading cause of death for both women and men in the US
- **B.** An approximation of efficacy of therapy is that there is a *1% reduction in risk of coronary artery disease (CAD)* for every *1% decrease in LDL*

II. ETIOLOGY
- **A. Total cholesterol** is influenced by genetic predisposition, concomitant disease, certain meds, and lifestyle
- **B. Genetic connection:** Autosomal dominant familial hypercholesterolemia—present in 1 in 500 patients with myocardial infarction

III. CHOLESTEROL SCREENING
- **A. In all adults > 20,** check a *fasting* lipoprotein profile (total cholesterol, HDL, LDL, triglycerides) every 5yrs
- **B. If the testing is non-fasting,** then only the values for total cholesterol and HDL will be usable. If the total cholesterol is > 200 or the HDL is < 40, then check a *fasting* profile
- **C. If any of the above abnormal,** recheck in 1–8 weeks and use the average of the 2 values to guide management
- **D. Cholesterol screening in children**
  1. Indications: Children > 2yrs

      a. With a parent with total cholesterol > 240mg/dL

      b. With a family history of premature (< 55) cardiovascular disease

  2. For screening purposes, finger-stick capillary technique is adequate

  3. Recommendations for checking full fasting lipid-profile is screening cholesterol > 170mg/dL

E. Cholesterol screening in the elderly

  1. No age limit for screening

  2. Elderly patients who are otherwise in good health and who can expect a reasonably long life in absence of coronary artery disease should not be excluded from cholesterol-lowering therapy. Level of aggressiveness in cholesterol-lowering depends on assessment of CAD risk. Stabilization of atherosclerotic lesions is very important in elderly patients who inherently have higher risk of coronary events

  3. Secondary prevention trials in those > 65 have shown significant risk reduction with statin therapy

F. Clinical pearls for cholesterol screening

  1. Patients who are acutely ill, losing weight, pregnant, or breast-feeding should not be screened (results will not be representative)

  2. If patient has had an MI in the last 3 months, cholesterol will be *lower* than the actual value. Should be rechecked

  3. Patient should be fasting 12hrs prior to blood draw (water and black coffee are okay)

  4. Cholesterol levels should be measured on *venous* samples

  5. Total cholesterol may be 10% higher in winter compared to summer

G. Classification of cholesterol

ATP III Classification of LDL, Total, and HDL Cholesterol (mg/dL)	
LDL Cholesterol	
< 100	Optimal
100 - 129	Near optimal/above optimal
130 - 159	Borderline high
160 - 189	High
≥ 190	Very High
Total Cholesterol	
< 200	Desirable
200 - 239	Borderline high
≥ 240	High
HDL Cholesterol	
< 40	Low
≥ 60	High

Source: Third Report of the National Cholesterol Education Program (NCEP) Expert Panel on Detection, Evaluation, and Treatment of High Blood Cholesterol in Adults (Adult Treatment Panel III), Executive Summary. NIH pub. no. 01-3670, May 2001. Table 2, p. 3. http://www.nhlbi.nih.gov/guidelines/cholesterol/atp3xsum.pdf

IV. INDICATIONS FOR THERAPY

A. Assess major risk factors per the table below (an HDL > 60 is a "negative" risk factor)

Major Risk Factors (Exclusive of LDL Cholesterol) That Modify LDL Goals*
• Cigarette smoking
• Hypertension (BP ≥ 140/90 mmHg or on antihypertensive medication)
• Low HDL cholesterol (< 40 mg/dL)†
• Family history of premature CHD (CHD in male first degree relative < 55 years; CHD in female first degree relative < 65 years)
• Age (men ≥ 45 years; women ≥ 55 years)*

* In ATP III, diabetes is regarded as a CHD risk equivalent.

† HDL cholesterol ≥ 60 mg/dL counts as a "negative" risk factor; its presence removes one risk factor from the total count.

Source: Third Report of the National Cholesterol Education Program (NCEP) Expert Panel on Detection, Evaluation, and Treatment of High Blood Cholesterol in Adults (Adult Treatment Panel III), Executive Summary. NIH pub. no. 01-3670, May 2001. Table 3, p. 3. http://www.nhlbi.nih.gov/guidelines/cholesterol/atp3xsum.pdf

B. Assess cholesterol levels in conjunction with risk category (see table below)

LDL Cholesterol Goals and Cutpoints for Therapeutic Lifestyle Changes (TLC) and Drug Therapy in Different Risk Categories			
Risk Category	LDL Goal	LDL Level at Which to Initiate Therapeutic Lifestyle Changes (TLC)	LDL Level at Which to Consider Drug Therapy
CHD or CHD Risk Equivalents (10-year risk > 20%)	< 100 mg/dL	≥ 100 mg/dL	≥ 130 mg/dL (100-129 mg/dL: drug optional)*
2+ Risk Factors (10-year risk ≤20%)	< 130 mg/dL	≥ 130 mg/dL	10-year risk 10-20% ≥ 130 mg/dL
			10-year risk < 10%: ≥ 160 mg/dL
0-1 Risk Factor†	< 160 mg/dL	≥ 160 mg/dL	≥ 190 mg/dL (160-189 mg/dL: LDL-lowering drug optional)

* Some authorities recommend use of LDL-lowering drugs in this category if an LDL cholesterol < 100 mg/dL cannot be achieved by therapeutic lifestyle changes. Others prefer use of drugs that primarily modify triglycerides and HDL, e.g., nicotinic acid or fibrate. Clinical judgment also may call for deferring drug therapy in this subcategory.

† Almost all people with 0-1 risk factor have a 10-year risk < 10%, thus 10-year risk assessment in people with 0-1 risk factor is not necessary.

Source: Third Report of the National Cholesterol Education Program (NCEP) Expert Panel on Detection, Evaluation, and Treatment of High Blood Cholesterol in Adults (Adult Treatment Panel III), Executive Summary. NIH pub. no. 01-3670, May 2001. Table 5, p. 8. www.nhlbi.nih.gov/guidelines/cholesterol/atp3xsum.pdf

V. MANAGEMENT: Correct secondary causes of lipid disorders (see related chapters)

    A. Diabetes

    B. Obesity

    C. Sedentary lifestyle

    D. Hypothyroidism

    E. Liver (obstructive jaundice)

    F. Renal disease (Nephrotic syndrome, dialysis)

    G. Smoking

    H. Hypertension

    I. Alcoholism

    J. Menopause: The ATP III guidelines (May, 2001) state that recent trials cast doubt on the use of hormone replacement therapy to reduce CHD risk in post-menopausal women

    K. Drug induced: Thiazide diuretics, Cimetidine (Tagamet), progestins, steroids (anabolic and corticosteroids), β-blockers, oral contraceptives, Chlorpromazine, bile salts

VI. LIFESTYLE MODIFICATION

    A. The daily American diet usually contains between 400–500mg of cholesterol. Intake of < 200mg/day is needed to reduce total cholesterol through diet alone

    B. Saturated fats increase LDL and HDL cholesterol levels. Reducing dietary saturated fats results in greater decrease in total cholesterol than does just restricting overall cholesterol intake

    C. NCEP ATP III Therapeutic Lifestyle Changes (TLC)

        1. Stress reduction of saturated fat (< 7% total calories) and total cholesterol (< 200mgs/day) in diet

        2. Also stress weight reduction and physical activity if high triglycerides, low HDL, or if metabolic syndrome is present

        3. Options for lowering LDL include increasing plant stanols/sterols (2g/day) and increasing viscous (soluble) fiber (10–25g/day) if LDL goal not met in 6 weeks

        4. May increase unsaturated fats so total fat is 25–35% of total calories. This can help decrease triglycerides and increase HDL especially in persons with metabolic syndrome

        5. Consider referral to dietician at any point

CARD

D. Evaluation after dietary management
1. If LDL goal is met, monitor lipid panel and adherence to TLC every 4–6 months
2. If LDL goal is not met with TLC after 12 weeks, consider adding drug therapy

E. Weight loss/Exercise
1. Decreases total cholesterol, decreases triglyceride levels, increases HDL levels, decreases BP, decreases risk of diabetes mellitus, improves metabolic syndrome, and decreases LDL in some people
2. Aerobic activity involving large muscle groups is most beneficial

VII. TYPES OF LIPID DISORDERS: Most common types of lipid disorders (80–90%) are types IIA, IIB, and type IV. Use this table as a guide to find a logical medication to start with. Always use dietary management concurrently

Lab Results	Type	Pharmacologic Management
Elevated LDL (no change or minimal change in triglycerides or HDL)	Type IIA	1) HMG CoA Reductase Inhibitors 2) Niacin 3) Resins
Elevated LDL (VLDL) and Triglycerides Decreased HDL	Type IIB	1) HMG CoA Reductase Inhibitors 2) Niacin 3) Fibrates
Elevated Triglycerides and LDL (VLDL) Decreased HDL	Type IV	1) Niacin 2) Fibrates
Elevated Triglycerides (chylomicrons) (Treat if > 500 to prevent pancreatitis)	Type I	1) Fibrates 2) Niacin

VIII. DRUG THERAPY
A. HMG CoA Reductase Inhibitors
1. Action: Inhibit rate limiting step in cholesterol biosynthesis. Up-regulates LDL receptors in liver, which increases clearance of LDL. Maximum effect is achieved after approximately 4–6 weeks of therapy
2. All should be taken QHS
3. Stop treatment in patients with transaminase levels > 3 × normal
4. Effect: At maximum recommended dose, all decrease LDL by 18–55%, increase HDL by 5–15% and decrease triglycerides by 7–30%

B. Niacin (Nicotinic Acid)
1. Action: Decreases the synthesis of LDL cholesterol by reducing the hepatic synthesis of VLDL cholesterol, by increasing the synthesis of HDL cholesterol, by inhibiting lipolysis in adipose tissue, and by increasing lipase activity
2. Effect: Decrease LDL 5–25%, decrease triglycerides up to 20–50%, increase HDL 15–35%, decrease lipoprotein A up to 50%

C. Bile Acid sequestrants
1. Action: Bind cholesterol-containing bile acids in the intestines, producing an insoluble complex that prevents reabsorption
2. Decrease LDL up to 15–30%, increase HDL by 3–5%, no effect on triglycerides
3. Good choice in young patients, women of child-bearing age, and in patients with hepatic disease. Avoid if triglycerides > 400. Caution if triglycerides > 200

D. Fibric Acid derivatives (Fibrates)
1. Action: Increase the clearance of VLDL cholesterol by enhancing lipolysis and reducing hepatic cholesterol synthesis
2. Drug of choice in patients with normal cholesterol and increased triglycerides
3. Effect: Decreases LDL 5–20%, decreases triglycerides 20–50%, increases HDL 10–20%
4. **Fenofibrate (TriCor)** is the most potent fibrate available to lower triglycerides and LDL. It is preferred over **Gemfibrozil** in diabetic patients with combined hyperlipidemia

Drugs Affecting Lipoprotein Metabolism				
Drug Class, Agents and Daily Doses	Lipid/Lipoprotein Effects	Side Effects	Contraindications	Clinical Trial Results
HMG CoA reductase inhibitors (statins)*	LDL ↓ 18-55% HDL ↑ 5-15% TG ↓ 7-30%	Myopathy Increased liver enzymes	Absolute: • Active or chronic liver disease Relative: • Concomitant use of certain drugs[†]	Reduced major coronary events, CHD deaths, need for coronary procedures, stroke, and total mortality
Bile acid Sequestrants[‡]	LDL ↓ 15-30% HDL ↑ 3-5% TG No change or increase	Gastrointestinal distress Constipation Decreased absorption of other drugs	Absolute: • dysbeta-lipoproteinemia • TG > 400 mg/dL Relative: • TG > 200 mg/dL	Reduced major coronary events and CHD deaths
Nicotinic acid[¥]	LDL ↓ 5-25% HDL ↑ 15-35% TG ↓ 20-50%	Flushing Hyperglycemia Hyperuricemia (or gout) Upper GI distress Hepatotoxicity	Absolute: • Chronic liver disease • Severe gout Relative: • Diabetes • Hyperuricemia • Peptic ulcer disease	Reduced major coronary events, and possibly total mortality
Fibric acids[§]	LDL ↓ 5-20% (may be increased in patients with high TG) HDL ↑ 10-20% TG ↓ 20-50%	Dyspepsia Gallstones Myopathy Unexplained non-CHD deaths in WHO study	Absolute: • Severe renal disease • Severe hepatic disease	Reduced major coronary events

*   Lovastatin (20-80 mg), pravastatin (20-40 mg), simvastatin (20-80 mg), fluvastatin (20-80 mg), atorvastatin (10-80 mg), cerivastatin (0.4-0.8 mg).

†   Cyclosporine, macrolide antibiotics, various antifungal agents and cytochrome P-450 inhibitors (fibrates and niacin should be used with appropriate caution).

‡   Cholestyramine (4-16 g), colestipol (5-20 g), colesevelam (2.6-3.8 g).

¥   Immediate release (crystalline) nicotinic acid (1.5-3 g), extended release nicotinic acid (Niaspan ®) (1-2 g), sustained release nicotinic acid (1-2 g).

§   Gemfibrozil (600 mg BID), fenofibrate (200 mg), clofibrate (1000 mg BID).

Source: Third Report of the National Cholesterol Education Program (NCEP) Expert Panel on Detection, Evaluation, and Treatment of High Blood Cholesterol in Adults (Adult Treatment Panel III), Executive Summary. NIH pub. no. 01-3670, May 2001. Table 7, p. 13. http://www.nhlbi.nih.gov/guidelines/cholesterol/atp3xsum.pdf

- Doses are QD unless otherwise noted
- Monitoring of LFTs should be obtained at baseline, at 6 and 12 weeks, and semiannually after initiating HMG CoA reductase therapy
- Monitoring of LFTs should be obtained at baseline and then intermittently after initiation of nicotinic acid and fibric acids
- Monitoring does not need to be performed for bile acid sequestrants, but consideration should be given to medication whose absorption may be affected by resins (or take care not to administer at same time as resins)

IX. COMBINATION THERAPY

   A. Combination therapy should be considered if cholesterol goals are not met

   B. HMG CoA reductase inhibitors should be taken 1hr before or at least 4hrs after sequestrant (bile acid sequestrant decreases bioavailability of HMG CoA reductase inhibitors)

   C. Caution with combination with fibrate-type drugs (Gemfibrozil) and Niacin due to risk of myopathy and rhabdomyolysis

POSSIBLE COMBINATION THERAPIES IF SINGLE-AGENT THERAPY IS NOT EFFECTIVE IN REDUCING LIPID LEVELS

Lipid levels	First drug → drug to add
Elevated LDL level and triglyceride level <200 mg per dL	Statin → bile acid-binding resin Nicotinic acid* → statin* Bile acid-binding resin → nicotinic acid
Elevated LDL level and triglyceride level 200 to 499 mg per dL	Statin*‡ → nicotinic acid* ‡ Statin* → fibrate Nicotinic acid → bile acid-binding resin Nicotinic acid → fibrate

LDL=low-density lipoprotein.
*—Possible increased risk of myopathy and hepatitis.
†—Increased risk of severe myopathy.
‡—The combination of nicotinic acid and lovastatin (Mevacor) may induce rhabdomyolysis, a rare adverse drug interaction.
Adapted from National Cholesterol Education Program. Cholesterol lowering in the patient with coronary heart disease. Bethesda, Md.: National Institutes of Health, National Heart, Lung, and Blood Institute, 1997; DHHS publication no. (NIH) 97-3794.

CARD

Adapted from National Cholesterol Education Program. Cholesterol lowering in the patient with coronary heart disease. Bethesda, Md.: National Institutes of Health, National Heart, Lung, and Blood Institute, 1997; DHHS pub. no. (NIH) 97-3794.

CLINICAL PEARLS

- 50% of patients with xanthelasma (localized lipid-containing infiltrate—commonly occur around eyelids) will have hypercholesterolemia
- Intertriginous planar xanthoma (web spaces of digits) is pathognomic for homozygous familial hypercholesterolemia
- NCEP-ATP III Guidelines can be found at www.nhlbi.nih.gov
- "Smoker" means any cigarette smoking in past month
- Metabolic Syndrome is defined as 3 or more of the following: abdominal obesity (waist > 40 inches in men and > 35 inches in women), triglycerides ≥ 150mg/dL, HDL < 40mg/dL in men and < 50 in women, blood pressure ≥ 130/≥ 85, and fasting glucose ≥ 110mg/dL
- Use cholesterol-lowering drug sparingly in young adult men and premenopausal women who are without risk factors
- Prescription for isolated low HDL is exercise, weight loss, and smoking cessation. No benefit exists in increasing *normal* HDL levels

References
Third Report of the National Cholesterol Education Program (NCEP) Expert Panel on Detection, Evaluation, and Treatment of High Blood Cholesterol in Adults (Adult Treatment Panel III), Executive Summary. NIH pub. no. 01-3670, May 2001.
    http://www.nhlbi.nih.gov/guidelines/cholesterol/atp3xsum.pdf
Pignone MP, et al. Use of lipid lowering drugs for primary prevention of coronary heart disease: meta-analysis of randomised trials. BMJ 2000;321:1–5.
Berg AO. Screening adults for lipid disorders. Recommendations and rationale. Am J Prev Med 2001;20(3 Suppl):73–6, 77–89.
Jick H, et al. Statins and the risk of dementia. Lancet 2000;356:1627–31.
Cholesterol screening in children; adapted from the U.S. Public Health Service "Clinician's Handbook of Preventive Services." Am Fam Phys 1995;51:1923–7.

Daniel M. Neides, MD
Michael B. Weinstock, MD
Kathy Provanzana, MD

41. HYPERTENSION

I. INTRODUCTION

   A. Hypertension (HTN) affects 50 million people in the US and 1 billion people worldwide
   B. There is a continuous, consistent relationship between blood pressure (BP) and risk of cardiovascular disease (CVD) which is independent of other risk factors
   C. The risk of CVD begins at 15/75 and doubles with each incremental rise of 20 (systolic)/10(diastolic) in patients 40–70
   D. Systolic BP (SBP) is more important CVD risk factor than diastolic BP (DBP) in patients > 50
   E. Antihypertensive therapy is associated with a 35–40% decreased incidence of stroke, a 20–25% decreased incidence of myocardial infarction, and a 50% decreased incidence of heart failure
   F. HTN is the most common diagnosis in the US with 35 million office visits/yr. 30% of people with HTN are unaware of their diagnosis

II. HISTORY

   A. Previous history of HTN with previous levels and previous therapies attempted (note if these therapies were successful or not). Adverse effects of previous therapies
   B. Symptoms of morbidity related to HTN including coronary artery disease, heart failure, cerebrovascular disease, peripheral vascular disease, dyslipidemia, renal disease, and diabetes mellitus
   C. Symptoms suggestive of secondary hypertension (see VI. below)
   D. Recent changes in weight, physical activity, smoking or other tobacco use, intake of sodium, alcohol, saturated fat, and caffeine
   E. Prescribed and over-the-counter meds, herbal remedies, and illicit drugs
   F. Other factors which may affect adherence with medication regimen including psychosocial and environmental factors such as employment status, educational levels, understanding of HTN, and importance of control
   G. Family history of conditions listed in II. B. above

III. PHYSICAL EXAM

   A. General: 2 or more blood pressure measurements at least 2 minutes apart with the patient seated, measurement in the other arm (if values are different, take the higher of the 2), weight, height, waist circumference
   B. Neck: Thyroid enlargement or nodules, carotid bruits, JVD
   C. Eyes: Funduscopic exam for hypertensive retinopathy, papilledema
   D. Lungs: Crackles or other signs of heart failure
   E. CV: Rhythm, rate, gallop, murmur
   F. Abdomen: Bruits (renal artery stenosis), abdominal aneurysm, truncal obesity or striae, enlarged kidneys, masses
   G. Extremities: Edema, pulses in the extremities (coarctation), femoral bruits
   H. Neurological exam

IV. EVALUATION

   A. Routine tests before initiating therapy: ECG, urinalysis, hematocrit, potassium, creatinine, calcium and fasting lipid profile (to include LDL, HDL, and triglycerides)
   B. Optional tests: Urinary albumin excretion or albumin/creatinine ratio
   C. Measurement of blood pressure
      1. Based on the average of 2 or more readings taken during at least 2 separate visits
      2. Measuring BP—Patient should be seated in chair and BP should be checked with appropriately sized cuff after 5 minutes of rest
   D. Ambulatory monitoring
      1. The BP recorded with ambulatory monitoring correlates with target organ injury

better than office measurement of blood pressure
2. Ambulatory BP > 135/85 is generally considered to be hypertensive
3. Indications
    a. Suspected white coat HTN
    b. Apparent drug resistance
    c. Hypotensive symptoms with meds
    d. Episodic HTN
    e. Autonomic dysfunction

V. CLASSIFICATIONS AND MANAGEMENT OF BLOOD PRESSURE

Classification and Management of Blood Pressure for Adults*					
				Initial Drug Therapy	
BP Classification	SBP‡ mmHg	DBP‡ mmHg	Lifestyle Modification	Without Compelling Indication	With Compelling Indications (See VII. C.)
Normal	<120	and <80	Encourage	No antihypertensive drug indicated.	Drug(s) for compelling indications.‡
Prehypertension	120–139	or 80–89	Yes		
Stage 1 Hypertension	140–159	or 90–99	Yes	Thiazide-type diuretics for most. May consider ACEI, ARB, BB, CCB, or combination.	Drug(s) for the compelling indications. ‡ Other antihypertensive drugs (diuretics, ACEI, ARB, BB, CCB) as needed.
Stage 2 Hypertension	>160	or >100	Yes	Two-drug combination for most † (usually thiazide-type diuretic and ACEI or ARB or BB or CCB).	

DBP, diastolic blood pressure; SBP, systolic blood pressure.

Drug abbreviations: ACEI, angiotensin converting enzyme inhibitor; ARB, angiotensin receptor blocker; BB, beta-blocker; CCB, calcium channel blocker.

* Treatment determined by highest BP category.

† Initial combined therapy should be used cautiously in those at risk for orthostatic hypotension.

‡ Treat patients with chronic kidney disease or diabetes to BP goal of<130/80 mmHg.

Source: The Seventh Report of the Joint National Committee on Prevention, Detection, Evaluation, and Treatment of High Blood Pressure. National Institutes of Health. NIH pub. no. 03–5233 (May 2003), Table 1, p. 3 & JAMA 2003;289(19):2561. www.nhlbi.nih.gov/guidelines/hypertension/express.pdf

VI. SECONDARY HYPERTENSION—CONSIDER EVALUATION WITH:

A. Patients whose age, history or physical exam, severity of hypertension, or initial lab findings suggest a secondary cause. Examples:
    1. Abdominal bruits—RAS
    2. Paroxysms of HTN accompanied by headache, palpitations perspiration—Pheochromocytoma
    3. Abdominal or flank masses—Polycystic kidneys
    4. Delayed or absent femoral pulses—Coarctation of the aorta
    5. Truncal obesity with abdominal striae—Cushing's or steroid therapy
    6. Unprovoked hypokalemia—Primary aldosteronism
    7. Hypercalcemia—Hyperparathyroidism
    8. Elevated creatinine—Renal parenchymal disease

B. **Other causes of secondary HTN:** Sleep apnea, drug-induced or drug-related thyroid disease, oral contraceptives, drug or alcohol-related sympathomimetics (decongestants, anoretics)

C. Poor response to conventional anti-HTN meds after an adequate trial

D. HTN which has suddenly worsened (well controlled hypertension has begun to increase)

E. Patients with stage 3 HTN or sudden onset of HTN

F. Patients who have renal failure after administration of ACE inhibitors/Angiotensin II receptor antagonists

VII. MANAGEMENT OF HYPERTENSION
A. Algorithm for treatment of hypertension

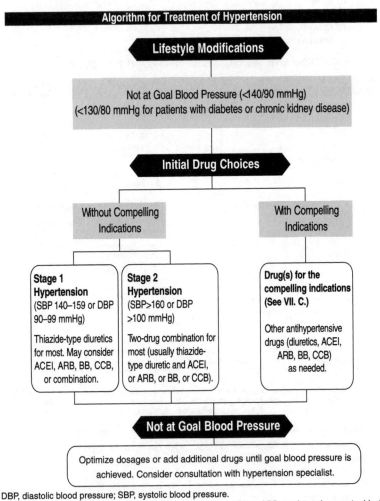

Algorithm for Treatment of Hypertension

Lifestyle Modifications

Not at Goal Blood Pressure (<140/90 mmHg)
(<130/80 mmHg for patients with diabetes or chronic kidney disease)

Initial Drug Choices

Without Compelling Indications

With Compelling Indications

Stage 1 Hypertension
(SBP 140–159 or DBP 90–99 mmHg)

Thiazide-type diuretics for most. May consider ACEI, ARB, BB, CCB, or combination.

Stage 2 Hypertension
(SBP>160 or DBP >100 mmHg)

Two-drug combination for most (usually thiazide-type diuretic and ACEI, or ARB, or BB, or CCB).

Drug(s) for the compelling indications (See VII. C.)

Other antihypertensive drugs (diuretics, ACEI, ARB, BB, CCB) as needed.

Not at Goal Blood Pressure

Optimize dosages or add additional drugs until goal blood pressure is achieved. Consider consultation with hypertension specialist.

DBP, diastolic blood pressure; SBP, systolic blood pressure.
Drug abbreviations: ACEI, angiotensin converting enzyme inhibitor; ARB, angiotensin receptor blocker; BB, beta-blocker; CCB, calcium channel blocker.

Source: The Seventh Report of the Joint National Committee on Prevention, Detection, Evaluation, and Treatment of High Blood Pressure. National Institutes of Health. NIH pub. no. 03–5233 (May 2003), Figure 1, p. 13 & JAMA 2003;289(19):2561. www.nhlbi.nih.gov/guidelines/hypertension/express.pdf

B. Lifestyle modifications

Lifestyle Modifications to Manage Hypertension*†		
Modification	**Recommendation**	**Approximate SBP Reduction (Range)**
Weight reduction	Maintain normal body weight (body mass index 18.5–24.9 kg/m^2).	5–20 mmHg/10 kg weight loss
Adopt DASH eating plan	Consume a diet rich in fruits, vegetables, and lowfat dairy products with a reduced content of saturated and total fat.	8–14 mmHg
Dietary sodium reduction	Reduce dietary sodium intake to no more than 100 mmol per day (2.4 g sodium or 6 g sodium chloride).	2–8 mmHg
Physical activity	Engage in regular aerobic physical activity such as brisk walking (at least 30 min per day, most days of the week).	4–9 mmHg
Moderation of alcohol consumption	Limit consumption to no more than 2 drinks (1 oz or 30 mL ethanol; e.g., 24 oz beer, 10 oz wine, or 3 oz 80-proof whiskey) per day in most men and to no more than 1 drink per day in women and lighter weight persons.	2–4 mmHg

DASH, Dietary Approaches to Stop Hypertension.
* For overall cardiovascular risk reduction, stop smoking.
† The effects of implementing these modifications are dose and time dependent, and could be greater for some individuals.

CARD

Source: The Seventh Report of the Joint National Committee on Prevention, Detection, Evaluation, and Treatment of High Blood Pressure. National Institutes of Health. NIH pub. no. 03–5233 (May 2003), Table 5, p. 8 & JAMA 2003;289(19):2561. www.nhlbi.nih.gov/guidelines/hypertension/express.pdf

C. Compelling indications

Clinical Trial and Guideline Basis for Compelling Indications for Individual Drug Classes						
	Recommended Drugs[†]					
Compelling Indication[*]	Diuretic	BB	ACEI	ARB	CCB	Aldo ANT
Heart failure	•	•	•	•		•
Postmyocardial infarction		•	•			•
High coronary disease risk	•	•	•		•	
Diabetes	•	•	•	•	•	
Chronic kidney disease			•	•		
Recurrent stroke prevention	•		•			

[*]Compelling indications for antihypertensive drugs are based on benefits from outcome studies or existing clinical guidelines; the compelling indication is managed in parallel with the BP.

[†]Drug abbreviations: ACEI, angiotensin converting enzyme inhibitor; ARB, angiotensin receptor blocker; Aldo ANT, aldosterone antagonist; BB, beta-blocker; CCB, calcium channel blocker.

Source: The Seventh Report of the Joint National Committee on Prevention, Detection, Evaluation, and Treatment of High Blood Pressure. National Institutes of Health. NIH pub. no. 03–5233 (May 2003), Table 8, p. 15 & JAMA 2003;289(19):2561. www.nhlbi.nih.gov/guidelines/hypertension/express.pdf

D. Pharmacologic management of HTN: The 7th Report of the Joint National Committee on Prevention, Detection, Evaluation, and Treatment of High Blood Pressure (JNC VII) recommends initial therapy for most patients with thiazide-type diuretics, either alone or in combination with ACE inhibitors, ARBs, β-blockers, or CCBs:

1. For stage 1 HTN, initiate therapy with 1 agent
2. For stage 2 HTN, consider initial therapy with 2 agents. Use caution for those at risk for orthostatic hypotension, diabetics, patients with autonomic dysfunction, and some older persons
3. Follow-up at monthly intervals until goal is achieved (BP < 140/90 for most and < 130/80 for diabetics and those with renal disease). More frequent visits for those with stage 2 HTN or complicating comorbid conditions
4. Monitor serum potassium and creatinine 1–2 times/yr

VIII. SPECIAL CONSIDERATIONS

A. Ischemic heart disease: Initial therapy with β-blocker or may use long acting CCB

B. Post myocardial infarction: ACE inhibitor, β-blockers, aldosterone antagonists

C. Heart failure
1. Asymptomatic—ACE inhibitor or β-blocker
2. Symptomatic—ACE, β-blocker, ARB, aldosterone antagonist along with loop diuretics

D. Diabetics: Usually will need 2 agents. May use thiazide diuretics, β-blockers, ACE inhibitors, ARBs or CCBs

E. Chronic kidney disease: Use ACE inhibitors or ARBs. With advanced renal disease (GFR < 30), loop diuretics are often needed in combination with other drugs

F. African Americans: Better response to diuretics or CCBs and reduced response to β–blockers, ACE inhibitors and ARBs

G. Older individuals: HTN occurs in more than $2/3$ of individuals > 65. Goal is the same as younger patients, consider lower doses initially. Multiple drugs are often needed

IX. ORAL ANTIHYPERTENSIVE DRUGS, SINGLE AND COMBINATION AGENTS

Oral Antihypertensive Drugs* Part A		
Class	**Drug (Trade Name)**	**Usual Dose Range in mg/day (Daily Frequency)**
Thiazide diuretics	chlorothiazide (Diuril)	125–500 (1)
	chlorthalidone (generic)	12.5–25 (1)
	hydrochlorothiazide (Microzide, HydroDIURIL†)	12.5–50 (1)
	polythiazide (Renese)	2–4 (1)
	indapamide (Lozol †)	1.25–2.5 (1)
	metolazone (Mykrox)	0.5–1.0 (1)
	metolazone (Zaroxolyn)	2.5–5 (1)
Loop diuretics	bumetanide (Bumex†)	0.5–2 (2)
	furosemide (Lasix†)	20–80 (2)
	torsemide (Demadex†)	2.5–10 (1)
Potassium-sparing diuretics	amiloride (Midamor †)	5–10 (1–2)
	triamterene (Dyrenium)	50–100 (1–2)
Aldosterone receptor blockers	eplerenone (Inspra)	50–100 (1–2)
	spironolactone (Aldactone †)	25–50(1–2)
Beta-blockers	atenolol (Tenormin†)	25–100 (1)
	betaxolol (Kerlone†)	5–20 (1)
	bisoprolol (Zebeta †)	2.5–10 (1)
	metoprolol (Lopressor†)	50–100 (1–2)
	metoprolol extended release (Toprol XL)	50–100 (1)
	nadolol (Corgard†)	40–120 (1)
	propranolol (Inderal†)	40–160 (2)
	propranolol long-acting (Inderal LA †)	60–180 (1)
	timolol (Blocadren†)	20– 40 (2)
Beta-blockers with intrinsic sympathomimetic activity	acebutolol (Sectral †)	200–800 (2)
	penbutolol (Levatol)	10–40 (1)
	pindolol (generic)	10–40 (2)
Combined alpha- and beta-blockers	carvedilol (Coreg)	12.5–50 (2)
	labetalol (Normodyne, Trandate†)	200–800(2)

Chart continued on following page

CARD

Oral Antihypertensive Drugs* Part B		
Class	**Drug (Trade Name)**	**Usual dose range in mg/day (Daily Frequency)**
ACE inhibitors	benazepril (Lotensin†)	10–40 (1–2)
	captopril (Capoten†)	25–100 (2)
	enalapril (Vasotec†)	2.5–40 (1–2)
	fosinopril (Monopril	10–40 (1)
	lisinopril (Prinivil, Zestril†)	10–40 (1)
	moexipril (Univasc)	7.5–30 (1)
	perindopril (Aceon)	4–8 (1–2)
	quinapril (Accupril)	10–40 (1)
	ramipril (Altace)	2.5–20 (1)
	trandolapril (Mavik)	1–4 (1)
Angiotensin II antagonist	candesartan (Atacand)	8–32 (1)
	eprosartan (Teveten)	400–800 (1–2)
	irbesartan (Avapro)	150–300 (1)
	losartan (Cozaar)	25–100 (1–2)
	olmesartan (Benicar)	20–40 (1)
	telmisartan (Micardis)	20–80 (1)
	valsartan (Diovan)	80–320 (1)
Calcium channel blockers—non-Dihydropyridine	diltiazem extended release (Cardizem CD, Dilacor XR, Tiazac†)	180–420 (1)
	diltiazem extended release (Cardizem LA)	120–540 (1)
	verapamil immediate release (Calan, Isoptin†)	80–320 (2)
	verapamil long acting (Calan SR, Isoptin SR†)	120–360 (1–2)
	verapamil—Coer (Covera HS, Verelan PM)	120–360 (1)
Calcium channel blockers—Dihydropyridines	amlodipine (Norvasc)	2.5–10 (1)
	felodipine (Plendil)	2.5–20 (1)
	isradipine (Dynacirc CR)	2.5–10 (2)
	nicardipine sustained release (Cardene SR)	60–120 (2)
	nifedipine long-acting (Adalat CC, Procardia XL)	30–60 (1)
	nisoldipine (Sular)	10–40 (1)

Chart continued on following page

Oral Antihypertensive Drugs* Part C		
Class	**Drug (Trade Name)**	**Usual Dose Range in mg/day (Daily Frequency)**
Alpha₁-blockers	doxazosin (Cardura)	1–16 (1)
	prazosin (Minipress†)	2–20 (2–3)
	terazosin (Hytrin)	1–20 (1–2)
Central alpha₂-agonists and other centrally acting drugs	clonidine (Catapres†)	0.1–0.8 (2)
	clonidine patch (Catapres-TTS)	0.1–0.3 (1wkly)
	methyldopa (Aldomet†)	250–1,000 (2)
	reserpine (generic)	0.05‡–0.25 (1)
	guanfacine (generic)	0.5–2 (1)
Direct vasodilators	hydralazine (Apresoline†)	25–100 (2)
	minoxidil (Loniten†)	2.5–80(1–2)

* These dosages may vary from those listed in the "Physicians' Desk Reference."

† Are now or will soon become available in generic preparations.

‡ A 0.1 mg dose may be given every other day to achieve this dosage.

Source: The Seventh Report of the Joint National Committee on Prevention, Detection, Evaluation, and Treatment of High Blood Pressure. National Institutes of Health. NIH pub. no. 03–5233 (May 2003), Table 6, p. 9–11 & JAMA 2003;289(19):2561. www.nhlbi.nih.gov/guidelines/hypertension/express.pdf

Combination Drugs for Hypertension		
Combination Type*	**Fixed-Dose Combination,mg†**	**Trade Name**
ACEIs and CCBs	Amlodipine/benazepril hydrochloride (2.5/10, 5/10, 5/20, 10/20)	Lotrel
	Enalapril maleate/felodipine (5/5)	Lexxel
	Trandolapril/verapamil (2/180, 1/240, 2/240, 4/240)	Tarka
ACEIs and diuretics	Benazepril/hydrochlorothiazide (5/6.25, 10/12.5, 20/12.5, 20/25)	Lotensin HCT
	Captopril/hydrochlorothiazide (25/15, 25/25, 50/15, 50/25)	Capozide
	Enalapril maleate/hydrochlorothiazide (5/12.5, 10/25)	Vaseretic
	Lisinopril/hydrochlorothiazide (10/12.5, 20/12.5, 20/25)	Prinzide
	Moexipril HCl/hydrochlorothiazide (7.5/12.5, 15/25)	Uniretic
	Quinapril HCl/hydrochlorothiazide (10/12.5, 20/12.5, 20/25)	Accuretic
ARBs and diuretics	Candesartan cilexetil/hydrochlorothiazide (16/12.5, 32/12.5)	Atacand HCT
	Eprosartan mesylate/hydrochlorothiazide (600/12.5, 600/25)	Teveten/HCT
	Irbesartan/hydrochlorothiazide (150/12.5, 300/12.5)	Avalide
	Losartan potassium/hydrochlorothiazide (50/12.5, 100/25)	Hyzaar
	Telmisartan/hydrochlorothiazide (40/12.5, 80/12.5)	Micardis/HCT
	Valsartan/hydrochlorothiazide (80/12.5, 160/12.5)	Diovan/HCT
BBs and diuretics	Atenolol/chlorthalidone (50/25, 100/25)	Tenoretic
	Bisoprolol fumarate/hydrochlorothiazide (2.5/6.25,5/6.25,10/6.25)	Ziac
	Propranolol LA/hydrochlorothiazide (40/25, 80/25)	Inderide
	Metoprolol tartrate/hydrochlorothiazide (50/25, 100/25)	Lopressor HCT
	Nadolol/bendrofluthiazide (40/5, 80/5)	Corzide
	Timolol maleate/hydrochlorothiazide (10/25)	Timolide
Centrally acting drug and diuretic	Methyldopa/hydrochlorothiazide (250/15,250/25,500/30,500/50)	Aldoril
	Reserpine/chlorothiazide (0.125/250, 0.25/500)	Diupres
	Reserpine/hydrochlorothiazide (0.125/25, 0.125/50)	Hydropres
Diuretic and diuretic	Amiloride HCl/hydrochlorothiazide (5/50)	Moduretic
	Spironolactone/hydrochlorothiazide (25/25, 50/50)	Aldactone
	Triamterene/hydrochlorothiazide (37.5/25, 50/25, 75/50)	Dyazide,Maxzide

*Drug abbreviations: ACEI, angiotensin converting enzyme inhibitor; ARB, angiotensin receptor blocker; BB, beta-blocker; CCB, calcium channel blocker.

†Some drug combinations are available in multiple fixed doses. Each drug dose is reported in milligrams.

Source: The Seventh Report of the Joint National Committee on Prevention, Detection, Evaluation, and Treatment of High Blood Pressure. National Institutes of Health. NIH pub. no. 03–5233 (May 2003), Table 7, p. 12 & JAMA 2003;289(19):2561. www.nhlbi.nih.gov/guidelines/hypertension/express.pdf

CARD

CLINICAL PEARLS
- HTN is "the silent killer" and the goal of treatment is prevention of cardiovascular disease, stroke, nephropathy, and retinopathy
- Compliance is a major factor in treating HTN. Therapy should be individualized
- Patients started on ACE inhibitors should have BP checked in 1 week and serum K^{++} creatinine checked in 1 week
- Patients with hypertension and *unexplained* hypokalemia (K < 3.5) have 50% incidence of primary hyperaldosteronism (Conn's syndrome). Approximately 0.5% of HTN is caused by Conn's syndrome
- No direct relationship has been found between caffeine intake and HTN
- About 5% of women on oral contraceptives will have a rise in BP to > 140/90
- Short acting calcium channel blockers should not be used in the management of HTN
- Low dose aspirin should not be used with uncontrolled HTN as risk of hemorrhagic stroke is increased

References

The Seventh Report of the Joint National Committee on Prevention, Detection, Evaluation and Treatment of High Blood Pressure (JNC-VII). National Institutes of Health, NIH pub. no. 03–5233 (May 2003) & JAMA 2003;289:2560–2572. www.nhlbi.nih.gov/guidelines/hypertension/express.pdf

Vasan RS, et al. Residual lifetime risk for developing hypertension in middle-aged women and men: The Framingham Heart Study. JAMA 2002;287:1003–10.

Hyman DJ, Pavlik VN. Characteristics of patients with uncontrolled hypertension in the United States. N Engl J Med 2001;345:479–86.

Sacks FM, et al. Effects on blood pressure of reduced dietary sodium and the dietary approaches to stop hypertension (DASH) diet. N Engl J Med 2001;344:3–10.

Vasan RS, et al. Impact of high-normal blood pressure on the risk of cardiovascular disease. N Engl J Med 2001;345:1291–7.

Perry HM, et al. Effect of treating isolated systolic hypertension on the risk of developing various types and subtypes of stroke: the systolic hypertension in the elderly program (SHEP). JAMA 2000;284:465.

Michael B. Weinstock, MD
Joe DeRosa, MD
Beth Weinstock, MD
Mrunal Shah, MD

42. Coronary Artery Disease

Note: This chapter is for management of patients with known coronary artery disease. For diagnosis of patients with chest pain or evaluation with stress testing, see Chapters 38 and 46

I. ETIOLOGY: Clinical manifestations are usually caused by fissuring, hemorrhage, and thrombosis of plaque in epicardial coronary arteries. Plaque is comprised of subintimal collections of abnormal fat, cells, and debris

II. CLINICAL PRESENTATION
- A. When ischemic cardiac events are transient, the patient may experience angina pectoris; if prolonged, can lead to myocardial necrosis and scarring with or without the clinical picture of MI
- B. Patients can also present with cardiomegaly and heart failure secondary to ischemic damage of left ventricle; may have caused no symptoms prior to development of congestive heart failure

III. HISTORY
- A. **Description of pain:** Character (tightness, squeezing, pressure), location, radiation (neck,

shoulder(s), arm(s), jaw), onset, duration, exacerbating and relieving factors. May be more important to ask about chest discomfort rather than *pain*

B. Associated symptoms: Dyspnea, diaphoresis, dizziness, syncope, palpitations, nausea with or without vomiting, peripheral edema, orthopnea, paroxysmal nocturnal dyspnea. Negative symptoms include pain associated with motion or deep breathing and positional pain (pericarditis is worse when supine and relieved when sitting forward)

C. Cardiac risk factors
1. Absolute: Family history, smoking, diabetes, hypertension, hyperlipidemia (LDL > 130, HDL < 35), Age (male > 45, female > 55)
2. Relative: Obesity, sedentary lifestyle, stress, postmenopausal state
3. Other: History of cerebrovascular, peripheral vascular disease

D. History of heart disease: CAD/MI, arrhythmia, valvular disease, previous heart catheterization or stress test, PTCA or CABG. Obtain old EKGs

E. Medications for angina and which may worsen angina

F. 5 questions recommended to be asked during follow up of patients with angina:
1. Have you decreased your physical activity since the last visit?
2. Have your anginal symptoms increased?
3. How are you tolerating therapy?
4. How successful have you been at reducing risk factors?
5. Have you developed any comorbid illness which may worsen your angina?

CARD

IV. PHYSICAL EXAM

A. Vital signs: Blood pressure, heart rate and rhythm, respiratory rate, oxygen saturation
B. HEENT: Hypertensive or diabetic retinopathy, JVD, carotid bruit, thyromegaly
C. Lungs: Rales, pleural effusions
D. Cardiovascular: Arrhythmia, murmur, rub, gallop, click, abnormal apical impulse
E. Abdomen: Hepatomegaly (CHF/hepatojugular reflux)
F. Extremities: Cyanosis, clubbing, edema, shiny hairless legs (PVD)
G. Skin: Xanthomas, diabetic skin changes

V. EVALUATION

A. Laboratory
1. **Lipid profiles:** See Chapter 40, Hyperlipidemia
2. **Cardiac enzymes:** For patient whose ambulatory presentation suggests acute MI (concerning symptoms lasting longer than 15–20 minutes), cardiac enzymes should be ordered in an acute care setting. CPK peaks at 6–8hrs and then falls within 24hrs. Troponin level peaks in 2–4hrs and falls in 10–14 days
3. Other: Thyroid panel

B. Chest XR: The presence of cardiomegaly, LV aneurysm, or pulmonary edema is associated with poorer long term prognosis

C. EKG
1. Normal EKG does not exclude the diagnosis of CAD; 12-lead EKG recorded at rest is normal in approximately half of patients with angina pectoris
2. With angina ST segments are usually depressed, but may be elevated in early stages of acute MI and in Prinzmetal's angina
3. T-wave and ST segment changes are nonspecific and may occur in pericardial, valvular, and myocardial disease, or with anxiety, changes in posture, meds, or esophageal disease

D. Echocardiography: To assess LV function in patients with history of MI, pathological Q waves, signs or symptoms of heart failure, systolic murmur suggesting mitral regurgitation, or patient with complex ventricular arrhythmias

E. Cardiac stress testing (radionuclide or echocardiography): See Chapter 46, Cardiac Stress Testing. Indications for patients with diagnosis of myocardial ischemia:
1. Patient with significant change in cardiac symptoms to identify extent, severity, and location of ischemia
2. ECG abnormalities including WPW, paced rhythm, > 1mm resting ST depression, LBBB
3. After cardiac catherization to identify if ischemia is present in the distribution of the coronary lesion identified

F. Coronary angiography: Indications for patients with diagnosis of myocardial ischemia
1. Patients with a significant change in symptoms or with severe angina despite medical therapy
2. Patients with high risk criteria on noninvasive testing regardless of angina severity
3. Clinical characteristics which indicate high likelihood of severe CAD or high probability of left main or triple vessel disease
4. Non-diagnostic noninvasive testing
5. Patients who have survived sudden cardiac death or serious ventricular arrhythmia
6. Patients with angina and heart failure
7. Patients suspected of having a non-atherosclerotic cause of myocardial ischemia (coronary artery anomaly, Kawasaki disease, primary coronary artery dissection, radiation induced vasculopathy
8. Suspected coronary artery vasospasm

VI. MANAGEMENT

A. Correction of reversible risk factors (smoking, hypertension, uncontrolled diabetes, obesity, sedentary lifestyle, stress). See related chapters for diagnosis and management

CORRECTION OF REVERSIBLE RISK FACTORS		
Intervention	*Cardiovascular event reduction (%)*	*Total mortality reduction (%)*
Smoking cessation	—	43
Lipid lowering	42	30
Exercise	25	20
Blood pressure control	21	12

B. Minimize meds which may exacerbate angina including sympathomimetics, thyroid meds
C. Treat associated conditions which may exacerbate angina including hypoxemia, anemia, diabetes, valvular heart disease
D. Exercise training program (may result in reduction of ischemia, improvement in lipids and blood glucose, and decrease in obesity) and weight reduction in obese patients
E. Anti-platelet meds
1. **Aspirin:** 160–325mg PO QD. Associated with 33% decrease in risk of adverse cardiac events
2. **Clopidogrel (Plavix):** 75mg PO QD. Should be used in those who failed ASA, cannot tolerate ASA, or are allergic to ASA
F. β-Blockers: Preferred as initial therapy. All are equally effective. Decrease heart rate and BP and onset of angina and ischemia. Adjust dose to decrease heart rate to 55–60
1. **Metoprolol (Lopressor):** 25–50mg PO BID
2. **Atenolol (Tenormin):** 50mg PO BID or 100mg PO QD
3. **Timolol (Blocadren):** 10mg PO BID
4. **Carvedilol:** 25–50mg BID
5. **Propranolol (Inderal):** 60–80mg PO TID
6. Avoid β-blockers with intrinsic sympathomimetic activity like **Acebutolol**, **Pindolol**, **Labetalol**
G. Calcium channel blockers: Decrease coronary resistance and increase coronary blood flow. Use in patients with contraindications or unacceptable side effects of β-blockers or in combination with β-blockers when initial therapy with β-blockers is not effective. **Note:** *Do not use short acting dihydropyridine calcium antagonists as they may increase cardiac events*
1. **Amlodipine (Norvasc):** 5mg PO QD initially, may increase to 10mg QD
2. **Nicardipine (Cardene):** 20mg PO TID initially, may increase to 120mg in 3 divided doses
3. **Nifedipine (Adalat CC):** 30mg PO QD, maximum 90mg QD; **(Procardia XL)** 30–60mg PO QD, maximum 90mg QD
4. **Diltiazem (Cardizem SR):** 60–120mg BID; **(Cardizem CD)** 120–300mg QD;

(**Dilacor XR**) 180–240mg PO QD initially, maximum 480mg QD
   5. **Verapamil (Calan SR):** 180mg PO QAM initially, maximum 480mg QD, elderly or small patients immediate-release 40 mg TID; (**Isoptin SR**) 120–180mg PO QAM initially, maximum 240mg Q12hrs

   Note: *Nifedipine is the most likely to cause reflex tachycardia*
 H. **Nitrates:** Have been shown to improve exercise tolerance, time to onset of angina and work well in combination with β-blockers and calcium channel antagonists. Nitrates do not decrease mortality
   1. **Short acting: Nitroglycerin spray** (0.4mg) or **SL NTG** 1/150 grain (0.4mg), 1/100 grain (0.6mg), or 1/200 grain (0.3mg)—1 SL Q5 minutes × 3 PRN angina. Should be taken 5 minutes before any activity likely to precipitate angina. If pain persists after 3 doses, patient should be evaluated in ER to rule out MI. Patients who require more doses of nitrates or who are not responding as well as they had previously should be re-evaluated
   2. **Long acting**
      a. **Transdermal NTG:** 0.1, 0.2, 0.4, 0.6mg/hr—should be removed for 8hrs per day
      b. **Isosorbide Dinitrate (Isordil):** 20–80mg PO TID
      c. **Isosorbide Mononitrate:**
         i. **Imdur:** 60mg PO QD
         ii. **Ismo:** 20mg PO BID 7hrs apart
   3. **NTG** deteriorates with exposure to air, moisture, and sunlight. If sublingual administration does not cause a slight burning/tingling, NTG may be inactive
 I. **Combination therapy:** Meds may be additive in effect. Exercise caution in giving a β-blocker and negative inotropic calcium channel blocker as this has a greater chance of leading to heart block. Particularly potent combination may be a β-blocker and a calcium channel blocker with a small amount of negative inotropic effect
 J. **Follow-up** every 4–12 months

VII. MEDICAL THERAPY VS. REVASCULARIZATION

 A. **With stable angina**, medical therapy is comparable to angioplasty. Medical therapy reduces the risk on MI and angioplasty results in more rapid relief of symptoms. Patients with left main stenosis > 70% and multivessel CAD with proximal LAD stenosis > 70% have better survival with CABG
 B. **Indications for revascularization procedures** (PTCA, STENT, CABG)
   1. Failed medical therapy (intolerable symptoms despite maximal medical therapy)
   2. Left main coronary artery stenosis > 50% (with or without symptoms)
   3. Triple vessel disease and LV dysfunction (EF < 50% or previous MI)
   4. 2 vessel disease with significant LAD CAD and either EF < 50% or ischemia on noninvasive testing
   5. Unstable angina symptomatic on stress testing despite maximal medical therapy
   6. Post-MI patient continuing to have angina or ischemia
   7. Relative indications include patients with anatomically critical lesions (> 90%), especially in the LAD, or physiologic evidence of severe ischemia by stress testing or ambulatory monitoring
 C. **PTCA vs. CABG:** 2 main comparative trials are the Bypass Angioplasty Revascularization Investigation (BARI) and the Emory Angioplasty versus Surgery Trial (EAST). They showed similar 5yr survival in all patients except diabetics who had a survival advantage with CABG (with multiple severe lesions)

CLINICAL PEARLS

 • Patients who are low risk and do not have indications for CABG have a 1% annual mortality
 • Most patients who die suddenly from ischemic heart disease do so as a result of ischemia-induced malignant ventricular tachycardia
 • In variant (Prinzmetal's) angina, the chest discomfort characteristically occurs at rest or awakens the patient from sleep. Condition is caused by focal spasm of proximal coronary arteries
 • PTCA is more effective than medical therapy for the relief of angina in patients with

                single-vessel coronary artery disease
- Cholesterol (LDL and TG) are falsely lowered after an acute MI

References

Gibbons RJ, et al. ACC/AHA/ACP–ASIM guidelines for the management of patients with chronic stable angina. Circulation 1999;99:2829. Available at: http://www.acc.org/clinical/guidelines/June99/exec.htm

1999 ACC and AHA update guidelines for coronary angiography and angina available at: http://www.acc.org and at: http://www.americanheart.org

Cohen JD. ABCs of secondary prevention of CHD: easier said than done. Lancet 2001;357:972–3.

Serruys PW, et al. Comparison of coronary-artery bypass surgery and stenting for the treatment multivessel disease. N Engl J Med 2001;344:1117–24.

Smith SC, et al. AHA/ACC guidelines for preventing heart attack and death in patients with atherosclerotic cardiovascular disease. Circulation 2001;104:1577. Available at: http://www.acc.org/clinical/guidelines/atherosclerosis/atherosclerosis_pdf.pdf

Parker JD, Parker JO. Nitrate therapy for stable angina pectoris. N Engl J Med 1998;338:520–31.

Smith SC. The challenge of risk reduction therapy for cardiovascular disease. Am Fam Phys 1997;55:491–8.

Michael B. Weinstock, MD
Joe DeRosa, MD
Melissa Harris, MD

43. HEART FAILURE

I. DEFINITION
    A. Dysfunction of myocardium resulting in decreased cardiac output Dysfunction may be:
        1. Systolic: Dilated, eccentrically hypertrophied ventricle with EF < 45%
        2. Diastolic: Thick walled, concentrically hypertrophied ventricle with normal or small cavity, EF > 50%
    B. Disease progression may be slowed or reversed by appropriate management

II. ETIOLOGY
    A. Ischemic
    B. Hypertensive
    C. Valvular dysfunction
    D. Alcoholic
    E. Diabetes
    F. Viral myocarditis
    G. Drug induced
    H. Hypo-/hyperthyroid
    I. Pulmonary hypertension
    J. Familial
    K. Other: Infiltrative disease (sarcoidosis, hemochromatosis, amyloidosis), TB
    L. Idiopathic

III. HISTORY
    A. Symptoms of pulmonary edema: Dyspnea with or without exertion, orthopnea, paroxysmal nocturnal dyspnea (PND), chronic non-productive cough (may be worse when supine)
    B. Fatigue, weight gain, nausea, anorexia, nocturia, peripheral/dependent edema, RUQ abdominal pain (hepatic congestion with right heart failure)
    C. Diet including salt intake, any changes in diet
    D. History of or symptoms of hypertension, ischemic heart disease, diabetes, thyroid disease
    E. Alcohol use/abuse
    F. Adherence to meds prescribed for heart failure
    G. Use of meds which may cause heart failure

IV. PHYSICAL EXAM

A. Vitals: Tachypnea, tachycardia, hypotension, low pulse oximetry

B. Neck: Jugular venous distention, assessment of thyroid gland

C. Pulmonary: Rales/crackles (may be difficult to hear in patients with COPD because of decreased lung parenchyma), decreased breath sounds secondary to pleural effusions, wheezing

D. CV: Murmurs, gallop rhythm, parasternal lift (RVH secondary to pulmonary HTN), displaced left ventricular impulse (LV dilation/hypertrophy)

E. GI: Hepatojugular reflux

F. Extremities: Dependent pitting edema (pretibial/sacral)

V. LAB AND OTHER TESTING

A. Laboratory: CBC, electrolytes (monitor potassium if patient is on diuretics), TSH, Digoxin level. Hyponatremia is a poor prognostic finding

B. Chest x-ray: Cardiomegaly, "fluffy" peri-hilar infiltrates (pulmonary edema), pleural effusion (bilateral or right sided), pulmonary venous congestion

C. ECG: Check for evidence of old MI, arrhythmia, bundle branch block (BBB), left ventricular hypertrophy (LVH), digoxin effects

D. ECHO: Suggested for patients with a new diagnosis of CHF to differentiate systolic from diastolic dysfunction, evaluate valvular function, and to check for pulmonary hypertension. ECHO will reveal wall motion abnormalities, old MI, ventricular and atrial hypertrophy or dilation, valvular dysfunction, shunts and pericardial effusion

E. Cardiac catheterization: Helpful when valvular disease must be excluded and when determining presence and extent of CAD

VI. NEW YORK HEART ASSOCIATION (NYHA) CLASSIFICATION OF CARDIAC LIMITATION

Class I: No limitation of physical activity. Ordinary physical activity does not cause undue fatigue, dyspnea, or anginal pain

Class II: Slight limitation of physical activity. Ordinary physical activity results in symptoms

Class III: Marked limitation of physical activity. Comfortable at rest, but less than ordinary activity causes symptoms

Class IV: Unable to engage in any physical activity without discomfort. Symptoms may be present even at rest

VII. MANAGEMENT OF HEART FAILURE WITH SYSTOLIC DYSFUNCTION

APPROACH TO THE PATIENT WITH HEART FAILURE

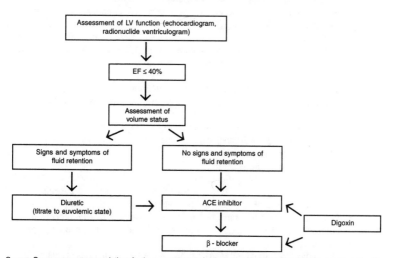

Source: Consensus recommendations for the management of chronic heart failure. On behalf of the membership of the advisory council to improve outcomes nationwide in heart failure. Am J Cardiol Jan 21 1999; 83(2A):24A (Fig 1). © 1999 Excerpta Medica.

A. Correct reversible causes
1. Prevent new cardiac injury
   a. Smoking cessation
   b. Weight reduction
   c. Control of HTN, hyperlipidemia, and DM
   d. Control of alcohol abuse
2. Control of selected cardiac problems: Rate control of atrial fibrillation or SVTs, anticoagulation of atrial fibrillation (if indicated), management of myocardial ischemia (medical vs. invasive/surgical), management of valvular disease
3. Assessment for meds which may worsen heart failure
   a. Calcium channel blockers
   b. Antiarrhythmic drugs
   c. NSAIDS

B. Diet and activity: Sodium restriction to 3g per day. Fluid restriction should include fluid with meals. Activity should include a regular exercise program such as walking 20–30 minutes a day, 4–5 × per week as tolerated

C. Aspirin: 325mg PO QD should be given if patient has CAD, dilated cardiomyopathy, atrial fibrillation, or valvular dysfunction

D. MEDICATIONS AND INTERVENTIONS WHICH HAVE BEEN SHOWN TO *DECREASE* MORTALITY
1. **Angiotensin converting enzyme inhibitors and angiotensin II receptor blockers**
   a. Work by inhibiting renin-angiotensin-aldosterone system by inhibiting conversion of angiotensin I to angiotensin II. This decreases vasoconstriction (normally mediated by angiotensin II) and decreases sodium retention (normally mediated by aldosterone)
   b. First line management. Result in a decrease in mortality (about 20% in symptomatic patients), decrease in hospitalizations and improvement in exercise tolerance and symptoms
   c. Start with a low dose and gradually increase dose especially in patients with low blood pressure, hypovolemia, prerenal azotemia and hyponatremia. Check renal function tests and potassium within several weeks of starting these meds
   d. Use limited by side effect of cough. Early data indicate that angiotensin II receptor blockers have similar efficacy without side effect of cough
   e. Examples include **Captopril (Capoten), Enalapril (Vasotec), Lisinopril (Prinivil, Zestril), Ramipril (Altace), Quinapril (Accupril), Benazepril (Lotensin), Fosinopril (Monopril), and Trandolapril (Mavik)**
   f. Angiotensin II receptor blockers are used when ACE inhibitors are contraindicated or not able to be tolerated (e.g., cough). They are not more efficacious than ACE inhibitors and should not be added to a regimen which includes an ACE. Examples include **Candesartan (Atacand), Irbesartan (Avapro), losartan (Cozaar), Telmisartan (Micardis), Valsartan (Diovan)**

2. **ß-blockers**
   a. New recommendations state that ß-blockers should be used in stable patients with class II or class III systolic dysfunction (and possibly class IV as well), in combination with diuretics and an ACE
   b. Recent large trial indicates ß-blockers can lessen symptoms of heart failure, decrease risk of death, and decrease combined risk of hospitalization and death. ß-blockers produce ejection fraction increase of about 10% and reduction in left ventricular size and mass
   c. Consider ß-blockers in patients with stable LV dysfunction with EF < 40%, stable circulation, NYHA class II or III heart failure. Do not use in patients with SBP < 90, bradycardia or second or third degree heart block
   d. ß-blocker should be started at a low dose and gradually increased. Dose is normally doubled every 2–4 weeks as tolerated until target dose is reached
   e. **Carvedilol**
      i. Study: US Carvedilol Heart Failure Study Group included 1,094 patients with Class II or III heart failure and found 65% reduction in mortality compared to

placebo and 29% decrease in hospitalization
    ii. Dose: Slowly increase from 3.125mg PO BID to 25–50mg PO BID by doubling every 2 weeks if tolerating well (higher doses appear to be more effective)
  f. **Metoprolol**
    i. Study: Metoprolol CR/XL Randomized Intervention Trial in Congestive Heart Failure (MERIT-HF) studied 3,991 patients with Class II–IV heart failure who had EFs < 40% and were optimized on standard therapy who received **Metoprolol** CR/XL or placebo. **Metoprolol** CR/XL group had improved survival (34% reduction in mortality), reduced need for hospitalizations due to worsening heart failure, and improved NYHA functional class
    ii. Dose: Previously mentioned study started with 12.5mg per day in Class III and IV failure and 25mg per day in Class II failure, and titrated for 6–8 weeks up to a target of 200mg per day
  g. **Bisoprolol**
    i. Study: Cardiac Insufficiency Bisoprolol Study (CIBIS II) treated with **Bisoprolol** up to 10mg QD in Class II and III heart failure was associated with a 34% reduction in mortality, 32% decrease in risk of hospitalization for CHF
    ii. Dose: Begin with 1.25mg PO QD
  3. **Aldosterone antagonists**
    a. RALES study showed **Spironolactone (Aldactone)** reduced mortality by 27% and decreased hospitalization by 36% in Class IV patients who were also receiving ACE inhibitors and diuretics
    b. Current recommendations state that use of this drug merits consideration in patients with Class IV heart failure
    c. Potassium should be checked 1–4 weeks after initiating therapy
    d. Dose—12.5–25mg QD
  4. **Hydralazine and Nitrates** combination should only be used in those who cannot take an ACE–I (should not be substituted for an ACE–I)
    a. **Isosorbide Dinitrate (Isordil):** 20–80mg PO Q6–8hrs—*and*—
    b. **Hydralazine (Apresoline):** Initially 10mg PO TID, increase to 25–100mg TID–QID
  5. **Surgical**
    a. Heart transplantation
    b. Coronary revascularization
E. **MEDICATIONS WHICH HAVE BEEN SHOWN TO *IMPROVE SYMPTOMS*, BUT HAVE NOT BEEN SHOWN TO IMPROVE MORTALITY**
  1. **Diuretics:** Have been shown to improve symptoms, but not mortality. Used in conjuction with meds listed above in mass trials
    a. **Furosemide (Lasix):** 20–320mg PO divided QD–QID
    b. **Bumetanide (Bumex):** 1–8mg PO QD or in divided doses
    c. Concurrent potassium replacement
    d. Note that **Hydrochlorothiazide (HCTZ)** is not effective in severe CHF
  2. **Nitrates:** Have been shown to reduce mortality when used with **Hydralazine**, but not when used alone. Effective for symptom relief. **Isosorbide Dinitrate (Isordil):** 20–80mg PO Q6–8hrs
  3. **Digitalis Glycosides**
    a. Digitalis Investigation Group recently published its results from 6800 patients with ejection fractions of 0.45 or less randomized to **Digoxin** or placebo, both in addition to diuretics and ACE inhibitors. They conclude:
      i. **Digoxin** did reduce the rate of hospitalization both overall and for CHF
      ii. **Digoxin** did not reduce overall mortality
    b. **Digoxin** has also been shown to decrease symptoms of heart failure and increase exercise tolerance
    c. **Digoxin (Lanoxin):** 0.125–0.250mg PO QD
  4. **Anticoagulants**
    a. Indicated for patients with risk of thromboembolism, such as patients with atrial fibrillation, history of emboli or LV aneurysms (situations where anticoagulation

would be used even without history of CHF). Risk of thromboembolism is low in stable patients (1–3% /yr) even in patients with very low EF

b. There are no definitive trials. Anti-coagulation with Coumadin is most justified in patients with atrial fibrillation or a previous embolic event

F. MEDICATIONS WHICH HAVE NOT BEEN SHOWN TO BE HELPFUL, AND *MAY BE HARMFUL*

1. **Calcium channel blockers:** Produce little benefit and may accelerate the progression of heart failure. Second generation calcium channel blockers (including **Norvasc**) have not been shown to be harmful or helpful

2. **Antiarrhythmic agents** when used to treat asymptomatic arrhythmias. Up to 70% of patients with heart failure can have asymptomatic episodes of nonsustained ventricular tachycardia (VT) less than 30 seconds. Symptomatic ventricular arrhythmias should be treated with drugs or an implantable cardiovascular defibrillator

3. **Milrinone:** PROMISE study showed that **Milrinone** infusion at 40mg QD increased mortality by 35% in patients with NYHA Class III or IV heart failure

4. **Periodic Dobutamine infusion:** Symptoms may be improved, but mortality is increased

VIII. MANAGEMENT OF HEART FAILURE WITH DIASTOLIC DYSFUNCTION

A. Take patients off Digoxin (unless prescribed for arrhythmia) and ACE inhibitors

B. The goal of therapy is to slow the rate to *allow time for ventricular filling.* Few meds are available to treat diastolic dysfunction, and they should be used with caution

1. ß-blockers
   a. **Propranolol (Inderal):** 60–80mg PO TID–QID
   b. **Metoprolol (Lopressor):** 50–100mg PO BID
   c. **Timolol (Blocadren):** 10mg PO BID
   d. **Atenolol (Tenormin):** 50mg PO BID or 100mg PO QD

2. Calcium channel blockers
   a. **Diltiazem (Cardizem, Cardizem SR, Cardizem CD, Dilacor XR):** 60mg PO TID initially, may increase to 360mg QD in 3 divided doses
   b. **Verapamil (Calan, Isoptin, Calan SR, Isoptin SR, Verelan):** 80mg PO TID initially, may increase to 480mg in 3 divided doses

C. The efficacy of therapy will be determined by sequential clinical examination. Meds should be adjusted accordingly

CLINICAL PEARLS

- Most common cause of right heart failure is left heart failure
- Frequent causes of CHF exacerbations are medication non-compliance or change in diet (salt)
- Patients who are bedridden will manifest their edema as sacral (dependent) edema as opposed to edema of the lower extremities
- Patients with stable CHF should continue to exercise as tolerated
- Diuretic resistance may be caused by NSAIDs
- An S4 gallop is often heard in patients with diastolic dysfunction

References

ACC/AHA guidelines for the evaluation and management of chronic heart failure in adult: executive summary: a report of the American College of Cardiology/American Heart Association Task Force on Practice Guidelines (Committee to revise the 1995 Guidelines for the Evaluation and Management of Heart Failure. J Am Coll Cardiol 2001;38(7):2101–13; Circulation 2001;104(24):2996–3007; J Heart Lung Transplant 2002;21(2):189–203.

Nohria A, et al. Medical management of advanced heart failure. JAMA 2002;287:628–40.

Pitt B, et al. The effect of spironolactone on morbidity and mortality in patients with severe heart failure. Randomized Aldactone Evaluation Study (RALES) Investigators. N Engl J Med 1999;341:709–17.

Bonet S, et al. Beta-adrenergic blocking agents in heart failure: benefits of vasodilating and non-vasodilating agents according to patients' characteristics: a meta-analysis of clinical trials. Arch Intern Med 2000;160:621–7.

Foody JM; et al. Beta-blocker therapy in heart failure. Scientific Review. JAMA 2002;287:883–9.

Michael B. Weinstock, MD
Bill Gegas, MD
Darrin Bright, MD
Beth Weinstock, MD

44. ATRIAL FIBRILLATION

I. DEFINITION

Irregular supraventricular tachyarrhythmia caused by simultaneous discharges from multiple atrial foci. If the AV node does not block, or if accessory pathways are present there may be a rapid ventricular response (pulse > 100)

II. INCIDENCE

A. Most common chronic disturbance of heart rhythm
B. Incidence increases with age: 50–59: 0.5%; 60–69: 3.8%; 70+: 9%
C. Chronic disease: Recurrence rate is extremely high, even if treated aggressively with DC or pharmacologic cardioversion

III. ETIOLOGY

An attempt should be made to diagnose the underlying cause, as acute intervention may be necessary even after ventricular rate is controlled

A. Cardiac: Cardiothoracic surgery, cardiomyopathy, congenital heart disease, hypertension with LV hypertrophy, lipomatous hypertroph, myocardial ischemia/infarction, pericarditis, preexcitation syndromes, tachycardia-Bradycardia syndrome, tumors, valvular heart disease: most often mitral, ventricular hypertrophy, ventricular pacing
B. Systemic: Alcohol/"Holiday Heart", cerebrovascular disease, chronic pulmonary disease, drugs (Ophthalmic Atropine, Digoxin, Theophylline, sympathomimetics, Adenosine, antidepressants, Nicotine gum), electrocution, electrolyte abnormalities, fever/hypothermia, hypovolemia, pneumonia/sepsis, pregnancy, sudden emotional change (heightened vagal or adrenergic tone), thyrotoxicosis, trauma
C. Lone atrial fibrillation: Occurs in persons < 60 years old, with no discernible etiology, and no clinical or echocardiographic evidence of heart disease. Favorable prognosis, may be related to myocarditis

IV. HISTORY

A. New onset vs. chronic or paroxysmal
B. Chest discomfort, palpitations
C. Dyspnea, fatigue, lightheadedness
D. Weight loss, sleeplessness, rapid speech, tremor (thyrotoxicosis)
E. Alcohol history: Acute ingestion (holiday heart) vs. alcoholism (alcoholic cardiomyopathy)
F. Medications
G. History of ischemic, valvular or other heart disease

V. PHYSICAL EXAM

A. Vital signs: temperature, O_2 saturation, pulse, blood pressure, and respiration
B. Neck: JVD, thyromegaly
C. Pulmonary: Wheezing, rhonchi
D. CV: Friction rub, murmur, gallop, variation in loudness of first heart sound

VI. OTHER TESTS

A. Laboratory: Thyroid studies, serial cardiac enzymes with initial onset, electrolytes
B. ECG: Irregularly irregular rhythm with absence of P waves (special attention to Lead II). Check for rapid rate, LVH, bundle-branch block, pre-excitation
C. CXR: Heart size, lung disease
D. Echocardiogram (transesophageal or transthoracic): To evaluate valves, atrial size, hypoakinesis, thrombus, pericardial effusion

VII. MANAGEMENT

A. Asymptomatic/minimal symptoms
　　1. A large proportion of recent-onset AF will spontaneously cardiovert within 24–48hrs
　　2. Outpatient initiation of anti-arrhythmics often acceptable, but should be done with a cardiology consult
B. Rate control (between 60–80 BPM at rest) *All agents can lead to heart block, bradycardia, and hypotension
　　1. **Calcium channel blockers:** Prolongation of AV node conduction. Good if LV function is normal. In elderly patients or patients with decreased LV function, use **Diltiazem**
　　　　a. **Diltiazem (Cardizem):** 120–360mg PO QD (use long-acting formulation). Onset 2–4hrs

b. Verapamil (Calan, Iso 120-360mg PO QD (use long acting formulatio
   2hrs
2. ß-blockers Use with caution or use cardioselective agent in COPD
   lar Disease, and CHF
   a. Metoprolol (Lopressor) 25-100mg PO BID. Onset 4-6hrs
   b. Atenolol (Tenorm 25-100mg PO QD
   c. Propranolol (Inder 80-160mg PO in divided doses. Onset 60-9
3. Digitalis Glycosides Effects include centrally mediated vagal activation
   ing of AV nodal conduction and direct action on atrial myocardium.
   20% of patients will convert to NSR with Digoxin (Lanoxin) 0.125-0.250mg
   PO QD
4. Ventricular pacing Can reduce irregularity and rate of ventri
   See below
5. AV nodal ablation and permanent pacemaker implantation These patients s
   need anticoagulation

C. Conversion to normal sinus Anticoagulation with Warfarin for 3 w
   and 4 weeks after elective cardioversion is necessary to pre
   Patients alternating between sinus rhythm and atrial fibrillatio
   risk for thromboembolism and should be converted (chemically c
   sultation with a cardiologist is recommended before initiation

Table A: Typical Doses of Drugs Used to Maintain Sinus Rhythm in Patients With Atrial Fibrillation**

Drug*	Daily Dosage	Potential Adverse Effects
Amiodarone†	100-400 mg	Photosensitivity, pulmonary toxicity, polyneuropathy, GI upset, bradycardia, torsade de pointes (rare), hepatic toxicity, thyroid dysfunction
Disopyramide	400-750 mg	Torsade de pointes, HF, glaucoma, urinary retention, dry mouth
Dofetilide‡	500-1000 mcg	Torsade de pointes
Flecainide	200-300 mg	Ventricular tachycardia, congestive HF, enhanced AV nodal conduction (conversion to atrial flutter)
Procainamide	1000-4000 mg	Torsade de pointes, lupus-like syndrome, GI symptoms
Propafenone	450-900 mg	Ventricular tachycardia, congestive HF, enhanced AV nodal conduction (conversion to atrial flutter)
Quinidine	600-1500 mg	Torsade de pointes, GI upset, enhanced AV nodal conduction
Sotalol‡	240-320 mg	Torsade de pointes, congestive HF, bradycardia, exacerbation of chronic obstructive or bronchospastic lung disease

GI indicates gastrointestinal; AV atrioventricular; and HF, heart failure.
*Drugs are listed alphabetically.
**The drugs and doses given here have been determined by consensus based on published studies.
†A loading dose of 600 mg per day is usually given for one month or 1000 mg per day over 1 week.
‡Dose should be adjusted for renal function and QT-interval response during in-hospital initiation phase.

Source: Fuster, et al. ACC/AHA/ESC Guidelines for management of patients with atrial fibrillation: Executive summary.
J Am Coll Cardiol 2001;38:1231–65, table 3. Used with permission from American College of Cardiology Foundation.

Note: QTc should remain < 520mg, and follow periodically

VIII. ANTICOAGULATION—See IX. Paroxysmal Atrial Fibrillation
   A. Anticoagulation of patients with chronic atrial fibrillation
      1. The overall risk of ischemia in patients with atrial fibrillation w
         coexisting risk factors
      2. Among all patients with nonrheumatic AF, the rate of ischemic stro

Factors Increasing the Risk of Stroke in Patients with Atrial Fibrillation

Increasing age
Rheumatic heart disease
Poor left ventricular function or recent congestive heart failure
Enlarged left atrium
Previous myocardial infarction
Hypertension
History of previous thromboembolic events
Diabetes mellitus
Female sex

Source: Akhtar W, Reeves W, Movahed A. Indications for anticoagulation in atrial fibrillation. Am Fam Phys
July 1998;58:131.

      3. Thrombus associated with AF arises most frequently in the l

Annual Rate of Stroke Based on Five Randomized Studies of Patients with Nonrheumatic Atrial Fibrillation

Category	Rate of stroke per year (%)*	
	Placebo	Warfarin
Independent risk factors		
Age < 65 years		
No risk factors	1.0	1.0
One or more risk factors	4.9	1.7
Age 65 to 75 years		
No risk factors	4.3	1.1
One or more risk factors	5.7	1.7
Age > 75 years		
No risk factors	3.5	1.7
One or more risk factors	8.1	1.2
History of hypertension	5.6	1.9
History of diabetes	8.6	2.8
History of prior stroke or transient ischemic attack†	11.7	5.1
Risk factors in any of the 5 traits‡		
History of congestive heart failure	6.8	1.6
History of angina pectoris	6.7	0.9
History of myocardial infarction	8.2	3.3
History of congestive heart failure, angina pectoris and myocardial infarction	6.1	1.6
Other		
History of peripheral vascular disease	6.0	1.8
Women	5.8	0.9
Paroxysmal or intermittent AF	5.7	1.7
Atrial fibrillation duration > 1 year	4.4	1.5

CARD

NOTE: *The five studies are the Atrial Fibrillation, Aspirin, Anticoagulation Study from Copenhagen, Denmark (AFASAK), the Stroke Prevention in Atrial Fibrillation Investigators (SPAFI) study, the Boston Area Anticoagulation Trial in Atrial Fibrillation (BAATAF), the Canadian Atrial Fibrillation Anticoagulation (CAFA) study and the Veterans Stroke Prevention in Nonrheumatic Atrial Fibrillation (SPINAF) study.*

*— Rates of stroke are based on the pooled results of five randomized studies the included 3,691 patients with nonrheumatic AF. They received placebo or warfarin.

†— In a separate randomized study of patients with AF who had a stroke or transient ischemic attack within 3 month before enrollment, rate of stroke was 12 percent and 4 percent with placebo and warfarin, respectively (Lancet 1993; 342: 1255-62).

‡— Selection criteria differed somewhat for the randomized trails. These factors were determined to be independent risk factors for stroke in any one of the five randomized studies. The rate of stroke, however, are tabulated from the pooled analysis.

Adapted with permission from Risk factors for stroke and efficacy of antithrombotic therapy in atrial fibrillation. Analysis of pooled data from five randomized controlled trials. Arch intern Med 1994; 154: 1449-57 (Published erratum in Arch Intern Med 1994; 154: 2254) and EAFT (European Atrial Fibrillation Trial) Study Group. Secondary prevention in non-rheumatic atrial fibrillation after transient ischemic attack or minor stroke. Lancet 1993; 342: 1255-62.

Source: Table 3. Annual Rates of Stroke Based on Five Randomized Studies of Patients with Nonrheumatic Atrial Fibrillation. Risk factors for stroke and efficacy of antithrombotic therapy in atrial fibrillation. Analysis of pooled data from five randomized controlled trials. Arch Intern Med 1994;154:1149-57. Used with permission.

4. **Risks of anticoagulation:** Rate of intracranial hemorrhage in Warfarin-treated patients is 0.3% /yr. In the subgroup of elderly patients (mean 80 yrs) the risk increased to 1.8% /yr from 0.8% for age matched Aspirin controls. Patient age and the intensity of anticoagulation are the most powerful predictors of major bleeding
5. **Recommendations for anticoagulation of patients in atrial fibrillation**

Table B: Recommendations for Antithrombotic Therapy in Patients with Atrial Fibrillation Based on Thromboembolic Risk Stratification

Patient Features	Antithrombotic Therapy	Grade of Recommendation
Age less than 60 years No heart disease (lone AF)	Aspirin (325 mg daily) or no therapy	I
Age less than 60 years Heart disease but no risk factors*	Aspirin (325 mg daily)	I
Age greater than or equal to 60 years No risk factors*	Aspirin (325 mg daily)	I
Age greater than or equal to 60 years With diabetes mellitus or CAD	Oral anticoagulation (INR 2.0-3.0) Addition of aspirin, 81-162 mg daily is optional	I IIb
Age greater than or equal to 75 years especially women	Oral anticoagulation (INR ≈ 2.0)	I
HF LV ejection fraction less than or equal to 0.35 Thyrotoxicosis Hypertension	Oral anticoagulation (INR 2.0-3.0)	I
Rheumatic heart disease (mitral stenosis) Prosthetic heart valves Prior thromboembolism Persistent atrial thrombus on TEE	Oral anticoagulation (INR 2.5-3.5 or higher may be appropriate)	I

*Risk factors for thromboembolism include HF, LV ejection fraction less than 0.35, and history of hypertension. AF indicates atrial fibrillation; CAD, coronary artery disease; HF, heart failure; INR, international normalized ratio; LV, left ventricular; and TEE, transesophageal echo.

Source: Fuster, et al. ACC/AHA/ESC Guidelines for management of patients with atrial fibrillation: Executive summary. J Am Coll Cardiol 2001;38:1231–65, table 14. Used with permission from American College of Cardiology Foundation.

6. Patients with history of TIA or minor CVA have a 12% risk of CVA/yr. The risk is reduced to 4% /yr with anticoagulation. The risk of major bleeding is increased 0.3% /yr. In absolute terms, for every 1000 patients with a history of TIA or minor CVA treated with anticoagulation, ~80 vascular events (mainly strokes) will be prevented/yr. The decrease is 40/yr with Aspirin
7. Inquire about contraindications (recent or scheduled surgery, pregnancy, bleeding tendencies) and med use which may affect Warfarin levels
8. INR should be kept between 2.0 and 3.0

B. Anticoagulation before cardioversion (Electrical or Chemical)
1. Atrial fibrillation of short duration (< 48hrs): The data are unclear. Conservative recommendations include IV Heparin with or without transesophageal echocardiography (TEE) prior to cardioversion
2. Atrial Fibrillation of longer duration (> 48hrs)
   a. Warfarin at therapeutic levels for 3 weeks prior to cardioversion
   b. Alternative management: IV Heparin for 12hrs followed by TEE. If TEE negative for atrial thrombi then proceed with cardioversion

C. Anticoagulation after cardioversion (Electrical or Chemical)
1. Continued for 4 weeks following cardioversion regardless of the duration prior to conversion
2. Prevents thrombus formation during recovery of atrial mechanical contractility

D. Drugs used for anticoagulation
1. **Warfarin:** Maintain the International Normalized Ratio (INR) between 2–3. Risk reduction dependent on age and coexisting risk factors
2. **Aspirin**—325mg QD

IX. PAROXYSMAL ATRIAL FIBRILLATION

A. Definition: Intermittent episodes of atrial fibrillation that usually cease spontaneously. When patient is not in atrial fibrillation, the baseline rhythm is usually NSR

B. The risk of thromboembolic disease appears independent of whether atrial fibrillation is chronic or paroxysmal. Several recent trials reported the risk of stroke to be similar in patients with chronic persistent and paroxysmal atrial fibrillation

C. Combined analyses (SPAF and Boston Area Anticoagulation Trial for Atrial Fibrillation) show that the annual stroke rate in patients with paroxysmal atrial fibrillation was 5.7% in the control group and only 1.7% in the Warfarin group. The use of chronic anticoagulation seems to be supported by this data

D. In patients who have, self-limited episodes of paroxysmal atrial fibrillation, anti-arrhythmic drugs to prevent recurrences are usually unnecessary, unless symptomatic

CLINICAL PEARLS

- 70–80% of patients with new onset atrial fibrillation will spontaneously convert to NSR within the first 24hrs
- The sooner atrial fibrillation is converted, the better the chances of success
- The loss of coordinated atrial contraction that occurs with atrial fibrillation causes a 10–20% decrease in cardiac output at a normal rate, and a reduction in diastolic filling time when the response is rapid < 100–120
- In the presence of atrial fibrillation without mechanical valves, anticoagulation can be interrupted for up to 1 week for surgical procedures

References

ACC/AHA/ESC Guidelines for management of patients with atrial fibrillation: Executive summary. J Am Coll Cardiol 2001;38:1231–65.

Aronow WS. Management of atrial fibrillation, ventricular arrhythmias and pacemakers in older per-sons. Management of the older person with atrial fibrillation. J Am Geriatr Soc Jun 1999;47:740–8.

Connolly S. Evidence-based analysis of amiodarone efficacy and safety. Circulation Nov 1999; 100:2025–34.

Ezekowitz M, Levine J. Preventing stroke in patients with atrial fibrillation. JAMA May 1999;281: 1830–5.

Akhtar W, Reeves W, Movahed A. Indications for anticoagulation in atrial fibrillation. Am Fam Phys Jul 1998; 58:130–6.

CARD

Michael B. Weinstock, MD
Mrunal Shah, MD

45. AMBULATORY POST-MI MANAGEMENT

I. IDENTIFY PATIENTS AT HIGH RISK FOR FUTURE EVENTS POST-MYOCARDIAL INFARCTION (MI): Patients at high risk, consider cardiology referral and cardiac catheterization

A. **Poor left ventricular (LV) function** (EF < 45%): By ECHO or cardiac catheterization. Patients with an EF of 20–44% have a 12% 1-yr mortality

B. **Recurrent ischemia post-MI**

C. **Multiple cardiac risk factors:** Post-MI patients with 4 risk factors have ~ 60% 2-yr mortality

D. **Location and extent of infarct:** Anterior infarct has highest 1-yr mortality

E. **Ventricular arrhythmias:** If a patient has > 10 PVCs/hr compared to < 1 PVC/hr, the 1-yr mortality is 18% compared to 3% (indication of poor LV function)

F. **Number of vessels with atherosclerotic disease:** 1-yr mortality is increased from 2% to 12% with triple vessel disease compared to single vessel disease

II. DIAGNOSTIC TESTING

Most patients will have at least 1 of these 3 tests before hospital discharge

A. **Stress testing:** Performed prior to hospital discharge. Submaximal testing 4–6 days post-MI or symptom limited at 10–14 days. See Chapter 46, Cardiac Stress Testing. This should be followed with a maximal stress test 3–6 weeks post-MI. If either is positive, cardiac catheterization should be strongly considered

B. **Cardiac ECHO:** To assess LV function and ejection fraction, wall motion, valves, septal defects, papillary muscle function. If the prehospital discharge ECHO shows LV dysfunction (EF < 45%), patients should be strongly considered for cardiac catheterization

C. **Cardiac catheterization:** The gold standard test recommended for patients at high risk of future events (see I. above) or if above tests are positive

III. INDICATIONS FOR CARDIAC CATHETERIZATION/STATISTICS

Of 100 patients admitted with acute MI:

A. 20 patients will have severe ischemia or severe pump failure during their hospital admission **Recommendation: Cardiac catheterization**

B. 20 patients will become symptomatic during a submaximal stress test prior to hospital discharge **Recommendation: Cardiac catheterization**

C. 10 patients will become symptomatic during maximal stress testing 3–6 weeks post-discharge **Recommendation: Cardiac catheterization**

D. The remaining 50 patients will be at low risk with a 0–5% 1-yr mortality. One half of the remaining 50 patients will undergo cardiac catheterization within 1yr. Medical management and risk factor modification should be aggressively pursued

IV. MANAGEMENT

A. **Risk factor modification post-MI:** Strongly encourage treatment, compliance, and/or behavioral modification of the following risk factors. Patients with 4 risk factors have a 2-yr mortality which is 60% compared to 5% in patients with 1 risk factor (see related chapters)

   1. Smoking
   2. Hypertension: Reduction of mortality by 20% with successful reduction of blood pressure
   3. Diabetes: Presence of diabetes increases 1-yr mortality post-MI by 25%
   4. High cholesterol: Target LDL post-MI is < 100mg/dL
   5. Sedentary lifestyle, obesity, depression

B. **Cardiac rehabilitation:** Most post-MI patients will benefit, although the extent of rehabilitation will have to be tailored to a patient's specific situation. Mortality may be decreased by up to 25% with participation in cardiac rehab

C. **Medical management post-MI** (Meds with proven efficacy to decrease mortality include aspirin, ß-blockers, ACE inhibitors, and HMG-CoA reductase inhibitors/statins)

1. **Aspirin:** Indicated for all patients unless allergic. Peptic ulcer disease is *not* a contraindication

   a. The *ISIS 2* trial showed that Aspirin reduced vascular death by 23% and reduced nonfatal infarctions by 49% post-MI

   b. **Aspirin** would save 5,000 lives/yr if given to all post-MI patients, yet as many as 28% of post-MI patients do not receive it. Aspirin has an approximate cost of $13 per life saved

   c. Dose at 160–325mg PO QD with meals

2. **ß-blockers:** Although their efficacy is proven, only 20–30% of post-MI patients are prescribed ß-blockers

   a. The ß-blocker Heart Attack Trial (BHAT) showed that ß-blockers (which reduce the heart rate) reduced sudden death by 32%, recurrent infarction by 27%, and overall cardiac mortality by 22% post-MI. The benefit is more pronounced in patients with co-morbid factors of angina, prior heart failure or arrhythmia

   b. Should be administered *within hours* post-MI

   c. Avoid **Labetalol** and intrinsic sympathomimetics such as **Acebutolol** and **Pindolol**

3. **Angiotensin converting enzyme (ACE) inhibitors:** Studies suggest a reduction in incidence of sudden cardiac death and nonfatal subsequent infarctions following myocardial infarction. ACC/AHA guidelines recommend that ACE inhibitors should be started within 24hrs post-MI and continued 4–6 weeks in patients without LV dysfunction and at least 3 years in patients with LV dysfunction

4. **Statins**

   a. The goal for post-MI patients with hypercholesterolemia is LDL< 100mg/dL

   b. For further guidelines and drug doses/side effects, etc., see Chapter 40, Hyperlipidemia

5. **Anticoagulants:** Indicated when there are other conditions that would benefit from treatment with oral anticoagulation (example: atrial fibrillation)

6. **Nitrates:** If a patient has to use PRN nitrates post-MI, strong consideration should be given to cardiac catheterization if it has not been performed

7. **Calcium channel blockers**

   a. Should not be used for secondary prevention post-MI except possibly in non-Q-wave MI where the EF has been preserved and there is no evidence of CHF. A Danish study *(DAVIT II)* suggested that **Verapamil** may be used for Q wave MIs without associated heart failure

   b. **Nifedipine** should not be used post-MI as it has been shown to *increase* mortality

   c. Although calcium channel blockers are not beneficial post-MI, they *are* beneficial for hypertension and angina (See Chapter 42, Coronary Artery Disease)

8. **Antiarrhythmics:** Although effective at suppressing ventricular ectopy, the *CAST* study showed that certain antiarrhythmics increased mortality post-MI. Therefore, they should not be routinely used post-MI

CLINICAL PEARLS

- In first year after an acute myocardial infarction (MI), mortality ranges from 6–19%. Subsequent mortality is 3–4% /yr
- There is early evidence that stopping a statin on admission to the hospital for acute MI increases mortality

References

Ryan TJ, et al. 1999 update: ACC/AHA guidelines for the management of patients with acute myocardial infarction: Executive summary and recommendations: A report of the American College of Cardiology/American Heart Association Task Force on Practice Guidelines (Committee on Management of Acute Myocardial Infarction). Circulation 1999;100:1016–30.

Muhlestein JB. Post-hospitalization management of high-risk coronary patients. Am J Cardiol

CARD

2000;85:13B-20B.

Chen J, et al. Beta-blocker therapy for secondary prevention of myocardial infarction in elderly diabetic patients. Results from the National Cooperative Cardiovascular Project. J Am Coll Cardiol 1999;34:1388–94.

Domanski MJ, et al. Effect of angiotensin converting enzyme inhibition on sudden cardiac death in patients following acute myocardial infarction. A meta-analysis of randomized clinical trials. J Am Coll Cardiol 1999;33:598–604.

Freemantle N, et al. ß Blockade after myocardial infarction: systematic review and meta regression analysis. BMJ 1999;318:1730–7.

Michael B. Weinstock, MD
Beth Weinstock, MD

46. CARDIAC STRESS TESTING

CARD

I. INDICATIONS FOR EXERCISE STRESS TESTING

(Those listed below do not address patients who have had a recent MI). Before ordering the test, assess the pretest and posttest likelihood of a positive result. If a positive test on an asymptomatic patient will be dismissed as a false positive, then do not perform the test. If a patient with symptoms suggestive of angina and multiple risk factors has a negative test and cardiac catheterization will be performed anyway, consider proceeding directly to the catheterization

A. Initial evaluation in patients with suspected or known CAD

B. Patients with suspected or known CAD with a significant change in clinical status

C. Low risk unstable angina patients who have been symptom free for 8–12hrs

D. Intermediate risk unstable angina patients with normal cardiac markers for 12hrs after onset of symptoms and normal repeat ECG

E. Patients with resting ECG abnormalities including WPW, paced rhythm, 1mm resting ST depression, LBBB or intraventricular conduction delay with QRS > 120ms

F. Stable patients undergoing periodic monitoring to guide treatment

G. Asymptomatic patients with diabetes mellitus who plan to start vigorous exercise

H. Asymptomatic men > 45 and women > 55 who:

1. Plan to start vigorous exercise
2. Are in occupations where impairment might endanger public safety
3. Are at high risk for CAD due to other diseases (PVD, CRF)

I. Chronic aortic regurgitation with equivocal symptoms, before participation in exercise, before valve replacement

J. Evaluation of exercise capacity in patients with valvular heart disease

II. TYPES OF EXERCISE AND OTHER TESTS

A. Exercise EKG: A graded exercise protocol with continuous EKG monitoring

1. Advantages: Inexpensive, fast, objective assessment of exercise-induced symptoms
2. Disadvantages: Requires ability to exercise, reduced accuracy in patients with abnormal baseline EKG, does not localize disease
3. Can be non-diagnostic in many situations: Resting ST-T wave abnormalities, LVH, pre-excitation, **digoxin** therapy, female gender (stress ECHO more cost-effective), mitral valve prolapse, LBBB, ventricular pacer
4. Sensitivity 50–67% and specificity 72–90%

B. Stress ECHO: Transthoracic ultrasound imaging of wall motion, valves, and ejection fraction before and after heart is stressed by exercise or pharmacological techniques (adrenergic stimulating, e.g., **Dobutamine**, or vasodilator agents). Changes in wall motions suggest myocardial ischemia

1. Advantages: No radiation exposure, less expensive/time-consuming than nuclear scans, able to localize disease, results are immediately available, can assess valvular and aortic disease

2. Disadvantages: Interpretation is subjective, slightly lower sensitivity for CAD than SPECT scanning, not a feasible test in 5–10% due to obesity or COPD
3. Sensitivity about 83–85% and specificity about 70–90%
4. **Dobutamine** stress echocardiography has a higher sensitivity than vasodilator stress echocardiography for detecting coronary stenoses

C. **SPECT perfusion imaging**: Direct visualization of myocardial perfusion with tracers such as **Sestamibi (Cardiolite)**. **Cardiolite** has largely replaced **Thallium** as tracer of choice. EF can be calculated using gated images
   1. Advantages: Localization of disease, better able to identify "borderzone" ischemia, quantification of EF, can be combined with pharmacologic stress (vasodilators such as **Adenosine** or **Persantine** have less side effects than **Dobutamine)**
   2. Disadvantages: More expensive than stress ECHO, more time-intensive, radiation exposure, inability to assess valvular/aortic/pericardial disease
   3. Nuclear imaging is the preferred modality for patients with expected suboptimal ECHO windows, or with LBBB or pacer. Also preferred in those patients with prior revascularization or prior MI
   4. Sensitivity and specificity about 83–85% and specificity about 70–90%

D. **Electron Beam Computed Tomography (EBCT)**: Multiple consecutive thin images using scanning electron beam during a single breath-hold. Images done in synchrony with heart rate at end-diastole. Quantifies a calcium score which has been shown to predict future cardiac risk. Clinical applications include evaluation of asymptomatic "intermediate risk" patients for risk stratification. Can predict future cardiac risk but not necessarily the presence of obstructive CAD. In symptomatic patients, stress imaging is preferable

CLINICAL PEARLS
- Failure to achieve 80–85% of predicted maximum heart rate (or rate adjusted to MET level) is associated with 84% increase in all cause mortality over the next 2 years
- Abnormal heart rate recovery is associated with increased all cause mortality at 6 years

References

Gibbons RJ, et al. ACC/AHA 2002 guideline update for exercise testing: a report of the American College of Cardiology/American Heart Association Task Force on Practice Guidelines (Committee on Exercise Testing) 2002 Amer Coll Cardiol Web site: http://www.acc.org/clinical/guidelines/exercise/exercise_clean.pdf

Nishime EO, et al. Heart rate recovery and treadmill exercise score as predictors of mortality in patients referred to exercise ECG. JAMA 2000;284:1392–98.

O'Rourke RA, et al. American College of Cardiology/American Heart Association expert consensus document on electron-beam computed tomography for the diagnosis and prognosis of coronary artery disease. J Am Coll Cardiol 2000;36:326–40.

Pollock ML, et al. AHA science advisory. Resistance exercise in individuals with and without cardiovascular disease: benefits, rationale, safety, and prescription. An advisory from the Committee on Exercise, Rehabilitation, and Prevention, Council on Clinical Cardiology, American Heart Association; Position paper endorsed by the American College of Sports Medicine, Circulation 2000;101:828–33.

Crawford MH, et al. ACC/AHA guideline for ambulatory electrocardiography: a report of the American College of Cardiology/American Heart Association Task Force on Practice Guidelines (Committee to Revise the Gluidelines for Ambulatory Electrocardiography): developed in collaboration with the North American Society for Pacing and Electrophysiology. J Am Coll Cardiol 1999;34:912–48.

Younis LT, Chaitman BR. The prognostic value of exercise testing. Cardiology Clinics 1993; 11(2):229–39.

American College of Sports Medicine. Guidelines for exercise testing and prescription. 4th ed. Philadelphia: Lea & Febiger, 1991:8.

CARD

David Sharkis, MD
Michael B. Weinstock, MD
Daniel M. Neides, MD
Loren Leidheiser, DO

47. SHORTNESS OF BREATH

I. DIFFERENTIAL DIAGNOSIS
A. Upper airway causes
1. Tracheal obstruction (cancer, foreign body, mucous plug)
2. Infectious: epiglottitis, croup
3. Angioedema/anaphylaxis
4. Retropharyngeal abscess

B. Pulmonary causes
1. Obstructive lung disease (COPD: asthma, chronic bronchitis, emphysema)
2. Infection (pneumonia, bronchitis, TB)
3. Pneumothorax
4. Pulmonary embolism, fat, air, or amniotic fluid embolism
5. Pleural effusion
6. Lung masses, metastatic disease
7. Restrictive lung diseases
   a. Extrathoracic: Chest wall restriction (kyphoscoliosis, obesity, ascites), diaphragmatic dysfunction, abdominal distention, pregnancy
   b. Intrathoracic: Infiltrate, infiltrative process (sarcoidosis, amyloidosis, pulmonary fibrosis), pneumonectomy, parenchymal process
8. Pulmonary hypertension
9. Adult respiratory distress syndrome (ARDS)
10. Carbon monoxide toxicity
11. Cystic fibrosis

C. Cardiac causes
1. Congestive heart failure (pulmonary edema)
2. Acute MI/anginal equivalent/myocardial ischemia
3. Cardiac arrhythmias (atrial fibrillation, ventricular tachycardia)
4. Cardiac valvular disease
5. Pericarditis/pericardial tamponade/myocarditis
6. Hypertensive crisis

D. Systemic causes
1. Noncardiogenic pulmonary edema: Drug OD, pancreatitis, trauma, sepsis, inhalation of toxic chemicals
2. Anemia
3. Diabetic ketoacidosis (DKA)/metabolic acidosis
4. Gastroesophageal reflux (GERD)
5. Hyper-/hypothyroidism
6. Deconditioning
7. Carbon monoxide poisoning, methemoglobinemia

E. Central causes
1. Panic disorder/anxiety
2. Acute hyperventilation
3. Cheyne-Stokes (rapid breathing): Seen in coma from intracerebral pathology
4. CNS/systemic neuromuscular disorders, such as CVA, phrenic nerve paralysis, Guillain Barre, tick paralysis, botulism
5. Multiple sclerosis
6. Phrenic nerve dysfunction
7. Sleep apnea

II. HISTORY
A. History of Present Illness (HOPI)

CARD

   1. General: Fever, night sweats, or weight loss
   2. ENT: Sore throat, dysphonia, dysphagia, acuity of onset, drooling/inability to handle secretions, recent pharyngitis
   3. Respiratory
      a. SOB: Acuity of onset and duration of symptoms, exacerbaters, and relievers, relation to exertion or environmental exposure, relation to chest discomfort, associated orthopnea/paroxysmal nocturnal dyspnea
      b. Other: Cough (productive vs. dry, duration, exacerbaters, and time of day), hemoptysis
   4. Cardio: Chest discomfort, heart racing, or palpitations
   5. Extremities: Peripheral edema
   6. Other: Work and travel exposures, anxiety/depression
 B. Past Medical/Surgical History
   1. Previous diagnoses of shortness of breath, cardiac or pulmonary disease, CAD risk factors, history of diabetes, history of previous DVT/PE, prolonged immobility, or oral contraceptive use
   2. Recent infections
   3. Medications
   4. Smoking history
   5. Home oxygen use

III. PHYSICAL EXAMINATION
 A. Vital signs: Fever, tachypnea, tachycardia/bradycardia, hypotension, oxygen saturation
 B. HEENT: Assess JVD, tracheal deviation, periorbital cyanosis, glossal deviation, peritonsillar/retropharyngeal abscess, other upper airway obstruction
 C. Chest: Rales/crackles, rhonchi, increased A-P chest wall diameter (COPD), dullness to percussion/decreased breath sounds, wheezing (asthma, pulmonary edema, foreign body), stridor, palpable crepitus
 D. Cardiac: Gallop, murmur, rub, distant heart sounds (pericardial tamponade), loud P_2 (pulmonary HTN), jugular venous distention (JVD)
 E. Extremities: Clubbing, cyanosis, edema, unilateral edematous or tender leg (DVT)

IV. TESTS
 A. Radiology: Obtain PA and lateral CXR
   1. Pleural effusions are best seen at the costophrenic angle on the lateral film
   2. Pneumonia is a *clinical diagnosis* as CXR findings of pneumonia may lag behind clinical findings
   3. Assess for pneumothorax, heart size, rib fracture, mediastinal widening/deviation, or free air under the diaphragm
   4. *Lateral neck films* should be considered to evaluate for upper airway compromise
 B. ABG: Assess pH, pO_2, pCO_2
 C. ECG: Should be performed in any patient > 30 and all patients with history of CAD or diabetes with undiagnosed dyspnea. In addition to signs of ischemia/infarction and arrhythmias, look for signs of pericarditis, pericardial effusion/tamponade, pulmonary embolism, and COPD
 D. Pulse oximetry: *Measures oxygenation only.* Rest and exercise oximetry may reveal oxygen desaturation (early finding in interstitial lung disease and pulmonary HTN, pneumocystis pneumonia.) The pulse oximetry may be limited by nail polish, hypothermia, severe vasoconstriction, carboxyhemoglobins, or methemoglobinemias, shock
 E. Pulmonary function testing
   1. Indications
      a. Evaluation of pulmonary dysfunction: Obstructive vs. restrictive impairment
      b. Evaluation of dyspnea and cough
      c. Evaluation of response to therapy
      d. To determine if there is bronchial reactivity: Methacholine challenge
      e. To determine if there is a reversible component to obstructive lung disease
      f. Preoperative evaluation in selected patients (see Chapter 101, Preoperative Evaluation)
      g. Evaluation of upper airway obstruction with a flow-volume loop

2. Examples of changes in PFTs with various pulmonary disorders:

Tests*	Obstructive†	Emphysema	Restrictive†
FEV$_1$ (Liters)	↓↓	↓↓	↓
FVC (Liters)	↓	↓	↓↓
FEV$_1$ / FEV%	↓	↓	Normal or ↑
RV (Liters)	↑	↑↑	↓
TLC (Liters)	Normal or ↑	↑↑	↓
DL$_{CO}$	Normal or ↑	↓↓	Normal or ↓

† For examples of obstructive/restrictive lung diseases, see Section I, Differential Diagnosis
FEV$_1$ (forced expiratory volume in 1 second), FVC (functional residual capacity), RV (residual volume), TLC (total lung capacity), DL$_{CO}$ (diffusing capacity of carbon monoxide)

*Source: Adapted from Williams DO, Cugell DW. Pulmonary function tests: indications and Interpretation. Hosp Med 1988;24(5):48.

F. Chest CT: Used primarily as a follow-up of abnormal CXR

G. Ventilation-perfusion scan/helical CT/pulmonary angiography: See below for evaluation for PE

H. Laboratory: Based on history and physical
1. CBC (elevated WBC, anemia, etc.), electrolytes, BUN/creatinine, glucose
2. Thyroid functions tests
3. Alpha-anti-trypsin

I. Bronchoscopy indications
1. Evaluation of hemoptysis
2. Diagnosis and staging of bronchogenic carcinoma, biopsy of tracheal or 2nd–4th generation bronchial tumors
3. Diagnosis of lung infiltrates and certain pulmonary infections including PCP and TB
4. Removal of foreign bodies

J. Cardiopulmonary exercise testing: If clinical presentation suggests cardiac etiology or if workup is negative

V. EVALUATION FOR PULMONARY EMBOLUS

A. Estimated 650,000 cases/yr in the US with 200,000 deaths

B. Deep venous thrombosis (DVT) is the etiology in 80–90% of cases

C. The classic triad of dyspnea, hemoptysis, and pleuritic chest pain occurs in < 20% of patients. See table below for signs and symptoms in patients with PE

D. ECG: Sinus tachycardia is the most common finding, plus new RBBB, p-pulmonale, S1Q3T3 (rarely), and 40% have non-specific ST-T wave changes

E. CXR: Usually normal or with non-specific findings. May have infiltrate or atelectasis in 50%. Beware of a normal CXR in the setting of dyspnea and hypoxia. Hampton's hump (a wedge shaped pleural based infiltrate) and Westermark's sign (relative oligemia distal to engorged pulmonary arteries with massive PE) are uncommon

F. ABG: PaO$_2$ may be normal but is often decreased, may see hypocapnia or increased A-a gradient (see Chapter 118, Formulas)

G. Laboratory: D-Dimer test may be a useful test in the future. There are 2 different tests used to determine the D-Dimer. These tests should be used in conjunction with the estimated pretest probability of PE
1. **ELISA test** has a sensitivity of 98% and a specificity of 30–40% and can be used to exclude PE (especially in a low-risk patient)
2. **Latex agglutination test:** Sensitivity is only 30% and the specificity is 30%. This test cannot be used reliably to exclude PE

H. Ventilation Perfusion (V/Q) scan: Should also be used in conjunction with the estimated

CARD

pretest probability of PE. False positives are increased in patients who have an infiltrate on CXR, preexisting cardiopulmonary disease, and history of previous PE. Will give 1 of 4 different categories including:

1. Normal: No perfusion defects
2. Low probability: < 20% chance of PE
3. Intermediate probability: 20–80% chance of PE
4. High probability: > 80% chance of PE

I. Helical CT: The sensitivity for proximal PE is 82–90% and the specificity is 93–96%, but these numbers are lower for subsegmental PEs

J. Pulmonary angiography: The gold standard with a negative test basically excluding the diagnosis of PE. Should be used when other studies are inconclusive or might produce false results (see above)

K. Note: Combining venous duplex exams of bilateral lower extremities with D-dimer, V/Q, or CT greatly increases sensitivity

Symptoms and Signs of 327 Patients with Angiographically Proven PE	
Symptoms and Signs	**Total Series, %**
Symptom	
Chest pain	88
Pleuritic	74
Non-pleuritic	14
Dyspnea	84
Apprehension	59
Cough	53
Hemoptysis	30
Sweats	27
Syncope	13
Sign	
Respirations > 16/min	92
Rales	58
P2 > S2	53
Pulse > 100/min	44
Temperature > 37.8°C	43
Phlebitis	32
Gallop	34
Diaphoresis	36
Edema	24
Murmur	23
Cyanosis	19

Source: Adapted from Bell WR, Simon TL, DeMets DL: The clinical features of submassive and massive pulmonary emboli. *Am J Med* 62:355, 1977. With permission from Elsevier.

CARD

CLINICAL PEARLS

- Tachypnea is the most common sign of pneumonia in the elderly
- Virchow's triad includes venous stasis, hypercoagulability, and endothelial damage and are factors contributing to the development of DVT
- In immunocompromised patients, dyspnea is often the initial manifestation of *Pneumocystis* pneumonia
- Steroids should be given early to asthmatics to minimize their chances of hospital admission
- Note that *orthopnea* may be seen in patients with severe dyspnea *regardless of etiology* as diaphragmatic mechanics are improved in the upright position
- Retropharyngeal abscess and epiglottitis are emergency situations requiring immediate pharyngeal examination by ENT specialists
- Patients with alcoholism and seizure disorders are at risk for aspiration
- A normal pulse oximetry does not exclude the possibility of pulmonary emboli
- Subcutaneous Epinephrine or Terbutaline should be used with caution in patients > 30yrs

References

American Thoracic Society. Dyspnea. Mechanism, assessment, and management: a consensus statement. Am J Respir Care Med 1999;159:321–40.

Mulrow CD, et al. Discriminating causes of dyspnea through clinical examination. J Gen Intern Med 1993;8:383.

Morgan WC, Hodge HL. Diagnostic evaluation of dyspnea. Am Fam Phys 1998;15:711.

Manning HL, Schwartzstein RM. Pathophysiology of dyspnea. N Engl J Med 1995;333:1547.

PIOPED. Value of the ventilation/perfusion scan in acute pulmonary embolism: results of the prospective investigation of pulmonary embolism diagnosis. JAMA 1990;263:2753.

Cannon CP, Goldhaber SZ. Cardiovascular risk stratification of pulmonary embolism. Am J Cardiol 1996;78:1149.

Morgenthaler TI, Ryu JH. Clinical characteristics of fatal pulmonary embolism in a referral hospital. Mayo Clin Proc 1995;70:417.

Beth Weinstock, MD
William Oley, MD

CARD

48. COMMUNITY–ACQUIRED PNEUMONIA (CAP)

I. DEFINITION

A. An acute infection of the pulmonary parenchyma associated with:
1. Symptoms of acute infection—*and*—
2. Physical examination and clinical findings consistent with pneumonia and/or presence of an acute infiltrate on CXR

B. Pneumonia is considered nosocomial (not community-acquired) if the patient has been hospitalized or treated in an ECF for 14 days prior to presentation of current illness

II. SIGNIFICANCE

A. Up to 5.6 million cases/yr with as many as 1.1 million hospitalizations

B. Annual incidence in children < 5 is 34–40 cases/1000 in Europe and North America

C. Annual incidence of pneumonia in patients > 65 is approx. 1%

D. Combination of community acquired pneumonia (CAP) and influenza ranks as the sixth leading cause of death in the US. Mortality has remained fairly consistent at approx. 25% over the last 4 decades, despite advances in ATBs and critical care medicine. Mortality in outpatients is less than 1%

III. ETIOLOGY

A. Neonate: *Group B Streptococcus, Listeria monocytogenes,* Gram negative enteric bacteria, *(E.Coli, Klebsiella), Chlamydia trachomatis* (neonate to 3 months), Viral pathogens, (CMV, HSV, Rubella)

B. < 1 year: Viral pathogens, (RSV, parainfluenza, influenza, adenovirus, rhinovirus), *Streptococcus pneumoniae, Haemophilus influenzae, Staphylococcus aureus*

C. > 1 year: *Streptococcus pneumoniae, Haemophilus influenzae. Staphylococcus aureus,* Viral pathogens, (influenza, parainfluenza, adenovirus, rhinovirus), *Chlamydia pneumoniae, Mycoplasma* (school-age children)

D. Adult: *Streptococcus pneumoniae, Haemophilus influenzae, Moraxella catarrhalis, Mycoplasma pneumoniae,* Gram-negative bacilli, Viruses, *Staphylococcus pneumoniae, Legionella pneumoniae, Chlamydia pneumoniae, Mycobacterium tuberculosis, Pneumocystis carinii*

E. Elderly, ECF resident: *Streptococcus pneumoniae, Haemophilus influenzae, Klebsiella pneumoniae, Pseudomonas aeruginosa,* Anaerobic organisms, (in cases of suspected/possible aspiration), MSSA, MRSA

F. Immunocompromised: *Streptococcus pneumoniae, Haemophilius influenzae, Klebsiella pneumoniae, Pseudomonas aeruginosa,* Anaerobic organisms (in cases of suspected/

possible aspiration), Fungal organisms *(histoplasmosis, coccidioidomycosis, cryptococcus,* etc.), *Pneumocystis carinii, Mycobacterium spp., cytomegalovirus*

IV. DIAGNOSIS
A. History
  1. Symptoms
     a. General: Fever/chills/rigors, fatigue, generalized malaise
     b. Respiratory: Cough—productive or nonproductive, dyspnea pleuritic chest pain
     c. Musculoskeletal: Myalgia/arthralgia
  2. Timing and temporal relationship of preceding symptoms
     a. Sudden onset: Indicative of "classic" pneumococcal pneumonia
     b. Preceding influenza pneumonia: "Classic" precedent to staphylococcal pneumonia
  3. Risk Factors for pneumonia: Extremes of age, smoker, severe illness or immunocompromised state, ECF resident, EtOH abuse, HIV/AIDS, aspiration risk factors
B. Physical examination
  1. Vitals signs: Febrile, tachypneic, tachycardic, check for hypoxia
  2. Assess hydration: Mucous membranes, skin turgor, urine output
  3. Lung exam
     a. Inspection: Retractions, accessory muscle use, asymmetry in inspiration secondary to splinting
     b. Auscultation
        i. Rales (Crackles) most common finding in CAP
        ii. Rhonchi
        iii. Bronchial breath sounds due to consolidation
        iv. Whispered pectoriloquy, present at consolidation
        v. Egophony, present at consolidation
     c. Palpation
        i. Tactile fremitus presents at consolidation
        ii. Percussion asymmetry present secondary to consolidation (dull over consolidation)
  4. Additional findings to lead diagnosis and therapy
     a. Signs of immunocompromised state (lymphadenopathy, thrush, Kaposi's sarcoma, wasting)
     b. Signs of malignancy (as above plus weight loss, smoking history, clubbing)
C. Radiographic findings
  1. Recommended for all patients suspected of pneumonia
  2. Helps to predict severity of disease: Multilobar infiltrates and pleural effusions are associated with increased mortality
  3. CXR may be falsely negative in dehydrated patients
  4. "Classic" findings
     a. Lobar infiltrate: Most commonly associated with *Streptococcus pneumoniae*
     b. Pleural effusion: Streptococcal, staphylococcal, or anaerobic infection
     c. Nodular or reticular infiltrates: *Mycoplasma* or Chlamydial atypical organisms
     d. Cavity with air-fluid level: Anaerobic lung abscess
     e. Upper-lobe cavitary lesion: Mycobacterium tuberculosis
     f. Diffuse bilateral infiltrates: Pneumocystis carinii pneumonia, viral
D. Laboratory evaluation
  1. Oxygenation
     a. Pulse oximetry: Admit patients with hypoxia
     b. Arterial blood gas: Consider ordering in patients with history of COPD, suspicion of pulmonary embolus, or hypoxia. $pO_2 < 60mmHg$ is predictive of increased mortality
  2. Sputum stain/culture: Often not useful in ambulatory CAP, because of high number of negative gram stains and cultures
  3. Blood culture: Not necessary for outpatient therapy. Only 11% of hospitalized patients with CAP will have positive blood cultures and do not usually result in a change in therapy

CARD

4. CBC: Leukocyte count should not guide diagnosis or treatment—it has not been shown to affect mortality
5. Electrolytes
    a. Hyponatremia occurs with CAP, most commonly with *Legionella pneumonia*. Na < 130mEq/L predictive of increased mortality
    b. BUN > 20mg/dL, creatinine > 1.2, and serum glucose > 250, all predictive of increased mortality
6. HIV status: Check in any patient with risk factors or suspected opportunistic pneumonia, (PCP, fungal, etc.)
7. Urine Legionella antigen—warranted in severe CAP

V. ADMISSION CRITERIA—Consider admission for the following:
A. **Age > 50** with co-morbid conditions
B. **Admit all patients < 20 days old** with pneumonia
C. **Social Factors**
    1. Elderly patients with poor social support
    2. Alcoholics
    3. Psychiatric illnesses
    4. Homelessness
D. **Physical examination criteria**
    1. Altered mental status
    2. Hypoxia
    3. Pulse > 125 bpm
    4. RR > 30/minute
    5. SBP < 90mmHg
    6. T < 35° C or > 40° C
E. **Laboratory criteria**
    1. pH < 7.35
    2. BUN > 30mg/dL
    3. Na < 130mEq/L
    4. Glucose > 250mg/dL
    5. Hematocrit < 30%
    6. Arterial pO_2 < 60mmHg
    7. Pleural effusion
F. **Radiographic criteria**—Multilobar involvement

VI. OUTPATIENT MANAGEMENT
A. **Adults** (> 18)
    1. Antibiotic Selection for Community-Acquired Pneumonia (ASCAP) 2002 consensus report
        a. First line: **Azithromycin (Zithromax)**
        b. Alternative: **Moxifloxacin (Avelox), Levofloxacin (Levaquin), Clarithromycin (Biaxin)** or **Gatifloxacin (Tequin)**
    2. Infectious Disease Society of America (ISDA) 2000 guidelines
        a. Initial (not in any particular order): **Doxycycline**, a Macrolide, a Fluoroquinolone
        b. Notes: Selection should be influenced by regional ATB susceptibility patterns for *S. pneumoniae*; PCN resistant pneumococci may be resistant to Macrolides and/or **Doxycycline**; for older patients and those with underlying disease a Fluoroquinolone may be a preferred choice
    3. Centers for Disease Control Drug-Resistant *Streptococcus pneumoniae* Therapeutic Working Group (CDC-DRSPTWG) 2000 guidelines:
        a. Initial therapy: Oral Macrolide (Azithromycin, Clarithromycin, or Erythromycin) or β-lactam monotherapy or Doxycycline
        b. Recommend that Fluoroquinolones be reserved for elderly patients who have failed Cephalosporin plus Macrolide, patients allergic to first line agents, patients who have documented infection with highly drug-resistant pneumococci (MIC > 4)
B. **Children**
    1. Birth–20 days: Admit patient

    2. 3 weeks–3 months: If afebrile oral **Erythromycin** (30–40mg/kg/day divided in 4 doses) or oral **Azithromycin** (1 dose 10mg/kg then 5mg/kg/day for 4 days). Patients with fever or hypoxia mandate admission

    3. 4 months–4yrs: Oral **Amoxicillin** (80–100mg/kg/day divided in 3 or 4 doses)

    4. 5–15yrs: Oral **Erythromycin** (30–40mg/kg/day in 4 divided doses), oral **Clarithromycin** (15mg/kg/day in 2 divided doses) or oral **Azithromycin** (1 dose 10mg/kg then 5mg/kg/day for 4 days). In children > 8yrs, consider oral **Doxycycline** (4mg/kg/day in 2 divided doses)

VII. OUTPATIENT FOLLOW-UP

    A. Advise patient to call or return to office for fever > 102°, worsening shortness of breath, inability to swallow meds or remain hydrated, chest pain, hemoptysis, or failure to improve after 2 days of therapy

    B. **Follow up CXR not necessary**: CXR findings may take weeks or months to return to normal. Follow-up CXR is warranted if suspicion of underlying pathology (e.g., malignancy)

VIII. PREVENTION

    A. Pneumococcal polysaccharide antigen vaccine: Risk for acquiring complications of pneumonia is reduced by ⅔ following vaccination, indicated for:

      1. Asplenic patients

      2. Immune-competent patients > 65

      3. Diabetes

      4. COPD

      5. Chronic renal failure

      6. Malignancy

      7. CAD and CHF

      8. Chronic liver disease

      9. HIV/AIDS

      10. Consider in any chronic, debilitating illness

    B. Pneumococcal conjugate vaccine in pediatric population—effective in decreasing pediatric pneumococcal pneumonia

    C. Influenza vaccine: Indicated yearly for all patients at risk for pneumonia

CLINICAL PEARLS

    • *Pneumococcus* remains the number-1 agent of bacterial pneumonia in children and adults

    • Presence of dementia or confusion in an elderly patient increases the likelihood of a chest film being positive for pneumonia. Dementia/confusion may be the only symptom in elderly patients with pneumonia

    • Most common pneumonia in patients with HIV is pneumococcal pneumonia. Ask about risk factors and evaluate for signs of HIV including thrush, oral hairy leukoplakia, seborrheic dermatitis

    • Treat early—delay in ATB therapy associated with increased mortality

    • Treat empirically: Gram stains are not helpful

References

Niederman MS, et al. Guidelines for the management of adults with community-acquired pneumonia: Diagnosis assessment of severity, antimicrobial therapy, and prevention. Am J Respir Crit Care Med 2001;163:1730–54.

Bernstein JM. Treatment of community-acquired pneumonia. IDSA guidelines. Chest Mar 1999:115:9S–13S.

McIntosh K. Community-acquired pneumonia in children. N Engl J Med 2002;346(6):429–37.

Fine MJ, et al. A prediction rule to identify low-risk patients with community-acquired pneumonia. N Engl J Med 1997;336(4):243–50.

Fine MJ, et al. The hospital admission decision for patients with community-acquired pneumonia. Results from the pneumonia Patient Outcomes Research Team cohort study. Arch Intern Med 1997;157(1):36–44.

Daniel M. Neides, MD
Ann M. Aring, MD
Michael B. Weinstock, MD

49. ASTHMA IN ADULTS

I. GENERAL
A. Affects 5% of the population, resulting in almost 500,000 admissions/yr and 5,000 deaths/yr
B. Death rates are highest for blacks 15–24yrs

II. PATHOGENESIS AND LONG TERM CONTROL
A. Chronic inflammatory condition resulting in airway obstruction and airway hyperresponsiveness to various stimuli (see below)
B. Asthma may be precipitated by sinusitis, gastroesophageal reflux, URIs, exercise, post nasal drip, or exposure to tobacco smoke
C. Asthma changes over time
D. 4 factors to consider in long term control of asthma
   1. Assessment and monitoring
   2. Control of factors contributing to asthma
   3. Pharmacologic therapy
   4. Patient education

III. HISTORY
A. **Symptoms:** Wheezing, cough (may be the only manifestation), shortness of breath, chest tightness, nocturnal symptoms
B. **Duration of symptoms**
C. **Frequency of symptoms** (how many days/nights per week or month)
D. **Medications attempted** in the past and response to meds
E. **Exacerbating factors:** Smoking, household with dust/mites, cockroaches, exercise
F. **Associated medical conditions**: Atopic dermatitis, allergic rhinitis, Aspirin/NSAID allergy
G. **Family history**: Asthma, allergy, sinusitis, rhinitis

IV. PHYSICAL EXAM
A. **General:** Pulse, respiratory rate, temperature
B. **ENT:** Nasal mucosa swelling, increased nasal secretions, nasal polyps, vocal wheezing
C. **Respiratory:** Tachypnea, retractions, wheezing (may elicit by having patient perform a forced expiration), hyperexpansion of thorax, rhonchi
D. **Skin:** Eczema, atopic dermatitis

V. DIFFERENTIAL DIAGNOSIS
A. **Upper airway disorders:** Vocal cord paralysis or dysfunction, foreign body aspiration, upper airway mass, tracheal narrowing, tracheomalacia, airway edema (angioedema/ inhalation)
B. **Lower airway disorders:** COPD, bronchiectasis, cystic fibrosis, eosinophilic pneumonia, bronchiolitis obliterans
C. **Systemic vasculitides:** Churg-Strauss syndrome
D. **Psychiatric disorders**: Conversion disorder, emotional laryngeal wheezing

VI. DIAGNOSIS
A. History of episodic symptoms of airway obstruction including wheezing, shortness of breath, tightness in chest, or cough
B. Reversibility of airway obstruction
   1. Spirometry
      a. Performed before and after inhaled bronchodilator therapy
      b. Establish obstruction: FEV_1 < 80% predicted or FEV_1/FVC ratio < 65% predicted
      c. Establish reversibility: FEV_1 increases > 12% or 200mL after use of a short-acting inhaled β_2-agonist
   2. Peak expiratory flow meters: There is variability depending on which is used, but good correlation to follow and assess the severity of symptoms. 20% variability from morning to afternoon suggests asthma
C. Exclude other diagnosis

VII. MANAGEMENT

A. Stepwise approach for adults and children > 5 years of age

Stepwise Approach for Managing Asthma in Adults and Children Older Than 5 Years of Age: Treatment

Classify Severity: Clinical Features Before Treatment or Adequate Control			Medications Required to Maintain Long-Term Control
	Symptoms/Day **Symptoms/Night**	**PEF or FEV₁** **PEF Variability**	**Daily Medications**

Step 4 Severe Persistent	Continual Frequent	≤ 60% > 30%	• Preferred treatment:
			 – High-dose inhaled corticosteroids
			     AND
			 – Long-acting inhaled beta₂-agonists
			     AND, if needed,
			 – Corticosteroid tablets or syrup long term (2 mg/kg/day, generally do not exceed 60 mg per day). (Make repeat attempts to reduce systemic corticosteroids and maintain control with high-dose inhaled corticosteroids)

Step 3 Moderate Persistent	Daily > 1 night/week	> 60% – < 80% > 30%	• Preferred treatment: – Low-to-medium dose inhaled corticosteroids and long-acting inhaled beta₂-agonists • Alternative treatment: – Increase inhaled corticosteroids within medium-dose range OR – Low-to-medium dose inhaled corticosteroids and either leukotriene modifier or theophylline If needed (particularly in patients with recurring severe exacerbations): • Preferred treatment: – Increase inhaled corticosteroids within medium-dose range and add long-acting inhaled beta₂-agonists • Alternative treatment: – Increase inhaled corticosteroids within medium-dose range and add either leukotriene modifier or theophylline
Step 2 Mild Persistent	> 2/week but < 1x/day > 2 nights/month	≥ 80% 20-30%	• Preferred treatment: – Low-dose inhaled corticosteroids • Alternative treatment: cromolyn, leukotriene modifier, nedocromil, OR sustained release theophylline to serum concentration of 5-15 mcg/mL
Step 1 Mild Intermittent	≤ 2 days/week ≤ 2 nights/month	≥ 80% < 20%	• No daily medication needed • Severe exacerbations may occur, separated by long periods of normal lung function and no symptoms. A course of systemic corticosteroids is recommended

Quick Relief All Patients	• Short-acting bronchodilator: 2–4 puffs **short-acting inhaled beta₂-agonists** as needed for symptoms • Intensity of treatment will depend on severity of exacerbation; up to 3 treatments at 20-minute intervals or a single nebulizer treatment as needed. Course of systemic corticosteroids may be needed • Use of short-acting beta₂-agonists >2 times a week in intermittent asthma (daily, or increasing use in persistent asthma) may indicate the need to initiate (increase) long-term control therapy

Step down Review treatment every 1 to 6 months; a gradual stepwise reduction in treatment may be possible **Step up** If control is not maintained, consider step up. First, review patient medication technique, adherence, and environmental control	**Note** • The stepwise approach is meant to assist, not replace, the clinical decision making required to meet individual patient needs • Classify severity: assign patient to most severe step in which any feature occurs (PEF is % of personal best; FEV₁ is % predicted) • Gain control as quickly as possible (consider a short course of systemic corticosteroids); then step down to the least medication necessary to maintain control • Provide education on self-management and controlling environmental factors that make asthma worse (e.g., allergens and irritants) • Refer to an asthma specialist if there are difficulties controlling asthma or if step 4 care is required. Referral may be considered if step 3 care is required

Goals of Therapy: Asthma Control	
• Minimal or no chronic symptoms day or night • Minimal or no exacerbations • No limitations on activities; no school/ work missed	• Maintain (near) normal pulmonary function • Minimal use of short-acting inhaled beta₂-agonist (< 1x per day, < 1 canister/month) • Minimal or no adverse effects from medications

Source: Quick Reference of the NAEPP Expert Panel Report: Guidelines for the diagnosis and management of asthma—update on selected topics 2002. NIH Pub. No 02–5075 (July 2002). www.nhlbi.nih.gov/guidelines/asthma/execsumm.pdf

CARD

B. Dosages for long term control meds

Usual Dosages for Long-Term-Control Medications for Adults		
Medication	**Dosage Form**	**Adult Dose**
Inhaled Corticosteroids *(See Estimated Comparative Daily Dosages for Inhaled Corticosteroids)*		
Systemic Corticosteroids		*(Applies to all three corticosteroids)*
Methylprednisolone	2, 4, 8, 16, 32 mg tablets	• 7.5–60 mg daily in a single dose in
Prednisolone	5 mg tablets,	a.m. or QOD as needed for control
	5 mg/5 cc,	• Short-course "burst" to achieve
	15 mg/5 cc	control: 40–60 mg per day as
Prednisone	1, 2.5, 5, 10, 20, 50 mg tablets;	single or 2 divided doses for 3–10
	5 mg/cc, 5 mg/5 cc	days
Long-Acting Inhaled Beta$_2$-Agonists (Should not be used for symptom relief or for exacerbations. Use with inhaled corticosteroids)		
Salmeterol	MDI 21 mcg/puff	2 puffs Q 12 hours
	DPI 50 mcg/blister	1 blister Q 12 hours
Formoterol	DPI 12 mcg/single-use capsule	1 capsule Q 12 hours
Combined Medication		
Fluticasone/Salmeterol	DPI 100, 250, or	1 inhalation BID; dose depends on
	500 mcg/50 mcg	severity of asthma
Cromolyn and Nedocromil		
Cromolyn	MDI 1 mg/puff	2–4 puffs TID-QID
	Nebulizer 20 mg/ampule	1 ampule TID-QID
Nedocromil	MDI 1.75 mg/puff	2–4 puffs BID-QID
Leukotriene Modifiers		
Montelukast	4 or 5 mg chewable tablet	10 mg Qhs
	10 mg tablet	
Zafirlukast	10 or 20 mg tablet	40 mg daily (20 mg tablet BID)
Zileuton	300 or 600 mg tablet	2,400 mg daily (give tablets QID)
Methylxanthines *(Serum monitoring is important [serum concentration of 5–15 mcg/mL at steady state])*		
Theophylline	Liquids, sustained-release tablets, and capsules	Starting dose 10 mg/kg/day up to 300 mg max; usual max 800 mg/day

Source: Quick Reference of the NAEPP Expert Panel Report: Guidelines for the diagnosis and management of asthma—update on selected topics 2002. NIH Pub. No 02–5075 (July 2002). www.nhlbi.nih.gov/guidelines/asthma/execsumm.pdf

C. Estimated comparative daily dosages for inhaled steroids: home treatment

Estimated Comparative Daily Dosage for Inhaled Corticosteroids for Adults		
Drug	**Low Daily Dose Adult**	**Medium Daily Dose Adult**	**High Daily Dose Adult**
Beclomethasone CFC 42 or 84 mcg/puff	168–504 mcg	504–840 mcg	> 840 mcg
Beclomethasone HFA 40 or 80 mcg/puff	80–240 mcg	240–480 mcg	> 480 mcg
Budesonide DPI 200 mcg/inhalation	200–600 mcg	600–1,200 mcg	> 1,200 mcg
Flunisolide 250 mcg/puff	500–1,000 mcg	1,000–2,000 mcg	> 2,000 mcg
Fluticasone MDI: 44, 110, or 220 mcg/puff	88–264 mcg	264–660 mcg	> 660 mcg
DPI: 50, 100, or 250 mcg/inhalation	100–300 mcg	300-600 mcg	> 600 mcg
Triamcinolone acetonide 100 mcg/puff	400–1,000 mcg	1,000–2,000 mcg	> 2,000 mcg

Source: Quick Reference of the NAEPP Expert Panel Report: Guidelines for the diagnosis and management of asthma—update on selected topics 2002. NIH Pub. No 02–5075 (July 2002). www.nhlbi.nih.gov/guidelines/asthma/execsumm.pdf

CARD

D. Management of asthma exacerbations: home treatment

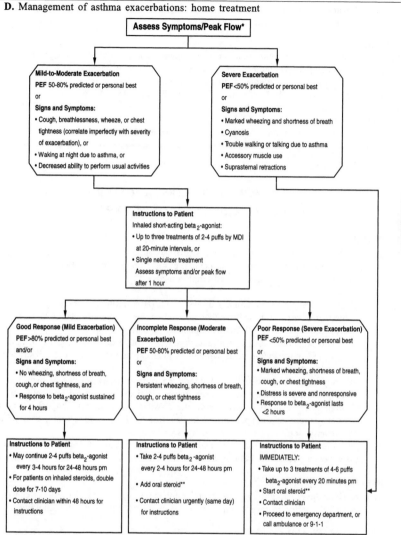

```
                        ┌─────────────────────────────┐
                        │  Assess Symptoms/Peak Flow*  │
                        └─────────────────────────────┘
```

Mild-to-Moderate Exacerbation
PEF 50-80% predicted or personal best
or
Signs and Symptoms:
• Cough, breathlessness, wheeze, or chest tightness (correlate imperfectly with severity of exacerbation), or
• Waking at night due to asthma, or
• Decreased ability to perform usual activities

Severe Exacerbation
PEF <50% predicted or personal best
or
Signs and Symptoms:
• Marked wheezing and shortness of breath
• Cyanosis
• Trouble walking or talking due to asthma
• Accessory muscle use
• Suprasternal retractions

Instructions to Patient
Inhaled short-acting beta $_2$-agonist:
• Up to three treatments of 2-4 puffs by MDI at 20-minute intervals, or
• Single nebulizer treatment
Assess symptoms and/or peak flow after 1 hour

Good Response (Mild Exacerbation)
PEF >80% predicted or personal best and/or
Signs and Symptoms:
• No wheezing, shortness of breath, cough, or chest tightness, and
• Response to beta $_2$-agonist sustained for 4 hours

Incomplete Response (Moderate Exacerbation)
PEF 50-80% predicted or personal best
or
Signs and Symptoms:
Persistent wheezing, shortness of breath, cough, or chest tightness

Poor Response (Severe Exacerbation)
PEF <50% predicted or personal best
or
Signs and Symptoms:
• Marked wheezing, shortness of breath, cough, or chest tightness
• Distress is severe and nonresponsive
• Response to beta $_2$-agonist lasts <2 hours

Instructions to Patient
• May continue 2-4 puffs beta $_2$-agonist every 3-4 hours for 24-48 hours prn
• For patients on inhaled steroids, double dose for 7-10 days
• Contact clinician within 48 hours for instructions

Instructions to Patient
• Take 2-4 puffs beta $_2$-agonist every 2-4 hours for 24-48 hours prn
• Add oral steroid**
• Contact clinician urgently (same day) for instructions

Instructions to Patient
IMMEDIATELY:
• Take up to 3 treatments of 4-6 puffs beta $_2$-agonist every 20 minutes prn
• Start oral steroid**
• Contact clinician
• Proceed to emergency department, or call ambulance or 9-1-1

* Patients at high risk for asthma-related death should receive immediate clinical attention after initial treatment. More intensive therapy may be required.
** Oral steroid dosages:
    Adult: 40-60 mg, single or 2 divided doses for 3-10 days.
    Child: 1-2 mg/kg/day, maximum 60 mg/day, for 3-10 days.

Source: Practical guide for the diagnosis and management of asthma. NIH Pub. No. 97–4053, Oct. 1997. www.nhlbi.nih.gov/health/prof/lung/asthma/practgde.htm

CLINICAL PEARLS

- During a severe exacerbation, wheezing may not be present
- Exercise-induced asthma usually begins within 3 minutes of the completion of the exercise and peaks in 10–15 minutes
- Most effective meds for controlling long term outcomes in children are inhaled corticosteroids. Potentially small risk of delayed growth (but benefit seems to outweigh risk)
- No benefit to adding ATBs for acute asthma exacerbations (unless infectious etiology suspected)
- With severe asthma exacerbation, the $PaCO_2$ returns to normal and is a marker for possible impending respiratory failure

CARD

• Duration of symptoms prior to presentation predicts duration of symptoms from institution of treatment to resolution

References

Executive Summary of the National Asthma Education and Prevention Program (NAEPP) Expert Panel Report: Guidelines for the diagnosis and management of asthma—Update on selected topics 2002. Available at: http://www.nhlbi.nih.gov/guidelines/asthma/index.htm

Naureckas ET, Solway J. Mild asthma. N Engl J Med 2001;345:1257–62.

Woodruff PG, Fahy JV. Asthma: Prevalence, pathogenesis, and prospects for novel therapies. JAMA 2001;286:395.

Holgate ST. Therapeutic options for persistent asthma. JAMA 2001;285:2637.

Michael B. Weinstock, MD
David P. Buck, M.D.

50. Chronic Obstructive Pulmonary Disease (COPD)

CARD

I. GENERAL

A. COPD classically encompasses several diffuse pulmonary diseases including chronic asthma, bronchiectasis, chronic bronchitis, cystic fibrosis, and emphysema. This section focuses on chronic bronchitis and emphysema

B. Definitions

1. Chronic obstructive pulmonary disease (COPD) is defined as the progressive development of airflow limitation that is not fully reversible (American Thoracic Society). Most patients will have components of both processes

2. Chronic bronchitis: A recurrent and productive cough on most days for 3 months or more in 2 consecutive years without another explanation. Caused by obstruction of small airways

3. Emphysema: The destruction of interalveolar septa characterized as having abnormal, permanent enlargement or air spaces distal to the terminal bronchiole without obvious fibrosis. It involves both the airways and lung parenchyma. Caused by enlargement of air spaces and destruction of lung parenchyma, loss of lung elasticity, and closure of small airways

C. COPD affects 30 million Americans and is the 4th leading cause of death in the US. Airway obstruction is present in 14% of white, male smokers compared to 3% of non-smokers

II. HISTORY

Inquire about fever, cough, dyspnea, exercise tolerance (current and baseline), chest pain, peripheral edema, history of environmental exposures, and cigarette smoking

III. PHYSICAL EXAMINATION

Increased A-P diameter, decreased lung sounds, prolonged expiration, dyspnea at rest, wheezing, pursed lip breathing, periorbital cyanosis, use of accessory muscles to breathe, rales and rhonchi, pedal edema, ascites, pink puffer (emphysema) vs. blue bloater (chronic bronchitis)

IV. COPD EXACERBATING FACTORS (in order of frequency)

BIRCHES—Bronchospasm, Infection (respiratory), Retained secretions, CHF, Hypoventilation (meds, neuromuscular), Emboli, Systemic illness (fever, MI, non-pulmonary infection)

V. DIAGNOSTIC PROCEDURES

A. **Chest x-ray:** In later stages may show flattening of the diaphragms, increased lung volumes, bullae and blebs, small heart (secondary to vertical orientation), increased retrosternal clear space. May see increased bronchovascular markings with chronic bronchitis

B. **Laboratory**

1. **ABG:** Useful for patients suspected of having moderate to severe lung disease

2. **α-1 antitrypsin levels:** Obtain if patient presents with emphysema at < age 50 or if there is a family history of early onset emphysema, or if < 20 pack/yr smoking history

C. **Pulmonary function testing:** Perform spirometry pre- and post-bronchodilator and/or DLCO and lung volumes in selected patients. For a table of Interpretation of PFTs, see Chapter 47, Shortness of Breath

VI. DIFFERENTIAL DIAGNOSIS

Acute bronchitis, acute viral infection, asthma, bronchiectasis, bronchogenic carcinoma, chronic pulmonary embolism, sleep apnea, primary alveolar hypoventilation, and chronic sinusitis

VII. MANAGEMENT OF COPD

A. **Smoking cessation** (see Chapter 35, Smoking Cessation)

B. **Bronchodilators**

1. **Ipratropium Bromide MDI (Atrovent)**
   a. *First line therapy.* Provides the same or greater bronchodilation when compared with the β₂ agonists. Few side effects. Minimal systemic absorption
   b. Dosage: 2 inhalations QID—not to exceed 12 inhalations per day
   c. Peak effect occurs in 1.5–2hrs; thus must use on a continuous basis

2. **β₂-adrenergic agonists:** *Second line.* Usually will be added to **Ipratropium**
   a. **Albuterol MDI (Proventil, Ventolin):** 2 puffs Q4–6hrs PRN
   b. **Albuterol** nebulized solution **(Ventolin nebules):** 2.5mg TID–QID
   c. **Metaproterenol MDI (Alupent, Metaprel):** 2–3 puffs Q3–4hrs
   d. **Metaproterenol** nebulized solution **(Alupent, Metaprel inhalant solution):** 0.2–0.3mL of 5% solution in 2.5mL of normal saline TID–QID
   e. **Pirbuterol MDI (Maxair):** 1–2 puffs Q4–6hrs
   f. **Terbutaline MDI (Brethaire):** 2 puffs Q4–6hrs
   g. **Levalbuterol** nebulized solution **(Xopenex):** 0.63–1.25mg nebulized Q6–8hrs
   h. **Salmeterol MDI or Diskus (Serevent):** For long-term maintenance therapy, 2 puffs Q12hrs only. Not for acute bronchospasm
   i. **Formoterol Aerolizer:** 12μg BID

3. **Combination Ipratropium** (21mcg) and **Albuterol** (120mcg)—**Combivent Inhaler,** Dose: 2 puffs QID, max 12 puffs/24hrs. Available as nebulizer solution **(DuoNeb)**

4. **Oral Methylxanthine (Aminophylline, Theophylline):** For use in selected patients who do not respond to other bronchodilators. Target Theophylline levels should be *8–12μg/mL* to minimize side effects. Increased serum levels can be expected with concomitant use of **Tagamet, Cipro,** or **Erythromycin**
   a. **Theophylline** immediate release tablets: 10mg/kg/day in 4 divided doses
   b. **Theophylline** sustained release tablets: 10mg/kg/day in 1–3 doses
   c. Adjust dose in older patients, patients with cor pulmonale or CHF

C. **Corticosteroids:** May be attempted concurrently with bronchodilators if patient has not shown sufficient improvement, but several recent studies have shown that inhaled steroids do not slow the progression of COPD. They may slightly reduce the severity of acute exacerbations

1. **Oral corticosteroids: Prednisone** 40–60mg PO QD for 5–7 days
   a. Have shown improved clinical outcomes and reduced length of hospitalization
   b. If there is no improvement, then discontinue steroids
   c. If there is improvement, initiate **Prednisone** taper and decrease to lowest effective dose. No benefit to continuing **Prednisone** > 2 weeks after exacerbation

2. **Inhaled corticosteroids**
   a. **Beclomethasone Dipropionate MDI (Beclovent, Vanceril, Vanceril DS):** Regular strength: 2 puffs TID/BID or 4 puffs BID. Double strength: 2 puffs BID
   b. **Budesonide (Pulmicort Turbuhaler):** 1–2 puffs QD/BID
   c. **Flunisolide MDI (Aerobid):** 2–4 puffs BID
   d. **Fluticasone MDI (Flovent):** 2–4 puffs BID
   e. **Triamcinolone MDI (Azmacort):** 2 puffs QID or 4 puffs BID

CARD

   D. Antibiotics: Exacerbations may be due to bacterial, viral, or URI infections
      1. Antibiotics have been shown to have an effect on clinical recovery and outcome in acute exacerbations of COPD
      2. Therapy should be directed at *S. pneumoniae, H. influenzae,* and *M. catarrhalis.* Consider *C. pneumoniae* and *Mycoplasma pneumoniae*
      3. **Doxycycline, Bactrim DS,** or **Augmentin** are appropriate first line agents
      4. Prophylactic ATB have not been shown to be helpful
   E. Adjunctive therapy: Consider use of mucolytic-expectorant as adjunct to chronic or acute COPD if the history suggests thick or viscous sputum or difficulty with expectoration. Examples are **Iodinated Glycerol** 60mg PO QID and **Guaifenesin (Robitussin, Humibid LA)** 1–2 PO BID
   F. Nonpharmacologic management
      1. Pulmonary rehabilitation: Shown to decrease hospital mortality and increase quality of life. No change in mortality
      2. Nocturnal ventilation with **BiPAP**
      3. Lung volume reduction surgery: Most useful in patients with localized upper-lobe emphysema. Improvements include increased FEV_1, improved exercise capacity, and improved quality of life which persist for at least 1yr
      4. Lung transplantation

VIII. VACCINATIONS
   A. Influenza vaccine: Annually
   B. Pneumococcal vaccine: Should be given at least once with consideration of re-vaccination every 5 to 10yrs

IX. INDICATIONS FOR SUPPLEMENTAL OXYGEN
   A. Resting PaO_2 < 55mm Hg or O_2 saturation < 88% at rest, with exercise or during sleep
   B. pO_2 55–59mm Hg with concurrent cor pulmonale ≥ than 16hrs/day
   C. Goal: PaO_2 60–80mm Hg

X. PULMONARY REHABILITATION
   A. Goals are to enhance standard medical therapy, maximize functional capacity, increase exercise tolerance, and improve quality of life
   B. No change in mortality
   C. Shown to decrease hospitalizations

CLINICAL PEARLS
   • For patients requiring chronic oral corticosteroids, remember to monitor for osteoporosis and DM
   • Genetic factors may determine which smokers will develop airflow limitation

References

Stoller JK. Acute exacerbations of chronic obstructive pulmonary disease. N Engl J Med 2002;346:988.

Hunter MH, King DE. COPD: Management of acute exacerbations and chronic stable disease. Am Fam Phys 2001;64:603–12,621–2.

Sayiner A, et al. Systemic glucocorticoids in severe exacerbations of COPD. Chest 2001;119:726–30.

Snow V, et al. The evidence base for management of acute exacerbations of COPD. Clinical practice guideline, part 1. Chest 2001;119:1185–9.

Barnes PJ. Chronic obstructive pulmonary disease. N Engl J Med 2000;343:269.

The Lung Health Study Research Group. Effect of inhaled triamcinolone on the decline in pulmonary function in chronic obstructive pulmonary disease. N Engl J Med 2000;343:1902–9.

American Thoracic Society. Standards for the diagnosis and care of patients with chronic obstructive pulmonary disease. Am J Respir Crit Care Med 1995;152:S77–S121.

CARD

Michael B. Weinstock, MD
Diane Minasian, MD
Daniel M. Neides, MD
David Buck, MD

51. ACUTE BRONCHITIS

I. GENERAL

    A. Definition: A respiratory tract infection which causes inflammation of the trachea-bronchial tree

    B. Approximately 90–95% of cases are viral in origin

    C. The cough generally lasts for 1–3 weeks. May persist for weeks to months after infection has resolved due to inflammatory changes. Up to 25% of patients may have a cough which persists longer than 1 month

    D. Up to 60% of patients have decreased FEV_1 and peak flows to less than 80% of predicted

    E. Cigarette smokers are predisposed to the development of acute bronchitis secondary to direct injury to airway epithelium, less cilia present, and delayed mucociliary clearance. Smokers have infections that are more frequent, more severe, and last longer

II. ETIOLOGY

    A. Viral (most common): *Influenza A & B, Parainfluenza, RSV, Adenovirus, and Rhinovirus*

    B. Bacteria: *Mycoplasma pneumonia, Chlamydia pneumonia, Moraxella catarrhalis, Bordetella pertussis, Legionella pneumophila, or Haemophilus influenzae* (most common cause in smokers)

III. DIFFERENTIAL DIAGNOSIS

    A. Reactive airway disease, asthma, COPD, bronchiectasis

    B. Occupational exposures, inhalation injuries

    C. Upper respiratory infection, common cold, sinusitis, influenza, pneumonia

    D. Congestive heart failure

    E. Gastroesophageal reflux disease

    F. Lung cancer

    G. Foreign body

IV. CLINICAL FEATURES

    A. Symptoms may vary depending on the etiologic agent and host factors including age, smoking history, and comorbidities such as asthma and/or COPD

    B. Common signs and symptoms

        1. Cough, initially dry and non-productive, then productive of mucopurulent sputum

        2. Preceding URI with sore throat, myalgias, chills, malaise, coryza, etc.

        3. Fever

        4. Fatigue and malaise

        5. Occasional dyspnea, rales, rhonchi, wheezing

V. DIAGNOSIS: Usually based on symptoms and physical exam. Culture of the sputum is generally unhelpful. Exclude pneumonia and non-pulmonary causes

VI. TREATMENT: Symptomatic (see Chapter 119, Symptomatic Medications)

    A. β_2-agonist metered dose inhaler. Multiple studies suggest a benefit including decreased duration of cough and earlier return to work

    B. Cough suppression

    C. Expectorants/Mucolytics: Widely prescribed but probably do not alter the course of the disease

CARD

D. Adequate hydration

E. Encourage *smoking cessation* if patient smokes

F. Antibiotics

1. Most cases are viral but ATBs are very frequently prescribed, usually because of physicians' perceptions of patients' expectations. At least one study has shown that when physicians explain the diagnosis and rationale for treatment, patients who did not receive ATBs were as satisfied as those who did

2. Studies of ATB use have found that there may be a slight improvement in duration of cough (0–1 day less cough) and feeling ill (0–1 day). There was no change in night cough, productive cough, or activity limitation. The patients treated with ATB had more adverse effects including nausea/vomiting, headache, skin rash, or vaginitis. Number needed to treat for benefit was 5–14 and the number needed to harm was 17. The CDC recommends against treating acute bronchitis with ATBs

CLINICAL PEARLS

- Antibiotics are prescribed at 70–90% of office visits for acute bronchitis despite the fact that about 90% are caused by viruses
- Purulent secretions from the nares or throat do not predict bacterial infection or benefit from ATB treatment
- Pulmonary function testing for asthma may yield false positive results in patients with acute bronchitis due to transient PFT obstructive abnormalities
- 10th most common diagnosis in the US
- Use of widespread ATBs has led to an increase in emergence of resistant bacteria

References

Snow V, et al. Principles of appropriate antibiotic use for treatment of nonspecific upper respiratory tract infections in adults. Clinical Practice Guideline, part 1. Ann Intern Med 2001;134:487–9.

Knutson D, Braun C. Diagnosis and management of acute bronchitis. Am Fam Phys 2002;65:2039–44.

Gonzales R, et al. Uncomplicated acute bronchitis. Arch Int Med 2000;133:981–91.

Smucny J, et al. Antibiotics for acute bronchitis (Cochrane Review). The Cochrane Library, 1, 2002. Oxford: Update Software

Mangione-Smith R, et al. The relationship between perceived parental expectations and pediatrician antimicrobial prescribing behavior. Pediatrics 1999;103:711–18.

VI. Management of Common Ambulatory Conditions

52. Diabetes Mellitus 173
53. Thyroid Disease & Testing 182
54. Headache: Diagnosis & Management 189
55. Evaluation & Management of Dizziness 192
56. Prevention & Management of CVAs 195
57. Seizures Disorders 199
58. Concussion Evaluation 202
59. Liver Function Tests 205
60. Diagnosis & Management of Hepatitis B 208
61. GERD and PUD 211
62. Evaluation of Diarrhea in Adults 216
63. Constipation in Adults 219
64. Hemorrhoids 220
65. Anemia 222
66. Ocular Disorders & Screening 225
67. Allergic Rhinitis/Seasonal Allergies 229
68. Acute Sinusitis 232
69. Differential Diagnosis of Arthritis 235
70. Osteoarthritis 238
71. Rheumatoid Arthritis 239
72. Gouty Arthritis 243
73. Osteoporosis 246
74. Urinary Tract Infections 249
75. Hematuria 252
76. Proteinuria 255
77. Benign Prostatic Hyperplasia 257
78. Calcium Disorders 260
79. Potassium Metabolism 263
80. Adverse Drug Interactions & Prescribing Errors 266
81. Medication Adherence 270

GEN

Michael B. Weinstock, MD
Steve Markovich, MD
Daniel M. Neides, MD
Rugen Alda, MD

52. DIABETES MELLITUS

I. GENERAL

A. As of the year 2000, 20 million people in the US have a form of diabetes mellitus, and only about ½ are diagnosed

B. By the year 2010, the number of people with diabetes worldwide will double. Increased prevalence of diabetes mellitus in the US stems largely from an increase in type 2 diabetes, which is a result of an aging population, an increasing prevalence of obesity, and a more sedentary population

C. The Diabetes Control and Complication Trial (DCCT) compared conventional treatment of type 1 diabetes with intensive treatment. Median HbA1c was 9.1% with conventional treatment compared to 7.3% with intensive treatment. It proved that intensive treatment reduced the risks of retinopathy, nephropathy, and neuropathy by 35–90%. For each 10% decrease in HbA1c, there was a 39% decreased risk of retinopathy, and a 25% decreased risk of nephropathy

D. In the US, it is has been estimated that $100 billion, or 1 out of every 7 health care dollars, is spent on patients with diabetes

II. COMPARISON OF TYPE 1 AND TYPE 2 DIABETES

	Type 1 diabetes	Type 2 diabetes
Age of Onset	Usually < 30 yr.	Usually > 40 yr.
Ketosis	Common	Rare
Body Weight	Nonobese	Obese (80%)
Prevalence	0.2-0.3%	2-4%

Genetics
   HLA Association
   Monozygotic twin studies
	Yes
	 Concordance rate 40-50%
		No
		 Concordance rate near 100%

Associated other autoimmune diseases	Occasional	No
Treatment with Insulin	Always	Sometimes
Insulin Secretion	Severe deficiency	Variable: mild-moderate deficiency to hyperinsulinemia
Insulin Resistance	Less common	Usually
Pathogenic process	Autoimmune destruction of beta cells of the pancreas with consequent absolute insulin deficiency	Resistance to insulin action and an inadequate compensatory insulin secretory response

III. SYMPTOMS OF DIABETES

A. Symptoms of marked hyperglycemia include polyuria, polydipsia, polyphagia, weight loss, and blurred vision

B. Symptoms of chronic hyperglycemia may include impairment of growth and susceptibility to certain infections

C. Type 1 diabetes mellitus

1. Uncomplicated onset: Progressive osmotic diuresis causes dehydration, thirst, and if glucose losses are extensive, weight loss despite polyphagia. In children the onset of

these symptoms often occurs over a short period

2. Acute decompensation: Diabetic Ketoacidosis (DKA)

D. Type 2 diabetes mellitus

1. Uncomplicated onset: Most patients are asymptomatic and the diagnosis is made by the detection of hyperglycemia or glycosuria on routine exam

2. Acute decompensation: Nonketotic hyperosmolar coma (a syndrome of extreme hyperglycemia and dehydration). Hyperosmolar coma most frequently occurs in older patients in whom an intercurrent illness increases glucose production secondary to stress hormones and impairs the capacity to ingest fluids

IV. TESTING AND DIAGNOSIS—AMERICAN DIABETES ASSOCIATION RECOMMENDATIONS JANUARY, 2002

    A. Criteria for testing for diabetes

Criteria for Testing for Diabetes in Asymptomatic, Undiagnosed Individuals

1. Testing for diabetes should be considered in all individuals at age 45 and above and, if normal, should be repeated at 3-year intervals

2. Testing should be considered at a younger age or be carried out more frequently in individuals who:
   - Are overweight (BMI ≥25 kg/m^2)
   - Have a first-degree relative with diabetes
   - Are members of a high-risk ethnic population (e.g., African-American, Hispanic American, Native American, Asian American, Pacific Islander)
   - Have delivered a baby weighing >9 lb or have been diagnosed with GDM
   - Are hypertensive (≥140/90)
   - Have an HDL cholesterol level ≤35 mg/dl (0.90 mmol/l) and/or triglyceride level ≥250 mg/dl (2.82 mmol/l)
   - On previous testing, had IGT or IFG

The OGTT or FPG test may be used to diagnose diabetes; however, in clinical settings the FPG test is greatly preferred because of ease of administration, convenience, acceptability to patients, and lower cost

    B. Criteria for diagnosis of diabetes

Criteria for the Diagnosis of Diabetes Mellitus

1. Symptoms of diabetes plus casual plasma glucose concentration ≥ 200 mg/dl (11.1 mmol/l). Casual is defined as any time of day without regard to time since last meal. The classic symptoms of diabetes include polyuria, polydipsia, and unexplained weight loss

        or

2. FPG ≥ 126 mg/dl (7.0 mmol/l). Fasting is defined as no caloric intake for at least 8 h

        or

3. 2-h PG ≥ 200 mg/dl (11.1 mmol/1) during an OGTT. The test should be performed as described by WHO, using a glucose load containing the equivalent of 75-g anhydrous glucose dissolved in water

In the absence of unequivocal hyperglycemia with acute metabolic decompensation, these criteria should be confirmed by repeat testing on a different day. The third measure (OGTT) is not recommended for routine clinical use.

Note: HbA1c is not recommended for diagnosis

GEN

C. Criteria for impaired fasting glucose/impaired glucose tolerance

1. Impaired fasting glucose: Fasting plasma glucose (FPG) ≥ 110mg/dl (6.1 mmol/L) and < 126mg/dl (7.0 mmol/L)
2. Impaired glucose tolerance: 2hr value in OGTT of ≥ 140mg/dl (7.8 mmol/L) and < 200mg/dl (11.1 mmol/L)

D. Gestational diabetes: See Chapter 18, Prenatal Care

V. COMPONENTS OF INITIAL VISIT

A. Medical history

1. Symptoms, results of laboratory tests (including prior A1C records), and special examination results related to the diagnosis of diabetes
2. Eating patterns, nutritional status, weight history; growth and development in children and adolescents
3. Details of previous treatment programs, including nutrition and diabetes self-management education, attitudes, and health benefits
4. Current treatment of diabetes, including meds, meal plan, and results of glucose monitoring and patients' use of data
5. Exercise history
6. Frequency, severity, and cause of acute complications such as ketoacidosis and hypoglycemia
7. Prior or current infections, particularly skin, foot, dental, and genitourinary infections
8. Symptoms and treatment of chronic eye; kidney; nerve; genitourinary (including sexual), bladder, and gastrointestinal function; heart; peripheral vascular; foot; and cerebrovascular complications associated with diabetes
9. Other meds that may affect blood glucose levels
10. Risk factors for atherosclerosis: smoking, hypertension, obesity, dyslipidemia, and family history
11. History and treatment of other conditions, including endocrine and eating disorders
12. Family history of diabetes and other endocrine disorders
13. Lifestyle, cultural, psychosocial, educational, and economic factors that might influence the management of diabetes
14. Tobacco, alcohol and/or controlled substance use, contraception, and sexual history

B. Physical examination

1. Height and weight measurement (and comparison to norms in children and adolescents)
2. Blood pressure determination, including orthostatic measurements when indicated, and comparison to age-related norms
3. Funduscopic, oral, thyroid exam
4. Cardiac examination
5. Abdominal examination (e.g., for hepatomegaly)
6. Evaluation of pulses by palpation and with auscultation
7. Hand/finger examination, foot examination
8. Skin examination (for acanthosis nigricans and insulin-injection sites)
9. Neurological examination
10. Signs of diseases that can cause secondary diabetes (e.g., hemochromatosis, pancreatic disease)

C. Laboratory evaluation

1. A1C
2. Fasting lipid profile, including total cholesterol, HDL cholesterol, triglycerides, and LDL cholesterol
3. Test for microalbuminuria in type 1 diabetic patients who have had diabetes for at least 5 years and in all patients with type 2 diabetes. Some advocate beginning screening of pubertal children before 5yrs of diabetes
4. Serum creatinine in adults (in children if proteinuria is present)
5. Thyroid-stimulating hormone (TSH) in all type 1 diabetic patients; in type 2 if clinically indicated
6. Electrocardiogram in adults
7. Urinalysis for ketones, protein, sediment

D. Referrals
1. Eye exam, if indicated
2. Family planning for women of reproductive age
3. Diabetes educator, if not provided by physician or practice staff
4. Behavioral specialist, as indicated
5. Foot specialist, as indicated

Source: Adapted from American Diabetes Association: Clinical Practice Recommendations 2002. Report of The Expert Committee on the Diagnosis and Classification of Diabetes Mellitus. Diabetes Care Jan 2002;25(1):S36, Table 5. Copyright© 2002, American Diabetes Association. Used with permission. http://care.diabetesjournal.org/cgi/content-nw/full/25/suppl_1/s33/T5

VI. MANAGEMENT
A. Diet
1. Caloric requirements can be estimated by multiplying IBW × 10
2. Weight loss may decrease the need for medication
3. Follow guidelines established by the ADA for caloric restriction
4. Arrange a consultation with a dietician if possible

B. Exercise
1. Regular exercise improves blood glucose control, reduces cardiovascular risk, contributes to weight loss and improves well-being
2. Before beginning an exercise program, patients should have a medical evaluation and appropriate diagnostic studies
3. Diabetics should try to exercise 20–30 minutes 3 ×/week. Insulin or med requirements may decrease with exercise. Warn patients of the possibility of exercise-induced hypoglycemia and monitor blood glucose levels before and after exercise

C. Monitoring of blood glucose
1. Blood glucose: Self monitoring of blood glucose in patient with type 1 diabetes should be 3 or more × a day, usually performed before meals and before bed. For patients with type 2 diabetes, the optimal frequency of testing is not known, but should be sufficient to allow for reaching of glycemic goals. Testing should be more frequent when adding or modifying therapy
2. HbA1c: Measures the average glycemia over the last 2–3 months. Perform twice a year in patients meeting treatment goals and every 3 months in patients with a change in therapy of who have not met treatment goals

D. Goals for glycemic control

Glycemic Control for Nonpregnant Individuals with Diabetes			
	Normal	Goal	Additional action suggested*
Plasma values†			
Average preprandial glucose (mg/dl)	< 110	90-130	< 90/ >150
Average bedtime glucose (mg/dl)	< 120	110-150	< 110/ >180
Whole blood values‡			
Average preprandial glucose (mg/dl)	< 100	80-120	< 80/ >140
Average bedtime glucose (mg/dl)	< 110	100-140	< 100/ >160
A1C (%)	< 6	< 7	> 8

The values shown in this table are by necessity generalized to the entire population of individuals with diabetes. Patients with comorbid diseases, the very young and older adults, and others with unusual conditions or circumstances may warrant different treatment goals. These values are for nonpregnant adults.
*Values above/below these levels are not "goals" nor are they "acceptable" in most patients. They are an indication for a significant change in the treatment plan. "Additional action suggested" depends on individual patient circumstances. Such actions may include enhanced diabetes self-management education, comanagement with a diabetes team, referral to an endocrinologist, change in pharmacological therapy, initiation of or increase in SMBG, or more frequent contact with the patient. A1C is referenced to a nondiabetic range of 4.0-6.0% (mean 5.0%, SD 0.5%). †Values calibrated to plasma glucose, ‡ measurement of capillary blood glucose.

Source: American Diabetes Association: Clinical Practice Recommendations 2002. Report of The Expert Committee on the Diagnosis and Classification of Diabetes Mellitus. Diabetes Care Jan 2002;25(1):S37, Table 6. Copyright© 2002, American Diabetes Association. Used with permission. http://care.diabetesjournal.org/cgi/cont/full/25/suppl_1/s33

GEN

E. Prevention, screening, and management of complications

1. Blood pressure (BP) control
   a. Data: Elevated BP affects 20–60% of patient with diabetes
   b. Screening: Measure BP at every visit and measure orthostatic BP to assess for autonomic neuropathy
   c. Goal: Target BP is < 130/80. Use lifestyle/behavioral therapy with SBP 130–139 and DBP 80–89 and meds if > 140/90
   d. Management: Antihypertensive meds shown to reduce cardiovascular events include angiotensin converting enzyme (ACE) inhibitors, angiotensin receptor blockers (ARBs), β-blockers, and diuretics. Use ACE inhibitors, ARBs, or β-blockers as initial therapy

2. Lipid management
   a. Data: Reducing lipid abnormalities has been shown to reduce macrovascular disease and mortality in type 2 diabetics
   b. Screening: Testing annually and in adults with low risk lipid values, repeat every 2yrs
   c. Goal: LDL < 100, triglycerides < 150 and HDL > 45 in men and > 55 in women
   d. Management: Statins should be used as first line therapy for lowering LDL (see Chapter 40, Hyperlipidemia)

3. Aspirin therapy
   a. Data: 30% decrease in MI and 20% decrease in stroke in young and middle aged patients both with and without CV disease, in males and females and patients with HTN
   b. Management: Use **Aspirin** 75–325mg PO QD in all adult patients over 30yrs with diabetes and macrovascular disease, in patients > 40yrs with diabetes and 1 or more CV risk factors, and consider in patients 30–40yrs with other CV risk factors

4. Smoking cessation
   a. Data: Heightened risk in diabetic smokers of morbidity and premature death. May have a role in development of type 2 diabetes
   b. Screening: Question all patients about smoking
   c. Goal: Smoking cessation in all patients
   d. Management: Counseling and other forms of treatment. See Chapter 35, Smoking Cessation

5. CV screening
   a. Data: No current data that exercise testing in asymptomatic patients with risk factors improves prognosis
   b. Screening: Assess CV risk factors annually
   c. CV risk factors include: dyslipidemia, HTN, smoking, family history of premature coronary disease, presence of micro- or macroalbuminuria
   d. Management: ADA recommendations for exercise stress testing
      i. Typical or atypical angina symptoms
      ii. Abnormal resting ECG
      iii. History of carotid or peripheral vascular disease
      iv. Sedentary lifestyle, age > 35 and plans to begin a vigorous exercise program
      v. Patients with 2 or more risk factors

6. Nephropathy
   a. Data: Diabetic nephropathy occurs in 20–40% of diabetics and is the leading cause of end stage renal disease (ESRD)
   b. Screening: Annually, measure in patients with type 1 diabetes after 5yrs and in type 2 diabetics starting at time of diagnosis
   c. There are 3 methods to screen for microalbuminuria:
      i. Microalbumin to creatinine ratio in random collection
      ii. 24hr collection with creatinine
      iii. Timed (e.g., over 4hrs) collection. If abnormal, then repeat. Must have 2 of 3 abnormal over 6 month period
   d. Definitions of abnormalities in albumin excretion

GEN

| Definitions of Abnormalities in Albumin Excretion ||
Category	Spot collection (µg/mg creatinine)
Normal	< 30
Microalbuminuria	30-299
Macro (clinical) albuminuria	≥ 300
Because of variability in urinary albumin excretion, two of three specimens collected within a 3- to 6- month period should be abnormal before considering a patient to have crossed one of these diagnostic thresholds. Exercise within 24 h, infection, fever, congestive heart failure, marked hyperglycemia, and marked hypertension may elevate urinary albumin excretion over baseline values.	

Source: Diagnosis and Classification of Diabetes Mellitus. Diabetes Care 2002:25(1):S43. Copyright © 2002, American Diabetes Association. Used with permission. http://care.diabetesjournal.org/cgi/content/full/25/suppl_1/s33

   e. Management
      i. Type 1 diabetics: Use ACE inhibitors as initial agents in patients with microalbuminuria or clinical albuminuria
      ii. Type 2 diabetics: Use ARBs as initial agents in patients with microalbuminuria or clinical albuminuria
      iii. If one class not tolerated, substitute for the other
      iv. Protein restriction with overt nephropathy at ≤0.8g/kg/day
7. Foot care
   a. Data: Early recognition of risk factors (diabetes > 10yrs, male, poor glucose control, CV/retinal/renal complications, peripheral neuropathy, increased pressure, bone deformity, PVD, nail pathology, history of ulcers or amputation) may prevent foot ulceration and amputation
   b. Screening: Comprehensive exam annually and a visual inspection at every visit
   c. Goal: Prevention of ulcers and amputation
   d. Management: Based on diagnosis
8. Retinopathy
   a. Data: Strongly related to duration of diabetes. Intensive management of blood sugar prevents or delays retinopathy
   b. Screening: Examine type 1 diabetics within 3–5yrs of diagnosis and type 2 diabetics shortly after diagnosis. Subsequent annually thereafter
   c. Goal: Prevention of retinopathy and blindness
   d. Management: Per ophthalmologist or optometrist experienced in diagnosing diabetic retinopathy

F. Hospital admission guidelines
   1. Life threatening complications including DKA, hyperglycemic hyperosmolar coma, hypoglycemia with neuroglycopenia (blood glucose < 50) with continuing confusion despite treatment, coma/seizures/altered behavior, hypoglycemia caused by a sulfonylurea drug without continuing supervision
   2. New diagnosis of diabetes in children and adolescents
   3. Poor control with need for close monitoring to determine the cause
   4. Severe complications that require intensive treatment
   5. Uncontrolled or newly diagnosed diabetes during pregnancy
   6. Institution of insulin pump therapy

VII. MEDICATIONS USED IN THE TREATMENT OF TYPE 2 DIABETES: See chart below
   A. General guidelines: Ultimate goal is control of HbA1c
      1. There are 5 classes of oral hypoglycemics and these are listed in the chart below
      2. All are equally effective (except for the α-glucosidase inhibitors and **Nateglinide (Starlix)**) and reduce HbA1c 1–2% when used as monotherapy
      3. Reasonable initial choices for monotherapy are **Metformin** or a **Sulfonylurea (SU)**
      4. The most commonly prescribed is **Metformin (Glucophage)** as it is associated with weight loss (or weight neutrality), a decrease in lipid levels, and very low risk of hypoglycemia. Optimal dose is 1,000mg BID. Contraindications include creatinine ≥ 1.5 in men and ≥ 1.4 in women, hepatic dysfunction, CHF, metabolic acidosis, dehydration, and alcoholism. Lactic acidosis occurs 1 in every 30,000 patient years

GEN

5. Second generation SUs are more potent and probably safer than first genration SUs, but with equal efficacy. SUs have a loss of efficacy over time with a 5% yearly failure rate. SUs should not be used with non-SU secretagogues

6. **Thiazolidinediones (TZDs)** cause an increase in HDL levels, decrease in triglycerides, and a slight decrease in blood pressure. They are contraindicated in patients with advanced CHF or hepatic dysfunction and do require LFT monitoring. May not exert full effect for weeks or months

7. Head-to-head trials have shown equal efficacy between Metformin, SUs, and TZDs with HbA1c decreases of 1–2% when used as monotherapy

8. The α-glucosidase inhibitors reduce HbA1c 0.5–1%

B. Combination therapy

1. After 3yrs only 50% of patients are controlled on 1 drug, and after 9yrs only 25% are adequately controlled

2. Generally, it is better to add 1 drug to a failing drug than to change drugs as the effect of the additional drug is additive

3. Most common combinations are SU and Metformin, Metformin and TZD, SU and TZD, but no combination has been shown to be superior. SUs should not be combined with non-SU secretagogues

4. One trial showed improved glycemia with triple therapy, but it is not formally approved by the FDA

5. Insulin should be used in combination with a failing regimen (preferred) or alone

C. Comparison of oral therapy for type 2 diabetes

Currently Available Oral Therapeutic Options for Type 2 Diabetes Mellitus				
Sulfonylureas (SUs)	**Non-SU Secretagogues**	**Biguanides**	**α-Glucosidase Inhibitors**	**Thiazolidinediones**
Mechanism of action Increased pancreatic insulin secretion	Increased pancreatic insulin secretion	Decreased hepatic glucose production	Decreased gut carbohydrate absorption	Increased peripheral glucose disposal
Advantages Well established Decreases microvascular risk Convenient daily dosing	Targets postprandial glycemia Possibly less hypoglycemia and weight gain than with SUs	Well established Weight loss No hypoglycemia Decreases microvascular risk Nonglycemic benefits (decreased lipid levels, increased fibrinolysis, decreased hyperinsulinemia) Convenient daily dosing	Targets postprandial glycemia No hypoglycemia Nonsystemic	No hypoglycemia Reverses prime defect of type 2 diabetes Nonglycemic benefits (decreased lipid levels, increased fibrinolysis, decreased hyperinsulinemia, improved endothelial function) Possible beta cell preservation Convenient daily dosing
Disadvantages Hypoglycemia Weight gain Hyperinsulinemia (role uncertain)	More complex (3 times daily) dosing schedule Hypoglycemia Weight gain No long-term data Hyperinsulinemia (role uncertain)	Adverse gastrointestinal effects Many contradictions Lactic acidosis (rare)	More complex (3 times daily) dosing schedule Adverse gastrointestinal effects No long-term data	Liver function test monitoring Weight gain Edema Slow onset of action No long-term data
Food and Drug Administration Approval status Monotherapy Combination with insulin metformin, thiazolidinedione, α-glucosidase inhibitors	Monotherapy Combination with metformin	Monotherapy Combination with insulin, SU, non-SU secretagogue, thiazolidinedione	Monotherapy Combination with SU	Monotherapy Combination with insulin (pioglitazone only), SU, metformin

D. Dosing and cost comparison of therapy for type 2 diabetes

DOSING AND COST COMPARISON OF THERAPY FOR TYPE 2 DIABETES

	USUAL DAILY DOSAGE	DURATION	SUPPLY	MONTHLY RETAIL COST (2001)
Sulfonylureas: Glimepiride (Amaryl)	I-4 mg QD	24 hrs	I, 2, 4mg	$60 (Two 4mg QD #60)
Glipizide (Glucotrol)	5-15mg QD or 5-40mg QD in divided doses	18-30 hrs	5, 10mg	$111 (Two 10mg BID #120)
Generic Glipizide				$46 (Two 10mg BID #120)
Glipizide (Glucotrol XL)	5-10mg QD	24 hrs	2.5, 5, 10mg	$50 (Two 10mg QD #60)
Glyburide (Diabeta) (Micronase) (Glynase) Generic Glyburide	5-20mg QD or in divided doses 1.25-20mg QD or in divided doses 0.75-12mg QD or in divided doses	10-30 hrs 10-30 hrs 24 hrs	1.5, 2.5, 5mg 1.5, 2.5, 5mg 1.5, 3, 6mg	$101 (Two 5mg BID #120) $112 (Two 5mg BID #120) $86 (One 6mg BID #60) $52 (Two 5mg BID # 120)
Biguanides: Metformin (Glucophage)	500-2,550mg in 2-3 divided doses	18 hrs	500, 850, 1000mg	$102 (Two 500mg BID #120)
Metformin ext. rel. (Glucophage XR)	500-2,000mg QD or in 2 divided doses		500mg ext. rel. tabs	$88 (Four 500mg QD # 120)
α-Glucosidase Inhibitors: Acarbose (Precose)	50-100mg TID with meals	Not absorbed	25, 50, 100mg	$78 (One 100mg TID #90)
Miglitol (Glyset)	50mg TID with meals	Not absorbed	25, 50, 100mg	$73 (One 50mg TID #90)
Thiazolidinediones: Rosiglitazone (Avandia)	4-8mg QD or in 2 divided doses	N/A	2, 4, 8mg	$175 (One 4mg BID #60)
Pioglitazone (Actos)	15–30 mg QD	16–24 hrs	15, 30, 45mg	$169 (One 45mg QD #30)
Non SU Secretagogues: Repaglinide (Prandin)	0.5-4mg 2-4 x/day within 30 min of meals	1 hr	0.5, 1, 2mg	$165 (Two 2mg TID #180)
Nateglinide (Starlix)	120mg before meals TID			$103 (One 120mg TID #90)
Combination Glyburide/Metformin (Glucovance)	2.5/500mg BID to 2 x 5/500mg BID		1.25/250mg, 2.5/500mg, 5/500mg tabs	$105 (Two 5mg/500mg BID #120)
Insulin (1 vial/ 100 U) Novolin or Humulin NPH Lantus Humalog Humalog 75/25	See VIII. below	See VIII. below	See VIII. below	$24 $44 $45 $46

Source: Adapted from Inzucchi SE. Oral antihyperglycemic therapy for type 2 diabetes. Scientific Review. JAMA 2002;287:365.

VIII. INSULIN THERAPY

A. Consider formal diabetes education prior to initiating

B. Type 1 diabetics

  1. Physiologic insulin secretion is 20–40U/day

  2. Start with 0.25–1.0U/kg/day human N insulin (pediatric less, adolescents more)

C. Type 2 diabetics—May combine any of below with oral therapy

  1. Check blood glucose AC and HS

  2. Options include:

    a. Begin with 10–20 U **NPH** 30 minutes before bedtime

    b. 70/30 QAM, **Humalog** at dinner and **NPH** at HS

    c. 70/30 QAM and before dinner

    d. Custom split dosing with intermediate N- and short acting R insulin

      i) AM dose: 2/3 daily dose. Of this 2/3 will be NPH and 1/3 will be regular

      ii) PM dose: 1/3 of daily dose. Of this 2/3 will be NPH and 1/3 will be regular

      iii) Adjust by 2–4U/day as needed

GEN

      e. **Lantus** QHS

      f. **Lantus** QHS and **Humalog** QAC with aggressive calorie counting

      g. **Humalog** QAC and long acting insulin QHS

D. Properties of various insulin types

CLASS	BRAND	ONSET	PEAK	DURATION
Rapid Acting	Humalog	15 min	30–90 min	1.5–3 hrs
Short Acting	Humulin/Novolin R (human)	0.5–1 hrs	2–4 hrs	6–12 hrs
Intermediate Acting	Humulin/Novolin N (human)	1–2 hrs	4–6 hrs	10–16 hrs
	Humulin/Novolin L (human)	2–3 hrs	8–12 hrs	12–18 hrs
Long Acting	Humulin U (Ultralente)	4–6 hrs	10–14 hrs	23–36 hrs
	Insulin Glargine (Lantus)	2–4 hrs	peakless	2–4 hrs
Mixed	Novolin/Humulin 50/50	30 min	2–4 hrs	24 hrs
	Novolin/Humulin 70/30	30 min	3–4 hrs (1st) 10–12 hrs (2nd)	10–16 hrs

IX. THE DIABETIC FLOW SHEET: A flow sheet on the front of the patient's chart can make each visit easier and help avoid overlooking potential problems

DIABETIC FLOW SHEET

Name: _____

Date of onset: _____

Age of onset: _____

Parameter and Frequency	Date	Date	Date	Date	Date
History					
Weight (each visit)					
BP (each visit)					
Heart and Lung exam (each visit)					
Feet (each visit)					
Fundi & Neuro (every other visit)					
Lab Random BS (each visit)					
Urine Dipstick (each visit)					
HgbA1C (Q 3–6 months)					
BUN/Cr (Q year)					
Lipid profile (Q year)					
TSH/T4 (Q 2–3 years)					
Referrals (including Ophtho)					
Medications Oral agent and dose Insulin: A.M. P.M.					
Diet					
Education/Questions					

GEN

CLINICAL PEARLS
- Diabetic nephropathy accounts for close to half of the patients receiving long-term renal dialysis in the US, 20–30% of type 2 diabetes will develop nephropathy
- Between 1–5% of patients with impaired glucose tolerance will go on to develop symptomatic diabetes or diagnostically abnormal glucose tolerance per year. Treatment with oral hypoglycemics does not delay the development of diabetes, but weight loss and exercise may
- Gestational diabetes occurs in 1–2% of pregnancies. These patients have a 30% risk of developing diabetes within 5–10yrs postpartum
- Up to 20% of type 2 diabetics have retinopathy when they are diagnosed
- In high risk patients, exercise may help prevent type 2 diabetes
- Patients who have autoimmune destruction of β-cells are also prone to other autoimmune diseases including Grave's disease, Hashimoto's thyroiditis, Addison's disease, vitiligo, and pernicious anemia
- Dosing adjustments may be needed for changes of activity, stress, change in diet, or infection
- For morning hyperglycemia, check a 2 AM glucose to rule out the Somogyi effect (rebound hyperglycemia secondary to hypoglycemia)

References

Inzucchi SE. Oral antihyperglycemic therapy for type 2 diabetes. Scientific review. JAMA 2002;287:360–72.

Holmboe ES. Oral antihyperglycemic therapy for type 2 diabetes: clinical applications. JAMA 2002;287:373–6.

Report of the Expert Committee on the Diagnosis and Classification of Diabetes Mellitus. Diabetes Care 2002;25(1):S5–S20.

American Diabetes Association. Implications of the diabetes control and complications trial (Position Statement). Diabetes Care 2002;25:S25–S27.

American Diabetes Association. Diabetic nephropathy (Position Statement). Diabetes Care 2002;25(1):S85–S89.

American Diabetes Association. Standards of medical care for patients with diabetes mellitus (Position Statement). Diabetes Care 2002;25:S33–S49.

Michael B. Weinstock, MD

53. THYROID DISEASE & TESTING

Note: These recommendations are for nonpregnant patients

I. INTRODUCTION/BACKGROUND
A. **Thyroid-stimulating hormone (TSH):** Secreted by the pituitary. Stimulates the steps of thyroid hormone production
B. **The thyroid gland:** Secretes mostly T_4 and a small amount of T_3
C. **The most active thyroid hormone** is T_3. About 90% of circulating T_3 is derived from peripheral deiodination of T_4
D. **Over 99% of circulating thyroid hormones** are bound to proteins, mostly thyroid-binding globulin (TBG)
E. **Approximately 2% of the adult population** has hypothyroidism and another 5–17% have mild/subclinical hypothyroidism (elevated TSH, normal serum free thyroxine)
F. **Approximately 0.2% of the adult population** has hyperthyroidism and 0.1–6.0% has mild/subclinical hyperthyroidism (decreased TSH, normal free throxine)
G. **Screening:** The American Thyroid Association recommends that adults be screened for thyroid dysfunction by measurement of the TSH beginning at age 35yrs and every 5yrs thereafter. Patients at high risk for thyroid disease should be screened more often

II. DIFFERENTIAL DIAGNOSIS

A. Hyperthyroidism

1. Toxic diffuse goiter (Graves' disease)—most common cause
2. Iatrogenic illness: Excessive administration of **Thyroxine** or **Triiodothyronine** (second most common cause)
3. Autonomous toxic adenoma (toxic nodular goiter)
   a. Single adenoma (Plummer's disease)
   b. Multiple adenomas (toxic multinodular goiter)
4. Thyroiditis: Inflammation induced release of thyroxine. May be subacute, silent (nontender gland) or post-partum
5. Iodine-induced hyperthyroidism: Jod-Basedow disease may occur in patients with multinodular goiter who take large amounts of iodine; health food preparations; Amiodarone
6. Excessive pituitary TSH (TSH secreting pituitary adenoma) or trophoblastic disease
7. Excessive ingestion of thyroid hormone (Thyrotoxicosis factitia)
8. Rarely: Thyroid cancer, choriocarcinoma, hydatidiform mole, embryonal testicular carcinoma, struma ovarii

B. Hypothyroidism

1. Primary hypothyroidism
   a. Autoimmune thyroiditis (Hashimoto's thyroiditis/Chronic lymphocytic thyroiditis): Most common cause in the US
   b. Surgical removal of the thyroid gland
   c. Radioactive iodine thyroid gland ablation
   d. External irradiation
   e. Thyroid gland iodine organification defect
   f. Idiopathic
2. Secondary (central) hypothyroidism
   a. Pituitary disease
   b. Hypothalamic disease

III. SIGNS AND SYMPTOMS AND LAB ABNORMALITIES

A. Hyperthyroidism: Severity of symptoms may vary (age of patient, duration of illness, magnitude of hormone excess)

1. General: Weight loss, poor sleep, alterations in appetite, fatigue, heat intolerance, increased sweating, mental disturbances
2. Eye: Vision change, photophobia, diplopia, exophthalmos
3. Neck: Possibly thyroid enlargement
4. Cardio: Palpitations and tachycardia, exertional intolerance/dyspnea on exertion
5. Neuro: Tremor, sudden paralysis
6. GYN: Menstrual disturbance (decreased flow), impaired fertility
7. Extremities: Pretibial myxedema (Graves' disease)

B. Hypothyroidism

1. General: Weight gain, poor sleep, alterations in appetite, fatigue, cold intolerance, hypothermia, dry or yellow skin, loss of hair, constipation
2. ENT: Thick tongue
3. Neck: Possibly thyroid enlargement (goiter)
4. Cardio: Bradycardia, cardiomyopathy
5. Neuro: Reflex delay, ataxia, memory and mental impairment, decreased concentration, depression, myalgias
6. GYN: Menstrual disturbance (increased flow), impaired fertility
7. Extremities: Myxedema
8. Lab abnormalities: In addition to abnormal thyroid tests (see below), increased cholesterol, increased liver enzymes and CPK, increased prolactin, hyponatremia, hypoglycemia, anemia (normal or increased MCV)

IV. TECHNIQUE FOR PHYSICAL EXAMINATION OF THE THYROID GLAND

A. Inspection: Located below the cricoid cartilage, observe while patient is swallowing water
B. Palpation

GEN

1. Examine from behind the patient
2. Palpate with 3 fingers on either side of the lower trachea (index fingers just below the cricoid) for size, shape, consistency, tenderness or nodularity

C. Examination during swallowing: The thyroid gland moves upward with swallowing and may be more easily palpated

V. INTERPRETATION OF LAB TESTS

A. Introduction

1. Primary screening test for thyroid abnormalities is TSH (third generation) (see below)
2. Free T_4 can be measured directly
3. FTI (free thyroxine index) is a calculation of the T_4 and T_3RU (see below) and is an estimation of the free T_4. Used because the T_4 level may not be a true indication of a patient's thyroid status because it is affected by altered states of protein binding
4. If the free T_4 is measured, FTI (which is an *approximation of free T_4*) does not need to be measured

B. Definition of commonly obtained thyroid tests

1. TSH
   a. Third generation assays measure TSH as low as 0.01mU/L. Second generation assays measure to 0.1mU/L
   b. TSH levels are decreased with:
      i. Primary hyperthyroidism (see II. A. Differential diagnosis of hyperthyroidism)
      ii. Thyroid hormone replacement
      iii. Severe nonthyroidal illness, pregnancy (1st trimester)
      iv. Dopamine, dopamine agonists (Levodopa) and glucocorticoids
      v. Mild/subclinical hyperthyroidism (decreased TSH and normal free level T_4)
   c. TSH levels are elevated with:
      i. Primary hypothyroidism (see II. B. Differential diagnosis of hyperthyroidism)
      ii. Hyperthyroidism secondary to pituitary neoplastic secretion of thyrotropin
      iii. Recovery from nonthyroidal illness
      iv. With dopamine antagonists (Metoclopramide), phenothiazines, Lithium, Amiodarone, and some antipsychotics
      v. Mild/subclinical hypothyroidism (elevated TSH and normal free T_4)
2. Free T_4: Measures the actual free T_4. May be falsely elevated in patients receiving Heparin (especially with dialysis), with depressed patients or with severe nonthyroidal illness
3. T_4: Measures thyroxine by radioimmunoassay and is affected by states of altered thyroxine binding. It measures both circulating thyroxine bound to protein and active (unbound) thyroxine
4. T_3RU: Measures the *percentage* of T_4 *not bound* to protein. If normal, thyroid binding proteins are not significantly altering the T_4 measurement, and T_4 will usually be an accurate estimation of *free T_4*. If T_3RU is abnormal, then look at FTI
5. T_3: For diagnosis of T_3 thyrotoxicosis (thyrotoxicosis with normal T_4 values). Like T_4, only measures *bound* T_3. Not useful in hypothyroidism. Obtain when suspect thyrotoxicosis in patients with low TSH and normal or low T_4 (T_3 toxicosis)
6. FTI: The FTI = $T_4 \times T_3RU/100$. The FTI *usually* corrects for abnormalities of thyroxine binding and is a good approximation of the amount of active (unbound) thyroxine
7. Reverse T_3 (RT_3): RT_3 is an inactive isomer of T_3. Level is increased in hyperthyroidism, by drugs that block conversion of T_4 to T_3 (Amiodarone, Propranolol), and in nonthyroid illnesses that decrease the T_3 concentration
8. Serum thyroglobulin: Storage site for thyroid hormones. Elevated in hyperthyroidism and thyroiditis. Reduced or undetectable in thyrotoxicosis factitia (exogenous thyroid hormone suppresses endogenous production)
9. Thyroid antibodies: Found in 5–10% of normal subjects and 20% of hospitalized patients
   a. Antimicrosomal antibodies: Elevated in Hashimoto's thyroiditis or Graves' disease
   b. Antithyroglobulin antibodies: Elevated in Hashimoto's thyroiditis or Graves' disease

GEN

VI. OTHER TESTS

   A. Calcitonin assay: Useful serum marker in medullary thyroid carcinoma. May also be elevated in azotemia, hypercalcemia, pernicious anemia, thyroiditis, and pregnancy as well as other malignancies

   B. Radioiodine (^{123}I) Uptake and scan of thyroid gland: Provides a picture of thyroid uptake

   1. Elevated: *Graves' disease, toxic nodular goiter, toxic adenoma,* dietary iodine deficiency, pregnancy, early Hashimoto's thyroiditis, nephrotic syndrome, recovery from thyroid hormone suppression, recovery from subacute thyroiditis, some thyroid enzyme deficiencies

   2. Decreased: Administration of iodine (including drugs, contrast dyes, etc.), antithyroid drugs, subacute thyroiditis, thyroid hormone administration, severe (high turnover) Graves' disease, thyroid gland damage (thyroiditis, surgery, radioiodine), ectopic functioning thyroid tissue

   C. Ultrasound: To differentiate solid from cystic nodules. Purely cystic are usually not cancer

   D. Fine-needle aspiration (FNA) thyroid biopsy: See X. D. below

VII. ALGORITHM FOR EVALUATION OF THYROID STATUS IN AMBULATORY PATIENTS

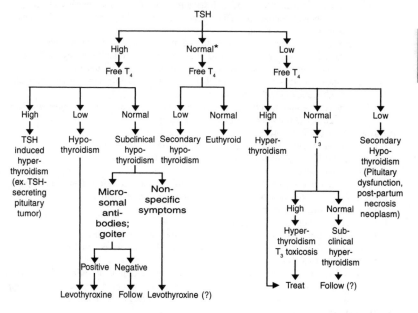

GEN

—Serum TSH may be in normal range in patients with hyperthyroidism secondary to hypothalamic or pituitary disease

Table adapted from: Pittman JG. Evaluation of patients with mildly abnormal thyroid function tests. Am Fam Phys 1996;54:962. Used with permission.

VIII. MANAGEMENT OF HYPERTHYROIDISM

   A. Graves' disease (Basedow's disease): Guidelines below are for non-pregnant patients
   1. Diagnosis
      a. Caused by thyroid stimulating antibodies which bind to and activate the thyrotropin receptor on thyroid cells
      b. Symptoms of hyperthyroidism, low TSH, high free T_4, elevated antithyroglobulin and antimicrosomal antibodies, diffusely enlarged thyroid gland
   2. ß-blockers (**Propranolol**)
      a. Symptomatic relief until hyperthyroidism is resolved. It has no effect on thyroid hormone secretion
      b. Dose: Begin with 10mg PO QD and increase. Usual dose is 20mg PO QID

3. **Antithyroid drugs**
  a. Indications include hyperthyroidism in pregnancy, "pretreatment" in elderly or cardiac patients, patients with mild disease or in patients with fear of isotopes. Decreased chance of post-treatment hypothyroidism
  b. **Methimazole (Tapazole)**
    i. Less frequent dosing than PTU and lower incidence of acute hepatic necrosis
    ii. Initially 30–60mg PO QD and then decrease dose as symptoms resolve and free T_4 returns to normal
  c. **Propylthiouracil** (PTU)
    i. Drug of choice in breast-feeding or pregnancy (use lower doses)
    ii. Blocks peripheral conversion of T_4 to T_3
    iii. Dose 300–600mg PO QD in 4 divided doses and then decrease dose as symptoms resolve and free T_4 returns to normal
  d. Side effects: Minor skin rashes, rarely agranulocytosis, acute hepatic necrosis
4. **Radioactive iodine**: Treatment of choice
  a. May be given in an ablative dose (with life-long thyroid replacement therapy necessary) or in a smaller dose to attempt to induce a euthyroid state
  b. Elderly or patients with cardiac history may benefit from treatment with antithyroid drugs before radioactive iodine therapy (to deplete the gland of stored hormone)
  c. Contraindicated in pregnancy
  d. Patients usually become hypothyroid by 3 months. May require partial thyroid replacement 2 months after radioactive iodine treatment. Note: TSH may not be a good indicator of thyroid status for the first several months after treatment
  e. Frequency of follow-up: 3 months, 6 months, 1yr, then, if thyroid status has normalized (with replacement therapy), every 1–2yrs
5. Surgery: Not commonly performed in the US, but may be appropriate with pregnant women intolerant of antithyroid drugs or pediatric patients

B. Toxic solitary thyroid nodules
1. Definition: A single hyperfunctioning thyroid nodule causing hyperthyroidism
2. Symptomatic: **Propranolol** with doses as above in Graves' disease
3. Definitive treatment
  a. Radioactive iodine: Permanent hypothyroidism occurs in less than 10% of patients
  b. Surgery: If radioactive iodine is contraindicated or < 40

C. Toxic multinodular goiter
1. General: Usually affects older patients
2. Symptomatic: **Propranolol** with dose as above in Graves' disease
3. Antithyroid meds: 95% recurrence rate after thioureas are stopped
4. Definitive treatment
  a. Radioactive iodine: Thiourea treatment before iodine. Requires high doses of radioactive iodine. Recurrences are common—patients need close follow-up
  b. Surgery: Reserved for cosmetic purposes or pressure symptoms

D. Subacute thyroiditis
1. General: Painless inflammation of the thyroid gland lasting weeks to months causing transient hypo-or hyperthyroidism. Subsides spontaneously
2. Symptomatic hyperthyroidism: **Propranolol** 10–40mg PO QID
3. Treat transient hypothyroidism with **Thyroxine** 0.05–0.1mg PO QD if symptomatic
4. Antithyroid medication and radioactive iodine are ineffective as thyroid hormone production is low

E. Suppurative (bacterial) thyroiditis
1. Often occurs during course of systemic infection
2. ATBs: **Empiric**
3. Surgical drainage if fluctuant

F. Thyrotoxicosis factitia
1. Occurs from exogenous ingestion of thyroid hormone
2. If it is suspected, then check serum thyroglobulin. The thyroglobulin level is reduced or undetectable in thyrotoxicosis factitia (exogenous thyroid hormone suppresses endogenous production)
3. Manage with patient education or psychiatric referral

G. **Mild/subclinical hyperthyroidism** (also called compensated hypothyroidism, decreased thyroid reserve, and prehypothyroidism)
   1. Definition: Low TSH and normal free T_4
   2. These patients have a 3 fold higher risk of developing atrial fibrillation within 10yrs and some may be at risk of developing thyroid induced osteoporosis
   3. Should be treated if associated with toxic goiter, toxic adenoma or toxic multinodular goiter. If asymptomatic, should probably not be treated. Follow closely

IX. MANAGEMENT OF HYPOTHYROIDISM

A. **Autoimmune thyroiditis (Hashimoto's thyroiditis):** Chronic lymphocytic thyroiditis
   1. Most common thyroid disorder in the US. Thyroid gland is usually diffusely enlarged, firm and finely nodular
   2. Thyroid autoantibodies (antithyroid peroxidase) are positive 95% of the time. Antithyroglobulin antibodies are increased 60% of the time
   3. Management
      a. Elderly or patients with coronary disease: Start with **Levothyroxine (Synthroid, Levothroid)** 0.025 PO QD (This dosage can be increased in the increments of 0.025–0.050 mg every 4–6 weeks until TSH level returns to normal)
      b. Young patients/healthy patient: Start with **Levothyroxine (Synthroid)** 0.05–0.1mg PO QD, with the dosage increased as indicated by TSH levels
      c. Note: Older patients generally require $^2/_3$ the amount as younger patients
   4. Follow-up: Once TSH normalizes and patient is asymptomatic, then check TSH every 1–2yrs
   5. Half-life of T_4 is about 7 days. Check TSH level 6–8 weeks after a change in dosage of thyroid replacement. Early testing may lead to over-treatment
B. **Surgical removal of the thyroid gland**
   1. Hypothyroidism develops in 25% at 8–12yrs post-op in patients with subtotal thyroidectomy
   2. Management as above
C. **Radioactive iodine thyroid gland ablation**
   1. Hypothyroidism develops at rate of 2–5% /yr (30–70% at 10–15yrs after treatment)
   2. Management as above
D. **Subclinical hypothyroidism**
   1. Normal free T_4 and high TSH
   2. Longitudinal progression to hypothyroidism of 5–8% /yr in patients with high TSH and significant titer of antimicrosomal antibodies. Incidence of hypothyroidism in patients over age 65 is 80% over 4yrs
   3. Indications for **Levothroid** replacement therapy
      a. All patients with elevated TSH and a significant titer of antimicrosomal antibodies
      b. Elderly patients with TSH greater than 20 µU/mL (20mU/L) and a negative antimicrosomal antibody test
      c. Patients with elevated TSH and goiter (+/- antimicrosomal antibodies)
      d. History of radioiodine treatment for thyrotoxicosis and elevated TSH
      e. Consider in symptomatic patients with elevated TSH: Start at sub-therapeutic dose of 0.05–0.075mg PO QD
   4. If treatment is not initiated, then follow closely

X. DIAGNOSIS AND MANAGEMENT OF SOLITARY THYROID NODULES

A. **Enlargement of the thyroid gland may be diffuse or nodular** and is detectable in 4% of adults. Most thyroid nodules are benign, less than 5% are malignant. If an incidental nodule > 1 cm is found, then consider fine needle aspiration. Solitary nodules are associated with higher incidence of malignancy
B. **Risk factors for thyroid cancer**
   1. History: Age < 20 or > 45, male, exposure to ionizing radiation (especially in childhood), family history
   2. Physical exam: Cervical lymphadenopathy, vocal cord paralysis, very firm nodule, rapid tumor growth, fixation to adjacent structures

GEN

C. **Factors which *do not* differentiate benign from malignant nodules:**
  1. History and physical exam
  2. Thyroid function tests
  3. Antithyroglobulin and antimicrosomal antibodies
  4. Ultrasound: May differentiate solid from cystic, but either may be malignant
  5. Thyroid radioiodine uptake and scan: May differentiate between a "cold" (nonfunctioning) nodule which is more likely to be malignant, and a "hot" (functioning nodule) which is less likely to be malignant, but does not *definitively* distinguish between benign and malignant nodules

D. **Fine needle aspiration (FNA):** Test of choice
  1. Safe, reliable, inexpensive and is performed as an outpatient
  2. Technique
    a. No anesthesia necessary
    b. Aspiration with 25 gauge needle. Success is increased by ultrasound guidance

E. **Results**
  1. If positive (suspicious or malignant), then referral for definitive therapy (surgery)
  2. If indeterminate, then consider:
    a. Repeat FNA—*or*—
    b. Radionuclide scanning: If "hot" then follow and if "cold" then surgery—*or*—
    c. Trial of suppression therapy with monthly follow-up over 6 months
      i. If size increases, then surgery
      ii. If size decreases, then follow
      iii. If size does not change, then consider surgery or repeat FNA
  3. If inadequate, consider referral for surgical excision in patients with one or more risk factors
  4. If benign, then trial of suppression therapy with monthly follow-up over 6 months

XI. GOITER

A. **Differential diagnosis**
  1. Hashimoto's thyroiditis
  2. Iodide deficiency
  3. Genetic thyroid hormone defects
  4. Drug goitrogens: Lithium, iodide, PTU, Methimazole, Phenylbutazone, Sulfonamides, Amiodarone
  5. Infiltrating diseases: Cancer, sarcoidosis

B. **Evaluation**
  1. History and physical exam as above
  2. Obtain TSH, Free T_4
  3. Consider thyroid radioiodine uptake and scan
  4. Consider ultrasound and FNA if nodule(s) are present

C. **Management:** Per specific diagnosis

CLINICAL PEARLS

- Approximately 5% of the world's population have goiter, mostly from iodine deficiency
- Free T_4 represents about 0.025% of total T_4 (bound and unbound)
- Amiodarone causes clinically significant hypothyroidism in about 8% of patients and asymptomatic hypothyroidism in another 17% of patients due to the high iodine concentration (TSH high and T_4 low or normal)
- Use caution with diagnosis of hospitalized patients. Up to 70% of moderately ill hospitalized patients will have thyroid function abnormalities
- Symptoms of thyrotoxicosis vary with age and may be atypical, especially in the elderly

References

Welker MJ, Orlov D. Thyroid nodules. Am Fam Phys 2003;67:559–66, 73–4.

Burman KD, Shrier D. Subclinical hyperthyroidism: Controversies in management. Am Fam Phys 2002;65:431–8.

Heuston WJ. Treatment of hypothyroidism. Am Fam Phys 2001;64:1717–24.

Ladenson PW, et al. American Thyroid Association guidelines for detection of thyroid dysfunction. Arch Int Med 2000;160:1573–5.

Weetman AP. Medical progress: Graves' disease. N Engl J Med 2000; 343:1236–48.

Woeber KA. The year in review: the thyroid. Ann Intern Med Dec 21, 1999;131:59–62.

Helfand M, Redfern CC. Clinical guideline, part 2. Screening for thyroid disease: an update. Am Coll Phys Ann Intern Med 1998;129:144–58.

Mazzaferri EL, et al. Management of a solitary thyroid nodule. N Engl J Med 1993;328:553–9

Geoffrey Eubank, MD
Michael B.Weinstock, MD
Elizabeth Walz, MD
Kathleen Provanzana, MD

54. HEADACHE: DIAGNOSIS & MANAGEMENT

GEN

I. EPIDEMIOLOGY

Most common pain problem seen in the ambulatory setting (greater than 10 million office visits/yr). Over 4 billion dollars are spent annually on over-the-counter meds for headaches. This does not include time missed from work, prescription meds, or physician visits

II. HISTORY

The cornerstone of diagnosis is to determine which headaches are more dangerous (secondary to medical problems) by classifying as a primary (migraine, tension, cluster, etc.) or secondary (CNS mass lesions, infections/meningitis, etc.) headache

A. **Headache characteristics:** Age of headache onset, location, frequency, severity, quality, speed of onset, or triggers (foods, stress, hunger, menstrual cycle, cough/exertion, position changes, etc.)

B. **Associated symptoms:** Photophobia, phonophobia, nausea/vomiting, sinus symptoms, fever, stiff neck, focal neurologic complaints, visual changes

C. **Meds:** Past and present meds and response to treatment. Consider both abortive and prophylactic therapies. OTC meds, caffeine use, and foods may be triggers (MSG, red wine). Chronic analgesic use/abuse may lead to rebound headaches. Meds which may cause headaches (nitrates, Reserpine, Indomethacin, Minoxidil, Apresoline, oral contraceptives)

D. **Past medical and surgical history:** Malignancy, stroke, head trauma, neurosurgery, psychosocial history, hypertension, hematologic abnormalities, polymyalgia rheumatica

E. **Family History:** Migraines tend to be hereditary and begin in childhood or early adult life; other headaches less so

III. PHYSICAL EXAM

A. **Vital signs:** Fever (meningitis, sinusitis, viral syndromes), BP

B. **Ophthalmologic:** Pupils, funduscopic

C. **HEENT:** Tympanic membrane, nares and sinus exams, TMJ exam, temporal artery swelling and tenderness (especially over age 50), scalp exam, neck exam (nuchal rigidity, paraspinal tenderness or spasm, range of motion)

D. **Neurologic:** Visual fields, cranial nerves, motor, sensory, coordination, gait, and mental status changes

IV. DIFFERENTIAL DIAGNOSIS

A. Primary headaches (benign)
  1. Tension-type headache (related to physical, mental and/or emotional stress): 47%
  2. Migraine headache (with or without aura): 31%
  3. Cluster headache: 7%
  4. Mixed headache (usually migraine/tension)
  5. Rebound headache: Caffeine, Butalbital, and narcotics
  6. Neuralgias (trigeminal, occipital) characterized by brief electrical/lanceting pains
  7. Uncommon syndromes (chronic paroxysmal hemicrania, hemicrania continua, cough/exertional headache, coital headache)
  8. Miscellaneous: TMJ dysfunction, chronic sinus/allergies

B. **Secondary headaches** (not so benign)
  1. CNS mass lesions (tumor, abscess)
  2. Vascular (cerebral/subarachnoid hemorrhage, arteriovenous malformations, stroke/TIA)
  3. Infectious (meningitis, sinusitis)
  4. Traumatic (epidural/subdural hematoma, subarachnoid/intracranial hemorrhage)
  5. Temporal arteritis: greater than age 50, increased sedimentation rate, jaw claudication, pain centered about one temple, visual symptoms
  6. Pseudotumor cerebri: headache with papilledema, visual loss and elevated CSF pressure (typically occurs in young, overweight females)
  7. Miscellaneous: Post lumbar puncture, sleep apnea (morning headaches), carbon monoxide poisoning, glaucoma, hypertensive

V. Red flags: Worrisome features that indicate need for further workup

A. First severe headache over 50 (temporal arteritis, mass lesion, stroke)
B. Intense headache without prior history of headache (subarachnoid hemorrhage)
C. Fever, nuchal rigidity, Kernig's/Brudzinski's sign (meningitis)
D. Papilledema
E. Diplopia
F. New/persistent neurologic signs
G. Elevated BP (diastolic > 110)
H. Unexplained vomiting
I. Exertional/cough headache (need MRI to rule out posterior fossa lesion)
J. Sudden change in headache pattern (Note: prior history of benign headache does not rule out development of new cause for headache)
K. History of head trauma, malignancy or coagulopathy

VI. TESTING: Consider testing as appropriate when any of the "red flags" above are present

A. **Neuroimaging, including:**
  1. Computed tomography (CT) scan: Best for detection of acute bleed (non-contrast)
  2. Magnetic resonance imaging (MRI): Best for detection of posterior fossa disease, more sensitive than CT for most conditions, except acute bleed
  3. Magnetic resonance angiography (MRA): Aneurysm or other vascular lesion, other

B. **Lumbar puncture:** Evaluating meningitis or subarachnoid hemorrhage, increased intracranial pressure (assuming neuroimaging shows no mass lesion)

C. **Electroencephalogram (EEG):** Rarely helpful

D. **Other diagnostic tests** including CBC, sed. rate, thyroid panel, drug levels (Lithium)

VII. MANAGEMENT
A. General

DIAGNOSIS AND MANAGEMENT OF PRIMARY HEADACHES

Character	Tension-type headache	Migraine headache	Cluster Headache
Location	Bilateral intense about the neck	Usually unilateral	Strictly unilateral, retroorbital
Quality	Pressure, "vise-like"	Throbbing, aching	Sharp, stabbing
Severity	Mild to moderate	Moderate to severe	Extremely severe
Frequency	Variable, may be constant or intermittent	Intermittent (<15/month), not typically daily	Episodic, 1–4/day for weeks to months, same time each day, esp. night
Duration	Several hours/days, fluctuating	4–48 hours, gradual build-up and decline	15–120 minutes, rapid onset and decline
Aura	None	Occasional (16%), esp. visual(zig-zag scotoma,etc.)	None
Activity level	Variable	Passive, rest in dark room	Active, pacing
Precipitants	Stress	Numerous (foods, chocolate, menstrual cycle, etc.)	Alcohol
Associated symptoms	Muscular tenderness, mild photo/phonophobia	Photo/phonophobia, nausea/vomiting, diarrhea	Horner's syndrome, rhinorrhea, lacrimation
Therapy: Abortive	Acetaminophen NSAIDs ASA Muscle relaxants Relaxation, exercise Butalbital/narcotics* *Be careful with prolonged use (rebound, dependence)	Acetaminophen NSAIDs Midrin 2 at onset, repeat Q 1 hr to max of 5 Triptans (see below) DHE-45 1 mL IV/IM, may repeat x 1 in 1 hr Intranasal Dihydroergotamine	Sumatriptan 6mg SQ 100% O_2 NRB mask for 15 minutes DHE-45 1 mL IV/IM, may repeat x 1 in 1 hr
Therapy: Prophylactic	Amitriptyline/Nortriptyline 10-100mg Qhs SSRIs (less effective) Depakote 250mg BID Neurontin 100-600mg TID Biofeedback/relaxation	Inderal 60-240mg QD (or other Beta blockers) Depakote 250mg BID Amitriptyline/Nortriptyline 10-100mg Qhs Verapamil 180-240mg QD Naproxen 500mg BID Neurontin 100-600mg TID	Prednisone 60mg QD and taper over 2-3 weeks for new/recurrent cluster Add prophylactic to continue 2 wks after headache controlled Verapamil 180-240mg QD, Lithium 900mg QD Depakote 250mg BID

B. Triptans: Very effective for migraine, but contraindicated in coronary disease, uncontrolled hypertension, history of stroke and complicated migraine (hemiplegic, basilar)

Drug	mg	Speed of Onset	Efficacy	Rebound	Side Effects	Cost
Sumatriptan Imitrex/ IM	6	++++	++++	+++	++++	+++++
Sumatriptan Imitrex/ nas	10-20	+++	+++	+++	+++	++++
Sumatriptan Imitrex/ po	25-100	++	++	+++	++	++++
Zolmitriptan Zomig	2.5-5	++	++	++	+++	++++
Naratriptan Amerge	2.5	+	+	+	+	++++
Rizatriptan Maxalt	10 (5 w/ Inderal)	+++	+++	++	++	++++

Adapted from: National Headache Foundation. Standards of Care for Headache Diagnosis and Treatment. Chicago, Il: National Headache Foundation; 1996:6–7.

GEN

CLINICAL PEARLS
- Myofascial pain, difficulty in concentration, emotional lability, divorce and job loss frequently accompany post-traumatic headache
- Headaches typically worse in the morning are: pseudotumor cerebri, sleep apnea, carbon monoxide poisoning, and hypertensive
- Frequent use of Ergotamine, caffeine/Butalbital containing products, NSAIDs, and Excedrin can cause rebound headaches

References

Goadsby PJ, et al. Migraine—current understanding and treatment. N Engl J M 2002;346:257–70.

Clinch CR. Evaluation of acute headaches in adults. Am Fam Phys 2001;63:685–92.

Holroyd KA, et al. Management of chronic tension-type headache with tricyclic antidepressant therapy, stress management therapy, and their combination: a randomized controlled trial. JAMA 2001;285:2208.

Parsekyan D. Migraine prophylaxis in adult patients. West J Med Nov 2000;173:341–5.

National Headache Foundation. Standards of Care for Headache Diagnosis and Treatment. Chicago, IL: National Headache Foundation; 1996;6–7.

Michael B. Weinstock, MD
Geoffrey Eubank, MD

55. EVALUATION & MANAGEMENT OF DIZZINESS

I. EVALUATION: Initial step is to define type of dizziness

    A. Vertiginous dizziness: Illusion that either their body or the environment is moving (sensation of room spinning around the patient, sensation of standing on a ship) often associated with nausea (see next table, Evaluation and Management of Vertiginous Dizziness)

        1. Peripheral lesions of the vestibular nerve and inner ear

            a. Benign paroxysmal positional vertigo (PPV): Calcium carbonate crystals which have fallen against the cupula of the posterior semicircular canal

            b. Ménière's disease (Endolymphatic hydrops)

            c. Vestibular neuronitis

            d. Labyrinthitis (serous or suppurative)

            e. Cerebellopontine angle tumors (acoustic schwannoma)

            f. Traumatic vertigo (labyrinthine concussion): Following head trauma

        2. Central lesions of the CNS

            a. Brain stem or cerebellar infarct: The 4 Ds—Dizziness, Diplopia, Dysarthria and Dysphagia. Also, change in motor and/or sensory function

            b. Vertebrobasilar insufficiency: Same symptoms as above but occur transiently (seconds to minutes)

            c. Multiple sclerosis: Disease onset in young adulthood. MRI is abnormal in a majority of cases

            d. Migraine: Can have dizziness in addition to other associated symptoms, including dysarthria, paresthesias, and visual disturbances. Even without headache, patients with migraines have higher than normal rate of episodic dizziness (which is otherwise unexplained)

            e. Tumors of the posterior fossa or brainstem/cerebellar: Often have other signs of brainstem dysfunction

            f. Other

                i. CNS infection

                ii. Trauma: Intracranial bleed

                iii. Temporal lobe epilepsy

    B. Presyncope/syncope: Lightheadedness, graying of vision with sitting/standing, diaphoresis

        1. Orthostatic hypotension: Sensation of light-headedness/vision going gray when standing or sitting up. Results from abnormal regulation of blood pressure

            a. Dehydration, blood loss

GEN

  b. Reflexive: Cough, valsalva, micturition
  c. Abnormal carotid baroreceptor response
 2. Cardiac: Valvular dysfunction, outflow obstruction, arrhythmia, ischemia
 3. Neuropathy (autonomic): Diabetic or alcoholic neuropathy, Guillain-Barre syndrome, nutritional
 4. Meds: Antihypertensives, vasodilators, anti-Parkinson drugs
C. Imbalance and ataxia (disequilibrium): Imbalance, abnormal gait, lack of coordination
 1. Neuropathy (peripheral): Diabetes, B_{12} deficiency, tabes dorsalis
 2. Vascular: Carotid insufficiency, CVA, migraine, anemia
 3. Age related: Unfamiliar surroundings, poor lighting at night, sedative meds, cognitive defect
 4. Poor vision: Diplopia, decreased acuity
 5. Other
  a. Neoplastic
  b. Metabolic disorders: Hypoglycemia
  c. Trauma: Intracranial bleed, postconcussive syndrome
  d. Infectious: CNS infection
D. Psychogenic dizziness: Symptoms are vague and imprecise (feeling apart from environment, fatigue, fullness in the head). Often associated with anxiety, panic disorders, hyperventilation syndrome. Diagnosis of exclusion

II. HISTORY
 A. Define the type of dizziness
 B. Provoking factors: Positional changes, changes in head positions
 C. Acuity of onset
 D. Aural symptoms: Hearing loss, tinnitus
 E. Focal neuro symptoms
 F. Visual symptoms: Diplopia, decreased acuity
 G. Cardiac symptoms: Palpitations, chest pain, shortness of breath
 H. Infectious symptoms
 I. Past medical history: Diabetes, alcohol, syphilis, migraine headaches, cardiac disease
 J. Meds
 K. Trauma
 L. Recent travel history (cruises and long plane flights can induce dizziness)

III. PHYSICAL EXAM
 A. Orthostatic BP and pulse
 B. Neuro exam: Cranial nerves, finger to nose, dysdiadochokinesia and Romberg—distinguish central from peripheral lesions
 C. Eye: Visual acuity, extra-ocular muscles, fundi and discs
 D. Ear: Tympanic membrane, external ear. Hearing test
 E. Neck: Nuchal rigidity or pain with movement. Reproduction of symptoms with movement. Carotid bruits
 F. Cardiac: Murmurs, signs of ischemia
 G. Gait
 H. Hallpike maneuver: Patient sits on bed while clinician supports head. Patient rapidly assumes supine position first with head straight, then turned 45° left then 45° right. With reproduction of symptoms, vertigo and nystagmus, benign positional vertigo is suggested. Also vertigo duration less than 1 minute, latency 2–20 seconds, unidirectional nystagmus, fatigability

IV. OTHER TESTS—As indicated by history and physical
 A. Caloric testing: Inject 5cc (then 10cc or 20cc if no response) of ice water over 5 seconds at posteroinferior quadrant of TM and observe for nystagmus, nausea and vertigo. If no response then vestibular apparatus is not functioning
 B. Audiography: Low frequency loss in Ménière's disease
 C. Electronystagmography (ENG): Most helpful in Ménière's disease and benign positional vertigo. Helpful in cases with medicolegal implications and psychogenic vertigo

GEN

D. **Brain MRI or CT:** MRI is much more sensitive than CT for dizziness since the region of the brain to be evaluated is usually the posterior fossa. Usually performed with contrast to help pick up acoustic neuromas

E. **Lumbar puncture:** Helpful when suspect multiple sclerosis, meningitis, or subarachnoid bleed

F. **Cardiac evaluation** if presyncope: Consider ECG, ECHO, EPS depending on symptoms

EVALUATION AND MANAGEMENT OF VERTIGINOUS DIZZINESS

Condition	Vertiginous symptoms	Nystagmus	Comments	Associated symptoms	Management
Benign positional vertigo	Vertigo: Positional, provoked by certain head positions.	Postional with latency, brief duration and fatigability. Horizontal.	Usually idiopathic, may result from head trauma, ear surgery, or sequelae of vestibular neuronitis.	None.	Positioning maneuvers to rid the posterior semicircular canal of debris.
Ménière's disease	Vertigo: Often with nausea and vomiting that lasts hours (not days or weeks).	Spontaneous during critical stage, postural in 25% of patients during first few weeks after an attack. Caloric testing reveals loss or impairment of thermally induced nystagmus on involved side.	Triad: Vertigo, tinnitus, hearing loss. Both ears affected in 30–50% of patients.	1. Tinnitus (louder during attacks). 2. Sensorineural hearing loss (low frequency). 3. Fullness in ear during attack.	Goal: To lower endolymphatic pressure. 1. Low salt diet (<2g Na$^+$/day). 2. Diuretics (HCTZ 50–100mg/day). 3. Surgical decompression.
Vestibular neuronitis	Vertigo accompanied by nausea and vomiting lasting days to weeks. Acute onset.	Increases when gaze is directed away from affected ear and is suppressed with visual fixation.	Auditory function *not* affected. BPV may develop as sequelae.	Antecedent or concomitant acute viral illness. Does not recur.	Symptomatic.
Labyrinthitis	Acute onset of vertigo *and* hearing loss which lasts 3–5 days. Rapid head movements may bring on vertigo.	Same as vestibular neuronitis.	Hearing loss may be total and permanent. Need to differentiate viral (serous) from bacterial (suppurative) labyrinthitis.	Antecedent or concomitant acute viral illness. Does not recur.	Tapered oral prednisone may be helpful. Suppurative labyrinthitis must be treated with antibiotics.
Acoustic schwannoma (acoustic neuroma)	Vertigo: Usually late, more often a progressive feeling of imbalance. Occasionally provoked by sudden head movements.	Spontaneous type frequently present.	Asymmetric sensorineural hearing loss. Usually unsteadiness and imbalance. Vertigo occurs in <20% of cases. Tinnitus is common. Diagnosed with MRI scanning.	1. Facial weakness. 2. Diplopia. 3. Headache. 4. Elevated CSF protein. 5. Hyperesthesia or hypoesthesia in distribution of eighth or fifth cranial nerve.	Surgery.
CNS vertigo	Vertigo: Nearly always positional — provoked by certain head positions.	Usually accompanies the vertigo.		1. Usually in the elderly. 2. Symptoms associated with arteriosclerosis, brainstem ischemia (visual symptoms), or cervical arthritis.	Directed to specific etiology.

V. SYMPTOMATIC MANAGEMENT OF TRUE VERTIGO

A. **Acute vertigo:** First few days
1. Vestibular suppressants
   a. **Meclizine**: 12.5–25mg PO Q6hrs PRN
   b. **Valium**: 2–5mg PO Q6hrs PRN
2. Antiemetics: **Compazine** or **Phenergan**. PO or rectal
3. Bedrest
4. Hospitalize if dehydrated or for other medical reasons
B. **Subacute vertigo**
1. Stop vestibular suppressants

2. Vestibular exercises
C. Benign paroxysmal positional vertigo (BPPV): Perform Epley maneuver. Maneuver is 80+% effective for this condition and has been demonstrated effective in the primary care setting. Don't use with known severe cervical spine disease or high grade carotid/vertebrobasilar disease

1. Step A: Perform the Dix-Hallpike test with the patient's head rotated 45° toward the affected (right) ear, the neck slightly extended, and the chin pointed slightly upward
2. Step B: When the vertigo and nystagmus provoked by the Dix-Hallpike test stop, rotate the patient's head about the rostral-caudal body axis until the unaffected ear is downward
3. Step C: Further rotate the head and body until the patient is face down, and maintain this position for 10 to 15 seconds
4. Step D: Keeping the head facing toward the shoulder on the unaffected side, bring the patient to a seated position and keep the head tilted so that the chin points slightly downward
5. Have patient sleep at 45–90⁰ angle for next 1–2 nights

CLINICAL PEARLS

- Patients with BPPV (especially those who respond favorably to maneuvers) do not generally need further testing. BPPV recurs about 30% of the time over the next 30 months
- Gait disturbance can be seen in central and peripheral vertigo
- In patients with multiple sclerosis, vertigo is the initial complaint in 5% and ultimately occurs in 50% of patients
- Symptoms of Ménière's disease may be mimicked in secondary and tertiary syphilis. Consider screening all patients with Ménière's disease with VDRL or RPR
- The average time from onset of symptoms to diagnosis of acoustic neuroma is 4yrs with an incidence of 1 case in 100,000 persons

References

Froehling DA, et al. The canalith repositioning procedure for the treatment of benign paroxysmal positional vertigo: a randomized controlled trial. Mayo Clin Proc 2001;75:695–700.

Kapoor WN. Primary care: syncope. N Engl J Med 2000;343:1856.

Furman JM, Cass SP. Primary care: benign paroxysmal positional vertigo. N Engl J Med 1999;341:1590.

King WM. Dizziness, hearing loss, and tinnitus. Arch Neurol 1999;56:1533.

Lawson J, et al. Diagnosis of geriatric patients with severe dizziness. J Am Geriatr Soc Jan 1999;47:12–7.

Baloh RW. Vertigo. Lancet Dec 5, 1998;352: 1841–6.

Hotson JR, Baloh RW. Acute vestibular syndrome. N Engl J Med 1998;339:680–5.

John A. Vaughn, MD

56. Prevention & Management Of CVAs

I. INTRODUCTION
A. Approximately 750,000 strokes occur/yr in the US
B. Cost of all strokes is $40 billion annually
C. Stroke is the third leading cause of death

II. TYPES OF STROKE
A. Ischemic infarct (80%): Results from decrease in bloodflow to a specific area of brain. In transient ischemic attack (TIA), symptoms last < 24 hrs
B. Intracranial hemorrhage (15%): Results from rupture of a blood vessel into specific area of brain
C. Subarachnoid hemorrhage (5%): Results from rupture of a blood vessel into subarachnoid space

Types of Stroke			
	Headache	**Decreased level of consciousness**	**Focal deficits**
Ischemic infarct	- (+ with embolism)	-	+
Intracranial hemorrhage	+	+	+
Subarachnoid hemorrhage	+	+	-

III. ETIOLOGY OF ISCHEMIC STROKE
  A. Embolic (20%): Cardiac (atrial fibrillation, MI, valvular disease), aortic
  B. Large vessel (20%): Carotid, vertebrobasilar
  C. Small vessel (lacunar) (25%)
  D. Cryptogenic/unusual (35%): Vasculitis, hypercoagulability, HIV, etc.

IV. RISK FACTORS
  A. Non-modifiable: Age, gender, race/ethnicity, family history
  B. Modifiable: Hypertension is strongest risk factor for stroke; others include diabetes mellitus, hyperlipidemia, smoking, excessive ETOH intake, cardiac disease (especially atrial fibrillation), oral contraceptives, hormone replacement therapy
  C. Risk factor management is the cornerstone of prevention

V. HISTORY
  A. Prior TIAs (amaurosis fugax, etc.) often are harbingers of future stroke
  B. Severe headache or decreased level of consciousness suggests hemorrhage
  C. Type of symptoms (and exam) should help localize lesion
    1. Anterior circulation (carotid circulation and branches)—contralateral numbness, weakness, visual field defect. Left sided cortical lesions often have language difficulties (aphasia), while right side lesions often have neglect
    2. Posterior circulation (vertebrobasilar circulation)—often times have "crossed signs" (e.g., right sided weakness, left sided numbness). Diplopia, dizziness, dysarthria, dysphagia (the "four D's") and gait ataxia are also seen

VI. EXAMINATION: Complete neuro exam, cardiac exam (rhythm, murmurs), vascular exam (especially carotid bruits), ophthalmologic (retinal emboli), and vital signs

VII. DIFFERENTIAL DIAGNOSIS: Todd's paralysis (postepileptic paralysis), hypoglycemia, complicated migraine, conversion disorder or malingering, brain tumor, drug overdose, Bell's palsy

VIII. EVALUATION: To evaluate stroke and rule out stroke "mimics" (migraine, seizure, mass lesions, multiple sclerosis, hypoglycemia, etc.)
  A. Neuroimaging
    1. CT head: Usually first step
      a. Quick, rules out hemorrhage easily
      b. Not sensitive for posterior fossa strokes or early infarcts
    2. MRI head
      a. Relatively slow (problem for claustrophobic or those that can't stay still)
      b. Visualization of posterior fossa stroke
      c. Use restricted in patients with pacemakers, aneurysm clips, etc.
      d. Routine MRI more sensitive for acute stroke than for CT
      e. Diffusion and perfusion techniques extremely sensitive for acute stroke and can localize areas of poor perfusion
  B. Laboratory
    1. Routine: CBC with platelets, glucose, PT/PTT, lipid profile, electrolytes, BUN/Cr,

liver enzymes can help establish other medical illnesses/issues
2. Vasculitis or hypercoagulable state (especially in young patients without risk factors): ESR, ANA, protein C & S, antiphospholipid antibodies, RPR, antithrombin III, Factor V and II

C. Cardiac
1. Rhythm: EKG and Holter monitor
2. Structural: ECHO to evaluate for structural heart disease. A TEE most sensitive, especially for unexplained stroke, stroke in the young

D. Vascular
1. Carotid Doppler/ultrasound: Safe/non-invasive, though operator dependent and difficulty with total vs. subtotal carotid occlusion. It only measures narrowing in the cervical carotid artery
2. MRA: Can evaluate cervical carotid, vertebrobasilar and intracranial circulation
3. CT angiography: Useful especially for those who cannot have MRA, can be done in the acute setting
4. Cerebral angiography
   1. Gold standard
   2. Invasive, with 0.5 to 3% complication rate (groin hematoma, dye reaction, stroke)

IX. PREVENTION

A. Cardiac source: Coumadin is recommended for prevention of stroke in atrial fibrillation. See Chapter 44, Atrial Fibrillation

Atrial Fibrillation		
Age (years)	**Risk factors***	**Treatment**
< 65	No	Aspirin
< 65	Yes	Warfarin
65-75	No	Aspirin or Warfarin
65-75	Yes	Warfarin
> 75	Yes or No	Warfarin
* Hypertension, LV dysfunction, prior TIA/stroke, systemic embolism. Goal INR should be 2.0 to 3.0 when warfarin is used		

B. Carotid disease: All patients should have risk factor modification and antiplatelet therapy
1. Symptomatic (unilateral amaurosis fugax or hemispheric TIA referable to the stenosed carotid artery)
   a. 70–99% stenosis: Clear benefit over medical therapy
   b. 50–69% stenosis: Less clear benefit, especially if surgical complication rate is not low
   c. < 50% stenosis, no benefit
2. Asymptomatic
   a. Slight reduction in risk of stroke with > 60% stenosis
   b. Benefit not realized if surgical complications > 3%
   c. Medical
      i. **Aspirin:** 50–325mg PO QD
      ii. **Clopidogrel (Plavix):** 75mg QD—slightly superior to Aspirin in preventing vascular events (peripheral, cardiac, or stroke) in patients that had a vascular event, stroke subset analysis less impressive, though not the primary endpoint of study. No need for routine lab monitoring. Can use in Aspirin- intolerant patients
      iii. **Aggrenox (Aspirin** 25mg and **Extended-Release Dipyridamole** 200mg): 1 PO BID. There is a > 20% reduction vs. Aspirin alone
      iv. **Ticlopidine (Ticlid):** 250 mg BID—demonstrated > 20% reduction in recurrent stroke vs. aspirin. Use limited by risk of hematologic abnormalities and need to monitor CBC (Q 2 weeks for 3 months and periodically thereafter)
      v. **Warfarin (Coumadin):** Found to be equivalent to **Aspirin** for recurrent stroke (after eliminating cardiac sources and significant carotid disease). Will likely be used less for routine stroke prophylaxis given safety issues and monitoring hassles

GEN

vi. As with all stroke patients, risk factor modification is essential

C. Hypertension: See Chapter 41, Hypertension

D. Hyperlipidemia: See Chapter 40, Hyperlipidemia

X. MANAGEMENT OF STROKE

A. Medical complications: Prevention is key

1. DVT: Prevent in patients at risk with **Heparin** 5000 U SQ Q12 hrs or low molecular weight **Heparin (Lovenox)** 1mg/kg SQ Q12hrs. Sequential compression devices and TED hose are recommended also (in addition to Heparin and especially those with Heparin contraindications)

2. Pneumonia: Evaluate and monitor swallowing function in all patients, especially those with speech or swallowing problems. Speech therapy and modified barium swallow if necessary, watch for fall risk, decubiti, UTI (especially with indwelling Foley, discontinue or avoid if possible)

B. Rehabilitation

1. Physical, occupational, and speech therapy as indicated

2. Transition to either inpatient (rehabilitation facility, nursing facility) or outpatient rehabilitation (therapists, social services can help guide appropriate choices)

3. Continued vigilance for medical complications, while maximizing functional improvements

4. Bowel/bladder programs

5. Need to involve caregivers from outset

CLINICAL PEARLS

- Acute stroke treatments are still being investigated (intra-arterial thrombolysis, neuroprotective agents). Angioplasty and stenting of carotid and other arteries are actively being studied, but still investigational
- While 10% of stroke patients are candidates for t-PA, only 1% receive treatment presently
- Lipid lowering agents (particularly HMGs) help prevent stroke, even in patients with normal lipid profiles (possibly by a different mechanism than lipid management)
- Non-US studies have suggested antihypertensive treatments (ACE inhibitors and diuretics) decrease the risk of recurrent stroke, even in normotensive individuals
- Isolated dizziness, confusion, or syncope is unlikely indicator of TIA/stroke

References

Alamowitch S, et al. Risk, causes, and prevention of ischaemic stroke in elderly patients with symptomatic internal-carotid-artery stenosis. Lancet 2001;357:1154–60.

American Heart Association Scientific Statement. Primary prevention of ischemic stroke. A statement for healthcare professionals from the Stroke Council of the American Heart Association. Circulation 2001;103:167.

Mohr JP, et al. A comparison of warfarin and aspirin for the prevention of recurrent ischemic stroke. N Engl J Med 2001;345:1444–51.

Inzitari D, et al. The causes and risk of stroke in patients with asymptomatic internal-carotid-artery stenosis. The North American Symptomatic Carotid Endarterectomy Trial Collaborators. N Engl J Med 2000;342:1693–1701.

Lees KR, et al. Secondary prevention of transient ischemic attack and stroke. West J Med Oct 2000;173:254–8.

Medical Letter Consultants. Aggrenox: a combination of antiplatelet drugs for stroke prevention. Med Lett Drugs Ther 2000;42:11–2.

Biller MD, et al. Guidelines for carotid endarterectomy: a statement for healthcare professionals from a special writing group of the Stroke Council, American Heart Association. Stroke 1998;29:554–62.

Boult C, Brummel-Smith K. Post-stroke rehabilitation guidelines. The Clinical Practice Committee of the American Geriatrics Society. J Am Geriatr Soc 1997;45(7):881–3.

Daniel M. Neides, MD
Steve Markovich, MD
Miriam Chan, PharmD
Geoffrey Eubank, MD

57. SEIZURE DISORDERS

I. DEFINITIONS
A. Seizure: A brief, sudden, excessive discharge of electrical activity in the brain that alters behavior
B. Epilepsy: Recurrent seizures without clear precipitating factors (such as alcohol withdrawal, hypoglycemia)

II. EPIDEMIOLOGY
A. 1 in 11 will have at least 1 seizure
B. US 1.5 million with active epilepsy
C. 7 million with epilepsy at some time
D. Peaks in infancy and again later in life

III. SEIZURE CLASSIFICATION
A. Reactive: Abnormal reaction of an otherwise normal brain (febrile, hypoglycemia)
B. Symptomatic: Secondary to underlying structural or biochemical abnormality
C. Idiopathic: No known cause, except for possibly genetic

IV. PRINCIPAL TYPES OF SEIZURES

PRINCIPAL TYPES OF SEIZURES

TYPE OF SEIZURE	CLINICAL FEATURES
Generalized Absence seizures (petit mal)	Seizure begins rapidly, with a brief period of unresponsiveness (average, 10 seconds} and rapid recovery; there may be increased or decreased muscle tone, automatisms, or mild clonic movement— Seizure can be precipitated by hyperventilation; age at first seizure, 3-20 yr
Primarily generalized tonic-clonic seizures (grand mal)	Loss of consciousness occurs without warning or is preceded by myoclonic jerks; clinical features are similar to those of a secondarily generalized partial seizure
Partial Simple partial seizures (focal)	Signs and symptoms may be motor, sensory, autonomic, or psychic, depending on the location of the electrical discharge; consciousness is not impaired
Complex partial seizures (temporal lobe or psychomotor)	Seizure may begin with no warning or with motor, sensory, autonomic, or psychic signs or symptoms; consciousness is impaired automatisms (automatic acts of which the patient has no recollection) may occur; seizure is often followed by a period of confusion
Secondarily generalized partial seizures (tonic-clonic, or grand mal)	Seizures may begin with motor, sensory, autonomic or psychic signs or symptoms; consciousness is lost, with tonic increase in muscle tone; subsequent rhythmic (clonic) jerks -subside slowly; patient is comatose after seizure and recovers slowly; tongue biting or incontinence, or both may occur

Table modified from Brown TR, Holmes GL. Epilepsy. N Engl J Med 2001;344:1145. Used with permission.
Copyright 2001 Massachusetts Medical Society. All rights reserved.

GEN

V. ETIOLOGY

A. Infection: Meningitis, encephalitis, intracranial abscess

B. Trauma: Concussion, subdural/epidural hematoma, subarachnoid hemorrhage

C. Intoxication: Amphetamine, cocaine, PCP, Propoxyphene, Tricyclics, Phenothiazines, Wellbutrin, Theophylline, alcohol (withdrawal), Aspirin, Romazicon, Organophosphates, carbon monoxide, Lithium

D. Metabolic: Hyper/hypoglycemia, hyper/hyponatremia, hypocalcemia, hypomagnesemia, kernicterus, hypoxia, uremia, inborn errors of metabolism, pyridoxine deficiency

E. Degenerative: Alzheimer's, Huntington's, Tay-Sachs, leukodystrophies

F. Congenital: Abnormal brain development, cerebral palsy, neuronal migrational defects, tuberous sclerosis, etc.

G. Neoplasms: Primary or metastatic

H. Vascular: Ischemic or hemorrhagic stroke, hypertensive encephalopathy, eclampsia, global cerebral hypoperfusion

I. Idiopathic: Mesial temporal sclerosis, genetic, etc.

J. Febrile seizures: See VII. I. below

VI. EVALUATION

A. History: Provoking factors, meds, premonitory symptoms, eyewitness accounts. Focal features, tongue biting/blood in the mouth, incontinence, post-ictal state

B. Physical examination: Complete neurologic exam, skin lesions (rash, neurocutaneous stigmata), fever, infection in ears or sinuses, trauma, congenital anomalies

C. Laboratory (as indicated for initial seizure)

1. CBC/blood cultures (for febrile patients), glucose, electrolytes (including calcium/magnesium)
2. Drug tests (look for intoxications, antiepileptic levels, ETOH)
3. Lumbar puncture (in selected patients)

D. Neuroimaging

1. CT head: For emergent evaluation/new onset seizures (trauma, vascular)
2. MR head: Provides more detail, for more in depth evaluation of etiology
3. PET/SPECT scans: Primarily for presurgical evaluation

E. Electrodiagnostics

1. Routine EEG (yield for single EEG approximately 50% in patients with epilepsy
2. Sleep deprived EEG (more sensitive, combined with routine EEG, 80% sensitive)
3. EEG monitoring (for refractory epilepsy or evaluation of pseudoseizures)

F. Differential diagnosis: Panic attacks, syncope, breath holding spell, pseudoseizures, sleep disorders (narcolepsy), migraine, TIA, episodic dyscontrol syndrome (rage attacks), Ménière's disease, movement disorders

VII. MANAGEMENT

A. Indications for meds

1. Two or more unprovoked seizures
2. Single seizure with risk factors (abnormal EEG, certain neuroimaging abnormalities, certain hereditary epilepsies including family history of seizures

B. Usual starting meds—(choose med based on seizure type)

1. Generalized tonic-clonic seizures
   a. **Divalproex Sodium (Depakote)**
   b. **Phenytoin (Dilantin)**
2. Absence (petit mal) seizures
   a. **Ethosuximide (Zarontin)**
   b. **Divalproex Sodium (Depakote)**
3. Partial seizures
   a. **Carbamazepine (Tegretol)**
   b. **Divalproex Sodium (Depakote)**
   c. **Oxcarbazepine (Trileptal)**
   d. **Phenytoin (Dilantin)**

C. Common side effects with all meds are sedation, dizziness, ataxia, headache, nausea, and rash

D. Usual doses of antiepileptic drugs in patients ≥ age 16

GEN

USUAL DOSAGES OF ANTIEPILEPTIC DRUGS IN PATIENTS 16 YEARS OF AGE OR OLDER*

DRUG	STARTING DOSE mg/day	DOSE FREQUENCY	DOSE INCREASE	MAINTENANCE DOSE mg/day	THERAPEUTIC RANGE OF PLASMA CONCENTRATIONS µg/ml
Carbamazepine (Carbatrol, Tegretol, Tegretol-XR)	400	Carbatrol or Tegretol-XR, twice a day; Tegretol or generic, three times a day	200 mg/day at 1-wk intervals	600-1200	4-12
Divalproex sodium (Depakote)	500-1000	Twice a day	250 mg/day at 1-wk intervals	1000-3000	50-150
Ethosuximide (Zarontin)	500	Twice a day	250 mg/day at 1-wk intervals	1000-2000	40-120
Gabapentin (Neurontin)	900	Three times a day	300 mg/day at 24-hr intervals	900-3600	Not established
Lamotrigine† (Lamictal)	50	Twice a day	50 mg/day at 2-wk intervals‡	300-500	Not established
Levetiracetam (Keppra)	1000	Twice a day	1000 mg/day at 2-wk intervals	1000-3000	Not established
Oxcarbazepine (Trileptal)	600	Twice a day	600 mg/day at 1-wk intervals	600-2400	Not established
Phenobarbital	90	Daily	30 mg/day at 4-wk intervals	90-120	10-40
Phenytoin (Dilantin)	300	Daily	100 mg/day at 4-wk intervals§	300-500	10-20
Primidone (Mysoline, Neurosyn)	100-125	Three times a day	Days 1-3, 100-150 mg daily at bedtime; days 4-6, 100-125 mg twice a day; days 7-9, 100-125 mg three times a day; day 10, 250 mg three times a day	750-1000	5-12
Tiagabine (Gabitril)	4	Twice a day to four times a day	4-8 mg/day at 1-wk intervals	32-56	Not established
Topiramate (Topamax)	25-50	Twice a day	25-50 mg/day at 1-wk intervals	200-400	Not established
Zonisamide (Zonegran)	100	Twice a day	100 mg/day at 2-wk intervals	400-600	Not established

*Data are from Browne and Holmes.⁵ Information on dosages for younger patients is also available from this source.

†The information shown is for persons who are taking lamotrigine in combination with an enzyme-inducing antiepileptic drug (carbamazepine, phenobartial, phenytoin, or primidone) and who are not taking valproic acid. For persons who are not taking an enzyme-inducing antiepileptic drug or who are taking valproic acid, the dose schedule is different. Consult the package insert.

‡After four weeks, the daily dose can be increased by 100 mg every two weeks.

§The dose should be increased at a rate of 30 to 50 mg per day at four-week intervals when the phenytoin plasma concentration is higher than 10 µg per milliliter.

E. Women's issues
   1. Many seizure meds can increase failure rate for oral contraceptives (an additional barrier method is an option)
   2. Many seizure meds increase the risk of birth defects (especially **Valproic Acid** and **Carbamazepine** which increase risk of neural tube defects)

F. Discontinuing therapy
   1. Continue meds for 2yrs after starting (even if patient is seizure free during this time)
   2. Risk of recurrent seizures is 25% for patients without risk factors, 50% for patients with risk factors

G. Surgery
   1. Refractory seizures with identifiable seizure focus—may benefit from surgical resection (especially mesial temporal epilepsy)
   2. Vagal nerve stimulator—refractory patients

H. Driving: Laws vary state to state, but most range from 6–12 months seizure free—it is usually the physician's responsibility to report patient to BMV or inform patient of obligations

I. Febrile Seizures
   1. The most common seizure of childhood
   2. Diagnosis: Tonic-clonic movements associated with temperature > 100.4° F (38.0° C)
     a. Generally in children between 6 months and 5yrs
     b. Duration of seizure activity < 15 minutes
     c. Seizure activity within 24hrs of onset of fever
     d. Normal development and neurologic exam
     e. No family history of epilepsy
     f. Diagnosis of febrile seizure is a diagnosis of exclusion
   3. Appropriate laboratory tests, including lumbar puncture, should be considered in any child with a seizure, especially if < 18 months old
   4. If child with febrile seizure meets all of the criteria listed above (Section VII. I. 2) *and* child appears fine, an antipyretic may be given and no further studies or treatment are necessary. Risk of recurrence is 25–30% with simple febrile seizures

CLINICAL PEARLS
   • Epilepsy peaks in childhood (75% begin in childhood) and again in later adulthood
   • Most common reason for seizure recurrence (and status epilepticus) is med noncompliance
   • After meds are discontinued, 80% of recurrences will occur during first 4 months and

GEN

90% within first year
- Recurrence rate for a single, unprovoked seizure is 30 to 70% (higher for abnormal tests or exam)
- In 50% of children with seizures, the etiology will be undetermined despite an appropriate work-up
- Breath-holding spells, benign paroxysmal vertigo, and syncope are often confused with seizures and should be considered in differential diagnosis

References

Silverman IE, et al. Poststroke seizures. Arch Neurol 2002;59:195.

Van Ness PC. Therapy for the epilepsies. Arch Neurol 2002;59:732.

Browne TR, Holmes GL. Epilepsy. N Engl J Med 2001;344:1145.

Engel J, Jr. A proposed diagnostic scheme for people with epileptic seizures and with epilepsy: report of the ILAE Task Force on Classification and Terminology. Epilepsia 2001;42:796–803.

Begley CE, et al. The cost of epilepsy in the United States: an estimate from population-based clinical and survey data. Epilepsia 2000;41:342.

Hirtz D, et al. Practice parameter: evaluating a first nonfebrile seizure in children: report of the Quality Standards Subcommittee of the American Academy of Neurology, the Child Neurology Society, and the American Epilepsy Society. Neurol 2000;55:616–23.

Jason J. Diehl, MD
Michael B. Weinstock, MD

GEN

58. CONCUSSION EVALUATION

DEFINITION: A concussion is a transient post-traumatic alteration in mental status that may or may not involve loss of consciousness

I. GENERAL
   A. Concussion may go unrecognized by coaches as the athlete may feel pressure to continue sports participation
   B. Multiple concussions may result in cumulative neurophysiologic deficits
   C. Concussion sustained while patient is still symptomatic from an earlier concussion may result in progressive cerebral edema
   D. Brain injuries are sustained by approximately 10% of high school and 20% of college football players

II. PATHOPHYSIOLOGY: Possible causes of altered level of consciousness
   A. Axonal shear injury: Often not evident in CT or MRI
   B. Cortical contusion: May result in cerebral edema, ischemia, and mass effect
   C. Intracranial hemorrhage

III. HISTORY
   A. Confusion and/or disorientation currently or at the time of event
   B. Amnesia to event and length of time of amnesia
   C. Headache, duration, frequency, exacerbating factors, etc.
   D. Dizziness/vertigo
   E. Nausea/vomiting
   F. Vision disturbances (blurred, double, photophobia)
   G. Sensitivity to noise or tinnitus
   H. Fatigue or sleep disturbances
   I. Memory dysfunction/poor attention and concentration, irritability
   J. Anxiety/depression
   K. Intolerance of bright lights or difficulty focusing
   L. Exacerbation of symptoms with exertion

IV. PHYSICAL EXAM
  A. Altered levels of consciousness
  B. Dazed appearance
  C. Unsteady gait
  D. Slurred speech or incoherent speech
  E. Vacant facial expression
  F. Inappropriate behavior
  G. Pupillary concordance/accommodation, papilledema or retinal hemorrhages
  H. Poor concentration/forgetting plays
  I. Apprehension
  J. Incoordination

V. CLASSIFICATION

Commonly Used Classification Systems			
System	**Grade 1 (mild)**	**Grade 2 (moderate)**	**Grade 3 (severe)**
Colorado	Confusion No PTA or LOC	Confusion and PTA No LOC	Any LOC
Cantu	No LOC PTA < 30 min	LOC < 5 min PTA > 30 min	LOC > 5 min PTA > 24 hrs
AAN	Confusion, no LOC Symptoms < 15 min	Confusion, no LOC Symptoms > 15 min	Any LOC

LOC = loss of consciousness; PTA = post-traumatic amnesia;
Note: 1. The Colorado Medical Society guidelines (1991) have been adopted by the
            National College Athletic Association (NCAA)
         2. Cantu guidelines (1986) have been adopted by the American College of Sports
            Medicine
         3. AAN = American Association of Neurology; published guidelines in 1997

VI. RETURN TO PLAY

Return to Play			
System	**Grade 1**	**Grade 2**	**Grade 3**
Colorado	1st May RTP if no Sx for 20 min	RTP if no Sx for 1 wk	RTP in 1 mo (if no Sx last 2 wks of the mo)
	2nd RTP in 1 wk if no Sx	RTP if no Sx for 1 mo	Terminate season
	3rd Terminate season	Terminate season	
Cantu	1st May RTP same day if totally asymptomatic	No RTP that day, may RTP if no Sx for 1 wk	RTP in 1 mo (if no Sx for last wk of the mo)
	2nd RTP in 2 wk if no Sx for last wk	RTP in 1 mo if no Sx for 1 wk	Terminate season
	3rd Terminate season	Terminate season	
AAN	1st May RTP if no Sx for 15 min	RTP if no Sx for 1 wk	If LOC brief (seconds), RTP if no Sx 1 wk If LOC prolonged, may RTP if no Sx 2 wks
	2nd RTP if no Sx for 1 wk	RTP if no Sx for 2 wks	RTP if no Sx for 1 mo
	3rd No recommendation	No recommendation	

RTP = return to play; Sx = symptoms

Sources: Practice parameter: the management of concussion in sports (summary statement). Report of the Quality Standards
        Subcommittee. Neurology 1997;48:581–5.
     Guidelines for the management of concussion in sports. Colorado Medical Society Guidelines of 1991. American Academy of
        Neurology.
     Cantu RC. Guidelines for return to contact sports after a cerebral concussion. Phys Sports Med 1986;14(10):75–6, 79, 83.

VII. IMAGING

A. CT scan is the initial imaging modality of choice. Consider acute CT with:
   1. Focal neurological changes/mental status changes
   2. Loss of consciousness greater than 1 minute (some recommend CT with any loss of consciousness)
   3. Lethargy, vomiting, or amnesia
   4. Weakness of paresthesias
   5. Incontinence
   6. Seizure

B. CT scan chronically indicated for:
   1. Persistent headaches
   2. Difficulty concentrating or other signs of post-concussive syndrome
   3. Any of the symptoms/signs listed above

C. If symptoms persist or progress despite a negative head CT, MRI may be useful in detection of small areas of contusion

VIII. ASSOCIATED CONDITIONS

A. **Second-impact Syndrome:** Condition can be seen in athletes that return to play prior to full resolution of concussion symptoms and experience second, even mild head trauma. Pathophysiology involves loss of vascular autoregulation, vascular engorgement, and subsequent brain herniation. Syndrome is usually fatal

B. **Postconcussive Syndrome**
   1. Continuation of symptoms (headache, dizziness, fatigue, irritability, depression, anxiety, apathy, and impaired concentration) for days to months after any grade of concussion. Approximately 10% will have continued symptoms after 1yr
   2. Patient should be evaluated with a CT or MRI scan and neuropsychiatric testing

C. **Intracranial hemorrhage/hematoma:** Any patient with prolonged loss of consciousness, deterioration of symptoms, or other signs and symptoms of intracranial pathology needs immediate evaluation and imaging

CLINICAL PEARLS

- 20 to 50% of patients with epidural hemorrhage will have a "lucid interval" before the onset of neurologic deterioration
- Epidural hemorrhage usually results from tearing of middle meningeal artery; subdural hemorrhage results from tearing of bridging veins or dura
- MRI is more sensitive than CT is showing small areas of axonal shear injury and cerebral contusion. CT is more sensitive at showing an acute bleed

References

Aubry M, et al. Summary and agreement statement of the 1st International Symposium on Concussion in Sport. Vienna 2001. Clin J Sports Med 2002;12(1):6–11.

Kushner DS. Concussion in sports: minimizing the risk for complications. Am Fam Phys 2001;64:1007–14.

Cantu RC. Return to play guidelines after a head injury. Clin Sports Med 1998:17(1):45–59.

Practice parameter: the management of concussion in sports (summary statement). Report of the Quality Standards Subcommittee Neurology 1997;48:581–5.

Guidelines for the management of concussion in sports. Colorado Medical Society Guidelines of 1991. American Academy of Neurology.

Cantu RC. Guidelines for return to contact sports after a cerebral concussion. Phys Sports Med 1986;14(10):75–6, 79, 83.

GEN

Daniel M. Neides, MD
Michael B. Weinstock, MD   Hut / Slistra / Sengupto / Lumen

59. LIVER FUNCTION TESTS

I. INTRODUCTION

A. LFTs typically include ALT, AST, alkaline phosphatase, bilirubin, and GGT. They are indirect measures of liver function. Protime/INR and albumin are a more accurate (but still indirect) measurement of the liver's function

B. First step in evaluation of abnormal test result in asymptomatic patient is to repeat the test

C. Ultrasound is the most useful *initial* radiographic study of the liver, especially for cholestasis

II. HISTORY

A. Abdominal pain/discomfort

B. Nausea/vomiting/diarrhea, color of stools and urine

C. Weight loss, fever, fatigue, anorexia, amenorrhea

D. Jaundice

E. Arthralgias (autoimmune hepatitis, hemochromatosis), pruritus (primary sclerosing cholangitis, primary biliary cirrhosis)

F. Meds

G. Past medical history: History of hepatitis, COPD (α-1 anti-trypsin deficiency), transfusions

H. Social history: Alcohol and drugs, sexual history, travel history

I. Family history

III. PHYSICAL EXAM

A. General: Fever

B. Eyes: Scleral icterus or Kayser-Fleischer rings (Wilson's disease)

C. Abdomen: Tenderness, enlargement of liver or spleen, ascites, palpable gall bladder (Courvoisier's sign)

D. Skin: Spider angioma or palmar erythema, jaundice and Dupuytren's contracture

E. Other: Signs of hypo/hyperthyroidism, gynecomastia, fetor hepatica, asterixis

IV. LIVER ENZYMES

A. Aminotransferases (ALT/AST)

1. Useful in diagnosing acute *hepatocellular disease*. There is poor correlation between liver damage and levels of aminotransferases

2. ALT is present in high concentrations in the liver whereas AST is found in liver, cardiac muscle, skeletal muscle, kidneys, brain, pancreas, lungs, leukocytes, and erythrocytes

3. Increases in both ALT and AST indicate hepatocellular necrosis or inflammation

4. Etiology

   a. Hepatic causes of elevated aminotransferases: Alcohol-related liver injury, chronic hepatitis B and C, autoimmune hepatitis, meds (see below), hepatic steatosis (fatty infiltration of liver), nonalcoholic steatohepatitis, hemochromatosis, Wilson's disease, α-1-antitrypsin deficiency

   b. Non-hepatic causes of elevated aminotransferases: celiac sprue, inherited and acquired muscle diseases, exercise

5. In liver disease secondary to alcohol, the transaminase values rarely exceed 300 U/L. Levels that are markedly increased in an alcoholic patient suggest another etiology. AST/ALT > 2 is suggestive of alcohol-induced liver disease

6. Initial evaluation

   a. Obtain other LFTs if not done yet. If Alk Phos and GGT are elevated, consider obstructive etiology

   b. Consider meds as etiology, see V. below

   c. Evaluate for alcohol use and if AST/ALT are minimally increased or AST:ALT > 2:1, consider trial of abstinence and recheck in 4 weeks

   d. Testing for acute viral hepatitis including HAAb IgG, HAAb IgM, HBsAB, HBsAg, HBc IgG, HBc IgM, and possibly HC Ab or HC PCR. Viral hepatitis may show an increase in ALT and AST about 1 week preceding the onset of jaundice

   e. Consider other tests including:

      i. Ferritin and possibly iron saturation (hemochromatosis)

      ii. Serum ceruloplasmin (decreased levels in Wilson's disease)

      iii. Serum protein electrophoresis (autoimmune hepatitis, α-1 antitrypsin deficiency)

      iv. Serum antiendomysial and antigliadin antibodies (celiac sprue)

      v. Creatine kinase and aldolase (disorders of striated muscle)

  f. Ultrasound evaluation for obstructive picture of hepatic steatosis or nonalcoholic steatohepatitis

  g. If etiologies are not evident after history, physical, and further testing, consider liver biopsy

  h. If aminotransferases are elevated but less than 2 × upper limit of normal, then observation alone may be sufficient (as opposed to liver biopsy)

B. Alkaline Phosphatase (Alk Phos)

1. Elevation usually indicates cholestatic liver disease (defined as intra- or extrahepatic biliary obstruction)
2. Primarily found in liver, bone, intestines, kidney, WBCs, and placenta
3. Hepatic causes of elevated Alk Phos include:
  a. Cholestatic diseases or conditions include partial obstruction of bile ducts—primary biliary cirrhosis, primary sclerosing cholangitis, adult bile ductopenia, and cholestasis induced by the use of drugs such as anabolic steroids
  b. Infiltrative diseases include sarcoidosis, other types of granulomatous diseases, and less often, unsuspected metastasis of cancer to the liver
4. Is normally elevated in 3rd trimester of pregnancy
5. Initial evaluation
  a. If the Alk Phos is elevated, order a GGT to help differentiate liver vs. bone. If the GGT is normal, the elevation is most likely due to non-hepatic causes
  b. Initial tests include RUQ ultrasound (to assess for obstruction and to assess hepatic parenchyma) and antimitochondrial antibodies (to assess for primary biliary cirrhosis)
  c. If above tests are negative and Alk Phos is < 50% of upper limit of normal, may observe and follow
  d. If above tests are negative and Alk Phos is > 50% of upper limit of normal, consider liver biopsy and either endoscopic retrograde cholangiopancreatography (ERCP) or magnetic resonance cholangiopancreatography

C. Gamma-glutamyl Transpeptidase (GGT)

1. Elevated often seen in *cholestatic liver disease* (along with concurrent increased Alk Phos). Test is sensitive for liver disease or alcohol use, but not specific
2. Found in hepatocytes and biliary epithelial cells
3. Elevated in pancreatic disease, myocardial infarction, renal failure, chronic obstructive pulmonary disease, diabetes, alcoholism, and with drugs such as Phenytoin (Dilantin), and barbiturates
4. A GGT level which is disproportionately higher than the AST, ALT, or Alk Phos in a patient not taking Dilantin or barbiturates is likely secondary to alcohol
5. GGT may be increased in thyrotoxicosis, renal failure, status post myocardial infarction, pancreatitis, diabetes, and prostate CA

D. Bilirubin (Bili)

1. Bilirubin is an end-product of destruction of red blood cells. Unconjugated bili is bound to albumin in serum. When it gets to the liver, it is conjugated, becomes water-soluble, and is excreted in the bile. Bilirubin may be elevated from increased production, decreased uptake by the liver, decreased conjugation, decreased secretion from the liver, or blockage of the bile ducts
2. Direct (conjugated) hyperbilirubinemia is almost always due to hepatobiliary disease, whereas indirect (unconjugated) hyperbilirubinemia has many causes
3. Etiology
  a. Elevated indirect (unconjugated) hyperbilirubinemia
    i. Increased bilirubin production: Hemolytic anemias, hemolytic reactions, hematoma, pulmonary infarction
    ii. Impaired bilirubin uptake and storage: Posthepatitis hyperbilirubinemia, Gilbert's disease, Crigler-Najjar syndrome, drug reactions
  b. Elevated direct (conjugated) hyperbilirubinemia
    i. Hereditary cholestatic syndromes: Faulty excretion of bilirubin conjugates such as Dubin-Johnson syndrome, Rotor's syndrome
    ii. Hepatocellular dysfunction: Biliary epithelial damage (hepatitis, hepatic

GEN

cirrhosis), intrahepatic cholestasis (drugs, biliary cirrhosis, sepsis, postoperative jaundice), miscellaneous (spirochetal infections, mononucleosis, cholangitis, sarcoidosis, lymphomas, toxins)

   iii. Biliary obstruction: Choledocholithiasis, biliary atresia, carcinoma of bile duct, sclerosing cholangitis, pancreatitis, and pancreatic neoplasms

  4. Evaluation: Assess whether bilirubin elevation is direct or indirect and whether other LFTs are elevated. Determine if elevation is secondary to hepatocellular cause vs. obstructive vs. benign cause (Gilbert's disease or recurrent jaundice of pregnancy)

  5. Gilbert's disease: Benign, asymptomatic elevation of indirect bilirubin. Bili level is usually < 3mg/dL. Patients with Gilbert's disease have no evidence of hemolysis and other LFTs are normal. May be present in 7–10% of the population

E. Albumin

  1. Is synthesized in liver and excreted in blood. Good indicator (along with the Protime) of the liver's ability to function properly and make protein

  2. Is decreased with cirrhosis and with significant liver damage in addition to malnutrition, certain kidney diseases, and other rarer causes

  3. Trauma, sepsis, or severe burns may rapidly lower the albumin level secondary to fluid shifts

F. Prothrombin Time (Protime)/INR

  1. The liver makes all of the clotting factors, except factor VIII. With severe liver disease, the ability of the blood to clot may be compromised

  2. Elevated PT/INR may also be caused by *hepatocellular disease or Vitamin K deficiency*

  3. To determine the etiology of increased PT in patients with cholestasis, give **Vitamin K 10mg IM** and recheck PT/INR in 24hrs. If hepatocellular function is satisfactory, PT will improve by at least 30%

V. MEDICATIONS WHICH MAY CAUSE ELEVATIONS IN LIVER ENZYME LEVELS

  A. Antibiotics: Synthetic penicillins, Ciprofloxacin, Nitrofurantoin, Ketoconazole, Fluconazole, Isoniazid

  B. Antiepileptic drugs: Phenytoin, Carbamazepine

  C. HMG CoA reductase inhibitors: Simvastatin, Pravastatin, Lovastatin, Atorvastatin

  D. NSAIDS

  E. Sulfonylureas: Glipizide

  F. Herbal/homeopathic: Chaparral, Chinese herbs (Jin Bu Huan and Ephedra), gentian, germander, Alchemilla, senna, shark cartilage, Scutellaria

  G. Drugs: Anabolic steroids, cocaine, MMDMA (Ecstasy), phencyclidine (angel dust), glues and solvents

	General Patterns of Biochemical Liver Tests					
Test	**Hepatocellular Necrosis**			**Biliary Obstruction**		**Hepatic Infiltration**
	Toxin/Ischemia	**Viral**	**Alcohol**	**Complete**	**Partial**	
	Acetaminophen or shock liver	Hepatitis A or B		Pancreatic carcinoma	Hilar tumor, primary sclerosing cholangitis	Primary or metastatic carcinoma tuberculosis, *Mycobacterium avium-intracellulare* infection
Aminotransferases	50-100x	5-50x	2-5x	1-5x	1-5x	1-3x
Alkaline phosphatase	1-3x	1-3x	1-10x	2-20x	2-10x	1-20x
Bilirubin	1-5x	1-30x	1-30x	1-30x	1-5x	1-5x
Prothrombin time	Prolonged and unresponsive to vitamin K in severe disease			Often prolonged and responsive to parenteral vitamin K		Usually normal
Albumin	Decreased in chronic disease			Usually normal; decreased in advanced disease (i.e., cirrhosis)		Usually normal

*Table includes illustrative disorders for each category

Source: Feldman M, et al. Sleisenger & Fordtran's gastrointestinal and liver disease, 6th ed., Philadelphia: W. B. Saunders. Copyright © 1998. With permission from Elsevier.

CLINICAL PEARLS

- Jaundice is usually not clinically evident until bilirubin level is > 3
- In patients with AST>ALT by 2:1, 90% was from alcoholic liver disease. If the ratio is > 3:1, then 96% is from alcoholic liver disease. An alcohol user/abuser with elevated transaminases who stops drinking for 2–4 weeks should significantly lower those levels
- In patients who consume > 50g alcohol (about 4 drinks per day), incidence of alcoholic cirrhosis is 8–15% over 10yrs
- Abnormalities associated with drug-induced liver injury should resolve once drug has been stopped
- Most common causes of asymptomatic liver enzyme elevation are obesity and alcohol
- In an asymptomatic middle aged female with elevated liver enzymes, consider primary biliary cirrhosis and obtain a serum AMA
- In evaluating cholestasis, consider ultrasound early in the work-up to rule out bile duct enlargement
- Consider nonalcoholic steatohepatitis (NASH) in older, obese diabetics

References

Pratt DS, Kaplan MM. Evaluation of abnormal liver-enzyme results in asymptomatic patients. N Engl J Med 2000;342:1266–71.

Daniel S, et al. Prospective evaluation of unexplained chronic liver transaminase abnormalities in asymptomatic and symptomatic patients. Am J Gastroenterol 1999;94:3010–14.

Grant A, et al. Guidelines for the use of liver biopsy in clinical practice. Gut 1999;45 (suppl 4):IV1.

Kamath PS. Clinical approach to the patient with abnormal liver function test results. Mayo Clin Proc 1996;71:1089–94.

Michael B. Weinstock, MD
Dawn Mattern, MD

60. DIAGNOSIS & MANAGEMENT OF HEPATITIS B

I. BACKGROUND

- **A.** One of the major vaccine-preventable diseases
- **B.** Chronic hepatitis affects 400 million people worldwide and 1.25 million in the US
- **C.** Transmitted by blood or blood products (injection drug use, sexual activity, occupational exposure, vertical transmission)
- **D.** Incubation period is 3–180 days
- **E.** Of adult patients infected with hepatitis B:
  1. 95% recover completely
  2. 5% develop chronic hepatitis or chronic carrier state. 20% of those with chronic HBV develop cirrhosis within 20yrs
  3. Fulminant hepatitis in < 1% with a mortality rate of about 60%

II. INTERPRETATION OF LAB TESTS

- **A. Overview:** First look at HBsAg and HBsAb (see table below)
  1. *If the HBsAg is positive*, patient usually has either acute hepatitis B or chronic infection
  2. *If the HBsAb is positive*, patient usually has either had past infection (and is noninfectious and protected from hepatitis B) or has received the HBV vaccine
  3. If both are negative (rare), patient may be in the "window phase" (see below)
  4. If both are positive (rare), see below
- **B. Tests**
  1. **HBsAg:** First manifestation of HBV infection and persists throughout clinical illness. Persistence associated with chronic hepatitis and implies infectivity
  2. **HBsAb:** Occurs in most patients after clearance of HBsAg and implies noninfectivity and protection from recurrent HBV infection. (Occasionally, the appearance of HBsAb is delayed until clearance of HBsAg and during this "window phase," both HBsAb and HBsAg may be negative—see below)

3. **HBcAb IgM:** Appears during acute hepatitis B and indicates a diagnosis of acute hepatitis B
4. **HBcAb IgG:** Appears during acute hepatitis B and persists indefinitely
5. **HBeAg:** Indicates viral replication and infectivity
6. **HBeAb:** Follows HBeAg and signifies diminished viral replication
7. **HBV DNA:** Usually parallels the presence of HBeAg, but is a more precise marker of viral replication and infectivity

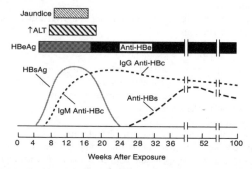

Source: Harrison's principles of internal medicine, 13th ed. New York, NY: McGraw-Hill, 1994:1458–83. Used with permission.

GEN

Common Serologic Patterns in Hepatitis B Virus Infection and Their Interpretation					
HBsAg	Anti-HBs	Anti-HBc	HBeAg	Anti-HBe	Interpretation
+	–	IgM	+	–	Acute hepatitis B
+	–	IgG[1]	+	–	Chronic hepatitis B with active viral replication
+	–	IgG	–	+	Chronic hepatitis B with low viral replication
+	+	IgG	+ or –	+ or –	Chronic hepatitis B with heterotypic anti-HBs (about 10% of cases)
–	–	IgM	+ or –	–	Acute hepatitis B
–	+	IgG	–	+ or –	Recovery from hepatitis B (immunity)
–	+	–	–	–	Vaccination (immunity)
–	–	IgG	–	–	False-positive; less commonly, infection in remote past

[1]Low levels of IgM anti-HBc may also be detected

Source: Tierney LM, et al. Current medical diagnosis and treatment, 2002. Stamford, CT: Appleton & Lange, 2002:680. Used with permission.

III. EVALUATION AND MANAGEMENT

A. Acute hepatitis B

1. Acute illness usually subsides over 2–3 weeks and lab values are normalized within 16 weeks unless patient develops chronic hepatitis
2. Clinical picture is variable, with symptoms ranging from asymptomatic (30%) to general malaise, myalgia, arthralgia, easy fatigability, anorexia, nausea/vomiting, diarrhea, fever/chills, jaundice
3. Physical exam: Hepatomegaly (> 50%), splenomegaly (15%), lymphadenopathy
4. Lab: Low WBC, elevated ALT or AST, elevated bilirubin and alkaline phosphatase, elevated prothrombin time (in severe hepatitis), mild proteinuria, and bilirubinuria
5. Management
   a. Acute disease: Symptomatic: rest, good diet, avoidance of hepatotoxins (alcohol, acetaminophen) and behaviors that transmit hepatitis B
   b. Long-term management: Follow LFTs and HBsAg every month until disappearance of HBsAg. When this occurs, check for appearance of HBsAb. If HBsAg is still positive after 6 months, patient has chronic hepatitis

   6. Indications for hospital admission
      a. Encephalopathy
      b. Prothrombin time prolonged > 3 seconds
      c. Intractable vomiting
      d. Hypoglycemia
      e. Age > 45yrs
      f. Immunosuppression
B. Chronic hepatitis B
   1. Definition: Persistent HBsAg > 6 months, chronic liver inflammation and character-
      istic histologic findings
      a. Chronic active hepatitis (replicative phase)
         i. Persistent HBsAg > 6 months
         ii. Persistent presence of HBV DNA or HBeAg
         iii. Liver injury (persistent elevation of LFTs > 6 months)
      b. Chronic persistent hepatitis (nonreplicative phase)
         i. Persistent HBsAg > 6 months
         ii. Absence of HBV DNA
         iii. Minimal liver injury (modest LFT elevation)
      **Remissions are characterized by the disappearance of HBV DNA and HBeAg
      (HBsAg persists). This means that the virus is in a nonreplicative phase, and
      patient is classified as having chronic persistent hepatitis—an important distinc-
      tion from chronic active hepatitis, which is characterized by higher infectivity
      and greater risk from progression to cirrhosis. Likelihood of converting from
      replicative to nonreplicative disease is approx. 10–15% /yr
   2. Symptoms and signs
      a. Chronic active hepatitis: Asymptomatic to severe constitutional symptoms, especially
         fatigue. Possibly jaundice, arthralgias, anorexia. End-stage includes ascites,
         edema, bleeding varices, hepatic encephalopathy, coagulopathy
      b. Chronic persistent hepatitis: Range from asymptomatic to mild symptoms; fatigue,
         anorexia, nausea, hepatomegaly
   3. Lab: Aminotransferase elevations (usually 100–1000 units), minimally elevated alkaline
      phosphatase, hyperbilirubinemia, hypoalbuminemia, prolongation of prothrombin time
   4. Medications
      a. Indicated for patients with active viral replication (positive HBeAg and HBV
         DNA) and chronic hepatitis (elevated aminotransferases)
      b. **Interferon α–2b (Intron A):** 5 million units daily or 10 million units 3 × a week
         SQ for 16 weeks; induces remission in up to 40% (normalization of aminotrans-
         ferase levels, disappearance of HBeAg and HBV DNA, and improved survival); sig-
         nificant side effects (the most frequent side effects are flu-like symptoms, particularly
         fever, headache, chills, myalgia, and fatigue)
      c. **Lamivudine (Epivir-HBV):** 100mg/day for 1–2yrs, induces remission in ~20%
         after 1yr, ~40% after 2yrs, better tolerated
   C. Patient has recovered from hepatitis B or has been vaccinated and is immune: No further
       action required

IV. INDICATIONS FOR HB IMMUNE GLOBULIN
   A. Sexual contacts of persons with HBV infection
   B. Individuals exposed to HBsAg containing material via mucous membranes or breaks in the skin
   C. Newborn infants of HBsAg positive mothers. Dose: 0.5mL IM at birth and first dose of hepatitis
       B vaccine concurrently at a separate site. Give 2nd and 3rd HB vaccine 1 month and 6 months
       after 1st dose
   D. Dose: 0.06 mL/kg IM within 7 days of exposure. Institute HB vaccine series

V. VACCINATIONS
   A. Timing: Initial, 1 month, 6 months
   B. Recombivax HB or Energerix-B

CLINICAL PEARLS

- Mortality rate with acute hepatitis B is 0.1–1%. It is higher with superimposed hepatitis D
- Risk of chronic infection in a neonate is 90% (when transmitted at the time of delivery by HBsAg positive mothers). They must receive the HB immune globulin, followed by the vaccine series
- HDV is a defective virus that only causes hepatitis in the presence of HBV infection. In US, infection is primarily with IV drug users
- There has been a 60% reduction in occupationally acquired hepatitis B infection due to immunization programs
- Hepatitis B vaccine series induces protective antibodies in 95% of healthy volunteers ages 20–39
- Incidence of hepatocellular carcinoma increases 200–300 fold in patients with chronic hepatitis B

References

Befeler AS, DiBisceglie AM. Hepatitis B. Inf Dis Clin North Amer 2000;14:3.

Hunt CM, et al. Clinic relevance of hepatitis B viral mutations. Hepatology 2000;31:1037.

Malik AH, et al. Chronic hepatitis B virus infection: Treatment strategies for the new millennium. Ann Intern Med 2000;132:723.

Chan HLY, Lok ASF. Hepatitis B in adults: a clinical perspective. Clin Liver Dis 1999;3:2.

Kienstag JL, et al. Lamivudine as initial treatment for chronic hepatitis B in the United States. N Engl J Med 1999;341:1256.

Daniel M. Neides, MD
Deb Frankowski, MD

61. Gastroesophageal Reflux Disease & Peptic Ulcer Disease

— PART ONE: GASTROESOPHAGEAL REFLUX DISEASE (GERD) —

I. SYMPTOMS OF REFLUX of gastric, biliary, pancreatic secretions into the esophagus: Heartburn, regurgitation, dyspepsia, chest pain

II. ETIOLOGY

- **A. Incompetent lower esophageal sphincter (LES):** Exacerbating factors include foods such as onion, fats, mint, ETOH, chocolate, caffeine as well as meds such as anticholinergics, ß-blockers, progesterone containing oral contraceptives, NSAIDs, Prednisone
- **B. Impaired esophageal peristalsis:** Associated diseases include CREST, scleroderma, Raynaud's, reflux-induced injury
- **C. Decreased salivation:** Associated conditions include Sjögren's, cigarette use, and anticholinergic meds
- **D. Delayed gastric emptying:** Associated conditions include gastroparesis, gastric outlet obstruction
- **E. Increased secretion of gastric acid:** Associated conditions include gastrinoma, Zollinger-Ellison syndrome
- **F. Direct irritants:** Citrus, tomato, cola, coffee (caffeine will decrease LESP)

III. EVALUATION

- **A. Empiric treatment** may be attempted in patients with typical "uncomplicated" symptoms (see V. Table 1)
- **B. Further evaluation,** as below, is required in patients with:
    1. Atypical symptoms (early satiety, anorexia, dysphagia, odynophagia, cough, chest pain, asthma, laryngitis)
    2. Patients > 50 with new onset symptoms
    3. Patients whose symptoms persist after 8 weeks of treatment
    4. Patients presenting with complications (anemia, guaiac positive stool, weight loss, stricture)

C. Patients treated empirically who do not respond in 2 weeks or whose symptoms recur after 6 weeks of treatment should undergo further evaluation

D. Evaluations include:

1. Upper endoscopy with biopsy: Best assessment of extent of mucosal damage, Barrett's esophagus, stricture
2. Esophageal pH monitoring: For diagnosing reflux and especially useful in patients with atypical symptoms of chronic cough, chest pain, asthma, laryngitis
3. Upper GI: May identify ulcers or stricture, but is insensitive for reflux
4. Esophageal motility: Useful assessment of motor function of the esophagus, especially preoperatively
5. Gastroesophageal scintigraphy: Noninvasive evaluation of esophageal emptying, especially useful in pediatric population
6. Although slightly controversial, there is currently no indication for *H. pylori* testing in uncomplicated GERD

Algorithm for Initial Evaluation and Treatment of Patients with Gastroesophageal Reflux Disease Symptoms

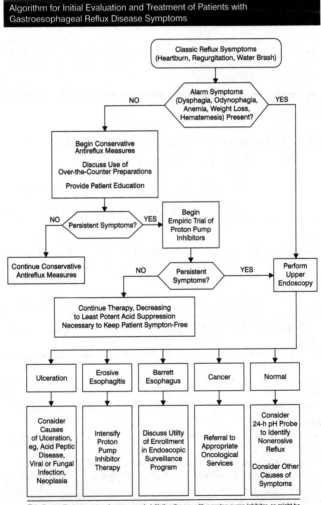

This diagram illustrates a step-down approach, initiating therapy with a proton pump inhibitor, as might be used for patient 1. Initial therapy with H₂ receptor antagonists in patients not previously receiving these medications is also acceptable (a step-up approach). Source: JAMA, April 17, 2002 - Vol 287, No. 15

Shaheen N, Ransohoff DF. Gastroesophageal reflux, Barrett esophagus, and esophageal cancer. Clinical applications. JAMA 2002;287:1982, 1984. Copyright 2002. American Medical Association. Used with permission.

IV. MANAGEMENT

A. Behavior modification

1. Avoid foods that are direct irritants or decrease LES pressure (see above)
2. Stop smoking and avoid alcohol
3. Avoidance, if possible, of drugs that may injure the esophageal mucosa (tetracycline, quinidine, potassium chloride tablets, NSAIDs) or decrease sphincter tone (Theophylline, calcium channel blockers, anticholinergics)
4. Avoidance of large evening meals near bedtime or before exercise
5. Weight loss
6. Avoid tight fitting clothes
7. Remain upright for 3hrs after eating
8. 4–8 inch blocks under head of bed

B. Antacids provide symptom relief but do not heal esophagitis

C. H_2 blockers: See V. Table 1

D. Proton pump inhibitors: See V. Table 1

E. Prokinetic agents aid in the competence of LES. They are approximately equivalent to H_2 blockers for mild GERD and maintenance: **Metoclopramide (Reglan):** 10mg PO QID, significant side effects

F. Mucosal protective agents: See PUD, IV.A.3

G. Combinations: PPIs plus Reglan are more effective than PPIs alone

H. Surgery: Nissen fundoplication is the therapy of choice for patients with strictures requiring repeated dilation or for patients who fail medical therapy. Surgery has a 90% efficacy and is especially effective in patients with atypical symptoms such as chronic cough, asthma, etc. Laparoscopic methods have lower morbidity than the standard open technique

V. COMPLICATIONS

A. Degree of injury is poorly correlated with degree of symptoms
B. Specific complications include:

1. **Barrett's Esophagus:** In 10% of patients with chronic reflux, esophageal squamous cells may undergo metaplasia to columnar cells. Esophageal adenocarcinoma may develop in up to 10% of patients with metaplasia. If multiple foci of high grade dysplasia are found on EGD, elective esophagectomy versus Q6 month EGDs with biopsy must be considered. For Barrett's esophagus metaplasia without dysplasia, EGD with biopsy must be performed Q1–2yrs
2. **Stricture:** EGD should confirm the stricture (usually at the GE junction) and dilation may be performed at the same time. Long term proton pump therapy should follow dilation
3. **Extra-esophageal complications** include asthma (aspiration versus vagal), laryngitis, chronic cough, sleep apnea

Table 1—Common Medications Used in GERD/PUD

	Famotidine (Pepcid) H_2 blocker	Ranitidine (Zantac) H_2 blocker	Cimetidine (Tagamet) H_2 blocker	Nizatidine (Axid) H_2 blocker	Omeprazole (Prilosec) Proton pump inhibitor	Lansoprazole (Prevacid) Proton pump inhibitor	Rabeprazole (AcipHex) Proton pump inhibitor	Esomeprazole (Nexium) Proton pump inhibitor	Pantoprazole (Protonix) Proton pump inhibitor
Acute duodenal ulcer	20mg BID or 40mg hs × 6–8 wks	150mg BID or 300mg hs × 6–8 wks	800mg hs × 6–8 wks or 400mg BID	150mg BID or 300mg hs × 6–8 wks	20mg QD × 4–8 wks	15mg QD × 4–8 wks	20mg QD × 4 wks	—	—
Maintenance duodenal ulcer	20mg hs	150mg hs	400mg hs	150mg hs	20mg QD	15mg QD	20mg QD		—
Acute gastric ulcer	40mg hs × 6–8 wks	150mg BID or 300mg hs × 6–8 wks	800mg hs × 6–8 wks	300mg hs × 6–8 wks	40mg QD ×4–8 wks	30mg QD × 4–8 wks	20mg QD × 4-8 wks	—	—
GERD symptoms	20mg BID	150mg BID	400mg BID	150mg BID	20mg QD	15mg QD	20mg QD	20mg QD	40mg QD
Esophageal lesions	40mg BID	150mg BID	800mg BID or 400mg QID	200mg BID	20mg QD	30mg QD	20mg QD	20–40mg QD × 40 weeks	20–40mg QD × 8 weeks
Maintenance esophageal ulcers / severe GERD		150mg BID			20mg QD	15mg QD	20mg QD	20mg QD	40mg QD

Note: Doses listed are for FDA approved indications

— PART TWO: PEPTIC ULCER DISEASE (PUD) —

I. SYMPTOMS
A. Duodenal ulcers frequently present with burning epigastric pain relieved by antacids. Symptoms may awaken the patient
B. Gastric ulcers often present with nausea, vomiting, pain made worse by food, early satiety
C. Nonspecific symptoms include dyspepsia, bloating, gas
D. Alarm symptoms for underlying malignancy or complicated ulcer disease include: age > 45yrs, rectal bleeding or melena, weight loss, anemia, dysphagia, abdominal mass, jaundice, family history of gastric cancer, previous history of PUD and anorexia/early satiety

II. ETIOLOGY
A. *Helicobacter pylori:* See below
B. NSAID use: Clinical ulcers (usually gastric) develop in 1% of patients per year of NSAID use. Risks of complications include increased age, prior GI disease, concomitant steroid or anticoagulant use, female sex, increased dose of NSAIDs. Cytotec (Misoprostol) provides some protection
C. Hypersecretory state: Zollinger Ellison Syndrome, gastrinoma
D. Exacerbating factors
  1. Tobacco: One study showed that the risk of duodenal ulcer, failure to heal, and recurrence was directly proportional to number of cigarettes
  2. Alcohol is a strong stimulant of acid secretion
  3. Corticosteroids
  4. Diet (controversial)

III. TREATMENT
A. Acute ulcers
  1. Testing and treatment for *H. pylori* (see IV.)
  2. Antisecretory meds per table 1
  3. Mucosal protective agents
    a. **Sucralfate (Carafate)**
      i. Forms a barrier at the ulcer base and stimulates production of mucous, HCO_3, and prostaglandins
      ii. Comparable to H_2 blockers in healing duodenal ulcers and in GERD
      iii. Dose: 1g PO QID × 6–8 weeks
    b. Antacids
      i. Help relieve symptoms and are comparable to H_2 blockers in healing duodenal ulcers and in GERD
      ii. Example: Mylanta
    c. **Bismuth (Pepto-Bismol)** stimulates production of HCO_3 and prostaglandins
B. Maintenance therapy
  1. Duodenal ulcers: H_2 blockers (or proton pump inhibitors) given at HS at half treatment dose (full dose in smokers or complicated disease)—*or*—**Carafate** 1g PO BID
  2. Gastric ulcers: No approved maintenance therapy
  3. NSAID ulcers: **Misoprostol (Cytotec)** acts as a prostaglandin analog and stimulates HCO_3 and mucous production. It is dosed at 200mcg PO QID with meals. Diarrhea and miscarriage induction limit its use
  4. Patients successfully treated for *H. pylori* may attempt discontinuation of antisecretory therapy

IV. HELICOBACTER PYLORI
A. General
  1. Approximately 30–40% of US population is infected with *H. pylori*. This bacteria is a cofactor in 75% of ulcers
  2. Infection causes histological gastritis in almost 100% of patients, PUD, and is a risk factor in the development of gastric adenocarcinoma (risk increased 9 fold) and lymphoma
  3. Patients infected have lifetime risk for PUD of approximately 15%
  4. Cure is associated with a reduction of ulcer recurrence and ability to stop antisecretory therapy
  5. Duodenal ulcers recurred in 6% of those cured of *H. pylori* and in 67% of those who remained positive for *H. pylori*

GEN

B. Indications for testing
1. Patients newly diagnosed (endoscopically or radiographically) with ulcer disease
2. Patients with history of ulcer disease on antisecretory therapy
3. Patients with ulcer-like dyspepsia
4. Patients with mucosa-associated lymphoid tissue lymphoma
5. Screening to prevent gastric cancer

C. Methods of *H. pylori* detection
1. Histological examination (after EGD)
2. Blood antibody tests
   a. Tests for IgG antibodies to *H. pylori*
   b. Most convenient but are less accurate
   c. Not able to distinguish active infection (cannot use to monitor efficacy of therapy) as it may stay positive for years after successful treatment
3. Urea breath tests (UBTs)
   a. A measure of current infection with a sensitivity of 80-100%
   b. May be falsely negative in patients receiving PPIs or *H. pylori* therapy. Prior to testing, stop PPIs for 2 weeks and ATBs/bismuth for 4 weeks
4. Stool antigen: Highly sensitive and specific, comparable to UBT

D. Other
1. In patients with new onset PUD, if the initial test for *H. pylori* is negative, another test should be performed
2. Factors affecting cure rate include patient compliance, duration of therapy, and presence of resistance to the ATBs
3. Resistance to Metronidazole is 28–39% and to Clarithromycin is 11%. Amoxicillin and Tetracycline resistant strains are rare

E. Confirmation of eradication
1. May be helpful after course of therapy
2. Use nonendoscopic methods including UBT (antibody test may remain positive for years after eradication)
3. Wait 4–6 weeks after completion of therapy

V. ERADICATION OF *H. PYLORI:* For **Omeprazole**—may substitute **Nexium (Esomeprazole)** if needed

Table 2: *H. pylori* Treatment Regimens from JAMA Consensus Statement (Feb 1996)

KEY:	Meds	Comments	Adverse Effects
	Bismuth (Pepto-Bismol)	2 tabs or 1tsp QAC+HS, works topically	black stools
	Metronidazole (Flagyl)	*H. pylori* easily develops resistance	nausea, metallic taste
	Tetracycline	500mg QAC+HS, works topically	metallic taste
	Omeprazole (Prilosec)		
	Clarithromycin (Biaxin)		
	Amoxicillin (Amoxil)	works topically, can't use Ampicillin IV	allergic reactions

Regimen #	Regimen	Length of treatment	Cure rate
1	**B** 2 tabs QAC+HS **M** 250mg QAC+HS **T** 500mg QAC+HS	1–2 weeks	88%
2	Add **O** 20mg BID with meals to Regimen 1	1 week	94–98%
3	**B** 2 tabs QAC+HS **M** 250mg QAC+HS **A** 500mg QAC+HS	1 week	75–81%
		2 weeks	80–86%
4	**M** 500mg BID with meals **O** 20mg BID with meals **C** 500mg BID with meals	1 week	87–91%
		2 weeks	slightly increased
5	**A** 1000mg BID with meals **O** 20mg BID with meals **C** 500mg BID with meals	1 week	86–91%
		2 weeks	slightly increased
6	**M** 500mg BID with meals **O** 20mg BID with meals **A** 1000mg BID with meals	2 weeks	77–83%

GEN

VI. COMPLICATIONS OF PUD

A. **Hemorrhage:** Symptoms include coffee ground emesis, hematemesis, melena, or hematochezia. Up to 20% of patients with PUD may develop bleeding

B. **Perforation:** Seen in up to 5% of ulcer patients. Usually occurs from ulcers on the anterior wall of the stomach or duodenum. Patients will usually have absent bowel sounds, rebound tenderness, and a very rigid abdomen. Upright or decubitus plain abdominal films will aid in diagnosis (free intraperitoneal air)

C. **Gastric outlet obstruction:** Occurs in 2% of ulcer patients due to edema or scarring of the pylorus or duodenal bulb. Upper endoscopy is necessary to define the extent of obstruction and to rule out carcinoma

CLINICAL PEARLS

- Costs in US of treating *H. pylori* related diseases is $3–5.6 billion/yr
- Patient education regarding Aspirin and NSAID use is important. Patients should be made aware of common signs and symptoms of PUD and instructed to inform the physician if they should develop (bleeding may be the first sign of PUD in patients taking NSAIDs)
- Smoking cessation is imperative in patients with PUD
- If patients need to continue NSAIDs despite being diagnosed with PUD, consider cox-2 inhibitors (Celebrex, Vioxx) or shorter acting NSAIDs (so that dosage can be titrated) rather than the potent once-a-day NSAIDs
- Consider Cytotec for prevention of PUD in chronic NSAID users

References

Meurer LN, Bower DJ. Management of Helicobacter pylori infection. Am Fam Phys 2002;65:1327–36,1339.

Shaheen N, Ransohoff DF. Gastroesophageal reflux, Barrett esophagus, and esophageal cancer. Clinical applications. JAMA 2002;287:1982.

Laine L, et al. Therapy for Helicobacter pylori in patients with non-ulcer dyspepsia. Ann Intern Med 2001;134:361–9.

Spechler SJ, et al. Long-term outcome of medical and surgical therapies for gastroesophageal reflux disease: Follow-up of a randomized controlled trial. JAMA 2001;285:2331.

Peterson WL, et al. Helicobacter pylori-related disease. Guidelines for testing and treatment. Arch Int Med 2000;160:1285.

American Gastroenterological Association. Medical position statement: Evaluation of dyspepsia. Gastroenterology 1998;114:579–81.

Daniel M. Neides, MD

62. EVALUATION OF DIARRHEA IN ADULTS

I. INTRODUCTION

A. Infectious diarrhea causes 200–375 million illnesses/yr in the US with 3,100 deaths and is the second leading cause of morbidity and mortality worldwide

B. Approximately $6 billion/yr is spent on medical care and lost productivity due to foodborne illnesses in US

C. Definitions
1. Diarrhea: Alteration in normal bowel movement characterized by increase in water content, volume or frequency of stools
2. Acute diarrhea: Episode < 14 days in duration
3. Persistent diarrhea: Episode > 14 days in duration
4. Infectious diarrhea: Diarrhea from an infectious etiology

II. DIFFERENTIAL DIAGNOSIS

A. **Viral:** Rotavirus, Norwalk, Adenovirus, Enterovirus, HIV

B. **Bacterial**: *Salmonella, Shigella, Yersinia, Campylobacter, E. coli, Vibrio cholerae, Vibrio parahaemolyticus, Staphylococcus aureus, Clostridium perfringens*

GEN

    C. Parasitic: *Giardia lamblia, Entamoeba histolytica, Cryptosporidium*

    D. Drugs: Laxatives, ATBs, caffeine, alcohol, digitalis

    E. Inflammatory: Ulcerative colitis, Crohn's disease, Ischemic colitis, Pseudomembranous colitis (*C. difficile*)

    F. Malabsorption: Sprue, lymphoma, Whipple's disease, pancreatic insufficiency, lactose intolerance

    G. Tumors: Intestinal carcinoma, carcinoid, islet-cell tumors, medullary carcinoma of the thyroid, villous adenoma

    H. Functional: Irritable bowel syndrome, diverticulosis

    I. Postsurgical: Postgastrectomy dumping syndrome, parasympathetic denervation, short bowel syndrome, enteroenteric fistulas

    J. Other: Cirrhosis, diabetes mellitus, Addison's disease, scleroderma, amyloidosis, radiation enteritis

III. HISTORY

    A. General: Fever, tenesmus, symptoms of dehydration (i.e., light-headedness, decreased urine output, lethargy), onset (abrupt vs. gradual), duration

    B. Stool characteristics: Frequency, quantity, consistency, volume, blood, pus, mucus, greasy stools

    C. Abdominal pain

    D. Exposure: Travel history (developing areas, camping), day care, exposure to persons who are ill, ingestion of raw or undercooked meat or seafood, raw milk, sexual contacts (oral-anal, receptive anal intercourse), visit to farm or petting zoo

    E. Med/Drug history: Recent ATBs, laxative use, antacids, excessive alcohol, caffeinated beverages, sorbitol (sugar-free gum or candy)

    F. Past medical history: Immunosuppression, HIV/AIDS, prior gastrectomy

    G. Other: Headaches, myalgias, confusion

IV. PHYSICAL EXAMINATION

    A. General: Temperature, blood pressure, pulse, weight

    B. Oral: Dry membranes

    C. Skin: Decreased skin turgor, rash, jaundice

    D. Abdomen: Guarding, rebound tenderness, hypo- or hyperactive bowel sounds, hepatomegaly, ascites, or masses

    E. Rectal: Guaiac stool, note any fistulas

V. EVALUATION

    A. Features which are common for infectious diarrhea

        1. History: Fever, abdominal pain, tenesmus, bloody stool, nausea/vomiting

        2. Physical: Abdominal pain, bloody or heme-positive stool

        3. Laboratory: Fecal WBCs > 50 HPF, fecal lactoferrin

    B. Indications for stool studies

        1. There have been numerous approaches recommended. In numerous studies yield in all cultures is between 1% and 5%

        2. Yield may be increased by selective use of studies. Conditions which increase likelihood for infectious diarrhea are listed above

        3. Infectious Disease Society of America issued recommendations in 2001 which recommend testing patients with diarrhea lasting > 1 day especially if accompanied by fever, bloody stool, systemic illness, recent use of ATBs, day care center attendance, hospitalization, or dehydration

        4. Stool studies may include culture and sensitivity (notify lab if evaluating for *E. coli 0157*), *Shigella, Salmonella, Yersinia, Campylobacter,* ova and parasites, *C. difficile* toxin

    C. Additional studies should be tailored to the signs and symptoms and may include CBC, electrolytes, BUN, creatinine, urinalysis, abdominal radiography, anoscopy, flexible sigmoidoscopy, and colonoscopy

    D. In patients with persistent diarrhea, consider further evaluation for other entities including inflammatory bowel disease (ulcerative colitis or Crohn's disease), irritable bowel syndrome, ischemic bowel disease, laxative abuse, partial obstruction, and other entities as mentioned in II. B. above

GEN

VI. MANAGEMENT OF INFECTIOUS DIARRHEA   (**Note**: Management of other etiologies mentioned in II. above, is tailored to specific diagnosis. Duration of treatment below is for immunocompetent patients)

   A. Replace fluid loss orally if possible. In patients with mild diarrhea use clear juices and soups and with more severe diarrhea or dehydration use oral rehydration solutions

   B. Avoid antimotility agents in patients with bloody diarrhea or infection with Shiga toxin-producing *E. coli*. In patients without these entities, consider **Imodium** 4mg PO initially, then 2mg after each unformed stool to maximum of 16mg/day or use **Pepto-Bismol** 2 tabs or 30mL up to Q10

   C. Institute therapy for:
      1. Traveler's diarrhea: **Fluoroquinolone** or **Trimethoprim-Sulfamethoxazole** × 3 days (may reduce duration of symptoms from 3–5 days to < 1–2 days
      2. Shigellosis: **Trimethoprim-Sulfamethoxazole** or **Quinolone** × 5 days
      3. Campylobacter: **Erythromycin** 500mg PO BID × 5 days
      4. Giardia: **Metronidazole (Flagyl)** 250–750mg PO TID × 7–10 days
      5. Cholera: **Doxycycline** or **Tetracycline** × 3 days or 1 dose of **Fluoroquinolone**
      6. Clostridium difficile: Stop offending ATB. **Metronidazole (Flagyl)** 250mg PO QID or 500mg PO TID × 10 days

   D. Not routinely recommended for:
      1. Salmonella: Unless patient is > 50yrs or has prosthesis, valvular heart disease, severe atherosclerosis, malignancy, or uremia
      2. Yersinia: ATB not usually required unless severe infection or immunocompromised
      3. E. coli 0157: Treatment with ATBs has been shown to increase production of Shiga toxin and may increase likelihood of hemolytic uremic syndrome (HUS). Treatment with ATBs has not been shown to ameliorate illness

   E. Decrease risk of transmission to contacts with hand washing and good hygiene

CLINICAL PEARLS
   • Treatment of salmonella with ATBs may prolong the carrier state. Institute therapy when systemic spread is considered, but not to reduce secondary transmission (can be accomplished with hand washing)
   • Traveler's diarrhea can occur from contaminated ice cubes or water used to wash fruits or vegetables
   • Patients taking Flagyl for an infectious diarrhea should avoid alcohol (may cause an Antabuse-like reaction)
   • Test for HIV in patients diagnosed with *Cryptosporidium*

References

Fass R, et al. Evidence- and consensus-based practice guidelines for the diagnosis of irritable bowel syndrome. Arch Int Med 2001;161:2081.

Guerrant RL, et al. Practice guidelines for the management of infectious diarrhea (ISDA guidelines). Clin Inf Dis 2001;32:331.

Horwitz BJ, Fisher RS. Current concepts: the irritable bowel syndrome. N Engl J Med 2001; 344:1846–50.

Mylonakis E, et al. Clostridium difficile-associated diarrhea: a review. Arch Int Med 2001;161:525.

Lipsky MS. Chronic diarrhea: evaluation and treatment. Am Fam Phys 1993;48:1461.

GEN

Linda Stone, MD
Michael B. Weinstock, MD
Daniel M. Neides, MD

63. Constipation In Adults

I. DEFINITION: Defecation which occurs < 2 ×/week

II. HISTORY AND PHYSICAL EXAM
  A. History
      1. Frequency of stools, consistency, need to strain, and pain with defecation
      2. Rectal bleeding (melena vs. bright red blood mixed with stool), weight loss, and abdominal bloating or cramping
      3. Past medical history
          a. Previous patterns of bowel activity
          b. Current meds
          c. History of malignancy or radiation therapy
          d. Previous surgeries
  B. Physical exam
      1. **Abdomen:** Note any surgical scars. Palpate for masses (stool) and hepatosplenomegaly. Check for hernia. Examination results are often normal
      2. **Neurologic:** Neuro exam if necessary
      3. **Rectal:** Digital examination to assess rectal tone and presence of pain (anal fissure). Palpate for rectal masses, stool impaction. Hemoccult stool

III. ETIOLOGIES
  A. Medications: Opiate analgesics, antihypertensives (calcium channel blockers), iron, calcium, barium, antidepressants, antipsychotics, antispasmodics, antiparkinson meds, antacids
  B. Neurologic dysfunction: Hirschsprung's disease, neurofibromatosis, autonomic neuropathy, Chagas disease, spinal cord lesions, multiple sclerosis, CVA, Parkinson's disease
  C. Metabolic and endocrine: Diabetes Mellitus, hypothyroidism, hypercalcemia, hypocalcemia, hypokalemia, pregnancy
  D. Collagen vascular diseases: Amyloidosis, systemic sclerosis, myotonic dystrophy
  E. Mechanical difficulties: Colorectal cancer, hernia, diverticulitis, irritable bowel, hemorrhoids, anal fissure, or stricture

IV. EVALUATION: Direct evaluation based on findings in history and physical examination
  A. Blood chemistry: Blood glucose, serum electrolytes, calcium, and TSH
  B. Fecal occult blood test: Perform during examination and send 3–4 home for patient to check and return
  C. Radiology
      1. Barium enema: To detect toxic megacolon and Hirschsprung's disease
      2. Sigmoidoscopy or colonoscopy: To detect colon cancer, obstructive lesions, and evidence of laxative abuse (melanosis coli)
      3. Transit study: Radiopaque markers are taken along with a high fiber diet. X-rays are obtained over the subsequent 3 days. Normal patients will pass the marker before 72hrs. Markers still present ≥ 4 days suggest a colonic problem
      4. Anorectal manometry: Measures sphincter tone; helps to differentiate patients with Hirschsprung's disease from other neurologic problems

V. MANAGEMENT
  A. Lifestyle
      1. Exercise (walking, jogging, swimming, etc.)
      2. Increase fluids intake: 6–8 glasses (8 oz) of water or fruit juice per day
      3. Increase fiber intake to 20–30g of dietary fiber per day

B. **Medications**

Laxatives for the Treatment of Constipation	
Laxative Class	**Recommendation for Adults**
Emollient	Docusate (Colace), 50–200 mg/d in divided doses
Fiber	Psyllium (Metamucil), 20–30 g/d
Hyperosmolar agents	70% Sorbitol, 15–45 mL/d
Lavage solutions	Polyethylene glycol–electrolyte solution (GoLYTELY), 250–500 mL/d
Lubricants	Mineral oil, 15–45 mL/d
Saline cathartics	Milk of magnesia, 15–45 mL Qhs
Stimulant cathartics	Bisacodyl (Dulcolax), two to four 5-mg tablets Qhs

Source: Rakel and Bope ET., eds. Conn's current therapy 2002, 54th ed., Philadelphia: W.B. Saunders, 2002. Table 3. With permission from Elsevier.

CLINICAL PEARLS
- New onset of constipation is a warning sign for cancer. Screen for colon cancer with selected patients
- Consider irritable bowel syndrome (IBS) as the cause of constipation
- Fecal impaction is often a common cause of constipation in the elderly

References
Fass R, et al. Evidence- and consensus-based practice guidelines for the diagnosis of irritable bowel syndrome. Arch Int Med 2001;161:2081.
Horwitz BJ, Fisher RS. Current concepts: The irritable bowel syndrome. N Engl J Med 2001;344:1846–50.
Yuan Chun-Su, et al. Methylnaltrexone for reversal of constipation due to chronic methadone use: A randomized controlled trial. JAMA 2000;283:367.
Brisinda G, et al. A comparison of injections of botulinum toxin and topical nitroglycerin for the treatment of chronic anal fissure. N Engl J Med 1999:341:65–9.

Michael B. Weinstock, MD
Linda Stone, MD

64. HEMORRHOIDS

I. DEFINITION: Hemorrhoids (piles) are varicosities of the rectal venous plexus. Can occur internally (above the pectinate line) or externally (below the pectinate line)
    A. **Internal hemorrhoids** are covered by viscerally innervated mucosa. Uncomplicated internal hemorrhoids are not painful. Internal hemorrhoids are referred to as complicated when the patient presents with painless bleeding, prolapse or thrombosis. Internal hemorrhoids may occasionally become strangulated (massive prolapse and thrombosis, necrosis and ulceration) and the patient presents with severe pain and inability to sit down or defecate
    B. **External hemorrhoids** are covered by somatic innervated mucosa. May be painful or painless. Complications include acute thrombosis or rupture with hematoma formation

II. CLASSIFICATION OF INTERNAL HEMORRHOIDS
    A. **First degree:** Do not protrude, cannot be palpated by digital rectal exam (DRE), require anoscopy for diagnosis
    B. **Second degree:** Protrude, reduce spontaneously
    C. **Third degree:** Protrude, require manual reduction
    D. **Fourth degree:** Prolapsed, irreducible

III. HISTORY AND PHYSICAL EXAMINATION
    A. **History**
        1. Rectal itching (from stool residue left secondary to poor wiping because of pain)

GEN

    2. Straining with stool

    3. Lump at the rectum

    4. History of constipation

    5. Rectal bleeding

    6. Pain: May be caused by fissure, thrombosis, ulceration or infection

B. Physical examination

    1. Inspect the rectum for external hemorrhoids or prolapsed internal hemorrhoids with the patient at rest and while straining. Hemorrhoids are usually painless, red or purplish, and protruding from the anus

    2. Examine for fissures, dermatitis, fungal infection and herpes. May use Q-tip to gently separate the edges of the anus to look for fissures

    3. Digital rectal examination (DRE): Detects only thrombosed internal hemorrhoids, but may detect anal cancer/masses which may be confused with hemorrhoids

IV. EVALUATION

A. Anoscopy: May be performed routinely or if diagnosis is in question

    1. Gently insert a lubricated anoscope

    2. Ask the patient to "bear down" (not too forcefully)

    3. Slowly withdraw the anoscope

    4. Watch for internal hemorrhoids to bulge into the anorectal lumen

B. Rectal bleeding: Consider evaluation with colonoscopy or flexible sigmoidoscopy and air contrast barium enema to exclude other sources of GI bleeding including colon cancer, neoplastic polyps, AV malformation, and inflammatory bowel disease

GEN

V. MANAGEMENT

A. Initial management: For first to third degree hemorrhoids. If these conservative measures are unsuccessful, then consider definitive management

    1. Lifestyle changes to avoid constipation (see Chapter 63, Constipation in Adults)

        a. Defecation: Patients should not suppress the urge to defecate and should not strain while defecating

        b. Diet: Modify diet to increase intake of fiber, fluids, and fruit juices. Decrease fats and meats

        c. Exercise: Increase aerobic exercise

    2. Sitz bath: Sitting in a warm or cool tub for 20 minutes BID–TID in the acute phase

    3. **Anusol-HC** cream or suppositories (**Hydrocortisone Acetate**): 1 PR BID × 2 weeks. For severe cases, may increase to TID

B. Definitive management: Patients with acute thrombosis and prolapse of internal hemorrhoids may require hospitalization and treatment with bed rest, analgesics, stool softeners and often hemorrhoidectomy. Definitive therapy is indicated for fourth degree hemorrhoids and first to third degree hemorrhoids which are not amenable to the above measures

    1. **Sclerotherapy:** For first degree and small second degree bleeding *internal* hemorrhoids. A sclerosing agent (e.g., quinine urea hydrochloride or phenol) is injected into the superior aspect of the hemorrhoid *above the pectinate line*. Injection may need to be repeated in several months

    2. **Ligation:** Best suited for third and fourth degrees *internal* hemorrhoids. Should *not* be used for external hemorrhoids or internal hemorrhoids complicated by abscess, thrombosis, cryptitis or anal fissure. Cure rates about 80–90%. The hemorrhoid is strangulated by placing a rubber band at the base. Complications include pain (6%), bleeding (3%), and perianal hematoma (3%). May require 2–3 separate ligations. Fatal septicemia has been reported after ligation and may present with triad of perianal pain, fever and urinary hesitancy

    3. **Excision and evacuation:** Indicated for large painful thrombosed external hemorrhoids (small thrombosed external hemorrhoids may respond to conservative management)

        a. Patient is placed in fetal position or on knees with buttocks taped open (the tape pulls one buttock laterally and then goes around abdomen and then placed so that it pulls the other buttock laterally)

        b. Hemorrhoid is anesthetized with 1% **Lidocaine** with **Epinephrine**. Use **Lidocaine** around the edges of hemorrhoid

    c. An elliptical incision is made over lateral edges of hemorrhoid. Hemorrhoid and clot are removed

    d. Sutures are not necessary. Wound is left open to heal by secondary intention

CLINICAL PEARLS

- Simple incision has higher recurrence rate compared to using an elliptical incision to completely excise clotted hemorrhoid
- About ½ of Americans over 50 will seek medical advice for hemorrhoids
- Most common cause of painless rectal bleeding is internal hemorrhoids
- Hemorrhoids are unusual in children and should be viewed with eye toward other disease
- Rectal pruritus may be initial complaint with hemorrhoids, but consider other causes such as fissures, dermatitis (contact or seborrheic), psoriasis, pinworm, *Candida*, herpes, neurodermatitis, and squamous cell cancer

References

Zuber TJ. Hemorrhoidectomy for thrombosed external hemorrhoids. Am Fam Phys 2002;65:1629.

Pfenninger JL, Surrell J. Nonsurgical treatment options for internal hemorrhoids. Am Fam Phys 1995;52:821,839–41.

The Standards Task Force of American Society of Colon and Rectal Surgeons. Practice parameters for the treatment of hemorrhoids. Dis Colon Rectum 1993;36:1118–20.

MacRae HM, McLeod RS. Comparison of hemorrhoidal treatment modalities. A meta-analysis. Dis Colon Rectum 1995;38:687–94.

GEN

Daniel M. Neides, MD
Michael B. Weinstock, MD

65. ANEMIA

I. GENERAL: Hemoglobin < 12g/dL in women and < 13g/dL in men (WHO criteria). Classically divided into microcytic (MCV < 83 mcm^3), normocytic (MCV 83–100 mcm^3), or macrocytic (MCV > 100 mcm^3)

II. PHYSIOLOGY OF NORMAL IRON METABOLISM

    A. Iron is required for hemoglobin and DNA synthesis. Daily dietary intake of iron in US is approximately 10–20mg/day

    B. Most iron absorption takes place in the small intestine

    C. Mucosal iron is stored as ferritin and the mucosal transport protein is transferrin

    D. Iron storage (as ferritin) is primarily found the bone marrow, spleen, liver, and skeletal muscle

III. HISTORY

    A. Many patients are asymptomatic. May have fatigue, weakness, lightheadedness, headache, irritability, palpitations, paresthesias, gait disturbances, sore tongue, brittle nails, or PICA (desire to eat dirt, ice, paint). Inquire about rectal bleeding, weight loss

    B. Alcohol use

    C. Meds: Zidovudine (AZT), Dilantin, Phenobarbital, OCPs, Sulfa, Trimethoprim, Colchicine, Neomycin

    D. Medical history including history of malabsorption syndromes or inflammatory bowel disease

    E. Surgeries—partial or total gastrectomy predisposes patient to B$_{12}$ deficiency—pernicious anemia

    F. Chemical or radiation exposure (myelodysplasia)

    G. Diet: Strict vegetarians are susceptible to developing B$_{12}$ deficiency; patients with a high carbohydrate diet (and nothing else) are susceptible to folate deficiency

IV. PHYSICAL: Physical exam may be normal or may include murmur, CHF, papillary atrophy of the tongue, retinal hemorrhages, glossitis, brittle nails, gait disturbance (B$_{12}$ deficiency) or splenomegaly/ascites/jaundice (liver disease), signs of chronic alcohol abuse

V. EVALUATION: May be considerable overlap, but the evaluation is generally initiated by first determining if it is microcytic (MCV < 80 mcm^3), macrocytic (MCV > 100 mcm^3), or normocytic (MCV 80–100 mcm^3)

A. Microcytic anemia
1. Differential diagnosis
   a. Iron deficiency anemia (the most common cause of microcytosis)
   b. (Anemia of) chronic disease
   c. Thalassemia
   d. Sideroblastic anemia
   e. Lead toxicity
2. Labs
   a. Serum iron, total iron binding capacity (TIBC), ferritin
   b. WBC (low count suggests marrow production problem and high count could suggest infection or leukemia)
   c. Peripheral smear: Burr cells (chronic renal failure), spherocytes (hemolytic diseases), dysplastic changes, basophilic stippling (thalassemia, iron deficiency, lead poisoning), Howell-Jolly bodies (asplenia, pernicious anemia, severe iron deficiency)
   d. Reticulocyte count: If < 1% this suggests inadequate production. If > 1%, then calculate the reticulocyte index (% reticulocytes × patient's hematocrit/normal hematocrit). Reticulocyte index should be > 2 with the presence of anemia

ETIOLOGY	SERUM Fe	TIBC	FERRITIN	BONE MARROW Fe STORES	HgbA$_2$ AND F (FETAL)
Iron Deficiency	Decreased	Increased	Decreased	NONE	Normal
Chronic Disease	Decreased	Normal or Decreased	Normal or *Increased*	Normal or Increased	Normal
Thalassemia	Normal	Normal	Normal or Increased	Normal	Increased in b-thal; Normal in a-thal
Sideroblastic anemia	Normal or Increased	Normal or Increased	Normal or Increased	Increased	Normal

3. Etiology of iron deficiency anemia
   a. Blood loss: Gastrointestinal (ulcer, malignancy), menstruation, blood donation
   b. Decreased ingestion or increased requirements (pregnancy, lactation)
   c. Decreased absorption: Malabsorption syndromes, partial gastrectomy
   d. Pulmonary hemosiderosis, polycythemia
4. Management of iron deficiency anemia
   a. Determine etiology and direct initial therapy toward correction
   b. Evaluation of the GI tract in adults (see below)
   c. Adults: **FeSO$_4$** 325mg PO BID-TID; children: 3–6mg elemental **Fe**/kg/day PO divided TID (e.g., Fer-in-sol). Side Effects: Cramping, nausea, constipation and/or diarrhea
5. Evaluating the gastrointestinal tract in iron deficiency anemia
   a. Idiopathic iron deficiency anemia in adults is commonly from blood loss in GI tract—obtain fecal occult blood test
   b. History and physical directed toward potential areas of blood loss
   c. Endoscopic evaluation (EGD or colonoscopy) depending on patient's symptoms
   d. For asymptomatic adults, perform colonoscopy first

B. Macrocytic anemia
1. Differential diagnosis
   a. Alcohol abuse
   b. B$_{12}$ or folate deficiency
   c. Hemolysis or bleeding
   d. Liver disease
   e. Hypothyroidism
   f. Myelodysplasia
   g. Chemotherapeutic agents or other drugs

2. Labs (as indicated)
   a. WBC and peripheral smear—target cells (liver disease), hyposegmented cells (myelodysplasia), hypersegmented cells (B_{12} or folate deficiency)
   b. B_{12} and folate (RBC folate is more reliable)
   c. Reticulocytes
   d. TSH and free T_4
   e. LFTs
   f. Consider bone marrow aspirate
3. Management: Directed toward underlying disorder
   a. Causes of B_{12} deficiency include decreased intake (strict vegan), decreased absorption (pernicious anemia, gastrectomy, gastric atrophy, Crohn's disease, ileal resection, celiac disease, tropical sprue, chronic pancreatitis, bacterial overgrowth) and decreased utilization (nitrous oxide inhalation, inborn errors of metabolism)
   b. Treatment of B_{12} deficiency includes oral therapy with **Vitamin B_{12}** 1,000–2,000 micrograms PO QD (equivalent to parenteral therapy) or 1,000mcg IM once per week
   c. Causes of folate deficiency include decreased intake, decreased absorption (tropical sprue, celiac disease, short gut syndrome), meds (Dilantin, Phenobarbital, alcohol, OCs, Trimethoprim, Sulfa), increased demands (pregnancy, infancy, hemolytic anemia)
   d. Treatment of folate deficiency—**Folate** 1mg PO QD. Note: Ensure that concomitant B_{12} deficiency does not exist since neurologic symptoms of B_{12} deficiency may worsen if treated only with folic acid

C. Normocytic anemia
1. Differential diagnosis
   a. Early iron deficiency anemia
   b. Anemia of chronic disease
   c. Chronic renal insufficiency
   d. Endocrine disorders: Thyroid disease, hyperparathyroidism, adrenal insufficiency
   e. Bone marrow failure: Radiation, drugs (chemotherapy), viruses (HIV, Hepatitis B)
   f. Bone marrow replacement: Metastatic cancer, myelofibrosis, leukemia
2. Normocytic anemia may be present due to some of the etiologies which have caused microcytic and macrocytic anemia
3. Labs (as indicated)
   a. WBC and peripheral smear
   b. B_{12} and folate (RBC folate is more reliable)
   c. Reticulocytes
   d. TSH and free T_4
   e. LFTs
   f. Consider bone marrow aspirate

CLINICAL PEARLS
- Most common causes of anemia in the elderly are anemia of chronic disease and iron deficiency anemia
- Neurologic symptoms in patients with B_{12} deficiency may precede the onset of anemia
- Patients with B_{12} deficiency may have normocytic or microcytic anemia
- Full term newborns have a 6 month supply of iron, therefore iron deficiency is rarely a cause of anemia in children < 6 months
- G6PD deficiency is present in 13% of black males and 2% of black females
- AAP recommends using iron fortified infant formulas and not to drink whole cow's milk during child's first year (may cause occult GI bleeding)

References
Abelson HT. Complexities in recognizing and treating iron deficiency anemia. Arch Ped Adolesc Med 2001;155:332.
Irwin JJ, Kerchner JT. Anemia in children. Am Fam Phys 2001;64:1379-86.
Brill JR, Baumgardner DJ. Normocytic anemia. Am Fam Phys 2000;62:2255-64.
Abramson SD, Abramson N. "Common" uncommon anemias. Am Fam Phys 1999;59:851-8.
Izaks GJ, et al. The definition of anemia in older persons. JAMA 1999;281:1714–7.

GEN

Beth Weinstock, MD
Frank J. Weinstock, MD
Ken Griffiths, MD

66. OCULAR DISORDERS & SCREENING

I. INDICATIONS FOR REFERRAL TO OPHTHALMOLOGIST

A. Immediate referral

1. **Penetrating trauma:** History of missile type injury, high velocity, metal on metal, irregular pupil
2. **Acute glaucoma:** Red and painful eye, pupil semi-dilated and fixed, hazy cornea decreased vision. May have nausea and abdominal pain
3. **Corneal ulcer:** Red and painful eye, photophobia, fluorescein staining on cornea. Usually associated with trauma, poor lid apposition, or contact lens wear
4. **Postoperative infection/endophthalmitis:** Pain, decreased vision, white cell level in anterior chamber, purulent drainage. Can result from any invasive ophthalmologic procedure
5. **Iritis:** Limbal flush, photophobia, small pupil, sore eye. Usually post-traumatic
6. **Floaters or flashes:** Differential includes retinal detachment or hole, posterior vitreous detachment
7. **Sudden decreased vision:** Occlusion of the retinal vein or artery, trauma, or stroke
8. **Orbital cellulitis:** Fever, pain or restriction of eye movements, endophthalmitis, periorbital swelling
9. **Chemical exposure with alkali**

B. Referral within several days: Poor healing of corneal abrasion, unresponsive conjunctivitis, double vision or any visual problem that does not improve with treatment

II. HISTORY

A. Onset and duration of symptoms (sudden, gradual), and associated symptoms including pain, redness, itching, burning, crusting/matting
B. Change in vision: Floaters, halos, scotoma (zigzags), photopsia (flashing lights), specific visual field defects
C. Photophobia
D. Pain, with or without eye movement
E. Diplopia (double vision)
F. Systemic symptoms of CVA/TIA, nausea, vomiting, abdominal pain (from the severe pain), fever, temporal pain
G. Contact lens wear
H. Night blindness or vision decrease (combined with myopia, cataracts, retinitis pigmentosa)
I. Recent eye surgery or trauma (if so, was the patient wearing safety glasses)

III. PHYSICAL EXAMINATION

A. **Check visual acuity** of each eye with correction. If corrective lenses not available, use pinhole (patient reads visual acuity chart through a pinhole which should compensate for any uncorrected refractive errors)
B. **Check pupils**
1. Size: Anisocoria (unequal pupils) may be acute or chronic (secondary to old trauma, surgery or a normal variant)
2. Reactivity: Sluggish versus rapidly reactive
3. Swinging flashlight test: Checks consensual response in opposite pupil (evaluation for optic nerve damage, i.e., glaucoma, retrobulbar neuritis)
C. **Inspect lids** for lid eversion (ectropion), lid inversion (entropion), lash growth toward the cornea (trichiasis), chalazion (see below). Also check for lash loss (hypothyroid) or crusting. May need to evert lid to check for foreign body, signs of blepharitis
D. **Extraocular muscle function:** Motility and position
1. Cranial nerve III: Innervates medial, inferior, and superior rectus and inferior oblique as well as levator muscle of lid
2. Cranial nerve IV: Innervates superior oblique

3. Cranial nerve VI: Innervates lateral rectus
4. Strabismus: Misalignment of the eyes

E. Fluorescein staining: Will stain areas of denuded or damaged epithelium (corneal abrasion, ulceration, etc.)

F. Tonometry: Average intra-ocular pressure is < 21 mmHg

G. Funduscopic Exam

1. Dilation: Eyes may be dilated if anterior chamber is not shallow (observed by shining light beam across the anterior chamber). Dilate with **Neo-Synephrine** 2.5% or 1% **Mydriacyl** (avoid Atropine due to long duration of action). Dilation causing an attack of acute angle closure glaucoma is extremely uncommon

2. Exam
   a. Red reflex: If unequal, consider cataract, vitreous hemorrhage, tumor
   b. Hemorrhages (e.g., diabetes, hypertension, trauma or renal disease)
   c. Retinal detachment
   d. Cotton wool spots: Infarctions of nerve fibers
   e. Cherry red spot in macula: Central retinal artery occlusion
   f. Papilledema, A-V nicking, cup/disc ratio (average is 0.3)

H. Confrontation visual field: To detect peripheral vision defects

I. Slit lamp exam: To examine anterior segment of eye, remove foreign bodies, and check for inflammatory cells in anterior chamber:

Hyphema: Blood in anterior chamber
Hypopyon: Layered white cells in anterior chamber (seen in iritis or infection)
Flare: Light scatter caused by inflammatory cells or proteins in the aqueous fluid

IV. MANAGEMENT

A. Conjunctivitis

1. Bacterial: Purulent drainage, red eye, minimal pain, no change in vision. Use 1 drop to affected eye Q 2hrs while awake × 2 days, then QID × 3–5 days. Many choices including:
   a. **Aminoglycosides** such as **Tobramycin** or **Gentamicin**
   b. **Quinolone** such as **Ofloxacin** (**Ocuflox**) or **Ciprofloxacin** (**Ciloxan**) for more severe infections
   c. **Neosporin** containing drops (**Neomycin, Polymyxin B,** and **Gramicidin**) may cause allergic reactions
   d. Encourage hand washing

2. Viral: No treatment necessary except infection control

3. Allergic: Itchy, red eyes. Bilateral. Many options, including:
   a. Antihistamine/decongestant: **Vasocon-A**
   b. Mast cell stabilizer: **Crolom Solution 4%, (Cromolyn Sodium)** 1 GTT QID, **Alamast (Pemirolast 0.1%)** 1–2 GTTS QID, **Alomide (Lodoxamide 0.1%)** 1–2 GTTS QID, **Alocril (Nedocromil 2%)** 1–2 GTTS BID
   c. Histamine antagonist: **Levocabastine** (**Livostin**) 1 GTT QID
   d. Anti-histamine/Mast-cell stabilizer: **Patanol** 1–2 GTTS BID
   e. Antihistamine/Mast-cell stabilizer/Eosinophil inhibitor: **Zaditor** 1 GTT Q8–12hr
   f. NSAID: **Ketorolac** (**Acular**), 1 GTT QID
   g. Steroid eye drops, not for extended use
   h. Systemic antihistamines: See Chapter 67, Allergic Rhinitis/Seasonal Allergies

B. Corneal abrasion: History of mild trauma (e.g., fingernail scratch, tree branch, contact lens), photophobia, conjunctival injection, involuntary lid closure, increased tearing, decreased vision if abrasion is located at center of cornea. Distinguish from corneal foreign body, herpes simplex (dendritic appearance to corneal stain), or corneal ulcer (infiltrate around corneal defect)

1. Use slit lamp to facilitate exam. If no slit lamp available, magnification of ophthalmoscope may be used for direct observation or by localizing the abrasion or foreign body against red reflex

2. Topical anesthetic (to relieve discomfort and facilitate examination): 1 drop of **Tetracaine** or **Proparacaine** will lead to immediate relief of pain. *Do not send anesthetic drops home with patient*

3. Prophylactic eye drops (ATBs) may be prescribed. If severe discomfort, may also give **Cycloplegic** drops (**1% Cyclopentolate** or **Homatropine 2% or 5%** TID) which will make patient more comfortable
4. Patient should follow-up in 1–2 days if not healed

C. Corneal foreign body
1. Topical anesthetic as used in corneal abrasion (see IV. B. above.)
2. Remove corneal foreign body with blunt instrument, cotton swab, or forceps
3. Patient may return to normal activities immediately. No need to patch eye
4. If a rust ring remains or foreign body cannot be removed, then refer

D. Conjunctival foreign body
1. No anesthetic necessary
2. Evert upper eyelid and remove foreign body with cotton swab
3. May see linear, vertical corneal abrasions (ice-skate track abrasions) indicating retained foreign bodies in the superior tarsal conjunctiva

E. Blepharitis: History of burning, excessive tearing (epiphora), foreign body sensation with erythema of lid margin, dandruff-like deposits on lashes, fibrinous scales around individual lashes (collarettes), lash loss, recurrent mild conjunctivitis. Caused by seborrhea, staph infection, and/or meibomian gland dysfunction and frequently recurs
1. Antibacterial eye drops, treat 7–10 days (chronic cases may require intermittent ATB/steroid drops)
2. Wash lids every day with baby shampoo (eyes closed)
3. Warm compresses to eye TID
4. Wash hands after touching eyes

F. Sudden onset double vision: Distinguish monocular from binocular double vision; binocular will resolve when either eye is covered. Monocular is secondary to uncorrected refractive error, dry eye, corneal scar, or cataract. Binocular diplopia may be secondary to nerve palsies (III, IV, or VI), decompensated strabismus, diabetes, cerebral aneurysm, tumor, myasthenia gravis, thyroid eye disease, orbital blow-out fractures
1. Patch either eye for symptomatic relief while awaiting definitive diagnosis
2. Evaluate for above mentioned entities and refer to ophthalmologist

G. Chalazion: Firm well-demarcated nodule just below lid margin; may have grayish discoloration on conjunctival surface which is secondary to a lipogranulomatous inflammation of meibomian gland
1. May be symptom-free, or nodule may be tender and erythematous
2. Treatment includes frequent warm compresses and ATB drops initially. After 1 month ophthalmologist may inject, lance, or excise the chalazion

H. Stye (hordeolum): Painful, erythematous, often pointed nodule on surface of skin (external stye) or on conjunctival surface (internal stye) which is usually caused by a staph infection of a sebaceous gland of the lid. Treatment includes warm compresses and topical ATB drops

I. Open-angle glaucoma
1. Refers to a group of diseases with progressive optic nerve damage and visual field loss, usually with associated elevations in intraocular pressure. Prevalence 0.5% of the population. More severe in African-Americans. Increased incidence with positive family history
2. Average intraocular pressure is < 21mmHg
3. Damage from glaucoma is manifested by optic nerve "cupping" (caused by loss of neurons and glial tissue). Cup-to-disc ≥ 0.6 or greater is one sign of glaucoma
4. Visual field loss over time (usually spares the central visual field until late)

J. Angle-closure glaucoma: Women > men, may have acute severe eye pain and blurry vision, with associated nausea, vomiting, diaphoresis, abdominal pain. May see halos around lights. *Requires immediate medical therapy followed by laser iridectomy*

V. PRIMARY/PREVENTIVE OPHTHALMOLOGY SCHEDULE
A. Neonates
1. Ophthalmologic screen for retinopathy of prematurity if birth weight <1500g, <33 weeks gestation, or received O_2 therapy for > 48hrs at birth
2. In all other neonates, red reflexes should be checked at birth and every visit thereafter

GEN

to screen for congenital cataracts, retinoblastoma, congenital glaucoma. Cataracts should be treated before the age of 3 months to prevent amblyopia. In more darkly pigmented individuals, the red reflex may look dull orange or whitish orange—make sure this is symmetric and uniform across entire reflex

B. Preschool

1. Screen for strabismus (exotropia and esotropia) with cover-uncover test and pupillary light reflex test (normally both light reflexes should be centered in each pupil). Begin screening at birth—prior to 4 months of age infants may show variable crossing or drifting out of the eyes due to underdevelopment of the macula. If strabismus not picked up early, it may lead to amblyopia (decreased vision in 1 eye). Refer for ophthalmololgic evaluation

2. Vision screening is feasible at around age 3½yrs; will initially use the Allen test (pictures) until child is able to read numbers or letters

C. School-aged children: Should have vision screen at least every 2–3yrs if asymptomatic

D. Adults

1. Routine "glaucoma" exam (Funduscopic exam and IOP) at 35 then every 2yrs (yearly if family history of glaucoma)

2. Funduscopic exam at least yearly in patients at increased risk—diabetes mellitus, family history of retinal detachments, or glaucoma corticosteroid therapy, **Plaquenil, Mellaril, Ethambutol** (visual acuity)

3. Age > 65; full eye exam every 1–2yrs regardless of risk factors

4. African-American (Recommendation of the Comprehensive Adult Eye Evaluation)—Comprehensive eye evaluation by an ophthalmologist:

   a. 20–39: Every 3–5yrs

   b. 40–64: Every 2–4yrs

   c. 65 or older: Every 1–2yrs

E. Diabetes: Examine type 1 diabetics within 3–5yrs of diagnosis and type 2 diabetics shortly after diagnosis. Subsequent exams annually

VI. SPECIFIC PEDIATRIC OPHTHALMOLOGIC DISORDERS

A. Conjunctivitis

1. In neonates, may be toxic conjunctivitis from routine perinatal prophylaxis

2. Infectious conjunctivitis may be caused by staph, chlamydia, herpes virus, gonorrhea. If discharge is purulent and excessive, gonorrhea is probable; *blindness can result in 24–48hrs, should be immediately referred*

B. Nasolacrimal duct obstruction (congenital)

1. Obstruction is common. It is usually unilateral which is often congenital due to lack of patency of the inferior ostium of the nasolacrimal duct. The tear lake is elevated, and the eye appears weepy

2. May get bacterial superinfection: Eyelids will be adherent with purulent matter on awakening. Lids are red with tearing of the eye. Infections will recur in spite of topical ATBs, unless duct opens or is opened up with massage and/or probing

3. Approximately 75% spontaneously open within first 6 months of life. Should be referred for duct probing after 6 months if no resolution. If persistent purulent drainage, then refer earlier

4. Can put pressure on nasolacrimal sac with a cotton swab or finger; if expression of mucopurulent material is seen from the puncta, then nasolacrimal duct obstruction is the diagnosis

5. Parent should massage over the duct 3–4 ×/day; this will relieve most obstructions

C. Strabismus (see under Preventive schedule)

1. Inward, outward, or upward deviation of 1 or both eyes; pupils are misaligned

2. Any patient with constant deviation, or deviation that develops after the first 3–4 months of life, should be referred to ophthalmologist

4. Therapy usually involves patching of good eye and/or corrective lenses (after evaluation to rule-out tumor, cataract, etc.)

5. Ideally, eyes should be straightened before age 2 to increase chance of stereopsis (normal depth perception)

GEN

CLINICAL PEARLS

- Vertically oriented, linear corneal abrasions may indicate a conjunctival foreign body under the upper lid. Evert the upper lid with a cotton swab
- Never send anesthetic eye drops home with patients with corneal abrasions; they delay healing by preventing re-epithelialization of the cornea, and may damage the cornea, resulting in blindness
- Always check vision before examination and treatment
- Be alert for herpes simplex; dendritic appearance under fluorescein staining
- **Neomycin** can cause allergic reaction in up to 10% of patients

References

Simon JW, Kaw P. Commonly missed diagnoses in the childhood eye examination. Am Fam Phys 2001;64:623–8.

American Diabetes Association: Diabetic retinopathy (Position Statement). Diabetes Care 23 2000;(Suppl. 1):S73–S76.

Leibowitz HM. Primary care: the red eye. N Engl J Med 2000;343:345.

Quilen D. Common causes of vision loss in elderly patients. Am Fam Phys 1999;60:99–108.

Olitsky SE. Common ophthalmologic concerns in infants and children. Pediatr Clin North Am 1998;45:993–1012.

Weinstock FJ, Weinstock MB. Common eye disorders: six patients to refer. Postgrad Med Apr 1996;99(4):107–10, 113–6.

American Diabetes Association: Clinical Practice Recommendations 2002. Position Statement, Jan 1998. Diabetic Retinopathy. Diabetes Care 2002;25(Suppl 1):S1–147.

Morrow GL, Abbott RL. Conjunctivitis. Am Fam Phys 1998;57:735.

Weinstock FJ, Assaad MH. Recurrent corneal erosions. Management by the primary care physician. Postgrad Med Nov 1995;98(5):155,159–60.

Ryan Hanson, MD
Michael B. Weinstock, MD

67. ALLERGIC RHINITIS/SEASONAL ALLERGIES

I. OVERVIEW

- **A.** Allergic rhinitis is an immunologically mediated disease. It is initiated by a type I antigen-antibody reaction. Inhaled allergens interact with T and B cell lymphocytes to produce IgE antibodies which then attach to mast cells and basophils resulting in the release of histamine and chemotactic factors and allergic rhinitis symptoms
- **B.** Allergic rhinitis is one of the most common primary care problems and affects 10–30% of adults and up to 40% of children
- **C.** Guidelines from the Joint Task Force on Practice Parameters in Allergy, Asthma and Immunology defines rhinitis "… as inflammation of the membranes lining the nose, and is characterized by nasal congestion, rhinorrhea, sneezing, itching of the nose and/or postnasal drainage."
- **D.** Rhinitis may be caused by allergic, non-allergic, infectious, hormonal, occupational, or other factors

II. HISTORY

- **A.** Seasonal prevalence
- **B.** Paroxysmal sneezing, rhinitis, dry, watery or pruritic eyes, pharyngeal itch, cough
- **C.** Triggering exposures
- **D.** Anosmia (decreased sense of smell)
- **E.** Age at onset
- **F.** Med use (inquire specifically about intranasal decongestants, also see list below)
- **G.** History of atopy
- **H.** Family history of allergies
- **I.** Nasal polyps: Often unilateral and associated with asthma and aspirin sensitivity. May mimic allergic rhinitis

III. PHYSICAL EXAM

A. Rhinorrhea and/or nasal congestion

B. Pale, boggy, blue-gray, edematous nasal turbinates which may be coated with clear secretions

C. Nasal crease ("allergic salute")

D. Infraorbital venous dilation (dark circles under eyes/allergic shiner)

E. Mouth breathing

F. Skin folds under eyes (Denies lines)

G. Cobblestoning of posterior pharynx

H. Scleral/conjunctival injection and/or edema

IV. LABS/TESTING

A. **Percutaneous testing (prick testing):** Small amount of antigen is pricked into the skin; can easily be done in office if supply of antigens is available. Preferred for initial testing because more rapid, less painful, less expensive, and less likely to cause systemic reactions

B. **Intradermal testing:** Antigen is injected into the dermis. Greater reproducibility and greater sensitivity than prick testing. Higher false positive rate than prick testing

C. **RAST (radioallergosorbent testing):** Blood is analyzed for specific anti-IgE antibodies to known antigens; useful for patients with extensive eczema, dermatographism or prior anaphylaxis, young, or cannot discontinue antihistamines

D. **Nasal smears:** Eosinophilia can be supportive but is not diagnostic

V. DIFFERENTIAL DIAGNOSIS: May mimic symptoms of allergic rhinitis

A. **Vasomotor rhinitis:** Related to autonomic dysfunction and more common in women

B. **Infectious rhinitis:** Viral URI, bacterial or viral sinusitis

C. **Rhinitis medicamentosa:** Tachyphylaxis after use of nasal decongestant. Nasal mucosa bright red and swollen

D. **Nonallergic rhinitis with eosinophilia syndrome (NARES):** Nasal eosinophils in patients who have perennial symptoms and occasionally loss of sense of smell

E. **Hormonal rhinitis:** Pregnancy (usually second trimester to term, resolving after delivery) and hypothyroidism

F. **Drug-induced rhinitis:** Aspirin, Clonidine, Hydralazine, Labetalol, Propranolol, Methyldopa, Prazosin, Terazosin, Reserpine, Viagra, NSAIDS, oral contraceptives

G. **Gustatory rhinitis:** Exposure to hot, spicy foods

H. **Nasal polyps:** May be associated with asthma and aspirin sensitivity

I. **Other:** Alcoholism, cocaine abuse, nasal septal deviation, tumors, adenoidal hypertrophy, hypertrophy of the nasal turbinates

VI. MANAGEMENT

A. **Environmental controls**

1. Indoor: Avoid active and passive tobacco smoke, remove bedroom carpet, foam pillows, enclose mattress and box springs in plastic, use air conditioning

2. Dust mites: Control bedroom: wash bedding weekly, impermeable covers on pillows and mattresses, keep humidity below 50%, HEPA (high density particulate air) filter

3. Molds: Remove any visible mold/mildew, treat with a retardant, frost-free refrigerator, keep firewood outside, avoid house-plants, clean heating and cooling systems, remove old books

4. Animals: Avoid furry animals and birds or eliminate carpeting and keep floors polished and upholstery frequently cleaned, HEPA vacuum. Animals should stay out of the bedroom

B. **Pharmacotherapy**

1. **Local meds:** Often helpful in conjunction with oral antihistamines

a. Steroid nasal inhalers: First line treatment

   i. **Beclomethasone Dipropionate (Vancenase/Beconase)** 1 spray in each nostril BID to QID. May decrease to QD once therapeutic

   ii. **Fluticasone Propionate (Flonase):** 2 sprays in each nostril QD or 1 spray in each BID

   iii. **Triamcinolone (Nasacort):** 2 sprays per nostril QD

   iv. **Flunisolide (Nasalide, Nasarel):** 2 sprays in each nostril BID

   v. **Budesonide (Rhinocort):** 2 sprays in each nostril BID

GEN

      vi. **Mometasone Furoate (Nasonex):** 2 sprays in each nostril QD
- b. Intranasal antihistamine—**Azelastine (Astelin):** 2 sprays each nostril BID
- c. Mast cell stabilizers—**Cromolyn Sodium (NasalCrom):** 1 spray in each nostril 3–6 ×/ day
- d. Saline nasal spray—Safe, inexpensive, helps thin mucous, use 3–6 ×/day, e.g., **Salinex, Ocean Nasal Mist, NaSal**
- e. Nasal vasoconstrictors—Should not use more than 3–4 days secondary to rebound vasodilatation and worsening of symptoms (Rhinitis medicamentosa). May be helpful in acute sinusitis or for airplane flights
  - i. **Neo-Synephrine (Phenylephrine):** 0.25, 0.5 or 1.0%: 2–3 sprays in each nostril Q 4hrs PRN
  - ii. **Oxymetazoline (Afrin)**
2. **Non-sedating antihistamines:** Slower onset of action than sedating antihistamines
   - a. **Fexofenadine (Allegra)**
     - i. 60mg PO BID or 180mg QD
     - ii. Approved for children 6–11yrs at 30mg PO BID
     - iii. Onset of action: 60 minutes
     - iv. Also available as **Allegra D** (60mg **Fexofenadine** and 120mg **Pseudoephedrine**) PO BID
   - b. **Cetirizine (Zyrtec)**
     - i. Dose: 5–10mg PO QD (slightly sedating in some patients)
     - ii. Approved for children 2–5yrs, 2.5mg QD with increases to 5mg QD (available 5mg/5cc). Dose for children 6–11yrs is 5–10mg QD
     - iii. Onset of action: 15–30 minutes
   - c. **Loratadine (Claritin)**
     - i. Dose: 10mg PO QD
     - ii. Approved for children 2–5 years: 5mg QD, > 6yrs, 10mg QD (available 5mg/5cc)
     - iii. Onset of action: 1–3hrs
     - iv. Also available as **Claritin D** 12hr (5mg **Loratadine**/120mg **Pseudoephedrine**) BID and **Claritin D** 24hr (10mg **Loratadine**/240mg **Pseudoephedrine**) QD
   - d. **Desloratadine (Clarinex)**
     - i. Dose: 5mg PO QD
     - ii. Approved for patients > 12yrs
3. **Sedating antihistamines:** Caution in patients with BPH and in the elderly secondary to urinary retention and risk of glaucoma
   - a. **Diphenhydramine (Benadryl, Banophen, Diphenhist)**
     - i. Adults: 25–50mg PO TID–QID
     - ii. Children >9 kg: 5mg/kg/24hrs divided TID to QID PRN
   - b. **Chlorpheniramine (Chlor-Trimeton, Chloamine, Allerchlor)**
     - i. Adults: 4mg PO TID–QID PRN
     - ii. Children 6–11yrs: 2mg PO Q 4–6hrs
     - iii. Children 2–5yrs: 1mg PO Q 4–6hrs
   - c. **Hydroxyzine (Atarax, Vistaril):** 25mg PO QID PRN
4. **Oral decongestants:** Stimulatory CNS effects may offset sedative effects of sedating antihistamines
   - a. **Phenylephrine**
   - b. **Pseudoephedrine**—e.g., **Sudafed**
5. **Ophthalmic solutions**—Note: **Levocabastine, Ketorolac** and **Lodoxamide** should not be used with soft contact lenses
   - a. **Cromolyn Sodium (Crolom)**—mast cell stabilizer: 1–2 GTTS OU 4×/day
   - b. **Lodoxamide (Alomide)**—mast cell stabilize: 1–2 GTTS OU 4×/day
   - c. **Levocabastine (Livostin)**—antihistamine: 1 GTT OU QID for up to 2 weeks
   - d. **Naphcon-A** (vasoconstrictor/antihistamine): 1 GTT OU Q 3–4hrs PRN—Should not be used for a prolonged time due to rebound
   - e. **Ketorolac (Acular)**—Anti-inflammatory: 1 GTT QID/7 days
6. **Systemic steroids:** Rarely necessary, but may be helpful in severe cases of complete nasal obstruction. Short course of **Prednisone** for 1 week or less

GEN

C. Immunotherapy
1. Indications
   a. Unable to manage symptoms with environmental modification or meds
   b. Patients who require meds for greater than 6 months of the year
   c. Intolerable side effects to meds
2. Perform RAST testing or skin testing to identify the offending allergen
3. Weekly injections are initiated with a small amount of antigen, which is gradually increased. Length of time between injections is also gradually increased to once every 3–4 weeks
4. Often able to discontinue after 3–5 seasons

CLINICAL PEARLS
- It may often be helpful with copious rhinitis to give an oral decongestant (Pseudoephedrine, Phenylephrine) along with an antihistamine and intranasal med
- Allergic rhinitis symptoms may worsen during pregnancy
- Intranasal meds are much more effective if patient blows nose before using
- Onset of allergic rhinitis is before age 30 in 70% of patients
- Pharmacotherapy is much more effective when used at the onset of symptoms or before symptoms begin
- Therapy for rhinitis medicamentosa involves weaning the intranasal decongestant over 1 week and combining with oral steroids (0.5–1.0mg/kg/day) tapered over 7–10 days
- Cystic fibrosis should be considered in the differential diagnosis in children with nasal polyps

References

Kaszuba SM. Superiority of an intranasal corticosteroid compared with an oral antihistamine in the as-needed treatment of seasonal allergic rhinitis. Arch Int Med 2001:161:2581.

American Academy of Allergy, Asthma and Immunology (AAAAI). The allergy report. Milwaukee, WS: AAAAI; 2000.

Corren J. Allergic rhinitis: Treating the adult. J Allergy Clin Immunol 2000;105:S610–5.

Fireman P. Therapeutic approaches to allergic rhinitis: Treating the child. J Allergy Clin Immunol 2000;105:S616–21.

Dykewicz MS, et al. Diagnosis and management of rhinitis: Complete guidelines of Joint Task Force on Practice Parameters in Allergy, Asthma and Immunology. Ann Allergy Asthma Immunol 1998;81:478–518.

Daniel M. Neides, MD

68. ACUTE SINUSITIS

I. GENERAL
A. **Definition:** Inflammation of the mucosa of 1 or more of the paranasal sinuses. The term rhinosinusitis has been suggested to replace acute sinusitis. Acute bacterial rhinosinusitis is usually a secondary infection resulting from sinus ostia obstruction or impairment of mucus clearance mechanisms caused by an acute viral upper respiratory tract
B. Rhinosinusitis is 1 of the 10 most common diagnoses in ambulatory care and resulted in approximately 25 million US physician office visits in 1995. Most common sinuses involved are the maxillary and ethmoid sinuses
C. This chapter is based on a clinical practice guideline published in the Annals of Internal Medicine in 2001 and endorsed by the Centers for Disease Control and Prevention, the American Academy of Family Physicians, the American College of Physicians–American Society of Internal Medicine, and the Infectious Diseases Society of America
D. 4 principles are discussed in these recommendations:
   1. Most cases presenting in the ambulatory setting are caused by viruses and not bacteria
   2. Since it is difficult to differentiate between bacterial and viral etiologies, the diagnosis of bacterial rhinosinusitis should be reserved for patients with 7 days of symptoms and maxillary pain or tenderness in the face or teeth and purulent nasal secretions. Rarely, patients may present with symptoms of shorter duration

3. Sinus radiography is not recommended
4. Most cases resolve without ATB treatment. ATBs should be reserved for those with severe symptoms, especially for those with unilateral facial pain. The most narrow spectrum ATB against *S. pneumoniae* and *H. influenzae* should be used

II. ETIOLOGY

A. Bacterial pathogens: *S. pneumoniae, H. influenzae, S. aureus, M. catarrhalis,* and *S. pyogenes*
B. Viral: Multiple pathogens

III. HISTORY: Features which increase the chances of acute bacterial rhinosinusitis are purulent nasal discharge along with maxillary tooth or facial pain (especially when unilateral), unilateral sinus tenderness, and worsening of symptoms after initial improvement. These symptoms however, are not specific

IV. PHYSICAL EXAMINATION

A. Purulence in the nares or nasopharynx (not always visible)
B. Irritation of the nasal mucosa: Leads to inflammation with a bright red, irregular appearance
C. Nasal polyps: Prolonged nasal inflammation may lead to polypoid degeneration of nasal mucosa and formation of polyps
D. Facial tenderness to palpation or percussion
1. Maxillary: Subzygomatic over cheek and upper teeth
2. Ethmoid: Periorbital
3. Frontal: Forehead above eyebrow
4. Sphenoid
a. Usually retrobulbar, often not well localized
b. Infection in sphenoid sinus may lead to pain and tenderness over vertex of skull, mastoid bones, and occipital portion of head
E. Periorbital tissue swelling or erythema of skin overlying affected sinus may be seen

V. CLASSIFICATION

A. Acute: Symptom duration < 4 weeks
B. Subacute: Symptom duration 4–12 weeks
C. Chronic: Symptom duration > 12 weeks

VI. DIAGNOSTIC PROCEDURES

A. Radiography
1. Plain films. No longer recommended due to the poor sensitivity and specificity
2. Sinus CT Scan
a. In general, high sensitivity but poor specificity as many patients with viral rhinosinusitis and viral URIs will have positive sinus CTs. However, 1 study found that when characteristic CT findings are combined with a high clinical likelihood (see III. above), the positive predictive value is about 90%
b. Not necessary to obtain in an uncomplicated acute sinusitis. Should be performed when diagnosis is in question
B. Rhinoscopy (flexible): Allows a detailed examination of the upper nasal cavities and posterior nasopharynx. Technique is also valuable in identifying polyps in the high nasal vault, and structural abnormalities
C. Transillumination: Technique has been unreliable in diagnosing acute sinusitis

VII. MEDICAL TREATMENT

A. There is controversy about ATB therapy for management of acute rhinosinusitis and there have been numerous recommendations for therapy. As previously stated, the clinical practice guidelines recently published recommend initial therapy with a narrow spectrum ATB. In 2001, a study (Piccirillo JF, et. al.) which retrospectively evaluated the efficacy of first and second line ATBs was published. It looked at 29,102 patients in 1996–1997 and found that the success rate for first line ATB was 90.1% and second line ATB was 90.8%. There were 2 cases of periorbital cellulitis in each group. Cost difference was $66.19 and was entirely attributed to ATB cost. Concluded that patients did not have clinically significant differences in outcomes based on the ATB used

GEN

B. Patients with complicated sinusitis with possible meningitis, cavernous sinus thrombosis, or periorbital cellulitis should be further evaluated before prescribing oral ATB

C. Initial therapy: May use any of these for 10–14 days

    1. **Amoxicillin**

        a. Adults: 500mg PO TID or 875mg PO BID

        b. Children: 40mg/kg/day in 2–3 divided doses

    2. **Trimethoprim-Sulfamethoxazole (Bactrim)**

        a. Adults: 1 double-strength tablet Q12hrs

        b. Children: (pediatric suspension) 8mg/kg/day **TMP** and 40mg/kg/day **SMX** in 2 divided doses Q12hrs

    3. **Doxycycline (Vibramycin)**: 100mg PO BID

D. Subsequent therapy for treatment failure involves a second line ATB

E. Adjunctive therapies

    1. **Nasal steroid spray**

    2. **Antihistamines and decongestants**

        a. Limited studies of decongestants show that they decrease nasal-airway resistance; however, their overall effect on the clinical course of acute sinusitis is not well known

        b. Antihistamines should probably be reserved for patients with known allergies

    3. Nasal irrigation

        a. May be used for patients with increased mucus drainage

        b. Bulb syringe is used to irrigate nasal passage with saline, TID–QID PRN

F. Failure despite above approaches

    1. Radiologic studies to obtain definitive diagnosis

    2. ATBs: Consider using a different second line agent for 4–6 weeks in conjunction with nasal steroids and a decongestant

    3. Referral to an allergist or ENT

VIII. RECURRENT OR CHRONIC SINUSITIS

A. In children the most common cause of recurrent sinusitis is recurrent viral upper respiratory infection

B. Other conditions predisposing patients to chronic sinusitis include allergic inflammation, cystic fibrosis, immunodeficiency disorders (insufficient or dysfunctional immunoglobulins), ciliary dyskinesia (immotile cilia syndrome, Kartagener's syndrome), nasal polyps, or an anatomical problem

C. Evaluation of children with recurrent or chronic sinusitis may include consulting an allergist, a sweat test, measurement of immunoglobulins and their subclasses, and possibly a mucosal biopsy (to assess ciliary function and structure)

IX. COMPLICATIONS OF ACUTE SINUSITIS (AND THEIR TREATMENT)

A. Periorbital cellulitis: Manifested by eye swelling, exophthalmos, and imparted/painful extraocular movements

B. Intracranial abscess: Manifested by signs of increased intracranial pressure, meningeal irritation, and focal neurologic deficits

C. Meningitis

X. INDICATIONS FOR SURGERY OR REFERRAL

A. Patients with chronic or recurrent sinusitis who have failed an extended course of ATBs, nasal steroids and allergy management

B. Patients with chronic sinusitis and worsening pulmonary disease

C. Patients with severe asthma which is exacerbated by recurrent sinus symptoms

CLINICAL PEARLS

- Before committing a patient to the diagnosis of *chronic* sinusitis, consider radiologic studies
- 3 most common causes of chronic cough (90–95%) are post-nasal drip (often secondary to sinusitis), asthma and gastroesophageal reflux disease (GERD)
- Acute rhinosinusitis is often viral in origin. Physicians prescribe an ATB 85–98% of the time
- *Pseudomonas* may be a pathogen in patients with cystic fibrosis
- Patients with HIV can present with recurrent sinusitis

GEN

References

Hirschmann JV. Antibiotics for common respiratory tract infections in adults. Arch Int Med 2002;162:256.

Hickner JM, et al. Principles of appropriate antibiotic use for acute rhinosinusitis in adults: Background. Ann Intern Med 2001;134:498–505 (Clinical practice guideline).

Osguthorpe JD. Acute rhinosinusitis: Diagnosis and management. Am Fam Phys 2001;63:69–76.

Piccirillo JF, et al. Impact of first-line vs second-line antibiotics for the treatment of acute uncomplicated sinusitis. JAMA 2001;286:1849–56.

Snow V, et al. Principles of appropriate antibiotic use for acute sinusitis in adults. Ann Intern Med 2001;134:495–7 (Clinical practice guideline).

Michael B. Weinstock, MD
Daniel M. Neides, MD

69. DIFFERENTIAL DIAGNOSIS OF ARTHRITIS

I. EVALUATION WITH HISTORY, PHYSICAL EXAM, AND COMMON CONDITIONS

Differentiate between mono-arthritis (1 joint involvement) and polyarthritis (> 1 joint involved)—see II. Differential Diagnosis below and V. Lab Tests for Polyarthritis below

GEN

A. Mechanical vs. inflammatory

1. Mechanical (Internal derangement, fracture, trauma, or loose body) is suggested by rapid onset of pain (over seconds or minutes), pain that occurs only after use, improves with rest, and involves weight-bearing joints

2. Inflammatory arthritis is suggested by onset from hours to days, intermittent pain unrelated to patterns of use, including fluctuations of pain and swelling, and morning stiffness

B. Exclude infectious arthritis

1. Joint sepsis produces dramatic inflammation followed quickly by irreversible destruction of cartilage and bone. Most develop from hematogenous spread

2. Infection should be suspected with the presence of systemic risk factors such as corticosteroid therapy, immunodeficiency or immunosuppression, diabetes, or intravenous drug abuse and local pathology such as effusions, penetrating trauma, previous injection of corticosteroids, prosthetic joint

3. Patient complains of intense local pain and may resist attempts to examine the affected joint. Infected peripheral joints are swollen, warm, very tender, and sometimes red, and they have markedly restricted range of motion; large joints are more frequently affected than small ones in the absence of local trauma or peripheral vascular disease

4. Gonococcal infection tends to manifest as an inordinately painful monarthritis or polyarthritis and often is preceded by a migratory arthritis

5. Lyme arthritis occurs weeks to months after initial exposure and after the development of the early syndrome of fevers, arthralgias, lymphadenopathy, and rash

C. Crystal induced arthritis

1. Usually a history of recurrent, self-limited attacks of inflammation of the same joint. Clinical features include extremely rapid onset of severe pain and inflammation with extension of the inflammatory process into surrounding tissues, producing appearance of cellulitis

2. Gout is present when urate crystals are identified in synovial fluid or confirmed by documentation of urate crystals in a tophus

3. Pseudogout: Calcium pyrophosphate dihydrate (CPPD) deposition is associated with acute or chronic inflammatory arthritis

D. Other—Non-inflammatory monoarticular arthritis

1. Osteoarthritis frequently manifests as monoarthritis, particularly in the knee, hip, acromioclavicular joint, first radiocarpal joint, or first metatarsophalangeal joint

2. Hip symptoms in a young patient suggest congenital dysplasia of hip or slipped capital femoral epiphysis
3. Osteochondritis dissecans should be suspected in a child or teenager who, after minor trauma, has relatively severe knee pain followed by mechanical dysfunction
4. Osteonecrosis is a common cause of monoarthritis of the hip, shoulders, and knees in young people with systemic diseases who require corticosteroid therapy
5. Hemarthrosis may occur in patients with clotting disorders or on anticoagulant therapy

II. DIFFERENTIAL DIAGNOSIS—MONOARTICULAR VS. POLYARTICULAR ARTHRITIS
(common presentations)

A. Monoarticular
1. Septic arthritis: Bacterial, tuberculous, fungal, Lyme disease
2. Crystal disease: Gout, pseudogout
3. Mechanical: Internal derangement, trauma, overuse, loose body, osteochondritis dissecans, stress fracture
4. Ischemic necrosis
5. Hemarthrosis: Coagulopathy, Warfarin (Coumadin)
6. Pauciarticular juvenile: Rheumatoid arthritis
7. Neoplastic: Osteogenic sarcoma, metastatic tumor
8. Other: Congenital hip dysplasia, reflex sympathetic dystrophy, Paget's disease involving joint, osteomyelitis

B. Polyarticular
1. Rheumatoid arthritis
2. Osteoarthritis
3. Psoriatic arthritis
4. Reiter's syndrome (idiopathic and human immunodeficiency virus)
5. Calcium pyrophosphate deposition disease
6. Chronic articular hemorrhage
7. Most juvenile rheumatoid arthritis and juvenile spondylitis
8. Erythema nodosum/sarcoid
9. Serum sickness: Acute hepatitis B, rubella
10. Henoch-Shönlein purpura
11. Systemic lupus erythematosus
12. Lyme disease
13. Parvovirus

III. DIAGNOSTIC STUDIES

A. **Synovial fluid analysis:** To differentiate between inflammatory, non-inflammatory and septic arthritis in patients with monoarthritis. See table below
B. **Cultures:** Culture synovial fluid if septic arthritis is suspected. If gonococcal arthritis is a consideration, cervicourethral, rectal, and pharyngeal samples should be obtained
C. **X-rays:** Plain radiographs of the affected joints should be obtained; common findings are soft tissue calcification, osteoarthritis, chondrocalcinosis, loose bodies, fracture, malignancy, osteomyelitis, or Paget's disease
D. **Nuclear Medicine:** Useful when it is important to search for a site of infection that cannot be detected or localized, fibrocartilaginous joints in which range of motion is poorly tested, or the spine
E. **MRI:** Superior to other imaging modalities in the diagnosis of ischemic necrosis of bone; occult fractures, meniscal and cruciate ligament injuries
F. **Ultrasound:** Useful for aspirating almost any joint
G. **Synovial biopsy:** May play a role in the diagnosis of chronic, unexplained monoarticular arthritis; tuberculous or fungal synovitis is more frequently identified by staining and culture of open biopsy material than by similar studies of synovial fluid
H. **Laboratory tests for polyarthritis**—see V. table below

GEN

IV. EXAMINATION OF JOINT FLUID

Examination of Joint Fluid				
Measure	Normal	Group I (Noninflammatory)	Group II (Inflammatory)	Group III (Purulent)
Volume (mL) (knee)	< 3.5	Often > 3.5	Often > 3.5	Often > 3.5
Clarity	Transparent	Transparent	Translucent to opaque	Opaque
Color	Clear	Yellow	Yellow to opalescent	Yellow to green
WBC (per µL)	< 200	200–300	3000-50,000	> 50,000[1]
Polymorphonuclear leukocytes	< 25%	< 25%	50% or more	75% or more [1]
Culture	Negative	Negative	Negative	Usually positive
Glucose (mg/dL)	Nearly equal to serum	Nearly equal to serum	> 25, lower than serum	< 25, much lower than serum

[1]Counts are lowered with infections caused by organisms of low virulence or if antibiotic therapy has been started.

Source: Tierney LM, et al., *Current medical diagnosis & treatment*, 41st ed. Lange Medical/McGraw-Hill, 2002;20:834.

GEN

V. LABORATORY TESTS FOR POLYARTHRITIS

Laboratory Tests for Polyarthritis		
Test	Significance	
	Positive	Negative
Rheumatoid factor	Helpful in young persons, in whom background positivity is low	Prognostic significance only, not helpful in individual cases
Antinuclear antibody	High titer, suggestive of a rheumatic disease	Virtually rules out active systemic lupus
Uric acid	Elevated levels, indicating that gout is possible	If repeated levels are normal, gout unlikely
Antistreptolysin O	Recent streptococcal exposure	Rheumatic fever unlikely
HLA-B27	Possibly marginally useful in early- onset ankylosing spondylitis	No benefit
Anti-*Borrelia*	Only helpful if pretest probability is high	Chronic Lyme disease unlikely

Source: Ruddy S, et al. *Kelly's textbook of rheumatology*, 6th ed. Copyright © 2001 W. B. Saunders. With permission from Elsevier.

CLINICAL PEARLS

- *Rapid* development of OA symptoms—consider the possibility of fracture related to osteopenia, an adjacent destructive process such as metastatic tumor, or avascular necrosis
- Untreated infectious arthritis can destroy a joint in 1–2 days
- Intravenous drug abuse increases the risk of septic arthritis through the introduction of infectious material into the intravascular space with subsequent hematogenous spread to the joints; most commonly caused by *Staphylococcus aureus* and *Pseudomonas*

References

Hani SE, et al. Evaluating patients with arthritis of recent onset: Studies in pathogenesis and prognosis. JAMA 2000;284:2368.

Pinals RS. Current concepts: Polyarthritis and fever. N Engl J Med 1994;330:769.

Baker DG, et al. Current concepts: Acute monoarthritis. N Engl J Med 1993;329:1013.

Linda Stone, MD
Michael B. Weinstock, MD
Edward T. Bope, MD

70. OSTEOARTHRITIS

I. INTRODUCTION
A. Osteoarthritis, also called degenerative joint disease (DJD), is the most common form of joint disease affecting 20 million in US. Marked loss of cartilage and joint space is characteristically found. Joint margin changes are also seen

B. Etiology is not known but it is more frequent with aging, has a genetic component, and is more common in the presence of other disorders such as RA, gout, Paget's and trauma including old sports injuries. By age 65, 80% will have some x-ray evidence and 5–10% will be symptomatic

C. 2 types
   1. Primary: Affects the DIP, PIP, the hip, knee, MTP joint of the great toe and the cervical and lumbar spine
   2. Secondary: May occur at any joint after an articular injury

II. SYMPTOMS AND SIGNS
A. Pain worsens with weight bearing and later with movement of the affected joint
B. Pain improves with rest
C. Joints enlarge and are tender to palpation
D. Often have crepitus and limited ROM, possibly with minimal effusions
E Heberden's nodes (DIP joints) and Bouchard's nodes (PIP joints)
F. Note: Systemic signs should prompt exploration for other causes
G. Patients at increased risk: Advancing age, family history of osteoarthritis, old joint injuries, participation in competitive sports, obesity

III. X-RAY: Used to confirm. Findings not always correlated with pain
A. Joint space narrowing
B. Osteophyte formation
C. Bony sclerosis
D. Cyst formation
E. Joint space collapse

IV. MANAGEMENT
A. Nonpharmacologic
   1. Routine exercise (walking, swimming) and stretching
   2. Weight loss and joint protection
   3. Muscle strengthening
   4. Patellar taping, lateral insole
   5. Support: Groups and telephone
   6. Ambulation assistive devices
   7. Surgery for knee and hip replacement for end stage knee and hip arthritis
B. Pharmacologic
   1. **Acetaminophen** is equally effective compared to NSAIDs for knee OA. Should be tried first line due to side effects associated with NSAIDs
   2. NSAIDs with GI protection (**Misoprostol**) if indicated
   3. COX-2 inhibitors for patients at high risk of GI complications
   4. Capsaicin cream
   5. Intra-articular steroids
   6. Intra-articular hyaluronan
   7. Glucosamine
   8. Estrogen replacement therapy may reduce knee and hip arthritis

CLINICAL PEARLS
   • Approximately 90% of all people will have evidence of osteoarthritis in weight bearing joints by 40

GEN

- There is no increased incidence of OA in recreational runners
- Although OA usually spares the wrist and MCP joints, it may involve these joints at the thumb
- Watch for side effects of NSAIDs, especially in the elderly patient: Inquire about signs of GI bleed and renal compromise. Monitor renal labs
- Discuss prognosis so that patient can have realistic expectations of future

References

Moreli V, et al. Alternative therapies for traditional disease states: osteoarthritis. Am Fam Phys 2003;67:339–44.

Hinton R, et al. Osteoarthritis: diagnosis and therapeutic considerations. Am Fam Phys 2002;65:841-8.

Mitka M. Arthritis pain guidelines. JAMA 2002;287:2067. http://www.ampainsoc.org

Felson DT, et al. Osteoarthritis: New insights. Part 1: The disease and its risk factors. Ann Intern Med 2000;133:635.

Felson DT, et al. Osteoarthritis: New insights. Part 2: Treatment approaches. Ann Intern Med 2000;133:726.

Creamer P, et al. Management of osteoarthritis in older adults. Clin Geriatr Med 1998;14:435–54.

Lane NE, Thompson JM. Management of osteoarthritis in the primary-care setting: an evidence-based approach to treatment. Am J Med 1997;103:25S–30S.

Laurie Dangler, MD
Michael B. Weinstock, MD
Miriam Chan, PharmD

GEN

71. RHEUMATOID ARTHRITIS

I. DEFINITION: A chronic, systemic inflammatory connective tissue disease characterized by symmetric, erosive synovitis and sometimes multisystem involvement. Etiology is unknown

II. EPIDEMIOLOGY

A. Estimated prevalence of 0.5–1% of US population

B. Prevalence increases with age

C. Women 2 × as often as men

D. Much higher concordance in monozygotic twins compared to dizygotic twins, suggesting genetic predisposition; also higher incidence with certain HLA subtypes (DR4 and DR1)

III. SIGNS AND SYMPTOMS

A. Insidious development of symptoms over several weeks

B. Symmetric inflammation of smaller joints, esp. MCP, PIP, and MTP joints, but may also affect large joints, particularly later in the disease (involvement of DIP joints is more typical of osteoarthritis and psoriatic arthritis)

C. Morning stiffness often lasting over 1hr

D. Joint deformity: Caused by laxity of ligaments and tendons around the joints
   1. Swan-neck: flexion of PIP and hyperextension at DIP joints
   2. Ulnar deviation of MCP joints
   3. Atlantoaxial subluxation of cervical spine: May cause myelopathy or even death (esp. if in car accident or other trauma with subluxation)

E. Joint destruction: Often not apparent on x-ray until 1yr after onset of disease; initially osteopenia followed by erosion of bone and decalcification

F. Rheumatoid nodules: Occur over pressure points and may be confused with tophi

G. Sjögren's syndrome: May occur secondarily, especially in older patients with long-standing disease

H. Anemia: Often have mild normochromic, normocytic anemia

I. Other: May also have vasculitis, pulmonary manifestations, nerve entrapment syndromes (e.g., carpal tunnel), low-grade fever, malaise, fatigue, and weight loss

IV. DIAGNOSIS

A. Rheumatoid Factor: Nonspecific but present in up to 90% of patients with RA, usually associated with more severe, erosive disease

    B. **Inflammatory markers:** ESR and C-reactive protein elevated but very nonspecific, however, may be used to clinically follow disease with changes in treatment

    C. **Synovial fluid analysis:** WBC count typically 10,000–20,000 with 60–75% PMNs

    D. **Diagnosis:** Based on American College of Rheumatology Criteria

The 1987 American College of Rheumatology Revised Criteria for Classification of Rheumatoid Arthritis (Traditional Format)

CRITERION	DEFINITION
1. Morning stiffness	Morning stiffness in and around the joints lasting at least one hour before maximal improvement
2. Arthritis of three or more joint areas	At least three joint areas with simultaneous soft tissue swelling or fluid (not bony overgrowth alone) observed by a physician. The 14 possible joint areas are right or left PIP, MCP, wrist, elbow, knee, ankle and MTP joints
3. Arthritis of hand joints	At least one joint area swollen as above in a wrist, MCP or PIP
4. Symmetric arthritis	Simultaneous involvement of the same joint areas on both sides of the body; bilateral involvement of PIP, MCP or MTP joints is acceptable without absolute symmetry
5. Rheumatoid nodules	Subcutaneous nodules, over bony prominences, or extensor surfaces, or juxta-articular regions, observed by a physician
6. Serum rheumatoid factor	Demonstration of abnormal amounts of rheumatoid factor by any method that has been positive in less than 5% of normal control subjects
7. Radiologic changes	Radiologic changes typical of rheumatoid arthritis on postanterior hand and wrist roentgenograms, which must include erosions or unequivocal bony decalcification localized to or most marked adjacent to the involved joints (osteoarthritis changes alone do not qualify)

NOTE: For classification purposes, a patient shall be said to have rheumatoid arthritis if at least 4 of the 7 criteria are present. Criteria 1 through 4 must have been present for at least 6 weeks. Patients with 2 clinical diagnoses are not excluded. Designation as "classic," "definite" or "probable" rheumatoid arthritis is not made

PIP = proximal interphalangeal joint; MCP = metacarpophalangeal joint; MTP = metatarsophalangeal joint

Source: Arnett FC. Revised criteria for the classification of rheumatoid arthritis. Bull Rheum Dis 1989;38(5):1–6. Used with permission.

V. MANAGEMENT

    A. **Goals**

        1. Relief of symptoms

        2. Preservation of function

        3. Prevention of structural damage and deformity

        4. Maintenance of a normal life-style

    B. **Education:** Explain goals of therapy and chronic disease course to patients; enroll help of family members and other support groups

    C. **Physical and occupational therapy**

    D. **Systemic rest:** Depends on the severity of disease (e.g., mild disease may require only 2hrs of rest per day)

    E. **Articular rest:** Relaxation and stretching of the hip and knee muscles to prevent contractures

    F. **Exercise:** To preserve joint motion, and enhance muscular strength and endurance

    G. **Assistive devices:** Raised toilet seat, gripping bar, cane, crutches, etc. (see Chapter 108, Falls in the Elderly)

    H. **Weight loss:** Will aid with arthritis of the lower extremities

    I. **Local therapies**

GEN

1. Heat and cold: For analgesic effects (heat or cold) and muscle-relaxing effects (prior to exercising or stretching—local moist heat or warm tub baths)
2. Injections of corticosteroids (see Chapter 89, Corticosteroid Injection of Joints)
3. Splints: To provide joint rest, reduce pain, prevent contracture. Should be applied for the shortest period of time possible and should be removed at least twice per day for stretching and range of motion exercises. May coordinate with physical or occupational therapist

J. Medications: The 4 categories are NSAIDs, glucocorticoids, DMARDs, and analgesics. Current strategy involves immediate therapy to control disease activity and prevent irreversible changes. This replaces the older gradualist approach

1. **Non-steroidal anti-inflammatory drugs (NSAIDs):** Do not affect the outcome, but do help to control symptoms
   a. **Aspirin:** Inexpensive; 650–975mg QID. Use of enteric coated Aspirin helps to decrease GI side effects
   b. Other NSAIDs have not been proven to be more effective than Aspirin, but may have less side effects. Most common side effects are GI and renal toxicity
   c. COX-2 inhibitors (**Celebrex, Vioxx, Bextra**) have similar efficacy as traditional NSAIDs. Their advantage is a reduced rate of adverse events, especially upper GI bleeding. Dose: **Celebrex** 100–200mg BID, **Vioxx** 25–50mg QD, **Bextra** 10mg QD
   d. GI prophylaxis with chronic NSAID use: First line is **Misoprostol (Cytotec)**. Proton pump inhibitors may be used to prevent NSAID induced ulcer. H_2 blockers and **Carafate** do not reduce the frequency of gastric ulceration, but do reduce dyspepsia
   e. **Misoprostol (Cytotec)**
      i. Indications: Should be given to patients at high risk for GI toxicity
         1. Age > 75
         2. Concomitant use of steroids, use of NSAIDs > 3 months, use of > 1 NSAID or large doses of NSAIDs
         3. History of peptic ulcer disease or GI bleeding
         4. Significant cardiovascular disease
      ii. Dose: 200mcg PO QID (may decrease to 100mcg QID or 200mcg BID if not well tolerated)
      iii. Side effects: Diarrhea and bloating. Note: Absolutely contraindicated in pregnancy

2. **Glucocorticoids**
   a. Indications
      i. Used as a bridge between NSAIDs and until onset of action of the DMARDs (see below)
      ii. For refractory disease when the NSAIDs and DMARDs have failed
      iii. For severe extra-articular manifestations (pericarditis, perforating eye lesions, etc.)
   b. Dose: Use the lowest dose possible—10mg PO QD or less (preferably 5–7.5mg QD). When discontinued, should be slowly tapered down
   c. Patients on chronic prednisone (≥ 7.5mg/day) should receive **Fosamax** or **Actonel** 5mg QD to prevent steroid-induced osteoporosis

3. **Disease-modifying antirheumatic drugs (DMARDs)**
   a. Have potential for modifying course of disease. **Methotrexate** is most frequently prescribed for initial therapy
   b. Consider starting within 2 months of diagnosis to reduce the possibility of irreversible joint destruction
   c. Should be prescribed by someone with experience with this category of drugs
   d. Require several months before effect is seen and require close monitoring for side effects

GEN

Disease-Modifying Antirheumatic Drugs for the Treatment of Rheumatoid Arthritis*			
Drug	**Usual Maintenance Dose**	**Route of Administration**	**Clinically Important Adverse Effects**
Methotrexate	12.5-25 mg/wk	Oral, subcutaneous	Nausea, fatigue, stomatitis, leukopenia, pneumonitis, hepatic fibrosis
Leflunomide	10-20 mg/d	Oral	Diarrhea, abdominal pain, allergic reactions, hypertension, alopecia, rash, elevated serum transaminases
Sulfasalazine	2-3 g/d in divided doses	Oral	Nausea, rash, headache, agranulocytosis, hepatitis, Stevens-Johnson reaction
Cyclosporine	2.5-5 mg/kg daily	Oral	Hypertension, renal insufficiency, hirsutism, tremors, hypertrichosis, gingival hyperplasia, lymphoproliferative disease
Azathioprine	2-3 mg/kg daily	Oral	Bone marrow suppression, hepatitis, pancreatitis, hypersensitivity reaction
Gold sodium malate	50 mg/wk-50 mg/4 times per wk	Intramuscular	Rash, stomatitis, bone marrow suppression, proteinuria
D-Penicillamine	500-1000 mg/d	Oral	Rash, leukopenia, thrombocytopenia, proteinuria, autoimmune syndromes
Hydroxychloroquine†	400 mg/d	Oral	Nausea, abdominal pain, rash, headache, myopathy, retinopathy
Minocycline†	100 mg twice daily	Oral	Dizziness, rash, nausea, vomiting, dysgeusia, skin discoloration
Etanercept	25 mg twice weekly	Subcutaneous	Mild injection site reactions, infection, SLE-like reactions, demyelinating disorder
Infliximab	3 mg/kg per 8 wk	Intravenous	Infusion reactions, infections, SLE-like reactions, demyelinating disorder

*SLE indicates systemic lupus erythematosus.
†Treatment with these agents has not been shown to reduce progression of radiologic joint damage.

Source: Pisetsky DS, St.Clair EW. Progress in the treatment of rheumatoid arthritis. JAMA 2001;286(22):2788. ©2001 American Medical Association. Used with permission.

CLINICAL PEARLS

- Asking about length of morning stiffness, e.g., "How long does it take in the morning for you to feel as good as you'll be?", is a useful way of following the severity of the disease as the duration of morning stiffness correlates with the degree of joint inflammation
- Since Methotrexate is teratogenic, male patients should wait 3 months after stopping therapy, and female patients should wait at least 1 ovulatory cycle before attempting to get pregnant

References

Choy E, Panayi GS. Mechanism of disease: Cytokine pathways and joint inflammation in rheumatoid arthritis. N Engl J Med 2001;348:907.

Pisetsky DS, St. Clair EW. Progress in the treatment of rheumatoid arthritis. JAMA 2001;286:2787-90.

Möttönen T, et al. Comparison of combination therapy with single-drug therapy in early rheumatoid arthritis: a randomised trial. Lancet 1999;353:1568–73.

Pincus T, et al. Combination therapy with multiple disease-modifying antirheumatic drugs in rheumatoid arthritis: a preventive strategy. Ann Intern Med Nov 16, 1999;131:768–74.

American College of Rheumatology Ad Hoc Committee of Clinical Guidelines. Guidelines for the management of rheumatoid arthritis. Arthritis Rheum 1996; 39:723–31.

GEN

Steve Brook, MD
Thomas D. Armsey, Jr., MD
Phil Favia, MD

72. GOUTY ARTHRITIS

I. DEFINITION

A. Gout: A common inflammatory disease characterized by the deposition of monosodium urate crystals within the kidneys, subcutaneous tissues, or joints. Prevalence is same in men and women. May be classified as either primary (resulting from inborn errors of metabolism) or secondary (resulting from meds or other medical conditions). There are 4 stages of gout:

1. Asymptomatic hyperuricemia
2. Acute gouty arthritis
3. Interval gout
4. Chronic tophaceous gout

B. Hyperuricemia: Defined as a level > 7.0mg/dL and resulting from either overproduction or underexcretion of uric acid. Men are 6 × as likely as women to have a uric acid level > 7mg/dL

II. ETIOLOGY

A. Primary Gout

1. Underexcretion of uric acid (90% of patients): Primary idiopathic
2. Overproduction of uric acid (10% of patients)
   a. Primary idiopathic
   b. Hypoxanthine-guanine phosphoribosyltransferase deficiency
   c. Phosphoribosylpyrophosphate synthetase overactivity
   d. Glucose 6-phosphatase deficiency

B. Secondary Gout

1. Underexcretion of uric acid
   a. Renal disease (chronic renal failure, renal insufficiency, lead nephropathy, polycystic kidney disease)
   b. Meds (ASA, diuretics, Niacin, Levodopa, Ethambutol)
   c. Alcohol
   d. Dehydration
   e. Starvation/metabolic abnormalities
   f. Other: HTN, obesity, hypothyroidism, Down's syndrome
2. Overproduction of uric acid
   a. Purine-rich diet (organ meats, sardines, anchovies, bacon, turkey, venison, veal, scallops)
   b. Alcohol
   c. Obesity
   d. Exercise
   e. Other: Myeloproliferative disorders, lymphoproliferative disorders, hemolytic disorders, psoriasis, chemotherapy

III. DIFFERENTIAL DIAGNOSIS: Infectious arthritis, cellulitis, bursitis, tendonitis, osteoarthritis, rheumatoid arthritis, pseudogout, amyloidosis, type IIa hyperlipidemia

IV. SIGNS AND SYMPTOMS: Differ depending on the stage

A. Asymptomatic hyperuricemia

1. No symptoms present
2. Serum uric acid level elevated (> 7.0mg/dL)

B. Acute gouty arthritis

1. Classic presentation: Acute, nocturnal onset of pain, swelling, warmth, and erythema
2. Monoarticular involvement is most common, with the first MTP joint affected in 50% of cases. Other joints affected include the forefoot, heel, ankle, wrist, fingers, and elbow

GEN

3. Fever and chills may be present in severe attacks
4. Peak intensity occurs within 24–36hrs
5. Resolution of symptoms without treatment occurs in days to weeks
6. Absence of symptoms between acute attacks (termed interval gout)

C. Interval gout
1. The asymptomatic period between acute attacks. May last weeks to years (50% patients experience another acute attack within 1yr)
2. Tophi (subcutaneous or interosseous collections of urate crystals) may be present in up to 10% of patients if the disease has progressed to the chronic stage

D. Chronic tophaceous gout
1. Increasingly rare due to modern therapy
2. Locations include: Ear helix, proximal ulnar olecranon, Achilles tendon, and prepatellar bursa
3. Acute exacerbations are frequent and often polyarticular
4. Morning stiffness and joint deformity are common

V. EVALUATION
A. Joint aspiration
1. Joint aspiration should take place after acute attack has subsided to avoid patient discomfort. Include gram stain and culture of fluid to rule out infection
2. Presence of monosodium urate crystals confirms the diagnosis of gout
3. The white blood cell count may also be elevated within the synovial fluid (10,000–60,000) with neutrophils predominating

B. 24hr urine for uric acid
1. Important test to direct treatment and determine if patient is overproducer or underexcretor of uric acid. Perform after acute attack resolves
2. Patients on normal diet with 24hr uric acid excretion > 800mg are classified as overproducers. Value of < 600mg classifies patient as underexcretor

C. Other labs
1. Serum uric acid: Often not helpful in the diagnosis of acute gout (normal in 10% of patients). Useful in monitoring response to urate-lowering therapy
2. Creatinine, CBC, LFTs, lipid profile, and UA

D. Imaging
1. Plain radiographs are not useful in diagnosing acute gout. Usually only soft tissue swelling is seen
2. Classic radiographic findings in chronic gout: "punched-out" bony lesions, cortical erosions with overhanging margins, and joint space preservation
3. In general, gout must be inadequately treated for approximately 12yrs before x-ray changes are seen

VI. MANAGEMENT
A. Asymptomatic hyperuricemia
1. No medical treatment is indicated
2. Secondary causes of hyperuricemia should be sought and adjusted accordingly:
   a. Weight loss
   b. Reduction in dietary purines
   c. Reduction in alcohol consumption
   d. Avoidance of dehydration (diuretics) and repetitive trauma
   e. Control HTN and hyperlipidemia

B. Acute gouty arthritis
1. Treatment should be initiated as early as possible (preferably within 24hrs). Immobilization and ice are important adjuncts to medical therapy
2. NSAIDs: Drugs of choice, with the exception of ASA. Use with caution in the elderly and patients with PUD, renal, hepatic, and cardiac disease. Examples:
   a. **Indomethacin:** 50mg PO QID for 2 days then 25mg PO QID until complete resolution (usually within a week)
   b. **Naproxen:** 500mg PO BID for 2 days then 250mg PO BID until complete resolution

      c. **Ibuprofen:** 800mg PO QID for 2 days then 400mg PO QID until complete resolution

  3. Alternative therapies: use if NSAIDs contraindicated

      a. **Colchicine:** 1.2mg PO initially, then 0.6mg PO every hr until improvement (do not exceed 10 doses). Usually terminates acute attacks within 10hrs. Therapy should be stopped when the maximum dosage is reached, the acute attack subsides, or side effects occur (nausea, vomiting, diarrhea)

      b. **Corticosteroids: Oral Prednisone** 40–60mg PO QD for 5 days then tapered over 10 days. Alternatives to oral therapy are **Triamcinolone Acetonide** 60mg intramuscularly, or **Triamcinolone Acetonide** 10mg intra-articularly

C. Interval gout/Chronic tophaceous gout

  1. Indications for chronic therapy:

      a. 2 or more acute attacks

      b. Visible tophi

      c. Radiographic evidence of urate deposits

      d. Renal stones: May occur in 10–25% patients with primary gout

      e. Renal damage

  2. Overproducers of uric acid (>800mg uric acid in 24hr urine) should be treated with xanthine-oxidase inhibitors—

      Allopurinol: 100mg PO QD increased by 100mg every week until a serum uric acid level of 6mg/dL or lower is achieved. Maximum dose is 600mg/day, but response is typically seen at 300mg/day. Dosages above 300mg should be given BID. Adjust dose for creatinine clearance

  3. Underexcretors of uric acid (<600mg uric acid in a 24hr urine) should be treated with a uricosuric agent—

      Probenecid: 250mg PO BID increased by 500mg every 2 weeks until a serum uric acid level of 6mg/dL or lower is achieved. The maximum dose is 3g/day, but response is typically seen at 2 g/day. (**Allopurinol** should be used in underexcretors with a creatinine clearance of <50 mL/min or history of renal calculi)

  4. Low dose **Colchicine** (0.6mg PO BID) or low dose NSAIDs should be initiated a week before therapy as prophylaxis against acute attacks and continued for 3–6 months

D. Indications for rheumatologic referral

  1. Early onset

  2. For documentation of gout in difficult to aspirate joints

  3. Treatment of polyarticular gout

  4. Treatment of refractory gout

  5. Therapeutic guidance in patients with organ failure

CLINICAL PEARLS

- Although hyperuricemia and gout are frequently associated, the 2 conditions are not mutually exclusive—some patients with gout have normal uric acid levels, and some patients with hyperuricemia never develop gout
- Any therapy for gout should include lifestyle modifications such as weight loss, low purine diet, and reduction in alcohol consumption
- If patients currently treated with Allopurinol or Probenecid experience an acute attack do not adjust the doses. Treat with NSAIDs or Colchicine
- If gout is present in patients < 30, consider a genetic disorder

References

Davis JC, Jr. A practical approach to gout. Current management of an "old" disease. Postgraduate Medicine. 1999;106(4):115–6, 119–23.

Harris MD, et al. Gout and hyperuricemia. Am Fam Phys 1999;59:925–34.

Pittman JR, et al. Diagnosis and management of gout. Am Fam Phys 1999;59:1799–1806.

Buckley TJ. Radiographic features of gout. Am Fam Phys 1996;54:1232–8.

Laurie Dangler, MD
Miriam Chan, PharmD

73. OSTEOPOROSIS

I. GENERAL
   A. Osteoporosis affects 10 million persons in US and accounts for 1.3 million fractures/yr
   B. Hip fractures are a serious complication with mortality rate as high as 20% in first 6 months following hip fracture
   C. Osteoporosis results from poor bone mass acquisition during adolescence and accelerated bone loss in older persons. Most important determinant in lifelong skeletal health is the bone mass attained early in life. Improved with adequate nutrition and body weight, exposure to sex hormones at puberty, physical activity, and not smoking
   D. **WHO definition of osteoporosis:** Bone mineral density 2.5 standard deviations below the mean for young white adult women
   E. **WHO definition of osteopenia:** Bone mineral density between 1.0 and 2.5 standard deviations below the mean for young white adult women
   F. **Primary osteoporosis:** Bone mass deterioration that is related to aging and decreased gonadal function and is unassociated with other chronic illnesses
   G. **Secondary osteoporosis:** Results from chronic conditions that contribute to accelerated bone loss (see table below)
      1. In men 30–60% of osteoporosis is due to secondary causes and is usually from hypogonadism, use of glucocorticoids, or alcoholism
      2. In perimenopausal women, 50% of osteoporosis is due to secondary causes and is usually from hypoestrogenemia, use of glucocorticoids, thyroid hormone excess, or anticonvulsant therapy
      3. In postmenopausal women, the prevalence of primary vs. secondary causes is unknown

Secondary Forms of Osteoporosis	
Endocrine or metabolic causes	**Medications**
Acromegaly	Cyclosporine (Sandimmune)
Anorexia nervosa	Excess thyroid hormone
Athletic amenorrhea	Glucocorticoids
Diabetes mellitus (type 1—formerly	GnRH agonists*
known as insulin-dependent diabetes	Methotrexate (Rheumatrex)
mellitus)	Phenobarbital
Hemochromatosis	Phenothiazines
Hyperadrenocorticism	Phenytoin (Dilantin)
Hyperparathyroidism	Heparin, prolonged treatment
Hyperprolactinemia	**Nutritional**
Thyrotoxicosis	Alcoholism
Collagen/genetic diorders	Calcium deficiency
Ehlers-Danlo syndrome	Chronic liver disease
Glycogen storage diseases	Gastric operations
Homocystinuria	Malabsorption syndromes
Hypophosphatasia	Vitamin D deficiency
Marfan syndrome	
Osteogenesis imperfecta	

*GnRH = gonadotropin-releasing hormone.
Adapted with permission from Tresolini CP, Gold DT, Lee LS, eds. Working with patients to prevent, treat and manage osteoporosis: a curriculum guide for health professions. 2d ed. San Francisco: National Fund for Medical Education, 1998. With permission from Elsevier.

   H. **Risk factors for osteoporosis**: Female gender, increased age, estrogen deficiency/ postmenopausal status, white or Asian ancestry, low weight and body mass index (BMI), family history of osteoporosis, smoking, history of prior fracture, and possibly sedentary lifestyle/immobilization, high caffeine intake, and alcohol

II. HISTORY
   A. Evaluate if patient has any of the above listed risk factors or any medical history or symptoms consistent with the secondary causes of osteoporosis listed above

B. Physical examination
1. Patient's current height and weight
2. Physical findings of systemic disease
3. Kyphosis, scoliosis, loss of lordotic curve: Dorsal kyphosis (dowager's hump)—result of multiple anterior compression fractures of thoracic spine
4. Gait, balance, strength, vision

III. DIAGNOSIS: Controlled trials have yet to prove that women who receive bone density screening have better outcomes than women who are not screened

A. Measurement of the bone mineral density (BMD) correlates strongly with load-bearing capacity of the hip and spine and with the risk of fracture

B. Possible indications
1. Estrogen deficient women or women with premature menopause considering therapy
2. Patients with osteopenia or vertebral fractures revealed on radiographs
3. Patients with loss of height who are considering therapy
4. Patients on long term glucocorticoid therapy (> 1 month of therapy and > 7.5mg Prednisone QD)
5. Asymptomatic hyperparathyroidism where osteoporosis would suggest parathyroidectomy
6. Monitoring therapeutic response in patients undergoing treatment for osteoporosis if result of the test would change management
7. Note: Use for screening has not been defined since approximately 750 BMD tests in white women 50–59 would need to be ordered in order to prevent 1 hip or vertebral fracture over a 5yr period of treatment

C. Dual energy x-ray absorptiometry (DXA)
1. Most precise measure and diagnostic measure of choice. Less radiation exposure than a chest x-ray
2. Results: T-score is defined as the number of standard deviations above or below the average BMD value for young healthy white women
   a. T score higher than –1: A bone density that is not more than 1 standard deviation below the young adult mean (normal)
   b. T score between –1 and –2.5: A bone density that lies between 1 and 2.5 standard deviations below the young adult mean (osteopenia)
   c. T score less than –2.5: A bone density that is more than 2.5 standard deviations below the young adult mean (osteoporosis)

D. Plain radiography: May be diagnostic if shows vertebral fracture, but generally not sensitive enough as screening since bone loss not apparent until 50% or more of bone is lost

E. Labs: To screen for secondary causes if indicated
1. CBC, chemistry
2. Alkaline phosphatase and serum calcium, TSH, phosphorus
3. Urinalysis
4. If suggested by clinical findings: ESR, serum parathyroid hormone concentration, serum 25-hydroxyvitamin D concentration, 24hr urinary calcium excretion, serum/urine protein electrophoresis, bone marrow examination/biopsy, hepatic transaminases, serum albumin level, serum ferritin and iron levels
5. There are various surrogate markers of bone turnover which may be helpful in the future

IV. MANAGEMENT: Patients with osteopenia should be counseled and treated so that no further bone loss occurs. Patients with osteoporosis should receive active therapy aimed at increasing bone density and decreasing fracture risk (see table below)

A. Exclude secondary causes of osteoporosis (see I. G. above) and halt progression through prevention (i.e., stop smoking, decrease alcohol intake, modify risk factors)

B. Calcium and Vitamin D: Calcium, 1000–1500mg/day with Vitamin D, 400–800 IU daily should be taken in the diet or given as supplements concurrently with any of the above treatments. Both are inadequate alone in majority of patients

C. Exercise: Weight-bearing exercise maintains bone density and recommended for both prevention and treatment of osteoporosis (walk, jog, row, weight training)

D. Oral Bisphosphonate: Alendronate (Fosamax), Risedronate (Actonel)

GEN

    1. Mechanism: Inhibits osteoclast-mediated bone resorption; has been shown to achieve bone stabilization, increase bone density and decrease fracture risk when given continuously for 3 years. Reduced risk of vertebral fracture by 30–50%

    2. Contraindications

      a. Esophageal abnormalities which may delay esophageal emptying (achalasia, stricture)

      b. Creatinine clearance < 35mL/min

      c. Hypocalcemia

E. Raloxifene (Evista)

    1. A selective estrogen receptor modulator (SERM) which acts on the bone, but does not stimulate the endometrium or breast. Reduced risk of vertebral fracture by 36% in trials

    2. Side effects: Hot flashes, leg cramps, risk of thromboembolic events, vaginitis

F. Calcitonin-Salmon (Miacalcin)

    1. Mechanism: Thought to inhibit osteoclastic resorption of bone, but this is uncertain at dose of 200 U/day. Also produces an analgesic effect for bone pain

    2. Indications: Second line after Alendronate or Risedronate for postmenopausal osteoporosis. May be used to manage bone pain following osteoporotic fracture

G. Estrogen Replacement Therapy (ERT): See Chapter 29, Menopause & HRT

    1. Greatest benefit if begun early in menopause because greatest rate of bone loss is in first 5–7 years of menopause

    2. Contraindications: History of breast cancer, estrogen-dependent neoplasia, undiagnosed abnormal genital bleeding, history of or active thromboembolic disorder

    3. In light of the results of WHI, hormone therapy is currently considered as second-line therapy after non estrogen therapies have failed or caused intolerance to side effects

H. Teriparatide (Forteo)

    1. Mechanism: Teriparatide if a portion of human parathyroid hormone (PTH) which is the primary regulator of calcium and phosphorus metabolism in bones

    2. Dosage: 20mcg SQ daily

    3. Side effects: Nausea, dizziness, leg cramps and headache

GEN

Agents for Treating Osteoporosis			
Medication	**Dosage**	**Route**	**Cost***
Elemental calcium	1,000 to 1,500 mg per day	Oral	$13 to $20
Vitamin D	400 IU per day (800 IU per day in winter in northern latitudes)	Oral	$1
Alendronate (Fosamax)	Prevention: 5 mg per day or one 35 mg tab once weekly	Oral	$61 (5 mg)
	Treatment: 10 mg per day or one 70 mg tab once weekly		$61 (10 mg)
Raloxifene (Evista)	60 mg per day	Oral	$61
Calcitonin (Calcimar)	200 IU per day or 50 to 100 IU per day	Intranasal or subcutaneous/intramuscular	$36 to $59
Conjugated estrogens	0.625 to 1.25 mg per day	Oral	$16 to $23
Estradiol skin patch (Estraderm)	0.05 mg every week	Topical	$26 to $68

*Estimated cost to the pharmacist based on average wholesale prices for one month of therapy (rounded to the nearest dollar) in Red Book. Montvale, N.J.: Medical Economics Data, 2000. Cost to the patient will be greater, depending on prescription filling fee.

Source: South-Paul JE. Osteoporosis: Part II. Nonpharmacologic and pharmacologic treatment. Am Fam Phys 2001;63:1121–8. Used with permission.

CLINICAL PEARLS

- Risk of fracture increases 2 to 2.5-fold in the spine and hip, respectively, for each standard deviation of bone mineral density below the young adult mean
- With estrogen replacement therapy, the risk of hip and wrist fractures is reduced about 50% and the risk of vertebral fractures is reduced about 75%. This effect is lost if not continued beyond 5 years
- The best protection for osteoporosis is development of largest peak bone mass within individual genetic potential by maintaining adequate body weight, providing adequate calcium intake, and mechanical loading with weight-bearing exercise
- 1000–1500mg elemental calcium is equivalent to four 8 oz glasses of milk per day.

Only 50–60% of the population has a calcium intake at this level
- The chance that a 50-year-old white woman will have a hip fracture during her lifetime is 14% and for a white man it is 5% to 6%
- Approximately 30% of hip fractures in persons older than 65 occur in men

References

Cadarette SM, et al, for the Canadian Multicentre Osteoporosis Study. Evaluation of decision rules for referring women for bone densitometry by dual-energy x-ray absorptiometry. JAMA 2001;286:57–63.

NIH Consensus Development Panel on Osteoporosis Prevention, Diagnosis, and Therapy. Osteoporosis prevention, diagnosis, and therapy. JAMA 2001;285:785.

South-Paul JE. Osteoporosis: Part I. Evaluation and assessment. Am Fam Phys 2001;63: 897–904,908.

South-Paul JE. Osteoporosis: Part II. Nonpharmacologic and pharmacologic treatment. Am Fam Phys 2001;63:1121–8.

Torgerson DJ, Bell-Syer SE. Hormone replacement therapy and prevention of nonvertebral fractures: a meta-analysis of randomized trials. JAMA 2001;285:2891–7.

Osteoporosis in postmenopausal women: diagnosis and monitoring, at http:// www.ahrq.gov/ clinic/osteosum.htm and from the National Guideline Clearinghouse at http:// www.guideline.gov

Ivan Wolfson, MD
Michael B. Weinstock, MD
Joyce Miller, PA-C

GEN

74. Urinary Tract Infections

Note: For children, see Chapter 14, Urinary Tract Infection in Children

I. ACUTE UNCOMPLICATED URINARY TRACT INFECTION (UTI)

  A. General: Approximately 7 million office visits/yr with direct costs of $1.8 billion annually

  B. Etiology: *E. Coli 85%, Staph saprophyticus 10%, Proteus, Klebsiella, Pseudomonas*

  C. Upper tract disease: Since up to 30% of patients diagnosed with cystitis-like syndrome may have *subclinical upper tract disease*, they need to be questioned for symptoms of complicated UTI, including fever, back pain, symptoms > 1 week, vomiting, or hematuria

  D. Dysuria as chief complaint can also be *urethritis* or *vaginitis*

    1. Factors which increase the likelihood of UTI include urgency, frequency, hematuria, back pain, and costovertebral angle tenderness, suprapubic pain or pressure

    2. Factors which decrease the probability of UTI include absence of dysuria, absence of back pain, history of vaginal discharge or vaginal irritation, and vaginal discharge on exam

  E. Evaluation

    1. Urine dipstick/urinalysis (see table below): Cost effective and safe because causative organisms and susceptibility profiles are very predictable. Leukocyte esterase is sensitive but not specific. Nitrate is less sensitive but more specific. Note: Urine dipstick or screen is more accurate if combined with pretest and posttest probabilities based on history and physical

    2. Patient has UA suggestive of UTI if:

      a. Greater than 5 WBC per high power field

      b. Bacteriuria is present

      c. Nitrite is positive

      d. Note: False positives occur with leukocyte esterase because of vaginal leukocytes

    3. Urine culture: Only necessary if there is a strong likelihood of UTI despite negative urine dip, screen or micro, atypical clinical features, suggestion of a complicated

UTI, patient is a child, is immunosuppressed, has recurrent UTIs, or is status post ATB treatment of UTI

4. Follow-up: For uncomplicated UTIs, no follow-up culture or visit is necessary unless symptoms persist, recur, or patient is pregnant

Sensitivity and Specificity of Components of the Urinalysis, Alone and in Combination		
Test	**Sensitivity % (Range)**	**Specificity % (Range)**
Leukocyte esterase	83 (67-94)	78 (64-92)
Nitrite	53 (15-82)	98 (90-100)
Leukocyte esterase *or* nitrite positive	93 (90-100)	72 (58-91)
Microscopy: WBCs	73 (32-100)	81 (45-98)
Microscopy: bacteria	81 (16-99)	83 (11-100)
Leukocyte esterase *or* nitrite *or* microscopy positive	99.8 (99-100)	70 (60-92)

Source: American Academy of Pediatrics, Practice Guideline. The diagnosis, treatment, and evaluation of the initial urinary tract infection in febrile infants and young children (AC9830). Pediatrics 1999:103;843–852. Used with permission.

F. Management

1. Duration of therapy
   a. 3 day course is as effective as 7 days with half the number of side effects. Single dose therapy is not recommended
   b. A 7–14 day course is recommended for an uncomplicated UTI if patient is: diabetic, > 65, febrile, pregnant (7 days), has had a UTI within 6 weeks, has had symptoms > 7 days, diaphragm user

2. ATBs
   a. **TMP/SMX (Septra, Bactrim):** First line empiric therapy if resistance rates in community are < 20%. 1 DS tab PO BID
   b. **Trimethoprim (Proloprim, Trimpex):** 100mg PO BID
   c. **Fluoroquinolones**: More expensive. Use if local resistance to **TMP-SMX** is high and for patients with recurrent, chronic or complicated UTIs. Not for use in pregnant women or if < 18
      i. **Levofloxacin (Levaquin)** 250mg PO QD
      ii. **Norfloxacin (Noroxin)** 400mg PO BID
      iii. **Ciprofloxacin (Cipro)** 250mg PO BID
      iv. **Ofloxacin (Floxin)** 200mg PO BID
      v. **Lomefloxacin (Maxaquin)** 400mg PO QD
   d. **Nitrofurantoin (Macrodantin, Macrobid):** May use in pregnancy. **Macrobid** 100mg PO BID
   e. **Amoxicillin (Amoxil)** 500mg PO TID (*33% resistance*)—Use only in pregnancy or infants
   f. **Fosfomycin (Monurol):** A 3g single dose

3. Relief of dysuria
   a. **Pyridium:** 200mg PO TID
   b. **Urised:** 2 tabs PO QID (PC and HS)

II. ACUTE UNCOMPLICATED PYELONEPHRITIS

A. Signs and symptoms
1. Dysuria, frequency, urgency
2. CVA/back pain
3. Fever/chills
4. Abdominal pain
5. Nausea/vomiting

B. Etiology: *E. coli*—80%, also *Proteus, Klebsiella, Enterobacter*

C. Evaluation: Urinalysis and consider culture. Pyuria almost always present, gram negative bacteria, WBC casts may be present

D. Indications for hospitalization
1. Nausea/vomiting
2. Ill appearing/dehydrated
3. Age > 65
4. Pregnancy
5. Immunosuppression

E. Outpatient treatment: Fluoroquinolone or TMP-SMX. See I. F. 2. above (× 14 days in low resistance area)

III. COMPLICATED UTIs
A. Complicated UTIs occur in the presence of structural abnormalities and in certain patient populations. In these cases, pathogens are more variable and may be more resistant to ATBs
   1. Abnormalities may include vesicourethral reflux, stones or obstruction
   2. Patient populations at risk include patients with diabetes, sickle cell disease, polycystic kidneys, renal transplant recipients, patients on immunosuppressive therapy, pregnancy, neurologically impaired
B. **Evaluation:** Obtain urinalysis and urine cultures and sensitivities
C. Treatment with **Fluoroquinolone** or **TMP-SMX** (as above): Begin while awaiting culture and sensitivities
D. **Hospitalization:** Severely ill patients should be hospitalized and covered for *Pseudomonas* and *Enterococcus*

IV. RECURRENT UTIs
A. **Epidemiology:** Occur in ~20% of young women
   1. Etiology: 90% are due to exogenous reinfection, typically months apart. Since rarely due to anatomic or functional abnormalities or urinary tract, imaging studies are of little use. Inquire about hygiene, diaphragm use, wiping pattern (back to front) and use of hot tubs. If diaphragm/spermicide use, consider another form of contraception
   2. Evaluation: Obtain culture and sensitivity
B. **Management**
   1. Relapses:
      a. Recurrent infection is usually by original pathogen, usually within 2 weeks
      b. Seek occult source or urogenic abnormality
      c. Treat for 2–6 weeks
   2. If 3 or > UTIs per year, consult a urologist

V. UTIs IN YOUNGER MEN
A. Rare if < 50 years. It used to be thought that UTIs in men were caused by urologic abnormalities, but now studies suggest that these UTIs are due to the same strains of *E. coli* that affect women. Need to differentiate from prostatitis and STD by obtaining a good sexual history and performing a rectal exam
B. Patients present with symptoms of cystitis, but may mimic urethritis with urethral discharge. Obtain urine culture and sensitivity on all patients. If there is urethral discharge, obtain culture before obtaining urine specimen
C. Risk factors: Homosexuality, sexual partner with vaginal colonization by uropathogen, immunosuppressed patients, bladder outlet obstruction
D. Adult men who respond to ATBs with their first UTI do NOT need further urologic evaluation. Subsequent UTIs do need further work-up
E. If indicated, further workup includes renal ultrasound, IVP, helical CT, or cystourethrogram
F. Treat with 7 day course of ATBs

VI. UTIs ASSOCIATED WITH CATHETERS
A. **Prevention:** Sterile insertion, prompt removal, and use of a closed collecting system
B. **Bacteriuria:** If catheter is in > 30 days, most such patients will have bacteriuria
   1. Intermittent catheterization has resulted in lower rates of bacteriuria than long-term indwelling catheter
   2. Distinguish between bacteriuria and infection (pain, fever, CVA tenderness, etc.)

GEN

C. Management
1. Indicated for symptomatic patients with culture showing > 100,000 CFU. Treat with a **Fluoroquinolone** (as above) for 10–14 days
2. Asymptomatic bacteriuria: No treatment

VII. ASYMPTOMATIC BACTERIURIA: Occurs in approximately 5% of women. Screening is of little use except:

A. Prior to urologic surgery
B. Pregnancy (major cause of maternal and fetal morbidity)
1. If symptomatic, give a 7 day course of **Amoxicillin** or **Nitrofurantoin**, adjust therapy base on susceptibility data
2. If asymptomatic bacteriuria:
   a. 3 day course of **Amoxicillin** or **Nitrofurantoin** (see above)
   b. Screen with cultures every month
3. If ≥ 1 UTI or asymptomatic bacteruria: Need prophylaxis for duration of pregnancy

CLINICAL PEARLS
- Dysuria may also be secondary to urethritis infections, irritant, contact, vaginitis, prostatitis, renal stone, hematuria, or concentrated urine
- Children/infants may present with fever and/or irritability instead of urinary symptoms
- Leukocytes and/or leukocyte esterase may be from vaginal leukocytes and not from cystitis

References
Bremnor JD, et al. Evaluation of dysuria in adults. Am Fam Phys 2002;65:1589–96.
Bachur R, Harper MB. Reliability of the urinalysis for predicting urinary tract infections in young febrile children. Arch Ped & Adol Med 2001;155–60.
Manges AR, et al. Widespread distribution of urinary tract infections caused by a multidrug-resistant escherichia coli clonal group. N Engl J Med 2001;345:1007.
Delzell JE, LeFevre ML. Urinary tract infections during pregnancy. Am Fam Phys 2000;61:691–700.
Scholes D, et al. Risk factors for recurrent urinary tract infection in young women. J Infect Dis 2000;182:1177–82.
Tambyah PA, Maki DG. The relationship between pyuria and infection in patients with indwelling urinary catheters: A prospective study of 761 patients. Arch Intern Med 2000;160:673.

Daniel M. Neides, MD

75. HEMATURIA

I. DEFINITION: The presence of red blood cells (RBCs) in the urine

II. INDICATIONS FOR WORKING-UP HEMATURIA
A. > 3 RBCs/HPF on 2 of 3 clean catch specimens
B. 1 episode of gross hematuria
C. 1 episode of large microhematuria (> 100 RBCs/HPF)

III. DIFFERENTIAL DIAGNOSIS
A. ABC mnemonic:
   A = Anatomic (renal cysts, AV malformation, obstruction with hydronephrosis, BPH)
   B = Boulders (nephrolithiasis, hypercalciuria, hyperuricosuria)
   C = Cancer (renal cell, bladder, prostate in adults; Wilms' tumor or leukemia in children)
   D = Drugs (prescribed and illicit drugs)
   E = Exercise (contact and noncontact sports)
   F = Familial or foreign body (indwelling catheter, trauma, Alport's syndrome—family history of deafness and renal disease
   G = Glomerulonephritis (post-strep, Goodpasture's, SLE, Berger's, Henoch-Schönlein purpura)
   H = Hematology (hemoglobinopathies, coagulopathies)
   I = Infection (bacterial, viral or fungal)
B. Most common etiology in elderly: Men–BPH; women–squamous metaplasia of the trigone

IV. HISTORY
A. Genitourinary history
1. Dysuria, nocturia, or increased frequency
2. Vaginal or penile discharge (obtain sexual history)
3. Recent trauma or vigorous exercise
4. Previous urologic surgery
5. Flank pain or prior nephrolithiasis
6. Last menstrual period

B. Painful vs. painless hematuria
1. Etiologies of painful hematuria: UTI, endometriosis, nephrolithiasis, papillary necrosis, obstruction, passage of clots
2. Etiologies of painless hematuria: Bladder tumor, staghorn calculus, polycystic kidneys, hydronephrosis, sickle cell anemia, hypercalciuria, anticoagulation

C. Recent Infections
1. Fever, sore throat, or rash
2. Tooth extraction or other invasive procedures
3. Recent travel (schistosomiasis)

D. Relation of gross hematuria to urinary stream
1. Initial: Distal urethra
2. Terminal: Bladder neck or prostatic urethra
3. Total: Upper tract or bladder proper

E. Clots
1. Large and thick: Bladder
2. Small and stringy: Ureter (upper tract)

F. Family history
1. Renal disease
2. Sickle cell anemia
3. Deafness (Alport's syndrome—familial nephritis)
4. Bleeding disorders (hemophilia, von Willebrand's disease, Vitamin K deficiency, liver disease)

G. Meds: Many drugs may cause hematuria (including Cyclophosphamide, Warfarin (Coumadin), NSAIDs, Aspirin, PCN)

H. Risk factors for urologic cancer: Age > 40, tobacco use, exposure to rubber or aniline dyes, schistosomiasis, pelvic radiation, family history of urologic cancer, or analgesic abuse

V. PHYSICAL EXAMINATION
A. General: Temperature and vital signs
B. Oropharynx: Tonsillar enlargement
C. Abdomen: Masses, hepatomegaly, or suprapubic tenderness
D. Back: CVA tenderness
E. Extremities: Supraclavicular, axillary, or inguinal adenopathy
F. Skin: Rash or ecchymoses
G. Rectal: Masses and prostate size, guaiac stool

VI. EVALUATING HEMATURIA
Directed by results of the history and physical exam: Processes which may yield a false positive dipstick result include contamination of the urine specimen with menstrual blood, dehydration, exercise, ascorbic acid (Vitamin C) or vitamins, high concentrations of oxidants, foods (beets, rhubarb, fava beans, blackberries), meds (Rifampin, Pyridium, Quinine), and Porphyria

A. Asymptomatic microscopic hematuria
1. Obtain UA and screening chemistries (see below)
2. If negative UA and screening chemistries, repeat UA in 3 months
3. If microscopic hematuria persists, then obtain radiologic study (U/S or IVP, with tomograms) and urologic consult

B. Asymptomatic gross hematuria
1. Obtain UA and screening chemistries (see below)
2. Obtain radiologic study (IVP or U/S) and obtain urologic consult for cystoscopy

GEN

C. Laboratory
1. Urinalysis +/- culture and sensitivity
   a. Pyuria, WBC casts (infection)
   b. Proteinuria, RBC casts (glomerular disease)
2. Screening chemistries, as clinically indicated
   a. BUN, creatinine, electrolytes
   b. CBC, platelets, PT/PTT
   c. PSA
3. If evidence of glomerular disease (i.e., presence of proteinuria or RBC casts):
   a. Serum ANA, Anti-GBM (glomerular basement membrane—Wegener's disease), C3, C4, ASO titers (post-strep), ESR, and serum protein electrophoresis
   b. 24hr urine for protein and CrCl
4. If the microscopic examination indicates an absence of RBCs then an evaluation for hemoglobinuria or myoglobinuria should be initiated

D. Radiology
1. Helical CT: Sensitivity and specificity for evaluation of nephrolithiasis/ureterolithiasis possibly exceeding IVP without the need for IV contrast
2. Intravenous pyelography (IVP)
   a. Useful in defining the anatomy of the urinary tract and evaluation of obstruction. Also gives an estimation of function
   b. Increase sensitivity by adding tomograms or renal CT scan (will detect smaller lesions or those not encroaching the collecting system)
   c. Consider ultrasound if contrast nephropathy is a concern
3. Renal ultrasound: Good for evaluation of kidney (cystic or solid masses or hydronephrosis) but limited evaluation of ureteral disease

E. Endoscopy—Cystoscopy: Useful for evaluating the lower urinary tract

F. Pathologic
1. Urinary cytology (low sensitivity, high specificity)
   a. Useful in detecting transitional cell cancer of the bladder (high grade or CIS)
   b. With in situ bladder lesions, cytology can be positive before visualization via cystoscopy
   c. False positives can occur with nephrolithiasis or UTIs
2. Renal biopsy
   a. Indications are unclear
   b. May not affect prognosis or treatment unless hematuria is accompanied by HTN, proteinuria, or decreased CrCl

VII. FOLLOW-UP EXAMINATIONS
Patients with a negative initial work-up will need close follow-up

A. Urologic cancer has been found on follow-up exam in 1–3% of patients with microscopic hematuria and 18% of patients with recurrent gross hematuria

B. The following should be considered as long as hematuria persists:
1. Every 6 months: Urinalysis and cytology
2. Every year: IVP and cystoscopy

CLINICAL PEARLS
- Patients with gross hematuria have approximately 5 × the yield of life-threatening conditions when compared to those with microhematuria
- Hematuria will be present in about 85% of patients with renal stones
- *Serratia marcescens* may cause a "red diaper" in healthy infants. Performing a UA proves the absence of hemoglobin in the urine
- Consider factitious hematuria (narcotic seekers complaining of kidney stones or Münchausen's disease) in patients with persistent undiagnosed hematuria
- Pyridium may cause a red-orange discoloration of alkaline urine
- Most common etiology in elderly men is BPH and in women is squamous metaplasia of the trigone

References

Madaio MP, Harrington JT. The diagnosis of glomerular diseases: acute glomerulonephritis and the nephritic syndrome. Arch Int Med 2001:161:25.

Avidor Y, et al. Cinical significance of gross hematuria and its evaluation in patients receiving anticoagulant and aspirin treatment. Urology 2000;55:22.

Thaller TR, Wang LP. Evaluation of asymptomatic microscopic hematuria in adults. Am Fam Phys 1999;60:1143–54.

Neiberger RE. The ABCs of evaluating children with hematuria. Am Fam Phys 1994;49:623–8.

Sutton JM. Evaluation of hematuria in adults. JAMA 1990; 263(18):2475–9.

Beth Weinstock, MD

76. PROTEINURIA

I. DEFINITION

A. Normal excretion of protein in urine
1. ≤150mg/day
2. Total protein excretion comprised of 5–15mg albumin, >30 different plasma proteins, and glycoproteins from distal tubule cells, i.e., Tamm-Horsfall protein (most prevalent, excreted at 50–75mg/day)

B. "Pathologic" proteinuria: ≥ 150mg/day. Massive proteinuria is defined as > 3.5gm/day. This leads to large albumin loss and other manifestations of nephrotic syndrome (edema, hypoalbuminemia, hyperlipidemia)

II. MECHANISM OF PROTEIN LOSS

A. Tubular/Overflow: Low-molecular weight proteins (β_2 microglobulin, lysozyme, light chains, insulin) are usually filtered by glomeruli and reabsorbed by tubules. If tubules are damaged (tubular or interstitial disease), these proteins are excreted, usually in the range of 1–3g/24hrs. High serum protein levels can also "overwhelm" tubules and overflow into urine (i.e., Bence-Jones protein associated with multiple myeloma)

B. Glomerular: Normal glomeruli filter little albumin or globulin. Glomerular disease disrupts this barrier; excretion of mostly albumin on urine electrophoresis signifies a glomerular lesion. Urinary excretion of > 2g/24hrs is usually a result of glomerular disease

III. APPROACH TO EVALUATION AND MANAGEMENT

A. If Dipstick > 1(+) proteinuria, then collect 24hr urine

B. If proteinuria > 2g/24hr
1. History: Pre-existing disease, HIV risk factors, systemic complaints (fatigue, polydipsia, polyuria, back pain, joint pain, weight loss, rash), family history (diabetes, polycystic kidney disease)
2. Physical exam: Blood pressure, weight, funduscopic exam, edema, skin and joint exam (vasculitis/rheumatologic disease), ophthalmologic exam for diabetic retinopathy
3. Labs
   a. Microscopic exam of urine sediment (casts, crystals)
      i. Casts: Formed when proteins gel inside renal tubules, trapping WBCs and RBCs
         aa. Hyaline casts: Found with concentrated urine, fever, diuretic use
         bb. RBC casts: Glomerulonephritis
         cc. WBC casts: Pyelonephritis, interstitial nephritis
         dd. Renal tubular casts: ATN, interstitial nephritis
         ee. Coarse granular casts: Degeneration of cast with cellular elements, non-specific
         ff. Broad waxy casts: Chronic renal failure. Stasis in collecting tubule
      ii. Crystals: Should be visualized when urine is freshly voided and still warm. Uric acid, phosphate, and oxalate crystals are seen in normal patients as well as

stone formers
  b. BUN and creatinine, CBC
  c. Serum protein immunoelectrophoresis (SPE) to identify any paraproteins in the serum which could be overwhelming the tubules. Obtain urine protein electrophoresis simultaneously to quantify the amount of each protein type in the urine (important to consider in patient age > 40)
  d. ANA, Hepatitis B, Hepatitis C, cryoglobulins, complement levels (C3 and C4) to screen for vasculitis as etiology of glomerular damage (depending on patient's associated symptoms)
  e. HIV test
  f. Blood glucose, Hemoglobin A1C
  g. Blood cultures: Screen for subacute bacterial endocarditis (can cause only proteinuria and/or hematuria)

C. **If proteinuria < 2g/24hrs**
  1. History: Recent fever, increase in exercise, other systemic complaints (back pain or other bone pain, fatigue) to screen for multiple myeloma
  2. Physical: Same as above
  3. Labs: Same as above
  4. Transient proteinuria
    a. Associated with fever, stress, exercise (within last 48hrs)
    b. Recheck after confounding factors have resolved
    c. If < 150mg/24hrs, then no work-up
    d. If > 150mg/24hrs, then check yearly BP, UA, and Cr
  5. Orthostatic proteinuria: Usually a benign process
    a. < 1g/24 hrs; if greater, should consider other etiologies
    b. More common in children and adolescents
    c. Can obtain urine dipstick on first void in AM, then check again after patient has been upright for 2hrs. Or do a split 24hr urine collection (16hrs daytime specimen and an 8hrs overnight specimen)
    d. Should follow yearly BP, UA, and creatinine, especially in children

D. **Nephrotic syndrome**
  1. Definition: Proteinuria > 3.5g/24hrs, hypoalbuminemia (serum albumin < 3.0g/dL), edema, and hyperlipidemia (fasting level > 200)
  2. Common end point due to a variety of disease processes: DM, amyloidosis, SLE, idiopathic renal disease such as focal glomerular sclerosis, membranous nephropathy, nil disease, etc. Arises due to an alteration in the permeability of the glomerular capillary wall
  3. Common to all diseases causing nephrotic syndrome is the presence of oval fat bodies seen on microscopic exam of urine; caused by degenerating tubular epithelial cells filled with cholesterol esters. Under polarized light will appear as "Maltese Crosses"
  4. Loss of antithrombin III and other proteins can lead to a hypercoagulable state, particularly venous involvement (DVT, PE, renal vein thrombosis)

IV. SPECIFIC DISEASES

A. **Diabetes Mellitus**
  1. Most common cause of end-stage renal disease in US. Higher incidence of renal complications in Hispanics, blacks, and Native Americans
  2. 20–30% risk of developing diabetic nephropathy
  3. Early renal changes of increased GFR, increased renal blood flow, and renal hypertrophy can be reversed with good glycemic control. Sustained hyperglycemia and HgbA1$_c$ > 9 correlates with hyperfiltration and hypertrophy
  4. Recommendation: *Yearly urine microalbuminuria screening.* Allows for detection of small amounts of albumin which are not detected on routine urine dipstick test. Persistent or increasing microalbuminuria indicates early diabetic nephropathy
  5. 24hr urine should be obtained if urine microalbumin screen is positive
  6. ACE inhibitor should be initiated in both hypertensive and normotensive type 1 diabetic patients with urine microalbuminuria. Blood pressure should be aggressively reduced to < 130/80. Check creatinine and potassium 1 week after initiating ACE inhibitor. In hypertensive Type 2 diabetic patients with microalbuminuria, ACE inhibitors and ARBs have been shown

to delay progression to macroalbuminuria; ARBs have been shown to delay the progression of nephropathy in patients with Type 2 diabetes, hypertension, and macroalbuminuia

7. Blood glucose should also be aggressively controlled to delay progression to persistent proteinuria

8. Microalbuminuria is highly predictive for subsequent retinopathy development

B. Hypertension

1. Hypertensive patients constitute 20% of the dialysis population. The 2 groups at highest risk for hypertensive ESRD are blacks of all ages and the elderly

2. A complete urinalysis should be performed yearly on all hypertensive patients. If positive for protein, a 24hr urine should be obtained. Other causes of proteinuria should also be considered. In addition to aggressive blood pressure management, patient should follow a no-added salt restriction

3. Meds: Diuretics and ACE inhibitors are most beneficial for patients with renal damage secondary to hypertension

4. Consider renal artery stenosis as a possible diagnosis in elderly hypertensives with unexplained deterioration of renal function

CLINICAL PEARLS

- In patients with proteinuria and altered renal function, try to avoid NSAIDs
- Smoking cessation has been shown to decrease albumin excretion
- When to refer to a nephrologist: Proteinuria greater than 1g/24hrs, unless the etiology is known (i.e., diabetes mellitus) and already being aggressively treated
- Proteinuria on initial dipstick analysis is found in as high as 17% of selected populations; < 2% have serious and treatable urinary tract disorders

References

Carroll MF, Temte JL. Proteinuria in adults: A diagnostic approach. Am Fam Phys 2000;62:1333–40.

Orth SR, Ritz E. The nephrotic syndrome. N Engl J Med 1998;338:1202–11.

Giatris I, et al. ACE inhibitors and nondiabetic renal disease. Ann Intern Med 1997;127:337–45.

Bennett PH, et al. Screening and management of microalbuminuria in patients with diabetes mellitus: Recommendations to the Scientific Advisory Board of the National Kidney Foundation from an Ad Hoc Committee of the Council on Diabetes Mellitus of the National Kidney Foundation. Am J Kidney Dis 1995;25:107–12.

Daniel M. Neides, MD
Michael B. Weinstock, MD

77. BENIGN PROSTATIC HYPERPLASIA

DEFINITION: Nodular enlargement of the prostate occurring in the periurethral region of the gland generally among men > 50

I. GENERAL

A. Is present in 50% of men > 50 and 90% of men > 80

B. At 75, half of men have symptoms of BPH

C. Pathology of BPH is hyperplastic growth pattern of stroma and epithelium

II. HISTORY

A. Frequency of urination, nocturia, urgency, straining to void, weak stream, hesitancy, sensation of incomplete voiding, postvoid dribbling

B. Previous surgeries and other therapies used for BPH

C. Symptoms of UTI, cancer (blood in stool or urine, weight loss),

D. Meds which may increase symptoms including OTC sympathomimetics

E. See American Urological Association (AUA) Symptom Index Chart below

The AUA Symptom Index

Name: _____ Date of Birth: _____ Today's Date: _____

A. For each of the seven questions below, please check the one box that best describes your symptoms. (Note: Numbers within boxes are for health care provider's use only.)

Over the past month...	Not at All	Less Than 1 Time in 5	Less Than Half the Time	About Half the Time	More Than Half the Time	Almost Always
1. How often have you had a sensation of not emptying your bladder completely after you finished urinating?	0	1	2	3	4	5
2. How often have you had to urinate again less than 2 hours after you finished urinating?	0	1	2	3	4	5
3. How often have you found you stopped and started again several times when you urinated?	0	1	2	3	4	5
4. How often have you found it difficult to postpone urination?	0	1	2	3	4	5
5. How often have you had a weak urinary stream?	0	1	2	3	4	5
6. How often have you had to push or strain to begin urination?	0	1	2	3	4	5
7. How many times did you most typically get up to urinate from the time you went to bed at night until the time you got up in the morning?	0 (None)	1 (1 time)	2 (2 times)	3 (3 times)	4 (4 times)	5 (5 or more times)

Instructions to Health Care Provider: To calculate the patient's total AUA Symptom Score, add up the numbers for all boxes checked in questions 1 through 7.
AUA Symptom Score: _____ Degree of Severity: ☐ Mild ☐ Moderate ☐ Severe
(0-7) (8-19) (20-35)

Original source for information: Barry MJ, Fowler FJ Jr, O'Leary MP, et al. The American Urological Association symptom index for benign prostatic hyperplasia. J Urol. 1992;148:1549-1557. Used with permission from the American Urological Association.

III. PHYSICAL EXAM

A. **Abdominal exam** (distended bladder)
B. **Digital rectal exam** for enlargement. Note that prostate size on exam correlates poorly with symptoms. Consistency of prostate is rubbery, firm, but not hard or nodular
C. **Focused neurological exam**

IV. LABORATORY AND OTHER TESTING

A. **Urinalysis** (infection or hematuria)
B. **Consider serum creatinine**
C. **Prostatic specific antigen**—Optional test: Has not yet been shown to decrease outcomes from prostate cancer and risks and benefits should be discussed with the patient first. Overlap between BPH and prostate cancer
D. Consider renal US to evaluate for hydronephrosis

V. MANAGEMENT

A. **Behavioral:** No fluids after dinner, no caffeine after noon, decrease or stop alcohol; minimize potential exacerbating meds. Timed voiding and double voiding
B. **Watchful waiting:** Progression is not inevitable. 31–55% will improve with no therapy. Approximately 7% will develop urinary retention over the next 4yrs
C. **Medical therapy**
  1. α-adrenergic antagonists: Improvement in 59–86% of patients

   a. **Tamsulosin (Flomax)**: 0.4mg to be taken ½ hr after the same meal each day and may increase to 0.8mg after 2–4 wks
   b. **Doxazosin (Cardura)**: Start with 1mg QHS for 7 days. If well tolerated, gradually increase dose to 8mg QD
   c. **Terazosin (Hytrin)**: Start with 1mg QHS for 7 days. If well tolerated, gradually increase dose to 20mg QD
   d. Check orthostatic pressures before starting for elderly patients
   e. Side effects: Orthostatic hypotension, dizziness, fatigue, headache, retrograde ejaculation
2. 5 α-reductase inhibitors: Decrease conversion of testosterone to dihydrotestosterone. Improvement in 54–78%. Need 6 months of therapy for maximum improvement
   a. **Finasteride (Proscar)**: 5mg PO QD
   b. **Dutasteride (Avodart)**: 0.5mg PO QD

D. Surgical therapy
1. Transurethral resection of the prostate (TURP)—improvement in 75–96% with impotence in 5–10% and retrograde ejaculation in 75%
2. Transurethral incision of the prostate (TUIP)
   a. Patients with moderate to severe symptoms and small prostates
   b. Improvement in 78–83%, with less retrograde ejaculation than TURP (25%)
3. Open prostatectomy
   a. Usually done when prostate is too large to be done by TURP/TUIP
   b. Improvement in 94–100%
   c. Impotence in 5–39%, incontinence in < 1%, retrograde ejaculation in 36–95%

E. Minimally invasive therapy
1. Laser therapy: Advantages include less blood loss and outpatient surgery. Disadvantages include lack of tissue for pathology and more irritative voiding complaints
2. Transurethral needle ablation of the prostate (TUNA): A catheter is placed in the urethra and radiofrequencies are used to heat the tissue resulting in coagulative necrosis
3. Transurethral electrovaporization of the prostate: High current densities cause a cavity in the prostatic urethra
4. Hyperthermia: Microwave hyperthermia with transurethral catheter
5. High-intensity focused ultrasound (HIFU): Thermal tissue ablation
6. Intraurethral stents: For patients with poor surgical risk
7. Transurethral balloon dilation of the prostate: Most effective in small prostates

GEN

CLINICAL PEARLS
• Utilize the symptom assessment to quantitate and follow prostatism
• For mild symptoms, reassurance and reassessment are appropriate management

References
Arai Y, et al. Impact of interventional therapy for benign prostatic hyperplasia on quality of life and sexual function: a prospective study. J Urol 2000;164:1206.
Donovan JL, et al. A randomized trial comparing transurethral resection of the prostate, laser therapy and conservative treatment of men with symptoms associated with benign prostatic enlargement: The CLasP study. J Urol 2000;164:65-70.
Medina JJ, et al. Benign prostatic hyperplasia (the aging prostate). Med Clin North Am 1999;83:1213.
Physical activity and benign prostatic hyperplasia. Arch Int Med 1998;158:2349.
McConnell JD, et al. The effect of finasteride on the risk of acute urinary retention and the need for surgical treatment among men with benign prostatic hyperplasia. N Engl J Med 1998;338:557–63.

Ann Aring, MD
Beth Weinstock, MD

78. CALCIUM DISORDERS

— PART ONE: HYPERCALCEMIA —

I. DEFINITION: Total calcium > 10.5mg/dL or ionized calcium > 5.3mg/dL. False positives may be caused by hemoconcentration during blood collection or elevation in serum proteins, particularly albumin

II. ETIOLOGY
  A. Malignancy
    1. Osteolytic hypercalcemia: Tumor cell products, such as cytokines, act locally to stimulate osteoclastic bone resorption. Occurs with extensive bone involvement by tumor, usually due to breast cancer, myeloma, and lymphoma
    2. Humoral hypercalcemia: Tumor products act systemically to stimulate bone resorption and to decrease calcium excretion. Most often caused by squamous cell carcinoma of the lung, head and neck, or esophagus, or by renal, bladder, or ovarian cancer
  B. Primary hyperparathyroidism: Most common etiology in ambulatory care with annual incidence of 2 in 1000. 85% of cases are due to an adenoma of a single gland, 15% to hyperplasia of all 4 glands, and 1% to parathyroid carcinoma
  C. Sarcoidosis (occurs secondary to increased absorption of calcium) and other granulomatous diseases
  D. Paget's disease
  E. Immobilization (due to suppression of the parathyroid-vitamin axis)
  F. Vitamin D intoxication (due to increased absorption of calcium) and milk-alkali syndrome
  G. Meds: Thiazide diuretics (increased renal reabsorption of calcium) and Lithium
  H. Other causes: Addison's disease, renal failure, familial hypocalciuric hypercalcemia, hyperthyroidism, vitamin A intoxication, disseminated SLE, pheochromocytoma, prolonged immobilization
  I. Multiple endocrine neoplasias (MEN) syndromes
    1. MEN I: Parathyroid, pituitary and pancreatic islet cell adenoma
    2. MEN IIA: Hyperparathyroid, pheochromocytoma, medullary cell CA of the thyroid

III. HISTORY AND PHYSICAL EXAM: Most patients are asymptomatic at time of diagnosis. Symptoms vary with degree of hypercalcemia and rapidity of development, but usually evident when serum calcium > 12mg/dL
  A. General: Weakness, fatigue, pruritus, hypertension, myopathy, weight loss, night sweats (malignancy)
  B. Duration of symptoms (primary hyperparathyroidism is usually etiology of symptoms present > 6 months without obvious cause)
  C. Diet: Intake of milk and antacids (milk-alkali syndrome), thiazides, Vitamin A or D, Lithium
  D. Evidence of Neoplasm: (e.g., breast or ovarian) Ectopic soft tissue calcification (may be seen when calcium levels rise > 13mg/dL)
  E. CNS: Confusion, depression, psychosis, stupor, coma, headache, hyporeflexia, hypotonia, apathy, mental retardation (infants)
  F. GI: Constipation, nausea, vomiting, anorexia, abdominal pain (pancreatitis, PUD)
  G. GU: Nephrolithiasis, nocturia, polyuria, renal failure (may be seen when calcium levels rise > 13mg/dL)
  H. Musculoskeletal: Bone pain (metastatic disease, multiple myeloma), deformities, fractures, myopathy, pseudogout, muscle atrophy, bone pain with palpation, proximal muscle weakness
  I. Eye: Band keratopathy (found in medial and lateral margin of cornea)

J. **Family history:** MEN syndromes, familial hypocalciuric hypercalcemia

IV. DIAGNOSTIC TESTING

A. Lab tests
1. CBC, electrolytes, BUN, creatinine (renal insufficiency)
2. Ionized calcium, albumin, phosphate, magnesium, alkaline phosphatase
3. 24hr urine calcium
4. Parathyroid hormone (PTH) level: Elevated in more than 90% of patients with primary hyperparathyroidism. Serum PTH levels are suppressed in patients with hypercalcemia due to malignancy or other causes (except familial hypocalciuric hypercalcemia which is distinguished by documenting low urinary calcium clearance)
5. 1, 25-dihydroxyvitamin D level (with history of excessive ingestion of fat soluble vitamins such as Vitamin D
B. ECG: Shortening of QT interval, wide T waves, Digoxin sensitivity
C. Bone survey: May show subperiosteal bone resorption (PTH excess)
D. Bone scan: May show lytic lesions

V. MANAGEMENT: Differs between acute symptomatic hypercalcemia and chronic hypercalcemia
A. Acute hypercalcemia: Symptomatic patients or those with serum calcium > 13mg/dL are generally admitted for IV therapy and observation
B. Chronic hypercalcemia
1. High fluid intake: Should consume 3–5 L/day of fluids to increase renal calcium excretion
2. Glucocorticoids: Inhibit intestinal absorption of calcium and increases urinary calcium excretion. Effect usually evident after 48–72hrs. Effective in hypercalcemia due to myeloma, hematologic malignancies, breast cancer, vitamin D intoxication, and sarcoidosis
3. Oral phosphates: Promotes calcium deposition in bone and soft tissue as well as inhibiting GI calcium absorption. Use only in patients with normal renal function
   a. Dose: 1–3g/day in divided doses
   b. E.g., **Neutra-Phos, Phos-tabs, Fleets phospho-soda**
   c. Side effects: Diarrhea, nausea, soft tissue calcification
4. Dietary Calcium restriction
C. Hypercalcemia due to specific conditions
1. Vitamin D toxicity: Treat with a low calcium diet (< 400mg/day). May take up to 2 months for effects of Vitamin D to subside
2. Sarcoidosis: **Prednisone** 10–20mg/day
3. Primary hyperparathyroidism: Parathyroidectomy is the only effective treatment. Indications for surgery include symptoms of hypercalcemia, nephrolithiasis, bone mass reduction greater than 2 standard deviations, age < 50, serum calcium > 12mg/dL
4. Malignancy: Interval between detection of hypercalcemia and death is often < 6 months

— PART TWO: HYPOCALCEMIA —

I. DEFINITION: Serum calcium < 9mg/dL or ionized calcium < 4.6mg/dL

II. ETIOLOGY
A. Hypoalbuminemia: Most common cause of low total serum calcium. Each decrease of 1g in serum albumin will decrease serum calcium by 0.8mg/dL, but will not change free (ionized) calcium
B. Renal insufficiency: Decreased production of 1,25-dihydroxyvitamin D, increased serum phosphate levels cause calcium deposits in bone and soft tissue
C. Vitamin D deficiency: Malabsorption, decreased production of 1,25-dihydroxyvitamin D, inadequate intake

GEN

   D. **Hypomagnesemia:** Decreased PTH secretion
   E. **Hyperphosphatemia**
   F. **Drugs:** Pentamidine, Ketoconazole, Foscarnet, Cisplatin, Cytosine Arabinoside
   G. **Other:** Acute pancreatitis, rhabdomyolysis, tumor lysis syndrome, pseudohypo-
      parathyroidism (PTH resistance), multiple citrated blood transfusions, sepsis

III. HISTORY AND PHYSICAL EXAM
   A. **General:** Weakness, depression, lethargy
   B. **Neuro:** Paresthesias, impaired cognitive function, seizures
   C. **Psychiatric:** Depression
   D. **Musculoskeletal**
      1. Symptoms consistent with pseudohypoparathyroidism: Short metacarpals and short
         stature
      2. Symptoms consistent with idiopathic hypoparathyroidism: Hypothyroidism, can-
         didiasis, vitiligo, adrenal failure
      3. Soft tissue calcifications
   E. **Neurological:** Tetany, seizures, psychosis
      1. Chvostek's sign: Facial twitching after tapping the facial nerve
      2. Trousseau's sign: Carpopedal spasm after inflation of blood pressure cuff (over the
         patient's systolic blood pressure) for 2–3 minutes
   F. **Cardiovascular:** Dysrhythmias, CHF, hypotension
   G. **Ophthalmologic:** Cataracts
   H. **Meds** (listed above)
   I. **Past medical/surgical history:** Previous neck surgery, history of diseases associated with
      idiopathic hypoparathyroidism (hypothyroidism, adrenal failure) or Vitamin D
      deficiency
   J. **Family history of hypocalcemia:** Familial hypocalcemia, hypoparathyroidism, or
      pseudohypoparathyroidism

IV. LABORATORY
   A. Ionized calcium and magnesium
   B. Phosphorus: Usually elevated in hypocalcemia except in Vitamin D deficiency
   C. BUN/creatinine
   D. Parathyroid hormone (PTH)
   E. Alkaline phosphatase
   F. Albumin

V. MANAGEMENT
   A. **Severe acute hypocalcemia:** Admission
   B. **Chronic hypocalcemia:** Objective is to maintain serum calcium levels between 8–9mg/dL. If
      hypercalciuria develops at serum calcium levels < 8.5mg/dL, **Hydrochlorothiazide** 50mg PO
      QD can be used to reduce urinary calcium excretion
      1. PO: **Calcium Carbonate (Tums, Os-Cal, Biocal, Caltrate)** 500–1000mg PO TID
      2. Renal failure
         a. Use phosphate binding antacids to reduce hyperphosphatemia (e.g., **Amphojel**)
         b. Oral calcium supplementation 0.5–1.0g PO TID with meals. **Tums** provides 500mg
            elemental calcium and is the least expensive
         c. For long term therapy, Vitamin D supplementation with **Calcitriol (Rocaltrol)** is
            best choice for most patients due to its lower risk of toxicity. Initial dose is
            0.25µg PO QD. Most patients maintained with 0.5–2.0ug PO QD
      3. Hypoparathyroidism or Vitamin D deficiency: Vitamin D and oral calcium supplementation
         as noted above
   C. **Hypomagnesemia**
      1. Severe hypomagnesemia (with serum calcium < 0.8mg/dL): Treat as a medical
         emergency in hospital setting
      2. Chronic hypomagnesemia: **Magnesium Oxide** 400mg PO BID–QID

CLINICAL PEARLS

- Patients who take Digoxin and are hypocalcemic should be monitored on telemetry, as hypocalcemia potentiates Digoxin toxicity
- 20% of patients with gram negative sepsis have hypocalcemia
- Calcium is 2% of the normal body weight

References

Guise TA, et al. Evaluation of hypocalcemia in children and adults. J Clin Endocrinol Metab 1995;80(5):1473–8.

Kaye TB. Hypercalcemia: How to pinpoint the cause and customize treatment. Postgrad Med 1995;97:153.

Bourke E, et al. Assessment of hypocalcemia and hypercalcemia. Clin Lab Med 1993;13(1):157–81.

Michael B. Weinstock, MD

79. POTASSIUM METABOLISM

— PART ONE: HYPERKALEMIA —

I. DEFINITION: A serum potassium ≥ 5.5 mmol/L

II. SIGNS AND SYMPTOMS

    A. Patient may have weakness and flaccid paralysis, abdominal distension and diarrhea. Primarily diagnosed by laboratory and ECG changes (see below)

III. ETIOLOGY

    A. Increased potassium intake: May result from salt substitutes, foods with high potassium content, or iatrogenic parenteral replacement

    B. Decreased potassium excretion: Usually due to impaired secretion resulting from either:
        1. Impaired sodium re-absorption—decreased aldosterones (as seen in Addison's disease, use of potassium sparing diuretics, ACE inhibitors, NSAIDs, Heparin, or Cyclosporine)
        2. Increased chloride reabsorption: Renal insufficiency and diabetic nephropathy
        3. Decreased distal flow rate—seen in protein malnourished patients

    C. Intra/Extracellular shift: Metabolic acidosis, insulin deficiency, exercise-induced hyperkalemia, tumor lysis syndrome, rhabdomyolysis, ß-blockers, or Digoxin toxicity

    D. Tissue damage: Crush injuries, rhabdomyolysis

    E. Other causes (mechanism not clear): Lupus nephritis, chronic pyelonephritis, renal transplantation, acute glomerulonephritis

    F. Pseudohyperkalemia: Lab error, thrombocytosis and leukocytosis, hemolysis (tourniquets, finger stick, delay between blood draw and analysis in lab)

IV. EVALUATION: Electrocardiogram is single most important factor in determining seriousness of patient's hyperkalemia

    A. Review history looking for iatrogenic or physiologic reasons for hyperkalemia

    B. Obtain ECG
        1. Earliest changes are peaked T waves, with potassium level > 6.5 mEq/L
        2. Potassium level > 7–8 mEq/L results in loss of P waves and widening of QRS complex
        3. Potassium level > 8–10 mEq/L may result in cardiac arrest

    C. Repeat test if lab does not correlate with clinical picture

    D. Do not delay ECG and/or treatment while waiting for repeat labs to come back!

GEN

V. MANAGEMENT

A. Emergency management: Indicated for hyperkalemia associated with cardiac toxicity, muscular paralysis or with severe hyperkalemia (> 6.5–7.0) without ECG changes

Emergency Management				
Drug	**Dose**	**Onset**	**Duration**	**Action**
1. Calcium gluconate 10% or calcium carbonate 5%	1 ampule IV (10 mL = 1 g)	0-5 minutes	1 hour	Stabilizes cardiac membranes
2. Sodium Bicarbonate	1-2 ampules (44-88 mEq) IV	15-30 minutes	1-2 hours	Shifts K⁺ into cells
3. Regular Insulin	5-10 units IV	15-60 minutes	4-6 hours	Shifts K⁺ into cells
4. D50 (dextrose)	1 ampule (25 g) IV	15-60 minutes	4-6 hours	Works with insulin
5. **Kayexalate***	15-60 g in 20% sorbitol PR or PO	1-4 hours	This is the **definitive** treatment May repeat Q6 hours	
6. **Hemodialysis*** — Indicated for refractory cases or in patients with renal failure				

*These are the **definitive** treatments that will remove potassium from the body. Insulin and D50 should be used together.

B. Non-emergency management

Non-Emergency Management		
Drug	**Dose**	**Action**
Kayexalate	PO: 15-30g in 20% sorbitol Rectal: 15-60g in 20% sorbitol	Binds potassium in bowel
Loop diuretic	**Furosemide (Lasix)** 40-160mg IV or PO	Increased renal potassium excretion
Hemo or peritoneal dialysis — Patients in acute or chronic renal failure		

Source: Adapted from Cogan MG, Papadakis MA. Fluid and electrolyte disorders. In: Tierney LM, et al. Current medical diagnosis and treatment, 34th ed. Norwalk, CT: Appleton & Lange, 1995:751.

— PART TWO: HYPOKALEMIA —

I. DEFINITION: Potassium level < 3.5 mEq/L

II. SIGNS AND SYMPTOMS

A. Potassium of 2.0-2.5 mEq/L: Muscle weakness, hyporeflexia, fatigue, cramps

B. Potassium of < 2.0 mEq/L: May cause areflexic paralysis, and respiratory insufficiency may occur. Rate at which potassium declines has direct relationship to severity of muscular abnormality

III. ETIOLOGY OF HYPOKALEMIA

A. Excess renal loss

1. Mineralocorticoid excess: Primary or secondary aldosteronism, renovascular HTN, Bartter's syndrome
2. Diuresis
3. Chronic metabolic alkalosis
4. ATBs: **Gentamicin, Amphotericin B**
5. Renal tubular acidosis
6. Hypomagnesemia
7. Other: Acute leukemia, ureterosigmoidostomy

B. Gastrointestinal loses: Vomiting, diarrhea

C. ECF →ICF shifts: Acute alkalosis, hypokalemic periodic paralysis, barium ingestion, insulin therapy or increased postprandial secretion of insulin, Vitamin B$_{12}$ therapy

D. Inadequate intake

IV. EVALUATION

A. Review history looking for iatrogenic or physiologic reasons for hypokalemia

B. If *unexplained* hypokalemia (e.g., young patient taking no meds, no history of vomiting), obtain a urinary potassium before repleting (hyperaldosteronism). If patient is hypertensive, obtain a renin and aldosterone level (mineralocorticoid excess)

GEN

C. Consider checking ABG (pH and bicarbonate) in the *unexplained* hypokalemic patient
D. **ECG changes** associated with hypokalemia affect primarily repolarization segments of the electrocardiogram
   1. ST segment depression
   2. T wave inversion
   3. Elevation of the U wave
E. **Hypokalemia** greatly increases the incidence of Digitalis toxicity including junctional rhythms or heart block

V. MANAGEMENT

A. Mild hypokalemia which is *not* symptomatic can be treated with PO replacement
   1. **K-Dur** 20–40mEq PO QD—Sustained release: Not to be used in critical situations
   2. **Slow-K** 8mEq—Sustained release: Not to be used in critical situations
   3. **K-Lyte** (powder) 25–50mEq PO/NG: May be used for treating hypokalemia acutely
B. If patient is severely hypokalemic (< 3.0), or with evidence of cardiac symptoms, replacement should be IV (on telemetry) with frequent lab checks
C. Potassium deficit by level of serum potassium:
   1. K^+ = 3.0–3.5   Replace with 50–75mEq KCl
   2. K^+ = 2.5–3.0   Replace with 100–150mEq KC
   3. K^+ = 2.0–2.5   Replace with 150–250mEq KCl
D. If magnesium level is low, **Magnesium Oxide** 400mg PO TID × 3–5 days

CLINICAL PEARLS

- Consider replacing magnesium or calcium in patients with refractory hypokalemia because potassium replacement will be ineffective if patient is also hypomagnesemic or hypocalcemic
- Because ECG manifestations of hypokalemia are often subtle, electrocardiogram should not be used as a guide to replacement therapy
- Arrhythmias may be more likely to occur in patients with hypokalemia who are also taking Digoxin
- Total amount of potassium in the body is 50 mcg/kg. About 95% is intracellular

References

Charytan D, et al. Indications for hospitalization of patients with hyperkalemia. Arch Intern Med 2000;160:1605.

Cohn JN, et al. New guidelines for potassium replacement in clinical practice. Arch Intern Med 2000;160:2429.

Perazella MA. Drug-induced hyperkalemia: Old culprits and new offenders. Am J Med 2000;109:307.

Stewart OM. Mineralocorticoid hypertension. Lancet 1999;353:1341.

Gennari FJ. Hypokalemia. N Engl J Med 1998;339:451.

Halperin ML, et al. Potassium. Lancet 1998;352:135.

Miriam M. Chan, PharmD

80. ADVERSE DRUG INTERACTIONS & PRESCRIBING ERRORS

I. DRUG INTERACTION MECHANISMS

A. Absorption of 1 drug can be reduced by another drug, e.g., Cholestyramine

B. Protein/tissue binding displacement can be important especially if the displacing drug also reduces the elimination of the object drug

C. Metabolism of 1 drug can be enhanced by an "enzyme-inducing" agent, e.g., Phenobarbital

D. Many commonly prescribed meds interfere with or are metabolized by the hepatic cytochrome P-450 enzyme system. The Cyt P-450 system refers to a collection of iso-enzymes that are responsible for the oxidative metabolism of many endogenous and exogenous compounds

E. Altered renal excretion can be caused by reduced excretion or change in urinary pH

F. Pharmacodynamic interaction occurs when drugs with either additive or antagonistic properties are given concomitantly

II. SELECTED CLINICALLY RELEVANT DRUG INTERACTIONS

The following table is not comprehensive. Drugs in parentheses are important examples of that class of drug

Selected Clinically Relevant Drug Interactions		
Object Drug	**Precipitant Drug**	**Effect/Action**
ACE inhibitors, ARBs	K⁺ sparing diuretics (Amiloride Spironolactone), K⁺ supplements	↑ Serum K⁺, especially in the presence of significant renal impairment. Monitor serum K⁺
Antiarrhythmics, Type 1C: Encainide, Mexiletine, Propafenone	*Enzyme inhibitors:* Cimetidine, Quinidine, SSRIs (Fluoxetine, Paroxetine)	↑ Antiarrhythmics plasma levels. Monitor patient carefully if used concurrently
Antidiabetic agents: Insulin, Sulfonylureas	ß-blockers, e.g. Nadolol, Propranolol, Timolol	Alternation of glycemic control and/or masking of some signs of hypoglycemia (e.g. tachycardia, tremor)
Antifungal agents: Itraconazole, Ketoconazole	*Gastric alkalinizers:* H₂-blockers, antacids, Omeprazole	↓ Absorption of Itraconazole and Ketoconazole
Benzodiazepines: Alprazolam (Xanax), Triazolam (Halcion)	*Enzyme inhibitors:* Ketoconazole, Itraconazole, Nefazodone	↑ Benzodiazepine levels, may lead to unexpected CNS impairment or other toxic effect. Contraindication
ß -blockers	Diltiazem, Verapamil	↑ Risk of bradycardia and AV block. Avoid combination
ß -blockers, non-selective: Nadolol, Propranolol, Timolol	Epinephrine	Severe hypertension and bradycardia secondary to unopposed α-stimulation. Avoid use in patients prone to anaphylaxis because they might not respond to Epinephrine
Carbamazepine (CBZ)	*Enzyme inhibitors:* Cimetidine, Erythromycin, Diltiazem, Fluoxetine, INH, Propoxyphene, Verapamil	↑ Serum CBZ levels significantly within 2–3 days. Monitor serum CBZ levels and signs of CBZ toxicity (e.g. drowsiness, ataxia, nystagmus, blurred vision, nausea)
Digoxin	↓ *Renal and non-renal clearance:* Antiarrhythmics (Amiodarone, Propafenone, Quinidine), Ca-channel blockers (Verapamil)	↑ Digoxin serum levels. Amiodarone and Quinidine can cause a = 2-fold increase in Digoxin levels. Effects of Propafenone and Verapamil may be less. Patients starting on these drugs should have Digoxin dosage reduced by 50%. Additional dosage adjustment may be necessary. Monitor serum Digoxin concentrations and signs of toxicity (e.g. GI upset, CNS disturbances, arrhythmias)
Digoxin	K⁺ wasting diuretics (Furosemide, HCTZ)	Digoxin toxicity can occur secondary to hypokalemia. Monitor serum K⁺ level and replace K⁺ as needed
Dofetilide (Tikosyn)	↓ *Renal clearance:* Cimetidine (Tagamet), Trimethoprim (alone or TMP/SMZ), Ketoconazole (Nizoral), Megestrol (Megace), Prochlorperazine (Compazine)	Significantly ↑ Dofetilide plasma concentrations, leading to ↑ risk of torsade de pointes (TdP). Concomitant use of these drugs with Dofetilide is contraindicated
Dofetilide (Tikosyn)	Drugs that prolong QTc interval (e.g., Sotalol, Amiodarone, TCAs, Phenothiazine, Macrolides) Hydrochlorothiazide	↑ Risk of TdP. Withhold the drug for = 3 t₁/₂ prior to Dofetilide dosing
Dofetilide (Tikosyn)	K⁺ -depleting diuretic (e.g., HCTZ)	↑ Risk of TdP. Monitor K⁺ and Mg²⁺ closely
Dofetilide (Tikosyn)	Verapamil (Calan)	↑ Risk of TdP. Concomitant use with Dofetilide is contraindicated
HMG CoA reductase inhibitors (not Pravastatin)	Azoles (Itraconazole, Ketoconazole), Cyclosporine, Erythromycin, Fenofibrate (Tricor), Gemfibrozil (Lopid), Niacin	Myopathy, ↑ risk of rhabdomyolysis. Close monitoring is required

Chart continued on next page

Object Drug	Precipitant Drug	Effect/Action
Lithium	↓ *Renal clearance*: NSAIDs except Sulindac, Thiazide diuretics	↑ Serum Li⁺ levels within days. Monitor serum Li⁺ levels and signs of toxicity (e.g. muscle twitching, confusion)
MAO inhibitors	Cold/cough medicines (Dextromethorphan, Sympathomimetics), Meperidine, SSRIs (e.g. Fluoxetine, Paroxetine, Sertraline). Food rich in tyramine (e.g. cheese, red wine, smoked fish)	Severe reactions (shivering, seizures, agitation, delirium, and death). Avoid combination
Oral contraceptives	*Enzyme inducers*: Carbamazepine, Phenobarbital, Phenytoin, Primidone, Rifampin, ↓ *enterohepatic recycling*: Ampicillins, Tetracycline, Griseofulvin	↓ Efficacy of oral contraceptives, resulting in breakthrough bleeding or pregnancy. Use another method of contraception
Phenytoin	*Enzyme inhibitors*: Amiodarone, Cimetidine, Fluconazole, Fluoxetine, Isoniazid, Omeprazole	↑ Serum Phenytoin levels. Monitor serum Phenytoin levels and signs of toxicity (e.g. ataxia, nystagmus, mental impairment)
	Protease inhibitors: Ritonavir (Norvir), Indinavir (Crixivan), Saquinavir (Invirase), Nelfinavir (Viracept)	See chapter 113, Ambulatory HIV/AIDS Management, for further information
Quinidine	*Enzyme inducers*: Phenobarbital, Phenytoin, Rifampin	↓ Serum quinidine levels. Adjust Quinidine dose as needed when initiating or discontinuing enzyme inducers
Quinolones (e.g., Cipro, Floxin)	*Chelating effect*: Antacids, iron salts, Sucralfate	↓ Bioavailability of Quinolones. The antibiotic should be given 2 hrs before or 4 hrs after a dose of antacid
Quinolones: Gatifloxacin (Tequin), Moxifloxacin (Avelox), Sparfloxacin (Zagam)	Antiarrhythmic agents Class IA and III (e.g., Disopyramide, Procainamide, Quinidine, Sotalol)	↑ Risk of TdP. Concomitant use of Sparfloxacin with class IA and III agents is contraindicated
Sildenafil (Viagra)	Nitrates	Sildenafil potentiates the vasodilatory effect of circulating nitric oxide, resulting in a significant and potentially fatal fall in BP. Concomitant use is contraindicated
Theophylline	*Enzyme inhibitors*: Cimetidine, Ciprofloxacin, Erythromycin, Fluvoxamine, Tacrine, Ticlopidine, Verapamil, Zileuton (Zyflo)	↑Serum Theophylline concentrations, leading to toxicity within 2-3 days. Theophylline dose may need to be adjusted by 30-50%. Monitor serum Theophylline levels and signs of toxicity (e.g. tachycardia, nausea, tremor)
Theophylline	*Enzyme inducers*: Carbamazepine, Phenobarbital, Phenytoin, Primidone, Rifampin	↓ Serum Theophylline concentrations gradually over 1-2 weeks. Monitor serum Theophylline levels and adjust dose as needed
Tramadol (Ultram)	Carbamazepine (Tegretol)	↓ Analgesic effect of Tramadol. Seizure risk associated with Tramadol. Avoid combination
Tramadol (Ultram)	CNS depressants (e.g. alcohol, sedatives)	↑ Risk of respiratory depression. Reduce dose of tramadol
Tramadol (Ultram)	*CYP2D6 enzyme inhibitors*: Quinidine, Fluoxetine, Paroxetine, Amitriptyline	↑ Serum Tramadol levels and ↑ risk of seizures
Tramadol (Ultram)	MAO inhibitors, SSRIs, TCAs, other Opioids, Neuroleptics	↑ Risk of seizure. Also ↑ risk of Serotonin syndrome when use concomitantly with SSRIs or MAO inhibitors
Tricyclic antidepressants: Amitriptyline, imipramine, nortriptyline	*Enzyme inhibitors*: Cimetidine, Fluconazole, Propoxyphene, Quinidine, SSRIs (Fluoxetine, Paroxetine)	↑ Tricyclic antidepressant serum concentrations possibly leading to toxicity. Monitor closely
Warfarin (Coumadin)	Acetaminophen (Tylenol)	Inhibits Warfarin metabolism. ↑ INR monitoring in patients taking > 2 g/day regularly
Warfarin (Coumadin)	*Enzyme inhibitors*: Amiodarone, Antimicrobials (Quinolones, Erythromycin, Fluconazole, Itraconazole, Ketoconazole, Metronidazole, Rifampin, Sulfa antibiotics), Cimetidine, Cisapride, Disulfiram, Omeprazole, Propafenone, Zafirlukast (Accolate), Zileuton (Zyflo). *Inhibit platelet function*: NSAIDs, Salicylates *Unknown mechanism*: Androgens, Clofibrate, Gemfibrozil (Lopid), thyroid hormones	↑ Hypoprothrombinemic response of Warfarin and ↑risk of bleeding. Concurrent use of Clofibrate should be avoided if possible due to the difficulty in the management of these interactions. Amiodarone may produce a large increase in INR over a period of weeks. When Amiodarone is added to therapy, a 50% reduction in Warfarin dose may be needed. NSAIDs also increase the risk of GI bleeding in anticoagulated patients. Use conservative Warfarin dosing, monitor INR more frequently, and monitor for clinical sign of bleeding. It may take 7-10 days to reach new steady state anticoagulant response
Warfarin (Coumadin)	↓ *GI absorption*: Bile acid Sequestrants (Cholestyramine, Colestipol) *Enzyme inducers*: Carbamazepine, Phenobarbital, Phenytoin, Primidone, Rifampin ↑ *Vitamin K*: vitamin K rich foods (green vegetables, enteral feeding, green tea)	↓ Hypoprothrombinemic response of Warfarin. Monitor INR more frequently and watch for excessive anticoagulant effect when the inducer is discontinued. Avoid use of Rifampin with Warfarin if possible due to the difficulty in the management of these interactions
Ziprasidone (Geodon)	Antiarrhythmics Class 1A and III, Mesoridazine, Thioridazine, Chlorpromazine, Droperidol, Pimozide, Sparfloxacin, Gatifloxacin, Moxifloxacin, Halofantrine, Mefloquine, Pentamidine, Arsenic trioxide, Levomethadyl, Dolasetron, or Tacrolimus	↑ Risk of TdP. Concomitant use of these drugs with Dofetilide is contraindicated

GEN

III. PREVENTING MEDICATION PRESCRIBING ERRORS

A. Confirm that patient's weight is correct for weight-based dosages. Write patient's weight on the prescription

B. Identify drug allergies in patients and reconfirm each time writing a prescription

C. Give patient oral and written instructions without using abbreviations

D. Specify exact dosage strength. When writing for narcotics specify quantity in numerals and written out, e.g., #20 (twenty)

E. Avoid use of a terminal zero to the right of the decimal point (e.g., use 5 rather than 5.0) to minimize 10-fold dosing errors

F. Use a zero to the left of a dose less than 1 (e.g., use 0.1 rather than .1) to avoid 10-fold dosing errors

G. Spell out dosage units rather than using abbreviations

H. Ensure that prescriptions and signatures are legible

GEN

Selected Drugs that Cause QT Prolongation and Torsade de Pointes				
Drug Name (Brand)	↑ QTc	TdP	Warning in Label	Comments
Antiarrhythmics: very probable TdP risk				
Amiodarone (Cordarone)	X	X	X	TdP risk is regarded as low
Disopyramide (Norpace)	X	X	X	Case reports
Dofetilide (Tikosyn)	X	X	X	TdP risk is highest within first few days of therapy and at high doses
Flecainide (Tambocor)	X	X	X	Case reports (rare), possible TdP risk
Ibutilide (Corvert)	X	X	X	Black box warning
Procainamide (Pronestyl)	X	X	X	Risk is higher when the drug is given IV
Quinidine (Quinidex)	X	X	X	Higher risk when the drug is given IV
Sotalol (Betapace)	X	X	X	TdP risk is highest within first few days of therapy and at high doses
Antipsychotics				
Mesoridazine (Serentil)	X	X	X	Black box warning
Thioridazine (Mellaril)	X	X	X	Black box warning; very probable TdP risk
Pimozide (Orap)	X	X	X	Probable TdP risk
Ziprasidone (Geodon)	X		X	Probable TdP risk
Chlorpromazine (Thorazine)	X	X		Possible TdP risk in high risk patients
Haloperidol (Haldol)	X	X		Possible TdP risk in high risk patients
Risperidone (Risperdal)	X	X		Possible TdP risk in high risk patients
Antiemetics				
Droperidol (Inapsine)	X	X	X	Black box warning
Dolasetron (Anzemet)	X		X	Related to blood levels of active metabolite
Ondansetron (Zofran)	X			Limited documentation

Chart continued on next page

Selected Drugs that Cause QT Prolongation and Torsade de Pointes (continued)

Drug Name (Brand)	↑ QTc	TdP	Warning in Label	Comments
Calcium Channel Blockers				
Bepridil (Vascor)	X	X	X	Black box warning
Isradipine (DynaCirc)	X			Case reports of slight QT prolongation
Nicardipine (Cardene)	X			Case reports of slight QT prolongation
Macrolides				
Clarithromycin (Biaxin)	X	X	X	Possible TdP risk in high risk patients
Erythromycin	X	X	X	Possible TdP risk in high risk patients
Quinolines				
Gatifloxacin (Tequin)	X	X	X	Possible TdP risk in high risk patients
Sparfloxacin (Zagam)	X	X	X	Possible TdP risk in high risk patients
Moxifloxacin (Avelox)	X		X	Case reports of QT prolongation
Other Anti-infectives				
Halofantrine (Halfan)	X	X	X	Black box warning
Pentamidine (Pentam)	X	X		Case reports, possible TdP risk in high risk patients
Opioids				
Levomethadyl (Orlaam)	X	X	X	Black box warning
Methadone (Dolophine)	X	X		Case reports of TdP in patients taking high doses
Antidepressants				
SSRIs: citalopram (Celexa), fluoxetine (Prozac), paroxetine (Paxil), sertraline (Zoloft)	X	X		Case reports (very rare), TdP risk unlikely
TCAs: amitriptyline (Elavil), desipramine (Norpramin), imipramine (Tofranil)	X			Can affect cardiac conduction; case reports of increased QTc; TdP risk possible in high risk patients
Venlafaxine (Effexor)	X	X		Case reports (rare), TdP risk possible in high risk patients

GEN

IV. EXAMPLES OF DRUGS THAT MAY CAUSE RENAL TOXICITY

A. **NSAIDs:** decrease renal perfusion, may cause interstitial nephritis and nephrotic syndrome

B. **ACE inhibitors, ARBS:** cause renal failure in patients with bilateral renal artery stenosis

C. **Aminoglycosides:** direct tubular injury occurring 7–10 days after initiation of treatment

D. **Amphotericin B:** direct tubular injury

E. **Cyclosporine:** Prerenal, thrombotic thrombocytopenic purpura—hemolytic uremic syndrome, or chronic renal failure

F. **Radiographic contrast dye:** Prerenal and acute tubular necrosis

G. **Foscarnet, Ganciclovir, Pentamidine**

V. EXAMPLES OF DRUGS THAT MAY CAUSE HEPATIC TOXICITY

A. **Acetaminophen:** Direct toxic reactions

B. **Alcohol:** Cirrhosis

C. **Amiodarone:** Fatty liver and alcoholic hepatitis

D. Estradiol: Cholestatic reactions

E. Isoniazid: Idiosyncratic reactions

F. HMG CoA reductase inhibitors: Mild elevations in AST/ACT, cholestatic injury

G. Phenytoin: Allergic hepatitis

H. Sustained-release nicotinic acid: Ischemic damage

I. Vitamin A: Indolent cirrhosis

CLINICAL PEARLS

- Always be alert for potential drug interactions with drugs that have narrow therapeutic indexes. E.g., antiarrhythmics, anticonvulsants, Cisapride, Lithium, MAOIs, nonsedating antihistamines, Theophylline, and Warfarin
- If the patient is stabilized on the object drug, it may be necessary to adjust the dose when starting, stopping or altering the dose of the precipitant drug
- Monitoring of serum drug concentrations may be useful in adjusting drug dosage
- Educate patient regarding early signs of a possible drug interaction and monitor carefully the clinical response of the patient
- The onset of drug interactions may vary, depending on the time required to reach the steady-state concentration of the precipitant drug
- Alcohol may potentiate the CNS effects of antidepressants, antihistamines, antipsychotics, benzodiazepines, narcotics, and sedatives. Alcohol can cause a disulfiram-like reaction (flushing, palpitations, tachycardia, nausea etc.) when it is taken concurrently with Metronidazole or Chlorpropamide

References

Ament PW, et al. Clinically significant drug interactions. Am Fam Phys 2000; 61:1745-54.

Hansten PD, Hom JR. Drug interactions analysis and management. Applied Therapeutics, Inc., 1997.

Goldberg RJ. The P-450 system. Arch Fam Med 1996;5:406–12.

McEvoy GK, ed. The American hospital formulary service. Bethesda, MD: American Society of Health-System Pharmacists, 1996.

Lee WM. Drug-induced hepatotoxicity. N Engl J Med 1995;333:1118–27.

Michael B. Weinstock, MD

81. MEDICATION ADHERENCE

I. STATISTICS

A. Approximately 20% of patients do not fill their prescriptions and approximately 30% of patients do not take their prescribed meds. Common reasons given are:

1. Think their meds are unnecessary
2. Do not think the meds will work
3. Worried about side effects
4. Cost

B. Up to 5–10% of hospital admissions of the elderly may be associated with med non-adherence

II. FACTORS WHICH INCREASE THE RISK OF NON-ADHERENCE

A. Lives alone

B. Uses more than 1 pharmacy or more than 1 provider

C. Multiple daily doses

D. Frequently changed regimen

E. Large number of drugs

F. Lack of understanding of the diagnosis and the role of meds

G. Poor cognition, vision or dexterity

GEN

III. HINTS TO IMPROVE MEDICATION ADHERENCE

A. Minimize the number of meds patients are taking

B. Explain to patients what their meds do and why they need to take them

C. Prescribe meds with minimal side effects

D. Inform patients about potential side effects and how to best manage them

E. Review patients' meds at each visit to ensure the meds they are taking (or not taking) are the same meds you think they are taking (or not taking)

F. Locate patients at high risk for med non-adherence (illiterate, decreased mobility, ignorant, rebellious (teenagers), and patients on multiple meds). Spend extra time with these patients and/or enlist the help of ancillary medical personnel (nurses, pharmacists, social workers, home health workers) to help with adherence

G. Minimize the number of times per day that a patient needs to take meds. If a patient is on a TID med, when possible, prescribe another TID med instead of a Q6hr med

H. Instruct, then observe patient taking metered dose inhalers. Use a spacer to increase delivery of the med

I. Be aware of cost of meds. Often prescriptions will not even be filled when the pharmacist tells patient the cost. A brilliant diagnosis dims when a patient does not take the meds

J. Refill only enough meds to get the patient to the next appointment

K. Ask patients how many times per week they take the meds. Ask in a non-judgmental, non-threatening way such as: "Many patients feel it is difficult to take all of their medications every day. How many times per week do you take (or do you miss) your medications?"

CLINICAL PEARLS

- Be alert for med toxicity in patients recently admitted to a hospital or extra-care facility. A clinician may have increased the dose of a patient's med because it was thought that the med was not working at a lower dose when, in fact, the patient was not taking the med. When the patient is admitted and receives prescribed dose, toxic levels are achieved. Admission equals compliance!

- In women who begin hormone replacement therapy (HRT), 33% will have stopped taking the meds at 6 months and 75% will have stopped at 3 years

References

Bedell SE, et al. Discrepancies in the use of medicines: Their extent and predictors in an outpatient practice. Arch Int Med 2000;160:21–9.

Wagner EH, et al. Improving outcomes in chronic illness. Manag Care Q 1996;4(2):12–25.

Lowes R. Patient-centered care for better patient adherence. Fam Prac Mgt 1998;5.

Sullivan SD, et al. Noncompliance with medication regimens and subsequent hospitalizations: Literature analysis and cost of hospitalization estimate. Res Pharm Ec 1990;2(2):19–33.

Task Force for Compliance. Noncompliance with medications: An economic tragedy with important implications for health care reform. Baltimore, MD: Task Force for Compliance; 1994.

GEN

VII. Musculoskeletal/ Sports Medicine

82. Common Fractures/Describing Fractures 275

83. Ankle Injuries 277

84. Knee Injuries 281

85. Shoulder Injuries 285

86. Elbow Injuries 288

87. Carpal Tunnel Syndrome 291

88. Low Back Pain 292

89. Corticosteroid Injection of Joints 296

MUSC

Steve Markovich, MD
Jason J. Diehl, MD

82. COMMON FRACTURES/DESCRIBING FRACTURES

INTRODUCTION: The ability to describe fractures and dislocations is essential to all physicians for accurate documentation and for communication with other health providers

I. FRACTURES: Each fracture can be described using an organized system based on what is seen radiographically. Fracture nomenclature includes location, fracture type, the relationship of fragments to one another, and the relationship to surrounding tissues

  A. Anatomic location: Name bone involved and anatomic location

    1. Location along the bone (diaphysis, metaphysis, epiphysis, or intraarticular)

    2. Fractures in children may also involve the growth plate (physis)

    3. Long bones are generally divided into thirds (proximal, middle, distal)

    4. Special location may be used (e.g., intertrochanteric femur fracture)

  B. Fracture type: May include fracture line, fragments, and forces involved

    1. Fracture line describes direction of fracture

      a. Transverse: Fracture runs 90° to the long axis of the bone

      b. Oblique: Fracture runs less than 90° to the long axis of the bone

      c. Spiral: Torsion results in curved fracture around the bone

      d. Greenstick: Incomplete fracture in children, disrupted periosteum opposite the fracture

    2. Fragmented fractures

      a. Comminuted: More than 2 fracture fragments

      b. Segmental: Type of comminuted with large well-defined fragments

    3. Fracture forces

      a. Impacted: Force down the shaft, forcing 1 fragment into another

      b. Avulsion: Muscle contraction pulls a fragment off from its attachment site

      c. Compression: Usually seen in cancellous flat bones (vertebral bodies)

      d. Torus or buckle: Seen in children, similar forces to an impact fracture

      e. Stress fracture: Skeletal breaks resulting from overuse

  C. Relationship of fragments

    1. Alignment: Describes direction and angle of distal fragment relative to proximal fragment, e.g., distal femur fragment is angulated 15° laterally

    2. Displacement: Shifting of fragments in relation to one another. Usually described in terms of percentage of subluxation. Fracture with 100% displacement and shortening is referred to as a bayonette fracture

  D. Relationship to surrounding tissues

    1. Open: Skin broken by either outside forces or fracture fragment

    2. Closed: Skin intact

MUSC

Fracture Line Orientation

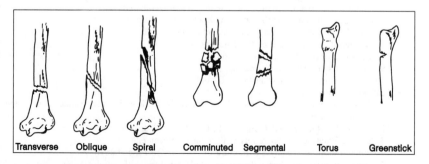

| Transverse | Oblique | Spiral | Comminuted | Segmental | Torus | Greenstick |

Source: Tintinalli JE, ed. Emergency Medicine. 5th ed. New York: McGraw-Hill, 2000: 1743 (figure 259-1). Used with permission.

II. DISLOCATION AND SUBLUXATION

A. Dislocation: Complete disruption of joint so that articular surfaces are no longer in contact
1. Description based on the position of distal bone relative to proximal bone, e.g., posterior elbow dislocation/displacement of ulnar olecranon, posterior relative to the humerus
2. May be associated with fractures
3. Bones often lie side-by-side, locked in that position until dislocation reduced

B. Subluxation: Incomplete disruption of a joint where articular surfaces are in contact but not perfectly aligned

III. TERMINOLOGY: Orthopedics has unique language to describe bony structures and relationships

A. Salter classification: Refers to physeal fractures in children
1. I-Fracture through the physis
2. II-Fracture through the physis with continuation towards the metaphysis
3. III-Fracture through the physis with continuation towards the epiphysis
4. IV-Fracture through the physis with continuation towards both the epiphysis and metaphysis
5. V-Crush injury to the physis

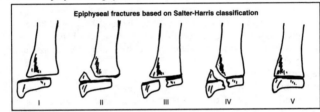

Epiphyseal fractures based on Salter-Harris classification

I II III IV V

Source: Tintinalli JE, ed. Emergency Medicine. 5th ed. New York: McGraw-Hill, 2000:1745 (figure 259-6). Used with permission.

B. Body parts
1. Genu: Knee
2. Hallux: Toe
3. Pes: Foot
4. Pollex: Thumb
5. Talipes: Ankle

C. Long bone locations
1. Diaphysis: Shaft of long bones
2. Metaphysis: Widened "neck" portion of bone adjacent to epiphysis
3. Epiphysis: Ossification center at the end of long bones, separated from the metaphysis by the physis in children
4. Physis: Cartilaginous growth plate

D. Other terminology
1. Ankylosis: Restricted motion in a joint
2. Apophysis: Ossification center at the insertion of a tendon
3. Arthrodesis: Surgical stiffening/fusion of a joint
4. Kyphosis: Curvature of the spine with posterior convexity
5. Lordosis: Curvature of the spine with anterior convexity
6. Spondylolisthesis: Slippage of 1 vertebra on another
7. Spondylolysis: Fracture of the pars interarticularis
8. Valgus: Distal part away from midline
9. Varus: Distal part toward midline
10. Volar: Towards palmar surface of hand

E. Unique fracture names
1. Boxer's Fracture: Fracture of the fifth metacarpal neck with volar displacement of the metacarpal head
2. Colles' Fracture: Distal radius fracture with dorsal displacement
3. Smith's Fracture: Distal radius with volar displacement
4. Jones' Fracture: Diaphyseal fracture of base of fifth metatarsal
5. Maisonneuve's Fracture: Proximal fibula fracture with syndesmosis rupture and associated medial malleolar fracture or deltoid ligament rupture

6. Monteggia's Fracture: Fracture of proximal third of ulnar shaft with radial head dislocation
7. Nightstick Fracture: Isolated fracture of ulna due to direct trauma
8. Rolando's Fracture: Y shaped intra-articular fracture of base of first metacarpal

References
Eiff MP, et al. Fracture management for primary care. Philadelphia: W. B. Saunders, 1998.
Rockwood CA, et al. Fractures in adults. 4th ed. Philadelphia: Lippincott, 1996.
Snider RK. Essentials of musculoskeletal care. Am Acad Ortho Surg 1999.

Brent Cale, MD

83. ANKLE INJURIES

I. INTRODUCTION: Although most ankle injuries are simple sprains of the lateral ligaments, a variety of other structures near the ankle may also be injured. Included in the differential diagnosis should be medial ankle sprains, trauma to the Achilles and peroneal tendons, tarsal tunnel syndrome, fractures, syndesmotic sprains and synovial impingement

II. ANATOMY
   A. Ligaments of the lateral ankle
      1. Anterior talofibular ligament
         a. Prevents forward subluxation of the talus/prevents inversion in plantar flexion
         b. Most frequently injured ligament with inversion injury
      2. Posterior talofibular ligament—strongest lateral ligament and rarely injured
      3. Calcaneofibular ligament—prevents inversion in neutral position
   B. Ligament of the medial ankle: Deltoid ligament
      1. Broad ligament with superficial and deep fibers
      2. Prevents eversion
   C. Tibiofibular joint/syndesmosis: The following ligaments connect the tibia and fibula. They form a fibrous joint between the distal tibia and fibula called the syndesmosis (see syndesmosis squeeze test below)
      1. Anterior tibiofibular ligament
      2. Posterior tibiofibular ligament
      3. Interosseous membrane
   D. Superficial posterior compartment of the leg: All of the following muscles insert at the calcaneus through the Achilles tendon
      1. Gastrocnemius muscle
      2. Soleus muscle
      3. Plantaris muscle

III. HISTORY
   A. General: Swelling, ecchymosis, abrasions, lacerations, paresthesias
   B. Mechanism of injury
      1. Was a "pop" felt or heard at the time of injury
      2. Ability to bear weight immediately following injury
      3. Inversion or eversion
      4. Force of injury
      5. Swelling or ecchymosis, abrasions or lacerations
   C. Previous injury to either ankle
   D. Type of employment and level of athlete

IV. PHYSICAL: Patients with acute ankle injuries will most likely have loss of range of motion (ROM) and decreased strength secondary to swelling and pain which may compromise the exam (drawer tests, etc). It may be helpful to reexamine after the swelling has decreased
   A. Inspection for swelling and ecchymosis to help localize the site of the injury. *Inspect the unaffected side for comparison.* Ecchymosis extending proximately from the ankle to the leg may indicate a syndesmotic injury
   B. Palpation: Gently palpate to find areas of greatest tenderness—start with examining the areas of least suspected tenderness. Particularly observe for tenderness of the malleoli, anterior talofibular ligament, anterior process of the calcaneous, calcaneofibular ligament,

MUSC

deltoid ligament, Achilles tendon, peroneal tendons, tibialis anterior tendon, navicular, and proximal fifth metatarsal

C. Range of motion: Normal is 13–16° of dorsiflexion and 31–44° plantar flexion

D. Pulses: Dorsal pedis and posterior tibial

E. Neurologic: Check sensation (L4:medial leg, L5:lateral leg and great toe, S1:heel)

F. Ankle stress testing: To assess ankle instability. Exam after acute injury may be limited by pain and swelling

  1. Anterior drawer test: To test for laxity or disruption of the anterior talofibular ligament

    a. Method: Have patient sit or lie flat with the legs unweighted. Grasp lower leg with one hand and the heel with the other hand and then, with the ankle in slight plantar flexion, apply anterior force to the calcaneus to displace the talus forward

    b. Results: Displacement of 8–10mm is noted with division of the anterior talofibular ligament, and 10–15mm displacement is noted with tearing of anterior and posterior talofibular ligament and calcaneofibular ligament

  2. Talar tilt (inversion test): To test for laxity or disruption of the calcaneofibular ligament

    a. Method: Have patient sit or lie flat with the legs unweighted. Place inversion stress on the ankle

    b. Results: Indicative of anterior talofibular ligament disruption if 10–20° of inversion is noted. If talar tilt greater than 20° then calcaneofibular ligament may also be torn

  3. Syndesmosis squeeze

    a. Method: 10cm above the lateral malleolus, compress the proximal fibula against the tibia

    b. Results: If the patient reports localized pain at the distal tibia and fibula during the syndesmosis squeeze, this may be indicative of a fibular fracture, interosseus membrane disruption or distal tibiofibular syndesmosis damage

  4. Thompson test

    a. Method: Have the patient lie prone with feet off the edge of the table. Compress the mid-calf and observe for plantar flexion

    b. Results: A positive test (no plantar flexion) helps to confirm the diagnosis of an Achilles tendon rupture

V. EVALUATION

A. Plain x-ray: Not all ankle injuries necessitate obtaining radiographic films. *The Ottawa ankle rules* apply to patients 18 or older and suggest that films be obtained:

  1. If the patient is unable to bear weight initially and when examined

  2. Bone tenderness at the posterior edge of the lower 6 cm of the distal tibia or fibula, proximal 5th metatarsal, or over the navicular bone

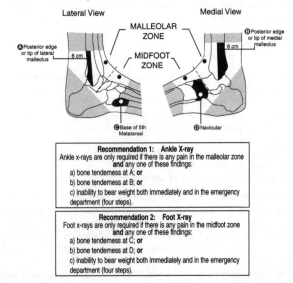

MUSC

B. CT: To localize osteochondritis dissecans, loose bodies and subchondral cysts
C. MRI: Osteochondral lesions such as osteochondritis dissecans and talar dome fractures, visualization of Achilles, peroneal and posterior tibial tendons
D. Technetium bone scan: To evaluate for stress fractures, infections or degenerative arthritis

VI. MANAGEMENT OF ANKLE SPRAINS

A. Incidence: 85% are lateral sprains, typically involving the anterior talofibular ligament, 10% are syndesmotic sprains, and 5% are medial sprains involving the deltoid ligament
B. Grade severity of ankle sprain

Severity	Pathophysiology	Symptoms	Signs	Weight-bearing
Grade I	Minimal tearing of fibers	Minimal pain or instability	Slight edema Anterior drawer and talar tilt test negative	Unimpaired
Grade II	Incomplete rupture of ligament	Moderate pain and disability	Moderate edema and ecchymosis Anterior drawer and talar tilt tests positive	Difficult
Grade III	Complete rupture of ligament	Severe pain with loss of function	Severe edema and ecchymosis Anterior drawer and talar tilt tests positive Possible avulsion fracture	Impossible

*Adapted from table 2—Ankle sprain grading system from Reisdorff, EJ. The injured ankle: New twists to a familiar problem. Emergency Medicine Reports 1995;16(5).

C. Management of Grade I and II sprains
   1. Support to prevent eversion and inversion and provide early mobilization
     a. Airsplint
     b. Gelsplint
     c. Swedo boot
     d. ROM boot cast
   2. RICE and meds (see below)
D. Management of Grade III sprains
   1. Non-weight bearing initially
   2. Immobilization
     a. Plaster posterior splint
     b. Sugar-tong splint
   3 Orthopedic evaluation
   4. RICE: See E. below
   5. Meds: See F. below
E. RICE
   1. **Rest:** Encourage weight bearing as tolerated; use crutches if needed
   2. **Ice:** 20 minutes Q2–3hrs × 48hrs or until edema and inflammation have subsided
   3. **Compression:** Elastic wrap from distal foot to mid calf will support ankle and decrease edema
   4. **Elevation:** Elevate foot to 15–25 cm above level of heart
F. Meds
   1. **NSAIDs: Ibuprofen** 600–800mg PO TID-QID, other NSAIDs should be equally efficacious
   2. **Acetaminophen:** 650–1000mg PO Q 4–6hrs. May be combined with NSAIDs to enhance analgesic effect
   3. **Narcotics** if necessary
     a. **Hydrocodone/Acetaminophen (Vicodin):** 1–2 tabs Q4–6hrs PRN #12–20
     b. **Oxycodone/Acetaminophen (Percocet):** 5mg–1–2 tabs Q4–6hrs PRN #12–20
   4. **Nonnarcotic analgesics: Tramadol/Acetaminophen (Ultracet)** 1–2 PO Q4–6hrs PRN
G. Rehabilitation: Physical therapy referral is appropriate
   1. Range of Motion
     a. Achilles tendon stretching
     b. Alphabet exercises: Moving the ankle in multiple planes by drawing the letters of the alphabet

MUSC

2. Muscle Strengthening Exercises: Start once full ROM obtained
    a. Start with isometric exercises and progress to dynamic exercises
    b. Perform in all 4 directions of ankle movement
3. Proprioception: Start once the patient can bear weight without pain. May involve toe raises with eyes closed or the use of devices such a wobble boards
4. Activity Specific Training: Graded progression to full activities which should be supervised by a therapist or trainer. The use of braces or athletic tape is useful early in the return to activities

VII. DIFFERENTIAL DIAGNOSIS OF THE NON-HEALING ANKLE INJURY
A. Incomplete rehabilitation
B. Chronic instability
C. Reflex sympathetic dystrophy (RSD)
D. Peroneal tendon pathology
E. Fractures (talar dome, 5th metatarsal, navicular, growth plate)
F. Anterior impingement
G. Neuroma
H. Accessory navicular bone
I. Osteochondritis dissecans (OCD)

CLINICAL PEARLS
- Prolonged immobilization may lead to slowed return to normal function
- If an ankle injury is not allowed to adequately heal and the ligaments are not allowed to adequately tighten, patients may be left with a "loose ankle", predisposing them to future ankle strains
- The typical mechanism of injury of a lateral ankle sprain is by inversion, which frequently occurs with some degree of plantar flexion
- Ecchymosis extending proximally from the ankle to the lower leg may indicate a tibiofibular syndesmotic injury. Syndesmotic sprains tend to require a more prolonged recovery time
- Tibiofibular syndesmosis is a commonly associated injury with injury to deltoid ligament
- Osteochondral fractures of the talar dome are typically diagnosed 4–6 weeks after an ankle "sprain" that does not heal
- In studies of patients with ankle sprains, no difference was found in the number of patient complaints or residual ankle stability between those who were casted and those who were not

References

Kerkhoffs GMMJ, et al. Immobilisation for acute lateral ankle ligament injuries in adults. In: The Cochrane Library, Issue 2, 2001. Oxford: Update Software.

Wolfe MW, et al. Management of ankle sprains. Am Fam Phys 2001;63(1):93–104.

Pijenburg AC, et al. Treatment of ruptures of the lateral ankle ligaments: a meta-analysis. J Bone Joint Surg (Am) 2000;82:761-773.

Garrick JG. Managing ankle sprains: keys to preserving motion and strength. The Phys & Sportsmed 1997;25(3):56–8.

Shrier I. Treatment of lateral collateral ligament sprains of the ankle: A critical appraisal of the literature. Clin J Sport Med 1995;5:187–95.

Michael B. Weinstock, MD
Ed Boudreau, DO
Shonna Reidlinger, PA-C

84. KNEE INJURIES

I. ANATOMY
A. Bursae: Provide lubrication between dynamic components
B. Cruciate ligaments
1. Anterior cruciate ligament (ACL): Stabilizes knee to prevent anterior motion of the tibia
2. Posterior cruciate ligament (PCL): Stabilizes knee to prevent posterior motion of the tibia
C. External tendons and ligaments
1. Patellar tendon
2. Medial collateral ligament (MCL) and lateral collateral ligament (LCL)
D. Muscles
1. Knee flexors: Hamstrings and gastrocnemius
2. Knee extensors: Quadriceps (continues on as the patellar tendon)
E. Articulations
1. Lateral and medial tibiofemoral articulations
2. Patellofemoral articulation

II. HISTORY
A. Acute trauma: Pain which began suddenly during a certain activity. Position of the knee when injured (flexed, extended, etc), or as a result of a direct blow
B. Chronic trauma: Activities
C. Swelling immediately after injury: Suggests meniscal or ligamentous injury
D. Locking/Buckling of the knee: Catching or "give way" episodes (meniscal injury)
E. History of patellar dislocation
F. Problems elsewhere in the lower extremity: One joint above and one joint below. Hip or foot problems, new shoes, etc.
G. Systemic illness: Polyarthralgia, fever, morning stiffness, history of gout, hyperuricemia, rheumatoid arthritis, or pseudogout
H. Past history: Knee injury, past surgeries of the knee

III. PHYSICAL: Compare to uninjured side
A. Visually inspect knee for swelling, evidence of past surgeries/injuries, abrasions, contusions, ecchymosis, erythema, patellar location. Visually inspect leg muscles for atrophy, leg length discrepancies, etc.
B. Range of motion, crepitus, gait, patellar grind, strength, reflexes
C. Patella
1. Palpate for effusion
    a. Inspection: With the patient seated and both knees flexed 90°, observe for a bulge on either side of the patellar ligament in the symptomatic knee
    b. Ballottement: The patient lies supine with knee extended and the examiner's first hand compresses from above and also on both sides of the patella then the examiner's other hand compresses the patella to see if it is ballottable
    c. Carlin maneuver: With patient supine, milk or squeeze the suprapatellar area and with the other hand place fingers on either side of the patellar tendon palpate for fluid redistribution or bulging of accumulated fluid
2. Evaluate for hypermobility of the patella by attempting to sublux the patella laterally
3. Apprehension sign: Pain and involuntary contraction of the quadriceps with deviation of the patella laterally
D. Lachman test: Test for ACL injury
1. Method: Have the patient supine and the leg in slight external rotation and the knee in 15° of flexion (often the foot is slightly off the edge of the table). Example for left knee: With the examiner on the patient's right, grasp the lateral aspect of the distal thigh with the

MUSC

left hand and the medial aspect of the proximal lower leg with the right hand and pull anteriorly on the lower leg (with the right hand)

 2. Results: The test is positive if there is anterior laxity. This is the most sensitive test for ACL injury

E. Drawer tests: Test for ACL or PCL injury

 1. Method: Anterior and posterior drawer tests—patient is supine with the hip flexed 45° and the knee flexed 90° and the plantar aspect of the foot resting on the table. The examiner sits on the patient's foot and then grasps the proximal aspect of the lower leg with both hands and attempts to anteriorly or posteriorly displace the tibia on the femur

 2. Results: Anterior subluxation of the tibia on the femur suggests injury to the ACL and posterior subluxation suggests injury to the PCL

F. Tibial sag test: Test for PCL injury

 1. **Method:** Place patient in the supine position with hips flexed to 45° and both knees flexed to 90°

 2. **Results:** Affected tibia sags on the femur suggesting PCL injury

G. Varus-valgus stress test: MCL or LCL injury

 1. Method: Patient is supine with knee flexed about 20° and a varus or valgus stress is placed on the knee with the examiner's hand

 2. Results: Laxity with valgus stress suggests injury to the MCL, and laxity with varus stress suggests injury to the LCL

H. McMurray test: Test for meniscus injury

 1. Method: With the patient supine and the knee flexed at 90°, externally rotate the foot and then extend the knee. Repeat with the foot internally rotated, and then extend the knee

 2. Results: A test is positive with pain and/or a palpable click at the medial or lateral joint lines

I. Apley grind test: Test for meniscus injury

 1. Method: With the patient prone and the knee flexed at 90°, push straight down on the foot and then rotate the foot (compresses the meniscus). Repeat by pulling up on the foot and then rotating the foot

 2. Results: If there is pain when the foot is pushed down, but no pain when the foot is pulled up, then consider a meniscus injury

IV. RADIOGRAPHY/SPECIAL TESTS

A. Radiography: Evaluate for fracture, osteochondritis dissecans, dislocation, Osgood-Schlatter's disease, etc.

B. MRI: Meniscus injury/internal derangement, occult fracture or bone bruise

C. Aspiration of knee effusion: Aspirate to evaluate for hemarthrosis, infection (septic joint), fat globules (fracture), and for relief of symptoms

V. DIFFERENTIAL DIAGNOSIS AND MANAGEMENT OF COMMON KNEE PROBLEMS

A. Fracture: Obtain x-ray with appropriate suspicion (mechanism, swelling, deformity, joint tenderness etc.) and orthopedic referral if positive

B. Meniscus injury

 1. History

  a. Twisting, flexion injury

  b. Inability to flex knee

  c. Difficulty in bearing weight

  d. Clicking or locking of the knee

  e. If chronic, may see intermittent effusions, locking, and possibly quadriceps wasting

 2. Physical

  a. Knee effusion

  b. Tenderness over joint line (medial with medial meniscus injury, lateral with lateral meniscus injury)

  c. McMurray test and Apley test: See above for method

 3. Acute management: Rigid knee immobilizer (short term), crutches, ice, rest

 4. Refer to orthopedist if still symptomatic after 14 days of conservative management

C. Ligament injuries

 1. History

        a. Pain immediately at time of injury (mechanism of injury)

        b. Knee stiffness and tenderness

        c. Knee swelling (occasionally)

        d. Decreased ability to ambulate

2. Physical

        a. Tenderness to palpation of ligament (MCL, LCL)

        b. Lachman test: Positive with ACL injury (see above)

        c. Drawer tests (Test for ACL, PCL injury) and tibial sag test (PCL injury)

        d. Tests for lateral instability (MCL, LCL)

3. Classification

        a. Grade I—Stretching of fibers without significant damage

        b. Grade II—Partial tear of fibers

        c. Grade III—Complete tear of fibers

4. Management

        a. Ice, elevation, rest

        b. Rigid knee immobilizer or posterior splint

        c. Crutches for grade II and III injuries

        d. Orthopedic/sports medicine referral/surgery

        e. Physical therapy

D. Patellofemoral syndrome

1. Etiology

        a. Lateral subluxation (Hypermobility of the patella)

           i. May be caused by increased angle between the quadriceps and patellar tendon (Q angle). This is called patella alta. Normal Q angle is up to 20° (women)

           ii. Patella alta can be identified on a lateral knee x-ray where the length of the patellar tendon exceeds the length of the patella by more than 1cm

           iii. Other causes include variation in hip anatomy that results in compensatory tibial torsion

        b. Chondromalacia: Damage to soft cartilage on posterior patella causing crepitus and pain

2. History

        a. Pain worsened by walking or running up or down hills, climbing stairs or kneeling

        b. Pain often disappears during activity and returns just after activity is completed

3. Physical

        a. Patella alta

        b. Hypermobility of the patella

        c. Pain or crepitus with patellofemoral movement

        d. Apprehension sign: Pain and involuntary contraction of the quadriceps with deviation of the patella laterally

        e. Patellar grind test

        f. Possible knee effusion

4. Evaluation includes lateral x-ray (to evaluate for patella alta or DJD) and sunrise view of the patella (to evaluate for lateral subluxation)

5. Management

        a. Rest with possible use of crutches, ice, NSAIDs

        b. Avoid sports until symptoms have subsided

        c. Physical therapy to strengthen quadriceps: Patellar realignment

        d. Consider orthotic to correct pronation of the foot

        e. Surgical consideration if conservative therapy fails

E. Osgood-Schlatter's Disease (Apophysitis of the tibial tubercle)

1. General

        a. Common cause of knee pain in adolescents

        b. Secondary to repetitive avulsions of the patellar tendon where it inserts into the growth plate of the tibial tubercle

        c. Pain is at the insertion of the patellar tendon on the tibial tubercle

2. History

        a. Pain with onset of activity

MUSC

      b. Often bilateral
3. Physical
    a. Enlargement and tenderness at the tibial tubercle
    b. Possible quadriceps atrophy
    c. Tightness of the quadriceps and hamstring muscles
4. Management
    a. Avoid activities that involve knee extension (running, climbing, jumping, kicking) until symptoms have subsided ~6–8 weeks
    b. Range of motion and stretching: Physical therapy
    c. Oral analgesics, ice after activity
    d. Surgical management if pain persists after ossification is complete

F. Osteochondritis dissecans (OCD): Occurs secondary to ischemia
1. General
    a. Loss of blood supply (avascular necrosis) to an area next to a joint surface
    b. The ischemic/dead bone and overlying cartilage gradually loosen and cause pain
    c. This osteochondral fragment may break loose into the joint and cause locking, sharp pain and effusion
    d. Rule out OCD in contralateral joint; 20–30% of cases are bilateral
2. History: Gradual onset of swelling and vague pain. Worse with activity. Insidious onset may be over several months
3. Physical: Often pain with palpation of the medial femoral condyle (most common site is the lateral portion of the medial condyle). Quadriceps wasting. Decreased ROM of the knee
    a. Radiologic diagnosis with plain films
    b. MRI needed to stage the lesion
    c. Orthopedic referral

G. Other: Prepatellar bursitis, retropatellar bursitis, patellar tendonitis, fat pad syndrome, pes anserinus bursitis, neoplasm, loose bodies

H. Arthritis: See Chapters 69–72

CLINICAL PEARLS
- Acetaminophen and NSAIDs are equally effective in osteoarthritis of the knee
- Tears of the medial meniscus are 10 times as common as tears of the lateral meniscus
- MRI is 90% sensitive for meniscus injury
- Following meniscectomy, patients may have joint space narrowing and arthritic changes
- Knee has highest prevalence of benign and malignant tumors than any other joint
- Osgood-Schlatter's disease occurs most commonly from age 11–15 and affects males more than females
- Osteochondritis dissecans predisposes to degenerative arthritis

References
Juhn MS. Patellofemoral pain syndrome: a review and guidelines for treatment. Am Fam Phys 1999;60:2012-22.
Cutbill JW, Ladly KO, Bray RC, Thorne P, Verhoef M. Anterior knee pain: a review. Clin J Sport Med 1997;7:40-5.
Smith BW, et al. Knee injuries: part I. History and physical examination. Am Fam Phys 1995;51:615.
Smith BW, et al. Acute knee injuries: part II. Diagnosis and management. Am Fam Phys 1995;51:799.

MUSC

Doug DiOrio, MD
Shonna Reidlinger, PA-C

85. SHOULDER INJURIES

I. SHOULDER ANATOMY AND BIOMECHANICS

A. Introduction: Normal shoulder function is a combination of the anatomic arrangement and the complex action of many muscles. The shoulder is the joint with the largest range of motion, but this allows for more instability. A single small injury to the shoulder may lead to functional deficit which potentiates damage to other structures

B. Anatomy
   1. Sternoclavicular joint (synovial joint)
   2. Acromioclavicular joint
   3. Glenohumeral joint (golf ball on a tee)
   4. Humeral head
   5. Glenoid fossa
   6. Glenohumeral ligaments
   7. Rotator cuff (SITS: Supraspinatus, infraspinatus, teres minor, subscapularis)
   8. Scapula rotators (trapezius, rhomboids, levator scapulae, serratus anterior)

C. History: See history under each specific diagnosis

D. Physical exam
   1. Inspect for asymmetry and deformity of shoulder girdle
   2. Palpate for tenderness and crepitus
   3. Range of motion
   4. Neck and elbow exam (to exclude referred pain)
   5. Neurovascular exam of bilateral upper extremities
   6. Apprehension test: Most sensitive finding with shoulder instability
      a. Method: With patient in supine position apply anterior force to the humerus with external rotation
      b. Result: Pain (apprehension) of impending subluxation suggests anterior instability
   7. Relocation test
      a. Method: With patient in supine position apply posterior force to the humerus with external rotation
      b. Result: Relief of pain or apprehension suggests anterior instability
   8. Sulcus sign
      a. Method: With patient in sitting position, apply downward traction to the humerus
      b. Result: Development of a sulcus between the greater tuberosity of the humerus and acromion suggests posterior instability
   9. Apley scratch test
      a. Method: Patient attempts to touch the superior and inferior aspects of the opposite scapula
      b. Result: Loss of range of motion suggests rotator cuff disease
   10. Supraspinatus test
      a. Method: Patient's arms are abducted 90% and internally rotated. Downward force is applied while patient attempts to maintain position against resistance
      b. Result: Inability to maintain the position against resistance suggests rotator cuff disease
   11. Drop arm test
      a. Method: Arms are passively abducted and patient slowly lowers arm to waist
      b. Result: If arm drops to side, suggests rotator cuff disease
   12. Neer's sign
      a. Method: The arm is forcibly forward flexed
      b. Results: If pain is invoked, suggests impingement
   13. Impingement test
      a. Method: 10cc of 1% **Lidocaine** is injected into the subacromial space and Neer's sign

MUSC

maneuver is repeated
  b. Results: Relief of pain after injection suggests impingement

II. SHOULDER INSTABILITY

A. Introduction: Shoulder instability (symptomatic abnormal glenohumeral translation) is common problem, especially in overhead athlete. Anterior instability is the most common and can range from subluxation to complete dislocation. Instability can also result from repetitive microtrauma as the ligaments are stretched

B. History
  1. Anterior: Shoulder is usually abducted and externally rotated. Force is applied to arm causing more external rotation and extension. This event is very painful and athlete may feel shoulder slide out of place. Athlete may have associated symptoms of a "dead arm" for seconds to minutes following the event
  2. Posterior: Shoulder is usually in flexed, adducted, and internally rotated position and a force applied to hand causes posterior dislocation. Happens with falls and in offensive linemen in football
  3. Multidirectional or recurrent: Pain is usual complaint that brings patients to see doctor. These injuries can masquerade as many other injuries because of disrupted biomechanics of shoulder

C. Physical exam
  1. Positive apprehension test and sulcus sign
  2. With recurrent injuries check for signs of nerve palsies. Also there may be a loss of internal rotation (10°) and crepitus with ROM. Think of impingement as a sign of instability (injection test)

D. Radiography
  1. Plain films
  2. MRI: Most useful with recurrent instability and determining associated complications (labral tears, chondral defects)

E. Management
  1. Shoulder dislocation
    a. Multiple techniques including modified hippocratic (traction-countertraction, Rowe maneuver (touch opposite ear). Stimson (prone with traction weights)
    b. Post-reduction repeat plain films and immobilize 2–6 weeks. Rehabilitation will include early isometrics
  2. Chronic instability
    a. Protect shoulder from provocative movements, and regain ROM and normal shoulder function with physical therapy. Gradual return to sport specific exercise and play. Plan 3–6 months of therapy
    b. Surgical indications: Irreducible acutely, displaced tuberosity fracture, unstable glenoid rim fracture, absolute stabilization needed prior to return to sport, and loss of time not an option

F. Clinical Pearls
  1. Need good on-field exam before reduction
  2. Shoulder pain is the most common symptom of shoulder instability
  3. When you think of impingement, think of chronic instability
  4. Asymptomatic laxity can be a normal variant, but may lead to chronic instability

III. ROTATOR CUFF DISEASE

A. History: Symptoms can range from minimal to marked pain limiting function and decreased range of motion. Special attention should be given to throwing athletes because they are prone to overuse injuries. Chronic tendonitis may present with night pain

B. Physical
  1. Tenderness over the greater tuberosity of humerus and painful abduction of arm. Positive drop arm test, supraspinator test, and impingement sign
  2. Weakness or pain with internal or external rotation

C. Radiography
  1. Plain films: AP and lateral films

2. MRI may be used in either the acute or chronic tear if rehabilitation has failed. MRI is 89–96% sensitive and 49–100% specific for rotator cuff tear

D. Management

1. Acute tears: Begin with conservative treatment (rest, ice, and NSAIDs). Rehabilitation program to be started in 1–2 weeks. If not improved, consider MRI and surgical referral

2. Chronic tears: Begin with a stretching and strengthening program, avoiding overhead activities. Consider ice, heat, massage and ionophoresis. Consider NSAIDs and/or corticosteroid injection. If patient improves, slowly work in overhead activities and then sport specific activities. With continued pain consider MRI and surgical referral

E. Clinical Pearls

1. Rehabilitation (physical therapy) is the most important part of treatment
2. A partial thickness tear may easily progress to full thickness tear
3. Age is one of the great dividers in this injury

IV. IMPINGEMENT

A. Introduction: There are 2 reasons for impingement: Increase in volume of the structures in the space (muscle hypertrophy, inflammation, trauma) and decreased available space (fibrositis, osteophyte, convex acromion)

B. History: Patients present with a toothache-like pain in shoulder. Worse with overhead movements. Inquire about past history of any injuries to the shoulder (subluxations or rotator cuff) and any medical problems (inflammatory diseases). Night pain is common

C. Physical exam: Findings are consistent with early rotator cuff disease. Patient should not have any weakness of the cuff muscles. Positive impingement sign and Neer's sign

D. Radiology: May indicate anatomic variations in acromions predisposed to impingement

E. Management: Relative rest with avoidance of overhead (greater than 90%) movements. Physical therapy for stretching and rehab of muscles. NSAIDs followed by injection of steroids in 2–4 weeks. Surgery may be needed in cases that do not improve or those that have osteophytes as the primary problem

MUSC

V. ADHESIVE CAPSULITIS (FROZEN SHOULDER)

A. Introduction: Capsular thickening and contraction of shoulder joint that results in pain and limited mobility. More common in middle age women and diabetics. Number one predisposing factor is a prolonged period of inactivity

B. History: Patient almost always has some history of prolonged immobilization of shoulder. This may have been in the remote past but the patient has a new job or demand on the shoulder. Other symptoms include nocturnal pain and pain with movement

C. Physical exam: Stiffness and limited active and passive ROM in all directions especially abduction. In abduction patient will rely on scapulothoracic movement to abduct arm. Patient may have tenderness around capsule and a thickened capsule to palpation, and muscle spasm

D. Radiology: A decrease volume of the glenohumeral joint will be present in most cases

E. Management: NSAIDs and ROM exercises. Patient should rest arm in between exercises and sometimes a sling is used. Frozen shoulder may resolve spontaneously but in most cases prolonged treatment is needed. Steroid injections are used commonly but do not always help. In difficult cases manipulation under anesthesia is used. Rarely surgical intervention is needed but it does not have a high success rate

CLINICAL PEARLS

• MRI is 89–96% sensitive and 49–100% specific for rotator cuff tear

References

Stevenson JH, Trojian T. Evaluation of shoulder pain. J Fam Prac 2002;51:605.

Woodward DW, Best TM. The painful shoulder: Part I. Clinical evaluation. Am Fam Phys 2000;61:3079–88.

Woodward DW, Best TM. The painful shoulder: Part II. Acute and chronic disorders. Am Fam Phys 2000;61:3291–300.

Miniaci A, Salonen D. Rotator cuff evaluation imaging and diagnosis. Orthop Clin North Am 1997;28:43–58.

Hawkins RJ, Kennedy JC, Impingement syndrome in athletes. Am J Sports Med 1980;8:151–7.

Winters JC, et al. Treatment of shoulder complaints in general practice: long-term results of a randomised, single blind study comparing physiotherapy, manipulation, and corticosteroid injection. BMJ May 22, 1999;318:1395–6.

Douglas L. Moore MD
Tim Scanlon, PA-C

86. ELBOW INJURIES

I. ANATOMY
   A. Olecranon humeral joint is a hinge joint
   B. Radius articulates with capitulum and the ulna with trochlea
   C. Lateral joint space is supported by radial and ulnar collateral ligament complexes
   D. Upper extremity is innervated by 5 nerve branches that originate at brachial plexus (axillary, radial, musculocutaneous, ulnar and median nerves). Ulnar nerve is found easily by palpation in groove behind medial epicondyle

II. PATHOPHYSIOLOGY
   A. In adults most injuries occur to ligaments, tendons, or bone itself
   B. In children, the weakest links are the growth plates, apophysis and epiphysis
   C. Tendon damage often occurs secondary to overuse and microrupture
   D. Repetitive strains may lead to ligament damage, chondromalacia, osteophytes, tendonosis, neuritis, loose bodies, or osteochondritis dissecans
   E. Overhead throwing can lead to medial tension overload, lateral compression, and posterior olecranon impaction

III. ELBOW PAIN BY ANATOMIC LOCATION
   A. Lateral elbow pain
      1. Lateral epicondylitis (Tennis elbow): Overload of forearm extensors, mainly extensor carpi radialis brevis causing microscopic ruptures and inflammation at the insertion to the bone
         a. History: Patient complains of pain, especially with combing hair, playing tennis or golf, shaking hands
         b. Physical exam: Pain over the tendon about 1–2cm distal to the lateral epicondyle. Pain is exacerbated by active extension of the wrist or passive flexion
         c. Management: Conservative therapy with ice, NSAIDs, and physical therapy is usually successful. If not better after 1–2 weeks consider steroid injection (see Chapter 89, Corticosteroid Injection of Joints). Other important therapies are enforced proper technique, decreased string tension on racquet, applying a cushioned grip, and use of counter force bracing. Strengthening of the muscle may be accomplished by extending the fingers with an elastic band stretched over them or by reverse wrist curls. If not better after 12–16 weeks, consider surgery
      2. Radial nerve entrapment
         a. History: Patient complains of local pain, paresthesias, dull ache
         b. Physical exam: Pain in forearm often with radiation proximal and distal. Pain exacerbated by supination and resisted extension of middle finger with wrist in neutral position. Tenderness often 2–3cm distal to lateral epicondyle. May be aggravated by counter bracing
         c. Management: Rest, NSAIDs, and rehabilitation. Surgical release for resistant cases
         d. Think of radial nerve entrapment in cases of resistant tennis elbow
      3. Radiocapitellar Overload Syndrome
         a. History: Pain with overhead throwing
         b. Caused by radial head impaction on the capitellum during valgus stress of the

elbow accompanied by medial instability. May consist of radiocapitellar chondromalacia, radiocapitellar degeneration, osteochondral fracture, or loose bodies

   c. Physical exam: Patient will have lateral pain and occasionally locking of the elbow

B. Medial elbow pain

1. Medial epicondylitis (Golfer's elbow)
   a. History: Sharp pain, trouble lifting objects
   b. Physical: Pain at the common flexor origin. Sometimes affects pronator teres and flexor carpi radialis as well. Pain with resisted flexion, pronation, and passive extension
   c. Management: If 1 week of conservative treatment (ice, NSAIDs) not helpful, consider steroid injection. Squeezing a soft ball or wrist curls help strengthen the muscles involved. Surgery only in resistant cases
2. Medial elbow instability
   a. History: Pain over medial elbow usually during acceleration phase of throwing
   b. Physical exam: Focal tenderness 2cm distal to medial epicondyle, decreased range of motion, pain with valgus stress, and asymmetric valgus laxity between elbows
   c. X-ray: May see small avulsion fracture on x-ray. Stress radiographs may help in diagnosis
   d. Management: In acute tears, conservative measures are treatment of choice for non-athletes. Elite athletes may respond better to surgery. About 50% of chronic tears will respond to conservative measures alone
3. Ulnar neuritis
   a. History: Localized pain with paresthesia
   b. Acute pain over medial elbow with radiation down arm caused by repeated traction, compression, or friction on nerve
   c. Physical exam: There may be numbness or tingling in the small and ring fingers. The nerve may feel doughy or thick and there may be a positive Tinel's sign
   d. Management: Conservative measures preferred. May splint at 30° if chronic subluxation of nerve present

C. Posterior elbow pain

1. Triceps tendonitis
   a. History and physical: Pain over triceps tendon exacerbated by resisted elbow extension
   b. Management: Initial management with ice, NSAIDs, physical therapy. Rupture is rare and treated by direct surgical repair
2. Valgus extension overload syndrome
   a. Insidious onset of pain with full extension exacerbated by valgus stress. Caused by impingement of the olecranon allowed by ulnar collateral instability and repetitive valgus stress
   b. Physical exam: May find tenderness at the tip of the olecranon with the elbow in 45° of flexion
   c. X-ray: May reveal osteophytes of the olecranon
   d. Management: Conservative measures preferred, but if osteophytes present, surgery is required
3. Stress fracture of the olecranon
   a. Pain over olecranon with throwing. Due to the repetitive sudden snap at full extension. May need bone scan or CT to diagnose if not seen on x-ray
   b. Management: Rest if the fracture is stable. Surgery if conservative measures fail
4. Triceps apophysitis
   a. Seen in children and is similar to Osgood-Schlatter's disease of the knee. Patient has pain with resisted extension and is tender over the olecranon
   b. Management: Internal fixation with bone grafting
5. Olecranon bursitis
   a. Presents with a distended soft posterior elbow
   b. Management: Ice and compression. May aspirate the bursa if elbow has decreased range of motion. Send for fluid analysis to ensure not infectious. Can inject with steroids

D. Anterior elbow pain

1. Anterior capsule stretch or tear: Can occur secondary to fall on extended elbow, resisted flexion, forceful supination, hyperextension, or direct trauma. Conservative

measures are recommended

2. Pronator teres syndrome: Radiating forearm pain with numbness and tingling in distribution of median nerve. Physical exam reveals pain with active pronation and resisted long finger extension

3. Distal biceps tendon rupture
   a. Most often occurs when the elbow is flexed to 90° and the contraction is overcome by a sudden extension force
   b. Physical exam will reveal a palpable deformity, balling of the biceps muscle, decreased strength in elbow flexion and supination, and ecchymosis in the antecubital fossa
   c. Acute surgical anatomic repair is treatment of choice

E. Subluxation of the radial head (nursemaid's elbow)

1. Definition and mechanism of injury
   a. Subluxation of radial head is common among preschool children. After age 7 radial head is larger than radial neck and subluxation is not common
   b. Mechanism of injury is sudden traction on the hand with the elbow extended and the forearm pronated. Forceful traction fibers, which encircle the radial neck, slip and become trapped between the radial head and capitellum

2. History
   a. Important to elicit a history of traction on the child's hand; the act may have been unrecognized by the parent or the history withheld because of a feeling of guilt
   b. About 50% of the radial head subluxations present with an atypical history

3. Physical exam
   a. Child may present irritable, playful or comfortably in parents' lap. Common symptom is unwillingness to use the extremity
   b. Any child not using an arm that is flexed and pronated and without signs of trauma should be considered to have a radial head subluxation, unless history strongly suggests another diagnosis

4. Evaluation: Radiographs are not necessary, unless another diagnosis is being considered or if reduction is not accomplished

5. Management
   a. Reduction is carried out by firmly placing the thumb over the radial head while the other hand is placed on the wrist. Forearm is fully supinated. If a "click" is not felt, elbow is flexed. Maneuver may be repeated if initial attempt does not reduce subluxation
   b. If a second attempt is not successful, then x-ray elbow
   c. Reduction as evidenced by a "click" is highly predictive and will result in relief from pain and, shortly thereafter, use of the affected arm
   d. After first subluxation, no immobilization is required. For recurrent subluxations, patient's arm should be immobilized in a sling. Should be referred for orthopedic consultation

CLINICAL PEARLS

- "Little League Elbow" is actually a constellation of diseases seen in skeletally immature athletes including medial epicondylar apophysitis, osteochondrosis of the radial head, osteochondrosis of the capitellum, and non-union of a stress fracture of the olecranon epiphysis. Due to overuse of overhead throwing
- If triceps tendonitis doesn't heal, consider an olecranon stress fracture
- Encourage proper sporting technique, stretching, strengthening, and proper fitting equipment

References

Chumbley EM, et al. Evaluation of overuse elbow injuries. Am Fam Phys 2000;61:691–700.

Hay EM, et al. Pragmatic randomised controlled trial of local corticosteroid injection and naproxen for treatment of lateral epicondylitis of elbow in primary care. BMJ Oct 9, 1999;319:964–8.

Safran MR. Elbow injuries in athletes. Clin Orthop 1995;310:257–77.

Foley AE. Tennis elbow. Am Fam Phys 1993;48:281.

MUSC

Michael B. Weinstock, MD
Jason J. Diehl, MD

87. CARPAL TUNNEL SYNDROME

I. DEFINITION: Syndrome caused by compression of the median nerve as it passes through the carpal tunnel. Increased pressure in the carpal tunnel presumably leading to intraneural ischemia. The most common entrapment neuropathy of the upper extremity

II. SIGNS AND SYMPTOMS
    A. The classic pattern includes pain and paresthesias affecting at least 2 of the first 3 digits. Symptoms may often affect the 4th and 5th digits (ulnar nerve) and the wrist with/without proximal radiation
    B. Symptoms often occur both with activity and at night and are relieved by shaking or rubbing hands (pronator syndrome presents with symptoms only with activity)
    C. *Tinel's sign:* Paresthesias (tingling) in fingers when the volar aspect of wrist is tapped by examiner's fingers
    D. *Phalen's sign:* Symptoms reproduced by full flexion of the wrist for 60 seconds
    E. *Direct median nerve compression test:* Symptoms reproduced with direct pressure over the carpal tunnel for 60 seconds
    F. Weakness of thumb abduction
    G. Atrophy of thenar eminence (late finding)
    H. Diminished 2-point discrimination and vibratory sensation of the index finger relative to the little finger

MUSC

III. ETIOLOGY
    A. Repetitive motion injury (flexor tenosynovitis)
    B. Trauma, Colles' fracture, degenerative joint disease, rheumatoid arthritis, ganglion cyst
    C. Hyperparathyroidism, hypocalcemia, associated with diabetes, hypothyroidism, pregnancy
    D. Poor work ergonomics

IV. DIAGNOSIS
    A. Clinical diagnosis: Patient history in correlation with physical findings. To exclude reversible causes consider obtaining thyroid studies and blood sugar
    B. Electromyography: Obtain when diagnosis is in doubt. May have up to a 20% false negative rate. Will show prolonged distal latency of the stimulated nerve with reduced sensory nerve action potential
    C. MRI: Imaging is reserved for special concerns including anomalous muscle bellies, severe synovitis, or nerve tumors

V. DIFFERENTIAL DIAGNOSIS: Cervical spondylosis/radiculopathy, generalized peripheral neuropathy, brachial plexus lesions, vascular insufficiency, thoracic outlet obstruction

VI. MANAGEMENT
    A. Non-operative: Reassess efficacy in 4–6 weeks
        1. Wrist splint (cock-up splint) usually worn at night but wearing during daily activities may have additional benefits
        2. NSAIDs: **Ibuprofen** 600–800mg PO TID–QID, **Naprosyn** 375–500mg PO BID, etc.
        3. Oral corticosteroid taper with failure of conservative therapies
        4. Intermittent icing: 20 minutes TID
        5. Corticosteroid injection: See Chapter 89, Corticosteroid Injection of Joints
    B. Operative: Recommended after failure of non-operative measures

       1. Open or endoscopically
       2. Provides relief in > 95% of patients
       3. Progress to full utilization in 4–6 weeks
  C. Prevention
       1. Hourly breaks while performing repetitive work
       2. Padded gloves to protect the carpal tunnel from vibration and trauma
       3. Ergonomic changes

References

D'Arcu CA, et al. Does this patient have carpal tunnel syndrome? JAMA 2000(283)23: 3110–7.

Retting AC. Wrist and hand overuse syndromes. Clin Sports Med 2000(20)3:591–611.

Rempel D, et al. Consensus criteria for the classification of carpal tunnel syndrome in epidemiologic studies. Am J Public Health 1998;88:1447–51.

Anonymous. Practice parameter for carpal tunnel syndrome (summary statement). Report of the Quality Standards Subcommittee of the American Academy of Neurology. Neurology 1993;43:2406–9.

O'Gradaigh D, Merry P. Corticosteroid injection for the treatment of carpal tunnel syndrome. Ann Rheum Dis 2000;59:918–9.

Michael B. Weinstock, MD
Chuck Levy, MD
Daniel M. Neides, MD
Sarita Salzberg, MD

88. Low Back Pain

I. INTRODUCTION

  A. Low back pain (LBP) is one of the most common ambulatory complaints, with a 60–70% lifetime incidence

  B. LBP is the second most common cause of repeat office visits and the most common cause of disability in patients < 45

  C. Red flags include: Age > 65, previous cancer history, unexplained weight loss, fever, chronic infection, failure to improve after 1 month of therapy or duration of pain > 1 month, nighttime pain, history of intravenous drug use (IVDU), trauma, morning stiffness, history of peripheral vascular disease

  D. For such a common problem, there are relatively few randomized, controlled trials to guide management. Most patients improve with conservative management and do not require diagnostic studies

II. HISTORY AND PHYSICAL EXAMINATION

  Goals are to exclude systemic disease, characterize neurologic deficits, determine the etiology of LBP, differentiate mechanical vs. non-mechanical pain, and evaluate for social or psychological distress which may amplify or prolong the pain

  A. History
       1. Determine mechanism of injury, onset, and duration
       2. Location and character of pain
       3. Constancy (intermittent, constant, or waxing and waning)
       4. Distribution (focal, extended, or radiating)
       5. Aggravating and relieving factors (positional, etc.)
       6. Presence (or absence) of sciatica
       7. Bowel or bladder dysfunction
       8. Fever, weight loss, trauma, morning stiffness
       9. Previous drug and therapeutic treatments (and their success or failure)
      10. Life stressors

11. History of cancer, IVDU
B. **Physical examination**
    1. Begin with observation of posture and gait, pain behavior
    2. Motor examination includes hip flexion (L2), knee extension (L3), ankle dorsiflexion (L4), great toe dorsiflexion (L5), and ankle plantarflexion (S1)

GRADING OF MUSCLE STRENGTH

Grade 0: No movement
Grade 1: Trace movement without joint motion
Grade 2: Partially or fully moves body part with gravity eliminated
Grade 3: Completely moves body part against gravity
Grade 4: Moves body part against moderate resistance through full range of motion
Grade 5: Normal

3. Reflex examination includes patella or knee jerk (L4), hamstring (L5), and Achilles or ankle (S1)
4. Because the sensory exam can be quite time consuming, instruct the patient to point out areas of sensory deprivation and compare to a dermatomal map
5. Limitation of lumbosacral range of motion should be noted in extension, flexion, side-bending, and rotation; palpation of the low back and buttocks can help localize pain and detect tender or "trigger points"
6. Straight leg raise test: Passive elevation of the lower extremity on the symptomatic side to less than 60° while the patient is supine; the test is positive with resulting radicular pain. Sensitivity is 95%, specificity is 40%
7. Abdominal exam for organomegaly, pulsatile abdominal mass
8. Look for Waddell signs (at least 3 indicate a psychologic or non-organic component of the pain)
   a. Inappropriate or widespread tenderness
   b. Pain on simulated physical maneuvers
   c. Inconsistent exam while patient is distracted
   d. Regional non-anatomic distribution of pain or weakness
   e. Overreaction to exam (excess moaning or grimacing)

III. DIAGNOSTIC STUDIES

A. **Radiologic studies:** Generally overused. *If a careful history and physical examination indicate acute musculoskeletal/radicular LBP in a patient age 20–50, radiologic imaging is unnecessary*
   1. Indications for radiographs
      a. Trauma to exclude fracture
      b. Possible neurologic deficits, fever, unexplained weight loss, history of cancer, corticosteroid use or IVDU, or suspicion of serious underlying illness based on "red flags" (see I. D., above). Note: If any of these diagnoses are being evaluated, the sensitivity of plain x-rays is very poor and other diagnostic testing such as CBC, ESR, or MRI should be considered
   2. Indications for MRI
      a. Suspicion of serious underlying cause of pain
      b. Progression of symptoms despite conservative management
      c. Prior to evaluation for surgery
      d. MRI and clinical symptoms do not always correlate. Studies on asymptomatic volunteers < 60 show that 22–54% have herniated or bulging disc and the prevalence in patients > 60 is 36–79%
   3. Bone scan: Indicated to evaluate osteomyelitis, neoplasm or occult fracture
B. **Electrodiagnostic studies (EMG)** assess the neurophysiologic status of the nerve fibers but do have some limitations and are not helpful for acute back pain
C. **Laboratory:** As indicated to screen for serious underlying illness (see, I. C., above)

IV. DIFFERENTIAL DIAGNOSIS OF LOWER BACK PAIN

Differential Diagnosis of Acute Low Back Pain					
Disease or condition	Patient age (years)	Location of pain	Quality of pain	Aggravating or relieving factors	Signs
Back strain	20 to 40	Low back, buttock, posterior thigh	Ache, spasm	Increased with activity or bending	Local tenderness, limited spinal motion
Acute disc herniation	30 to 50	Low back to lower leg	Sharp, shooting or burning pain, paresthesia in leg	Decreased with standing; increased with bending or sitting	Positive straight leg raise test, weakness, asymmetric reflexes
Osteoarthritis or spinal stenosis	>50	Low back to lower leg; often bilateral	Ache, shooting pain, "pins and needles" sensation	Increased with walking, especially up an incline; decreased with sitting	Mild decrease in extension of spine; may have weakness or asymmetric reflexes
Spondylolisthesis	Any age	Back, posterior thigh	Ache	Increased with activity or bending	Exaggeration of the lumbar curve, palpable "step off" (defect between spinous processes), tight hamstrings
Ankylosing spondylitis	15 to 40	Sacroiliac joints, lumbar spine	Ache	Morning stiffness	Decreased back motion, tenderness over sacroiliac joints
Infection	Any age	Lumbar spine, sacrum	Sharp pain, ache	Varies	Fever, percussive tenderness; may have neurologic abnormalities or decreased motion
Malignancy	>50	Affected bone(s)	Dull ache, throbbing pain; slowly progressive	Increased with recumbency or cough	May have localized tenderness, neurologic signs or fever

Source: Patel AT, Ogle AA. Diagnosis and management of acute low back pain. Am Fam Phys 2000;61:1779. Used with permission. www.aafp.org/afp/20000315/1779.html

V. TWO CATEGORIES OF LBP

A. Mechanical/discogenic

1. Acute undetermined soft tissue injury (LUMBOSACRAL SPRAIN): May present with lumbosacral pain following a traumatic injury or possibly accompanied by a tearing sensation while lifting
   a. History and physical examination reveal no evidence of radiculopathy
   b. The natural history of nonspecific LBP (often referred to as lumbosacral strain) is that $^1/_3$ are substantially better at 1 week and $^2/_3$ at 7 weeks. Reoccurrences are common
   c. Treatment
      i. NSAIDs, muscle relaxants and analgesics
      ii. Physical therapy emphasizes stretching hamstrings, gluteals, hip flexors, and tensor fascia lata
      iii. Instruction on strengthening of extensor muscles (walking, jogging, swimming) and proper lifting techniques
2. Acute discogenic LBP (HERNIATED DISC): Caused by either *disruption of the annular fibers of the disc* or *herniation of the disc* with resulting nerve root impingement (radiculopathy)
   a. Radiculopathy almost always involves the L5 or S1 nerve root
   b. The peak age for herniated disc disease is 30–55
   c. History: Usually includes a previous episode of similar LBP that resolved spontaneously in 3–5 days; patients often complain that pain is worse in a seated position; occurs after lifting or trauma
   d. The natural history of herniated disc is that $^2/_3$ have partial or complete resolution at 6 months, and 10% have sufficient pain that surgery may be considered after 6 weeks of conservative therapy
   e. Treatment
      i. In patients without progressive neuro deficit or cauda equina syndrome, use conservative management for at least 1 month
      ii. Bed rest for no more than 2–3 days if patient is unable to ambulate
      iii. A steroid taper or NSAIDs to decrease inflammation and provide relief

MUSC

iv. Pain control
3. Chronic LBP: Most episodes of acute LBP respond by 10–12 weeks. Pain beyond this time frame should result in the following actions
   a. Review the diagnosis to exclude systemic disease
   b. Determine patient compliance with activity modifications and meds
   c. Review the type of treatment patient is receiving in physical therapy
   d. Screen for an underlying depression (see Chapter103, Depression & Dysthymia) or myofascial pain/fibromyalgia

B. Non-mechanical
1. Cancer: Multiple myeloma, metastatic disease to bone from lung, prostate, kidney, or breast
2. Gynecologic
3. Renal: UTI/pyelonephritis, renal colic, renal artery occlusion
4. Rheumatoid arthritis: Morning stiffness > 1hr, improvement with exercise, gradual onset of symptoms, and pain duration > 3 months
5. Gastrointestinal: PUD, pancreatitis
6. Osteoporosis/compression fractures: See Chapter 109, Compression Fractures
7. Vascular: Abdominal aortic aneurysm (AAA)

VI. MANAGEMENT

A. Meds: NSAIDs, muscle relaxants and analgesics (narcotic or non-narcotic) may be effective (see Chapter 100, Pain Management)
B. Physical therapy: May be used in the acute phase and may include superficial heat, deep heat, ultrasound, cold packs, massage, instruction in stretching, lifting techniques and exercise
C. Chiropractic: Studies have suggested that chiropractic intervention may be useful
D. Psychologic: Most useful reliable predictor of return to work after a back injury is prior job satisfaction. Patients with depression or substance abuse may have difficulties with pain resolution. Pending litigation may affect return to work
E. Physical therapy: Communication
F. Surgery Note: There is no evidence from trials that surgery is effective unless patients have sciatica, pseudoclaudication, or spondylolisthesis

MUSC

Indications for Surgical Referral Among Patients with Low Back Pain

Sciatica and Probable Herniated Disks
The cauda equina syndrome (surgical emergency): characterized by bowel or bladder dysfunction (usually urinary retention), numbness in the perineum and medial thighs (i.e., in a saddle distribution), bilateral leg pain, weakness, and numbness
Progressive or severe neurologic deficit
Persistent neuromotor deficit after 4-6 weeks for nonoperative therapy
Persistent sciatica (not low back pain alone) for 4-6 weeks, with consistent clinical and neurologic findings (in this circumstance, and for persistent neuromotor deficit, surgery is elective, and patients should be involved in decision making)

Spinal Stenosis
Progressive or severe neurologic deficit, as for herniated disks
Back and leg pain that is persistent and disabling, improves with spine flexion, and is associated with spinal stenosis on imaging tests; surgery is elective, and patients should be involved in decision making

Spondylolisthesis
Progressive or severe neurologic deficit, as for herniated disks
Spinal stenosis with referral indications as above
Severe back pain or sciatica with severe functional impairment that persists for a year or longer

---

Source: Deyo RA, Weinstein JN. Low back pain. N Engl J Med 2001;344:363. Copyright 2001Massachusetts Medical Society. All rights reserved.

CLINICAL PEARLS
- In patients with spinal stenosis, 70% are stable at 4 years, 15% improved, and 15% worsen
- Low back pain in a patient taking long-term corticosteroids is a compression fracture until proven otherwise
- 98% of clinically significant lumbar disc herniations occur at either the L4–5 or L5–S1 level
- The single most reliable predictor of return to work is job satisfaction
- Scoliosis is 80% idiopathic. The presence of concurrent back pain is a red flag to look for other causes (cerebral palsy, muscular dystrophy, spina bifida, neurofibromatosis, tumor)
- For back pain in pregnancy: Can use Acetaminophen, maternity back supports, or physical therapy (except ultrasound)

References

Deyo RA, Weinstein JN. Low back pain. N Engl J Med 2001;344:363.

Bigos S, et al. Acute low back problems in adults. Rockville, MD: U.S. Dept of Health & Human Serv, Pub Health Serv. Agency for Health Care Policy & Research 1994;AHCPR 95-0642.

Bigos, et al. A prospective study of work perceptions and psychosocial factors affecting the report of back injury. Spine 1996;16:1–6.

Vroomen, et al. Diagnostic value of history and physical examination in patients suspected of sciatica due to disc herniation: A systematic review. J Neurol 1999;246:899–906. [Medline]

Gibson JNA, et al. The Cochrane review of surgery for lumbar disc prolapse and degenerative lumbar spondylosis. Spine 1999;24:1820–1832. [Medline]

Moffett JK, et al. Randomised controlled trial of exercise for low back pain: clinical outcomes, costs, and preferences. BMJ Jul 31, 1999;319:279-83.

Doug DiOrio, MD
Jason J. Diehl, MD

MUSC

89. CORTICOSTEROID INJECTION OF JOINTS

I. INTRODUCTION: Joint aspiration and injection can be a part of any primary care office. Aspiration can give symptomatic relief and a quick diagnosis with fluid analysis. Joint injection can be part of a diagnostic exam of a painful joint (Lidocaine) or part of a treatment plan (steroids)

II. GENERAL LIST OF CONDITIONS IMPROVED WITH STEROID INJECTION

A. Articular conditions: Rheumatoid arthritis, ankylosing spondylitis, arthritis associated with inflammatory bowel disease, psoriasis, Reiter's syndrome, gout, pseudogout, osteoarthritis

B. Nonarticular disorders: Fibrositis, bursitis, adhesive capsulitis, tenosynovitis/tendonitis, tennis elbow, golfer's elbow, plantar fasciitis, carpal tunnel syndrome, tarsal tunnel syndrome, costochondritis, Tietze's syndrome

III. CONTRAINDICATIONS TO JOINT INJECTION/ASPIRATION

A. Cellulitis or broken skin over the entry site
B. Coagulopathy or uncontrolled anticoagulation
C. Prostheses
D. Septic effusion, unstable joints, lack of response to previous injections (steroids)
E. Allergy to injected med

IV. SIDE EFFECTS

A. Steroid arthropathy
B. Tendon rupture
C. Skin atrophy, depigmentation
D. Iatrogenic infectious arthritis
E. Acceleration of cartilage attrition
F. Lipodystrophy
G. Transient hyperglycemia (most important for diabetics)

V. TECHNIQUE: Follow standard sterile procedure for any procedure where skin barrier is broken. Locate your landmarks and mark entry point with thumbnail or pen. Prep area and aspirate the joint. Use hemostat to hold needle in place if syringes are switched to inject joint. Never inject directly into a nerve or tendon

A. Knee: Place the knee in a slightly flexed position by placing a towel under the popliteal space. A lateral or medial approach may be used. Find the superior lateral (medial) border of the patella. Mark a point perpendicular to the border at a level just posterior to the patella. Insert needle at that point keeping the needle perpendicular to the axis of the knee and guide the needle under the patella. There should be no resistance

B. Subacromial bursa: Locate the lateral edge of the acromion just posterior to the AC joint. There is usually a soft spot just superior to the humeral head. Insert the needle through the deltoid muscle and under the acromion. Needle should move freely in the space

C. Plantar fascia: Medial approach is done by locating the most tender point of the fascia's insertion. From the medial side of the foot insert the needle perpendicular to the bottom of the heel and superior to the heel fat pad

D. Greater trochanter: Insert needle over the point of maximum tenderness making sure that the needle remains perpendicular to the femur. Patient will usually have pain when the needle enters the bursa

E. Olecranon bursa: Place the elbow at 90° of flexion and insert the needle into the area of most fluid. Tensing the bursa in your opposite hand may help you to localize the best insertion site

F. Carpal tunnel: Dorsiflex the wrist to 30° and locate the palmaris longus tendon. Insert the needle proximal to the carpal tunnel and radial to the palmaris longus. Advance the needle downward at a 45°angle toward the middle finger. Advance the needle 1–2 cm until there is no resistance. If there is any discomfort in the fingers pull back the needle and redirect

G. Acromioclavicular joint: With patient seated and arms relaxed to sides, the joint sulcus is identified. A superior approach is used to guide needle into posterior portion of joint. Need to fan out the medication in this space

H. DeQuervain's Tenosynovitis: Tendon identified by placing thumb in the hitchhiking position. With thumb relaxed, insert needle into the tendon sheath. Movement of thumb will identify if needle has been placed in tendon. Do not inject tendon directly. Injection will meet little resistance if needle is in proper position

I. Glenohumeral joint: A posterior approach is used. Location for needle insertion is approximately 2cm medial to posterior lateral corner of the acromion. Needle is inserted into joint while aiming at the coracoid process. Med should flow freely

VI. GENERAL GUIDELINES FOR EQUIPMENT AND STEROID DOSING
A. Technique
   1. Mark the injection site
   2. Clean with povidone iodine and then clean with alcohol prep
   3. Consider anesthetizing site with ethyl chloride spray
B. Meds
   1. Steroid (**Kenalog, Decadron, Depo-Medrol, Celestone**)
     a. **Kenalog** 40mg/mL (K-40)
     b. **Kenalog** 10mg/mL (K-10)
     c. **Depo-Medrol** 80mg/mL (D-80)
     d. **Depo-Medrol** 40mg/mL (D-40)
   2. Anesthetic (**Lidocaine, Xylocaine, Sensorcaine**)
     a. **Lidocaine 1%** without Epinephrine (L)
     b. **Sensorcaine 0.25%** (S)
C. Materials: Size of needle, type and amount of steroid and anesthetic
   1. AC joint
     a. 22 gauge, 1½" needle
     b. 1mL (K-40) + 1–2mL (L)
   2. Shoulder (subacromial bursa; joint)
     a. 22–27 gauge, ⅝"–1½" needle
     b. 1mL (K-40) + 5mL (L) or 1mL (D-40) + 1mL (K-40) or (K-10) + 3mL (L)
   3. Elbow (olecranon bursa; joint)
     a. 22 gauge, 1"–1½" needle

MUSC

         b. ½–1mL (K-40) + 1–2mL (L)
   4. Elbow (lateral epicondyle)
      a. 25 gauge, ⁵/₈" needle
      b. ½mL (D-80) + 1mL (L)
   5. Wrist (joint)
      a. 25 gauge, ⁵/₈" needle
      b. ½mL (D-80) + ½mL (L)
   6. Wrist (carpal tunnel)
      a. 25 gauge, ³/₈"–⁵/₈" needle
      b. ½mL (D-40) *only*
   7. Hip (pointer)
      a. 18–22 gauge, 1½" needle
      b. 2mL (K-40) + 10mL (L)
   8. Hip (femoral trochanter bursa)
      a. 22 gauge, 1½" needle
      b. 1mL (D-40) + 1mL (K-40 or K-10) + 3mL (L)
   9. Knee
      a. 22 gauge, 1½" needle
      b. 1mL (K-40) + 2–5mL (L)
  10. Ankle
      a. 20–22 gauge, 1½" needle
      b. 1mL (D-40) + 1mL (L)
  11. Heel (spur)
      a. 18–25 gauge, ⁵/₈"–1½" needle
      b. 1mL (K-40) + 2–3mL (L)
  12. Muscle (general trigger pain)
      a. 25 gauge, ⁵/₈" needle
      b. 1mL (D-40) + 2–3mL (L)

MUSC

References
Snider RK, et al. Essentials of musculoskeletal care. Amer Acad Orthoped Surg 1999.
Cardone DA, Tallia AF. Joint and soft tissue injection. Am Fam Phys 2002;66:283–8, 290.

VIII. Dermatology

90. Describing Dermatologic Lesions 301

91. Contact Dermatitis 303

92. Acne & Rosacea 305

93. Skin Biopsies 309

94. Topical Steroids 312

95. Warts, Scabies, Lice & Superficial Tinea Infection Management 313

96. Hair Changes & Balding 315

DERM

Michael B. Weinstock, MD
Ryan Hanson, MD

90. DESCRIBING DERMATOLOGIC LESIONS

I. TYPE OF LESION (see illustrations on next page)

A. Macule: A circumscribed area of skin in which the color is different from the surrounding skin. (Can differentiate from papule by oblique lighting). A macule is flat and may measure up to 1cm

B. Patch: A flat area of color change > 1cm in size (basically a macule >1cm)

C. Papule: A solid lesion, generally < 0.5cm in diameter, that is elevated above the plane of the surrounding skin. Confluence of papules leads to plaque formation

D. Nodule: A palpable, solid, round or ellipsoidal lesion that is deeper than a papule and is in the dermis or subcutaneous tissue (basically a large papule). These result from infiltrates, neoplasms or metabolic deposits and are often indicators of systemic disease

E. Vesicle: A circumscribed, elevated fluid-containing lesion (blister) < 0.5cm, often translucent

F. Bulla: A blister measuring greater than 0.5cm. Both bulla and vesicles are formed from a cleavage at various levels of the skin, i.e., epidermal layers or dermal-epidermal interface

G. Pustule: Blister filled with pus

H. Plaque: An elevation above the skin surface that occupies a relatively large area in comparison with its height above the skin

I. Wheal: An edematous pink papule or plaque that is characteristically evanescent, disappearing within hours

J. Crusts: Dried serum, blood or exudate on the surface of the skin

   1. Honey-colored: Impetigo

   2. Thick and adherent over entire epidermis: Ecthyma

K. Erosion: A break in the surface epithelium

L. Ulcer: A skin defect in which there has been loss of the epidermis and dermis. Describe the location, borders, base, discharge and any topographic features

M. Comedone: A plugged pilosebaceous opening, open (blackhead) vs. closed (whitehead)

N. Burrow: A linear trail produced by parasites

O. Atrophy: Loss of substance in the epidermis, dermis, and/or subcutaneous tissue

P. Telangiectasia: A superficial dilatation of blood vessels

Q. Purpura: Non-blanching red or violaceous lesions

R. Cyst: A cavity with a lining containing liquid or semisolid material

S. Scale: Superficial dead epidermal cells cast off from the skin

T. Fissure: Skin split extending into the dermis

U. Excoriation: Superficial skin erosion caused by scratching

V. Lichenification: Skin markings and thickening with induration secondary to chronic inflammation caused by irritation (such as scratching or pressure point)

DERM

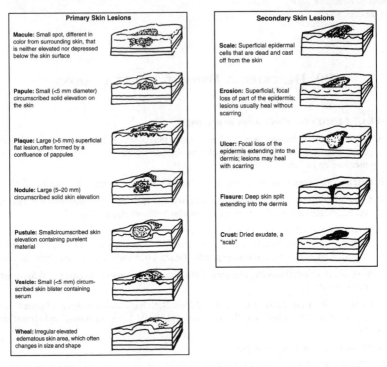

Primary Skin Lesions

Macule: Small spot, different in color from surrounding skin, that is neither elevated nor depressed below the skin surface

Papule: Small (<5 mm diameter) circumscribed solid elevation on the skin

Plaque: Large (>5 mm) superficial flat lesion, often formed by a confluence of pappules

Nodule: Large (5–20 mm) circumscribed solid skin elevation

Pustule: Small circumscribed skin elevation containing purelent material

Vesicle: Small (<5 mm) circumscribed skin blister containing serum

Wheal: Irregular elevated edematous skin area, which often changes in size and shape

Secondary Skin Lesions

Scale: Superficial epidermal cells that are dead and cast off from the skin

Erosion: Superficial, focal loss of part of the epidermis; lesions usually heal without scarring

Ulcer: Focal loss of the epidermis extending into the dermis; lesions may heal with scarring

Fissure: Deep skin split extending into the dermis

Crust: Dried exudate, a "scab"

Source: Goldstein BG, Goldstein AO, eds. Practical Dermatology, 2nd ed. St. Louis:Mosby, 1997; Tables 1–1, 1–2. With permission from Elsevier.

DERM

II. **COLOR:** Of either the skin (if diffuse involvement) or the lesion
   A. **White**
      1. Hypopigmented
      2. Depigmented (no pigment)
   B. **Erythema**
      1. Pink
      2. Violaceous
   C. **Brown**
      1. Hypermelanosis
      2. Hemosiderin
   D. **Black, blue, gray, orange, yellow**

III. **PALPATION**
   A. Soft, firm, hard, fluctuant, board-like
   B. Temperature difference
   C. Mobility of lesion
   D. Tenderness
   E. Depth

IV. **SHAPE**
   A. Round
   B. Oval
   C. Polygonal
   D. Polycyclic
   E. Annular
   F. Iris
   G. Serpiginous

   H. Umbilicated
   I. Grouped
      1. Herpetiform
      2. Zosteriform
      3. Arciform
      4. Annular
      5. Reticular (net-like)
      6. Linear
      7. Disseminated (scattered or diffuse)

V. DISTRIBUTION
   A. Extent
      1. Isolated
      2. Generalized
      3. Localized
      4. Regional or universal
   B. Pattern
      1. Symmetrical
      2. Exposed areas
      3. Pressure points
      4. Intertriginous areas
      5. Follicular
      6. Random
      7. Photo distribution

CLINICAL PEARLS
   • Persistent and unidentifiable nodules should be biopsied and a portion ground and
     cultured for fungi and bacteria
   • If a wheal remains longer than 72hrs, consider biopsy as this can be caused by
     urticarial vasculitis

Ryan Hanson, MD
John Rockwood, PA-C

DERM

91. CONTACT DERMATITIS

I. DEFINITION: Acute, subacute or chronic inflammation of the epidermis and dermis caused by
   external agents, toxicity or an allergic reaction and characterized by pruritus or burning

II. TYPES
   A. **Allergic contact dermatitis:** Cell-mediated type IV hypersensitivity reaction
   B. **Irritant contact:** Due to inflammation from a local toxic effect of a chemical on the skin
   C. **Contact photodermatitis:** A type of allergic contact dermatitis triggered by ultraviolet light
   D. **Contact urticaria:** Wheal and flare reaction—may be allergic (IgE) or nonallergic

III. HISTORY
   A. **Family history of atopy**
   B. **Exposure history:** Inquire about new exposures to common irritants (listed below)
      1. Nickel: Cheap jewelry, metal clothing fasteners, coins
      2. Potassium Dichromate: Cement, paper, leather, metal paint, detergent
      3. Paraphenylenediamine: Hair dyes, ink, fur dyes, radiographic fluid
      4. Chrome
      5. Formaldehydes: Permanent press fabrics, shampoos, smoke
      6. Rhus plants: Poison ivy, oak and sumac
   C. **Duration of lesions** and previous successful or unsuccessful therapy

IV. PHYSICAL EXAM

- A. **Acute contact dermatitis:** Vesicles and/or bullae filled with clear fluid or erythematous, edematous skin
- B. **Subacute contact dermatitis:** Erythema, minimal edema, multiple papules
- C. **Chronic contact dermatitis:** Lichenified plaques with minimal erythema, minimal edema, possible scales
- D. **Rhus dermatitis (poison ivy dermatitis—see below)**
- E. **Attempt to correlate the location of the eruption with exposure** (e.g., dermatitis due to nickel in cheap earrings is present on the earlobes)
- F. **Evaluate for secondary infection**

V. PATCH TESTING

- A. Patch testing may be performed in patients who are suspected of having contact allergy but no allergen can be elicited by history. This should be done *after* the episode of dermatitis has resolved
- B. Apply patch test to skin on back and occlude for 48hrs
- C. Interpret in 72hrs
- D. Positive test with the development of erythema, papules, vesicles

VI. MANAGEMENT

- A. **Identify and eliminate the offending agent,** i.e., remove exposure
- B. **Wet compresses for oozing and vesiculation**
- C. **Wash BID with soap and water**
- D. **Burrow's solution:** Aluminum Acetate tablets in water for wet compresses, then apply steroid cream to suppress inflammation
- E. **Topical steroid cream:** Use a stronger cream for areas of thick skin (back of arms, palms, etc.) (see Chapter 94, Topical Steroids, for a listing of different steroid creams.) Do not use fluorinated steroid creams on face as it may result in depigmentation of skin
- F. **Systemic (oral) corticosteroids** for extensive dermatitis. Begin with **Prednisone** 1–2mg/kg/day (40–60mg max) given QD or as a divided dose and taper over 2–3 weeks. An easy taper is to give #30, 10mg pills and use 40, 30, 20, 10mg/day for 3 days each. Shorter courses may result in a rebound phenomenon
- G. **Symptomatic meds**
  1. Adults
     a. **Hydroxyzine (Atarax):** 25mg PO TID–QID
     b. **Diphenhydramine (Benadryl):** 25–50mg PO TID–QID
  2. Children
     a. Younger than 6yrs: **Hydroxyzine** (10mg/5cc), 50mg/day PO in divided doses, **Benadryl** (2.5mg/5mL) 2–6yrs: 6.25mg Q 4hrs, not to exceed 25mg/24hrs; 6–12yrs: 12.5–25mg Q 4–6hrs
     b. Older than 6yrs: Same as adults

VII. RHUS DERMATITIS: POISON IVY, POISON SUMAC, ETC.

- A. **Hypersensitivity reaction** from exposure to *rhus* plants either directly (by contact with a plant) or indirectly (by contact with something which has been exposed to the plant and carries its oils—clothing, gloves, pets, shoelaces, etc.)
- B. **Exanthem** develops over 48–72hrs and consists of linear vesicles (with direct exposure) or grouped vesicles (with indirect exposure) which may be weeping. The fluid inside the vesicles is not contagious as it does not contain the plant oils
- C. **Complications:** Infection
- D. **Management**
  1. Wash lesions BID with soap and water
  2. Cold washcloth or shower will help decrease itching
  3. Symptomatic meds: See VI. G. above
  4. Topical steroid cream: See VI. E. above
  5. Oral steroids: Indicated for most rhus rashes unless small area (topical) or asymptomatic or contraindicated. See VI. F. above
  6. Cut fingernails short in children
  7. Patients (especially children) should be educated in identification of plants

DERM

CLINICAL PEARLS

- *A rash that seems to be spreading* may be caused by repeated exposure to the plant, exposure to clothes/pets which bear the oils, or different sensitivities of the skin which has been exposed (arm vs. face)
- Contact dermatitis is one of the most common reasons for worker's compensation claims for skin disease

References

Sevila A, et al. Contact dermatitis in children. Contact Dermatitis 1994 May;30(5):292–4.

Weston WL. Contact dermatitis in children. Curr Opin Pediatr 1997 Aug;9(4):372–6.

Schauder S, Ippen H. Contact and photocontact sensitivity to sunscreens. Review of a 15-year experience and of the literature. Contact Dermatitis 1997 Nov;37(5):221–32.

Oh-i T. Contact dermatitis due to topical steroids with conceivable cross reactions between topical steroid preparations. J Dermatol 1996 Mar;23(3):200–8.

Lee NP, Arriola ER. Poison ivy, oak, and sumac dermatitis. West J Med Nov/Dec 1999;177:354–5.

Klaus MV, Wieselthier JS. Contact dermatitis. Am Fam Phys 1993;48:629.

Ryan Hanson, MD
Steve Markovich, MD
Michael B. Weinstock, MD

92. ACNE & ROSACEA

I. DEFINITION

A. **Acne vulgaris:** Chronic inflammation of the pilosebaceous units, caused by increased sebum production, abnormal follicles, propionibacterium, and hormonal and immunological factors

B. **Rosacea:** Chronic acneform inflammation of the pilosebaceous units of the face coupled with an increased reactivity of the capillaries to heat, leading to flushing and telangiectasias

C. **Special forms of acne include:**
1. Acne conglobata: Severe cystic acne with coalescing nodules, cysts and abscesses
2. Acne fulminans: Acute, severe suppurative cystic acne with fever and generalized arthritis

— PART ONE: ACNE VULGARIS—

II. ETIOLOGY

A. **Caused by *Propionibacterium***

B. **Endocrine**
1. Premenstrual and androgenic disorders such as polycystic ovary, or Cushing's syndrome
2. Menstrual irregularities
3. Hirsutism

C. **Environment**
1. Humidity
2. Excessive sweating
3. Working in an environment with aerosolized fats (i.e., fast-foods)

D. **Mechanical**
1. Pressure
2. Constant rubbing of clothes
3. Picking/squeezing: May lead to scarring and worsening
4. Washing with harsh soaps, excessive scrubbing

E. **Cosmetics**

F. **Meds:** Steroids, ACTH, androgens, Dilantin, barbiturates, Lithium, Isoniazid, Cyclosporine, iodides and bromides, oral contraceptives with strong androgens and/or anti-estrogenic activity

DERM

III. HISTORY

   A. Duration and previous successful and unsuccessful therapies

   B. Relation to menses

   C. Presence of hirsutism

   D. Cleansing habits (vigorous scrubbing, etc.), cosmetics

   E. Mechanical factors: Tight clothing, constant rubbing of clothes, picking and squeezing

   F. Meds: Listed above

   G. Seasonal prevalence: Often worse in fall and winter

   H. Diet: No firm studies link diet to acne, but patients may notice worsening of acne after eating certain foods

IV. PHYSICAL

   A. Comedones: Sebum clogged sebaceous follicles, open (blackheads) or closed (whiteheads)

   B. Pustules: Erupting follicular contents

   C. Papules: Inflammatory raised lesions in dermis

   D. Cysts: Deep, intense inflammatory papule progressing to fluctuant, painful area

   E. Seborrhea may also be seen

   F. Inspect face, back, chest and buttocks for lesions and scarring

   G. Severity: To guide treatment

   1. **Type 1—Mild inflammatory acne:** Comedonal, less than 10 lesions, face only, no scarring

   2. **Type 2—Mild papular acne:** Less than 25 lesions, face and trunk, mild scarring

   3. **Type 3—Pustular acne:** More than 25 lesions with moderate scarring

   4. **Type 4—Severe cystic acne:** Nodulocystic with extensive scarring

V. LABS: Indicated in young women who don't respond to therapy

   A. Hormone testing: Androgens, plasma testosterone, dihydroepiandrosterone, partial 11- or 12-hydroxylase block

   B. Genetics: Severe acne in XYY

VI. MANAGEMENT: Listed by type of acne (see algorithm below)

   A. General

   1. Wash with mild soap (e.g., Dial, Ivory, Phisoderm, Panoxyl, Neutrogena). Do not scrub face to remove lesions as this could cause worsening of the condition

   2. There is no relationship to diet (e.g. pizza, chocolate or soda) or stress

   3. If any of the above factors (listed in etiology) are contributing to a worsening of acne, then modify as needed

   4. May try different therapies for different types of acne. Types 1–3 often respond to topical meds used first line and if not effective alone or in combination, consider oral meds. Cystic acne will not respond to topical therapy

   B. Mild inflammatory acne (Type 1): Topical meds—first line

   1. **Benzoyl Peroxide:** Many OTC preparations

   a. Has bactericidal (with bacteriostatic activity superior to topical ATBs) and comedolytic properties (increases epithelial cell turnover with desquamation)

   b. Apply to clean, dry skin QHS or BID. (Available in 2.5%, 5%, 10% creams, lotions, gels and soaps. Liquid and cream are less irritating, gel better for oily skin)

   c. Most common side effect is skin irritation. It is an oxidizing agent, and can bleach clothing and bed linens. May be best to apply to a clean, dry face in the AM and at dinnertime (as opposed to before bed)

   2. **Salicylic Acid:** Many OTC preparations

   a. Inhibits comedogenesis by promoting desquamation of follicular epithelium

   b. Is as effective as Benzoyl Peroxide with comedomal acne

   c. Apply QD or BID. Available OTC at 0.5% or 2% in creams and lotions

   3. **Azelaic Acid (Azelex)**

   a. Has antibacterial and antikeratinizing activity

      b. Is as effective as Benzoyl Peroxide or Tretinoin (Trans-retinoic acid, Retin-A) in treatment of mild to moderate acne

      c. Apply BID. Available as a 20% cream (**Avelox, Azelex**)

  4. **Retinoids:** Caution in pregnant patients

      a. Slows the desquamation process which decreases number of comedones and microcomedones—comedolytic

      b. Apply QD to clean, dry skin at bedtime. Start with the lowest strength and increase after a few weeks if necessary. Patients may experience a pustular flare during the first few weeks. Do not stop therapy as this is a sign of accelerated resolution of exiting acne.

      c. **Tretinoin (Retin A):** Cream is better for dry skin and least irritating (available in 0.025%, 0.05%, and 0.1% cream; 0.01%, 0.025%, and 0.1% gel; and 0.05% liquid). Avoid sun exposure. Also available as 0.1% Tretinoin microsphere gel which brings the medication more directly to the follicle and is less irritating than the 0.1% cream

      d. **Adapalene (Differin):** 0.1% gel or solution to be used QD in the evening

      e. **Tazarotene (Tazorac):** 0.05%, or 0.1% gel or cream for once daily application

  5. **Combination therapy:** May try **Benzoyl Peroxide** in the AM and **Retin-A** in the PM if single therapy fails. Combinations also available (e.g., **Benzamycin**—5% Benzoyl Peroxide and 3% Erythromycin—is mixed by the patient or the pharmacist and kept refrigerated)

C. Mild papular acne (Type 2)

  1. Topical ATBs as listed above

  2. **Clindamycin** 1% lotion or gel. Applied BID to clean and dry skin

  3. **Erythromycin** 2% gel or pledgettes. Applied BID

D. Pustular acne (Type 3): Consider starting first with topical agents as listed above; if not effective, then use oral ATBs plus topical agents. Taper ATBs after 7–10 days to lowest effective dose

  1. **Tetracycline**

      a. Dose: 250mg PO QID or 500mg PO BID

      b. Note: Do not use in pregnancy or children < 12yrs

  2. **Erythromycin**

      a. Dose: 250mg PO QID

      b. Note: Pustular acne is more resistant

  3. **Minocycline**

      a. Dose: 50mg PO BID or 100mg QD

      b. Note: Highly effective due to lipophilicity

      c. Side effects include dizziness and color changes

  4. **Trimethoprim/Sulfamethoxazole**

      a. Dose: 1 DS tablet QD

      b. Note: For refractory cases (may have severe eruptive reaction)

E. Severe cystic acne (Type 4): Topical therapy not effective

  1. **Isotretinoin (Accutane):** Decreases sebum production

      a. Many side effects, including teratogenic, thus negative pregnancy tests are required 1 month before starting and monthly during therapy

      b. Should only be prescribed by physicians with experience with the use of this very potent drug

  2. **Steroid injection:** Intralesional Triamcinolone can decrease cyst-size in 2–3 days. Use a minimal amount to avoid steroid-atrophy

  3. Systemic hormones

      a. OCPs for low-dose estrogen effect (e.g., **Ortho Tri-Cyclen**)

      b. **Prednisone** 5mg/day to decrease adrenal androgen production—*very short term only*

F. Treatment failure: If treatment fails after oral ATBs, consider dermatology referral due to the serious side effects of the latter therapies and the scarring

DERM

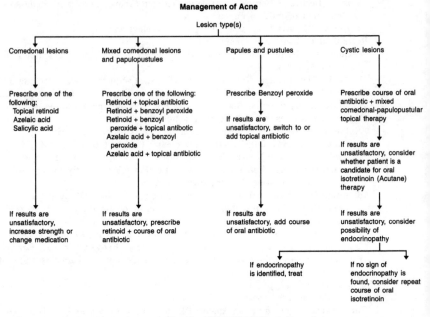

Management of Acne

Source: Russell J. Topical therapy for acne. Am Fam Phys 2000;61:357–66. Used with permission.

— **PART TWO: ROSACEA** —

DERM

I. HISTORY
  A. Usually ages 30–50
  B. Females > Males
  C. Celtic/Northern Europeans much more than pigmented races
  D. Hot liquids/heat may stimulate or worsen, alcohol increases flushing
  E. Emotional stress may be a factor
  F. Rosacea has now been associated with *H. pylori*. Treatment of *H. pylori* disease has improved co-existing rosacea

II. PHYSICAL
  A. Flushing
  B. Papular and papulopustular lesions
  C. Telangiectasias
  D. Nodules
  E. Absence of comedones
  F. Usually present on the **face only**: cheeks, chin, forehead, nose and rarely neck
  G. Associated rhinophyma
  H. Blepharitis, episcleritis and conjunctivitis may occur

III. DIFFERENTIAL DIAGNOSIS: Ethanol use, pheochromocytoma, mastocytosis, carcinoid tumor, Marfan's syndrome, homocystinuria

IV. MANAGEMENT
  A. Decrease alcohol and hot beverage intake
  B. Topical
  1. **Metronidazole 0.75% (MetroGel, MetroCream)**—Apply BID to clean, dry skin. May take 4–8 weeks
  2. **Azelaic Acid (Azelex) 20% cream**
  3. **Sodium Sulfacetamide**
  4. **Ketoconazole, Terbinafine, or Naftifine**

C. Systemic: If topical fails, then consider oral **Doxycycline** 100mg PO BID or **Minocycline** 100mg PO BID. Doses may be decreased after response

D. Avoid sun

CLINICAL PEARLS

- About 50% of patients with rosacea have ocular involvement with irritation, chalazia, styes or corneal damage
- Blepharitis can often be cleared with simple lid scrubs with baby shampoo and PO Tetracycline

References

Wilkin J, et al. Standard classification of rosacea: Report of the National Rosacea Society Expert Committee on the Classification and Staging of Rosacea. J Am Acad Dermatol 2002; 46:584–7.

Webster GF. Update on rosacea. Program of the 59th Annual Meeting of the American Academy of Dermatology; March 2–7, 2001; Washington, DC. Page 70.

Russell J. Topical therapy for acne. Am Fam Phys 2000;61:357–66.

White GM. Recent findings in the epidemiologic evidence, classification, and subtypes of acne vulgaris. J Am Acad Dermatol 1998;39(2 pt 3):S34–7.

Leyden JJ. Therapy for acne vulgaris. N Engl J Med 1997;336:1156–62.

Leyden JJ. New understandings in the pathogenesis of acne. J Am Acad Dermatol 1995;32(5 pt 3):S15-25.

Krowchuk DP, et al. The psychosocial effects of acne on adolescents. Pediatr Dermatol 1991;8:332–8.

Ryan Hanson, MD
Michael B. Weinstock, MD

93. SKIN BIOPSIES

DERM

I. INDICATIONS

A. Lesions suspected of being malignant or pre-malignant (i.e. actinic keratosis)

B. A persistent rash, unresponsive to topical meds

C. Lesions that are difficult to diagnose by clinical exam

D. Bullous disorders: Send for immunofluorescence

E. Congenital nevi: Increased incidence of developing into melanoma

F. Cosmetic purposes

II. INFORMED CONSENT: Patient should understand risk of scarring, bleeding, the indications and alternatives, general risks and that further treatment may be necessary

III. SITE

A. Choose well-developed lesions

B. If a lesion is ulcerated, then biopsy the border

C. Lesions to avoid (consider referral)
   1. Cosmetically sensitive areas
      a. Face
      b. Hypertrophic scarring areas like upper chest and deltoid region
   2. Excoriated lesions
   3. Secondarily infected areas
   4. High-infection areas: axilla and groin
   5. Lesions overlying vital structures (nerves, arteries, joints)

IV. ANESTHESIA

A. 1% Lidocaine (Xylocaine) is usually adequate. Use enough to make a good wheal under the skin

B. Lidocaine with **Epinephrine**: Useful if hemostasis is an issue or prolonged effect desired. *Do not use on fingers, toes, nose, clitoris or penis*

C. Adjuncts

1. Topical anesthetics, i.e., EMLA cream (2.5% **Lidocaine**, 2.5% **Prilocaine**): Applied thickly over area with occlusion for *at least* an hour. Not to be used on mucous membranes or broken skin
2. Cryotherapy

V. TYPES: Take care with handling so as not to crush sample, place immediately in formalin. Special studies such as immunofluorescence and electron microscopy require special handling and stains

A. Shave biopsy: If the blade is kept parallel to the skin, scarring should be slight

1. Indications: Removal of protruding portion of superficial raised papular or pedunculated lesions or superficial lesions on a convex surface (pinnae of the ear or nose) when full thickness specimens are not required (e.g., milia, warts, seborrheic keratosis, molluscum contagiosum, benign appearing nevi)
2. Should NOT be the technique of choice for any lesion suspicious for melanoma (need full thickness specimen for Breslow or Clark staging)
3. Technique
   a. Infuse local anesthetic intradermal to raise lesion
   b. Stretch skin on either side of the biopsy site
   c. Use a No. 15 scalpel or a No. 10 scalpel for larger lesions
   d. Keep blade parallel to skin with cutting edge upward to prevent penetration into dermis
   e. Hemostasis (see below)

B. Punch biopsy: Full thickness cylindric biopsies, 2–8mm in size

1. Indications: When full thickness specimen is required (e.g., sarcoidosis, granuloma annulare, sclerosing basal cell CA, psoriasis, *erythema multiforme*, connective tissue disorders, bullous skin diseases). Easy removal of small tumors or when multiple biopsies are needed. If suspicious of malignant melanoma, perform an excisional biopsy
2. Technique
   a. Determine the proper size instrument required to adequately obtain clear skin margins (will help to avoid repeat excision for atypical or dysplastic lesions)
   b. Stretching skin perpendicular to tension lines while performing biopsy will result in oval shaped skin defect which can more easily be closed with sutures
   c. While rotating the instrument in an alternating clockwise/counterclockwise fashion, apply perpendicular pressure until the subcutaneous tissue is reached
   d. Lift specimen with toothless Adson forceps (or 25 gauge needle) and cut the base
   e. Close biopsy sites > 4 mm (e.g., 4–0 or 5–0 Ethilon). If site is not sutured, then inform patient that there will be a scar—usually a 1–2 mm white depression at the site
   f. Sutures should be removed in 5 days if on face, 7 days on upper extremity, and 10–14 days on lower extremity

C. Excisional biopsy: Removal of the entire area of pathology

1. Indications: Removal of tumors of the skin for diagnosis and cure
2. Technique
   a. Elliptic excision oriented parallel to the skin tension lines (Langer's lines)
   b. Length is 3 times the width
   c. If suspicious of melanoma, then refer to physician experienced in skin cancer
   d. Undermining the wound may allow for easier closure (blunt dissection under wound edges to create a plane under the skin to allow the wound edges to be more easily brought together with minimum tension)
   e. Consider layered closure for large defects (absorbable suture such as Vicryl for deep and nylon or polypropylene sutures (4–0 to 5–0) for the skin edges)
   f. Hemostasis (see below)

DERM

D. Incision biopsy: Elliptic specimen taken from within a lesion
1. Indications: For examination of subcutaneous tissues (fibrous tumors, panniculitis) and when necessary to view transition from normal to abnormal tissue. In pigmented lesions, use only if there are contraindications to excisional biopsy (cosmesis or functional considerations)
2. Technique: Similar to excisional biopsy
   a. Narrow elliptic incision
   b. Choose location of most raised or most pigmented area of the lesion
   c. Technique as above
   d. Hemostasis (see below)

VI. HEMOSTASIS
A. Pressure
B. Pinpoint electrodesiccation
C. Topical solutions
1. Aluminum Chloride Hexahydrate (Drysol)
2. Absorbable gelatin powder (Gelfoam)
3. 30% Aluminum Chloride
4. Monsel's solution (Ferric Subsulfate): May leave raised pigmented lesion
5. Silver Nitrate

CLINICAL PEARLS
- Because of possibility of malignant transformation of congenital nevi, it is recommended that all congenital nevi be considered for prophylactic excision
- Never use a shave biopsy for pigmented lesions
- Allergy to Procaine (Novocain) is not a contraindication to use of Lidocaine
- The incidence of melanoma has nearly tripled in the last 3 decades, faster than any other cancer. The poor prognosis makes speed and accuracy of diagnosis essential. The ABCDE's of malignant melanoma are:
  - A—asymmetry
  - B—border irregularity
  - C—color variegation
  - D—diameter > 6mm
  - E—enlargement, rapid growth over weeks to months

DERM

References

Zuber TJ. Punch biopsy of the skin. Am Fam Phys 2002;65:1155–68.

Achar S. Principles of skin biopsies for the family physician. Am Fam Phys 1996;54(8):2411.

Arca M, et al. Biopsy techniques for skin, soft-tissue, and bone neoplasms. Surg Oncol Clin North Am 1995;1:157–74.

Koh HK. Cutaneous melanoma. N Engl J Med 1991;325:171–82.

94. TOPICAL STEROIDS

Classification of Topical Steroid Preparations by Potency

Low Potency

Alclometasone dipropionate 0.05% Aclovate (cream, ointment) **Fluocinolone acetonide 0.01%** Synalar (solution) **Hydrocortisone base or acetate 0.5%** Cortisporin* (cream)	**Hydrocortisone base or acetate 1%** Cortisporin* (ointment) Hytone (cream, lotion, ointment) Vytone* (cream)	**Hydrocortisone base or acetate 2.5%** Hytone (cream, lotion, ointment) **Triamcinolone acetonide 0.025%** Aristocort A (cream) Kenalog (cream, lotion, ointment)

Intermediate Potency

Betamethasone valerate 0.12% Luxiq (foam) **Desonide 0.05%** DesOwen (cream, lotion, ointment) **Desoximetasone 0.05%** Topicort-LP (emollient cream) **Fluocinolone acetonide 0.01%** Derma-Smoothe/FS (oil) Capex (shampoo) **Fluocinolone acetonide 0.025%** Synalar (cream, ointment) **Flurandrenolide 0.025%** Cordran-SP (cream) Cordran (ointment)	**Flurandrenolide 0.05%** Cordran-SP (cream) Cordran (lotion, ointment) **Fluticasone propionate 0.005%** Cutivate (ointment) **Fluticasone propionate 0.05%** Cutivate (cream) **Hydrocortisone probutate 0.1%** Pandel (cream) **Hydrocortisone butyrate 0.1%** Locoid (cream, ointment, solution) **Hydrocortisone valerate 0.2%** Westcort (cream, ointment)	**Mometasone furoate 0.1%** Elocon (cream, lotion, ointment) **Prednicarbate 0.1%** Dermatop e (emollient cream, ointment) **Triamcinolone acetonide 0.1%** Aristocort A (cream, ointment) Kenalog (cream, lotion) **Triamcinolone acetonide 0.2%** Kenalog (aerosol)

High Potency

Amcinonide 0.1% Cyclocort (cream, lotion, ointment) **Betamethasone dipropionate, augmented 0.05%** Diprolene AF (emollient cream) Diprolene (lotion) **Desoximetasone 0.05%** Topicort (gel)	**Desoximetasone 0.25%** Topicort (emollient cream, ointment) **Diflorasone diacetate 0.05%** Psorcon e (emollient cream, emollient ointment) Psorcon (cream) **Fluocinonide 0.05%** Lidex (cream, gel, ointment, solution) Lidex-E (emollient cream)	**Halcinonide 0.1%** Halog (cream, ointment, solution) Halog-E (emollient cream) **Triamcinolone acetonide 0.5%** Aristocort A (cream) Kenalog (cream)

Super High Potency

Betamethasone dipropionate, augmented 0.05% Diprolene (ointment, gel)	**Clobetasol propionate 0.05%** Olux (foam) Temovate (cream, gel, ointment, scalp application) Temovate-E (emollient cream)	**Diflorasone diacetate 0.05%** Psorcon (ointment) **Flurandrenolide 4mcg/sq cm** Cordran (tape) **Halobetasol propionate 0.05%** Ultravate (cream, ointment)

*Indicates that the product has more than one active ingredient.
The classification is based on vasoconstrictor assays and clinical studies. Potency varies according to the corticosteroid, its concentration, and the vehicle. In general, corticosteroids in lotions, creams, gels, and ointments are increasingly more potent due to increased absorption from these vehicles.
Absorption is increased by prolonged therapy, large areas of skin damage, and the use of occlusive dressings which may cause an increase in the incidence of side effects. (Revised 1/20/03)

Source: Monthly prescribing reference. Prescribing Reference, Inc., New York NY June 2003:108. Used with permission.

DERM

Michael B. Weinstock, MD
Steve Markovich, MD

95. WARTS, SCABIES, LICE & SUPERFICIAL TINEA INFECTION MANAGEMENT

I. TREATMENT OF WARTS

A. Cryotherapy: Scar formation is minimized
1. If the wart is large, then shave it first (e. g., #10 blade)
2. Plantar warts often require Q week applications at weekly or biweekly intervals

B. Medical: Shave the wart as closely as possible, then soak in warm water to moisten. Vaseline may be applied to areas surrounding the wart to prevent tissue injury
1. **Duofilm:** Apply to affected area QD × 3 months
2. **Trans-Ver-Sal** (Salicylic Acid in a transdermal delivery system): Apply QD × 6 weeks
3. **Topical Retinoids (Retin-A):** Apply BID × 4–6 weeks. Less scarring than other therapies, therefore, good for use on the face
4. Consider **Benzoyl Peroxide, Di- and Trichloroacetic Acid, Podophyllin**, occlusive therapy (occlusion with waterproof tape for 1 week)

II. TREATMENT OF SCABIES

A. Permethrin 5% (Elimite) cream: Apply from head to soles of feet. Rinse after 8–14hrs. 30g is adequate for adults. Drug of choice for children

B. Lindane (Kwell, Scabene) lotion, cream or shampoo. Apply lotion or cream to skin from neck down to feet and rinse in 8–12hrs. Some dermatologists recommend retreating in 7–14 days. Should not be used in children who are < 2yrs, malnourished, with underlying skin disease or seizure disorders

C. Treat all intimate contacts and family members. Bed linens, clothing and towels should be washed

III. TREATMENT OF PEDICULOSIS (LICE)

A. Head lice: 1% Permethrin (NIX) or **Lindane** (last resort)

B. Pubic lice: Lindane shampoo: Lather from neck to feet and leave on for 4 minutes. May also use **Permethrin** or **Lindane** creams—leave in place for several hours

C. Body lice: Permethrin or **Lindane** cream applied once and left on for several hours

D. Eyelash infestation: Manual removal of lice and nits or apply **Petroleum jelly (Vaseline)** to eyelids TID–QID for 8–10 days. Do not use pediculicides to treat eyelash infestations

IV. ANTIFUNGALS

A. Treatment of tinea pedis (4 weeks), **tinea cruris** (2–3 weeks), and **tinea corporis** (2–3 weeks). May require longer treatment based on clinical response
1. Topical agents: All should be applied to affected areas BID
   a. **Undecylenic Acid (Cruex, Desenex):** Available OTC
   b. **Tolnaftate 1% (Tinactin, Aftate, NP-27):** Available OTC
   c. **Ciclopirox 1% (Loprox)**
   d. **Imidazoles**
      i. **Clotrimazole 1% (Lotrimin, Mycelex):** Available OTC
      ii. **Miconazole 2% (Monistat-Derm, Micatin):** Available OTC
      iii. **Ketoconazole 2% (Nizoral)**
   e. **Allylamines**
      i. **Naftifine 1% (Naftin)**
      ii. **Terbinafine 1% (Lamisil)**
2. Oral agents (for extensive infections): **Microsize Griseofulvin (Fulvicin-U/F, Grifulvin V, Grisactin)** 10mg/kg/day PO × 4 weeks, usual adult dose is 500mg QD. Available as suspension 125mg/5mL and 250, 500mg tabs. Monitor renal, hepatic and hematopoietic

DERM

functions periodically and discontinue if granulocytopenia occurs

B. Treatment of *tinea capitis*: Microsize Griseofulvin (Fulvicin-U/F, Grifulvin V, Grisactin) 10mg/kg/day PO × 4–6 weeks (2 weeks beyond clinical resolution), usual adult dose is 500mg QD. Available in suspension 125mg/5mL and 250, 500mg tabs. Monitor renal, hepatic and hematopoietic functions periodically and discontinue if granulocytopenia occurs

C. Treatment of *tinea unguium*

　1. Oral agents (for cure): **Sporanox** or **Lamisil**

　　a. Fingernails

　　　i. **Terbinafine (Lamisil):** 250mg PO QD × 6 weeks

　　　ii. **Itraconazole (Sporanox):** pulse therapy 200mg PO BID × 7days, then off for 3 weeks and repeat × 1

　　b. Toenails

　　　i. **Terbinafine (Lamisil):** 250mg PO QD × 12 weeks; monitor LFT

　　　ii. **Itraconazole (Sporanox):** 200mg PO QD × 12 weeks; monitor LFT

　2. Topical agents (for treatment):

　　a. **Ciclopirox Topical solution 8% (Penlac nail lacquer):** Apply the lacquer evenly on the entire nail once daily. Once a week, remove the Penlac with alcohol and then apply Penlac once daily. May take 6 months of therapy before initial improvement of symptoms is noticed

　3. Topical agents (for control): Apply BID indefinitely

　　a. **Ciclopirox (cream, lotion)**

　　b. **Terbinafine (cream, gel)**

D. Treatment of oral candidiasis

　1. **Nystatin (Mycostatin** suspension): 5mL PO QID swish and swallow 5–7 days

　2. **Clotrimazole (Mycelex):** 10mg troches, dissolve in mouth 5 ×/day for 14 days

　3. **Fluconazole (Diflucan):** 200mg on day 1, then 100mg PO QD × 2 weeks. Esophageal candidiasis: Same dose for minimum of 3 weeks, continue for 2 weeks after symptoms resolve. Monitor renal and liver function

E. Treatment of tinea versicolor

　1. **Topicals**: Apply BID for 1–3 weeks

　　a. **Selenium Sulfide 2.5%**

　　b. **Ciclopirox 1%**

　　c. **Clotrimazole 1%**

　　d. **Miconazole 2%**

　　e. **Ketoconazole 2%**

　2. **Orals**

　　a. **Ketoconazole:** 200mg QD × 7 days (concentrates in sweat, use before exercise)

　　b. **Itraconazole:** 200mg/day × 7–10 days

　　c. **Fluconazole:** 150–300mg/day × 7–10 days

References

Gibbs S, et al. Local treatments for cutaneous warts: systematic review. BMJ Aug 31, 2002;325:461–4.

Chosidow O. Scabies and pediculosis. Lancet 2000;355:819.

Chaula EN, et al. Equivalent therapeutic efficacy and safety of ivermectin and lindane in the treatment of human scabies. Arch Dermatol Jun 1999;135:651–5.

Temple ME, et al. Pharmacotherapy of tinea capitis. J Am Board Fam Pract May-June 1999;12:236–41.

Gupta AK, et al. An overview of topical antifungal therapy in dermatomycoses. A North American perspective. Drugs 1998;55:645–74.

Benton EC. Therapy of cutaneous warts. Clin Dermatol 1997;15:449

DERM

Steve Markovich, MD
Michael B. Weinstock, MD

96. HAIR CHANGES & BALDING

I. GENERAL

A. Hair is a type of keratin generated by the *hair matrix*, which form the shaft and surrounding structures. The scalp has 100–150,000 hairs

B. **Types of hair**

1. Lanugo: Soft silky hair that covers fetus in utero; mostly shed before birth

2. Vellus: Short, fine hairs that cover the entire body except for the palms and soles

3. Terminal: Long, coarse pigmented hair; before puberty found only on the scalp and in eyebrows and eyelashes. After puberty in the axilla, pubic area and on the chest and face in men

C. **Growth Cycle:** Hair growth and loss is continuous and random, not cyclical or seasonal and can be defined by 3 discrete stages

1. Anagen: Active growth phase—1cm/month which decreases with age; plucked hair in this phase has a 2–3mm white sheath at the end

2. Catagen: Active follicular regression that signals end of anagen; plucked hair has a small white tip at end

3. Telogen: Resting phase, all cellular activity stops; represents 10% of all hair. 25–100 telogen hairs are normally shed each day; shampooing may increase this number

II. APPROACH TO PATIENT WITH HAIR LOSS—Signs and symptoms

A. Generalized versus discrete areas of hair loss and location

B. Rapid versus gradual hair loss

C. Partial versus complete balding

D. Changes in hair texture or breakage

E. Scarring

F. Meds/chemotherapy

G. Family history

III. PATTERNS OF HAIR LOSS AND MANAGEMENT

A. **Diffuse, rapid hair loss**

1. Telogen effluvium: Telogen (resting) hair loss often seen 3 months after pregnancy, fever or severe illness, major surgery or change in diet and resolves spontaneously over 1–2 months. No more than 50% of hairs are affected. Scarring and inflammation are absent

2. Anagen effluvium: Abrupt insult to active growth. Usually due to chemo-therapeutics. Only telogenic hairs remain

3. Management: Await resolution after insult is over

B. **Diffuse, gradual hair loss, often with thinning, restricted to top of scalp—Androgenic alopecia**

1. Male pattern baldness: Frontal recession or loss over the temples or crown

2. Female pattern baldness: Gradual loss on the central scalp with preservation of the frontal hair line

3. Management

a. **Minoxidil (Rogaine):** Available OTC as 2% solution and as 5% (extra strength) solution to be applied topically BID. Ineffective for frontal hair loss. Can grow moderate to dense hair in 50% of patients. Effects may not be apparent for 6 months and new hair is lost when treatment stopped

b. **Finasteride (Propecia):** 1mg PO QD. Approved for men only. May result in hair gain but some feel primary benefit is prevention of further hair loss. New hair lost when treatment stopped

c. Surgical options include hair transplants, scalp reductions and flaps, and hair weaves

DERM

C. **Diffuse, gradual hair loss, often with thinning, all over scalp**
1. Diffuse alopecia areata: Alopecia areata is rapid hair loss in sharply defined, usually round, areas. It rarely occurs in more diffuse distributions with poorer potential for regrowth
2. Etiology: Thyroid/iron deficiency, meds (Warfarin, Heparin, Propanolol, Vitamin A), secondary syphilis, lupus, gradual hair loss with age
3. Management: Directed toward underlying disorder

D. **Discrete balding areas without scarring or scalp inflammation**
1. Alopecia areata: Most common cause in both children and adults. Etiology is unknown. Check for ! shaped hairs at edge of balding areas. These are short, broken-off hairs where broken end is thicker and darker than where hair emerges from scalp. May be associated with nail pitting and longitudinal striations
   Management: Generally resolves spontaneously but can also be treated with intralesional steroids
2. Trichotillomania: Caused by the irresistible urge to pull out longer hairs leaving very short, fine hairs. Often seen in children

E. **Discrete balding areas with scarring or scalp inflammation**
1. Infection: Tinea capitis, kerion, bacterial infection, herpes zoster
2. Traumatic: Burns, radiation
3. Neoplastic: Basal cell carcinoma, metastatic disease
4. Systemic: S.L.E., psoriasis, eczema, lichen planus, scleroderma

CLINICAL PEARLS
- In US $900 million dollars spent each year on hair loss
- Androgenic alopecia (male pattern baldness) occurs in approximately $2/3$ of men

References
Walsh DS, et al. Improvement in androgenic alopecia (stage V) using topical minoxidil in a retinoid vehicle and oral finasteride. Arch Dermatol 1995;131:1373.
Savin RC. Use of topical minoxidil in the treatment of male pattern baldness. J Am Acad Dermatol 1987;16:696.

DERM

IX. Surgery

97. Evaluation of Abdominal Pain 319

98. Diverticulosis & Diverticulitis 323

99. Management of Wounds 325

100. Pain Management in Adults & Children 329

101. Preoperative Evaluation 332

SURG

1. 318
2. 321
75. 323
100. 326
120. 328

Daniel M. Neides, MD
Eric Bates, PA
Ryan Bowman, PA-C

97. EVALUATION OF ABDOMINAL PAIN

I. INTRODUCTION
  A. Abdominal pain accounts for 4–8% of adult emergency department visits
  B. Special considerations should be taken with the elderly, immunocompromised, patients on steroids, and women of childbearing age

II. HISTORY
  ### A. Pain
   1. Onset and duration: Abrupt (vascular, perforation, torsion, or colic) vs. gradual (inflammation, infection). Was patient awakened from sleep?
   2. Location: Site of onset/site presently (have patient point to area of worst pain)
   3. Quality/Character: Visceral pain (steady ache or vague discomfort or excruciating or colicky pain); parietal pain (more localized to specific site); referred pain (e.g., renal colic may refer pain to the testicles or labia, biliary pain may be referred to the right infrascapular region)
   4. Severity
   5. Constant vs. intermittent
   6. Aggravating/relieving (movement/coughing/respiration/food/vomiting/meds/lying still/car ride)
   7. Change of any variables over time (better/worse/same)
   8. Previous similar symptoms
  ### B. Associated symptoms
   1. Fever: Young patients are better able to mount a fever response compared to the elderly. Rectal temperatures generally more reliable. Temperature may be low due to antipyretics and oral temperature may register low in mouth breathing patient
   2. Vomiting: Relationship of abdominal pain and vomiting (e.g., pain usually precedes vomiting by 3–4hrs in patients with appendicitis but is just the opposite in gastroenteritis). Frequency of vomiting along with character (including color and content, i.e., bilious, bloody, coffee ground, etc.)
   3. Anorexia: Usually associated with acute abdominal pain: often precedes the onset of pain in appendicitis
   4. Bowels: Constipation, diarrhea, and recent change in bowel habits. Watery diarrhea with crampy pain suggests gastroenteritis. Large amount of loose stool suggests cause in lower GI. Smaller amounts of loose stools upper GI. Failure to pass flatus with crampy pain and vomiting suggests mechanical obstruction. Bloody diarrhea (infectious), bright red blood (lower GI causes—diverticulosis, neoplasm, infection, IBD, AVM, hemorrhoids, fissures, fistulae, or prolapse), melanic stools (upper GI causes—peptic ulcer, gastritis, varices, Mallory-Weiss)
   5. Urination: Dysuria, frequency, urgency, incontinence, hematuria, back pain
   6. Vaginal: Discharge (PID), bleeding (ectopic, miscarriage)
   7. Menstruation: Last menstrual period (exact dates), frequency, duration, the type of contraception and duration of use
  ### C. Past medical and surgical history
   1. Prior surgeries/hospitalizations
   2. History of similar pain suggests recurrent disease
   3. History of chronic diseases (diabetes, HIV, CNS disease, i.e., multiple sclerosis)
   4. Recent or current meds (including NSAIDs, steroids, pain meds, ATBs)
   5. Social history: tobacco, alcohol and other drugs of abuse, living circumstances, others with similar symptoms, occupation
   6. Recent out of country travel or exposure to lake, well, or stream water

SURG

III. PHYSICAL EXAMINATION

A. **General:** Patient's appearance, ability to answer questions, position in bed, and degree of discomfort. Dehydration may be suggested by dry mucous membranes, sunken eyes, and by rapid and shallow respirations. A patient writhing on the bed or pacing the room may have kidney stones, while a patient lying still is more likely to have peritoneal irritation. Facial expression may indicate pain of a crampy or constant nature. Pallor suggests anemia

B. **Vital signs:** Temperature, tachycardia, and hypotension may signify hypovolemia. A variant in blood pressure between the arms and legs may indicate aortic dissection. Increased respirations may signify metabolic acidosis, DKA, diaphragmatic irritation, or pain

C. **Inspection:** Scars, hernias, masses, distention, peristaltic waves, rash (herpes zoster), signs of liver disease (jaundice, spider angiomas, palmar erythema, ascites), pancreatitis (Grey Turner's sign—purple/red flanks; Cullen's sign—red umbilical)

D. **Auscultation:** Frequency and pitch of bowel sounds. High pitched bowel sounds may indicate obstruction. Presence or absence of abdominal bruits

E. **Percussion and palpation**
   1. Have patient point "with one finger" to area of greatest pain
   2. Begin in the quadrant free of pain and perform lightly (Note voluntary and involuntary guarding, rigidity and rebound). Study the face
   3. Organomegaly, and other masses including the bladder, and hernias. Pulsatile mass (AAA)
   4. Costovertebral angle tenderness

F. **Genitourinary**
   1. Umbilical hernia (and inguinal hernia)
   2. Examine the testicles for swelling and/or retraction
   3. Penis for discharge

G. **Pelvic examination**
   1. Both speculum and bimanual examination
   2. GC/*Chlamydia* cultures, Wet prep/Trichomoniasis evaluation if indicated
   3. Cervical motion tenderness (GU vs. peritonitis), adnexal tenderness, masses, discharge, bleeding or FBs

H. **Rectal examination**
   1. Probe for perirectal mass, fecal impaction, prostate enlargement or irregularity
   2. Guaiac stool
   3. Rectal tenderness 40% in appendicitis but rarely confirms or excludes the diagnosis

I. **Signs**
   1. **Psoas sign:** Pain on passive extension of the right hip. Suggestive of appendicitis
   2. **Obturator sign:** Pain with passive flexion and internal rotation of the right hip. Suggestive of appendicitis
   3. **Rovsing's sign:** Referred pain in the RLQ when palpating the LLQ. Suggestive of appendicitis
   4. **Murphy's sign:** Inspiratory arrest with deep palpation of the RUQ. Suggestive of cholecystitis
   5. **Carnett's sign:** Increased tenderness to palpation when abdominal muscles are contracted. Suggestive of abdominal wall pain

IV. DIAGNOSTIC STUDIES

A. **Plain abdominal radiograph:** Usefulness is limited and markedly overutilized. One study concluded that plain films should be used only for suspected obstruction, perforation, ischemia, peritonitis, or renal colic
   1. Both a supine and upright film of the abdomen should be obtained, as well as a PA (+/- lateral) chest film to exclude intrathoracic causes of acute abdominal pain (e.g., lower lobe pneumonia or aortic dissection)
   2. Conditions which may be diagnosed with acute abdominal series:
      a. Perforated viscus: May see free air under the diaphragms
      b. Bowel obstruction: Look for colonic haustra in order to distinguish large

            from small bowel
    c. Retroperitoneal inflammation: Psoas shadow is obscured
    d. Foreign body
    e. Kidney stone
B. Laboratory
    1. Complete blood count (CBC). Can indicate an infectious process, but if normal does not exclude one. Is potentially misleading and falsely reassuring. Up to 60% of patients with surgically proven appendicitis will have an initially normal WBC
    2. Electrolytes, BUN/creatinine
    3. Urinalysis: Urinary tract infection, renal or ureteral calculi. Patients with AAA may have some hematuria
    4. Serum amylase (sensitivity and specificity for acute pancreatitis is 80–90% and 75% respectively at 3 × upper limit of normal) and lipase (sensitivity and specificity for acute pancreatitis is 90% and 90% respectively at 2 × the upper limit of normal), ALT/AST, Alk Phos, β-HCG, lactic acid
    5. PT/PTT, type and screen (prior to surgery)
C. Ultrasonography: Cholelithiasis, fluid-containing cavities, intraabdominal masses, intrauterine or extrauterine pregnancy, ovarian cyst, and testicular torsion
D. Intravenous pyelogram (IVP) has been the test of choice for diagnosing kidney stones but has largely been replaced by helical CT which does not require administration of dye and can image other abdominal structures (AAA)
E. CT Scan: Useful in diagnosis of small bowel obstruction, mass, appendicitis, diverticular abscess, kidney stones, pancreatic necrosis, free air, AAA, and many other conditions. For evaluation of appendicitis, the helical CT with triple contrast (PO, IV, rectal) is about 98% sensitive. If a patient has a clinical diagnosis of appendicitis, do not do a CT as it may be a false negative. These patients need urgent surgical evaluation
F. Nuclear medicine: Helpful in diagnosing cholecystitis and testicular torsion

V. CAUSES OF ABDOMINAL PAIN IN PATIENTS PRESENTING TO AN ED

Final Diagnosis	≤ 50 years old	> 50 years old
Biliary tract disease	6%	21%
Nonspecific abdominal pain	40%	16%
Appendicitis	32%	15%
Bowel obstruction	2%	12%
Pancreatitis	2%	7%
Diverticular disease	<0.1%	6%
Cancer	<0.1%	4%
Hernia	<0.1%	3%
Vascular	<0.1%	2%
Acute gynecologic disease	4%	<0.1%
Other	13%	13%

SURG

Source: Gallagher J. Acute abdominal pain. In: Tintinalli J, ed. Emergency Medicine: a comprehensive study guide. 5th ed. New York: McGraw-Hill, 2000: 500.

VI. PRESENTATION OF COMMON CONDITIONS LEADING TO AN ACUTE ABDOMEN

DIAGNOSIS	PRESENTATION	EVALUATION
Peritonitis	Diffuse, severe tenderness; guarding or rigidity; absent bowel sounds; rebound	*Diagnosis is clinical;* upright chest film may show free intraperitoneal air
Appendicitis	Focal, lower right quadrant (McBurney's point) tenderness, with rebound; anorexia	*Diagnosis is clinical;* ultrasound, CT, spiral CT or barium enema may aid in diagnosis
Acute Pancreatitis	Diffuse upper abdominal tenderness radiating to the back; mild rebound; ileus; Grey Turner's sign (flank hematoma)	Serum amylase and Lipase; ultrasound or CT
Acute Cholecystitis	Right upper quadrant tenderness; muscle guarding; worse with inspiration	Ultrasound
Diverticulitis	Left lower quadrant tenderness; rebound; guarding; fever; quiet bowel sounds	CT; barium enema (Gastrografin should be used if a perforation is a possibility)
Small bowel obstruction — Proximal	Nausea, vomiting; alkalosis; normal or quiet bowel sounds; NO distension	Abdominal film; upper GI series; endoscopy
Small bowel obstruction — Distal	Nausea, vomiting; tenderness, distension; hyperactive bowel sounds	Abdominal film; angiogram; serum amylase
Cholangitis	Fever, jaundice; right upper quadrant pain	Ultrasound; ERCP; cholangiogram
Ectopic pregnancy	Peritonitis, hypotension; anemia; shock	B-hCG; vaginal ultrasound
Ruptured Aortic Aneurysm	Upper abdominal tenderness; back pain; pulsatile mass; hypovolemic shock	Angiogram; ultrasound, CT

VII. NONSURGICAL CAUSES OF ABDOMINAL PAIN

SYSTEM	DISEASE
Cardiac	Myocardial infarction, acute pericarditis
Pulmonary	Pneumonia, pulmonary infarction or embolus, pleural effusion
Gastrointestinal	Pancreatitis, gastroenteritis, hepatitis, inflammatory bowel disease (IBD), peptic ulcer disease (PUD), irritable bowel syndrome (IBS)
Endocrine	DKA, acute adrenal insufficiency, Addisonian crisis
Metabolic	Acute porphyria, familial Mediterranean fever
Musculoskeletal	Rectus muscle hematoma
Neurologic	Nerve root compression, tabes dorsalis
Genitourinary	Pyelonephritis, acute salpingitis, ovarian cyst, prostatitis, nephrolithiasis, endometriosis, dysmenorrhea
Psychologic	Depression, anxiety, somatization
Dermatologic	Herpes zoster

SURG

CLINICAL PEARLS
- Pain that is out of proportion to findings on exam may suggest ischemic bowel
- Most common etiologies of small bowel obstruction are adhesions, hernia, and tumor
- Most common etiologies of colonic obstruction are tumor, volvulus, and diverticular disease
- If an abdominal exam is difficult because of increased pain, peritoneal irritation can be demonstrated by having the patient cough and then asking to point to the area of maximum tenderness
- White blood cell count can be helpful, but may also be misleading. One study (1,800 patients) showed that a WBC > 10,000–11,000 only doubled the odds of appendicitis
- History and physical are almost worthless in excluding an ectopic pregnancy in a pregnant patient with abdominal pain and/or vaginal bleeding. An ectopic pregnancy

cannot be absolutely excluded based on quantitative hCG. A low (or high) hCG should NOT be reassuring to the clinician. Perform vaginal ultrasound in pregnant patients with abdominal pain and/or vaginal bleeding

References

Trowbridge, RL, et al. Does this patient have acute cholecystitis? JAMA 2003;289:80–86.

Gallagher J. Acute abdominal pain. In: Tintinalli, J ed. Emergency medicine: a comprehensive study guide. 5th ed. New York: McGraw-Hill, 2000: 497–512.

Lake AM. Chronic abdominal pain in childhood: Diagnosing and management. Am Fam Phys 1999;59:1823.

Dart RG, Kaplan B, Varaklis K. Predictive value of history and physical examination in patients with suspected ectopic pregnancy. Ann Emerg Med 1999;33:283–290.

Carrico CW, et al. Impact of sonography on the diagnosis and treatment of acute lower abdominal pain in children and young adults. Am J Roentgenol Feb 1999;172: 513–6.

Sfairi A, et al. Acute appendicitis in patients over 70 years of age. Presse Med Apr 27, 1999; 25(15):707–101.

Coleman C, et al. White blood cell count is a poor predictor of severity of disease in the diagnosis of appendicitis. Am Surg Oct 1998;64(10):983.

Balthazar EJ, et al. Appendicitis: the impact of computed tomography imaging on negative appendectomy and perforation rates. Am J Gastroent May 1998;93(5):768.

Martin, R. The acute abdomen: an overview and algorithms. Surgical Clinics of N Am 1997;77(6) 1227–43.

Parker JS, et al. Abdominal pain in the elderly: use of temperature and laboratory testing to screen for surgical disease. Fam Med Mar 1996; 28(3):193–7.

Deb Frankowski, MD
Daniel M. Neides, MD

98. DIVERTICULOSIS & DIVERTICULITIS

I. DEFINITION: Colonic diverticula are mucosal protrusions through the muscularis. Diverticulitis refers to inflammation in or around diverticula. 33% of the US population will have diverticular disease by age 45 and 67% by age 85. Diverticulitis occurs in 10–25% of people with diverticulosis

II. PATHOGENESIS

    A. High fat, low fiber diet "Western diet" results in decreased bulk of stool which leads to decreased colon diameter which leads to increased wall tension

    B. Retention of fecal material in a diverticular sac (obstruction of diverticuli) compromises blood flow to the sac and surrounding tissue which leads to inflammation

III. EPIDEMIOLOGY

    A. Incidence of diverticula increases with age, exponentially at age 50. Patients < 50 with symptomatic disease are most likely to require some form of surgical intervention

    B. Incidence in left colon is 3 × that of the right colon. Highest incidence is in the sigmoid colon

    C. Incidence in men > women

    D. Incidence in the US and Europe > Asia and Africa (genetic vs. diet)

IV. SIGNS AND SYMPTOMS: Patients present because of bleeding and complications of inflammation (obstruction)

    A. Diverticulosis: Usually asymptomatic, but may present with painless hematochezia

    B. Diverticulitis

        1. Fever

        2. Anorexia, nausea, vomiting

        3. Abdominal pain (usually LLQ)

        4. Rebound tenderness

        5. Hypoactive bowel sounds

        6. Rectal exam may demonstrate tenderness on the left side and may be heme positive

        7. Guaiac positive stools (rarely gross hematochezia)

        8. Constipation or diarrhea

        9. Tenesmus

        10. Urinary frequency (from irritation of the bladder or ureter)

SURG

C. Complications
1. Ruptured diverticula/perforation
2. Hemorrhage
3. Fistula between colon and bladder (pneumaturia, fecaluria)
4. Paralytic ileus
5. Small bowel obstruction (if loop of bowel becomes narrowed or kinked in the inflammatory mass)
6. Large bowel obstruction from stenosis

V. EVALUATION
A. Diverticulosis
1. If bleeding, then obtain barium enema, colonoscopy or angiography
2. Diverticulosis is often an incidental finding on colonoscopy, flexible sigmoidoscopy and barium enema

B. Diverticulitis
1. Laboratory
   a. WBC: Normal with diverticulosis, may be elevated with left shift in diverticulitis
   b. H/H: May be decreased with bleeding (chronic diverticulosis)
   c. Urinalysis: May include WBC or RBC with fistula formation
   d. Blood culture: May be positive
2. Other studies
   a. Acute abdominal series: Free air (perforation), mass, obstruction
   b. Barium enema: For diagnosis of diverticulosis
   c. Abdominal CT: Evaluate for abscess or fistula
   d. Colonoscopy
   e. Angiography: With bleeding

VI. DIFFERENTIAL DIAGNOSIS: Colon cancer, appendicitis, inflammatory bowel disease, ischemic colitis, urinary tract infection, incarcerated hernia, prostatitis, irritable bowel syndrome, ovarian pathology (torsion, cyst, mass), ectopic pregnancy

VII. MANAGEMENT
A. Asymptomatic diverticula
1. Low fat and high fiber vegetable diet
2. High fiber diet (Note: A high fiber diet has been associated with a lower risk of developing diverticular disease, but studies have not conclusively shown that high fiber diet helps with symptoms or prevents complications)
3. Avoiding seeds and nuts is controversial

B. Bleeding diverticulosis: Note—80% of bleeding will cease spontaneously
1. Bowel rest
2. Colonoscopy with cautery
3. Angiogram with vasoconstrictor injection
4. Surgery

C. Diverticulitis
1. Outpatient: No signs of peritonitis or systemic infection
   a. Bowel rest: Liquid diet for 48hrs
   b. ATBs: Need aerobic and anaerobic coverage. Use 1 of the following ATBs with **Metronidazole (Flagyl)** 500mg TID or **Clindamycin (Cleocin)** 300mg QID
      i. **Cephalexin (Keflex)** 500mg QID
      ii. **Quinolone (Levaquin** 500mg PO QD, **Ciprofloxacin** 500mg PO BID, etc.)
      iii. **TMP-SMX DS** BID
      iv. **Amoxicillin** 500mg TID or 875mg BID
2. Hospitalization
   a. Indications
      i. Systemic signs or symptoms of infection
      ii. Peritonitis/acute abdominal signs
      iii. Inability to take oral meds
      iv. Questionable diagnosis
   b. Bowel rest
   c. Broad spectrum ATBs

SURG

CLINICAL PEARLS
- Irritable bowel syndrome is often diagnosed as diverticular disease
- Bleeding occurs in 5–15% of patients with diverticulosis. Stops spontaneously in 75–95%
- Between 7 and 28% of people treated medically have recurrent bouts of diverticulitis

References

Thorn M, et al. Clinical and functional results after elective colonic resection in 75 consecutive patients with diverticular disease. Am J Surg 2002;183:7–11.

Chintapalli KN, et al. Diverticulitis versus colon cancer: differentiation with helical CT findings. Radiology Feb 1999;210:429–35.

Munson KD, et al. Diverticulitis. A comprehensive follow-up. Dis Colon Rectum 1996;39:318–22.

Smits BJ, et al. Lactulose in the treatment of symptomatic diverticular disease: a comparative study with high-fibre diet. Br J Clin Pract 1990;44:314–8.

Michael B. Weinstock, MD
Karen Hazelton, PA-C

99. MANAGEMENT OF WOUNDS

I. INTRODUCTION: The general goal of suturing is hemostasis, cosmesis, prevention of infection, and restoration of function

II. HISTORY: Crushing injuries and puncture wounds are at increased risk for infection
- **A.** How, when, and where did injury occur
- **B.** Mechanism of injury
- **C.** Clean or soiled environment
- **D.** What was the position of the extremity during the injury (position of a hand is important for locating tendon injury)
- **E.** Profession
- **F.** History of tetanus immunization

III. PHYSICAL EXAM
- **A.** Location, length, shape, depth and tension lines of the wound
- **B.** Associated tissue injury, such as joint, tendon or ligament involvement
- **C.** Contaminants and foreign bodies
- **D.** Neurovascular integrity and function

IV. LABORATORY AND RADIOLOGICAL STUDIES
- **A.** If wound appears clinically infected, consider aerobic and anaerobic cultures. The best way to obtain culture is with a quantitative tissue culture (tissue biopsy)
- **B.** Radiograph may be needed for suspected radiopaque foreign objects or fracture
- **C.** Consider x-ray for all lacerations secondary to broken glass as glass may remain in the wound even if it is not seen during exploration

V. INITIAL WOUND PREPARATION
- **A.** Wounds should generally not be closed after 6–12hrs, but in heavily vascularized areas such as the face, wound closure may be attempted up to 12–24hrs
- **B.** Anesthetize wound first so wound can be cleansed in a pain-free environment
- **C.** Massively contaminated wounds and wounds with extensive macerated tissue may require debridement in the operating room
- **D.** Adequate debridement and copious irrigation with normal saline or sterile water reduces risk of infection. Attach an 18–20 gauge needle to a 30–60cc syringe to irrigate heavily contaminated wounds. Irrigation from an IV bag is not adequate
- **E.** Hair should be cut and not shaved. Do not clip, cut, or shave the eyebrows
- **F.** Consider temporary short term placement of a tourniquet to obtain a bloodless field

VI. ANESTHESIA
- **A. Anesthetic agents**
  1. Topical: Contraindicated on mucous membranes and areas of end circulation such as digits, ears, tip of nose, penis
     a. **TAC: Tetracaine (0.5%), Adrenaline (1:2000), Cocaine (11.4%)**
     b. **EMLA cream**—Maximal effect may not be achieved for 1hr after application

SURG

        c. Topical **Lidocaine** (5%)

        d. **Epinephrine** (1:2000)

    2. Infiltrative

        a. **Lidocaine** (1% or 2%): Maximum dose is 5mg/kg (0.5cc/kg of 1%)

        b. **Lidocaine** with **Epinephrine** 1:2000

           i. Maximum dose is 7mg/kg (0.7cc/kg of 1%)

           ii. Contraindicated in areas of end circulation

        c. **Bupivacaine 0.25% (Marcaine):** Maximum dose is 3mg/kg (1.2cc/kg)

    3. Allergy to **Lidocaine**

        a. Usually due to an allergy to the PABA preservative

        b. Consider using a preservative-free Lidocaine

        c. Consider using **Diphenhydramine** 1% or 0.5% for infiltration

    4. Nerve blocks: Most commonly used for face, hands, and feet

  B. Techniques to reduce pain with infusion

    1. Use needle ≥ 25 gauge

    2. Inject slowly

    3. Inject through wound (as opposed to intact skin)

    4. Use a buffering agent: Mix 9cc of 1% **Lidocaine** with 1cc of **Sodium Bicarbonate** with a concentration of 44mEq/50mL. The acidity of an acute wound decreases the effectiveness of local non-buffered anesthesia

    5. Warm anesthetic to 98.6° F

    6. Use topical agents or sedation in children

    7. Regional nerve blocks in highly contaminated wounds, digital blocks for fingers and toes

VII. WOUND CLOSURE MATERIAL

  A. Sutures

SITE OF LACERATION	SUTURE*	SIZE OF SUTURE	SUTURE REMOVAL	COMMENTS
Eyelid	Nonabsorbable suture: Prolene monofilament (Prolene) Nylon monofilament (Ethilon)	6-0, 7-0	3 days	Prolene has the least amount of tissue reactivity
Cheek	same	5-0. 6-0	3–5 days	
Nose, forehead, neck	same	4-0, 5-0	5 days	
Ear	same	4-0, 5-0	4–5 days	
Scalp	same	3-0	5–7 days	
Arm, hand	same	3-0, 4-0	7–10 days	
Leg, foot, chest, back	same	3-0, 4-0	10–14 days	
Tendons	Prolene	3-0, 4-0	----	
Deep closure of wounds, intraoral	Absorbable suture: Vicryl Dexon PDS Chromic gut	3-0, 4-0, 5-0 5-0 (intra-oral)	----	Vicryl and Dexon lose 50% of their tensile strength in 14–20 days PDS loses 50% in 5 weeks Synthetic sutures: preferable to gut in acute wounds

*Despite its ease of tying, silk suture should generally not be used because of increased tissue reactivity and chance of infection

  B. Staples

    1. Advantage: Faster

    2. Precautions: Never use on face

    3. Potential indications: Consider use on scalp, trunk, upper and lower extremities

  C. Topical tissue adhesive

    1. Example: 2-octylcyanoacrylate (Dermabond)

    2. Technique: Approximate wound edges and 3 ever larger concentric circles over wound edges

    3. Use only with superficial wounds under low tensile stress

VIII. SUTURE TECHNIQUE

  A. Always use good lighting and be comfortable (easier to sit than stand or bend)

  B. Most common suture technique is simple interrupted

  C. Sutures should be placed with equal depth and width for best results. Sutures should be

SURG

placed to evert wound edges without gapping or pulling. Eversion may be accomplished by placing the needle through the skin at a 90° angle and not tangentially

D. Sutures should be used to approximate the wound edges and not to pull the wound together. For wounds with high tension, place deep sutures or mattress sutures

E. Simple sutures are placed closer together and with smaller bites on the face and neck to minimize scarring

F. When suturing lips, place first suture through vermilion border (junction of lip and skin)

G. Delayed primary closure is preferred in heavily contaminated wounds if no signs of infection are present after 3–5 days

H. Hints for special circumstances
1. Topical tissue adhesive for superficial lacerations with little tension
2. Staples for selected sites such as scalp
3. Continuous sutures for longer lacerations of the face and scalp
4. Deep sutures for high-tension wounds
5. Vertical mattress sutures for medium deep lacerations
6. Half buried mattress sutures for flap lacerations

IX. BITE WOUNDS

A. Initial evaluation
1. Generally, bite wounds are primarily closed in very vascular areas and if cosmetically necessary
2. Areas usually primarily sutured are face, scalp, and neck. Avoid deep sutures
3. Consider closing wounds of trunk, arm and legs
4. Avoid suturing any bite wounds of the hands and feet

B. Wound preparation: See above. Very important to use copious irrigation and debridement of devitalized tissue

C. High risk bite wounds
1. Location: Hand, foot, wrists, joints. In infants: Scalp or face
2. Type of wound: Puncture (cat bite) or crush
3. Patient: Age > 50, asplenic, alcoholic, immunocompromised, diabetic, peripheral vascular disease, chronic steroid use, prosthetic or diseased cardiac valve or joint

D. Human bites
1. Most common organisms include α-hemolytic *Streptococcus, Staphylococcus, Eikenella corrodens, Corynebacterium,* and *Bacteroides*
2. Carry the highest risk of infection on the hand. About 47% of human bites to hand become infected
3. If there is invasion of the MCP joint capsule (usually from injuries sustained during a fight), then refer to a hand surgeon for possible debridement in the operating room
4. Wound closure
   a. Human bites to the hand should not be closed
   b. Those in other areas may be closed if less than 6hrs old after adequate irrigation and debridement
5. ATB prophylaxis: **Amoxicillin/Clavulanate (Augmentin)** 875mg PO BID × 5 days

E. Dog bites
1. Most common organisms include *Strep viridans, Pasteurella multocida, S. aureus, E. corrodens, Bacteroides*
2. Dog bites tend to be more of an open, tearing type of wound
3. Wound closure
   a. Dog bites to the hand should not be closed
   b. Those in other areas may be closed if less than 6hrs old after adequate irrigation and debridement
4. ATB prophylaxis
   a. Risk of infection without ATBs is 9–16%
   b. Prophylaxis should be administered in high risk bite wounds (see above) and optional in other wounds
   c. Give prophylaxis as soon as possible (preferable before repair is done)
   d. ATB prophylaxis: **Amoxicillin/Clavulanate (Augmentin)** 875mg PO BID × 3–5 days if indicated
   e. Alternative
      i. Adults: **Clindamycin** 300mg PO QID plus **Fluoroquinolone** (e.g., **Cipro** 500mg BID)

SURG

ii. Children: **Clindamycin** plus **Bactrim**

F. Cat bites

1. Most common organisms include staph and strep species and *Pasteurella multocida*
2. Cat bites are usually deep puncture type wounds
3. Wound closure: Leave all cat bites open to heal by secondary intention
4. ATB prophylaxis
   a. Risk of infection is ~ 50% without ATBs
   b. Recommended: **Amoxicillin/Clavulanate (Augmentin)** 875mg PO BID × 3–5 days
   c. Alternative: **Cefuroxime (Ceftin)** 500mg PO BID or **Doxycycline** 100mg PO BID
   d. Caution: Do not use **Cephalexin (Keflex)** or **Dicloxacillin**

X. AFTERCARE INSTRUCTIONS

A. General

1. Topical ATBs
2. Dressings (non-adherent or sterile gauze)
3. Splint lacerations over joints

B. Wounds that should be rechecked in 24–48hrs

1. Hand wounds
2. Bite wounds
3. Heavily contaminated wounds
4. Other wounds requiring prophylactic ATBs

C. Tetanus prophylaxis

SUMMARY OF TETANUS PROPHYLAXIS FOR THE INJURED PATIENT

History of Adsorbed Tetanus Toxoid (Doses)	Nontetanus-Prone Wounds		Tetanus-Prone Wounds	
	Td[1]	TIG	Td[1]	TIG
Unknown or ≤ three	Yes	No	Yes	Yes
≥ Three[2]	No[3]	No	No[4]	No

1 For children younger than 7 years old: DTP (DT, if pertussis vaccine is contraindicated) is preferred to tetanus toxoid alone. For persons 7 years old and older, Td is preferred to tetanus toxoid alone
2 If only 3 doses of fluid toxoid have been received, a fourth dose of toxoid, preferably an adsorbed toxoid, should be given
3 Yes, if more than 10 years since last dose
4 Yes, if more than 5 years since last dose (more frequent boosters are not needed and can accentuate side effects)
Td Tetanus and diphtheria toxoids adsorbed—for adult use
TIG Tetanus immune globulin—human

CLINICAL PEARLS

- Lidocaine with Epinephrine should not be used in areas with poor blood supply (nose, fingers, toes, skin flaps, etc.)
- Wounds should generally not be closed after 6–8hrs, but may be primarily closed up to 24hrs in very vascular areas such as the face and scalp
- Subcutaneous suture in the hand and any silk suture is generally not used because of increased tissue reactivity and increased risk of infection
- Shaving the hair around a wound increases the chance of infection

References

Sanford JP, et al. Guide to antimicrobial therapy. 32th ed. Antimicrobial Therapy, Inc. 2002.

Burns TB, Worthington, JM. Using tissue adhesive for wound repair: a practical guide to Dermabond. Am Fam Phys 2000;61:1383–8.

Hollander JE, Singer AJ. Laceration management. Ann Emerg Med Sep 1999;34:356–67.

Eisenbud DE. Modern wound management. Columbus, OH: Anadem Publishing, 1998.

Presutti RJ. Bite wounds: early treatment and prophylaxis against infectious complications. Postgraduate Med 1997;101(4):243–54.

Noeller T. Laceration repair techniques. Emergency Med Rep 1996;17(21):207–18.

Lewis KT, Management of cat and dog bites. Am Fam Phys 1995;52:479.

SURG

Michael B. Weinstock, MD

100. PAIN MANAGEMENT IN ADULTS & CHILDREN

PAIN MANAGEMENT IN ADULTS AND CHILDREN

Medication	Equi-analgesic dose PO*	Equi-analgesic dose IM/SC	Duration of analgesia** (hours)	Recommended dose in adults and children*** (start with the lowest dose for pain control and then increase dose as needed)
Morphine sulfate	30mg	10mg	3–7	Adults — IM/IV: 2–10mg Q 2–3hrs Children — IM/IV: 0.1–0.2mg/kg/dose **Roxanol** 20mg/mL, 10mg/2.5mL — Titrate to effective dose Q 4 hours PO — Logical starting dose is 10–30mg Q 4hours PO **MS Contin/Oramorph SR** (Sustained release) — 15, 30, 60, 100mg tabs (MS contin has a 200mg tab)
Hydro-morphone (Dilaudid)	4–6mg	1.5–2mg	2–4	IM/IV/SC: 1–2mg Q 4–6 hours PO: 2–4mg Q 4–6 hours (2, 4, 8mg tabs or 5mg/5mL liquid) Rectal: One supp. PR Q 6–8 hours Available 3mg Not recommended for children
Methadone (Dolophine)	5–6mg	2.5–3mg	4–8	Adults — PO: 2.5–10mg Q 3–4 hours
Meperidine (Demerol)	300mg	75–100mg	2–4	Adults — IV/IM/PO: 50–100mg Q 3–4 hours (20, 100mg tabs) Children — IV/IM/PO: 1–1.5mg/kg/dose Q 3–4 hours (Elixir: 50mg/5mL)
Oxycodone (Oxyir, Percocet, Percodan OxyContin)	30mg	NA	4–6	**Oxyir** (oxycodone 5mg caps or 20mg/mL liquid) **OxyContin** (controlled release) — every 12 hours available 10, 20, 40, 80mg Percocet 2.5/325 (oxycodone 2.5mg/acetaminophen 325mg) Percocet 5/325 (oxycodone 5mg/acetaminophen 325mg) Percocet 7.5/500 (oxycodone 7.5mg/acetaminophen 500mg) Percocet 10/650 (oxycodone 10mg/acetaminophen 650mg) Percodan (oxycodone 4.5mg/aspirin 325mg)
Hydrocodone (Lorcet, Lortab, Vicodin, Vicoprofen)	30mg	NA	3–8	**Lorcet 10/650** (hydrocodone 10mg/acetaminophen 650mg) **Lorcet plus** (hydrocodone 7.5mg/acetaminophen 650mg) **Lortab 10/500** (hydrocodone 10mg/acetaminophen 500mg) **Lortab 7.5/500** (hydrocodone 7.5mg/acetaminophen 500mg) **Lortab 5/500** (hydrocodone 5mg/acetaminophen 500mg) **Lortab 2.5/500** (hydrocodone 2.5mg/acetaminophen 500mg) **Lortab elixir** (hydrocodone 7.5mg/acetaminophen 500mg/elixir 15mL) **Vicodin** (hydrocodone 5mg/acetaminophen 500mg) **Vicodin ES** (hydrocodone 7.5mg/acetaminophen 750mg) **Vicoprofen** (hydrocodone 7.5mg/ibuprofen 200mg)
Codeine (Tylenol #2, #3, #4, Empirin #2, #3, #4)	200mg	120mg	4–6	Note: Cough suppressant at 15–30mg Q4 hours Note: PO doses > 65 not recommended due to decreased incremental analgesia. **T#2** = codeine 15mg/acetaminophen 300mg **T#3** = codeine 30mg/acetaminophen 300mg **T#4** = codeine 60mg/acetaminophen 300mg **Elixir:** codeine 12mg/acetaminophen 120mg/5mL
Propoxyphene (Darvon, Darvon-N Darvocet-N 100)	130–200mg	NA	4–6	**Darvon** (propoxyphene 65mg) **Darvon-N** (propoxyphene 100mg) **Darvocet-N 100** (propoxyphene 100/acetaminophen 650mg)
Fentanyl (Duragesic)	Duragesic transdermal system patch 100mcg/hr = morphine 60mg IV/24 hours		72	Patches in doses of 25, 50, 75, 100mcg/hour Note: Should not be used to treat acute pain Dose – give every 3 days

* Consider reducing calculated parental dose when switching from PO to IV/IM to accommodate for cross sensitivity and absorption variation.
** Duration of action is immediate release preparations (not sustained release)
*** All doses are for adults unless otherwise specified. Maximum 4g acetaminophen per day. Medications are generally dosed every 4–6 hours unless otherwise specified.

SURG

I. GENERAL

    A. Pain can be divided into 3 main origins:

        1. Visceral pain: Poorly localized and usually either cramping, sharp or aching

        2. Somatic pain: Well localized and usually sharp, achy, throbbing or pressure-like

        3. Neuropathic pain: Radiating and usually burning or stabbing

    B. General principles in treating chronic pain (pain from chronic conditions such as cancer)

        1. Schedule dosing with PRN breakthrough doses of pain meds

        2. One method is to use an initial dose scheduled at an appropriate frequency (generally Q3–4hrs) and provide a 1hr PRN dose of ½ of the scheduled dose. If patient requires more than 2 breakthrough pain doses, adjust the scheduled dose by adding previous scheduled dose and previous breakthrough dose. Adjust new breakthrough dose of ½ of new scheduled doses. Continue with this method until pain is controlled

        3. Anticipate side effects

            a. When prescribing opiates, consider concomitantly prescribing laxatives

            b. Anticipate nausea when initiating high doses of opiates

            c. Discuss sedation and ways to prevent falls (lighting, hand rails, slow movement, (see Chapter 108, Falls in the Elderly)

II. SIDE EFFECTS OF OPIOIDS

    A. Respiratory depression/arrest

    B. Sedation

    C. Nausea and vomiting: May administer an anti-nausea med concurrently with opioid

    D. Constipation

    E. Tolerance and dependence

    F. Histamine reaction including hypotension and itching: Less with synthetic opioids (**Dilaudid** and **Fentanyl**). May be helped with **Benadryl**

III. NON-OPIOID PAIN MANAGEMENT (May use as adjunct to narcotics to decrease duration of narcotic use)

DRUG	ADULT DOSE	PEDIATRIC DOSE
Acetaminophen (Tylenol)	650–1000mg Q4–6 hours PRN (Max. daily dose is 4g)	10–15mg/kg/dose Q4–6 hours PRN Supplied: Drops — One dropper-full (0.8mL)=80mg Elixir — 160mg/5mL (One teaspoon) Chewable tablets — 80mg/tab
Ibuprofen	200–800mg Q8 hours (Max. daily dose is 3200mg)	5–10mg/kg/dose Q8 hours PRN Supplied: 100mg/5mL (One teaspoon)
Aspirin	325-650mg Q4–6 hours PRN (Max. daily dose is 3600mg)	For anti-rheumatic doses or for treatment of Kawasaki's dz., consult other sources
Ketorolac (Toradol)	IM: 30–60mg IM loading dose PO: 10mg Q4–6 hours PRN Do not exceed 5 days (injection plus oral)	Not recommended for children
Tramadol/ Acetaminophen (Ultracet)	1–2 PO Q4–6 hours PRN	Not recommended for children
Rofecoxib (Vioxx)	12.5–25mg PO QD For acute pain may give 50mg PO QD for a maximum of 5 days	Not recommended for children
Celecoxib (Celebrex)	100–200mg PO QD For acute pain may give 400–600mg PO on day 1 and 200mg PO QD afterward	Not recommended for children

Note:
1. Efficacy (analgesic effect) is equal between the cox-2 inhibitors and traditional NSAIDs
2. The patients taking cox-2 inhibitors had fewer symptomatic and complicated ulcers than the patients receiving traditional NSAIDS. This effect was negated in patients taking low dose aspirin.
3. The cox-2 inhibitors are better tolerated with less adverse effects including abdominal pain, dyspepsia and other GI side effects, but their cost is significantly higher
4. The "number needed to treat" (when treated for one year) to prevent one UGI event was 41 with Rofecoxib and 66 with Celecoxib vs. traditional NSAIDs

IV. OTHER MODALITIES TO TREAT PAIN
A. Neuropathic pain
1. Antidepressants: e.g., Amitriptyline (Elavil), Imipramine (Tofranil)
2. Anticonvulsants: e.g., Carbamazepine (Tegretol), Gabapentin (Neurontin), Divalproex (Depakote), Phenytoin (Dilantin)
3. Local anesthetics: Capsaicin (Zostrix)

B. Bone metastasis
1. Pamidronate (Aredia)
2. Calcitonin (Calcimar)

C. Generalized chronic pain: Antidepressants, e.g., Amitriptyline (Elavil), Imipramine (Tofranil)

D. Other: Physical therapy, exercise, massage, transcutaneous electrical nerve stimulation (TENS), radiation therapy, chemotherapy, psychotherapy, pastoral care

V. PREEMPTIVE ANALGESIA
A. Administration of local anesthetics, nerve blocks, epidural blocks, opiates, and anti-inflammatory drugs prior to noxious stimuli (i.e., surgery) can reduce the sensitization of pain receptors and lead to better post-op pain control
B. Administration of general anesthesia with a volatile drug such as Forane does not prevent sensitization

CLINICAL PEARLS:
- There is no maximum dose of opioid analgesics
- Endoscopic studies reveal gastric or duodenal ulcers in 15–30% of patients who regularly take NSAIDs, but many are asymptomatic
- Pain medicines are frequently underdosed. Pain medicines should generally be *scheduled* and given in doses adequate to relieve pain. This practice will reduce possibility of addiction
- To initiate pain management, begin with the most benign medicine which will still control the pain. Often involves starting with a non-opioid analgesic and titrating upward
- It is questionable whether acetaminophen with codeine is any more effective than acetaminophen without codeine

References

Buttgereit F, et al. Gastrointestinal toxic side effects of nonsteroidal anti-inflammatory drugs and cyclooxygenase-2-specific inhibitors. Am J Med 2001;110(3A):13S–19S.

Gottschalk A, Smith DS. New concepts in acute pain therapy: Preemptive analgesia. Am Fam Phys 2001;63:1979–84, 1985–6.

Hochberg MC. What have we learned from the large outcome trials of COX-2 selective inhibitors? The rheumatologist's perspective. Clin Exp Rheumatol 2001;19:S15–22.

WHO Cancer Program. Cancer pain and relief and palliative care in children. Available to order: http://www5.who.int/cancer/main.cfm?p=0000000509 (last update May 2002).

Vogt BA. Novel aspects of pain management: Opioids and beyond. N Engl J Med 2000;342:141–2.

American Pain Society. Principles of analgesic use in the treatment of acute pain and cancer pain, 4th ed. Glenview IL, 1999.

SURG

Michael B. Weinstock, MD
Beth Weinstock, MD

101. PREOPERATIVE EVALUATION

I. INTRODUCTION

Preoperative assessment is mandatory in all patients undergoing both cardiac and noncardiac surgery. Evaluation includes history and physical on all patients, with lab, EKG, cardiac stress testing, and PFTs added individually as needed. Preoperative evaluation should be performed within 1 month of surgery

II. HISTORY

A. Current symptoms: Emphasis is placed on cardiac and pulmonary symptoms, including chest pain at rest or with exertion, peripheral vascular symptoms, dyspnea with exertion, orthopnea, PND, palpitations, light-headedness, or syncope

B. Medications

1. Include over-the-counter meds, vitamins, and herbal supplements. Meds listed should be stopped 5–7 days preoperatively if possible: Aspirin and any related product, NSAIDs, Vitamin E, garlic (inhibits platelet aggregation), ginseng, ginkgo, St. John's Wort, kava, ephedra/Ma Huang

2. Patient should continue blood pressure medicines and any bronchodilators until morning of surgery

3. Patients on chronic corticosteroids should receive a stress dose of steroid (**Hydrocortisone**) about 30–60 minutes preoperatively

4. **Coumadin**: Anticoagulation can be interrupted for up to 1 week for surgical procedures in the absence of mechanical valves

5. Diabetes meds: Avoid oral hypoglycemics on AM of surgery. Patients on insulin pump should continue basal rate but avoid any bolus infusion. Sliding scale insulin will be used in hospital until post-op intake is resumed

C. Past medical history

1. Previous anesthesia reaction

2. History of DVT, PE, or clotting disorder

3. Previous stress testing or revascularization

4. Age > 70, history of MI/angina/LV dysfunction/arrhythmia, $pO_2 < 60mmHg$, $pCO_2 > 50mmHg$ are all clinical predictors of increased perioperative cardiac risk

D. Social history

1. Tobacco and alcohol use

2. Exercise: Helps to determine patient's functional capacity. Functional capacity can be expressed in metabolic equivalents (METs). Perioperative cardiac risk is increased in patients unable to meet a 4 MET demand
   a. 1–4 METs: Eating, dressing, walking around house
   b. 4–10 METs: Climbing a flight of stairs, walking briskly, running a short distance, playing golf
   c. > 10 METs: Swimming, tennis, football, jogging

III. PHYSICAL EXAMINATION

A. Vitals: Heart rate and rhythm, BP

B. HEENT: Dentition/dentures, neck examination (thyroid, carotid bruits, pulses)

C. Cardiac: Heart murmurs (AS), gallop, cardiomegaly, JVD, peripheral edema, orthopnea

D. Abdominal: Pulsatile mass, hepatosplenomegaly
E. Pulmonary: Rales (CHF), wheezes (COPD), rhonchi, pleural effusions, clubbing
F. Neurological: Mini-mental status examination if applicable, cranial nerve examination
G. General: Jaundice, cyanosis, anemia, dehydration

IV. INDICATIONS FOR LABORATORY, ECG, AND RADIOLOGICAL TESTING

To use the following table, order:

1. All tests recommended for patients by age — *plus* —
2. All tests recommended based on the type of surgery — *plus* —
3. All tests recommended based on patients' associated conditions

INDICATIONS FOR PREOPERATIVE TESTING

	Hb/ Hct	PT/ PTT	Type/ screen	Electro-lytes	Creat/ BUN	Glucose	CXR	ECG
1) Age < 40 y/o	X							
Age 40–65	X				X	X		X
Age > 65 y/o	X				X	X	X	X
2) All ages, major surgery *	X	X	X	X	X	X	X	X
3) *Associated conditions:*								
Cardiovascular					X		X	X
Pulmonary							X	X
Diabetes				X	X	X		
Renal	X			X	X			
Hypertension					X			X
Smoking (>20 pack years)	X						X	
Use of diuretics				X	X			
Use of digoxin				X	X			X
Use of anticoagulants	X	X						
Use of steroids				X		X		
Antiarrhythmics				X				X

* Major surgery—vascular, intrathoracic/intra-abdominal surgery

V. INDICATIONS FOR TESTING IN PATIENTS WITH CARDIOVASCULAR DISEASE
A. Elective surgery should be delayed for at least 6 months post-MI
B. Semi-elective surgery may be performed 4–6 months post-MI with intensive monitoring
C. Stable angina, CHF, and arrhythmias should be maximally medically managed prior to surgery
D. Indications for cardiac stress testing or cardiac catheterization prior to elective or semi-elective *noncardiac* surgery (see algorithm below)

SURG

ACC/AHA Guidelines

Stepwise Approach to Preoperative Cardiac Assessment

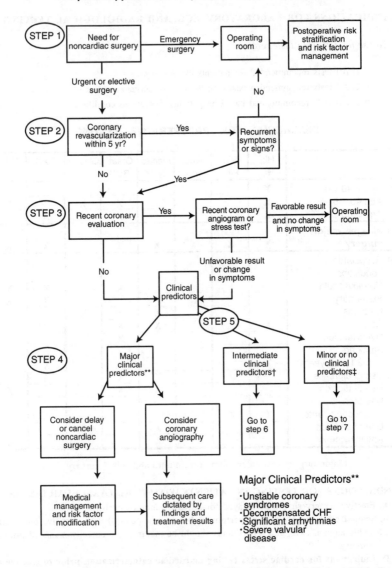

CHF indicates congestive heart failure; ECG, electrocardiogram; MET, metabolic equivalent; MI, myocardial infarction.

Continued on next page

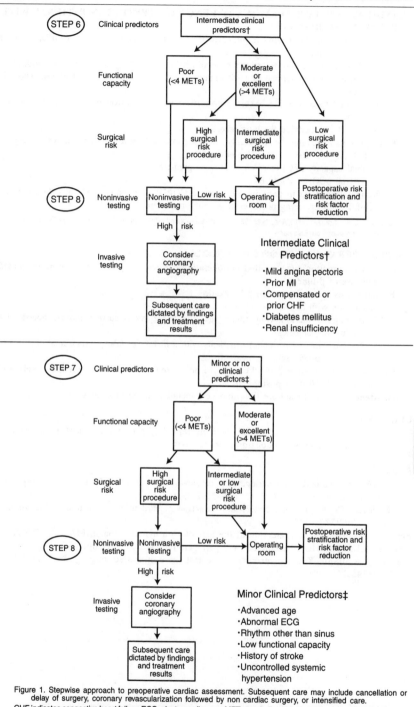

Figure 1. Stepwise approach to preoperative cardiac assessment. Subsequent care may include cancellation or delay of surgery, coronary revascularization followed by non cardiac surgery, or intensified care.

CHF indicates congestive heart failure; ECG, electrocardiogram; MET, metabolic equivalent; MI, myocardial infarction.

* Source: Eagle, et al. ACC/AHA Guideline Update for the Perioperative Cardiovascular Evaluation for Noncardiac Surgery. J Am Coll Cardiol 1996;27:910–48. Copyright © 1996 Amer Coll of Cardiol, Amer Heart Assoc., Inc. Used with permission. www.acc.org/clinical/guidelines/perio/update/periupdate_index.htm

VI. INDICATIONS FOR PULMONARY FUNCTION TESTING IN PATIENTS WITH PULMONARY DISEASE*

A. Pulmonary function testing is indicated if the patient has a history of COPD, SOB, or orthopnea —and—

1. There is a need to determine reversibility of bronchospasm with bronchodilators (reversibility is defined as a 15% improvement in the FEV_1 by the American Thoracic Society); —or—

2. A need to determine baseline condition in anticipation of post-op intubation; —or—

3. Patient is scheduled for lung resection

B. Test results indicating a significantly increased morbidity and mortality following surgery:

1. If FEV_1 < 2 liters or < 60% predicted

2. Vital capacity (VC) or MVV < 50% of predicted

3. Arterial pCO_2 > 45mm HG

C. Preoperative ABG in patients with severe COPD is recommended; this data may be helpful in determining postoperative ventilator settings

*Source: Adapted from Miller RD, Anesthesia 859:4/e. New York: Churchill Livingstone, 1994:859. © 1994 Elsevier Inc. Used with permission from Elsevier.

VII. PERIOPERATIVE USE OF β-BLOCKERS

A. New information suggests that perioperative cardiac complications may be prevented with use of β-blockers

B. Candidates for perioperative β-blockade

1. Patients with known coronary risk, —or—

2. Meeting 2 of the following criteria: age > 65, hypertension, current smoker, cholesterol > 240mg/dL, diabetes

3. Revised criteria also included patients with a history of CVA, serum creatinine > 2.0, or with known ischemic heart disease

C. Ideally perioperative β-blockers would be started at least 7 days preoperatively and continued 7–10 days postoperatively

D. **Atenolol** or **Bisoprolol** are the β-blockers included in recent studies

CLINICAL PEARLS

- Patients should be questioned routinely regarding need for endocarditis prophylaxis (see Chapter 36, Endocarditis Prophylaxis)

References

ACC/AHA guideline update for perioperative cardiovascular evaluation for noncardiac surgery—executive summary. J Am Coll Cardiol 2002;39:542–53.

Auerbach AD, Goldman L. β-blockers and reduction of cardiac events in noncardiac surgery. JAMA 2002;287:1445–7.

Fleisher LA. Preoperative evaluation of the patient with hypertension. JAMA 2002;287:2043.

Ang-Lee MK, et al. Herbal medicines and perioperative care. JAMA 2001;286:218.

Fleisher LA, Eagle KA. Lowering cardiac risk in noncardiac surgery. N Engl J Med 2001;345:1677–81.

SURG

X. Care of Patients with Psychiatric Disorders

102. Anxiety Disorders 339

103. Depression & Dysthymia 342

104. Sexual Dysfunction 347

105. Alcohol & Other Drugs of Abuse 352

PSY

3. Care of Patients with Psychiatric Disorders

Daniel M. Neides, MD
Christine Costanzo, MD
Budd Ferrante, EdD

102. ANXIETY DISORDERS

I. INTRODUCTION

A. Anxiety disorders, commonly seen in the general population, include:
1. Generalized anxiety disorder (GAD)
2. Panic disorder
3. Obsessive-compulsive disorder (OCD)
4. Adjustment disorder with mixed anxiety and depression
5. Phobic disorder
6. Post traumatic stress disorder (PTSD)
7. Social phobia
8. Substance induced anxiety disorder

B. Panic disorder is the most common of the anxiety disorders in which patients will seek treatment and can be very disabling with severe financial, social, and occupational consequences for the patient

C. Patients with panic disorder often have many physical complaints. Delineate between symptoms resulting from the panic disorder and those which are non-psychiatric in origin

D. Rule out organic causes for the patient's symptoms of anxiety

II. MEDICAL CAUSES OF ANXIETY

Before treating for anxiety disorder, a complete history and physical and lab work (if indicated) will be necessary to rule out other organic causes. New onset anxiety in an older patient should be a red flag to evaluate for other causes

A. Endocrine: *Hyperthyroid*, hypoglycemia, carcinoid syndrome, parathyroid dysfunction, pheochromocytoma, adrenal dysfunction

B. Inflammatory: Systemic lupus erythematosus (SLE), rheumatoid arthritis (RA), polyarteritis nodosa, temporal arteritis

C. Neurologic: CNS tumors, migraine, subarachnoid hemorrhage, syphilis, multiple sclerosis, Wilson's disease, Huntington's chorea, seizure disorders

D. Cardiopulmonary: *Angina*, pulmonary insufficiency

E. Nutritional: Pellagra, B_{12} deficiency

F. Metabolic: Porphyria

G. Pharmacologic: *Alcohol and drug abuse or withdrawal*, amphetamines, *caffeine*, sympathomimetics, tobacco

H. Assess for other psychiatric disorders such as depression

III. GUIDELINES FOR TREATMENT OF ALL ANXIETY DISORDERS

A. Consideration should be given to non-pharmacologic approaches (cognitive-behavior therapy is indicated regardless of pharmacologic or non-pharmacologic approaches)

B. Define underlying conflicts and stresses, coping mechanisms and support systems

C. Consider if psychosocial factors or the patient's personality place the patient at risk for abuse or addiction

D. Individualize anxiolytic therapy

E. Goal of therapy should be clearly discussed with the patient

F. In the elderly:
1. Start with half dose regimen
2. Avoid frequent dosing adjustments
3. Watch for signs of confusion, sedation, ataxia

PSY

— PART I: GENERALIZED ANXIETY DISORDER (GAD) —

I. EPIDEMIOLOGY
   A. Prevalence is 2–4% of the general population; female to male ratio is 2:1
   B. Age of onset is in the 20s, although there is a clear rise in diagnosis of children and adolescents
   C. 15–17% of first degree relatives have GAD

II. DIAGNOSTIC

Diagnostic Criteria for 300.02 Generalized Anxiety Disorder

Excessive anxiety and worry (apprehensive expectation), occurring more days than not for at least six months, about a number of events or activities (such as work or school performance).

The person finds it difficult to control the worry.

The anxiety and worry are associated with three (or more) of the following six symptoms (with at least some symptoms present for more days than not for the past six months). NOTE: Only one item is required in children.
   Restlessness or feeling keyed up or on edge
   Being easily fatigued
   Difficulty concentrating or mind going blank
   Irritability
   Muscle tension
   Sleep disturbance (difficulty falling or staying asleep, or restless unsatisfying sleep)

The focus of the anxiety and worry is not confined to features of an Axis I disorder, e.g., the anxiety or worry is not about having a panic attack (as in Panic Disorder), being embarrassed in public (as in Social Phobia), being contaminated (as in Obsessive-Compulsive Disorder), being away from home or close relatives (as in Separation Anxiety Disorder), gaining weight (as in Anorexia Nervosa), having multiple physical complaints (as in Somatization Disorder), or having a serious illness (as in Hypochondriasis), and the anxiety and worry do not occur exclusively during Post-traumatic Stress Disorder.

The anxiety, worry or physical symptoms cause clinically significant distress or impairment in social, occupational or other important areas of functioning.

The disturbance is not due to the direct physiological effects of a substance (e.g., a drug of abuse, a medication) or a general medical condition (e.g., hyperthyroidism) and does not occur exclusively during a Mood Disorder, a Psychotic Disorder, or a Pervasive Developmental Disorder.

Reprinted with permission from the American Psychiatric Association. Diagnostic and statistical manual of mental disorders. 4th ed. Washington, D.C.: American Psychiatric Association, 1994:435-6.

III. TREATMENT
   A. Remove exacerbating factors: Caffeine, tobacco, drugs, alcohol
   B. Psychotherapy: Cognitive-behavioral therapy or group psychotherapy may help in treating a generalized anxiety disorder
   C. Exercise: Aerobic exercise is 20 minutes of uninterrupted exercise with heart rate >120, performed a minimum of 3× a week
   D. Anxiolytic: Non-benzodiazepine
      1. **Buspirone (BuSpar)** 5mg PO BID–TID (gradually increase to 30–60mg/day). Does *not* have the sedative, *withdrawal*, or abuse potential seen with the Benzodiazepines. Effects of the drug may take several weeks to become evident
      2. Side effects: Dizziness, drowsiness, headache
   E. Benzodiazepines: Have the potential for abuse and dependence. Very effective for short-term treatment of anxiety or while waiting for other meds to start working. No evidence that they are more effective than no pharmacologic treatment when used for long periods of time. All are equally efficacious
      1. **Lorazepam (Ativan)** 0.5–1mg PO BID–TID

   2. **Clonazepam (Klonopin)** 0.5mg PO BID (may increase to 2–10mg/day)
   3. Side effects: Drowsiness, fatigue, ataxia, unsteadiness, memory impairment in elderly
F. Serotonin selective reuptake inhibitors (SSRIs)
   1. Efficacious without addictive properties. Consider starting at ½ the antidepressant dose to avoid initially exacerbating anxiety
   2. May use BDZ initially when starting SSRIs as the SSRI may not decrease symptoms for the first several weeks
   3. E.g. **Venlafaxine (Effexor)** Starting dose 37.5mg–75mg QD × 4–7 days, then increase by 37.5–75mg/day PRN up to 225mg/day. Most frequent side effects: nausea, anorexia, insomnia, headache, increased BP, especially in dose > 300mg/day
G. Propranolol (Inderal): Starting dose 10–20mg TID–QID. Useful for prominent and somatic (as opposed to psychotic) complaints (i.e., palpitations, trembling, restlessness, motor tension). Note: Not approved for anxiety or other psychiatric problems
H. Consider **Imipramine (Tofranil)**, **Trazodone (Desyrel)**, and **Nefazodone (Serzone)**

— PART II: PANIC DISORDER —

I. EPIDEMIOLOGY
   A. 2–4% prevalence in the general population
   B. Age of onset: Usually late 20s
   C. Female to male ratio: Without agoraphobia (irrational fear of being in open or public places), 1:1; with agoraphobia, 2:1
   D. Co-morbidity with depression

II. DIAGNOSIS OF PANIC DISORDER (ADAPTED FROM DSM-IV)
   A. Recurrent unexpected panic attacks (defined as a period of intense fear or discomfort in which 4 or more of the following symptoms develop abruptly and peak within 10 minutes: palpitations, tachycardia, sweating, trembling, shortness of breath, choking sensation, chest pain, nausea, dizziness, derealization, depersonalization, fear of losing control or of dying, paresthesias, chills, hot flushes)
   B. At least 1 of the attacks has been followed by 1 month or more of at least 1 of the following: persistent concern about additional attacks, worry about the implications of the attack, or a significant change in behavior related to the attacks
   C. Agoraphobia may be present or absent
   D. The panic attacks are not due to the direct psychological effects of a substance (alcohol, drugs of abuse, or meds) or a general medical condition
   E. The panic attacks are not better accounted for by another mental disorder

III. TREATMENT
   • Before initiating treatment, discuss previous therapies (psychotherapy or drugs) the patient may have encountered, and the results of the particular therapies
   • This condition may be chronic, so rapid resolution of symptoms may not occur
   A. Benzodiazepines: Used most often in the acute setting of panic disorder especially when symptoms are severely disabling. Long-term use of this class of drugs is not recommended due to the risks of abuse and/or dependence. Side effects: Drowsiness, ataxia, dizziness, cognitive impairment, hypotension
   B. Selective serotonin reuptake inhibitors (SSRIs): All generally started at ½ antidepressant dose
   1. **Sertraline (Zoloft):** Begin 25mg PO QAM × 1–2 weeks, then increase to 50mg QD
   2. **Paroxetine (Paxil):** Begin 10mg PO QD 1 week, then increase to 20mg QD
   3. **Fluoxetine (Prozac):** Begin 10mg PO QAM and gradually increase to 40mg QD
   4. **Citalopram (Celexa):** Begin 10mg PO QAM and gradually increase to 40mg QD
   C. Psychotherapy: Cognitive-behavioral therapy, cognitive therapy, or group therapy are some nonpharmacologic options for treating panic disorder
   D. Behavioral: Avoidance of places where attacks might occur or if this cannot be done, then brief exposure initially with increases over time. Avoidance should slowly be confronted. Continued avoidance could result in serious disability and increased anticipatory anxiety

PSY

CLINICAL PEARLS
- Separation anxiety disorder in childhood may predispose to panic disorder later in life
- Patients with panic disorder and other anxiety disorders are at increased risk for drug abuse, especially alcohol and anxiolytics
- Depression screening is helpful to reduce the high risk of co-morbidity with anxiety. Treatment of depression can help to reduce anxiety

References
Saeed SA, Bruce TJ. Panic disorder: effective treatment options. Am Fam Phys 1998; 57:2405–12.
Walley EJ, et al. Management of common anxiety disorders. Am Fam Phys 1994;50:1745–53.
American Psychiatric Association. Diagnostic and statistical manual of mental disorders (DSM-IV). 4th ed. Washington, D.C.: American Psychiatric Association, 1994.
Roy-Byrne, et al. Psychopharmacologic treatment of panic, generalized anxiety disorder, and social phobia. Psych Clin N Am 1993;16(4):719–33.

Michael B. Weinstock, MD
Peter P. Zafirides, MD
Daniel M. Neides, MD
Mary S. DiOrio, MD
Christine Costanzo, MD
Budd Ferrante, EdD

103. DEPRESSION & DYSTHYMIA

I. INTRODUCTION
A. Over 1 in 10 outpatients have major depression, but most are not recognized or not appropriately treated
B. Proven therapies (pharmacologic and psychotherapeutic) are available with 50–60% responding to any individual antidepressants and 80% responding to at least 1 medication
C. ⅓ of patients will have another episode within 1 year of stopping treatment and ½ will have another episode in their lifetimes

II. EPIDEMIOLOGY
A. Depression
1. 5% of the US population is affected by depression at any one time
2. 17–30% of the US population is affected in a lifetime
3. Female to male ratio is 2–3:1
4. Increased risk of developing depression for first degree relatives
B. Dysthymia
1. Lifetime prevalence is 6%
2. In children, occurs equally in both sexes
3. In adults, women are 2–3 times more likely to develop or to report
C. Screening
1. There are many validated short-screening questions
2. The following "2 question case finding instrument" has a 96% sensitivity, and a 57% specificity. If answers to either of the questions is positive, then proceed to establish diagnosis according to full DSM-IV criteria listed below
   (1) During the past month, have you often been bothered by feeling down, depressed, or hopeless?
   (2) During the past month, have you often been bothered by having little interest or pleasure in doing things?

III. DIAGNOSIS
A. DSM-IV Criteria for Major Depression
1. At least 5 of the following symptoms have been present during the same 2 week period and represent a change from previous functioning; at least 1 of the symptoms is depressed mood or loss of interest or pleasure

PSY

    a. Depressed mood most of the day

    b. Diminished interest or pleasure in all, or almost all, activities most of the day

    c. Significant weight loss or weight gain or a decrease or increase in appetite

    d. Insomnia or hypersomnia

    e. Psychomotor agitation or retardation

    f. Fatigue or loss of energy

    g. Feelings of worthlessness or excessive or inappropriate guilt

    h. Diminished ability to think or concentrate

    i. Recurrent thoughts of death, recurrent suicidal ideation without a specific plan, or a suicide attempt or a specific plan for committing suicide

2. The symptoms cause clinically significant distress or impairment in social, occupational, or other important areas of functioning
3. The symptoms are not due to the direct physiological effects of a substance (drug of abuse or prescribed medication) or a general medical condition
4. The symptoms are not better accounted for by bereavement

B. A mnemonic for symptoms of Major Depression is: **SIG E CAPS**:

    S   Sleep (insomnia or hypersomnia)

    I   Interest (loss of interest)

    G   Guilt

    E   Energy (feeling of fatigue)

    C   Concentration (inability to concentrate)

    A   Appetite (increased or decreased)

    P   Psychomotor (agitation or retardation)

    S   Suicidality (ideation, plan)

C. DSM-IV Criteria for Dysthymia

1. Depressed mood for most of the day, for more days than not, as indicated either by subjective account or observation by others, for at least 2 years. Note: In children and adolescents, mood can be irritable and duration must be at least 1 year
2. Presence while depressed of 2 or more of the following:

    a. Poor appetite or overeating

    b. Insomnia or hypersomnia

    c. Low energy or fatigue

    d. Low self-esteem

    e. Poor concentration or difficulty making decisions

    f. Feelings of hopelessness

3. During the 2-year period (1 year for children or adolescents) of the disturbance, the person has never been without the symptoms in Criteria 1 and 2 for more than 2 months at a time
4. No Major Depressive Episode has been present during the first 2 years of the disturbance (1 year for children and adolescents); i.e., the disturbance is not better accounted for by chronic Major Depressive Disorder or Major Depressive Disorder in partial remission
5. There has never been a Manic Episode, a Mixed Episode, or a Hypomanic Episode, and criteria have never been met for Cyclothymic Disorder
6. The disturbance does not occur exclusively during the course of a chronic Psychotic Disorder, such as Schizophrenia or Delusional Disorder
7. The symptoms are not due to the direct physiological effects of a substance (e.g., a drug of abuse, a medication) or a general medical condition (e.g., hypothyroidism)
8. The symptoms cause clinically significant distress or impairment in social, occupational, or other important areas of functioning

IV. MEDICAL CAUSES OF DEPRESSION

    A. Endocrine: Hypo- or hyperthyroidism, hyperparathyroidism, Cushing's disease, diabetes, Addison's disease, or menopause

    B. Infectious: AIDS, tertiary syphilis, tuberculosis, mononucleosis, or hepatitis

PSY

    C. **Inflammatory:** Systemic lupus erythematosus (SLE), rheumatoid arthritis and other connective tissue diseases

    D. **Neurologic:** Multiple sclerosis (MS), Parkinson's disease, complex partial seizures, CNS tumors, dementia, or stroke

    E. **Nutritional:** Vitamin deficiencies (B_{12}, folate, niacin, thiamine, or C)

    F. **Pharmacologic:** ß-blockers, corticosteroids, contraceptives, Cimetidine (Tagamet), Phenothiazines, α-methyldopa, or anticholinesterases

V. MANAGEMENT—General considerations

    A. **Antidepressant meds and structured psychotherapy** are both effective treatments and may be combined if not effective alone

    B. **Patients with dysthymia** may also respond to antidepressant therapy

    C. **Bereavement may lead to major depression** and patient with depressive symptoms persisting more than 2 months should be offered therapy

    D. **Other psychiatric disorders** such as anxiety, mania, psychosis, and substance use may co-exist with major depression

    E. **Patients should be assessed for suicidal tendencies** by asking: "Do you ever think of hurting yourself or taking your own life?" If the answer is yes, then ask: "Do you currently have a plan?" If the answer is yes, then ask "What is your plan?"

    F. **Risk factors for suicide** include age > 65, male, white or Native American, single, divorced, separated or widowed, unemployed, history of psychiatric admission, family or personal history of suicide attempt, drug or alcohol use, recent severely stressful life event, panic attacks or severe anxiety, severe physical illness, severe hopelessness or anhedonia, specific plan, access to firearms or other lethal means

    G. **Choice of antidepressant meds:** (See tables below). No specific meds have been proven most effective for major depression, but certain meds will also work for co-existing conditions (panic, obsessive-compulsive, pain) and some have more side effects than others. Selective serotonin reuptake inhibitors (SSRIs) have become widely prescribed secondary to their favorable side-effect profile.

    General considerations include:

      1. Select a med by taking into account side effects, interactions, treatment of co-existing conditions, and cost

      2. Start a med gradually and increase dose over 5–10 days

      3. Although the full therapeutic effect may not occur for 4–6 weeks, if there is no effect after 3–4 weeks, then increase dose

      4. Duration of therapy: Patients with 2 or more episodes of major depression lasting more than 2 years should continue meds for at least 2 years and possibly for life

      5. Failure to respond to a specific SSRI does not predict nonresponse to another SSRI. If stopping short-acting serotonergic meds (e.g., **Citalopram**, **Paroxetine**, **Sertraline**, or **Venlafaxine**) then gradually decrease dose to prevent a discontinuation syndrome which may include tinnitus, vertigo, or paresthesias

      6. Tricyclic antidepressants

        a. Avoid using in patients with ischemic heart disease or arrhythmias

        b. Obtain ECG before starting in patients > 50 and repeat ECG before increasing dose if first degree AV block or bundle branch block

      7. **Bupropion (Wellbutrin)** may increase the risk of seizures with daily dose exceeding 450mg or single doses > 200mg

      8. **Trazodone** may rarely cause priapism

      9. Discontinuing therapy: Meds should be slowly decreased over 2–3 months with monthly follow-up to telephone consultation. If depression recurs, then restart meds for additional 3–6 months

    H. **Follow-up:** At least 3 visits in the first 12 weeks to assess response, side effects, and adherence. Almost ½ of patients stop their meds in the first month

    I. **Other therapies**

      1. Exercise: A study of 156 patients (published in Arch Int Med in 1999—see References) compared 156 patients randomized to aerobic exercise, **Sertraline (Zoloft)**, or both (average age 50) and found at 16 weeks that there was no difference between the groups, though the groups receiving medication did show a faster

PSY

initial response. Conclusion: Exercise is a comparable antidepressant therapy to medication, though the initial response is not as rapid

2. Cognitive-behavioral therapy: Identifying any pessimistic or self-critical thoughts and decreasing behavior which causes depression
3. Problem-solving therapy: Identifying specific problems and taking steps to solve them
4. Interpersonal psychotherapy: Clarify/resolve interpersonal difficulties
5. Electroconvulsive therapy
   a. Useful for refractory depression
   b. Works well in the elderly population (especially when antidepressant side effects are not tolerated)

Selected Antidepressants for Use in Medical Outpatients*						
Category and Generic Name	Trade Name	Initial Dose†	Target Dose‡	Set-up Dose‡	Other Indications	Cost Per Month§
Serotonin - and norepinephrine-reuptake inhibitors						
Tricyclics (tertiary amines)						
Amitriptyline	Elavil, Endep	25 mg at bedtime	100 mg at bedtime	150 mg at bedtime	Chronic pain, delusions,¶ insomnia, migraine, postherpetic neuralgia	$8.43
Doxepin	Sinequan	25 mg at bedtime	100 mg at bedtime	150-200 mg at bedtime	Alcoholism,¶ insomnia, post-traumatic stress disorder	$11.85
Imipramine	Tofranil	25 mg at bedtime	100 mg at bedtime	150-200 mg at bedtime	Enuresis,¶ insomnia, panic disorder, post-traumatic stress disorder, obsessive-compulsive disorder	$42.24
Tricyclics (secondary amines)						
Desipramine	Norpramin	25 mg at bedtime	100 mg at bedtime	150-200 mg at bedtime	Attention-deficit disorder,¶ bulimia, diabetic neuropathy, postherpetic neuralgia	$32.98
Nortriptyline	Aventyl, Pamelor	25 mg at bedtime	50-75 mg at bedtime	100-150 mg at bedtime	Attention deficit disorder, chronic low back pain, irritable bowel syndrome, diabetic neuropathy	$45.88-$70.65
Bicyclic						
Venlafaxine	Effexor	37.5 mg twice daily	75 mg twice daily	100-150 mg twice daily	Anxiety disorder,¶ neuropathic pain, obsessive-compulsive disorder	$78.71
	Effexor XR	37.5 mg daily	75-150 mg daily	225 mg daily		$69.65-$75.86
Selective serotonin-reuptake inhibitors						
Citalopram	Celexa	20 mg daily	20 mg daily	40 mg daily	Obsessive-compulsive disorder, diabetic neuropathy, post-stroke depression,¶ panic disorder	$60.51
Fluoxetine	Prozac	20 mg every morning	20 mg every morning	40-60 mg every morning	Bulimia,¶ obsessive-compulsive disorder ¶	$67.36
Paroxetine	Paxil	20 mg daily	20 mg daily	50 mg daily	Obsessive-compulsive disorder,¶ panic disorder,¶ migraine, social phobia¶	$69.86
Sertraline	Zoloft	50 mg every morning	100 mg every morning	150-200 mg every morning	Obsessive-compulsive disorder, panic disorder,¶ post-traumatic stress disorder	$72.29

Chart continued on next page

PSY

Selected Antidepressants for Use in Medical Outpatients (continued)						
Category and Generic Name	Trade Name	Initial Dose†	Target Dose‡	Set-up Dose‡	Other Indications	Cost Per Month§
Serotonin antagonist						
Mirtazapine	Remeron	15 mg at bed-time	30 mg at bed-time	45 mg at bedtime	Anxiety, insomnia	$71.83
Norepinephrine and dopamine-reuptake inhibitor						
Bupropion	Wellbutrin	75 mg twice daily	150 mg twice daily	150 mg three times daily	Attention-deficit disorder, smoking cessation,¶ post-traumatic stress disorder	$96.11
	Wellbutrin SR	150 mg every morning	150 mg twice daily	200 mg twice daily		$91.64
Serotonin antagonists and reuptake inhibitors						
Nefazodone	Serzone	100 mg twice daily	150 mg twice daily	300 mg twice daily	Panic disorder, post-traumatic stress disorder	$74.11
Trazodone|	Desyrel	50 mg at bed-time	200 mg at bed-time	200 mg twice daily	Insomnia	$21.98

*The information provided in this table is intended only as a guide. Providers should refer to the package inserts or consult with a pharmacist for individual dosage recommendations, precautions, and drug interactions.
†The initial dose should be reduced in frail or elderly patients with hepatic or renal dysfunction.
‡The target dose is the dose likely to be effective for a typical patient. The set-up dose is the dose above which most patients would not derive additional benefit.[50]
§The average wholesale price in U.S. dollars for a 30-day supply of the target dose is given. Generic prices are used, when available. Data are from *2000 Drug Topics Red Book*.[51]
¶The drug is approved by the Food and Drug Administration for this indication.
| Trazodone is too sedating at therapeutic doses for depression; it is best used in lower doses (50-100 mg at bedtime) as adjunctive therapy for patients with insomnia.

Source: Whooley MA, Simon GE. Primary care: managing depression in medical outpatients. N Engl J Med 2000;343(26): 1946. Used with permission.

Frequency of Side Effects of Antidepressant Medications								
Medication	Sedation	Agitation	Anti-Cholinergic Effects†	Postural Hypoten-sion	Gastro-Intestinal Upset	Sexual Dysfunction	Weight Gain	Weight Loss
Serotonin-and norepinephrine-reuptake inhibitors								
Tricyclics (tertiary amines)								
Amitriptyline	++++	0	++++	+++	+	+	++	0
Doxepin	++++	0	++++	+++	+	+	+	0
Imipramine	+++	0	++++	+++	+	+	+	0
Tricyclics (secondary amines)								
Desipramine	+++	0	+++	++	+	+	+	0
Nortriptyline	+++	0	+++	++	+	+	+	0
Bicyclic								
Venlafaxine ‡	++	+	++	0	+++	++	0	+
Selective serotonin-reuptake inhibitors								
Citalopram	0	0	+	0	++	+	+	+
Fluoxetine	+	++	+	0	++	++	+	+
Paroxetine	++	0	+	0	++	++	+	+
Sertraline	+	+	+	0	++	++	+	+
Serotonin antagonist								
Mirtazapine	+++	0	++	+	0	0	++	0
Norepinephrine-and dopamine-reuptake inhibitor								
Bupropion	+	++	++	0	++	0	+	++
Serotonin antagonists and reuptake inhibitors								
Nefazodone	++	0	++	+	+	0	0	0
Trazodone	++++	0	++	+	+	0	+	+

*0 denotes none; +, minimal (<5 percent of patients); ++, low frequency (5-20 percent); +++, moderate frequency (21-40 percent); ++++, high frequency (>40 percent).
†Side effects may include dry mouth, dry eyes, blurred vision, constipation, urinary retention, tachycardia, or confusion.
‡Venlafaxine may cause a dose-related elevation in diastolic blood pressure; monitoring of blood pressure is recommended.

Source: Whooley MA, Simon GE. Primary care: managing depression in medical outpatients. N Engl J Med 2000;343(26): 1947. Used with permission.

CLINICAL PEARLS

- Differentiate between depression and bipolar disorder as therapies are different
- Indefinite antidepressant maintenance therapy may be necessary after a third episode of major depression
- Recurrence risk after the first, second, and third episodes of major depression is 50%, 70%, and 90% respectively

References

Olfson M, et al. National trends in the outpatient treatment of depression. JAMA 2002;287:203–9.

Kroenke K, et al. Similar effectiveness of paroxetine, fluoxetine, and sertraline in primary care: a randomized trial. JAMA 2001;286:2947–55.

Whooley MA, Simon GE. Primary care: managing depression in medical outpatients. N Engl J Med 2000;343:1942–50.

Son SE, Kirchner JT. Depression in childhood and adolescents. Am Fam Phys 2000;62:2297–308,2311–2.

Blumenthal JA, et al. Effects of exercise training on older patients with major depression. Arch Int Med 1999;159:2349.

Simon GE, et al. An international study of the relation between somatic symptoms and depression. N Engl J Med 1999;341:1329–35.

Anita Schwandt, MD
Daniel M. Neides, MD

104. SEXUAL DYSFUNCTION

— PART ONE: MALE —

I. INTRODUCTION

A. Definition: Consistent inability to achieve and/or maintain an erect penis which is adequate for satisfactory sexual performance

B. Affects 15–25% males > 65. About 80% of cases are secondary to organic disease. Affects 10–30 million men in US

C. May have negative impact on self esteem, relationships, and quality of life

II. DIFFERENTIAL DIAGNOSIS

A. Psychogenic: E.g., Performance anxiety, stress or relationship discord, anxiety/depression, etc.)

B. Organic

    1. Vasculogenic: Most common are arterial/inflow problems (e.g., DM, CAD, etc.)

    2. Neurogenic: E.g., Spinal cord injury, multiple sclerosis, herniated disc, etc.

    3. Hormonal: E.g., Hypogonadism, hyperprolactinemia, hypo/hyper-thyroidism

    4. Mechanical: Peyronie's disease, anatomic abnormalities

C. Iatrogenic

    1. Meds (see III. F. below)

    2. Environmental: E.g., Alcohol, cigarettes, drugs of abuse

III. HISTORY

A. Techniques to initiate discussion of sexual topics in a nonthreatening manner

    1. Consider asking: Many men (with diabetes, CHF, etc.) experience sexual problems. Has this happened to you?

    2. Are you currently sexually active? Do you or your partner have any sexual issues that you would like to discuss?

B. Distinguish loss of libido vs. loss of erections: If libido and erections are intact, the cause is usually psychogenic

C. Onset and duration of impotence: Gradual loss of erections over time suggests organic cause

D. Erections: Difficulty in obtaining or maintaining erections and presence of nocturnal erections. If normal erections do occur, then the cause is usually psychogenic

E. Past medical history: Diabetes mellitus, coronary artery disease, peripheral vascular disease, hypertension, hyperlipidemia, hypogonadism, multiple sclerosis, neurologic disease, thyroid disorders, renal failure, adrenal disorders

F. Medications

    1. Antihypertensives

        a. Diuretics: Thiazides, Spironolactone

        b. Sympatholytics: Methyldopa (Aldomet), Clonidine (Catapres), Reserpine, α-blockers

        c. β-blockers (especially non-selective β-blockers)

    2. Psychiatric meds: Tricyclics, SSRIs, MAOIs, anxiolytics (Benzodiazepines)

PSY

　　　　3. Antiandrogens: Digoxin, histamine H_2 receptor blockers
　　　　4. Others: Ketoconazole (Nizoral), Niacin, Phenobarbital, Phenytoin (Dilantin), anabolic steroids, corticosteroids, Finasteride (Proscar), Gemfibrozil (Lopid)
　　G. **Drugs:** Alcohol, nicotine, illicit drug use
　　H. **Past surgical history:** Pelvic surgery or spinal cord injury
　　I. **Social history:** Recent divorce, death of a spouse, new partner, marital/relationship discord, history of sexual abuse, increased stress (job change, move, death or illness in family, new baby, new diagnosis of concerning medical condition), substance, tobacco, or alcohol use

IV. PHYSICAL
　　A. **General:** Overt appearance/dress/speech may show signs of anxiety or depression
　　B. **Vascular disease:** Check blood pressure, auscultate vessels for bruits, signs of HTN or ischemic heart disease, lack of hair on legs may indicate peripheral vascular disease
　　C. **Secondary sexual characteristics:** Masculinization, beard, and body hair changes
　　D. **Neurological exam:** Peripheral sensory exam plus other (see rectal exam)
　　E. **Genital:** Penile scarring or plaque formation (Peyronie's disease), hypospadias, phimosis, hypogonadism, testicular abnormalities, tunics and erectile tissue
　　F. **Rectal**
　　　　1. Prostate exam (DRE)
　　　　2. Check rectal tone
　　　　3. Superficial anal reflex (to assess sacral cord function—perform by touching perianal skin and note contraction of external anal sphincter muscles
　　　　4. Bulbocavernosus reflex (to assess sacral cord function—perform by placing a finger in the rectum and then squeeze the glans penis and noting contraction of the anal sphincter and bulbocavernosus muscle)
　　G. **Consider psychological evaluation**—especially if younger male or psychogenic cause suspected

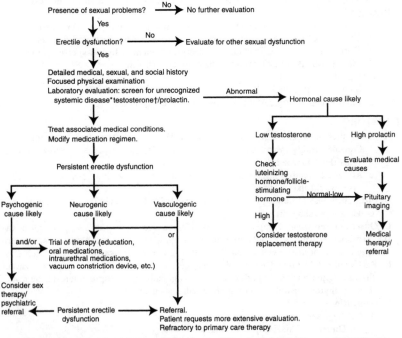

*Screening panel: complete blood count, urinalysis, renal function, lipid profile, fasting blood sugar, and thyroid function.
†First-morning, free testosterone level.

Source: Miller TA. Diagnostic evaluation of erectile dysfunction. Am Fam Phys 2000;61:95–104, 109–10. Used with permission.

PSY

V. LABORATORY AND DIAGNOSTIC TESTS (If necessary after history and physical exam):
See flow chart above

A. Labs: CBC, chemistry, glucose, $HgbA_{1C}$, lipid profile, PSA, testosterone, thyroid function tests, urinalysis

B. If testosterone is abnormal: Check FSH, LH, prolactin

C. Nocturnal penile tumescence testing: If erections are obtained, this suggests psychogenic etiology. Test is not necessary if the history indicates that patient has erections

D. Injection of vasoactive substance into penis: If results in erection, vascular cause is excluded; also done to determine therapeutic options

E. Color Doppler ultrasonography: If there is a suggestion of vascular disease

VI. TREATMENT OF ORGANIC IMPOTENCE (Listed in increasing order of invasiveness):
For treatment of psychogenic impotence, refer to other sources

A. Minimize meds with side effects of sexual dysfunction, or change to a different class of agents

B. Smoking cessation, alcohol in moderation, healthy diet, regular exercise

C. Sildenafil (Viagra)
   1. Dose: 50mg PO taken 30 minutes to 4hrs before sexual activity. May increase to 100mg if not effective. If > 65 or with hepatic or renal impairment, then start with 25mg
   2. Side effects: Headache (16%), flushing (10%), dyspepsia (7%), nasal congestion (4%)
   3. Interactions: Cytochrome P450 3A inhibitors: Erythromycin, Ketoconazole, Itraconazole, Cisapride. Contraindicated in patients on nitrates
   4. Trials: 21 randomized, double blind trials up to 6 months in duration with 3000 patients aged 19–89 showed improvement in 63% (25mg), 74% (50mg), and 82% (100mg) compared to 24% with placebo. Men with DM or radical prostrate surgery did not do as well
   5. Available: Tabs 25, 50, 100mg
   6. Cost: ~ $7 wholesale for all strengths

D. Testosterone supplementation: Use only for men who are hypogonadal and do not have prostate cancer after adequate evaluation. May speed up BPH in older men, follow-up every 6 months with DRE and PSA. Can be given intramuscularly or transdermal
   1. **Depo-Testosterone**: 200mg every 3 weeks of **Testosterone Cypionate**. Follow every 6 weeks with testosterone levels and liver function tests
   2. Transdermal patches include **Testoderm** or **Androderm** and should be changed daily; however absorption is erratic and higher risk of hepatotoxicity

E. Yohimbine
   1. α_2-adrenergic receptor antagonist
   2. Dose: 5.4mg PO TID
   3. Side effects mild and include agitation, anxiety, HA, increased urinary output, and GI upset

F. Urethral suppository
   1. **Muse (Alprostadil):** Supervise initial application
   2. Initially 125 or 250mcg suppository is inserted into urethra after urination. May adjust dose in stepwise increments on separate occasion. Maximum 2 suppositories/day

G. Vacuum constriction devices: Consist of a hollow cylinder placed over the penis, a vacuum is generated and a rubber ring is rolled onto the erect penis to the base to trap blood maintaining the erection. Often the choice of older men. Low cost but can be uncomfortable and may be associated with ecchymoses

H. Penile self-injection of vasoactive agents into corpora cavernosa, may use single agent or mixture, **Caverject (Alprostadil)**

I. Surgical options: Consider after less invasive treatments have failed
   1. Penile prosthesis: Either malleable or inflatable
   2. Vascular reconstruction

— PART TWO: FEMALE —

I. INTRODUCTION: Sexual dysfunction in women is common and should be brought up by the physician during the history. Estimated that 19–50% of women have at least occasional sexual dysfunction

II. DIFFERENTIAL DIAGNOSIS
A. Inhibited sexual desire

PSY

    B. Inhibited arousal
    C. Orgasmic dysfunction
    D. Pain with sexual intercourse: Dyspareunia/vaginismus

III. HISTORY

    A. **Family background:** Repressive background/upbringing
    B. **Onset and duration:** Primary vs. secondary
    C. **Relationship to stage of sexual intercourse:** Problems with lack of adequate lubrication, pain with deep thrusting (if this is causing the cervix to be moved it may indicate infection, pelvic mass, etc.)
    D. **Trauma:** Rape, abusive relationship, sexual abuse or incest (childhood or adult)
    E. **Sexual orientation**
    F. **Life changes in the past year:** Losses, pregnancy, stresses
    G. **Relationship with sexual partner(s):** New partner, marital/relationship discord, inexperience, inhibition
    H. **Menarche/menopause**
    I. **Pregnancy or post-partum**
    J. **Past medical history:** Chronic illness, sexually transmitted diseases, HIV/AIDS, cancer
    K. **Drugs:** Alcohol, nicotine, IV drugs
    L. **Meds**
      1. Psychoactive meds: E.g., BDZ, SSRIs, MAOIs, TCAs
      2. Cardiovascular and antihypertensives: E.g., β-blockers, Clonidine, Digoxin, Spironolactone, anti-lipids, Methyldopa (Aldomet)
      3. Hormonal preparations: Danazol, OCPs, GnRh agonists (Lupron, Synarel)
      4. Anticholinergics
      5. Antihistamines
      6. Others: Ketoconazole (Nizoral), Phenytoin (Dilantin), histamine H2 receptor blockers
    M. **Past surgical history:** Pelvic surgery (number and type) or spinal cord injury
    N. **Hormonal changes:** Postpartum, breast-feeding

IV. PHYSICAL

    A. **General:** Vital signs for HTN and signs of ischemic heart disease or other chronic medical condition
    B. **Genital:** Discharge, vulvar dystrophy, dermatitis, vaginismus, ulcerations (HSV)
    C. **Surgical changes:** Female circumcision, clitoral adhesions, episiotomy
    D. **Pelvic exam:** Adnexal tenderness and signs of endometriosis such as uterosacral nodularity and decreased pelvic organ mobility
    E. **Rectal exam:** Rectocele, infections/ulcerations, mass, blood/heme testing

PSY

V. MANAGEMENT: Treat secondary factors first and/or concurrently with the interventions listed below

    A. **Decreased libido:** See table below, C. 3.
      1. Estrogen replacement therapy if postmenopausal (or with surgical menopause)
      2. The short-term addition of androgens has been helpful in some women in restoring sexual desire
      3. If secondary to relationship or marital strife, address these problems or refer for therapy. Address other aspects (listed in history) including religious taboos, social restrictions, sexual identity conflicts, guilt, history of abuse, inexperience, stressors
      4. Consider altering or prolonging arousal phase, use of erotic materials, interventions to reduce anxiety
    B. **Orgasmic problems**
      1. Primary anorgasmia (never experienced orgasm in any situation)
        a. Causes: May be due to fear of pregnancy, satisfaction, losing control. Anxiety is often a factor
        b. Treatment
          i. Usually very successful
          ii. Extinguish the woman's subconscious over control and enhance sensory stimulation

  iii. Focus on erotic thoughts and fantasies. Consider "spectatoring" (observing oneself from a third-party perspective)

  iv. Self-stimulation or prolonged stimulation with partner (up to 1hr). Consider use of a vibrator

  v. Heighten arousal and lubrication before penetration

 2. Secondary anorgasmia

  a. In-depth exploration of differences in life situation now and in the past (when she was able to obtain an orgasm)

  b. Use the above techniques

C. Dyspareunia

 1. Superficial: Occurs with attempted penetration. May be due to irritative conditions such as infections/dermatitis or to vaginismus

  a. Vaginismus is painful reflex spasm of the perivaginal muscles due to fear of sex (young and inexperienced, often from strict homes) or prior rape or incest

  b. May be complete (occurs whenever there is penetration) or situational

  c. Gradual muscle relaxation and vaginal dilation. Have patient alternatively relax and contract pelvic muscles. Vaginal dilation may be with patient's finger, partner's finger, or commercial dilator (may use tampon). Success rates close to 90%

  d. Psychotherapy

 2. Vaginal: Pain related to friction and often secondary to irritation from inadequate vaginal lubrication (may be physiologic or from decreased arousal)

  a. Consider trial of prolonged arousal phase

  b. Lubricants such as K-Y jelly, Lubrin, Replens

  c. Vaginal creams containing estrogen can reverse vaginal atrophy in peri-menopausal women

  d. Low dose oral contraceptive therapy or hormone replacement therapy can alleviate vaginal dryness

 3. Deep: Pain related to thrusting, often from pelvic disease

  a. Endometriosis

  b. Ovarian cysts/mass

  c. May require further work-up

Basic Treatment Strategies for Female Sexual Dysfunction
Provided education
Provide information and education (e.g., about normal anatomy, sexual function, normal changes of aging, pregnancy, menopause). Provide booklets, encourage reading; discuss sexual issues when a medical condition is diagnosed, a new medication is started, and during pre- and postoperative periods; give permission for sexual experimentation.
Enhance stimulation and eliminate routine
Encourage use of erotic materials (videos, books); suggest masturbation to maximize familiarity with pleasurable sensations; encourage communication during sexual activity; recommend use of vibrators*; discuss varying positions, times of day or places; suggest making a "date" for sexual activity.
Provide distraction techniques**
Encourage erotic or nonerotic fantasy; recommend pelvic muscle contraction and relaxation (similar to Kegel exercise) exercises with intercourse; recommend use of background music, videos or television.
Encourage noncoital behaviors***
Recommend sensual massage, sensate-focus exercises (sensual massage with no involvement of sexual areas, where one partner provides the massage and the receiving partner provides feedback as to what feels good; aimed to promote comfort and communication between partners); oral or noncoital stimulation, with or without orgasm.
Minimize dyspareunia
Superficial: female astride for control of penetration, topical lidocaine, warm baths before intercourse, biofeedback. Vaginal: same as for superficial dyspareunia but with the addition of lubricants. Deep: position changes so that force is away from pain and deep thrusts are minimized, nonsteroidal anti-inflammatory drugs before intercourse.

NOTE: For a review, see Striar S, Bartlik B. Stimulation of the libido: the use of erotica in sex therapy. Psych Annals 1999;29:60-2.

*—Provide information for obtaining one discreetly.

**—Helpful in eliminating anxiety, increasing relaxation and diminishing spectatoring.

***—Also helpful if partner has erectile dysfunction.

Source: Philips NA. Female sexual dysfunction: evaluation and treatment. Am Fam Phys 2000;62:127–36, 141–2. Used with permission.

PSY

CLINICAL PEARLS
- Premature ejaculation is usually psychogenic (performance anxiety)
- 40% of men in their 40's report occasional difficulty in obtaining or maintaining an erection, this number rises to 70% at 70
- At 60, men have an average of 1 erection per week
- Most patients feel that sexual function is an appropriate topic to be addressed by their primary care providers
- 8–10% of adult women in the US have never had an orgasm. 10% achieve orgasm with fantasy alone

References

Heim LJ. Evaluation and differential diagnosis of dyspareunia. Am Fam Phys 2001:63:1535–44,1551–2.

Miller TA. Diagnostic evaluation of erectile dysfunction. Am Fam Phys 2000;61:95–104,109–10.

Phillips NA. Female sexual dysfunction: Evaluation and treatment. Am Fam Phys 2000;62:127–36,141–2.

American College of Obstetricians and Gynecologists. Sexual dysfunction. Technical bulletin no. 211. Washington, DC: ACOG,1995.

DeBusk R, et al. Management of sexual dysfunction in patients with cardiovascular disease: Recommendations of the Princeton Consensus Panel. Am J Cardiol 2000;86:175–81.

Goldstein I, et al. Oral sildenafil in the treatment of erectile dysfunction. N Engl J Med 1998;338:13.

NIH Consensus Conference: Impotence. JAMA 1993;270:83.

Douglas Knutson, MD
Michael B. Weinstock, MD
Daniel M. Neides, MD

105. ALCOHOL & OTHER DRUGS OF ABUSE

I. GENERAL
- **A.** 10% of Americans are affected by alcohol at some time in their lives
- **B.** Drug dependence costs the US about $67 billion/yr and alcoholism costs $166 billion/yr
- **C.** About 100,000 Americans die each year because of alcohol-related causes (including traffic accidents and cirrhosis)
- **D.** Concomitant medical disorders are high among substance abuse patients and include HTN, CAD, chronic liver disease, hepatitis C, depression, and anxiety

II. ALCOHOL
- **A. Definitions**
    1. **Abuse:** A pathological pattern of use involving social, occupational, or functional impairment
    2. **Dependence:** Abuse plus evidence of tolerance
- **B. Screening**
    1. Eliciting an alcohol and drug history
        - a. Ask patients: "Have you ever had a health, legal, or personal problem as a result of alcohol or drugs?" and "When was your last drink or use of drugs?"
        - b. Answering "yes" to the first question and "within the last 24 hours" to the second question is almost 95% sensitive for diagnosing alcoholism
        - c. Asking a patient "How much do you drink?" or "Do you use drugs?" often results in dishonest answers
    2. CAGE Questions: 2 out of 4 positive answers to the CAGE questions is also fairly sensitive and specific for alcoholism
        - a. Have you ever tried to **C**ut down?
        - b. Do you get **A**nnoyed when people question your drinking?
        - c. Do you feel **G**uilty about drinking?
        - d. Have you ever needed an **E**ye opener?
    3. Other: Inconsistent mild hypertension, insomnia or anxiety, unexplained hepatitis or

PSY

cirrhosis, pancreatitis without stones

C. Laboratory abnormalities in patients with alcoholism
1. Elevated GGT (> 35 units)
2. High or high-normal MCV (> 95)
3. AST/ALT >2 (suggests alcohol-induced liver disease)
4. Serum uric acid > 7mg/dL
5. Serum triglycerides > 180mg/dL

D. Signs and symptoms of withdrawal: Symptoms begin 5–10hrs after the last drink and peak at 2–3 days; usually improve by 4–5 days
1. Withdrawal: Tremor; increased pulse; blood pressure, or temperature; insomnia, or anxiety
2. Delirium tremens (DTs): Can occur in 5% of alcoholic withdrawals. Entails confusion, hallucinations, delusions, and/or grand mal seizures

E. Alcohol withdrawal and outpatient detoxification
1. Mild or moderate symptoms may be managed with supportive care and monitoring
2. Severe symptoms may be managed as an outpatient with initial doses every 6hrs of **Diazepam (Valium)** 5–10mg, **Lorazepam (Ativan)** 1–2mg, **Oxazepam** 15–30mg, or **Chlordiazepoxide** 50mg

F. Meds for alcohol dependence
1. **Disulfiram (Antabuse)**
   a. Inhibits aldehyde dehydrogenase which leads to elevated acetaldehyde levels which causes nausea, flushing, and hypotension when alcohol is consumed
   b. Dose: 250mg PO QD (Available: 250, 500mg tabs)
   c. Outcome measures of oral administration show modest evidence for reduction in drinking frequencies without significantly enhancing abstinence rates. Data for implant is less supportive
   d. May cause hepatitis, monitor LFTs
2. **Naltrexone (ReVia, Depade)**
   a. Opioid antagonist
   b. Dose: 50mg PO QD
   c. Reduces relapse rates and frequency and quantity of drinking in alcohol-dependent individuals and may decrease craving. Positive effect on abstinence only when combined with supportive psychotherapy. Note: Recent large study in NEJM (see References) found no effect in men with chronic, severe alcohol dependence
3. **Acamprosate**
   a. Mechanism of action unknown
   b. Enhances abstinence and reduces drinking rates in alcoholism
   c. *Available in Europe but not yet in US*
4. Serotonergic agents (SSRIs, **Buspirone, Ondansetron**): Limited data but do not seem effective except to treat the anxiety and depression in alcoholics
5. **Lithium**: Not effective

G. Rehabilitation oriented treatment: At 1yr about 40–60% are continuously abstinent and an additional 15–30% have not resumed dependent use. Predictors of poor adherence include low socioeconomic status, co-morbid psychiatric conditions, and lack of support system

III. BENZODIAZEPINES

A. Signs and symptoms of withdrawal are similar to those of alcohol, but they can persist longer

B. Outpatient detoxification with a long acting benzodiazepine (**Diazepam** commonly used). Start with 50% of total daily dose and decrease over 7–14 days. If patient has been using for several years, may taper over 8–12 weeks

IV. OPIATES

A. Withdrawal: Called "Jonesing"; symptoms include HTN, nausea, sweating, abdominal cramping, diarrhea, insomnia, and pain

B. Medications for dependence

1. Opioid agonist—**Methadone** taper (Methadone detox clinic): Methadone is an alternative opiate used to avoid symptoms. Determine amount of opiate used by the addict and give equivalent Methadone:

   1mg **Methadone** = 3mg **Morphine** = 1mg **Heroin** = 20mg **Demerol**

   Most start with 10–25mg **Methadone** twice every day

   Wean 10–20% of original dosage every day

2. Opioid partial agonist—**Buprenorphine Hydrochloride (Subutex)**

   a. Administered sublingually and is active for 24–36hrs.

   b. Trials have shown reductions in opioid use comparable to Methadone, but with fewer withdrawal symptoms on discontinuation.

   c. May work well with Naltrexone

3. Opioid antagonist: **Naltrexone (ReVia, Depade)**

   a. Blocks actions of heroin for 48–72hrs through competitive binding. Produced 70% less opiate use and 50% less reincarceration when added to standard federal program

C. Meds for relief of symptoms

1. Abdominal cramping: **Dicyclomine (Bentyl)** 20mg PO QID PRN

2. Pain relief: **Ibuprofen** and/or **Acetaminophen**

3. Diarrhea: **Kaopectate** 30cc PO QID PRN

4. Insomnia: **Diphenhydramine (Benadryl)** 25–50mg PO QHS PRN

V. COCAINE

A. Has no withdrawal syndrome, but does have intense cravings

B. Desipramine 200mg PO QHS may decrease cravings in some cases (for 4–6 weeks)

CLINICAL PEARLS

- There are potent, well tolerated meds for nicotine, opioid, and alcohol dependence, but not for marijuana or stimulant dependence
- Denial is an integral part of alcohol or drug abuse—family denial may be as strong as patient denial
- For every abuser there is an enabler—*both* need rehabilitation

References

Krystal JH, et al. Naltrexone in the treatment of alcohol dependence. N Engl J Med 2001;345:1734.

Weisner C, et al. Integrating primary medical care with addiction treatment: a randomized controlled trial. JAMA 2001;286:1715.

Holder HD, et al. Effect of community-based interventions on high-risk drinking and alcohol-related injuries. JAMA 2000;284:2341.

Kranzler HR. Medications for alcohol dependence—new vistas. JAMA 2000;284:1016.

Fiellin DA, et al. Outpatient management of patients with alcohol problems. Ann Intern Med 2000;133:815-27.

Swift RM. Drug therapy for alcohol dependence. N Engl J Med 1999;340:1482-90.

PSY

XI. Care of the Geriatric Patient

106. Periodic Health Screening in the Elderly 357

107. Drugs to be Cautious of in the Elderly 358

108. Falls in the Elderly 362

109. Compression Fractures 364

110. Urinary Incontinence in the Elderly 365

111. Evaluation of Mental Status Changes 368

112. Addressing Code Status 372

GERI

Edward T. Bope, MD

106. PERIODIC HEALTH SCREENING IN THE ELDERLY

I. HISTORY: "Yearly physical" should be more comprehensive than the episodic visits. Updating the history is perhaps most important component. Little agreement on how often the "yearly physical" should occur but it should be at some routine to avoid chaotic and episodic care. During visit note:

    A. Medical and family history
    B. Dietary intake
    C. Tobacco, alcohol and drug use
    D. Mental status changes
    E. Review of systems
    F. Physical activity
    G. Functional status at home
    H. Mood (depression screening)
    I. New diagnoses, meds or hospitalizations since last visit

II. PHYSICAL EXAMINATION

    A. Height, weight, blood pressure
    B. Visual acuity and fundus exam
    C. Ear exam and hearing test
    D. Thyroid exam
    E. Heart, Lungs and abdomen
    F. Breast exam
    G. Pelvic if indicated (see below)
    H. Digital rectal exam
    I. Neurologic exam
    J. Skin exam

III. LABORATORY

    A. Prostate specific antigen (PSA): US Preventive Services Task Force (USPSTF) recommends not screening asymptomatic men but several major organizations including the American Cancer Society and the American Urological Association do recommend screening

    B. Cholesterol: USPSTF recommends every 5yrs until 65. Research is unclear after 65 (see Chapter 40, Hyperlipidemia)

    C. Thyroid: Consider this in women and in anyone on Lithium or Amiodarone (Cordarone)

    D. Glucose: Obtain in obese patients or those with family history of DM or personal history of gestational diabetes (see Chapter 34, for ADA recommendations on screening)

    E. HIV: High risk populations only

IV. OTHER TESTING

    A. Colorectal screening: USPSTF recommends screening at 50 with fecal occult blood testing (FOBT) and/or sigmoidoscopy at unspecified intervals. Others recommend FOBT annually and/or sigmoidoscopy every 5yrs

    B. Mammogram: USPSTF recommends every 1–2yrs starting at 50. Others recommend starting at 40. Benefits of screening after 69 are not known

    C. Pap smears: USPSTF recommends screening every 3yrs after becoming sexually active. Others recommend every 1–3yrs

    D. EKG: Not recommended in asymptomatic patients

Recommendations for Screening by Age																										
AGE	6	6	6	6	6	6	6	6	6	6	7	7	7	7	7	7	7	7	7	7	8	8	8	8	8	8
	0	1	2	3	4	5	6	7	8	9	0	1	2	3	4	5	6	7	8	9	0	1	2	3	4	5
Cholesterol	R					R					R					R					R					R
FOBT	R	R	R	R	R	R	R	R	R	R	R	R	R	R	R	R	R	R	R	R	R	R	R	R	R	R
Sigmoidoscopy	R					R					R					R					R					R
Mammogram	R	x	R	x	R	x	R	x	R	x	R	x	R	x	R	x	R	x	R	x	R	x	R	x	R	x
Pap	R	x	x	R	x	x	R	x	x	R	x	x	R	x	x	R	x	x	R	x	x	R	x	x	R	X
BP	R		R		R		R		R		R		R		R		R		R		R		R		R	
PSA	x	x	x	x	x	x	x	x	x	x	x	x	x	x	x	x	x	x	x	x	x	x	x	x	x	x

R = recommended, x = some organizations recommend this interval
FOBT= Fecal occult blood testing, BP=Blood pressure, PSA=Prostate specific antigen

GERI

V. PREVENTIVE CARE

A. **History and physical:** USPSTF recommends periodic screening but gives no frequency

B. **Obesity:** USPSTF recommends periodic screening but gives no frequency

C. **Glaucoma:** USPSTF gives no recommendation for or against screening for glaucoma by the family doctor

D. **Immunizations:** USPSTF recommends using the schedule recommended by the Advisory Committee on Immunization Practices (endorsed by the AAFP)—dT every 10yrs, Influenza vaccine yearly, pneumococcal vaccine once, hepatitis B for high risk patients

E. **Fall prevention** (see Chapter 108, Falls in the Elderly)

F. **Nutrition:** Diet should be balanced and contain fresh fruits and vegetables. Consider calcium and Vitamin D supplementation and daily Aspirin if indicated

G. **Mental health:** Be aware of the high incidence of dementia and of depression particularly in the widowed (see Chapter 103, Depression & Dysthymia)

CLINICAL PEARLS

- Tailor preventive program to needs and desires of patient. Present recommendations that have good evidence (USPSTF) and try to get patient to follow them
- Approximately 25% of men and 38% of women between 65–75 are overweight
- Annual incidence of falls in people in the community between 70–75 is 25–35%; 5–10% of all falls result in serious injury
- Cerebrovascular disease is third leading cause of death in the US
- Screening for lung cancer in asymptomatic patients is not recommended
- The American College of Physicians (ACP), the Canadian Task Force (CTF), and the USPSTF have all *recommended against* screening asymptomatic patients without risk factors with resting ECGs or exercise stress tests
- Consider chemoprophylaxis with Aspirin if > 40 with risk factors for MI

References

Agency for Health Care Policy and Research—Put prevention into practice—www.ahcpr.gov/clinic/ppix.htm

USPSTF Report—http://odphp.osophs.dhhs.gov/pubs/guidecps/tcpstoc.htm

USPSTF guidelines available at: http://www.ahrq.gov/clinic/prevnew.htm

2001 Recommendations for adults—www.milwaukeemedicalsociety.org/default.cfm?t=47

Cancer screening in elderly patients—A framework for individualized decision making. JAMA 2001;285(Np 71):2750–6.

Miriam M. Chan, PharmD

107. DRUGS TO BE CAUTIOUS OF IN THE ELDERLY

I. GERIATRIC DRUG USE ISSUES

A. Approximately 13% of the US population are persons 65 years and older but they consume about $1/3$ of all prescribed medications

B. Elderly use more meds than any other age group because they often have multiple diseases that require treatment

C. The average home-dwelling elderly uses 4.5 different prescription drugs at the same time, while nursing home resident receives an average of 7 drugs

D. Polypharmacy and age-related physiological changes contribute to the increased incidence of adverse drug events and noncompliance in the elderly population

E. Approximately 10–17% of acute geriatric medical admission is due to adverse drug reactions. Subtle but important side effects such as sedation or cognitive impairment resulting in falls may go unrecognized

F. Elderly patients experience a large proportion of adverse drug effects as a result of drug interactions

II. EFFECTS OF AGING ON PHARMACOTHERAPY

A. **Altered absorption:** Drug absorption may decrease as a result of low acid production (e.g., Ketoconazole). The significance of changes in the GI tract during aging is not clear

B. **Changes in drug distribution**

GERI

1. Elderly persons have more body fat, less total body water and lean body mass than younger adults. Therefore, lipid-soluble drugs (e.g., Diazepam) will have increased body store and hence prolonged effects. On the other hand, water-soluble drugs (e.g., Cimetidine and Lithium) and drugs bound to muscle (e.g., Digoxin) will have higher serum concentrations and hence increased toxicity

2. Serum albumin concentration often declines, especially in frail elderly. Drugs that are highly protein bound (e.g., Phenytoin, Warfarin) will have increased pharmacologic action because there will be more drug available in free (active) form

C. Drug clearance and aging

1. Hepatic metabolism of certain drugs may diminish with age. Drugs that undergo Phase I metabolism (e.g., Diazepam, Alprazolam) will have a prolonged activity

2. Renal elimination of drugs is affected as renal function declines by approximately 10% each decade after 40. Serum creatinine may overestimate renal function in the elderly because of decreased muscle mass. Creatinine clearance (CrCl) is a more useful measurement of renal function (see Chapter 118, Formulas, for estimation of CrCl). Drugs that depend on renal elimination (e.g., aminoglycosides, Digoxin, H_2 blockers) will require dosage adjustment according to CrCl

D. Pharmacodynamics: Older patients appear to be more sensitive to Benzodiazepines, Opiates, Warfarin, and agents with anticholinergic side effects. The apparent increase in receptor sensitivity can result in greater therapeutic effect as well as an increased potential for toxicity

III. RECOGNIZING AND PREVENTING ADVERSE DRUG REACTIONS

A. Adverse drug reactions may mimic the characteristics of disease states. Drug induced cognitive impairment may be mistaken for senile dementia. Drugs with strong anticholinergic properties can cause many somatic symptoms such as dry mouth, constipation, confusion, and urinary retention

B. The susceptibility of older persons to adverse drug reactions can be assessed by determining the risk associated with specific drugs. For example, a recent study examined a cohort of 8127 elderly, community-dwelling women and concluded that antidepressant use and narcotic use are associated with increased risks for fractures (Ensrud KE, et al. Arch Intern Med 2003;163:949–57)

C. Use the acronym **MASTER** developed by Garnett and Barr as a guide for rational drug therapy in the elderly:

Minimize number of drugs used and simplify medication schedules. Discontinue drug whenever possible

Alternatives should be considered. Avoid drugs that pose high risk to older persons. Select the most cost-effective alternative

Start low, go slow. Start at the lowest possible dosage and increase slowly

Titrate the dose according to response. Monitor plasma levels if applicable. Monitor patients for adverse reactions

Educate patients about their drug therapy and their potential side effects. Be aware of visual, hearing and memory impairment and adjust instruction accordingly. Encourage and routinely check for compliance

Review regularly patient's meds, including OTC products and home remedies. Assess for drug-disease and drug-drug interactions

IV. COMMONLY PRESCRIBED DRUGS REQUIRING SPECIAL CONSIDERATIONS

DRUGS	ADVERSE EFFECTS	SPECIAL CONSIDERATIONS
Antiarrhythmics: e.g. Lidocaine, Procainamide, Quinidine, Disopyramide (Norpace)	↑ half-life and thus ↑ frequency of adverse events. Avoid Disopyramide if possible because it also has potent negative inotropic and anticholinergic effects	Reduce dose and use with close monitoring. Procainamide and Disopyramide will need dosage adjustment according to CrCl
Antihypertensive, α-blockers: Doxazosin (Cardura), Prazosin (Minipress), Terazosin (Hytrin)	Postural hypotension especially during initial therapy. Other common adverse effects are dizziness, headache, syncope, and incontinence	Give low dose at bedtime and titrate slowly. Monitor orthostatic blood pressure. Doxazosin and Terazosin may improve the symptoms of BPH in elderly hypertensive men
Antihypertensive, centrally acting agents: Clonidine (Catapres), Guanabenz (Wytensin), Methyldopa (Aldomet)	Adverse CNS effects (i.e. fatigue, sedation, dry mouth). Rebound hypertension may occur with abrupt cessation of Clonidine	Prescribe with caution in the elderly. Use lowest possible dose and monitor carefully. Avoid Methyldopa because it may cause bradycardia or exacerbate depression in elderly

Chart continued on next page

GERI

DRUGS	ADVERSE EFFECTS	SPECIAL CONSIDERATIONS
Antimicrobials, renally excreted: e.g. Acyclovir, Aminoglycosides, most Cephalosporins, Fluconazole, Imipenem, Ofloxacin, Ticarcillin, TMP/SMX, Vancomycin	↓ clearance, ↑ serum concentration and ↑ toxicity	Adjust dose according to creatinine clearance. Measure serum concentration if possible
Antipsychotic agents (Typical)	All cause sedation, hypotension, anticholinergic and extrapyramidal symptoms. Tardive dyskinesia can develop even with short-term, low-dose use	Start with a low dose and titrate slowly. Close follow-up is important. Low-potency drugs (Chlorpromazine, Thioridazine) are very sedating, hypotensive and anticholinergic, but produce less extrapyramidal symptoms. High-potency drugs (Haloperidol) have more prominent extrapyramidal symptoms but are less anticholinergic, sedating and hypotensive
Barbiturates: e.g. Phenobarbital, Secobarbital	Are fat soluble and thus have prolonged duration. Are enzyme inducers and may cause drug interactions with other concomitant medications. Highly addictive	Use safer alternatives
Benzodiazepines (BDZ), long-acting: e.g. Chlordiazepoxide (Librium), Clonazepam (Klonopin), Diazepam (Valium), Flurazepam (Dalmane)	Are lipid soluble and have active metabolites. ↑ half-life, leading to excess CNS effects (e.g. confusion, oversedation, falls and fractures)	Evaluate the need for a BDZ. When it is used, select a short or intermediate acting agent. Start with lowest possible dose and limit use to short term. Monitor closely. Short-acting BDZ: Triazolam (Halcion). Intermediate-acting BDZ: Alprazolam (Xanax), Lorazepam (Ativan), Oxazepam (Serax), Temazepam (Restoril)
β-blockers	↑ CNS adverse reactions (e.g. depression, fatigue), especially with more lipophilic agents (e.g. Propranolol, Metoprolol). Worsening diseases that are common in elderly, such as asthma, diabetes and PVD. May mask symptoms of hypoglycemia	Avoid Propranolol, use only to control violent behaviors. Agents with less lipid solubility (e.g. Atenolol) have less CNS side effects. Cardioselective agents (e.g. Atenolol, Metoprolol) in small doses cause less bronchoconstriction and less disturbance of glucose and lipid metabolism. Agents with intrinsic sympathomimetic activity (e.g. Pindolol) produce less peripheral vasoconstriction
β-blockers, Ophthalmic: Timolol (Timoptic), Betaxolol (Betoptic), Carteolol (Ocupress), Levobunolol (Betagan), Metipranolol (OptiPranolol)	Systemic absorption may occur from topical administration and can cause exacerbations of asthma and bronchospasm, confusion and heart block	Be cautious when using in elderly person who has glaucoma and other concomitant illness
Digoxin	↑ toxicity caused by ↓ clearance and ↓ muscle mass. In addition, elderly are more sensitive to Digoxin. Toxicity may be subtle and can occur even at normal serum concentrations	Evaluate the need for Digoxin. Reduce both loading and maintenance doses (rarely > 0.125mg/d). Watch for drug interactions especially with antiarrhythmics and diuretics. Monitor closely with serum concentrations and signs of toxicity (e.g. GI upset, CNS disturbances, arrhythmias)
Diphenhydramine (Benadryl)	Confusion, falls and urinary retention	Commonly used as a hypnotic, but its strong anticholinergic effects make it undesirable for use in the elderly
GI antispasmodics	Highly anticholinergic and generally produce substantial toxic effects in the elderly. Doses that are tolerated by the elderly may not be effective.	Avoid long-term use of Dicyclomine (Bentyl), Hyoscyamine (Levsin), Propantheline (Pro-Banthine), Belladonna Alkaloids (Donnatal), Clidinium-Chlordiazepoxide (Librax)
H₂ blockers Note: OTC products are now available	Adverse CNS effects (e.g. confusion, psychosis, hallucinations), especially with Cimetidine. ↑ risk of drug interaction	Adjust dose according to creatinine clearance. Monitor closely for drug interactions. Cimetidine (Tagamet) inhibits the hepatic metabolism of drugs such as Benzodiazepines, Carbamazepine, Quinidine, Theophylline, Terfenadine, and Warfarin. Ranitidine (Zantac) has less drug interactions than Cimetidine
Meprobamate (Miltown, Equanil)	Highly addictive and sedating	Avoid Meprobamate. Use safer alternative
Muscle relaxants/ antispasmodic drugs	Anticholinergic side effects, sedation, and weakness. Doses that are tolerated by the elderly may not be effective	Whenever possible, avoid Methocarbamol (Robaxin), Carisoprodol (Soma), Oxybutynin (Ditropan), Chlorzoxazone (Paraflex), Metaxalone (Skelaxin), and Cyclobenzaprine (Flexeril)

GERI

Chart continued on next page

DRUGS	ADVERSE EFFECTS	SPECIAL CONSIDERATIONS
Narcotics	↑ sensitivity to analgesic effects, respiratory depression, and CNS effects (e.g. confusion, somnolence). ↑ incidence of nausea and constipation	Start with smaller doses or longer dosing interval. Use bowel stimulants (e.g. Pericolace) as soon as narcotic therapy. Avoid Meperidine (Demerol) and Propoxyphene (Darvon) because they have active metabolites which can accumulate in patients with decreased renal function and cause seizures. Avoid Pentazocine (Talwin) because it has more CNS effects and it is also a mixed agonist/antagonist
NSAIDs Note OTC drug use	↑ gastric ulceration and hemorrhage. ↑ renal toxicity. ↑ CNS effects (e.g. dizziness, confusion). ↑ risk of drug interactions. Avoid Indomethacin because it oftens causes confusion. Avoid Phenylbutazone because of its serious hematological side effects	Recognize high-risk patient for gastropathy and acute renal failure. Reduce dosage/duration of therapy if feasible. Monitor closely for adverse reactions, drug interactions and compliance. Administer prophylactic therapy when appropriate or use COX-2 agents
OTC cold remedies: Most contain decongestants (sympathomimetics) and/or antihistamines	Decongestants may effect blood pressure control. Antihistamines are sedating and can produce anticholinergic side effects	Limit use to short term. Be aware of the alcohol content in some of the products
SSRIs: Fluoxetine (Prozac), Paroxetine (Paxil), Sertraline (Zoloft), Citalopram (Celexa)	Agitation and insomnia, nausea and GI discomfort, headache and weight loss. ↑ risk of drug interaction	Give dose in the morning to avoid sleep interruption. Fluoxetine has a long half-life and active metabolites. Both Fluoxetine and Paroxetine are potent enzyme inhibitors and are more likely to cause drug interactions with other concomitant medications
Sulfonylureas	Prone to hypoglycemia. Because the elderly often have a blunted metabolic response, hypoglycemia is more subtle in presentation. Avoid Chlorpropamide (Diabinese) because it has a long half-life	Start with a low dose and increase slowly. Use a second generation agent, i.e. Glipizide (Glucotrol), Glyburide (DiaBeta, Glynase), Glimepiride (Amaryl). Glipizide is metabolized to inactive metabolites and is preferable for patients with decreased renal function
Theophylline	↓ clearance, ↑ serum concentrations and ↑ toxicity	Reduce dose and monitor serum concentration and signs of toxicity. Watch for drug-drug interactions
Thiazide diuretics	Susceptible to fluid and electrolyte disturbances (↓K+, ↓Na+, ↑ uric acid, volume depletion) and glucose intolerance	Use HCTZ at doses of 6.25 to 12.5mg/day. Higher doses have more side effects without any significant increase in efficacy
Tricyclic antidepressants (TCAs)	Susceptible to adverse effects including anticholinergic effects, cardiac toxicity, cognitive decline, orthostatic hypotension, and sedation. This is particularly problematic in the very old and the more frail elderly patients	Reduce dose and titrate slowly. Of the TCAs, Desipramine (Norpramin) and Nortriptyline (Pamelor) are preferred agents because they have lower rate of side effects. Avoid Amitriptyline (Elavil) and Imipramine (Tofranil) which are highly anti-cholinergic, Doxepin (Sinequan), which is very sedating, and Protriptyline (Vivactil) which has a long half-life
Trimethobenzamide (Tigan)	High extrapyramidal effects and low efficacy	Use safer alternative for antiemetic therapy
Warfarin	Enhanced activity and prolonged duration	Start with a low dose and increase slowly. Monitor frequently. Watch for drug-drug interactions. Be aware of increased risk of falls and head trauma in the elderly

GERI

References

Chutka DS, et al. Drug prescribing for elderly patients. Mayo Clin Proc 1995;70:685–93.

Willcox SM, et al. Inappropriate drug prescribing for the community dwelling elderly. JAMA 1994;272:292–6.

Chrischilles EA, et al. Self-reported adverse drug reactions and related resource use: a study of community-dwelling persons 65 older. Ann Intern Med 1992;117:634–40.

Beers MH, Ouslander JG. Risk factors in geriatric drug prescribing a practical guide to avoiding problems. Drugs 1989;37:105–12.

Michael B. Weinstock, MD
Jim Cassady, MD

108. Falls In The Elderly

I. BACKGROUND/EPIDEMIOLOGY: Note: Falls due to reasons other than syncope
  - **A.** Falls in the elderly are a common problem which can often be avoided by taking a careful history, performing a complete physical examination and searching for factors contributing to falls (meds, alcohol, dehydration, environmental factors)
  - **B.** Falls are leading cause of injury related visits to the ER and are primary etiology of accidental deaths in persons > 65
  - **C.** 33% of community based adults and 60% of nursing home residents fall each year. 20–30% of falls result in moderate to severe injuries that reduce mobility and independence and increase risk for premature death
  - **D.** Fractures account for 75% of serious injuries. Most common sites are wrist, hip and vertebrae with hip fractures as most severe. 25% of elderly persons with hip fractures die within 6 months. 95% of hip fractures are due to falls
  - **E.** > 50% of those who fall have multiple episodes. Women are 3 × as likely to be hospitalized for fall-related injuries
  - **F.** Falls can be markers for poor health and functional decline. They may be non-specific presenting sign of many acute illnesses (pneumonia, UTI, MI)

II. RISK FACTORS
  - **A. Demographic:** Older age, white race, homebound, living alone
  - **B. Historical**
    1. Use of cane or walker
    2. Previous falls
    3. Acute illness
    4. Chronic conditions, especially neuromuscular disorders, anemia, CHF, chronic weakness secondary to cancer, etc.
    5. Meds/substances: May contribute to falls including; alcohol, benzodiazepines, narcotics, barbiturates, TCAs, anti-hypertensives, cardiac meds, steroids, NSAIDs, anticholinergic meds, hypoglycemic meds, phenothiazines, and diuretics
    6. Other: Postprandial hypotension, insomnia, urinary urgency, pedal/peripheral edema (increase in weight of legs may make them difficult to lift)
    7. History: **CATASTROPHE** mnemonic
        - **C** Caregiver and housing
        - **A** Alcohol (including withdrawal)
        - **T** Treatment (meds including compliance)
        - **A** Affect (depression or lack of initiative)
        - **S** Syncope (any episodes of fainting)
        - **T** Teetering (dizziness)
        - **R** Recent illness
        - **O** Ocular problems
        - **P** Pain with mobility
        - **H** Hearing (necessary to avoid hazards)
        - **E** Environmental hazards
  - **C. Physical Deficits**
    1. Cognitive impairment/dementia/delirium
    2. Reduced vision, hearing, proprioception and vestibular function
    3. Difficulty rising from chair
    4. Postural instability
    5. Foot problems
    6. Pain (osteoarthritis)

GERI

7. **I HATE FALLING** mnemonic
   - **I**   Inflammation of joints (or joint deformity)
   - **H**   Hypotension (orthostatic BP changes)
   - **A**   Auditory and visual abnormalities
   - **T**   Tremor (Parkinson's disease or other causes of tremor)
   - **E**   Equilibrium (balance) problem
   - **F**   Foot problems
   - **A**   Arrhythmia, heart block or valvular disease
   - **L**   Leg length discrepancy
   - **L**   Lack of conditioning (generalized weakness)
   - **I**   Illness
   - **N**   Nutrition (poor, weight loss)
   - **G**   Gait disturbance

D. Environmental hazards: Most falls are in or around home
   1. Poor lighting (change 60 watt to 100 watt bulbs)
   2. Unsafe stairways
   3. Loose rugs and other tripping hazards
   4. No bathroom grab bars or nonskid bathtubs

III. INTERVENTIONS: Treat medical conditions, minimize offending meds, minimize and alter environmental hazards, and pursue strength and balance training

A. Postural hypotension
   1. Decrease dose or discontinue meds causing orthostatic hypotension
   2. Rehydration
   3. Pressure stockings
   4. Dorsiflexion exercises
   5. Behavioral recommendations (elevate head of bed, rise slowly)
   6. If indicated, **Fludrocortisone (Florinef)** 0.1mg PO BID-TID

B. Sedative-hypnotic use
   1. Education regarding appropriate use
   2. Taper and discontinue if possible
   3. Switch to shorter acting agents if discontinuation not possible
   4. Non-benzodiazepine treatment of sleep disorders

C. Polypharmacy
   1. Review meds frequently, assess for risks and benefits
   2. Try to reduce number/dosage of meds being taken
   3. Change meds to those less centrally acting, shortest duration of action, and have less effect on postural hypotension

D. Environmental hazards
   1. Home safety assessment to identify modifiable risk factors
   2. Improve lighting (reduce glare, shadows; install nightlights)
   3. Remove tripping hazards (loose rugs, uneven floor surfaces, clutter)
   4. Improve stairway safety (secure handrails, contrasting tape on steps, nonskid surface)
   5. Improve bathroom safety (grab bars, nonskid bathtub, raised toilet seat)
   6. If patient is confined to bed, make sure bedrails up at all times

E. Gait impairment
   1. Balance and gait training, strengthening exercises
   2. Appropriate footwear, treat foot disorders (calluses, bunions)
   3. Assistive devices (cane, walker)
   4. Check for vitamin deficiency and cervical spondylosis

F. Reduced muscle strength or joint range of motion—muscle strengthening exercises (resistance training)

G. Reduced vision or hearing or vestibular dysfunction
   1. Refraction, cataract extraction
   2. Hearing aids, cerumen removal
   3. ENT evaluation

H. Dementia
   1. Increased supervision
   2. Orientation cues

GERI

IV. PREVENTION
A. Strategies
1. Eliminate environmental hazards
2. Improve home supports
3. Provide opportunities for socialization and encouragement
4. Modify meds
5. Provide balance and strength training
6. Hip protectors
7. Protective flooring
8. Involve family
9. Provide follow-up

CLINICAL PEARLS
- Falls most often multifactorial with influence from declining sensory function, strength and balance combined with coexistent medical conditions, medication side effects, and environmental hazards
- Elderly patients on benzodiazepines have a 29 × increased risk of falling
- In elderly women with hip fractures, mortality is approximately 20% in the first year
- Confusion may be reason for fall or result of fall. Subdural hematoma is treatable and often overlooked sequelae of falling

References
Fuller GF. Falls in the elderly. Am Fam Phys 2000;61:2159–68.
Ray WA, et al. Benzodiazepines and the risk of falls in nursing home residents. J Am Geratr Soc 2000;48:682–5.
Stevens JA, Olson S. Reducing falls and resulting hip fractures among older women. MMWR 2000;49(RR02):1–12.
Mahoney JE. Immobility and falls. Clin Geriatr Med 1998;14:699–726.

Charles Levy, MD
Marc Duerden, MD
Michael B. Weinstock, MD
Phil Favia, MD

109. COMPRESSION FRACTURES

I. GENERAL: For information of evaluation of back pain and diagnosis and management of osteoporosis, see Chapter 88, Low Back Pain and Chapter 73, Osteoporosis

II. HISTORY
A. Patient typically complains of low thoracic pain which began suddenly following activity involving flexion of the thoracic spine (bending, lifting) or simply after coughing or laughing
B. High risk groups include thin, Caucasian, post-menopausal women. Other risk factors include smoking, chronic alcoholism, treatment with steroids, Vitamin D or calcium deficiency, osteoporosis, advanced age, anticonvulsant meds, renal or hepatic insufficiency, hyperthyroidism, hyperparathyroidism, and cancer
C. Red flags that may suggest increased risk of neoplasm include history of cancer, constitutional symptoms (fever, weight loss), pain that is not diminished by rest, and age > 50

III. PHYSICAL EXAMINATION
A. Exam is often normal
B. Examine for focal neurologic deficits (strength, sensation)
C. Observe posture and gait, height, and spine
D. Palpate for point tenderness over painful area
E. Symptoms suggestive of cauda equina syndrome, which requires urgent surgical consultation, include saddle anesthesia, recent onset of bladder or bowel dysfunction, and severe or progressive lower extremity weakness

GERI

IV. MANAGEMENT

A. Pain relief with analgesics and/or NSAIDs. Caution in elderly. Consider trying Acetaminophen initially

B. Calcitonin: 100 units SQ 3 ×/week or 200 IU intranasally (**Miacalcin**) QD

   1. Provides effective *analgesia* and inhibits osteoclastic activity
   2. Duration of therapy can be for the symptomatic course (4–6 weeks) or as long as 12–18 months to treat the underlying disease process

C. Heat (heating pad) and massage

D. Braces: May be helpful in selected populations, but in general back braces not shown to be helpful in back pain and may be harmful

E. Rehabilitation/maintenance of conditioning

   1. Begin with isometric exercises and advance to exercises involving active lumbothoracic extension (walking, swimming). Avoid exercises in flexion, as they increase the incidence of new compression fractures
   2. Physical and occupational therapy will strengthen thoracolumbar extensors and minimize flexion
   3. Assistive devices such as long-handled "reachers" and shoehorns can decrease risky postures and minimize flexion
   4. Gait training with a cane can improve stability and decrease the risk of hip fractures

V. PREVENTION: Focused on prevention of osteoporosis, see Chapter 73; Osteoporosis

CLINICAL PEARLS

- Declines in physical function and changes in appearance contribute to social isolation and loss of self-esteem, impairing quality of life
- As many as 40% of symptomatic vertebral fractures are initially misdiagnosed
- Chronic pain can develop when kyphosis causes strain on muscles and ligaments, often does not respond to analgesics, but may diminish with exercise

References

NIH Consensus Development Panel on Osteoporosis Prevention, Diagnosis, and Therapy. Osteoporosis prevention, diagnosis, and therapy. JAMA 2001;285:785.

Cadarette SM, et al, for the Canadian Multicentre Osteoporosis Study. Evaluation of decision rules for referring women for bone densitometry by dual-energy x-ray absorptiometry. JAMA 2001;286:57–63.

Weinstein L, Ullery B. Identification of at-risk women for osteoporosis screening. Am J Obstet Gynecol 2000;183:547–9.

Ernst E. Exercise for female osteoporosis. A systematic review of randomised clinical trials. Sports Med 1998;25:359–68.

John M. Bertman, MD
Jim Cassady, MD

GERI

110. Urinary Incontinence In The Elderly

I. BACKGROUND/EPIDEMIOLOGY

A. Urinary incontinence affects 10–35% of older adults and 50–70% of nursing home population. Twice as common in females as in males. Fewer than 50% of patients report incontinence to physician because of stigma and misconception

B. Physiology

   1. **Two muscle groups**
      a. Sphincter muscles (pelvic floor and bladder neck muscles plus bladder-urethral angle). Controlled by sympathetic (α-adrenergic) innervation
      b. Detrusor muscles are smooth muscles surrounding bladder. Controlled by parasympathetic (cholinergic) innervation
   2. **Innervation:** Voiding is a reflex—when bladder fills to certain stretch point, voiding occurs unless inhibited by higher function centers in cerebral cortex

a. α-adrenergic (sympathetic) to sphincter provides increased tone and continued continence
b. Cholinergic to detrusor muscles causes contraction (and voiding) and to sphincter causes relaxation (and voiding)

C. Pharmacology
1. Andrenergics (decongestants) cause persistent sphincter tone and retention
2. α-adrenergic blockers (**Prazosin, Terazosin, Cardura**) decrease sphincter tone
3. Anticholinergics (antihistamines, tricyclics, antipsychotics) prevent both detrusor contraction and sphincter relaxation and thereby cause urinary retention

II. CLASSIFICATION/DIAGNOSIS—Note: These disorders are often mixed (e.g., stress and urge incontinence)

A. Stress incontinence
1. Urinary leakage associated with increased abdominal pressure (sneezing, coughing, laughing), generally caused by poor anatomic support of bladder neck and urethra (urethral hypermobility)
2. Often associated with multiple childbirths or prior surgery as well as vaginal atrophy, history of local radiation, and α-adrenergic blocking meds (sphincter is innervated by sympathetic/α-adrenergic innervation

B. Urge incontinence (overactive bladder)
1. Urinary leakage associated with an abrupt desire to void that cannot be suppressed. Loss of urine in large volume. Have an "urge" to urinate that cannot be suppressed
2. Caused by detrusor muscle (muscles surrounding bladder) instability/irritability. When detrusor muscle begins to contract, it contracts all the way and empties bladder
3. May be secondary to UTI, stones, or bladder cancer, but most often idiopathic inability to suppress detrusor contractions

C. Overflow incontinence
1. Urine loss from overdistended bladder
2. Most often seen with bladder outlet obstruction (e.g., BPH) or poorly contractile bladder (anti-cholinergic meds, stool impaction, pelvic organ prolapse secondary to surgery, diabetic nephropathy, low spinal cord injury, MS)

D. Functional incontinence (transient)
1. Urinary leakage seen in patients with mental or physical impairments (dementia, DJD) that impede toileting
2. Anatomy and physiology often normal

III. TRANSIENT CAUSES OF INCONTINENCE (DIAPPERS MNEMONIC)
D   Delirium/confusion
I   Infection—urinary (symptomatic)
A   Atrophy (urethritis or vaginitis)
P   Pharmaceuticals
P   Psychological disorders, especially depression
E   Excessive urine output (CHF, hyperglycemia, diuretics)
R   Restricted mobility
S   Stool impaction

IV. HISTORY
A. Identify reversible and nonreversible causes (DM, stroke, lumbar disc disease, chronic lung disease, fecal impaction, UTI, NPH, pain, cognitive impairment, meds)
B. OB-GYN history: Gravity, parity, number of vaginal, instrument-assisted, and Cesarean deliveries; previous hysterectomy and/or vaginal or bladder surgery; pelvic radiation; trauma; estrogen status
C. Stooling history: Frequency, straining, fecal incontinence
D. Medication review

V. PHYSICAL EXAMINATION: Complete physical focusing on coexistent medical disorders
A. Mental status exam

GERI

  B. Mobility and dexterity
  C. Neuro: Herniated disc, tumor, MS, NPH, B_{12} deficiency
  D. Abdominal exam (distended bladder, mass)
  E. Rectal: Tone, prostate exam, mass, stool impaction
  F. Pelvic: Inflammation, infection, atrophy, cystocele, pelvic floor laxity (strain or cough induced prolapse), urethral hypermobility

VI. LABS/SPECIAL TESTS: Perform if dictated by history and physical
  A. Urinalysis with culture if indicated
  B. BUN, creatinine, glucose (consider electrolytes and calcium)
  C. Post void residual (PVR): Ultrasound or catheterization. PVR > 50mL or < 20% of amount voided is abnormal and may indicate overflow incontinence
  D. Urodynamics
  E. Incontinence diary of voids and incontinent episodes (include triggers and volume)

VII. MANAGEMENT

Urinary Incontinence - Diagnosis and Management*			
Pathophysiology	History	Testing	Management
Stress Urinary leakage from poor anatomic support/weak sphincter – α-adrenergic innervation	Loss of small volumes of urine with increasesd abdominal pressure (cough, sneeze, etc.)	Large PVR, palpable bladder, incontinence with Valsalva maneuver (with full bladder), atrophic urethritis/vaginitis	1. Pelvic floor Exercises – Kegel (see below) 2. α-adrenergic agonists a. Pseudoephedrine (Sudafed) 60 mg Q 6-8 hrs b. Imipramine (Tofranil) 10 - 25 mg QD to TID 3. Estrogens – oral or topical 4. Pessaries 5. Surgeries (tension-free vaginal tape has up to 86% 5 year cure rate)
Urge Detrusor muscle instability/hyperreactivity – cholinergic innervation	Intense urgency followed by incontinence, nocturnal wetting, may be triggered by running water	Normal (PVR)	1. Timed voiding bladder training 2. Bladder relaxants a. Oxybutynin (Ditropan) 2.5 - 5.0 mg TID or Ditropan XL 10 mg QD b. Tolterodine (Detrol) 2 mg BID (or Detrol LA 4 mg QD) c. Flavoxate (Urispas) 100 - 200 mg TID-QID d. Imipramine (Tofranil) 10 - 25 mg QD to TID 3. Estrogen replacement therapy (Oral or topical) 4. Biofeedback
Overflow Urine loss from overdistended bladder – often from outlet obstruction or poorly contractile bladder	Frequent leaking of small amounts, dribbling, urgency, (prostatism), nocturnal wetting	Large PVR, palpable bladder, cystocele, enlarged prostate, neuropathy (diabetes, injury), fecal impaction, hydronephrosis	1. Remove obstruction – Eliminate offending agents (medications), medical management of obstruction if possible (BPH), or surgical correction 2. Timed voiding (every 4-6 hours) 3. Intermittent or chronic catheterization
Functional Urinary leakage in patients with mental or physical impairments	Functionally impaired patient (demented, sedated, arthritic, CVA, bed-ridden, restrained, acutely ill)	Impaired mobility	Improve environment (bedside commode, voiding reminder, easy access to bathroom or commode) Diapers, catheters

*Mixed types are common, various permutations are acceptable

  A. Timed-voiding bladder training schedule (patient instructions)
    1. Void every 2hrs while awake and every 2–4hrs during the night (individualize)
    2. Increase voiding schedule by 30 minutes each week until reasonable (Q4hr void)
    3. Even if patient feels need to void, have him or her make every effort to wait until scheduled time before voiding
    4. Have patient make every effort to void on schedule, even if there is no urge to void at that time
  B. Pelvic floor strengthening exercises (Kegel), (patient instructions)
    1. Identify pelvic floor muscles by practicing voiding teaspoon-like amounts. The muscles used to start and stop flow are the pelvic floor muscles
    2. 5 times a day (or with each void), practice contracting and holding these muscles tight for 5 seconds, 10 repetitions (total of 50 repetitions per day)
    3. Regular daily repetitions (weeks to months) are necessary for this technique to work
    4. Up to 38% of motivated patients cured after 3 months
  C. Additional patient information
    1. *Understanding Incontinence—A Patient's Guide* (AHCPR #96-0684) from US Public Health Service, Agency for Health Care Research Clearing House: Call (800) 358-9295
    2. National Association for Continence Resource Guide and Newsletter: 800-BLADDER; 864-579-7900; www.nafc.org

GERI

D. When to refer
1. Elevated PVR (>150–200) may indicate a significant underlying obstruction and further evaluation is warranted
2. Hematuria (gross or microscopic) needs to be evaluated for neoplasms or stones
3. If surgical intervention is likely (suspicion of prostate cancer, high grade cystocele, severe stress incontinence)
4. Unclear diagnosis or unsuccessful management

CLINICAL PEARLS
- Surgical correction should be considered in cases where obstruction is causing urinary retention with overflow, when lower urinary tract pathology (bladder stone or tumor) is contributing, and in women with stress urinary incontinence who have not benefited from pharmacologic or behavioral therapy
- Urge incontinence is the most common type of incontinence in the elderly, accounting for up to 70% of cases
- Many of the meds used to treat incontinence in elderly have potential adverse effects. Start low and titrate upward. Evaluate for adverse effects at each visit

References

Appell RA, et al. Prospective randomized controlled trial of extended-release oxybutynin chloride and tolterodine tartrate in the treatment of overactive bladder: results of the OBJECT study. Mayo Clin Proc 2001;76:358–63.

Schneider D, et al. Urinary incontinence in an elderly woman. Hosp Phys 2001;37:52–61,70.

Vapnek JM. Urinary incontinence: Screening and treatment of urinary dysfunction. Geriatrics 2001;56:25–9.

Culligan PJ, Heit M. Urinary incontinence in women: Evaluation and management. Am Fam Phys 2000;62:2433–44, 2447, 2452.

Bo K, et al. Single blind, randomized controlled trial of pelvic floor exercises, electrical stimulation, vaginal cones, and no treatment in management of genuine stress incontinence in women. BMJ Feb 20, 1999;318:487–93.

Michael B. Weinstock, MD
Edward T. Bope, MD
Jim Cassady, MD

111. Evaluation Of Mental Status Changes

I. DEFINITION
- **A. Delirium:** A disturbance of consciousness marked by agitation and confusion, possibly with hallucinations and delusions. Hallmark is fluctuating character and reversibility. Duration acute to subacute onset lasting hours to weeks
- **B. Dementia:** Organic loss of cognitive function demonstrated by memory loss and deterioration in several other cognitive domains including judgment, insight, executive functioning, language, communication, and visuospatial skills. Hallmark is chronic, progressive course often largely irreversible in nature. Onset is gradual with duration of months to years

II. GENERAL
- **A.** The most common causes of dementia are Alzheimer's disease (AD) (75%) and vascular injury (15%). Combination of the 2 may also occur (mixed dementia)
- **B.** Approximately 10% of people > 65 have AD; prevalence doubles every 5yrs after 60 and reaches nearly 50% in people over 85. Currently 4 million people in US have dementia; will more than double by 2030 as population ages
- **C.** Average time from diagnosis to death is 10yrs
- **D.** Marked changes in memory are not part of normal aging; patients may try to hide or minimize deficits
- **E.** Early intervention can slow the deterioration of cognitive function and the development of behavior problems, maintaining function for a longer period and delaying admission to a nursing home

GERI

III. RISK FACTORS

A. Advancing age
B. Family history
C. Down Syndrome (presents at earlier age)
D. Previous head trauma
E. Vascular disease risk factors (smoking, HTN, CVA, TIA, hyperlipidemia, DM, known CAD)
F. CABG (high prevalence and persistence of cognitive decline after CABG)
G. Genetic factors (APO-E4 allele on chromosome 19 associated with increased risk for late onset AD)
H. Mild cognitive impairment: Clinical state of individuals with memory impairment but who are otherwise functioning well and do not meet clinical criteria for dementia (progress to AD at 10–15% /yr compared to 1–2% /yr in cognitively normal elderly persons)
I. Possible negative risk factors include post-menopausal estrogen replacement, Vitamin E therapy, long-term anti-inflammatory medication, and statin therapy

IV. DIFFERENTIAL DIAGNOSIS OF DELIRIUM

A. **Drugs:** Anticholinergics, narcotics and benzodiazepines, H_2 receptor blockers, β-blockers, steroids and NSAIDs, ethanol (intoxication or withdrawal), Digoxin, Phenytoin
B. **Fluids and electrolytes:** Sodium, calcium or magnesium disorders, hyper/hypovolemia
C. **CNS:** Alzheimer's disease, CVA/Multi-infarct dementia, subdural/epidural hematoma/subarachnoid hemorrhage, hypertension, seizure, unmasked dementia
D. **Infectious:** HIV/AIDS dementia, syphilis, meningitis/encephalitis/brain abscess, Lyme disease, measles (subacute sclerosing panencephalitis). Note: In the elderly almost any infection (pneumonia, urosepsis, sepsis, etc.) can cause acute reversible mental status changes
E. **Metabolic:** Renal or hepatic failure, anemia, hyper/hypoglycemia, Wernicke's encephalopathy, hypoxemia/hypercapnia
F. **Endocrine:** Thyroid disorders, adrenal dysfunction
G. **Psychiatric:** Depression, psychosis, mania
H. **Miscellaneous:** Vitamin deficiency (B_{12}, folate, thiamine), hypo/hyperthermia, myocardial infarction, pulmonary embolus, change in environment, sundowner's, pain, sleep loss, depression

V. HISTORY

A. Obtain from patient and 1 or more family members
B. Evaluate for progressive decline in memory, decrease in ability to perform activities of daily living, personality changes, behavior problems, sleep history
C. Symptoms and mode of onset (abrupt vs. gradual), duration and progression (discrete, stepped events characteristic of vascular dementia vs. continuous decline characteristic of AD), and worsening vs. improving vs. fluctuating symptoms
D. Meds (prescription and OTC), alcohol use, drugs of abuse, dietary habits
E. Previous head trauma (causing loss of consciousness)
F. Psychiatric history and suicidal symptoms
G. Family history (e.g., Alzheimer's disease, Huntington's disease)
H. Non-Alzheimer causes of mental status changes including infectious, metabolic, mass, NPH, vascular—see IV. above

VI. PHYSICAL

A. General: Temperature and vital signs
B. Ophthalmologic exam for papilledema, meiotic pupils, Kayser-Fleischer rings
C. Neck: Carotid bruits, JVD, nuchal rigidity
D. Pulmonary: Rales, rhonchi, wheezing, decreased breath sounds
E. Cardiovascular: Murmur, irregularly irregular rhythm
F. Abdomen: Distension, mass, hepatomegaly, ascites
G. Skin: Dehydration, rash
H. Neuro: Complete neuro exam including cranial nerve exam and for focal neurological deficits muscle strength, cerebellar function, and mental status exam (see IX. below)

GERI

VII. LABS (when indicated)

A. CBC, electrolytes, glucose, BUN/creatinine, calcium and magnesium, liver function tests

   B. ABGs/oxygen saturation
   C. Blood alcohol level and toxicology screen
   D. HIV (selected patients)
   E. Syphilis serology
   F. Thyroid studies (TSH and free T_4)
   G. Vitamin B_{12}, folate
   H. Urinalysis
   I. Other: Heavy metals screen, HIV, ceruloplasmin, arylsulfatase, electrophoresis, Lyme disease titers, genetic testing for Alzheimer, other dementia genes, Apolipoprotein E, lead level

VIII. OTHER TESTS

   A. Brain imaging: Head CT or MRI (more sensitive)
   1. Will evaluate for vascular disease, tumor, subdural hematoma or normal-pressure hydrocephalus
   2. Controversial, but probably not necessary with gradual onset dementia without localizing neurologic signs
   B. Lumbar puncture: Not usually necessary except for evaluation of infection, syphilis or vasculitis
   C. Other: Carotid doppler, ECG, ECHO, CXR, EEG

IX. THE MINI-MENTAL STATUS EXAM (MMSE)

   A. Score < 24 is strongly suggestive of dementia
   B. Not used to diagnose dementia, but used to establish a baseline for future evaluations and to document change over time or response to therapy

Maximum Score	Score	
		ORIENTATION
5	( )	What is the (year) (season) (date) (day) (month) ?
5	( )	Where are we: (state) (county) (town or city) (hospital) (floor).
		REGISTRATION
3	( )	Name 3 common objects (e.g. "apple," "table," "penny"):] Take 1 second to say each. Then ask the patient to repeat all 3 after you have said them. Give 1 point for each correct answer. Then repeat them until he/she learns all three. Count trials and record. Trials:
5	( )	**ATTENTION AND CALCULATION** Spell "world" backwards. The score is the number of letters in correct order (D___ L___ R___ O___ W___).
3	( )	**RECALL** Ask for the 3 objects repeated above. Give 1 point for each correct answer. [Note: recall cannot be tested if all 3 objects were not remembered during registration.]
		LANGUAGE
2	( )	Name a "pencil," and "watch." (2 points)
1	( )	Repeat the following. "No ifs, ands, or buts." (1 point)
3	( )	Follow a 3-stage command: "Take a paper in your right hand, fold it in half, and put it on the floor." (3 points)
		Read and obey the following:
1	( )	Close your eyes. (1 point)
1	( )	Write a sentence. (1 point)
1	( )	Copy the following design (1 point)

Total score:_____

Adapted from Folucin MF, Folmein SE. Mini-Mental State. J Psychiatric Rev 1975; 12:196–8; and Coclurell JR and Folucin MF Mini-Mental State Examination (MMSE). Psychopharm Bull 1988; 24(4):689–92.

GERI

X. MANAGEMENT

A. Treatment of cognitive deficits in Alzheimer's disease

1. Pharmacologic: Acetylcholinesterase inhibitors (provide modest improvement; do not alter natural course). Used for mild to moderate disease
2. **Donepezil (Aricept):** Start at 5mg PO QD and may increase to 10mg after 4–6 weeks. Side effects include nausea, vomiting, diarrhea and may initially see an increase in agitation
3. **Galantamine (Reminyl):** Initially 4mg PO BID, may increase by 4mg BID every 4 weeks to maximum of 12mg BID. Side effects include nausea, vomiting, diarrhea
4. **Rivastigmine (Exelon):** Initially 1.5mg PO BID, may increase by 1.5mg every 4 weeks to maximum of 6mg BID. Side effects include nausea, vomiting, diarrhea, dizziness, abdominal pain, fatigue, agitation
5. Non-pharmacologic
   a. Control risk factors for vascular disease
   b. Correct nutritional deficiencies and weight loss
   c. Treat behavioral problems (orienting cues, structured routine and social environment)

B. Treatment of behavior and mood disorders in Alzheimer's disease

1. Problematic delusions, hallucinations, severe psychomotor agitation, and combativeness
   a. Antipsychotic agents: **Risperidone (Risperdal), Olanzapine (Zyprexa), Quetiapine (Seroquel)**
   b. Mood stabilizing: **Trazodone (Desyrel), Carbamazepine (Tegretol), Divalproex Sodium (Depakote)**
2. Insomnia, anxiety, and agitation
   a. Benzodiazepines: **Lorazepam (Ativan), Oxazepam (Serax), Temazepam (Restoril), Zolpidem (Ambien), Triazolam (Halcion)**
   b. Nonbenzodiazepines: **Buspirone (BuSpar)**
3. Antidepressants

CLINICAL PEARLS

- Less common types of dementia include Pick's disease, dementia of frontal lobe type, dementia with Lewy bodies, progressive supranuclear palsy, multiple-systems atrophy and normal-pressure hydrocephalus
- Hypertension should not be corrected too rapidly since could lead to cerebral hypoperfusion, especially during an acute CVA
- Hypoglycemia from insulin overdose may outlast effects of 1 amp of D50
- Effect of opiates may outlast 1 amp of Narcan

PATIENT RESOURCES FOR DEMENTIA

- Memory and aging: Alzheimer's disease and related disorders, and many other materials. Alzheimer's Association, 919 N. Michigan Av., Suite 1100, Chicago, IL, 60611; telephone (800) 272–3900, www.alz.org
- Memory loss: What's normal, what's not. American Academy of Family Physicians, 11400 Tomahawk Creek Parkway, Leawood, KS 66211-2672; telephone (800) 944–0000, www.familydoctor.org/healthfacts/124

GERI

References

Cummings JL, et al. Guidelines for managing Alzheimer's disease: Part I. Assessment. Am Fam Phys 2002;65:2263.

Cummings JL, et al. Guidelines for managing Alzheimer's disease: Part II. Treatment. Am Fam Phys 2002;65:2525.

Doody RS, et al. Practice parameter: management of dementia (an evidence-based review). Neurology 2001;56:1154–66.

Grundman M, Thal LJ. Treatment of Alzheimer's disease: Rationale and strategies. Neurol Clin 2000;18:807–28.

Petersen RC. Aging, mild cognitive impairment, and Alzheimer's disease. Neurol Clin 2000;17:789-806.

Michael B. Weinstock, MD
Adam Houg, MD

112. ADDRESSING CODE STATUS

Code status will need to be addressed with critically ill patients and patients with terminal conditions (such as cancer or end-stage AIDS). If there is a disagreement between patient and family, patient's wishes always come first!

IN THE AMBULATORY SETTING

I. Encourage all patients to have a living will and to decide on code status and a power of attorney. It is always better to establish patient's code status in the ambulatory setting ahead of time

II. Recent studies have shown that elderly, chronically ill patients are more satisfied with their primary care physician when advanced directives are discussed before the hospital setting

III. Discuss with patients (or family, if patient has granted them power of attorney) several options for intervention:

    A. Full code: Doing "everything" including chest compressions, intubation, and using vasopressors (ACLS meds)

    B. No code (Do not resuscitate—DNR). Includes providing continuing medical management, but no chest compressions or intubation

    C. Comfort care only

CLINICAL PEARLS

- Consider involving other physicians or other health care professionals
- Hospital ethics committees are often available for consultation for the most difficult situations
- $1/2$ of all patients survive the initial resuscitation, $1/3$ survive for 24hrs, and $1/8$ survive to leave the hospital

References

Tierney WM, et al. The effect of discussions about advance directives on patients' satisfaction with primary care. J Gen Inter Med Jan 2001;16:32–40.

Ebell MH. Practical guidelines for do-not-resuscitate orders. Am Fam Phys 1994; 50:1293–9.

Jayes RL, et al. Do-not-resuscitate orders in intensive care units: current practices and recent changes. JAMA 1993;270:2213–7.

GERI

XII. HIV & AIDS

113. Ambulatory HIV/AIDS Management 375

114. AIDS-Defining Conditions 383

115. CD4 Cell Counts & Associated Clinical Manifestations 384

116. Work-up in Patients with HIV/AIDS 385

117. Post-exposure Prophylaxis for HIV 390

HIV

Michael B. Weinstock, MD

113. Ambulatory HIV/AIDS Management

The optimal management of patients with HIV/AIDS is a constantly evolving process. These recommendations are intended for physicians with experience in treating patients with HIV/AIDS who have a baseline level of knowledge. These recommendations are for management of *adults* with HIV and AIDS. For diagnosis and management of symptoms, see Chapters 113—117. These recommendations are current as of June 2003

I. HISTORY

A. History of present illness: In addition to standard history, ask specifically about: Fatigue, weight loss, weakness, fever, chills, night sweats, lymphadenopathy, rash or skin changes, oral lesions, dysphagia/odynophagia, change in vision, cough, dyspnea, easy bruising, diarrhea, nausea/vomiting, abdominal pain, dysuria, vaginal/penile discharge, yeast infections, anal pain, headaches, confusion/seizures

B. Past medical history: Hospitalizations/operations, drug allergies, immunizations, meds, history of infectious diseases (varicella/zoster, TB or positive skin tests, HSV, hepatitis, STDs), date of initial diagnosis of HIV and AIDS

C. Social history: Possible mode of infection, current sexual practices, drug use, smoking and alcohol, diet, stressors, support systems.

II. PHYSICAL EXAMINATION

A. General exam (cachexia)
B. Ophthalmic exam (visual field defects, fundi)
C. Dermatologic exam (seborrheic dermatitis, Kaposi's sarcoma, tinea, varicella, HSV, etc.)
D. Oral and dental exam (candidiasis, oral hairy leukoplakia, HSV, KS)
E. Pulmonary
F. Cardiovascular
G. Abdominal exam
H. Neurologic exam (baseline)
I. Consider rectal exam (condyloma, perirectal HSV)
J. Genital exam (candida, HSV, chancre, HPV, etc.)

III. LABORATORY AND OTHER DIAGNOSTIC EVALUATIONS

TESTING AND IMMUNIZATIONS DURING THE INITIAL EVALUATION

Laboratory	Other tests	Immunizations
CBC with differential and platelets	Chest radiograph	Pneumococcal vaccine
Chemistry panel	PPD skin testing (no anergy screen necessary)	Hepatitis B vaccine (if seronegative)
Liver enzymes		Hepatitis A vaccine
Syphilis serology	PAP smear (cervical dysplasia risk increased 8–11 times)	Influenza vaccine
Hepatitis A, B, C screen		
Toxoplasma titer (IgG)		(Varicella vaccine *for household contacts* with no history of chickenpox)
CD4 count (cells/mm^3)		
Viral load (copies/cc)		
Consider resistance testing with acute HIV syndrome		

A. Laboratory and other tests—see V. below
B. Immunizations
  1. Pneumococcal vaccine (cost ~$10): Strongly recommended
    a. Recommended for all patients with HIV with CD4 counts over 200. Optional for patients with CD4 counts less than 200 as the response to vaccination is poor. A

HIV

one time follow-up vaccination recommended at 5 years

    b. Impact on viral load: May transiently increase the viral load. Viral load testing should be delayed for 4 weeks after the immunization

    c. General: Incidence of pneumococcal pneumonia is increased over 20 times in patients with HIV and the risk of pneumococcal bacteremia is increased 150–300 fold higher than age matched controls without HIV. Pneumococcal vaccine should be given at the earliest opportunity and repeated once at 5 years. 88% of asymptomatic HIV infected patients responded to at least 1 component of the 23-valent vaccines

 2. Influenza vaccine (cost ~ $5): Generally recommended

    a. Recommended by the centers for disease control (CDC)

    b. Impact on viral load: May raise the viral load, therefore, viral load testing should be delayed for 4 weeks after the immunization

    c. General: Patients with HIV do not have worse infections with influenza than non-infected patients, however, the advantage of preventing influenza is that the symptoms will not be confused with symptoms of an opportunistic infection and unnecessary evaluations will be avoided. Other advantages include the increased risk of persons with HIV for bacterial infections that may complicate influenza. Protective antibody titers develop in 52–89% of patients with asymptomatic disease and 13–58% of patients with AIDS

 3. Hepatitis B vaccine: Generally recommended

    a. Recommended for individuals who continue to engage in high risk behaviors and who do not have serologic evidence of past infection with hepatitis B.

    b. General: Patients with HIV and hepatitis B have a 19–37% risk of becoming chronic carriers (3–6 times higher risk than patients without HIV). Response rate to the vaccine is 25–60%

 4. Hepatitis A vaccine: Generally recommended for those who engage in anal intercourse and for travelers

 5. Hemophilis Influenzae type B, diphtheria/tetanus, MMR: Same as for non-infected patients

 6. Travel vaccines: Same as for non-infected patients, but no live vaccines

 7. Varicella

    a. Vaccine: Not recommended for persons infected with HIV secondary to the risk of disseminated viral infection. It is recommended for household contacts of persons with HIV if they have not had chickenpox

    b. Immune globulin: With significant exposure to chicken pox or shingles in patients without history of either condition (or negative antibody titer) give Varicella Zoster Immune Globulin (VZIG) 5 vials (1.25mL each) IM if < 96hrs post-exposure (preferable within 48hrs)

 8. Vaccines not to give: Oral polio vaccine (OPV), varicella vaccine, other live vaccines

C. Other information: Provide patient with written information on HIV/AIDS, support groups, unsafe and safe sexual and IV drug use practices. Certain sexual practices are safe for patient to continue to engage in (activities which do not exchange body fluids) and should be discussed explicitly with the patient. Past contacts should be notified, but this can be deferred until the doctor patient relationship has been better established. Explain to patient the need for frequent visits and blood tests

IV. PROPHYLAXIS

A. PCP prophylaxis

 1. Pneumocystis is (probably) a protozoa which is common in the environment. Most children have antibodies by age 2–3. Most common site is pulmonary, but infection may occur in extra-pulmonary sites as well (e.g., skin, lymph nodes, spleen, brain)

 2. **Trimethoprim/Sulfamethoxazole (TMP/SMX)** is first line for prophylaxis. It is low cost, effective, and it has activity against toxoplasmosis and many bacterial infections in addition to *Pneumocystis carinii*. If it is not tolerated due to rash, GI upset,

HIV

or fever, a desensitization protocol may be attempted

3. Indications for primary PCP prophylaxis
   a. CD4 < 200 cells/mm³
   b. HIV associated oral thrush
4. **TMP/SMX** initiation protocol: Tolerated better if started as a low dose (½ DS tab QOD) and gradually increased
5. **TMP/SMX** desensitization: Very slow initiation may be attempted for patients who had previous non-anaphylactic reactions to TMP/SMX
6. Patients who have CD4 count increase to > 200 for 3–6 months may discontinue *primary* PCP prophylaxis

PROPHYLAXIS OF PNEUMOCYSTIS PNEUMONIA (PCP)

MEDICATION	DOSE	COST/MO. (AWP 7/00)	RELAPSE RATE	SIDE EFFECTS
Trimethoprim-sulfamethoxazole DS	One PO QD (preferred) or One TIW or One SS QD	$10	<5%/yr	Rash, nausea/vomiting, fever, anemia neutropenia, Stevens-Johnson
Dapsone	100mg PO QD (preferred) or 50mg PO QD	$6	5–20%/yr	Rash, agranulocytosis, aplastic anemia, hemolytic anemia in G6PD deficiency
Aerosolized pentamidine	300mg per month administered over 30–45 minutes per Respirgard II nebulizer	$138 plus cost of administration	15–25%/yr	Bronchospasm (consider pre-treat with albuterol MDI), increased incidence of upper lobe disease and extra-pulmonary PCP
Atovaquone(Mepron)	1500mg PO QD Avail: 750mg/5cc	$890	5–20%/yr	Rash (20%), GI intolerance (20%), diarrhea (20%)

B. Mycobacterium avium complex (MAC) prophylaxis

1. Common in food and water. Causes disease in up to 40% of late stage patients with HIV infection who do not take MAC prophylaxis
2. Indications: CD4 < 50 cells/mm³
3. If Clarithromycin or Azithromycin (macrolides are preferred agents) are used, then screen for MAC first by obtaining a MAC culture. There is about a 27% incidence of resistance to macrolides in patients who develop MAC while on prophylaxis with macrolides)
4. Patients who have CD4 count increase to > 100 for 3 months may discontinue primary prophylaxis

PROPHYLAXIS OF MYCROBACTERIUM AVIUM COMPLEX (MAC)

Medication	Dose	Cost/yr. (AWP 7/00)	Side effects and precautions
Clarithromycin (Biaxin)	500mg BID	$2347	GI disturbances
Azithromycin (Zithromax)	1200mg per week (Two 600mg tabs with or without food)	$1635	GI disturbances
Rifabutin (Mycobutin)	300mg QD	$3743	Neutropenia, thrombocytopenia, rash and GI, uveitis, drug-drug interactions with protease inhibitors

C. Tuberculosis (see Chapter 37, Tuberculosis Screening)

D. Cryptococcus
1. Cryptococcus is a fungus, acquired by inhalation
2. Primary prophylaxis not recommended

E. CMV disease (retinitis)
1. CMV is a viral infection often causing blindness as a result of retinitis
2. Screening: Ophthalmologist exam every 6 months with CD4 counts less than 50 cells/mm³ or visual symptoms
3. Primary prophylaxis not recommended

HIV

V. ANTIRETROVIRAL THERAPY

Currently, 2 HIV enzymes can be inhibited with meds: reverse transcriptase and HIV protease. Nucleoside analogs, nucleotide analogs, and nonnucleoside analogs work to inhibit reverse transcriptase. Protease inhibitors work to inhibit HIV protease. See following table on antiretroviral meds

A. Pathogenesis of HIV

1. HIV is a retrovirus. It is incorporated into CD4 cells by the binding of the HIV envelope protein gp120 to the CD4 receptor and a second receptor (possibly a chemokine receptor). Once inside the cell the HIV RNA is converted into DNA by the enzyme *reverse transcriptase* and then incorporated into the host cell's DNA. Next, messenger RNA (mRNA) is made which is then translated to make the proteins that will eventually form into the virus. These proteins are cleaved into the active form of HIV by the enzyme *HIV protease*. These active viral components are then packaged and put into circulation as infectious virions

2. HIV pathogenesis is a very active process. Even during early, asymptomatic disease there are approximately 10 billion HIV viral particles produced and destroyed each day. The half life of plasma virus is about 6hrs

3. In addition to active viral replication in the blood, there is viral replication in the lymphoid system, CSF and other sites

4. Decreases in plasma viral load are not always paralleled by decreases in these other locations or in genital secretions. A patient with a non-detectable plasma viral load should not be considered to be noninfectious

B. Viral load testing (the level of HIV RNA in the plasma)

1. The viral load measures the amount of virus in 1 cc of plasma. It ranges from "non-detectable" (< 25 to < 400 copies/cc (depending on the lab) to > 750,000 copies/cc (the upper limit of the test). The viral load count *routinely varies by a factor of 3 (0.5 log)*. This variability may be decreased by multiple measurements

2. Uses

   a. Viral load is the strongest predictor of progression (should still be correlated with the CD4 count and the clinical picture)

   b. Useful for therapeutic monitoring: Decreases in viral load during therapy are strongly associated with a decrease in risk of subsequent disease progression

3. Limitations: Viral load testing does not test immune function, CD4 regenerative reserve, susceptibility to antiretroviral agents, infectivity, viral phenotype (syncytium vs. non-syncytium inducing forms), virus in lymph nodes, CNS, genital secretions

4. Cost: ~$80–292 per test

5. Method

   a. 2 baseline assays should be done 2–4 weeks apart

   b. Viral load should be checked 2–4 weeks after starting or changing therapy and then at 10–12 weeks

   c. Testing should be done by the same laboratory using the same test

   d. Wait 4 weeks after vaccinations to perform viral load testing

C. CD4 count

1. CD4 count = WBC × percent lymphocytes × lymphocytes that are CD4 cells. Therefore, anything which affects the WBC count may influence the CD4 count (infection, drugs, steroids). CD4 count normally *varies by 30%*, but this variation can be accounted for by multiple measurements of the CD4 count. Should be checked 2 weeks apart, by the same laboratory to reduce variation. The "% CD4" count stays fairly constant and should be looked at in conjunction with the CD4 count

2. Should be used in conjunction with the viral load and the clinical picture to make decisions about antiretroviral therapy

3. Is an independent risk factor for opportunistic infections

4. Cost: ~$100 per test

D. General considerations with antiretroviral therapy
1. Never use monotherapy
2. Don't add a protease inhibitor to a failing regimen (same as using monotherapy because the virus is likely resistant to the current agents)
3. At least 2 agents should be changed at once (add 2 agents, change 1 and add 1, etc.)
4. Emphasize adherence at every visit
5. Monitor drug interactions
6. Monitor viral load and CD4 counts
7. Think ahead about what you can change if resistance develops

E. Initiation of therapy

INDICATIONS FOR INITIATING ANTIRETROVIRAL THERAPY (DHHS Guidelines 5/17/02)
1. Symptomatic AIDS or severe symptoms regardless of CD4 count or viral load
2. Asymptomatic AIDS with CD4 < 200 and any value viral load
3. Asymptomatic HIV with CD4 > 200 and < 350 with any value viral load (offer treatment, but controversial)
4. Asymptomatic HIV with CD4 > 350 and viral load (PCR or bDNA) > 55,000 (Controversial—the risk of AIDS in 3 years is 30% with no treatment)

1. Initiation of therapy should be a lifelong commitment by the patient and the physician. The goal of treatment is to change HIV from a chronic disease that is always fatal into a chronic disease (similar to diabetes) where the virus is suppressed through the duration of a patient's life by the continual use of meds
2. 100% adherence should be repeatedly stressed. If this is not possible at the present time, then antiretroviral therapy should be delayed until this is possible
3. Decisions on the initiation of therapy should take into account the whole clinical picture including history and exam, CD4 count and viral load. If test results are discordant (e.g., high CD4 and high viral load), obtain expert consultation

F. Goal: To decrease viral load to non-detectable and to increase CD4 count

G. Choices for initial therapy
1. Strong consideration should be given to dosing frequency and side effects of the regimen, as these meds may be taken for the duration of the patient's life, and compliance issues are important
2. Consideration for cost, side effects and drug interactions (see table at VIII. below)

H. Correlation between virologic response at 6 months and adherence

Adherence to HAART	VL < 400 copies/ml
>95% adherence	78%
90-95% adherence	45%
80-90% adherence	33%
70-80% adherence	29%
<70% adherence	18%

HIV

I. Choices for initial antiretroviral therapy for patients who are antiretroviral naïve (see chart on next page)

Antiretroviral Regimens Recommended for Treatment of HIV-1 Infection in Antiretroviral Naïve Patients		
NNRTI-Based Regimens		# of pills per day
Preferred Regimens	**Efavirenz + Lamivudine + (Zidovudine or Tenofovir DF or Stavudine*)—except for pregnant women or women with pregnancy potential**	3-5
Alternative Regimens	Efavirenz + Emtricitabine + (Zidovudine or Tenofovir DF or Stavudine*)—except for pregnant women or women with pregnancy potential**	3-4
	Efavirenz + (Lamivudine or Emtricitabine) + Didanosine—except for pregnant women or women with pregnancy potential**	3
	Nevirapine + (Lamivudine or Emtricitabine) + (Zidovudine or Stavudine* or Didanosine)	4-5
PI-Based Regimens		# of pills per day
Preferred Regimens	**Lopinavir/Ritonavir (co-formulated as Kaletra®) + Lamivudine + (Zidovudine or Stavudine)**	8-10
Alternative Regimens	Amprenavir/Ritonavir† + (Lamivudine or Emtricitabine) + (Zidovudine or Stavudine)	12-14
	Atazanavir + (Lamivudine or Emtricitabine) + (Zidovudine or Stavudine*)	4-5
	Indinavir + (Lamivudine or Emtricitabine) + (Zidovudine or Stavudine*)	8-10
	Indinavir/Ritonavir† + (Lamivudine or Emtricitabine) + (Zidovudine or Stavudine*)	8-11
	Lopinavir/Ritonavir (co-formulated as Kaletra®) + Emtricitabine + (Zidovudine or Stavudine*)	8-9
	Nelfinavir§ + (Lamivudine or Emtricitabine) + (Zidovudine or Stavudine*)	6-14
	Saquinavir (sgc or hgc)φ /Ritonavir† + (Lamivudine or Emtricitabine) + (Zidovudine or Stavudine*)	14-16
Triple NRTI Regimen – Only when an NNRTI- or a PI-based regimen cannot or should not be used as first line therapy		# of pills per day
Only as alternative to NNRTI- or PI-based regimen	Abacavir + Lamivudine + Zidovudine (or Stavudine*)	2-6

* Higher incidence of lipoatrophy, hyperlipidemia, and mitochondrial toxicities reported with Stavudine than with other NRTIs
** Women with child bearing potential implies women who want to conceive or those who are not using effective contraception
† Low-dose (100–400 mg) Ritonavir
§ Nelfinavir available in 250 mg or 625 mg tablet
φ sgc = soft gel capsule; hgc = hard gel capsule

Source: U.S. Department of Health and Human Services. Panel on Clinical Practices for Treatment of HIV. Guidelines for the use of antiretroviral agents in HIV-1-infected adults and adolescents. Nov. 10, 2003, Nov. 10, 2003: Table 12a. http://aidsinfo.nih/guidelines/adult/AA_111003.pdf (most recent information is available at www.aidsinfo.nih.gov/guidelines)

VI. CHANGING THERAPY—Indications for changing therapy:

A. Treatment failure
  1. Clinically significant increase in viral load
  2. Failure to achieve desired reduction in viral load after initiation of therapy
  3. Declining CD4 count (Caution: CD4 counts may take 3–6 months or longer to increase after potent suppression of the viral load)
  4. Possible indications
      a. Discordance: Fall in viral load and continued fall in CD4 counts
      b. Clinical disease progression despite obtaining target viral burden
B. Unacceptable toxicity of regimen
C. Noncompliance due to difficulty of regimen (if there is noncompliance because a patient is unwilling to take the meds, then consider deferral of antiretroviral therapy until patient can make an absolute commitment)
D. If meds are held for toxicity, it is best to stop all meds at once and not just 1 med (to decrease chance of resistance)
E. Goal: To decrease viral load to non-detectable (ranges from less than 400 copies/mL to < 20 copies/mL depending on the assay used)
F. Empiric selection for changing antiretroviral regimens

HIV

Treatment Options Following Virologic Failure on Initial Recommended Therapy Regimens

Regimen Class	Initial Regimen	Recommended Change
NNRTI	2 nucleosides + NNRTI	• 2 nucleosides (based on resistance testing) + PI (with or without low-dose Ritonavir) (AII)
PI	2 nucleosides + PI (with or without low-dose Ritonavir)	• 2 nucleosides (based on resistance testing) + NNRTI (AII)
Triple nucleosides	3 nucleosides	• 2 nucleosides (based on resistance testing) + NNRTI or PI (with or without low-dose Ritonavir) (AIII) • NNRTI + PI (with or without low-dose Ritonavir) (CIII) • Nucleoside(s) (based on resistance testing) + NNRTI + PI (with or without low-dose Ritonavir) (CII)

Source: U.S. Department of Health and Human Services. Panel on Clinical Practices for Treatment of HIV. Guidelines for the use of antiretroviral agents in HIV-1-infected adults and adolescents, Nov. 10, 2003: Table 25. http://aidsinfo.nih/guidelines/adult/AA_111003.pdf (most recent information is available at www.aidsinfo.nih.gov/guidelines)

VII. RESISTANCE TESTING

A. Advantages
   1. Improves drug selection in "rescue regimens"
   2. Virologic outcome at 16–24 weeks is better
   3. Number of drugs changed is reduced
B. General
   1. Must be done while a patient is taking meds
   2. Results are limited to the dominant strains (>20% of the total population). A result of resistant is probably accurate, while a result of sensitive may or may not be accurate
   3. A viral load of > 1,000 is required
   4. Interpretation is complex and there are a multiplicity of mutations and differing levels of resistance
   5. Benefits compared to decisions based on antiretroviral history are modest
   6. Cost is $600–900 per test and results are not available for about 2 weeks

VIII. ANTIRETROVIRAL THERAPY: DOSING, SIDE EFFECTS, DOSE

Antiretroviral Medications					
Medication	**Adult dose**	**Monitoring**	**Side effects**	**AWP-6/03**	**Available**
—Nucleoside and nucleotide analog reverse transcriptase inhibitors (NRTIs)—					
Zidovudine (Retrovir) AZT	200mg TID or 300mg BID	CBC every 2-4 weeks for 3 months, then every 3 months	Anemia - Hb < 8.0 (1.8%), neutropenia - ANC < 750 (5.4%), headache (27%), fatigue (23%), nausea (29%), myalgia (6%)	$4008	Caps:100mg Tabs: 300mg Soln: 10mg/mL
Didanosine (Videx) ddI -or- Videx EC (enteric coated)	If > 60kg: 400mg QD If < 60kg: 250mg QD *-empty stomach*	Intermittent CBC and LFT's	Acute pancreatitis (5-9%), painful peripheral neuropathy (5-12%), nausea/vomiting, hepatic failure	$2972 $3667	Cap: 400mg, 250mg enteric coated Powder: 100, 167, 250mg Tabs: 25, 50, 100, 150, 200
Stavudine (Zerit) d4T	40mg BID if > 60kg 30mg BID if < 60kg	Intermittent creatinine and LFT's	Peripheral neuropathy, elevated liver enzymes	$4069 $3935	Caps: 15, 20, 30, 40mg Soln: 1mg/mL
Lamivudine (Epivir) 3TC	150mg BID -or- 300mg QD	Intermittent	3TC plus AZT: anemia - Hb < 8.0 (2.9%), neutropenia - ANC < 750 (7.2%), HA (35%), fatigue (27%), nausea (33%), myalgia (8%)	$3792	Tabs: 150, 300mg Soln: 10mg/mL
Emtricitabine (Emtriva) FTC	200mg QD	Intermittent	Minimal SE: lactic acidosis with hepatic steatosis	$3636	Cap: 200mg
Abacavir (Ziagen) ABC	300mg BID	Intermittent	Hypersensitivity (2-5%), n/v, malaise, morbilliform rash. DO NOT RECHALLENGE!	$4615	Tabs: 300mg Soln: 20mg/mL
Tenofovir (Viread)	300mg QD	Intermittent	Asthenia, HA, n/v/d, flatulence, lactic acidosis	$4896	Tabs: 300mg
Combivir (AZT/3TC)	One BID (AZT 300mg and 3TC 150mg)	Same as AZT and 3TC	Same as AZT, 3TC	$7894	Tabs
Trizivir (AZT/3TC/ABC)	One BID (AZT 300mg, 3TC 150mg, ABC 300mg)	Same as AZT, 3TC, ABC	Same as AZT, 3TC, ABC	$13,315	Tabs

HIV

Chart continued on next page

Antiretroviral Medications (continued)					
Medication	Adult dose	Monitoring	Side effects	AWP-6/03	Available
—Nonnucleoside reverse transcriptase inhibitors (NNRTIs)—					
Nevirapine (Viramune) NVP	200mg QD X 14 d. then 200mg BID	Intermittent LFT's	Rash (17%), increased GGT > 450 U/L (2.4%)	$4154	Tabs: 200mg Soln: 50mg/5mL
Delavirdine (Rescriptor) DLV	400mg TID	Intermittent CBC and LFT's	Rash (30%), increased LFT's, HA, nausea, diarrhea, fatigue, anemia, neutropenia	$3504	Tabs: 100, 200mg
Efavirenz (Sustiva) EFV	600mg QHS	Intermittent	Dizziness, disconnectedness, somnolence, insomnia, bad dreams, confusion, amnesia, agitation, poor concentration, rash (5%).	$5396	Caps: 50, 100, 200mg Tabs: 600mg
—Protease inhibitors (PIs)—					
Saquinavir (Fortovase) FTV	1200mg TID with food (400mg BID with RIT)	Intermittent glucose, cholesterol, triglycerides, LFT's	Diarrhea (19%), nausea (11%), fatigue (5%), headaches (5%)	$7702	Soft gel caps: 200mg
Ritonavir (Norvir) RIT	600mg BID (400mg BID with FTV)	Same	Monotherapy: nausea/vomiting (13-26%), abd. pain (3-7%), circumoral paresthesias (3-6%), increased LFT's, increased chol.	$8910	Caps: 100mg Soln: 600mg/7.5mL
Indinavir (Crixivan) IDV	800mg Q8 hours -empty stomach or light foods	Same	Monotherapy: nausea (12%), vomiting (4%), increased bilirubin (8%), abdominal pain (9%), nephrolithiasis (3%)	$6399	Caps: 200, 333, 400mg
Nelfinavir (Viracept) NFV	1250mg BID -or- 750mg TID	Same	Mild GI: Diarrhea (15-20%), flatulence (4-7%)	$9080	Tabs: 250mg Oral powder: 50mg/g
Amprenavir (Agenerase) AMP	1200mg BID	Same	GI (10-30%), rash (20-25%), Stevens-Johnson syndrome (1%), paresthesias-perioral or peripheral (10-30%)	$7994	Caps: 50, 150mg Soln:15mg/mL
Lopinavir + Ritonavir (Kaletra)	Three BID (Use four BID when taken with EFV)	Same	GI, n/v/d, asthenia, elevated LFT's, hyperglycemia	$8125	Caps: 133.3/33.3mg Soln: 80/20mg per mL
Atazanavir (Reyataz)	400mg QD Note: if taken with norvir, then 300mg QD and 100mg norvir QD	Same	Indirect hyperbilirubinemia, prolonged PR, hyperglycemia	$9696	Caps: 100, 150, 200mg
—Fusion inhibitors—					
Enfuvirtide (Fuzeon) ENF	90mg SQ Q12 hours	No additional	Local injection site reaction with pain (9%), erythema (32%), pruritus (4%), induration (57%), and nodules or cysts (26%)	$20,000	Vials for constitution: 90mg

CLINICAL PEARLS

- Using antiretrovirals during pregnancy can significantly decrease maternal transmission of HIV to the fetus
- Average fall in CD4 counts without therapy is about 50–80/yr
- CD4 counts and viral load both independently predict risk for HIV disease progression. Using both together can provide even more diagnostic information
- Openness and honesty are paramount. Most AIDS patients will also be getting information from sources other than their physician, including the internet and friends infected with HIV. Desperation makes a believer out of a cynic. Ask your patients what other interventions they are trying

NATIONAL RESOURCES:

1. National AIDS Hotline .... 800-342-2437(AIDS)
2. Experimental Drug Trial Information .... 800-874-2572 (TRIALS-A)
3. American Foundation for AIDS Research (AMFAR) ......800-392-6327; 212-806-1600; www.amfar.org
4. National Assoc. of People With AIDS (NAPWA) 202-898-0414;www.napwa.org
5. Body Positive (Support for people HIV+) 212-566-7333;www.thebody.com

References
CDC. Guidelines for using antiretroviral agents among HIV-infected adults and adolescents: Recommendations of the Panel on Clinical Practices for Treatment of HIV. MMWR 2002:51(No. RR–7):1–56.

CDC. USPHS/IDSA Guidelines for preventing opportunistic infections among HIV-infected persons. MMWR 2002;51(No. RR-08):1–46.

Bartlett JG. 2002 Medical management of HIV infection. Johns Hopkins Univ, Dept of infectious diseases. Baltimore, MD, 2002.

Note: Available at http://www.hopkins-aids.edu/publication/book/book_toc.html

Hogg RS, et al. Rates of disease progression by baseline CD4 cell count and viral load after

HIV

initiating triple-drug therapy. JAMA 2001;286:2568.

Lee LM, et al. Survival after AIDS diagnosis in adolescents and adults during the treatment era, United States, 1984–1997. JAMA 2001;285:1308.

Gallant JE. Strategies for long-term success in the treatment of HIV infection. JAMA 2000;283:1329–34.

114. AIDS-DEFINING CONDITIONS

INDICATOR CONDITIONS IN CASE DEFINITION OF AIDS (ADULTS)—1997*

Candidiasis of esophagus, trachea, bronchi, or lungs—3,846 (16%)

Cervical cancer, invasive[†‡] —144 (0.6%)

Coccidioidomycosis, extrapulmonary[†]—74 (0.3%)

Cryptococcosis, extrapulmonary—1,168 (5%)

Cryptosporidiosis with diarrhea >1 month—314 (1.3%)

CMV of any organ other than liver, spleen or lymph nodes; eye—1,638 (7%)

Herpes simplex with mucocutaneous ulcer >1 month or bronchitis, pneumonitis, esophagitis—1,250 (5%)

Histoplasmosis, extrapulmonary[†] —208 (0.9%)

HIV-associated dementia[†]: Disabling cognitive and/or dysfunction interfering with occupation or activities of daily living—1,196 (5%)

HIV-associated wasting[†]: Involuntary weight loss >10% of baseline plus chronic diarrhea (≥2 loose stools/day ≥30 days) or chronic weakness and documented enigmatic fever ≥30 days—4,212 (18%)

Isosporiasis with diarrhea >1 month[†] —22 (0.1%)

Kaposi's sarcoma in patient under 60 yrs (or over 60 yrs[†])—1,500 (7%)

Lymphoma, Burkitt's—162 (0.7%), immunoblastic—518 (2.3%), primary CNS—170 (0.7%)

Mycobacterium avium, disseminated—1,124 (5%)

Mycobacterium tuberculosis, pulmonary—1,621 (7%), extrapulmonary—491 (2%)

Pneumocystis carinii pneumonia—9,145 (38%)

Pneumonia, recurrent-bacterial (≥2 episodes in 12 months)[†‡]—1,347 (5%)

Progressive multifocal leukoencephalopathy—213 (1%)

Salmonella septicemia (non-typhoid), recurrent[†] —68 (0.3%)

Toxoplasmosis of internal organ—1,073 (4%)

Wasting syndrome due to HIV (as defined above—HIV-associated wasting) (18%)

*Indicates frequency as the AIDS-indicator condition among 23,527 reported cases in adults for 1997. The AIDS diagnosis was based on CD4 count in an additional 36,643 or 61% of the 60,161 total cases. Numbers indicate sum of definitive and presumptive diagnosis for stated condition. The number in parentheses is the percentage of all patients reported with an AIDS-defining diagnosis; these do not total 100%, since some had a dual diagnosis.

[†]Requires positive HIV serology.

[‡]Added in the revised case definition, 1993.

HIV

115. CD4 CELL COUNTS & ASSOCIATED CLINICAL MANIFESTATIONS

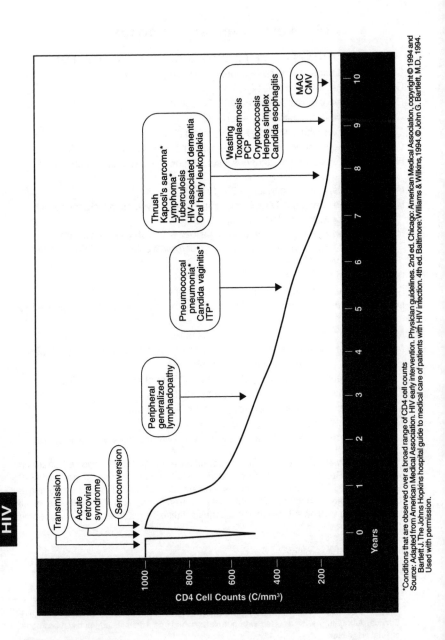

*Conditions that are observed over a broad range of CD4 cell counts
Source: Adapted from American Medical Association. Physician guidelines. 2nd ed. Chicago: American Medical Association, copyright © 1994 and Bartlett J. The Johns Hopkins hospital guide to medical care of patients with HIV infection. 4th ed. Baltimore: Williams & Wilkins, 1994. © John G. Bartlett, M.D., 1994. Used with permission.

HIV

116. Work-Up In Patients With HIV/AIDS

I. HEADACHE

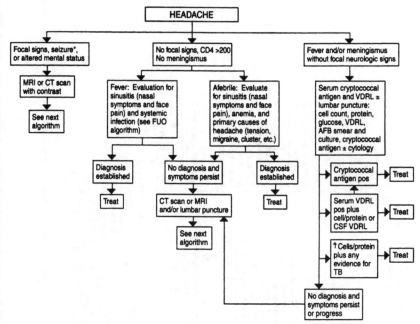

* Causes of seizures: HIV encephalitis (50%), toxoplasmosis (25%), cryptococcal meningitis (15%), lymphoma (5%), metabolic (5%)

Head Scan (CT With Contrast or MRI)

Disorder	Number	Pattern	Enhancement	Location
Toxoplasmosis	1–many	Ring mass	+ +	Basal ganglia
Lymphoma	1–several	Solid mass	+ + +	Periventricular
PML	1–several	No mass	0	Subcortical white
Cryptococcosis	0–many	Punctate	0	Basal ganglia
CMV	1–several	Confluent	+ +	Periventricular
HIV encephalitis	1–several	Confluent	0	Deep white

HIV

II. ACUTE DIARRHEA

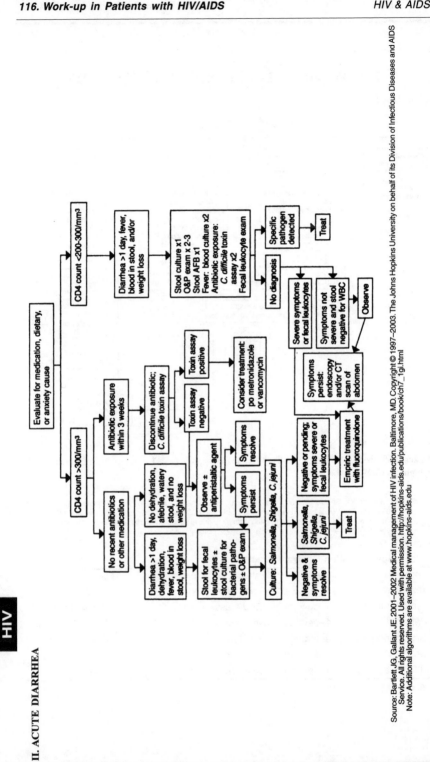

HIV

III. PULMONARY COMPLICATIONS

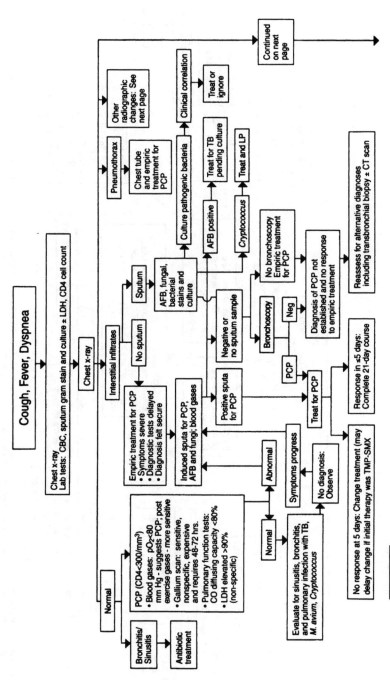

Cough, Fever, Dyspnea

Chest x-ray
Lab tests: CBC, sputum gram stain and culture ± LDH, CD4 cell count

Chest x-ray

Interstitial infiltrates

No sputum

Sputum

AFB, fungal, bacterial stains and culture

Culture pathogenic bacteria

AFB positive → Treat for TB pending culture

Cryptococcus → Treat and LP

Clinical correlation → Treat or ignore

Pneumothorax → Chest tube and empiric treatment for PCP

Other radiographic changes: See next page

Continued on next page

Empiric treatment for PCP
• Symptoms severe
• Diagnostic tests delayed
• Diagnosis felt secure

Induced sputa for PCP, AFB and fungi; blood gases

Positive sputa for PCP → Treat for PCP

Negative or no sputum sample

Bronchoscopy

PCP → Treat for PCP

Neg

No bronchoscopy: Empiric treatment for PCP

Diagnosis of PCP not established and no response to empiric treatment → Reassess for alternative diagnoses including transbronchial biopsy ± CT scan

Response in ≤5 days: Complete 21-day course

No response at 5 days: Change treatment (may delay change if initial therapy was TMP-SMX)

Normal

Bronchitis/Sinusitis → Antibiotic treatment

PCP (CD4 <300/mm³)
• Blood gases: pO₂ <80 mm Hg - suggests PCP; post exercise gases - more sensitive
• Gallium scan: sensitive, nonspecific, expensive and requires 48-72 hrs.
• Pulmonary function tests: CO diffusing capacity <80%
• LDH elevated >90% (non-specific)

Normal

Abnormal

Symptoms progress

No diagnosis: Observe

Evaluate for sinusitis, bronchitis, and pulmonary infection with TB, *M. avium, Cryptococcus*

HIV

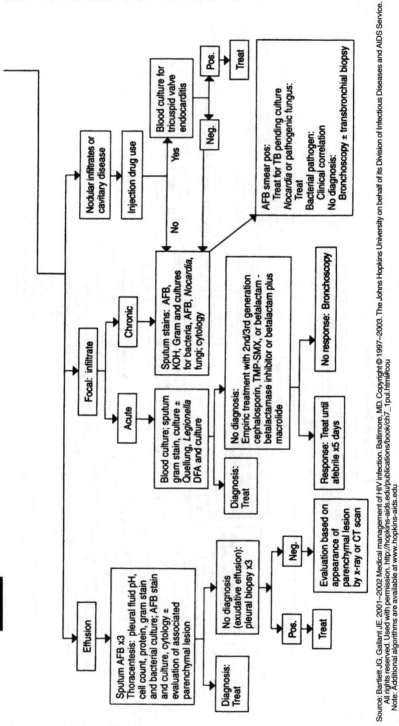

HIV

IV. FEVER OF UNKNOWN ORIGIN IN PATIENTS WITH AIDS

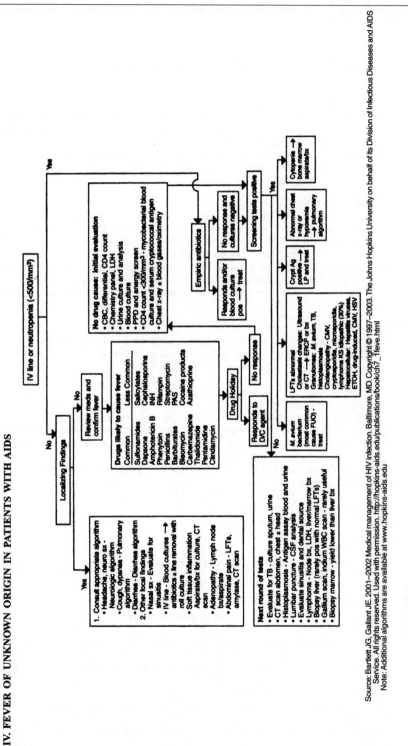

HIV

Michael B. Weinstock, MD

117. POST-EXPOSURE PROPHYLAXIS FOR HIV

I. TRANSMISSION: HIV is transmitted by transfer of blood or body fluids

    A. Body fluids that are documented to carry sufficient virus include blood, semen, vaginal secretions, cerebrospinal fluid (CSF), synovial fluid, pleural fluid, peritoneal fluid, pericardial fluid and amniotic fluid

    B. Body fluids *not considered* to be at risk include feces, nasal secretions, sputum, saliva, sweat, tears, urine and vomitus. The safest policy for health care workers is to use universal precautions with all body fluids

II. PREVALENCE/EPIDEMIOLOGY

    A. The 3 groups with the highest prevalence of HIV are gay men, IV drug abusers and hemophiliacs. Wives of hemophiliac men have a rate of 20–25%. The rate in prostitutes varies with location and with concomitant IV drug use. Other routes of infection include heterosexual transmission, blood transfusions, pregnancy, breast milk

    B. As of December 1995, all blood is screened for both HIV antibody and antigen. The use of this new technique has decreased the risk of HIV infected blood to less than one in 500,000 units of blood. Non-intimate contact and household exposure does not increase risk of transmission of HIV

III. RISK OF TRANSMISSION

    A. Occupational exposure: Pooled data from 23 prospective studies showed that risk after occupational exposure to needles and other contaminated devices was 0.33 percent (20 infections after 6,135 exposures). Risk is increased with:

        1. Deep injury

        2. Visible blood on the injuring device

        3. Injection directly into blood vessel

        4. Source patient with high viral titer (high viral load, end-stage AIDS, etc.)

    B. Risk with mucocutaneous exposures: 1 infection in 1,443 mucosal exposures (0.09%)

    C. Risk with exposure to intact skin: No conversions have been documented (no infections after 2,712 instances of exposure)

    D. Risk with single exposure from an HIV-infected source (Probability/10,000 exposures)

        1. Needle sharing: 67

        2. Percutaneous (occupational exposure): 30

        3. Receptive anal intercourse: 10–30

        4. Receptive vaginal intercourse: 8–20

        5. Insertive vaginal sex: 3–9

        6. Insertive anal sex: 3

IV. MANAGEMENT OF HEALTH CARE PERSONNEL

    A. Based on PHS statement of management of occupational exposures. (MMWR 2001;50:RR–11)

    B. Recommendations: Evaluate risk including exposure code (EC) and HIV status of body fluid/blood. Recommendations below are for a positive HIV status of body fluid/blood

        1. EC 1: Small volume exposure (few drops, limited time) to compromised skin (chapped skin, abrasion) or mucous membrane

           ➛ Offer, but toxicity of PEP may outweigh benefit

        2. EC 2: Larger volume exposure to compromised skin/mucous membranes OR less severe percutaneous exposure (superficial scratch, solid needle)

           ➛ Consider 2 drug regimen (see below) without protease inhibitor

HIV

3. EC 3: Severe percutaneous exposure (large bore hollow needle, deep puncture, etc.)
   → 3 drug regimen (see below)

C. Timing: Initiate as soon as possible, preferably within 1–2hrs postexposure. If > 36hrs, consult expert

D. Testing: Immediately after exposure, then at 6 weeks, 3 months, and 6 months. Testing at 1 year is optional (4% may seroconvert after 6 months). The antiretroviral syndrome (acute febrile illness) occurs 50–70% of the time and occurs within 2–4 weeks after exposure

E. Treatment regimen: (See Chapter 113, Ambulatory Management of HIV, for dosing)
  1. **2 drug**
     a. AZT + 3TC
     b. 3TC + d4T
     c. d4T + ddI
  2. **3 drug**—Use above 2 drug regimen plus 1 of the following:
     a. IDV
     b. NFV
     c. EFV
     d. ABC

F. Duration: The optimal duration is unknown. Recommendations are 4 weeks

V. MANAGEMENT OF NONOCCUPATIONAL EXPOSURES
A. Most recent DHHS guidelines are from 1998
B. Decision based on risk per III. D. above. Decision should be made by doctor and patient after discussion regarding risk of exposure, compliance with meds, and side effects of meds
C. Timing and duration of therapy same as above

CLINICAL PEARLS
- CDC does not recommend postexposure prophylaxis after exposure to urine
- Risk after exposure to Hepatitis B infected sharps is 23–62% and for Hepatitis C 1.8%
- Risk of sexual exposure to a person with *N. Gonorrhea* is 20–25% per contact
- Prevalence of AIDS in US prisons is 14 times that in the general population. Prison rape may represent a high risk exposure

References

Bartlett JG, Gallant JE. 2001–2002 Medical management of HIV infection. Copyright © 1997–2003. The Johns Hopkins University on behalf of its Division of Infectious Disease and AIDS Service. http://hopkins-aids.edu/publications/book/book_toc.html

US Public Health Service guidelines for the management of occupational exposure to HBV, HCV and HIV recommendations for postexposure prophylaxis. MMWR Recomm Rep 2001;50:RR–11.

Bamberger JD, et al. Postexposure prophylaxis for human immunodeficiency virus (HIV) infection following sexual assault. Am J Med March 1999;106:323–6.

Henderson DK. Postexposure chemoprophylaxis for occupational exposures to the human immunodeficiency virus. JAMA March 1999;281:931–6.

Kats MH, Gerberding JL. Postexposure treatment of people exposed to the human immunodeficiency virus through sexual contact or injection drug use. N Engl J Med 1997; 336:1097–1100.

HIV

XIII. Appendix

118. Formulas 395

119. Symptomatic Medications: Colds & Flu, Sinusitis, Bronchitis, etc. 396

120. Adult Advanced Cardiac Life Support (ACLS) Protocols 398

121. Common Adult Emergency Drug Dosage 407

122. Preparation of Infusion for Adult Emergency Drugs 408

APPX

Michael B. Weinstock, MD

118. FORMULAS

A. Anion gap:

$$AG = Na^+ - (Cl^- + HCO_3)$$

$$Normal = 8\text{--}16 \text{ mEq} / L$$

B. Creatinine clearance (CrCl):

1. $CrCl \text{ (male)} = \dfrac{(140 - age) \times weight \text{ (kg)}}{Serum\ creatinine \times 72}$

2. $CrCl \text{ (female)} = 0.85 \times CrCl \text{ (male)}$

C. Fractional excretion of sodium:

$$Fe_{Na} = \frac{U_{Na} / P_{Na}}{U_{Cr} / P_{Cr}} \times 100$$

D. Serum osmolality:

$$Osm = 2(Na^+ + K^+) + (Glucose / 18) + (BUN / 2.8)$$

E. A–a Gradient:

$$= (713 \times F_IO_2) - (PaCO_2 \times 1.2) - PaO_2$$
Note: Pressures are at sea level
F_IO_2 at room air is 0.21 (21%)
(Normal A–a Gradient = 5–15)

F. Corrected sodium with hyperglycemia:

$$Corrected\ Na^+ = Na^+ + [1.6 \times (Glucose - 140) / 100]$$

G. LDL Cholesterol:

$$LDL\ cholesterol = Total\ cholesterol - HDL\ cholesterol - \left(\frac{triglycerides}{5} \right)$$

Michael B. Weinstock, MD
Beth Weinstock, MD

119. SYMPTOMATIC MEDICATIONS: COLDS & FLU, SINUSITIS, BRONCHITIS, ETC.

DRUG	COMPONENTS	ADULT DOSE	PEDIATRIC DOSE	OTC/Rx
ANTITUSSIVES				
Hycodan	Hydrocodone bitartrate 5mg, Homatropine methylbromide 1.5mg, per tab or per 5mL	5mL or 1 tab PO Q4–6hrs PRN	Under 6 y/o: Not rec. 6–12 y/o: 2.5mL or 1 tab PO Q4–6hrs PRN — max dose 15mL/day	Rx (Class III)
Robitussin Pediatric	Dextromethorphan 7.5mg per 5mL	—	Under 2y/o: Not rec. 2–6 y/o: 5mL PO Q6–8hrs 6–12 y/o: 10mL PO Q6–8hrs	OTC
Tessalon Perles	Benzonatate 100mg	100mg PO TID — max dose 600mg/day	Under 10 y/o: Not rec. Over 10 y/o: Same as adult	Rx
ANTITUSSIVES, EXPECTORANTS				
Humibid DM	Dextromethorphan 30mg, Guaifenesin 600mg per tab, sustained release	1–2 tabs PO Q12hrs	Under 2 y/o: Not rec. 2–6 y/o: ½ tab PO Q12hrs 6–12 y/o: 1 tab PO Q12hrs	Rx
Hycotuss, VicodinTuss	Hydrocodone bitartrate 5mg, Guaifenesin 100mg per 5mL	5mL PO after meals and QHS, at least 4 hours apart — max dose 30mL/day	Under 6 y/o: Not rec. 6–12 y/o: 2.5–5mL PO Q4–6	Rx (Class III)
Tussi-Organidin	Codeine phosphate 10mg, Iodinated glycerol 30mg per 5mL	5–10mL PO Q4hrs	Under 6 y/o: Not rec. 6–12 y/o: 5mL PO Q4–6hrs	Rx (Class V)
Robitussin DM	Dextromethorphan 10mg, Guaifenesin 100mg per 5mL	10mL PO Q4hrs	Under 2 y/o: Not rec. 2–6 y/o: 2.5mL PO Q4hrs 6–12 y/o: 5mL PO Q4hrs	OTC
Robitussin A–C	Codeine phosphate 10mg, Guaifenesin 100mg per 5mL	10mL PO Q4hrs	Under 6 y/o: Not rec. 6–12 y/o: 5mL PO Q4hrs	Rx (Class V)
ANTITUSSIVES, EXPECTORANTS, SYMPATHOMIMETICS				
Duratuss HD	Hydrocodone bitartrate 5mg, Guaifenesin 100mg, Pseudoephedrine 30mg per 5mL	10mL PO Q4–6hrs	Under 6 y/o: Not rec. 6–12 y/o: 5mL PO Q4–6hrs	Rx (Class III)
Robitussin DAC	Codeine phosphate 10mg, Guaifenesin 100mg, Pseudoephedrine 30mg per 5mL	5–10mL PO Q4hrs — max dose 40mL/day	Under 6 y/o: Not rec. 6–12 y/o: 5mL PO Q4–6hrs — max dose 20mL/day	Rx (Class V)
ANTITUSSIVES, ANTIHISTAMINES, SYMPATHOMIMETICS				
Actifed with codeine	Codeine phosphate 10mg, Triprolidine 1.25mg, Pseudoephedrine 30mg per 5mL	10mL PO TID–QID	Under 2 y/o: Not rec. 2–6 y/o: 2.5mL PO TID–QID 6–12 y/o: 5–10mL PO TID–QID	Rx (Class V)
Bromfed-DM, Dimetane-DX	Dextromethorphan 10mg, Brompheniramine 2mg, Pseudoephedrine 30mg per 5mL	10mL PO Q4hrs	Under 2 y/o: Not rec. 2–6 y/o: 2.5mL PO Q4hrs 6–12 y/o: 5mL PO Q4hrs	Rx
Rondec-DM	Dextromethorphan 15mg, Carbinoxamine 4mg, Pseudoephedrine 60mg per 5mL	5mL PO QID	Under 18 months: Use Rondec-DM drops 18 mo.–6 y/o: 2.5mL PO QID Over 6 y/o: Same as adults	Rx
Triaminic Nite Light	Dextromethorphan 7.5mg, Chlorpheniramine 1mg, Pseudoephedrine 15mg per 5mL	20mL PO Q6hrs	Under 3 months: Not rec. 3–12 mo. (12–17 lbs): 1.25mL PO Q6hrs 1–2 y/o (18–23 lbs): 2.5mL PO Q6hrs 2–6 y/o: 5mL PO Q6hrs 6–12 y/o: 10mL PO Q6hrs	OTC

APPX

SYMPATHOMIMETICS				
Afrin	Pseudoephedrine 120mg SR	1 tab PO Q12hrs	Not recommended	OTC
Sudafed **Sudafed 12 HR** **Sudafed Liquid**	Pseudoephedrine 30, 60mg; 120mg (Sudafed 12HR); 30mg/5mL (liquid)	60mg PO Q4–6hrs or 1 12-hour tab Q12hrs — max dose 240mg/day	Under 2 y/o: Not rec. 2–6 y/o: 2.5mL PO Q4–6hrs 6–12 y/o: 5mL PO Q4–6hrs	OTC
EXPECTORANTS				
Organidin	Iodinated glycerol 30mg	2 tabs QID with liquid	Up to half adult dose	Rx
Robitussin	Guaifenesin 100mg per 5mL	10–20mL PO Q4hrs	Under 2 y/o: Not rec. 2–6 y/o: 2.5–5mL PO Q4hrs 6–12 y/o: 5–10mL PO Q4hrs	OTC
Humibid LA	Guaifenesin 600mg, sustained release, scored tabs	1–2 tabs PO Q12hrs	Under 2 y/o: Not rec. 2–6 y/o: ½ tab PO Q12hrs 6–12 y/o: 1 tab PO Q12hrs	Rx
Naldecon Senior EX	Guaifenesin 100mg per 5mL	10mL PO Q4hrs	Not recommended	OTC
ANTIHISTAMINES				
Allegra	Fexofenadine 60mg Fexofenadine 180mg	1 tab PO BID 1 tab PO BID	6–11y/o: 30mg PO BID	Rx
Allegra-D	Fexofenadine 60mg Pseudoephedrine 120mg	1 tab PO BID		
Atarax	Hydroxyzine 10mg/tab Hydroxyzine 10mg/5mL	25mg PO TID–QID	Under 6 y/o: 50mg PO daily Over 6 y/o: 50–100mg PO QD	Rx
Benadryl	Diphenhydramine 25, 50mg Diphenhydramine 12.5mg/5mL	25–50mg PO TID–QID	Over 20 lbs: 5–10mL PO TID–QID — max dose 5mg/kg/day	OTC
Chlor-trimeton	Chlorpheniramine 4mg tabs Chlorpheniramine 2mg/5mL	4mg PO Q4–6hrs	Under 2 y/o: Not rec. 2–5 y/o: 2.5mL PO Q4–6hrs 6–11 y/o: 5mL PO Q4–6hrs	OTC
Clarinex	Desloratadine 5mg	1 PO QD		Rx
Claritin	Loratadine 10 mg tabs	1 PO QD on empty stomach	Under 12 y/o: Not rec.	Rx
Zyrtec	Cetirizine 10mg	1 tab PO QD	2–5 y/o: 1 tsp (5mg/5cc) PO QD	Rx
Zyrtec-D	Cetirizine 10mg Pseudoephedrine 120mg	1 PO QD	6–11 y/o: 5–10mg PO QD	

— See Chapter 67, Allergic Rhinitis/Seasonal Allergies, for information on nasal inhalers and ophthalmic solutions

ANTIHISTAMINES, SYMPATHOMIMETICS				
Actifed **Actifed syrup**	Triprolidine 2.5mg, Pseudoephedrine 60mg Note: Syrup contains ½ amount per 5mL	1 tab or 10mL PO, Q4–6hrs PRN	Under 6 y/o: Not rec. Over 6 y/o: ½ tab or 5mL, Q4–6hrs PRN max. 4 doses/day	OTC
Dimetapp Allergy	Brompheniramine			OTC
Rondec	Carbinoxamine 4mg, Pseudoephedrine 60mg per tab or by 5mL	1 tab or 5mL PO QID	Under 18 mo.: Not rec. 18 mo.–6 y/o: 2.5mL PO QID	Rx
Rondec TR	Carbinoxamine 4mg, Pseudoephedrine 120mg per sustained release tab	1 tab PO Q12hrs	Not recommended	Rx

120. ADULT ADVANCED CARDIAC LIFE SUPPORT (ACLS) PROTOCOLS

Source: American Heart Association. Guidelines 2000 for cardiopulmonary resuscitation and emergency cardiac care. Circulation. 2000;102(suppl.):I1-1384.Copyright 2001, American Heart Association. Used with permission.

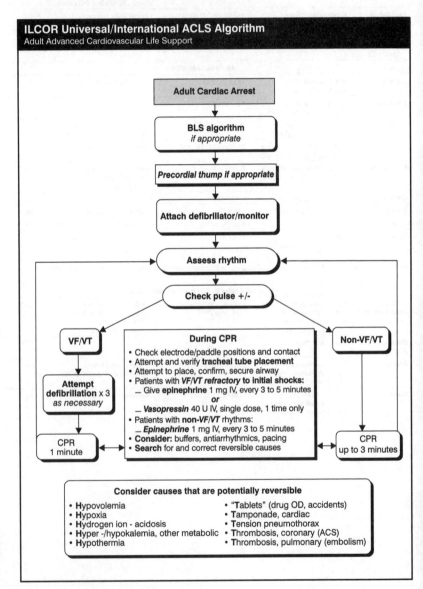

ILCOR Universal/International ACLS Algorithm
Adult Advanced Cardiovascular Life Support

Adult Cardiac Arrest

BLS algorithm
if appropriate

Precordial thump if appropriate

Attach defibrillator/monitor

Assess rhythm

Check pulse +/-

VF/VT

Attempt defibrillation x 3
as necessary

CPR
1 minute

During CPR
• Check electrode/paddle positions and contact
• Attempt and verify **tracheal tube placement**
• Attempt to place, confirm, secure airway
• Patients with *VF/VT refractory* to initial shocks:
  _ Give **epinephrine** 1 mg IV, every 3 to 5 minutes
    or
  _ *Vasopressin* 40 U IV, single dose, 1 time only
• Patients with **non-VF/VT** rhythms:
  _ *Epinephrine* 1 mg IV, every 3 to 5 minutes
• **Consider:** buffers, antiarrhythmics, pacing
• **Search** for and correct reversible causes

Non-VF/VT

CPR
up to 3 minutes

Consider causes that are potentially reversible
• Hypovolemia
• Hypoxia
• Hydrogen ion - acidosis
• Hyper -/hypokalemia, other metabolic
• Hypothermia
• "Tablets" (drug OD, accidents)
• Tamponade, cardiac
• Tension pneumothorax
• Thrombosis, coronary (ACS)
• Thrombosis, pulmonary (embolism)

ILCOR Universal/International ACLS Algorithm

APPX

Ventricular Fibrillation/Pulseless Ventricular Tachycardia (VF/VT) Algorithm
Adult Advanced Cardiovascular Life Support

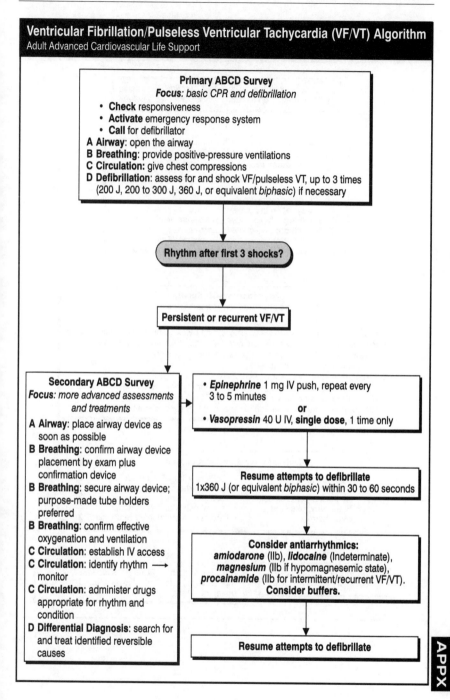

Ventricular Fibrillation/Pulseless Ventricular Tachycardia (VF/VT) Algorithm

Pulseless Electrical Activity Algorithm
Adult Advanced Cardiovascular Life Support

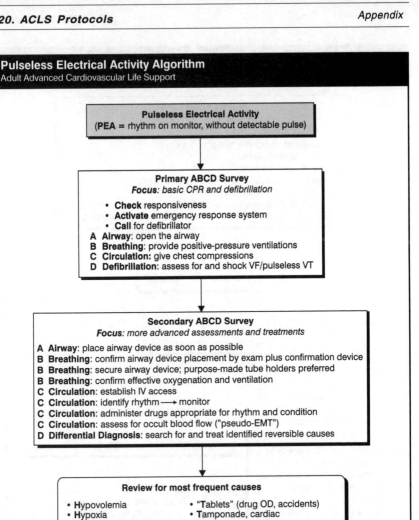

Pulseless Electrical Activity
(**PEA** = rhythm on monitor, without detectable pulse)

Primary ABCD Survey
Focus: basic CPR and defibrillation

- **Check** responsiveness
- **Activate** emergency response system
- **Call** for defibrillator
A **Airway**: open the airway
B **Breathing**: provide positive-pressure ventilations
C **Circulation**: give chest compressions
D **Defibrillation**: assess for and shock VF/pulseless VT

Secondary ABCD Survey
Focus: more advanced assessments and treatments

A **Airway**: place airway device as soon as possible
B **Breathing**: confirm airway device placement by exam plus confirmation device
B **Breathing**: secure airway device; purpose-made tube holders preferred
B **Breathing**: confirm effective oxygenation and ventilation
C **Circulation**: establish IV access
C **Circulation**: identify rhythm ⟶ monitor
C **Circulation**: administer drugs appropriate for rhythm and condition
C **Circulation**: assess for occult blood flow ("pseudo-EMT")
D **Differential Diagnosis**: search for and treat identified reversible causes

Review for most frequent causes

- Hypovolemia
- Hypoxia
- Hydrogen ion - acidosis
- Hyper -/hypokalemia
- Hypothermia

- "Tablets" (drug OD, accidents)
- Tamponade, cardiac
- Tension pneumothorax
- Thrombosis, coronary (ACS)
- Thrombosis, pulmonary (embolism)

Epinephrine 1 mg IV push, repeat every 3 to 5 minutes

Atropine 1 mg IV (if PEA rate is *slow*), repeat every 3 to 5 minutes as needed, to a total dose of 0.04 mg/kg

APPX

Pulseless Electrical Activity Algorithm (PEA)

Asystole: The Silent Heart Algorithm
Adult Advanced Cardiovascular Life Support

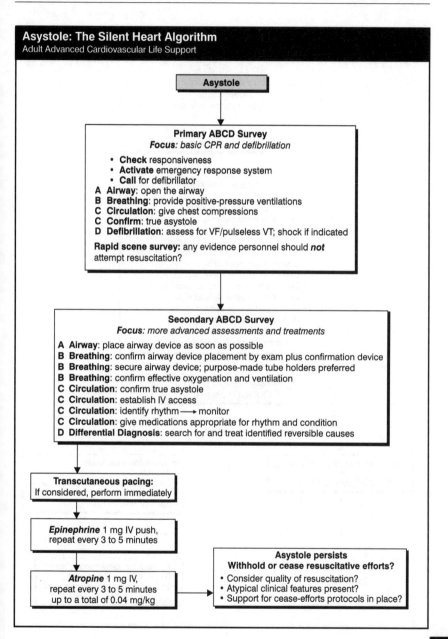

Asystole

Primary ABCD Survey
Focus: basic CPR and defibrillation

- **Check** responsiveness
- **Activate** emergency response system
- **Call** for defibrillator
A **Airway**: open the airway
B **Breathing**: provide positive-pressure ventilations
C **Circulation**: give chest compressions
C **Confirm**: true asystole
D **Defibrillation**: assess for VF/pulseless VT; shock if indicated

Rapid scene survey: any evidence personnel should *not* attempt resuscitation?

Secondary ABCD Survey
Focus: more advanced assessments and treatments

A **Airway**: place airway device as soon as possible
B **Breathing**: confirm airway device placement by exam plus confirmation device
B **Breathing**: secure airway device; purpose-made tube holders preferred
B **Breathing**: confirm effective oxygenation and ventilation
C **Circulation**: confirm true asystole
C **Circulation**: establish IV access
C **Circulation**: identify rhythm → monitor
C **Circulation**: give medications appropriate for rhythm and condition
D **Differential Diagnosis**: search for and treat identified reversible causes

Transcutaneous pacing:
If considered, perform immediately

Epinephrine 1 mg IV push,
repeat every 3 to 5 minutes

Atropine 1 mg IV,
repeat every 3 to 5 minutes
up to a total of 0.04 mg/kg

Asystole persists
Withhold or cease resuscitative efforts?
- Consider quality of resuscitation?
- Atypical clinical features present?
- Support for cease-efforts protocols in place?

APPX

Asystole: The Silent Heart Algorithm

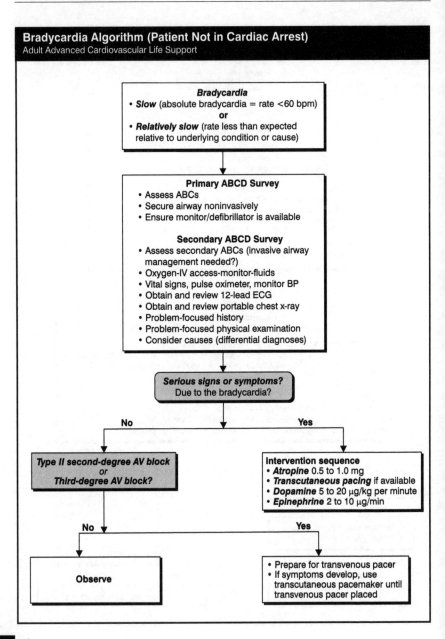

Bradycardia Algorithm (Patient Not in Cardiac Arrest)
Adult Advanced Cardiovascular Life Support

Bradycardia
- *Slow* (absolute bradycardia = rate <60 bpm)
  or
- *Relatively slow* (rate less than expected relative to underlying condition or cause)

Primary ABCD Survey
- Assess ABCs
- Secure airway noninvasively
- Ensure monitor/defibrillator is available

Secondary ABCD Survey
- Assess secondary ABCs (invasive airway management needed?)
- Oxygen-IV access-monitor-fluids
- Vital signs, pulse oximeter, monitor BP
- Obtain and review 12-lead ECG
- Obtain and review portable chest x-ray
- Problem-focused history
- Problem-focused physical examination
- Consider causes (differential diagnoses)

Serious signs or symptoms?
Due to the bradycardia?

No   **Yes**

Type II second-degree AV block
or
Third-degree AV block?

Intervention sequence
- *Atropine* 0.5 to 1.0 mg
- *Transcutaneous pacing* if available
- *Dopamine* 5 to 20 µg/kg per minute
- *Epinephrine* 2 to 10 µg/min

No   **Yes**

Observe

- Prepare for transvenous pacer
- If symptoms develop, use transcutaneous pacemaker until transvenous pacer placed

APPX

Bradycardia Algorithm (with the patient not in cardiac arrest)

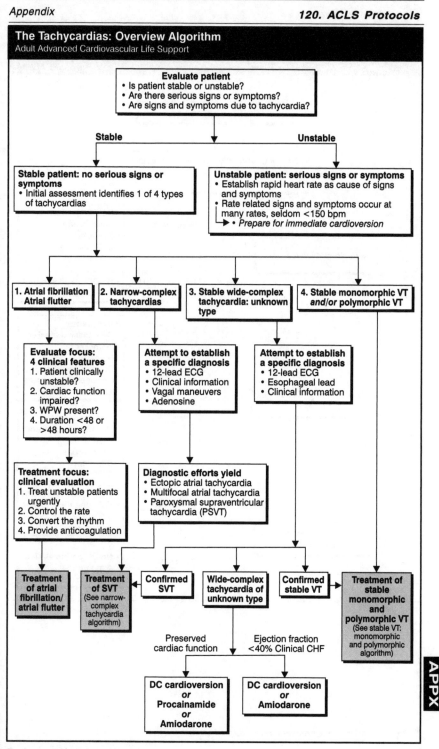

The Tachycardias: Overview Algorithm
Adult Advanced Cardiovascular Life Support

Evaluate patient
- Is patient stable or unstable?
- Are there serious signs or symptoms?
- Are signs and symptoms due to tachycardia?

Stable

Unstable

Stable patient: no serious signs or symptoms
- Initial assessment identifies 1 of 4 types of tachycardias

Unstable patient: serious signs or symptoms
- Establish rapid heart rate as cause of signs and symptoms
- Rate related signs and symptoms occur at many rates, seldom <150 bpm
  - *Prepare for immediate cardioversion*

1. Atrial fibrillation Atrial flutter

2. Narrow-complex tachycardias

3. Stable wide-complex tachycardia: unknown type

4. Stable monomorphic VT *and/or* polymorphic VT

Evaluate focus: 4 clinical features
1. Patient clinically unstable?
2. Cardiac function impaired?
3. WPW present?
4. Duration <48 or >48 hours?

Attempt to establish a specific diagnosis
- 12-lead ECG
- Clinical information
- Vagal maneuvers
- Adenosine

Attempt to establish a specific diagnosis
- 12-lead ECG
- Esophageal lead
- Clinical information

Treatment focus: clinical evaluation
1. Treat unstable patients urgently
2. Control the rate
3. Convert the rhythm
4. Provide anticoagulation

Diagnostic efforts yield
- Ectopic atrial tachycardia
- Multifocal atrial tachycardia
- Paroxysmal supraventricular tachycardia (PSVT)

Treatment of atrial fibrillation/ atrial flutter

Treatment of SVT (See narrow-complex tachycardia algorithm)

Confirmed SVT

Wide-complex tachycardia of unknown type

Confirmed stable VT

Treatment of stable monomorphic and polymorphic VT (See stable VT: monomorphic and polymorphic algorithm)

Preserved cardiac function

Ejection fraction <40% Clinical CHF

DC cardioversion *or* Procainamide *or* Amiodarone

DC cardioversion *or* Amiodarone

APPX

Tachycardias: Overview Algorithm

Narrow-Complex Tachycardia
Adult Advanced Cardiovascular Life Support

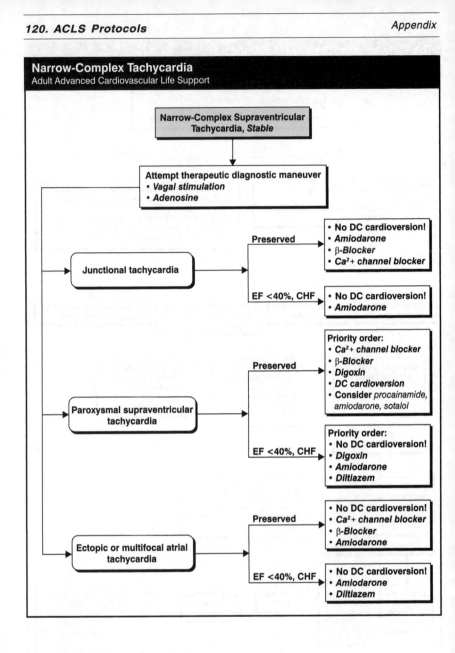

Tachycardias: Narrow-Complex Tachycardia

Stable Ventricular Tachycardia: Monomorphic and Polymorphic
Adult Advanced Cardiovascular Life Support

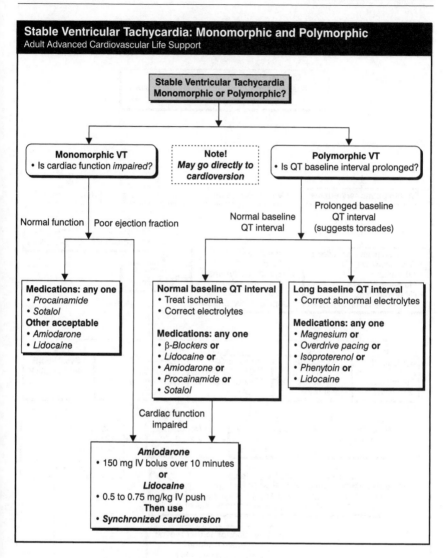

Tachycardias: Stable Ventricular Tachycardia: Monomorphic and Polymorphic

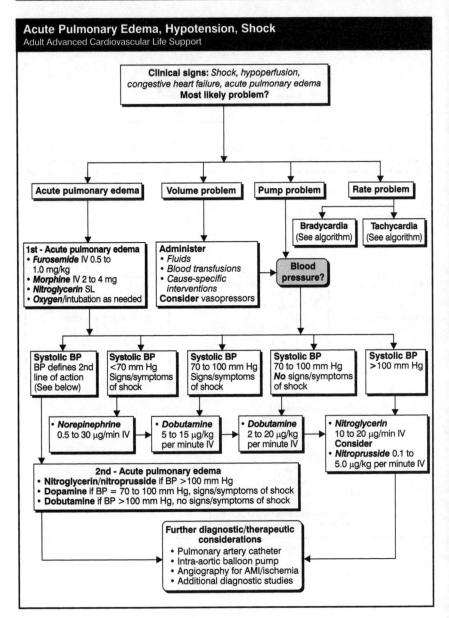

Acute Pulmonary Edema, Hypotension, Shock
Adult Advanced Cardiovascular Life Support

Clinical signs: *Shock, hypoperfusion, congestive heart failure, acute pulmonary edema*
Most likely problem?

| Acute pulmonary edema | Volume problem | Pump problem | Rate problem |

Bradycardia (See algorithm)   **Tachycardia** (See algorithm)

1st - Acute pulmonary edema
- *Furosemide* IV 0.5 to 1.0 mg/kg
- *Morphine* IV 2 to 4 mg
- *Nitroglycerin* SL
- *Oxygen*/intubation as needed

Administer
- *Fluids*
- *Blood transfusions*
- *Cause-specific interventions*

Consider vasopressors

Blood pressure?

| Systolic BP | Systolic BP | Systolic BP | Systolic BP | Systolic BP |
| BP defines 2nd line of action (See below) | <70 mm Hg Signs/symptoms of shock | 70 to 100 mm Hg Signs/symptoms of shock | 70 to 100 mm Hg *No* signs/symptoms of shock | >100 mm Hg |

- *Norepinephrine* 0.5 to 30 µg/min IV

- *Dobutamine* 5 to 15 µg/kg per minute IV

- *Dobutamine* 2 to 20 µg/kg per minute IV

- *Nitroglycerin* 10 to 20 µg/min IV
Consider
- *Nitroprusside* 0.1 to 5.0 µg/kg per minute IV

2nd - Acute pulmonary edema
- **Nitroglycerin/nitroprusside** if BP >100 mm Hg
- **Dopamine** if BP = 70 to 100 mm Hg, signs/symptoms of shock
- **Dobutamine** if BP >100 mm Hg, no signs/symptoms of shock

Further diagnostic/therapeutic considerations
- Pulmonary artery catheter
- Intra-aortic balloon pump
- Angiography for AMI/ischemia
- Additional diagnostic studies

Acute Pulmonary Edema, Hypotension, Shock

Miriam Chan, PharmD

121. Common Adult Emergency Drug Dosage[1]

Drug	Indications	Dosage	Comments
Adenosine	1. Narrow- Complex PSVT	6mg rapid IVP over 1–3 sec; if no response in 1–2 min, repeat 12mg rapid IVP. A third dose of 12mg may be given if needed	Common side effects: transient chest pain, flushing and dyspnea
Amiodarone	1. Ventricular fibrillation/pulseless VT	300mg rapid infusion diluted in 20–30mL D5W, may repeat 150mg infusion in 3–5 min. Max cumulative dose: 2.2g/24hr	Long half-life (45hr) Do not shake ampules and avoid foaming Use a large bore needle to draw up the drug Adheres to plastic; use glass bottles for continuous infusion
	2. Ventricular tachycardia 3. Atrial fibrillation/flutter (conversion of rhythm)	150mg over 10 min (15mg/min); repeat as needed. Maintenance infusion: 1mg/min x 6hr, then 0.5mg/min x 18hr Max cumulative dose: 2.2g/24hr	
Atropine	1. Symptomatic bradycardia 2. AV block at the nodal level	0.5–1.0mg IVP Q3–5 min	Maximum dose: 3mg (0.04mg/kg)
	3. Asystole Note: Will not work with cardiac transplant patients	1mg IVP Q 3–5 min	
Epinephrine	1. Cardiac arrest	Recommended dose: 1mg (1:10,000) IVP Q3–5 min If IV is not available, may give via tracheal tube at 2–2.5 x IV dose	May use continuous infusion via central line: 30mg/250mL at 100mL/hr (comparable to 1mg Q5 min)
	2. As a vasopressor in symptomatic bradycardia	2–10mcg/min IV infusion titrate to effect	
Isoproterenol	1. Refractory torsades de pointes 2. Symptomatic bradycardia	Use low doses: 2–10mcg/min IV infusion, titrate to effect	At high doses, it can exacerbate ischemia and arrhythmia
Lidocaine	1. VF/pulseless VT 2. PVCs, VT, wide-complex tachycardia of uncertain type, wide complex PSVT	1.5mg/kg IVP, repeat in 3–5 min 1.0–1.5mg/kg IVP, repeat with 0.5–0.75mg/kg IVP Q 5–10 min	1. Maximum dose: 3mg/kg 2. Maintenance drip: 2–4mg/min (Conc: 2g in 500mL D_5W or NS)
Magnesium Sulfate	1. Torsades de pointes 2. Suspected hypomagnesemia 3. Severe refractory VF/ pulseless VT	1–2g/100mL infuse over 1–2 min during cardiac arrest	In acute MI patient with documented Mg deficiency, $MgSO_4$ may be given as 1–2g / 50–100mL over 5–60 min, followed by an infusion of 0.5–1g/hr x 24 hr
Procainamide	1. PVCs, recurrent VT, wide-complex tachycardia of uncertain type 2. Refractory VF / pulseless VT	20–30mg/min IV infusion until effect, maximum dose = 17mg/kg. S/E Hypotension, or QRS > 50% its orignal width (May give as 1g in 50mL D_5W or NS)	1. Maintenance drip: 1–4mg/min (Conc: 2g in 500mL D_5W or NS) 2. Avoid use in patients with prolonged QT interval or torsades de pointes
Sodium Bicarbonate	1. Hyperkalemia 2. Not recommended for routine use during arrest (use appropriately according to clinical situation)	Use ABG to guide therapy. If ABG unavailable, 1mEq/kg IVP then ½ dose Q 10 min	Adequate ventilation and restoration of tissue perfusion are essential
Vasopressin	Cardiac Arrest	40 U IV one time only	Not recommended for asystole or PEA
Verapamil	1. To control ventricular rate in atrial fibrillation and atrial flutter 2. Narrow-complex PSVT	2.5–5mg IVP over 2 min, repeat PRN. 5–10mg Q 15–30 min to a maximum of 20mg	1. In elderly, give 2–4mg over 3–4 min 2. S/E — Hypotension

[1] This table is a summary of ACLS drug dosages from the 2000 AHA recommendations. It is intended to serve only as a quick reference. One should refer to appropriate references for detailed information.

APPX

Miriam Chan, PharmD

122. PREPARATION OF INFUSION FOR ADULT EMERGENCY DRUGS

Drug	Dosage Range	Infusion Concentration	Drip Rate (mL/hr) (assume a 70kg patient)
Amiodarone	1mg/min x 6hr 0.5mg/min x 18hr	600mg/300mL	1mg/min = 30mL/hr
Dobutamine	2.0–20mcg/kg/min	500mg/250mL	2mcg/kg/min = 4mL/hr
Dopamine	2.0–20mcg/kg/min	400mg/250mL	5mcg/kg/min = 13mL/hr
Epinephrine	2–10mcg/min	2mg/250mL	2mcg/min = 15mL/hr
Isoproterenol	2–10mcg/min	2mg/250mL	2mcg/min = 15mL/hr
Lidocaine	2–4mg/min	2g/500mL	2mg/mL = 30mL/hr
Nitroglycerin (IV)	start 10–20mcg/min	50mg/250mL	10mcg/min = 3mL/hr
Nitroprusside	0.1–5.0mcg/kg/min	50mg/250mL	0.1mcg/kg/min = 2mL/hr
Norepinephrine	0.5–30mcg/min	8mg/250mL	0.5mcg/min = 1mL/hr
Phenylephrine	start 25–40mcg/min	50mg/250mL	50mcg/min = 15mL/hr
Procainamide	1–4mg/min	2g/500mL	1mg/min = 15mL/hr

INDEX

Note: Chapter titles are in all capitals

A

A–a Gradient
  formulas 395
Abacavir
  HIV/AIDS 380, 381
ABC
  HIV/AIDS 381, 391
Abdominal aortic aneurysm
  back pain 295
ABDOMINAL PAIN 319–323
  diverticulitis 323
ABO incompatibility
  neonatal jaundice 13
Acamprosate
  alcohol & drug abuse 353
Acarbose
  diabetes 180
Accupril
  heart failure 142
  hypertension 134
Accuretic
  hypertension 135
Accutane
  acne 307
ACE inhibitors
  drug interactions 266, 269
  hypertension 134
Acebutolol
  breast-feeding 60
  coronary artery disease 138
  hypertension 133
Acenocoumarol
  breast-feeding 59
  pregnancy 58
Aceon
  hypertension 134
Acetaminophen
  alcohol & drug abuse 354
  ankle injuries 279
  back-pain 296
  breast-feeding 59
  drug interactions 269
  headache 191
  osteoarthritis 238
  otitis media 23
  pain management 330
  pharyngitis 27
  pregnancy 56, 58
Acetate
  steroids 312
Achilles tendon
  ankle injuries 277, 278
AcipHex
  GERD 213

Aclovate
  steroids 312
ACLS PROTOCOLS 398-407
ACNE & ROSACEA 305–309
Actifed 396, 397
Actinomyces
  PID 95
Activella
  menopause & HRT 85
Actonel
  osteoporosis 247
Actos
  diabetes 180
Acular
  allergic rhinitis 231
  ocular disorders 226
ACUTE SINUSITIS 232–235
Acyclovir
  medication use, elderly 360
  pregnancy 62
  rashes in children 43
  vaginitis/STDs 94
Adalat CC
  coronary artery disease 138
  hypertension 134
Adapalene
  acne 307
Adderall
  ADHD 47
Addison's disease
  potassium disorders 263
Adenomyosis
  uterine bleeding 79
Adenosine
  ACLS, tachycardia 404
  cardiac stress testing 153
  emergency drug dosage 407
Adenovirus
  diarrhea in children 31, 34
Adhesive capsulitis
  shoulder injuries 287
Adrenal dysfunction
  anxiety 339
Adrenaline
  wounds 325
ADULT ADVANCED CARDIAC LIFE SUPPORT
      PROTOCOLS 398-407
Aerobid
  COPD 167
Aerolized Pentamidine
  HIV/AIDS 377
Afrin 397
  allergic rhinitis 231
Aftate
  tinea pedis 313

Agenerase
  HIV/AIDS 382
Aggrenox
  CVAs 197
AIDS. *See* HIV/AIDS
AIDS MANAGEMENT 375–383
AIDS-DEFINING CONDITIONS 383
Alamast
  ocular disorders 226
Albumin
  liver function tests 207
Albuterol
  asthma in children 21
  COPD 167
Alclometasone Dipropionate
  steroids 312
Alcohol
  anxiety 339, 340
  drug interactions 269, 270
  GERD 213
  liver function tests 206, 208
  preoperative evaluation 332
  PUD 214
  sexual dysfunction 349
ALCOHOL & OTHER DRUGS OF ABUSE 352–354
  hyperlipidemia 124
  liver function tests 208
Aldactone
  hypertension 133, 135
Aldara
  vaginitis/STDs 94
Aldomet
  hypertension 135
  medication use, elderly 359
  sexual dysfunction 347
Aldoril
  hypertension 135
Aldosterone receptor blockers
  heart failure 143
  hypertension 132, 133
Aldosteronism
  hypertension 129
Alendronate
  osteoporosis 247, 248
Alesse
  contraception 70, 72
Alkaline Phosphatase
  liver function tests 206
Alkaloids
  medication use, elderly 360
Allegra 397
  allergic rhinitis 231
Allerchlor
  allergic rhinitis 231
Allergens
  asthma in children 21
ALLERGIC RHINITIS/SEASONAL ALLERGIES 229–32
  asthma 162
ALLERGIES, SEASONAL 229–232
Allopurinol
  gouty arthritis 245
Alocril
  ocular disorders 226
Alomide
  allergic rhinitis 231
  ocular disorders 226

Alora
  menopause & HRT 86
α-adrenergic-receptor antagonists
  pregnancy 56
α-blockers
  hypertension 133
  medication use, elderly 359
  sexual dysfunction 347
α-Glucosidase Inhibitors
  diabetes 179, 180
α-fetal protein
  prenatal care 52
α1-blockers
  hypertension 135
Alport's syndrome
  hematuria 252, 253
Alprazolam
  breast-feeding 60
  drug interactions 266
  medication use, elderly 360
Alprostadil
  sexual dysfunction 349
Altace
  heart failure 142
  hypertension 134
Aluminum Acetate
  pregnancy 56
Aluminum Chloride
  skin biopsies 311
Aluminum Hydroxide
  pregnancy 56
Alupent
  COPD 167
Alzheimer's disease
  mental status changes 368, 371
Amaryl
  diabetes 180
  medication use, elderly 361
Ambien
  mental status changes 371
Amcinonide
  steroids 312
AMENORRHEA 82–84
  breast disorders 90
  contraception 70
  menopause & HRT 84
Amerge
  headache 191
Amiloride
  hypertension 133, 135
Aminoglycosides
  drug interactions 269
  medication use, elderly 360
  ocular disorders 226
  pregnancy 58
Aminophylline
  COPD 167
Aminopterin
  pregnancy 57
Aminotransferases
  liver function tests 205
Amiodarone
  ACLS 399, 403, 404, 405
  atrial fibrillation 146
  breast-feeding 60

INDEX

drug interactions 268, 269
emergency drugs 407, 408
health screening, elderly 357
thyroid disease 188
Amitriptyline
depression & dysthymia 345, 346
drug interactions 267, 269
headache 191
medication use, elderly 361
pain 331
Amlodipine
coronary artery disease 138
hypertension 134, 135
Amniocentesis
prenatal care 53
Amoxicillin
bite wounds 327, 328
diverticulitis 324
fever in children 17
otitis media 22, 23
pharyngitis 27
pneumonia 161
prenatal care 52
PUD 215
rashes in children 43
sinusitis 234
UTI 250, 252
Amoxil
PUD 215
UTI 250
AMP
HIV/AIDS 382
Amphojel
calcium disorders 262
Amphotericin B
drug interactions 269
potassium disorders 264
Ampicillin
prenatal care 55
Amprenavir
HIV/AIDS 380, 382
Amyloidosis
heart failure 140
Anabolic steroids
sexual dysfunction 348
Analgesics
back pain 294, 295
breast-feeding 59
Andrenergics
urinary incontinence, elderly 366
Androderm
sexual dysfunction 349
Androgenic drugs
pregnancy 57
ANEMIA 222–225
Anesthesia
wounds 325
Angina
cardiac stress testing 152
Angiotensin converting enzyme inhibitors
heart failure 141, 142
hypertension 129, 130, 132, 135
post-MI 151
pregnancy 56, 57
Angiotensin II receptor blockers
drug interactions 266, 269

heart failure 142
hypertension 129, 130, 132, 134, 135
Anion gap
formulas 395
Ankylosing spondylitis
back pain 294
Ankylosis
fractures 276
Anorexia
abdominal pain 319
diverticulitis 323
Anovulation
amenorrhea 83
Antabuse
alcohol & drug abuse 353
Antacids
GERD 213
pregnancy 56
PUD 214
Anterior cruciate ligament 281
Anterior drawer test
ankle injuries 278
Antiarrhythmic agents
heart failure 144
medication use, elderly 359
post-MI 151
Antibiotics
bronchitis 170
contraception 69
dizziness 194
liver function tests 207
UTIs in children 39
wound management 327, 328
Anticholinergic drugs
pregnancy 57
Anticoagulants
atrial fibrillation 146, 148, 149
breast-feeding 59
heart failure 143
post-MI 151
Antiepileptics
breast-feeding 59
liver function tests 207
Antifibrinolytics
pregnancy 56
Antifungals
hyperlipidemia 126
Antihistamines
ADHD 46
medication use, elderly 361
sinusitis 234
urinary incontinence, elderly 366
Antihypertensives
medication use, elderly 359
Antipsychotics
medication use, elderly 360
urinary incontinence, elderly 366
Antiretroviral therapy
HIV/AIDS 378
Anusol-HC
hemorrhoids 221
Anxiety
shortness of breath 155
ANXIETY DISORDERS 339–342
Anxiolytics
breast-feeding 60

Anzemet
   drug interactions 268
Aorta coarctation
   hypertension 129
   newborn exam 3
Apley grind test
   knee injuries 282
Apresoline
   heart failure 143
   hypertension 135
Aredia
   pain 331
Aricept
   mental status changes 371
Aristocort A
   steroids 312
Arthritis
   back pain 295
ARTHRITIS, DIFFERENTIAL DIAGNOSIS 235–238
ARTHRITIS, GOUTY 243–246
ARTHRITIS, RHEUMATOID 239–243
ASA muscle relaxants
   headache 191
Aspirin
   asthma 162
   asthma in children 21
   atrial fibrillation 148
   breast-feeding 59
   coronary artery disease 138
   CVAs 197
   diabetes 177
   health screening, elderly 358
   heart failure 142
   hematuria 253
   pain management 330
   post-MI 151
   pregnancy 56
   rheumatoid arthritis 241
Astelin
   allergic rhinitis 231
Astemizole
   pregnancy 56
ASTHMA 162–166
   bronchitis 170
ASTHMA IN CHILDREN 18–22
Atacand
   heart failure 142
   hypertension 134, 135
Atarax 397
   allergic rhinitis 231
   contact dermatitis 304
Atenolol
   atrial fibrillation 146
   breast-feeding 60
   coronary artery disease 138
   heart failure 144
   hypertension 133, 135
   medication use, elderly 360
   preoperative evaluation 336
Ativan
   alcohol & drug abuse 353
   anxiety 340
   medication use, elderly 360
   mental status changes 371
Atomoxetin
   ADHD 48

Atopic dermatitis
   asthma 162
Atorvastatin
   hyperlipidemia 126
Atovaquone
   HIV/AIDS 377
ATRIAL FIBRILLATION 145–150
Atrophy
   dermatologic lesions 301
Atropine
   ACLS 400, 401, 402
   emergency drug dosage 407
Atrovent
   COPD 167
Augmentin
   bite wounds 327
   COPD 168
   fever in children 17
   otitis media 23
Auralgan
   otitis media 23, 24
Avalide
   hypertension 135
Avandia
   diabetes 180
Avapro
   heart failure 142
   hypertension 134
Avelox
   acne 307
   drug interactions 267, 269
   pneumonia 160
Aventyl
   depression & dysthymia 345
Avodart
   BPH 259
Axid
   GERD 213
Azathioprine
   rheumatoid arthritis 242
Azelaic acid
   acne 306
   rosacea 308
Azelastine
   allergic rhinitis 231
Azelex
   acne 306
   rosacea 308
Azithromycin
   HIV/AIDS 377
   otitis media 23
   pharyngitis 26
   pneumonia 160, 161
   vaginitis/STDs 93
Azmacort
   COPD 167
AZT
   HIV/AIDS 381, 391

B

BACK PAIN 292–296
   pregnancy 63
Back strain
   back pain 294

INDEX

Bacterial tracheitis
  croup 28
Bactrim
  COPD 168
  dog bites 328
  otitis media 23
  sinusitis 234
  UTI 250
  UTIs in children 39
BALDING 315–316
Ballottement
  knee injuries 281
Banophen
  allergic rhinitis 231
Barbiturates
  liver function tests 206
  medication use, elderly 360
  pregnancy 57
Barium enema
  constipation in adults 219
  diverticulitis 324
Barley malt extract
  constipation in children 37
Barlow test
  newborn exam 4
Barrett's esophagus
  GERD 213
Basedow's disease
  thyroid disease 185
Bayonette fracture 275
BCG
  tuberculosis screening 109
Beclomethasone
  allergic rhinitis 230
  asthma 164
  asthma in children 20
Beclomethasone Dipropionate
  COPD 167
Beclovent
  COPD 167
Beconase
  allergic rhinitis 230
Belladonna
  medication use, elderly 360
Benadryl 397
  alcohol & drug abuse 354
  allergic rhinitis 231
  contact dermatitis 304
  medication use, elderly 360
  rashes in children 43
Benazepril
  heart failure 142
  hypertension 134, 135
Bence-Jones protein
  proteinuria 255
Bendectin
  pregnancy 57
Benicar
  hypertension 134
BENIGN PROSTATIC HYPERTROPHY 257–260
Bentyl
  alcohol & drug abuse 354
  medication use, elderly 360
Benzamycin
  acne 307

Benzathine Penicillin
  pharyngitis 26
Benzodiazepines
  alcohol & drug abuse 353
  anxiety 340, 341
  falls in the elderly 364
  medication use, elderly 360
  PMS 89
  pregnancy 56, 57
Benzonatate 396
Benzoyl Peroxide
  acne 306, 307
  pregnancy 56
  warts 313
Bepridil
  drug interactions 269
β-blockers
  ACLS, tachycardia 404, 405
  atrial fibrillation 146
  coronary artery disease 138
  drug interactions 266
  headache 191
  heart failure 142, 144
  hypertension 129, 130, 132, 133, 135, 141
  medication use, elderly 360
  post-MI 151
  preoperative evaluation 336
  sexual dysfunction 347
β-lactam monotherapy
  pneumonia 160
β2-agonist
  asthma 165
Betagan
  medication use, elderly 360
Betamethasone
  steroids 312
Betapace
  drug interactions 268
Betaxolol
  hypertension 133
  medication use, elderly 360
Betoptic
  medication use, elderly 360
Bextra
  rheumatoid arthritis 241
Biaxin
  drug interactions 269
  HIV/AIDS 377
  otitis media 23
  pneumonia 160
  PUD 215
Bichloracetic Acid
  vaginitis/STDs 94
Bicillin
  pharyngitis 26
Biguanides
  diabetes 179, 180
Bile acid
  hyperlipidemia 125, 126, 127
Bilirubin
  liver function tests 205, 206
  neonatal jaundice 13
Biocal
  calcium disorders 262

Biofeedback
  headache 191
Biopsies, skin 309–312
BiPAP
  COPD 168
Bisacodyl
  constipation in adults 220
  constipation in children 37
  pregnancy 56
Bismuth
  pregnancy 56
  PUD 214, 215
Bisoprolol
  heart failure 143
  hypertension 133, 135
  preoperative evaluation 336
Bisphosphonate
  osteoporosis 247
Bite wounds 327
Black Cohosh
  menopause & HRT 86
Bladder training
  urinary incontinence, elderly 367
Blepharitis
  acne 309
  ocular disorders 227
Blocadren
  coronary artery disease 138
  heart failure 144
  hypertension 133
Bone scan
  back pain 293
Booster phenomenon
  tuberculosis screening 108
Boric acid
  vaginitis/STDs 93
Boxer's fracture 276
BPH 257–260
Bradyarrhythmia
  ECG 121
Bradycardia
  ECG 117, 122
Brain injury
  ADHD 45
Breast cancer
  menopause & HRT 87
BREAST MASS, BREAST PAIN & NIPPLE
  DISCHARGE 90–92
BREAST-FEEDING & INFANT FORMULA 10–13
Brethaire
  COPD 167
Brevicon
  contraception 72
Bromfed-DM 396
Brompheniramine 396, 397
Bronchiolitis
  asthma in children 18
Bronchitis 396–397
BRONCHITIS, ACUTE 169–170
Bronchopulmonary dysplasia
  asthma in children 18
Budesonide
  allergic rhinitis 230
  asthma 164
  asthma in children 20

COPD 167
Bulla
  dermatologic lesions 301
Bumetanide
  heart failure 143
  hypertension 133
Bumex
  heart failure 143
  hypertension 133
Bupivacaine
  wounds 326
Buprenorphine Hydrochloride
  alcohol & drug abuse 354
Bupropion
  depression & dysthymia 344, 346
  smoking cessation 102
Burrow's solution
  contact dermatitis 304
  dermatologic lesions 301
Bursitis
  knee injuries 284
Buserelin
  PMS 89
BuSpar
  anxiety 340
  mental status changes 371
Buspirone
  alcohol & drug abuse 353
  anxiety 340
  mental status changes 371
Butalbital
  headache 191
Bypass Angioplasty Revascularization Investigation
  coronary artery disease 139

C

Caffeine
  anxiety 339, 340
  breast disorders 91
  hypertension 136
  PMS 88
  pregnancy 63
CAGE questions
  alcohol & drug abuse 352
Calamine lotion
  pregnancy 56
Calan
  atrial fibrillation 146
  coronary artery disease 139
  heart failure 144
  hypertension 134
Calcaneofibular ligament
  ankle injuries 277
Calcimar
  osteoporosis 248
  pain 331
Calcitonin
  compression fractures 365
  osteoporosis 248
  pain 331
Calcitriol
  calcium disorders 262

Calcium
  calcium disorders 262
  menopause & HRT 86
  osteoporosis 247, 248
  potassium metabolism 264
  pregnancy 56
Calcium channel blockers
  ACLS, tachycardia 404
  atrial fibrillation 145
  coronary artery disease 138
  heart failure 144
  hypertension 129, 130, 132, 134, 135
  post-MI 151
CALCIUM DISORDERS 260–263
Caltrate 262
Campylobacter
  diarrhea in adults 216, 218
  diarrhea in children 31
Cancer
  uterine bleeding 79
CANCER SCREENING 99–102
Candesartan
  heart failure 142
  hypertension 134, 135
Candida
  vaginitis/STDs 92
Candidiasis
  HIV/AIDS 383
Capex
  steroids 312
Capoten
  heart failure 142
  hypertension 134
Capozide
  hypertension 135
Capsaicin
  osteoarthritis 238
  pain 331
Captopril
  heart failure 142
  hypertension 134, 135
Carafate
  PUD 214
  rheumatoid arthritis 241
Carbamazepine
  breast-feeding 59
  contraception 69
  drug interactions 266
  medication use, elderly 360
  mental status changes 371
  pain 331
  pregnancy 57, 58
  seizures 200, 201
Carbatrol
  seizures 201
Carbinoxamine 396, 397
Carcinoid syndrome
  anxiety 339
Cardene
  coronary artery disease 138
  drug interactions 269
  hypertension 134
Cardiac catheterization
  cardiac stress testing 152

  heart failure 141
  post-MI 150
  preoperative evaluation 333
Cardiac enzymes
  coronary artery disease 137
CARDIAC STRESS TESTING 152–154
Cardiolite
  cardiac stress testing 153
Cardiovascular
  breast-feeding 60
Cardizem
  atrial fibrillation 145
  coronary artery disease 138
  heart failure 144
  hypertension 134
Cardura
  BPH 259
  hypertension 135
  medication use, elderly 359
  urinary incontinence, elderly 366
Carisoprodol
  medication use, elderly 360
Carlin maneuver
  knee injuries 281
CARPAL TUNNEL SYNDROME 291–292
Carteolol
  medication use, elderly 360
Carvedilol
  coronary artery disease 138
  heart failure 142
  hypertension 133
Cat bites 328
Catapres
  ADHD 48
  hypertension 135
  medication use, elderly 359
  sexual dysfunction 347
Catheters
  UTI 251
CBZ
  drug interactions 266
CD4 CELL COUNTS/CLINICAL MANIFESTATIONS 384
  HIV/AIDS 378, 380
Cefdinir
  otitis media 23
Cefixime
  otitis media 23
  UTIs in children 39
  vaginitis/STDs 93
Cefotaxime
  PID 96
Cefoxitin
  PID 96
Cefpodoxime
  UTIs in children 39
Ceftin
  cat bites 328
  otitis media 23
Ceftizoxime
  PID 96
Ceftriaxone
  fever in children 16, 17
  PID 96
  vaginitis/STDs 93

Cefuroxime
   cat bites 328
   otitis media 23
   rashes in children 43
Celebrex
   pain management 330
   rheumatoid arthritis 241
Celecoxib
   pain management 330
Celestone
   joint injections 297
Celexa
   anxiety 341
   depression & dysthymia 345
   drug interactions 269
   medication use, elderly 361
   postpartum 66
Central α2-agonists
   hypertension 135
Cephalexin
   breast-feeding 11
   cat bites 328
   diverticulitis 324
   pharyngitis 26
   UTIs in children 39
Cephalosporins
   medication use, elderly 360
   pneumonia 160
   pregnancy 58
Cerivastatin
   hyperlipidemia 126
Cervical cancer
   HIV/AIDS 383
Cetirizine 397
   allergic rhinitis 231
CHEST PAIN 113–117
Chicken pox
   pregnancy 62
   rashes in children 43
CHILDHOOD IMMUNIZATION & HEALTH CARE 6–10
Chlamydia
   asthma in children 18
   vaginitis/STDs 93
Chloamine
   allergic rhinitis 231
Chlor-Trimeton 397
   allergic rhinitis 231
Chloramphenicol
   breast-feeding 59
   rashes in children 44
Chloraseptic spray/lozenges
   pharyngitis 27
Chlordiazepoxide
   alcohol & drug abuse 353
   medication use, elderly 360
Chlorothiazide
   hypertension 133
Chlorpheniramine 396, 397
   allergic rhinitis 231
Chlorpromazine
   drug interactions 268
   medication use, elderly 360
   pregnancy 56
Chlorpropamide
   medication use, elderly 361

Chlorthalidone
   hypertension 133
Chlorzoxazone
   medication use, elderly 360
Cholera
   diarrhea in adults 218
Cholesterol
   coronary artery disease 140
   formulas 395
   hyperlipidemia 122
   post-MI 150
   preoperative evaluation 336
Cholestyramine
   hyperlipidemia 126
Chondromalacia
   knee injuries 283
Chorionic villus sampling
   prenatal care 53
Chronic lung disease
   ECG 121
CHRONIC OBSTRUCTIVE PULMONARY DISEASE
     (COPD) 166–169
Chvostek's sign
   calcium disorders 262
Ciclopirox
   tinea pedis 313
   tinea unguium 314
   tinea versicolor 314
Ciloxan
   ocular disorders 226
Cimetidine
   GERD 213
   medication use, elderly 360
Cipro
   COPD 167
   dog bites 328
   drug interactions 267
   UTI 250
   vaginitis/STDs 93
Ciprofloxacin
   diverticulitis 324
   ocular disorders 226
   UTI 250
   vaginitis/STDs 93
Cirrhosis
   hepatitis B 208, 210
Cisapride
   drug interactions 270
Citalopram
   anxiety 341
   depression & dysthymia 344, 345, 346
   drug interactions 269
   medication use, elderly 361
   postpartum 66
Clarinex 397
   allergic rhinitis 231
Clarithromycin
   drug interactions 269
   HIV/AIDS 377
   otitis media 23
   pneumonia 160, 161
   PUD 215
Claritin 397
   allergic rhinitis 231
Cleft palate
   newborn exam 4

Cleocin
  diverticulitis 324
  vaginitis/STDs 93
Clidinium-Chlordiazepoxide
  medication use, elderly 360
Climara
  menopause & HRT 86
Clindamycin
  acne 307
  breast-feeding 11
  diverticulitis 324
  dog bites 328
  pregnancy 56
  prenatal care 55
  vaginitis/STDs 93
Clobetasol Propionate
  steroids 312
Clofibrate
  hyperlipidemia 126
Clonazepam
  anxiety 341
  medication use, elderly 360
Clonidine
  ADHD 48
  hypertension 135
  medication use, elderly 359
  menopause & HRT 86
  sexual dysfunction 347
  smoking cessation 103
Clopidogrel
  coronary artery disease 138
  CVAs 197
Clostridium difficile
  diarrhea in adults 218
  diarrhea in children 31
Clostridium perfringens
  diarrhea in adults 216
Clotrimazole
  oral candidiasis 314
  tinea pedis 313
  tinea versicolor 314
  vaginitis/STDs 93
CMV
  HIV/AIDS 377, 385
Cocaine
  alcohol & drug abuse 354
  wounds 325
Coccidioidomycosis
  HIV/AIDS 383
CODE STATUS 372
Codeine 396
  bronchiolitis 30
  pain management 329
  pregnancy 56
Codeine Phosphate 396
Codeine/Acetaminophen
  pain management 329
Cognitive impairment
  ADHD 46
Coitus interruptus 74
Colace
  constipation in adults 220
  constipation in children 35
  postpartum 65
Colchicine
  gouty arthritis 245

COLDS AND FLU, SINUSITIS, BRONCHITIS, ETC.
  medications 396–397
Colesevelam
  hyperlipidemia 126
Colestipol
  hyperlipidemia 126
Colles' fracture 276
  carpal tunnel syndrome 291
Colonoscopy
  constipation in adults 219
Colorectal cancer
  constipation in adults 219
Colorectal screening
  health screening, elderly 357
Combination therapy
  coronary artery disease 139
  diabetes 179
Combipatch
  menopause & HRT 86
Combivent Inhaler
  COPD 167
Combivir
  HIV/AIDS 381
Comedone
  dermatologic lesions 301
Compazine
  dizziness 194
COMPRESSION FRACTURES 364–365
Computed tomography
  abdominal pain 321
  concussion 204
Concerta
  ADHD 47
CONCUSSION EVALUATION 202–205
Condom 73
Condylox
  vaginitis/STDs 94
Congenital infections
  neonatal jaundice 13
Conjugated estrogen
  amenorrhea 83
  osteoporosis 248
Conjunctival foreign body
  ocular disorders 227
Connor's Parent Rating Scale
  ADHD 45
Conn's syndrome
  hypertension 136
Constipation
  diverticulitis 323
  neonatal jaundice 13
  pregnancy 63
CONSTIPATION IN ADULTS 219–220
CONTACT DERMATITIS 303–305
CONTRACEPTION 69–75
Contraceptives
  pregnancy 57
COPD 166–169
  preoperative evaluation 336
Copper Paragard T380A
  contraception 74
Cordarone
  drug interactions 268
  health screening, elderly 357
Cordran
  steroids 312

Coreg
  hypertension 133
Corgard
  hypertension 133
Corneal abrasion
  ocular disorders 226
Corneal foreign body
  ocular disorders 227
Corneal ulcer
  ocular disorders 225
Coronary angiography
  coronary artery disease 138
CORONARY ARTERY DISEASE 136–140
Corrected sodium with hyperglycemia
  formulas 395
CORTICOSTEROID INJECTION OF JOINTS 296–298
Corticosteroids
  carpal tunnel syndrome 291
  sexual dysfunction 348
  shoulder injuries 287
Cortisporin
  otitis media 23
  steroids 312
Corvert
  drug interactions 268
Corzide
  hypertension 135
Costochondritis
  breast, evaluation 91
Cough
  asthma 162
  HIV/AIDS 387
Coumadin
  CVAs 197
  drug interactions 267
  preoperative evaluation 332
Courvoisier's sign
  liver function tests 205
Covera HS
  hypertension 134
Cow's milk
  infant formulas 12
COX-2 agents
  medication use, elderly 361
Cozaar
  heart failure 142
  hypertension 134
Creatinine clearance (CrCl)
  formulas 395
Crigler-Najjar syndrome
  liver function tests 206
  neonatal jaundice 13
Crixivan
  drug interactions 267
  HIV/AIDS 382
Crohn's disease
  anemia 224
Crolom
  allergic rhinitis 231
  ocular disorders 226
Cromolyn
  allergic rhinitis 231
  asthma 164
  asthma in children 20
  ocular disorders 226
  pregnancy 56

CROUP (acute laryngotracheitis) 28–29
Cruex
  tinea pedis 313
Crusts
  dermatologic lesions 301
Cryotherapy
  vaginitis/STDs 94
Cryptococcosis
  HIV/AIDS 383, 385
Cryptococcus
  HIV/AIDS 377
Cryptosporidiosis
  HIV/AIDS 383
Cryptosporidium
  diarrhea in adults 217
  diarrhea in children 31
Cushing's disease
  depression & dysthymia 343
  hypertension 129
Cutivate
  steroids 312
CVAs, PREVENTION & MANAGEMENT 195–199
Cyanosis 3
Cyclessa
  contraception 72
Cyclizine
  pregnancy 56
Cyclobenzaprine
  medication use, elderly 360
Cyclocort
  steroids 312
Cyclopentolate
  ocular disorders 227
Cyclophosphamide
  breast-feeding 60
  hematuria 253
  pregnancy 57
Cycloplegic
  ocular disorders 227
Cyclosporine
  drug interactions 269
  hyperlipidemia 126
  osteoporosis 246
  rheumatoid arthritis 242
Cylert
  ADHD 47
Cyst
  dermatologic lesions 301
Cystic fibrosis
  asthma in children 18
  sinusitis 234
Cystoscopy
  hematuria 254
Cystourethrogram
  enuresis 41
Cytochrome P-450 inhibitors
  hyperlipidemia 126
Cytomegalovirus
  HIV/AIDS 383
  neonatal jaundice 13
Cytotec
  PUD 214, 216
  rheumatoid arthritis 241

INDEX

D

D-Penicillamine
    rheumatoid arthritis 242
d4T
    HIV/AIDS 381, 391
D50
    potassium disorders 264
Dalmane
    medication use, elderly 360
Danazol
    breast disorders 91
    PMS 89
    pregnancy 57
Dapsone
    HIV/AIDS 377
Darvocet-N 100
    pain management 329
Darvon
    medication use, elderly 361
    pain management 329
DDAVP
    enuresis 41
ddC
    HIV/AIDS 381
ddl
    HIV/AIDS 381, 391
Decadron
    joint injections 297
Decongestants
    medication use, elderly 361
    pregnancy 56
    sinusitis 234
    urinary incontinence, elderly 366
Dehydration
    diarrhea in children 32
Delavirdine
    HIV/AIDS 380, 382
Delirium
    mental status changes 368, 369
Delirium tremens
    alcohol & drug abuse 353
Deltoid ligament
    ankle injuries 277
Demadex
    hypertension 133
Dementia
    mental status changes 368, 370, 371
Demerol
    alcohol & drug abuse 354
    medication use, elderly 361
    pain management 329
Denver Development Screening Test
    developing child 6
Depade
    alcohol & drug abuse 353, 354
Depakote
    headache 191
    mental status changes 371
    pain 331
    seizures 200, 201
Depo-Medrol
    joint injections 297

Depo-Provera
    contraception 70, 73
    postpartum 65
    uterine bleeding 79
Depo-Testosterone
    sexual dysfunction 349
Depression
    back pain 295
    dysmenorrhea 89
    postpartum 65, 66
    shortness of breath 155
DEPRESSION & DYSTHYMIA 342–347
Depro-Lupron
    PMS 89
Derma-Smoothe/FS
    steroids 312
DERMATOLOGIC LESIONS 301–303
Dermatop e
    steroids 312
Desenex
    tinea pedis 313
Desipramine
    ADHD 48
    alcohol & drug abuse 354
    depression & dysthymia 345, 346
    drug interactions 269
    medication use, elderly 361
Desloratadine 397
    allergic rhinitis 231
Desmopressin
    enuresis 41
Desogen
    contraception 72
Desogestrel
    contraception 70
Desonide
    steroids 312
DesOwen
    steroids 312
Desoximetasone
    steroids 312
Desyrel
    anxiety 341
    depression & dysthymia 346
    mental status changes 371
Detrol
    urinary incontinence, elderly 367
DEVELOPING CHILD & NORMAL PEDIATRIC
        VITAL SIGNS 5–6
Dexamethasone
    croup 28
Dexedrine
    ADHD 47
Dextroamphetamine Sulfate
    ADHD 47
Dextromethorphan 396
    bronchiolitis 30
    pregnancy 56
Dextrostat
    ADHD 47
DHE-45
    headache 191
Diabeta
    diabetes 180
    medication use, elderly 361

Diabetes
  cardiac stress testing 152
  carpal tunnel syndrome 291
  constipation in adults 219
  hyperlipidemia 124
  hypertension 132
  lipid management 177
  ocular disorders 228
  preoperative evaluation 336
  proteinuria 256
  shoulder injuries 287
DIABETES MELLITUS 173–182
Diabinese
  medication use, elderly 361
Diaphragm 73
Diarrhea
  diverticulitis 323
  HIV/AIDS 383, 386
  infant formulas 12
  potassium disorders 263, 264
DIARRHEA IN ADULTS 216–219
DIARRHEA IN CHILDREN 31–35
Diazepam
  alcohol & drug abuse 353
  breast-feeding 60
  medication use, elderly 360
  pregnancy 57
Dichloroacetic Acid
  warts 313
Diclectin
  pregnancy 56
Dicloxacillin
  cat bites 328
Dicyclomine
  alcohol & drug abuse 354
  medication use, elderly 360
Didanosine
  HIV/AIDS 380, 381
Dienestrol
  menopause & HRT 86
Diethylstilbestrol
  pregnancy 57
Differin
  acne 307
Diflorasone Diacetate
  steroids 312
Diflucan
  oral candidiasis 314
  vaginitis/STDs 93
Digitalis
  atrial fibrillation 146
  ECG 121
  heart failure 143
Digoxin
  ACLS, tachycardia 404
  atrial fibrillation 146
  calcium disorders 263
  drug interactions 266
  heart failure 143, 144
  hypertension 141
  medication use, elderly 360
  potassium disorders 265
  sexual dysfunction 348
Dihydroergotamine
  headache 191

Dihydropyridines
  hypertension 134
Dilacor
  coronary artery disease 139
  heart failure 144
  hypertension 134
Dilantin
  contraception 69
  liver function tests 206
  osteoporosis 246
  pain 331
  seizures 200, 201
  sexual dysfunction 348, 350
Dilaudid
  pain management 329
Diltiazem
  ACLS, tachycardia 404
  atrial fibrillation 145
  coronary artery disease 138
  heart failure 144
  hypertension 134
Dimenhydrinate
  pregnancy 56
Dimetane 396
Dimetapp 397
Dioctyl Sodium Sulfosuccinate
  constipation in children 35
Diovan
  heart failure 142
  hypertension 134, 135
Diphenhist
  allergic rhinitis 231
Diphenhydramine 397
  alcohol & drug abuse 354
  allergic rhinitis 231
  contact dermatitis 304
  medication use, elderly 360
  pregnancy 56
  rashes in children 43
  wounds 326
Diplopia
  headache 190
  ocular disorders 225
Diprolene
  steroids 312
Dipyridamole
  CVAs 197
Disc herniation
  back pain 294
Disease-modifying antirheumatic drugs (DMARD)
  rheumatoid arthritis 241
Diskus
  COPD 167
Dislocation
  fractures 276
Disopyramide
  atrial fibrillation 146
  drug interactions 268
  medication use, elderly 359
Disseminated intravascular coagulation
  neonatal jaundice 13
Disulfiram
  alcohol & drug abuse 353

INDEX

Ditropan
  enuresis 41
  medication use, elderly 360
  urinary incontinence, elderly 367
Diupres
  hypertension 135
Diuretics
  dizziness 194
  heart failure 143
  hypertension 129, 130, 132, 133, 135, 141
Diuril
  hypertension 133
Divalproex
  mental status changes 371
  pain 331
  seizures 200, 201
Diverticulitis
  constipation in adults 219
Diverticulosis
  diarrhea in adults 217
DIVERTICULOSIS & DIVERTICULITIS 323–325
DIZZINESS 192–195
DLV
  HIV/AIDS 382
Dobutamine
  ACLS, acute pulmonary edema 406
  cardiac stress testing 152, 153
  emergency drugs, infusion 408
  heart failure 144
Docusate
  constipation in adults 220
Docusate Sodium
  pregnancy 56
Dofetilide
  atrial fibrillation 146
  drug interactions 266, 268
Dog bites 327
Dolasetron
  drug interactions 268
Dolophine
  drug interactions 269
  pain management 329
Donepezil
  mental status changes 371
Donnatal
  medication use, elderly 360
Dopamine
  ACLS, acute pulmonary edema 406
  ACLS, bradycardia 402
  emergency drugs, infusion 408
Doryx
  vaginitis/STDs 93
Down's syndrome
  prenatal care 53
Doxazosin
  BPH 259
  hypertension 135
  medication use, elderly 359
Doxepin
  breast-feeding 59
  depression & dysthymia 345, 346
  medication use, elderly 361
Doxorubicin
  breast-feeding 60

Doxycycline
  cat bites 328
  COPD 168
  diarrhea in adults 218
  PID 96
  pneumonia 160, 161
  rashes in children 43, 44
  rosacea 309
  vaginitis/STDs 93
Drawer tests
  knee injuries 282
Droperidol
  drug interactions 268
Drospirenone
  contraception 70
Drug abuse
  anxiety 339, 340
Drug clearance
  medication use, elderly 359
DRUG DOSAGE, EMERGENCY 407
DRUG INTERACTIONS 266–270
  medication use, elderly 358
Drug prescribing errors
  drug interactions 268
DRUGS OF ABUSE 352–354
DRUGS TO BE CAUTIOUS OF IN THE ELDERLY 358–361
Drysol
  skin biopsies 311
DSM-IV criteria
  ADHD 45
  depression & dysthymia 342, 343
Dubin-Johnson syndrome
  liver function tests 206
  neonatal jaundice 13
Ductus arteriosis 3
Dulcolax
  constipation in adults 220
Duofilm
  warts 313
DuoNeb
  COPD 167
Dupuytren's contracture
  liver function tests 205
Duragesic
  pain management 329
Duratuss HD 396
Dutasteride
  BPH 259
Dyazide
  hypertension 135
DynaCirc
  drug interactions 269
Dyrenium
  hypertension 133
Dysfunctional uterine bleeding
  uterine bleeding 79
Dysmenorrhea 89
Dyspareunia
  sexual dysfunction 350, 351
Dyspepsia
  PUD 214
Dyspnea
  acute bronchitis 169
  chest pain 114

COPD 166
heart failure 140
HIV/AIDS 387
shortness of breath 155
DYSTHYMIA 342–347
Dysuria
hematuria 253
UTI 249, 250

E

E. coli
diarrhea in adults 216, 218
ECG
heart failure 141
potassium disorders 265
preoperative evaluation 333
shortness of breath 155
ECG INTERPRETATION 117–122
ECHO
chest pain 114
heart failure 141
post-MI 150
Echocardiography
coronary artery disease 137
Ectopic pregnancy
contraception 69
PID 95, 96
Eczema
asthma 162
Edema
chest pain 114
COPD 166
heart failure 140
preoperative evaluation 332
shortness of breath 155
Efavirenz
HIV/AIDS 380, 382
Effexor
ADHD 48
anxiety 341
depression & dysthymia 345
drug interactions 269
menopause & HRT 86
EFV
HIV/AIDS 382, 391
EKG
cardiac stress testing 152
coronary artery disease 137
health screening, elderly 357
Elavil
depression & dysthymia 345
drug interactions 269
medication use, elderly 361
pain 331
ELBOW INJURIES 288–291
Elderly
cholesterol screening 123
compression fractures 364–365
drugs to be cautious of 358–361
falls 362–364
hypertension 132
periodic health screening 357–358
urinary incontinence 365–368
Electrocardiogram. See ECG

Electrodiagnostic studies
back pain 293
Electrolyte abnormalities
ECG 121
Electromyography
carpal tunnel syndrome 291
Electron Beam Computed Tomography (EBCT)
cardiac stress testing 153
Elimite
scabies 313
Elocon
steroids 312
EMERGENCY DRUG DOSAGE 407
EMERGENCY DRUGS, INFUSION 408
Emetrol
morning sickness 61
EMLA cream
wounds 325
Emory Angioplasty versus Surgery Trial
coronary artery disease 139
Empiric
thyroid disease 186
Empirin
pain management 329
Enalapril
heart failure 142
hypertension 134, 135
Encainide
drug interactions 266
Encephalopathy
hepatitis B 210
Endep
depression & dysthymia 345
ENDOCARDITIS PROPHYLAXIS 104–108
preoperative evaluation 336
Endometrial sampling
menopause & HRT 87
Endometriosis
contraception 69
hematuria 253
uterine bleeding 79
Endometritis
uterine bleeding 79
Endophthalmitis
ocular disorders 225
ENF
HIV/AIDS 382
Enfuvirtide
HIV/AIDS 382
Entamoeba histolytica
diarrhea in adults 217
diarrhea in children 31
Enterovirus
diarrhea in children 31
ENURESIS 40–42
Epidural hemorrhage
concussion 204
Epiglottis
croup 29
Epiglottitis
croup 28
shortness of breath 154, 157
Epinephrine
ACLS 398–402
emergency drug dosage 407
emergency drugs, infusion 408

hemorrhoids 221
  wounds 326, 328
Epispadias
  newborn exam 3
Epivir
  HIV/AIDS 381
  hepatitis B 210
Eplerenone
  hypertension 133
Epley maneuver
  dizziness 195
Eprosartan
  hypertension 134, 135
Epstein's pearls
  newborn exam 4
Equanil
  medication use, elderly 360
Erections
  sexual dysfunction 347
Ergotamine
  pregnancy 56
Erosion
  dermatologic lesions 301
Erythema
  breast disorders 91
  rashes in children 42
Erythromycin
  acne 307
  breast-feeding 11
  COPD 167
  diarrhea in adults 218
  drug interactions 269
  otitis media 23
  pharyngitis 26
  pneumonia 160, 161
  pregnancy 56
  prenatal care 55
Esomeprazole
  GERD 213
  PUD 215
Estrace
  menopause & HRT 86
Estraderm
  menopause & HRT 86
  osteoporosis 248
Estradiol
  drug interactions 270
  menopause & HRT 86
  osteoporosis 248
Estratab
  menopause & HRT 86
Estratest
  menopause & HRT 86
Estring
  menopause & HRT 86
Estrogen
  amenorrhea 82
  contraception 71
  menopause & HRT 86
  urinary incontinence, elderly 367
  vaginitis/STDs 93
Estrogen replacement therapy
  osteoarthritis 238
  osteoporosis 248
  urinary incontinence, elderly 367

Estrogen/Progesterone patch
  menopause & HRT 86
Estropipate
  menopause & HRT 86
Estrostep
  contraception 72
Etanercept
  rheumatoid arthritis 242
Ethinyl Estradiol
  contraception 70, 73
Ethosuximide
  breast-feeding 59
  seizures 200, 201
Etonogestrel
  contraception 73
Etretinate
  pregnancy 57
Evening primrose oil
  breast disorders 91
Evista
  osteoporosis 248
Exanthem
  contact dermatitis 304
Excoriation
  dermatologic lesions 301
Exelon
  mental status changes 371
Exercise
  asthma 162
Eye problems 225–229

F

FALLS IN THE ELDERLY 362–364
Famciclovir
  pregnancy 62
  vaginitis/STDs 94
Famotidine
  GERD 213
Famvir
  vaginitis/STDs 94
Fatigue
  bronchitis 169
  depression & dysthymia 343
  HIV/AIDS 375
  pneumonia 159
Febrile seizure
  seizures 201
Fecal impaction
  constipation in adults 220
Felodipine
  hypertension 134
FemHRT
  menopause & HRT 85
FemPatch
  menopause & HRT 86
Fenofibrate
  hyperlipidemia 125, 126
Fentanyl
  pain management 329
Ferric Subsulfate
  skin biopsies 311
Fertility based awareness
  contraception 74
FeSO4
  anemia 223

Fetal alcohol syndrome
  ADHD 45
Fetal exposure to drugs
  ADHD 45
Fetal heart tones
  prenatal care 52
Fever
  abdominal pain 319
  bronchiolitis 29
  bronchitis 169
  chest pain 114
  constipation in children 35, 37
  COPD 166
  croup 28
  diverticulitis 323
  headache 190
  hematuria 253
  hepatitis B 209
  HIV/AIDS 375, 383, 387, 389
  otitis media 22
  pharyngitis 25, 27
  pneumonia 159
  pregnancy 61
  rashes in children 43
  seizures 200, 201
  shortness of breath 155
  UTI 250
  UTIs in children 38
FEVER WITHOUT A SOURCE 15–18
Fexofenadine 397
  allergic rhinitis 231
Fibrates
  hyperlipidemia 126, 127
Fibric Acid
  hyperlipidemia 125, 126
Fibrocystic breast disease
  breast disorders 90
Fibroids
  uterine bleeding 79
Fibromyalgia
  back pain 295
Fifth disease
  pregnancy 62
  rashes in children 42
Finasteride
  BPH 259
  hair loss 315
  sexual dysfunction 348
Fine needle aspiration
  thyroid disease 188
Fissure
  dermatologic lesions 301
Fistula
  newborn exam 3
Flagyl
  diarrhea in adults 218
  diverticulitis 324
  PUD 215
  vaginitis/STDs 93
Flavoxate
  urinary incontinence, elderly 367
Flecainide
  atrial fibrillation 146
  drug interactions 268
Fleets phospho-soda
  calcium disorders 261

Flexeril
  medication use, elderly 360
Flomax
  BPH 259
Flonase
  allergic rhinitis 230
Florinef
  falls in the elderly 363
Flovent
  COPD 167
Floxin
  drug interactions 267
  UTI 250
  vaginitis/STDs 93
Flu
  medications 396–397
Fluconazole
  medication use, elderly 360
  oral candidiasis 314
  tinea versicolor 314
  vaginitis/STDs 93
Fludrocortisone
  falls in the elderly 363
Flunisolide
  allergic rhinitis 230
  asthma 164
  asthma in children 20
  COPD 167
Fluocinolone Acetonide
  steroids 312
Fluocinonide
  steroids 312
Fluoride
  care of children 9, 12
Fluoroquinolones
  diarrhea in adults 218
  dog bites 328
  otitis media 23
  pneumonia 160
  UTI 251, 252
Fluoxetine
  anxiety 341
  breast-feeding 59
  depression & dysthymia 345, 346
  drug interactions 269
  medication use, elderly 361
  PMS 89
  postpartum 66
  pregnancy 56
Flurandrenolide
  steroids 312
Flurazepam
  medication use, elderly 360
Flurbiprofen
  pregnancy 58
Fluticasone
  allergic rhinitis 230
  asthma 164
  asthma in adults 164
  asthma in children 20
  COPD 167
  steroids 312
Fluvastatin
  hyperlipidemia 126
Folate
  anemia 224

Folic Acid
　prenatal care 51
Forane
　pain 331
Foreign body aspiration
　croup 28
Formoterol
　asthma 164
　asthma in children 20
　COPD 167
FORMULAS 395–396
Forteo
　osteoporosis 248
Fortovase
　HIV/AIDS 380, 382
Foscarnet
　drug interactions 269
Fosfomycin
　UTI 250
Fosinopril
　heart failure 142
　hypertension 134
Fractional excretion of sodium
　formulas 395
FRACTURES 275–277
FRACTURES, COMPRESSION 364–365
FTV
　HIV/AIDS 382
Fulvicin-U/F
　tinea capitis 314
　tinea pedis 313
Fundal height
　prenatal care 52
Funduscopic exam
　ocular disorders 226
Furosemide
　ACLS, acute pulmonary edema 406
　heart failure 143
　hypertension 133
　potassium disorders 264
Fuzeon
　HIV/AIDS 382

G

G-6-PD deficiency 13
Gabapentin
　pain 331
　seizures 201
Gabitril
　seizures 201
Galactorrhea
　amenorrhea 82
　breast disorders 90
Galactosemia
　neonatal jaundice 13
Galantamine
　mental status changes 371
Gamma-glutamyl transpeptidase
　liver function tests 206
Ganciclovir
　drug interactions 269

Gardnerella
　vaginitis/STDs 92
Gastrinoma
　PUD 214
Gastrocnemius muscle
　ankle injuries 277
GASTROESOPHAGEAL REFLUX DISEASE
　& PEPTIC ULCER DISEASE 211–216
Gastroesophageal reflux
　asthma 162
Gatifloxacin
　drug interactions 267, 269
　pneumonia 160
Gelfoam
　skin biopsies 311
Gemfibrozil
　hyperlipidemia 125, 126
　sexual dysfunction 348
Generalized anxiety disorder 339, 340
Genital warts
　vaginitis/STDs 94
Gentamicin
　ocular disorders 226
　potassium disorders 264
Gentian violet
　vaginitis/STDs 93
Geodon
　drug interactions 267, 268
GERD & PUD 211–216
Geriatric drug use 358–361
GERIATRIC HEALTH SCREENING 357–358
Giardia
　diarrhea in adults 217, 218
　diarrhea in children 31
Gilbert's disease
　liver function tests 206, 207
　neonatal jaundice 13
Glaucoma
　health screening, elderly 358
　ocular disorders 225, 227
Glimepiride
　diabetes 180
　medication use, elderly 361
Glipizide
　diabetes 180
　liver function tests 207
　medication use, elderly 361
Glomerulonephritis
　hematuria 252
Glucocorticoids
　calcium disorders 261
　osteoporosis 246
　pregnancy 56
　rheumatoid arthritis 241
Glucola
　prenatal care 53
Glucophage
　diabetes 178, 180
Glucotrol
　diabetes 180
　medication use, elderly 361
Glucovance
　diabetes 180
Glyburide
　diabetes 180
　medication use, elderly 361

Glycerin
  constipation in children 37
  pregnancy 56
Glynase
  diabetes 180
  medication use, elderly 361
Glyset
  diabetes 180
GnRH agonists
  osteoporosis 246
Goiter
  thyroid disease 186, 188
Gold salts
  breast-feeding 59
Gold Sodium Malate
  rheumatoid arthritis 242
Golfer's elbow 289
GoLYTELY
  constipation in adults 220
Gonorrhea
  vaginitis/STDs 93
Goodpasture's syndrome
  hematuria 252
Gout
  arthritis 235, 236
  knee injuries 281
GOUTY ARTHRITIS 243–246
Gramicidin
  ocular disorders 226
Granulomatous diseases
  liver function tests 206
Graves' disease
  thyroid disease 183, 185
Grifulvin V
  tinea capitis 314
  tinea pedis 313
Grisactin
  tinea capitis 314
  tinea pedis 313
Griseofulvin
  contraception 69
  tinea capitis 314
  tinea pedis 313
Group B streptococcus
  prenatal care 54
Guaifenesin 396, 397
  COPD 168
Guanabenz
  medication use, elderly 359
Guanfacine
  hypertension 135
Guillain-Barre syndrome
  dizziness 193
Gyne-Lotrimin
  vaginitis/STDs 93

H

H2 blockers
  GERD 213
  medication use, elderly 360
Habitrol
  smoking cessation 103
HAIR CHANGES & BALDING 315–316
Halcinonide
  steroids 312

Halcion
  drug interactions 266
  medication use, elderly 360
  mental status changes 371
Haldol
  drug interactions 268
Halfan
  drug interactions 269
Hallpike maneuver
  dizziness 193
Halobetasol Propionate
  steroids 312
Halofantrine
  drug interactions 269
Halog
  steroids 312
Haloperidol
  drug interactions 268
  medication use, elderly 360
  pregnancy 56
Hand, foot & mouth disease
  rashes in children 43
Hashimoto's thyroiditis
  thyroid disease 183, 187, 188
HB Immune Globulin
  hepatitis B 210
HCTZ
  dizziness 194
  medication use, elderly 361
HEADACHE 189–192
  contraception 73, 74
  dysmenorrhea 89
  HIV/AIDS 385
  pharyngitis 25
Health care personnel
  HIV/AIDS 390
HEALTH SCREENING IN THE ELDERLY 357–358
Heart block
  ECG 117, 118
HEART FAILURE 140–145
  hypertension 132
Helicobacter pylori
  PUD 214, 215
HEMATURIA 252–255
  UTI 249
Hemochromatosis
  heart failure 140
HEMORRHOIDS 220–222
Hemostasis
  skin biopsies 311
Heparin
  breast-feeding 59
  CVAs 198
  osteoporosis 246
  pregnancy 56, 58
Hepatic toxicity
  drug interactions 269
Hepatitis
  depression & dysthymia 343
  liver function tests 205, 206
Hepatitis A vaccine
  HIV/AIDS 376
HEPATITIS B 208–211
Hepatitis B vaccine
  health screening, elderly 358
  HIV/AIDS 376

Herbal/homeopathic
    liver function tests 207
Hereditary hemolytic anemia
    neonatal jaundice 13
Herniated disc
    back pain 294, 295
Heroin
    alcohol & drug abuse 354
Herpes
    HIV/AIDS 383
    neonatal jaundice 13
    pregnancy 62
    vaginitis/STDs 94
Hirschsprung disease
    constipation in children 35, 37
Hirsutism
    acne 305
Histamine H2 receptor blockers
    sexual dysfunction 348, 350
Histoplasmosis
    HIV/AIDS 383
HIV/AIDS
    contraindications & drug interactions 381
    diarrhea, acute 386
    encephalitis 385
    fever of unknown origin 389
    headache 385
    pulmonary complications 387
HIV/AIDS MANAGEMENT 375–383
HIV/AIDS POST-EXPOSURE PROPHYLAXIS 390-391
HIV/AIDS, WORK-UP IN PATIENTS WITH 385
HIVID
    HIV/AIDS 381
HMG CoA reductase inhibitors
    drug interactions 266, 270
    hyperlipidemia 125, 126
    liver function tests 207
Homatropine 396
    ocular disorders 227
Hormonal patch
    contraception 73
Hormonal preparations
    sexual dysfunction 350
Hormone replacement therapy 85
    drug interactions 271
Hot flashes
    menopause & HRT 86
Humalog
    diabetes 180, 181
Human bites 327
Human papilloma virus
    Pap smears 78
    vaginitis/STDs 94
Humibid 396, 397
    COPD 168
Humulin
    diabetes 180, 181
Huntington's chorea
    anxiety 339
Hycodan 396
Hycotuss 396
Hydralazine
    heart failure 143
    hypertension 135
    pregnancy 56

Hydrocele
    newborn exam 3
Hydrochlorothiazide
    calcium disorders 262
    heart failure 143
    hypertension 133
Hydrocodone 396
    ankle injuries 279
    pain management 329
Hydrocortisone
    hemorrhoids 221
    preoperative evaluation 332
    steroids 312
Hydrodiuril
    hypertension 133
Hydromorphone
    pain management 329
Hydronephrosis
    hematuria 253
Hydropres
    hypertension 135
Hydroxychloroquine
    rheumatoid arthritis 242
Hydroxyurea
    HIV/AIDS 380
Hydroxyzine 397
    allergic rhinitis 231
    contact dermatitis 304
    pregnancy 56
Hyoscyamine
    medication use, elderly 360
Hypercalcemia
    calcium disorders 260, 261
    ECG 121
    hypertension 129
Hyperkalemia
    ECG 121
    potassium metabolism 263
HYPERLIPIDEMIA 122–128
Hyperparathyroidism
    calcium disorders 260
    carpal tunnel syndrome 291
    compression fractures 364
    hypertension 129
Hyperphosphatemia
    calcium disorders 262
HYPERTENSION 128–136
    contraception 69
    hyperlipidemia 124
    post-MI 150
    preoperative evaluation 336
    proteinuria 257
    shortness of breath 154
Hyperthyroidism
    compression fractures 364
    depression & dysthymia 343
    thyroid disease 183, 187
Hyperuricemia
    gout 243
    gouty arthritis 243, 244
    knee injuries 281
Hypoalbuminemia
    calcium disorders 261
Hypocalcemia
    calcium disorders 261
    carpal tunnel syndrome 291
    ECG 121

Hypoglycemia
  mental status changes 371
Hypoglycemic drugs
  pregnancy 57
Hypokalemia
  ECG 121
  potassium metabolism 264
Hypomagnesemia
  calcium disorders 262
Hypospadias
  newborn exam 3
Hypotension
  anxiety 341
  falls in the elderly 362
  heart failure 141
  neonatal jaundice 15
  shortness of breath 155
Hypothermia
  ECG 122
Hypothyroidism
  breast disorders 90
  carpal tunnel syndrome 291
  hyperlipidemia 124
  neonatal jaundice 13
  thyroid disease 183, 187
Hytone
  steroids 312
Hytrin
  BPH 259
  hypertension 135
  medication use, elderly 359
Hyzaar
  hypertension 135

I

Ibuprofen
  alcohol & drug abuse 354
  ankle injuries 279
  bronchiolitis 30
  carpal tunnel syndrome 291
  fever in children 16
  gouty arthritis 245
  otitis media 23
  pain management 330
  pharyngitis 27
  pregnancy 58
Ibutilide
  drug interactions 268
IDV
  HIV/AIDS 382, 391
Imaging
  fetal exposure 62
Imdur
  coronary artery disease 139
Imipenem
  medication use, elderly 360
Imipramine
  ADHD 48
  anxiety 341
  depression & dysthymia 345, 346
  drug interactions 267, 269
  enuresis 41
  medication use, elderly 361
  pain 331
  urinary incontinence, elderly 367

Imiquimod
  vaginitis/STDs 94
Imitrex
  headache 191
Immotile cilia syndrome
  sinusitis 234
Immunization schedule, child 6
Immunizations
  HIV/AIDS 375
Imodium
  diarrhea in adults 218
Impingement
  shoulder injuries 285, 286, 287
Impotence
  sexual dysfunction 347, 349
Inapsine
  drug interactions 268
Incontinence
  elderly 365–368
Indapamide
  hypertension 133
Inderal
  anxiety 341
  atrial fibrillation 146
  coronary artery disease 138
  headache 191
  heart failure 144
  hypertension 133
Inderide
  hypertension 135
Indinavir
  drug interactions 267
  HIV/AIDS 380, 382
Indomethacin
  gouty arthritis 244
  medication use, elderly 361
Infection
  back pain 294
Infertility
  PID 95, 96
Infliximab
  rheumatoid arthritis 242
Influenza
  care of children 10
  croup 28
  health screening, elderly 358
  otitis media 22
  pharyngitis 25
  pregnancy 63
Influenza vaccine
  HIV/AIDS 376
  prenatal care 52
Inhaled corticosteroids
  asthma 165
INJECTION OF JOINTS 296–298
Inspra
  hypertension 133
Insulin
  diabetes 180, 181
  drug interactions 266
  potassium disorders 264
  pregnancy 56, 58
Interferon
  hepatitis B 210

Intrauterine devices
  contraception 74
Intravenous pyelogram
  abdominal pain 321
Intron A
  hepatitis B 210
Invirase
  drug interactions 267
  HIV/AIDS 380
Iodide
  thyroid disease 188
Iodinated Glycerol 396, 397
  COPD 168
Ipratropium
  COPD 167
Irbesartan
  heart failure 142
  hypertension 134, 135
Iritis
  ocular disorders 225
Iron deficiency
  anemia 223, 224
Irritable bowel syndrome
  constipation in adults 219, 220
  diarrhea in adults 217
  diverticula 325
Ischemia/infarction
  ECG 119
Ischemic heart disease
  hypertension 132
  preoperative evaluation 336
Ismo
  coronary artery disease 139
Isoniazid
  drug interactions 270
  tuberculosis screening 109, 110
Isoproterenol
  ACLS, tachycardia 405
  emergency drug dosage 407
  emergency drugs, infusion 408
Isoptin
  atrial fibrillation 146
  coronary artery disease 139
  heart failure 144
  hypertension 134
Isordil
  coronary artery disease 139
  heart failure 143
Isosorbide
  coronary artery disease 139
  heart failure 143
Isosporiasis
  HIV/AIDS 383
Isotretinoin
  acne 307
  pregnancy 56, 57
Isradipine
  drug interactions 269
  hypertension 134
Itraconazole
  drug interactions 266
  tinea unguium 314
  tinea versicolor 314

J

Jaundice
  hepatitis B 209
  liver function tests 205, 207, 208
  neonatal 13–15
Jenest-28
  contraception 72
Joint aspiration
  joint injections 296
JOINT INJECTION 296–298
Jones' fracture 276
Jonesing
  alcohol & drug abuse 353

K

K-Dur
  potassium metabolism 265
K-Lyte
  potassium metabolism 265
K-Y jelly
  sexual dysfunction 351
Kaletra
  HIV/AIDS 382
Kaopectate
  alcohol & drug abuse 354
Kaposi's sarcoma
  HIV/AIDS 383
Kartagener's syndrome
  sinusitis 234
Karyotype
  prenatal care 53
Kawasaki's disease
  rashes in children 43
Kayexalate
  potassium disorders 264
Kayser-Fleischer rings
  liver function tests 205
Keflex
  breast-feeding 11
  cat bites 328
  diverticulitis 324
  pharyngitis 26
  UTIs in children 39
Kegel exercises
  urinary incontinence, elderly 367
Kenalog
  joint injections 297
  steroids 312
Keppra
  seizures 201
Kerlone
  hypertension 133
Kernicterus
  neonatal jaundice 15
Kernig's/Brudzinski's sign
  headache 190
Ketoconazole
  drug interactions 266
  medication use, elderly 358
  rosacea 308
  sexual dysfunction 348, 350
  tinea pedis 313
  tinea versicolor 314
  vaginitis/STDs 93

INDEX

Ketorolac
   allergic rhinitis 231
   ocular disorders 226
   pain management 330
   pregnancy 58
Kidney disease
   hypertension 132
Klonopin
   anxiety 341
   medication use, elderly 360
KNEE INJURIES 281–284
Kwell
   scabies 313
Kyphosis
   fractures 276

L

Labetalol
   coronary artery disease 138
   hypertension 133
   pregnancy 56, 58
Lacerations
   wounds 326
Lachman test
   knee injuries 281, 283
Lactation
   contraception 70
   drugs used during 58
Lactobacillus
   vaginitis/STDs 93
Lactose intolerance
   diarrhea in adults 217
Lactulose
   constipation in children 37
   pregnancy 56
Lamictal
   seizures 201
Lamisil
   tinea pedis 313
   tinea unguium 314
Lamivudine
   hepatitis B 210
   HIV/AIDS 380, 381
Lamotrigine
   seizures 201
Lanoxin
   atrial fibrillation 146
   heart failure 143
Lansoprazole
   GERD 213
Lantus
   diabetes 180, 181
Laryngotracheitis 28–29
Lasix
   heart failure 143
   hypertension 133
   potassium disorders 264
Lateral epicondylitis
   elbow injuries 288
LDL cholesterol
   formulas 395
Lead screening
   care of children 9
Lead toxicity
   anemia 223

Learning disability
   ADHD 46
Leflunomide
   rheumatoid arthritis 242
Leukoencephalopathy
   HIV/AIDS 383
Levalbuterol
   COPD 167
Levaquin
   diverticulitis 324
   pneumonia 160
   UTI 250
Levatol
   hypertension 133
Levetiracetam
   seizures 201
Levlen
   contraception 72
Levobunolol
   medication use, elderly 360
Levocabastine
   allergic rhinitis 231
   ocular disorders 226
Levofloxacin
   pneumonia 160
   UTI 250
Levomethadyl
   drug interactions 269
Levonorgestrel
   contraception 74
Levothroid
   thyroid disease 187
Levothyroxine
   pregnancy 58
   thyroid disease 187
Levsin
   medication use, elderly 360
Lexxel
   hypertension 135
Libido
   sexual dysfunction 347, 350
Librax
   medication use, elderly 360
Librium
   medication use, elderly 360
LICE 313
Lichenification
   dermatologic lesions 301
Lidex
   steroids 312
Lidocaine
   ACLS 399, 405
   emergency drug dosage 407
   emergency drugs, infusion 408
   hemorrhoids 221
   joint injections 296, 297
   medication use, elderly 359
   rashes in children 43
   shoulder injuries 285
   skin biopsies 309
   wounds 326, 328
Ligament injuries
   knee injuries 282
Lindane
   lice 313
   scabies 313

Lipid disorders 122–127
Lipid-soluble drugs
   medication use, elderly 359
Lisinopril
   heart failure 142
   hypertension 134, 135
Lithium
   alcohol & drug abuse 353
   breast-feeding 59
   drug interactions 267, 270
   headache 191
   health screening, elderly 357
   pregnancy 56, 57
   thyroid disease 188
LIVER FUNCTION TESTS 205–208
Livostin
   allergic rhinitis 231
   ocular disorders 226
Lo-Ovral
   contraception 72
Lochia
   postpartum 65
Locoid
   steroids 312
Lodoxamide
   allergic rhinitis 231
   ocular disorders 226
Loestrin
   contraception 70, 72
   menopause & HRT 84
Lomefloxacin
   UTI 250
Loniten
   hypertension 135
Lopid
   sexual dysfunction 348
Lopinavir
   HIV/AIDS 380, 382
Lopressor
   atrial fibrillation 146
   coronary artery disease 138
   heart failure 144
   hypertension 133, 135
Loprox
   tinea pedis 313
Lorabid
   otitis media 23
   UTIs in children 39
Loracarbef
   otitis media 23
   UTIs in children 39
Loratadine 397
   allergic rhinitis 231
   pregnancy 58
Lorazepam
   alcohol & drug abuse 353
   anxiety 340
   medication use, elderly 360
   mental status changes 371
Lorcet
   pain management 329
Lordosis
   fractures 276
Lortab
   pain management 329

Losartan
   heart failure 142
   hypertension 134, 135
Lotensin
   ACE inhibitors 134
   heart failure 142
   hypertension 135
Lotrel
   hypertension 135
Lotrimin
   tinea pedis 313
Lovastatin
   hyperlipidemia 126, 127
Lovenox
   CVAs 198
LOW BACK PAIN 292–296
Low-Ogestrel
   contraception 72
Lozol
   hypertension 133
Lubrin
   sexual dysfunction 351
Lumbosacral sprain
   back pain 294
Lung disease
   shortness of breath 154
Lupron
   PMS 89
Lupus erythematosus, systemic 344
   anxiety 339
Luxiq
   steroids 312
Lyme disease
   arthritis 235, 236
   rashes in children 43
Lymphoma
   HIV/AIDS 383, 385

M

Macrobid
   prenatal care 52
   UTI 250
   UTIs in children 39
Macrodantin
   UTI 250
Macrolides
   hyperlipidemia 126
   pneumonia 160
   pregnancy 58
Macular hemangiomas
   newborn exam 4
Macule
   dermatologic lesions 301
Maculopapular Exanthems
   rashes in children 42
Magnesium
   ACLS 399, 405
   PMS 89
Magnesium Citrate
   constipation in children 37
Magnesium Hydroxide
   constipation in children 37
   pregnancy 56

Magnesium Oxide
  calcium disorders 262
  potassium disorders 265
Magnesium Sulfate
  emergency drug dosage 407
Maisonneuve's fracture 276
Maltsupex
  constipation in children 35
Mammogram
  health screening, elderly 357
Mantoux test
  tuberculosis screening 108
MAO inhibitors
  drug interactions 267
Marcaine
  wounds 326
Mastalgia
  breast disorders 90
  contraception 74
Mastitis
  breast disorders 91
Maternal serum alpha fetal protein
  prenatal care 52
Mavik
  heart failure 142
  hypertension 134
Maxair
  COPD 167
Maxalt
  headache 191
Maxaquin
  UTI 250
Maxillary tooth or facial pain
  acute sinusitis 233
Maxzide
  hypertension 135
McMurray test
  knee injuries 282
Measles
  rashes in children 42
Meclizine
  dizziness 194
  pregnancy 56
MEDICATION COMPLIANCE 270–271
MEDICATION INTERACTIONS 266–270
Medication prescribing errors
  drug interactions 268
MEDICATIONS DURING PREGNANCY AND
    LACTATION 55–61
Medroxyprogesterone
  amenorrhea 83
  contraception 73
  menopause & HRT 86
  uterine bleeding 80, 81
Mefenamic Acid
  pregnancy 58
Megestrol Acetate
  menopause & HRT 86
Mellaril
  drug interactions 268
Menest
  menopause & HRT 86
Ménière's disease
  dizziness 193
Meningitis
  fever in children 17

Meningococcemia
  rashes in children 44
Meniscus injury 282
Menopause
  hyperlipidemia 124
MENOPAUSE & HORMONE REPLACEMENT
    THERAPY 84–88
Menstrual period
  amenorrhea 82
MENTAL STATUS CHANGES 368–372
Meperidine
  breast-feeding 59
  medication use, elderly 361
  pain management 329
Meprobamate
  medication use, elderly 360
Mepron
  HIV/AIDS 377
Mesoridazine
  drug interactions 268
Mestranol
  contraception 70
Metamucil
  constipation in adults 220
  pregnancy 63
Metaprel
  COPD 167
Metaproterenol
  COPD 167
Metaxalone
  medication use, elderly 360
Metformin
  diabetes 178, 179, 180
Methadone
  alcohol & drug abuse 354
  drug interactions 269
  pain management 329
Methimazole
  pregnancy 56, 57
  thyroid disease 186, 188
Methocarbamol
  medication use, elderly 360
Methotrexate
  breast-feeding 59, 60
  osteoporosis 246
  pregnancy 57
  rheumatoid arthritis 241, 242
Methyldopa
  hypertension 135
  medication use, elderly 359
  pregnancy 56
  sexual dysfunction 347
Methylphenidate
  ADHD 47
Methylprednisolone
  asthma 164
  asthma in children 20
Methylxanthine
  COPD 167
Metipranolol
  medication use, elderly 360
Metoclopramide
  GERD 213
  pregnancy 56
Metolazone
  hypertension 133

Metoprolol
  atrial fibrillation 146
  coronary artery disease 138
  heart failure 143, 144
  hypertension 133, 135
  medication use, elderly 360
MetroCream
  rosacea 308
MetroGel
  rosacea 308
  vaginitis/STDs 93
Metronidazole
  diarrhea in adults 218
  diverticulitis 324
  PID 96
  PUD 215
  rosacea 308
  vaginitis/STDs 93
Mevacor
  hyperlipidemia 127
Mexiletine
  drug interactions 266
Miacalcin
  compression fractures 365
  osteoporosis 248
Micardis
  heart failure 142
  hypertension 134, 135
Micatin
  tinea pedis 313
Miconazole
  tinea pedis 313
  tinea versicolor 314
  vaginitis/STDs 93
Microalbuminuria
  proteinuria 256
Microcytosis
  anemia 223
Microgestin 1/20
  contraception 72
Micronase
  diabetes 180
Micronor
  contraception 72
Microzide
  hypertension 133
Midamor
  hypertension 133
Midrin
  headache 191
Miglitol
  diabetes 180
Migraine
  contraception 69
  dizziness 192
Milk of Magnesia
  constipation in adults 220
Milrinone
  heart failure 144
Miltown
  medication use, elderly 360
Mineral oil
  constipation in adults 220
  constipation in children 37
  pregnancy 56

Mini-mental status exam
  mental status changes 370
Minipress
  hypertension 135
  medication use, elderly 359
Minocycline
  acne 307
  rheumatoid arthritis 242
  rosacea 309
Minoxidil
  hair loss 315
  hypertension 135
Mircette
  contraception 70, 72
Mirena
  contraception 74
  uterine bleeding 79
Mirtazapine
  depression & dysthymia 346
Misoprostol
  osteoarthritis 238
  pregnancy 57
  PUD 214
  rheumatoid arthritis 241
Mitral valve prolapse
  cardiac stress testing 152
  endocarditis prophylaxis 107
Modicon
  contraception 72
Moduretic
  hypertension 135
Moexipril
  hypertension 134, 135
Mometasone Furoate
  allergic rhinitis 231
  steroids 312
Mongolian spots
  newborn exam 4
Monistat
  vaginitis/STDs 93
Monistat-Derm
  tinea pedis 313
Mono-spot test
  pharyngitis 27
Monoarticular arthritis 236
Mononucleosis
  depression & dysthymia 343
  pharyngitis 27
Monopril
  heart failure 142
  hypertension 134
Monsel's solution
  skin biopsies 311
Monteggia's fracture 277
Montelukast
  asthma in children 20
Monurol
  UTI 250
Moro reflex
  newborn exam 4
Morphine
  ACLS, acute pulmonary edema 406
  alcohol & drug abuse 354
  breast-feeding 59
  pain management 329
  pregnancy 58

Moxifloxacin
  drug interactions 267, 269
  pneumonia 160
MPA
  amenorrhea 83
MRI
  back pain 293
  concussion 204
  HIV/AIDS 385
MS Contin/Oramorph SR
  pain management 329
Mucosal protective agents
  GERD 213
Multiple endocrine neoplasias
  calcium disorders 260
Multiple sclerosis
  anxiety 339
  constipation in adults 219
  depression & dysthymia 344
Münchausen's disease
  hematuria 254
Murmurs
  newborn exam 3
Muscle relaxants
  back pain 295
  low back pain 294
  medication use, elderly 360
Muse
  sexual dysfunction 349
Mycelex
  oral candidiasis 314
  tinea pedis 313
Mycobacterium avium complex
  HIV/AIDS 377, 383
Mycobacterium tuberculosis
  HIV/AIDS 383
Mycobutin
  HIV/AIDS 377
Mycostatin
  oral candidiasis 314
Mydriacyl
  ocular disorders 226
Mykrox
  hypertension 133
Mylanta
  PUD 214
Myofascial pain
  back pain 295
Mysoline
  contraception 69
  seizures 201

N

Nadolol
  breast-feeding 60
  drug interactions 266
  hypertensi on 133, 135
Naftifine
  rosacea 308
  tinea pedis 313
Naftin
  tinea pedis 313
Naldecon Senior EX 397
Nalidixic Acid
  UTIs in children 39

Naltrexone
  alcohol & drug abuse 353, 354
Naphazoline
  pregnancy 56
Naphcon-A
  allergic rhinitis 231
Naprosyn
  carpal tunnel syndrome 291
Naproxen
  gouty arthritis 244
  headache 191
Naratriptan
  headache 191
Narcan
  mental status changes 371
Narcotics
  headache 191
  medication use, elderly 361
Nasacort
  allergic rhinitis 230
NaSal
  allergic rhinitis 231
Nasal polyps
  sinusitis 233, 234
Nasal steroid spray
  acute sinusitis 234
NasalCrom
  allergic rhinitis 231
Nasalide
  allergic rhinitis 230
Nasarel
  allergic rhinitis 230
Nasonex
  allergic rhinitis 231
Nateglinide
  diabetes 180
Nausea
  alcohol & drug abuse 353
  anxiety 341
  chest pain 114
  concussion 202
  diverticulitis 323
  dysmenorrhea 89
  hepatitis B 209
  HIV/AIDS 375
  liver function tests 205
  PUD 214
  UTI 250
Necon
  contraception 72
Nedocromil
  asthma 164
  ocular disorders 226
Nefazodone
  anxiety 341
  depression & dysthymia 346
Nelfinavir
  drug interactions 267
  HIV/AIDS 380, 382
Nelova
  contraception 72
Neo-Synephrine
  allergic rhinitis 231
  ocular disorders 226
Neomycin
  ocular disorders 226, 229

INDEX

NEONATAL JAUNDICE 13–15
Neonatal sepsis
   newborn exam 5
Neosporin
   ocular disorders 226
Nephrolithiasis
   hematuria 253
Nephropathy
   diabetes 177
Nephrotic syndrome
   proteinuria 256
Neurontin
   headache 191
   pain 331
   seizures 201
Neurosyn
   seizures 201
Neutra-Phos
   calcium disorders 261
Nevirapine
   HIV/AIDS 380, 382
New York Heart Association Classification
   heart failure 141
NEWBORN EXAM 3–5
Nexium
   GERD 213
   PUD 215
NFV
   HIV/AIDS 382, 391
Niacin
   hyperlipidemia 125, 126
   sexual dysfunction 348
Niaspan
   hyperlipidemia 126
Nicardipine
   coronary artery disease 138
   drug interactions 269
   hypertension 134
Nicoderm
   smoking cessation 103
Nicorette
   smoking cessation 102
Nicotine gum
   smoking cessation 102
Nicotine inhaler
   smoking cessation 102
Nicotine nasal spray
   smoking cessation 102
Nicotine patch
   smoking cessation 103
Nicotinic Acid
   drug interactions 270
   hyperlipidemia 125, 126, 127
Nicotrol
   smoking cessation 102, 103
Nifedipine
   coronary artery disease 138, 139
   hypertension 134
Nightstick fracture 277
Nisoldipine
   hypertension 134
Nitrates
   coronary artery disease 139
   heart failure 143
   post-MI 151
   UTI 249

Nitrofurantoin
   neonatal jaundice 13
   prenatal care 52
   UTI 250, 252
   UTIs in children 39
Nitroglycerin
   ACLS, acute pulmonary edema 406
   chest pain 114
   coronary artery disease 139
   emergency drugs, infusion 408
Nitroprusside
   ACLS, acute pulmonary edema 406
   emergency drugs, infusion 408
NIX
   lice 313
Nizatidine
   GERD 213
Nizoral
   sexual dysfunction 348, 350
   tinea pedis 313
   vaginitis/STDs 93
Nocturia
   hematuria 253
Nodule
   dermatologic lesions 301
Non-Sulfonylureas secretagogues
   diabetes 179, 180
Nonsteroidal antiinflammatory drugs
   ankle injuries 279
   asthma 162
   back pain 294, 295
   breast-feeding 59
   compression fractures 365
   drug interactions 269
   elbow injuries 288, 289
   gouty arthritis 245
   headache 191
   hematuria 253
   liver function tests 207
   medication use, elderly 361
   osteoarthritis 238, 239
   pain 331
   pregnancy 56, 57
   PUD 214
   rheumatoid arthritis 241
   shoulder injuries 287
Nor-QD
   contraception 72
Nordette
   contraception 72
Norelgestromin
   contraception 73
Norepinephrine
   ACLS, acute pulmonary edema 406
   emergency drugs, infusion 408
Norfloxacin
   UTI 250
Norgestimate
   contraception 70
Norinyl
   contraception 72
Normodyne
   hypertension 133
Noroxin
   UTI 250

Norpace
  drug interactions 268
  medication use, elderly 359
Norplant
  contraception 73
Norpramin
  depression & dysthymia 345
  drug interactions 269
  medication use, elderly 361
Nortriptyline
  depression & dysthymia 345, 346
  drug interactions 267
  headache 191
  medication use, elderly 361
  smoking cessation 103
Norvasc
  coronary artery disease 138
  heart failure 144
  hypertension 134
Norvir
  drug interactions 267
  HIV/AIDS 382
Norwalk virus
  diarrhea in children 31
Novolin/Humulin
  diabetes 181
Novonin
  diabetes 180
NP-27
  tinea pedis 313
NPH
  diabetes 180, 181
NSAIDs. *See* Nonsteroidal antiinflammatory drugs
Nuchal rigidity
  headache 190
Nursemaid's elbow
  elbow injuries 290
NuvaRing
  contraception 73
  uterine bleeding 79
NVP
  HIV/AIDS 382
Nystatin
  breast-feeding 11
  oral candidiasis 314
  vaginitis/STDs 93

O

Obesity
  hyperlipidemia 124
  liver function tests 208
  shortness of breath 154
Obsessive-compulsive disorders
  anxiety 339
Occlusive therapy
  warts 313
Ocean Nasal Mist
  allergic rhinitis 231
Ocuflox
  ocular disorders 226
OCULAR DISORDERS 225–229
Ocupress
  medication use, elderly 360
Ofloxacin
  medication use, elderly 360

  ocular disorders 226
  PID 96
  UTI 250
  vaginitis/STDs 93
Ogen
  menopause & HRT 86
  vaginitis/STDs 93
Ogestrel
  contraception 72
Olanzapine
  mental status changes 371
Olmesartan
  hypertension 134
Olux
  steroids 312
Omeprazole
  GERD 213
  PUD 215
Omnicef
  otitis media 23
Ondansetron
  alcohol & drug abuse 353
  drug interactions 268
Oophorectomy
  menopause & HRT 87
Opiates
  alcohol & drug abuse 353
Opioids
  pain 330
  pregnancy 57
OptiPranolol
  medication use, elderly 360
Oral candidiasis 314
Oral contraceptives
  drug interactions 267
Oral phosphates
  calcium disorders 261
Orap
  drug interactions 268
Orbital cellulitis
  ocular disorders 225
Organidin 397
Orlaam
  drug interactions 269
Ortho-Cept
  contraception 72
Ortho-Cyclen
  contraception 72
Ortho-Est
  menopause & HRT 86
Ortho-Evra
  contraception 73
Ortho-Novum
  contraception 72
Ortho-Prefest
  menopause & HRT 85
Ortho-Tri-Cyclen
  acne 307
  contraception 72
Orthopedics 275–277
Orthopnea
  heart failure 140
  shortness of breath 155
Ortolani test
  newborn exam 4

INDEX

Os-Cal
  calcium disorders 262
Osgood-Schlatter's disease
  knee injuries 283, 284
OSTEOARTHRITIS 238–239
  back pain 294
Osteochondritis dissecans
  ankle injuries 279
  knee injuries 284
Osteopenia
  arthritis 237
  osteoporosis 246, 247
OSTEOPOROSIS 246–249
  back pain 295
  compression fractures 364
OTITIS MEDIA 22–25
Ovarian cysts
  contraception 69
Ovcon
  contraception 72
Ovral
  contraception 72, 75
Ovrette
  contraception 72
Oxazepam
  alcohol & drug abuse 353
  medication use, elderly 360
  mental status changes 371
Oxcarbazepine
  seizures 200, 201
Oxybutynin
  enuresis 41
  medication use, elderly 360
  urinary incontinence, elderly 367
Oxycodone
  ankle injuries 279
  breast-feeding 59
  pain management 329
Oxycontin
  pain management 329
Oxygen
  ACLS, acute pulmonary edema 406
  COPD 168
Oxyir
  pain management 329
Oxymetazoline
  allergic rhinitis 231
  pregnancy 56

P

Paget's disease
  breast disorders 91
  calcium disorders 260
PAIN MANAGEMENT 329–332
Pamelor
  depression & dysthymia 345
  medication use, elderly 361
  smoking cessation 103
Pamidronate
  pain 331
Pancreatic disease
  liver function tests 206
Pandel
  steroids 312

Panic disorder 339, 341
Pantoprazole
  GERD 213
PAP SMEARS 75–79
  cervical cancer 75
  health screening, elderly 357
  squamous intraepithelial lesion 77
Papilledema
  headache 190
Papule
  dermatologic lesions 301
Paraflex
  medication use, elderly 360
Paramethadione
  pregnancy 57
Parathyroid dysfunction
  anxiety 339
Parkinson's disease
  depression & dysthymia 344
Paroxetine
  anxiety 341
  depression & dysthymia 344, 345, 346
  drug interactions 269
  medication use, elderly 361
Paroxysmal atrial fibrillation 149
Patanol
  ocular disorders 226
Patch
  dermatologic lesions 301
Patella
  back pain 293
  knee injuries 281, 283
Patellofemoral syndrome
  knee injuries 283
Paxil
  anxiety 341
  depression & dysthymia 345
  drug interactions 269
  medication use, elderly 361
PCP prophylaxis
  HIV/AIDS 376
Peak expiratory flow meter
  asthma in children 18
Pedialyte
  diarrhea in children 32
Pediatric health care 6, 8
Pediazole
  otitis media 23
PEDICULOSIS 313
Pelvic floor strengthening exercises
  urinary incontinence, elderly 367
PELVIC INFLAMMATORY DISEASE (PID) 95–96
Pemirolast
  ocular disorders 226
Pemoline
  ADHD 47
Pen Vee K
  pharyngitis 26
Penbutolol
  hypertension 133
Penicillin
  pregnancy 58
  prenatal care 55
  rashes in children 43
Penlac nail lacquer
  tinea unguium 314

Pentam
  drug interactions 269
Pentamidine
  drug interactions 269
Pentazocine
  medication use, elderly 361
Pepcid
  GERD 213
PEPTIC ULCER DISEASE (PUD) 214–216
Pepto-Bismol
  diarrhea in adults 218
  PUD 214, 215
Percocet
  ankle injuries 279
  pain management 329
  postpartum 65
Percodan
  pain management 329
Perdiem
  pregnancy 63
Pericardial effusion
  ECG 121
Pericarditis
  ECG 122
Pericolace
  medication use, elderly 361
Perindopril
  hypertension 134
PERIODIC HEALTH EXAMINATIONS 101–102
Peripheral cyanosis
  newborn exam 3
Peripheral neuropathy
  carpal tunnel syndrome 291
Permethrin
  lice 313
  scabies 313
Persantine
  cardiac stress testing 153
Petechial rash
  rashes in children 44
Petroleum jelly
  lice 313
Phalen's sign
  carpal tunnel syndrome 291
PHARYNGITIS 25–28
Phenergan
  contraception 75
  dizziness 194
Phenindione
  breast-feeding 59
Phenobarbital
  ADHD 46
  breast-feeding 59
  contraception 69
  medication use, elderly 360
  osteoporosis 246
  seizures 201
  sexual dysfunction 348
Phenolphthalein
  pregnancy 56
Phenothiazines
  osteoporosis 246
Phenylbutazone
  medication use, elderly 361
  thyroid disease 188

Phenylephrine
  allergic rhinitis 231
  emergency drugs, infusion 408
  pregnancy 56
Phenytoin
  ACLS, tachycardia 405
  breast-feeding 59
  contraception 69
  drug interactions 267, 270
  liver function test 206
  osteoporosis 246
  pain 331
  pregnancy 57, 58
  seizures 200, 201
  sexual dysfunction 348, 350
Pheochromocytoma
  anxiety 339
Phobic disorder
  anxiety 339
Phos-tabs
  calcium disorders 261
Phosphate enemas
  constipation in children 37
Photodermatitis
  contact dermatitis 303
Pick's disease
  mental status changes 371
Pilonidal sinus tracts
  newborn exam 4
Pimozide
  drug interactions 268
Pindolol
  coronary artery disease 138
  hypertension 133
  medication use, elderly 360
Pioglitazone
  diabetes 180
Pirbuterol MDI
  COPD 167
Pituitary adenomas
  breast disorders 90
Plan B
  contraception 75
Plantar warts 313
Plaque
  dermatologic lesions 301
Plavix
  coronary artery disease 138
  CVAs 197
Plendil
  hypertension 134
PML
  HIV/AIDS 385
PMS
  contraception 69
Pneumococcal vaccine
  health screening, elderly 358
  HIV/AIDS 375
Pneumocystis carinii
  HIV/AIDS 383
PNEUMONIA, COMMUNITY ACQUIRED 158
Pneumothorax
  chest pain 113
Pneumovax. *See also* Pneumococcal vaccine
  care of children 10

Podofilox
    vaginitis/STDs 94
Podophyllin
    warts 313
Podophyllum
    vaginitis/STDs 94
Poison ivy
    contact dermatitis 303
Poison oak
    contact dermatitis 303
Polyarteritis nodosa
    anxiety 339
Polyarthralgias
    knee injuries 281
Polyarticular arthritis 236, 237
Polycystic ovarian syndrome
    uterine bleeding 79
Polyethylene glycol electrolyte solution
    constipation in adults 220
Polymyxin B
    ocular disorders 226
Polyps
    uterine bleeding 79
Polythiazide
    hypertension 133
Porphyria
    anxiety 339
Post-exposure prophylaxis
    HIV/AIDS 390–391
POST-MI MANAGEMENT 150–152
    hypertension 132
Post-strep
    hematuria 252
Postcoital contraception 74
Posterior cruciate ligament
    knee injuries 281
POSTPARTUM CHECKUP 66
Postpartum contraception 70
POTASSIUM METABOLISM 263–265
Potassium-sparing diuretics
    hypertension 133
Prandin
    diabetes 180
Pravastatin
    hyperlipidemia 126
Prazosin
    hypertension 135
    medication use, elderly 359
    pregnancy 56
    urinary incontinence, elderly 366
Precose
    diabetes 180
Prednicarbate
    steroids 312
Prednisolone
    asthma 164
    asthma in children 20
    pregnancy 58
Prednisone
    acne 307
    allergic rhinitis 231
    asthma 164
    asthma in children 20
    calcium disorders 261
    contact dermatitis 304
    COPD 167

dizziness 194
    gouty arthritis 245
    headache 191
    pregnancy 58
Preeclampsia
    prenatal care 52
Pregnancy
    back pain 296
    caffeine 63
    cardiac stress testing 154
    carpal tunnel syndrome 291
    contraception 69
    dental procedures 63
    diabetes 182
    medications during 55–61
    morning sickness 61
    PID 95
    prenatal care 51
    round ligament pain 63
    seat belts 63
    tuberculosis screening 109
    UTI 252
    vaginitis/STDs 92
Premarin
    contraception 73
    menopause & HRT 85, 86
    vaginitis/STDs 93, 94
Premature labor
    prenatal care 54
PREMENSTRUAL SYNDROME
    & DYSMENORRHEA 88–90
Premphase
    menopause & HRT 86
Prempro
    menopause & HRT 85
PRENATAL CARE 51
Prenatal labs
    prenatal care 64
Prentif cervical cap
    contraception 73
PREOPERATIVE EVALUATION 332–336
Presyncope
    dizziness 192
Prevacid
    GERD 213
Preven kit
    contraception 75
Prevnar
    care of children 9
    fever in children 17
Prilosec
    GERD 213
    PUD 215
Primary nocturnal enuresis 41
Primidone
    breast-feeding 59
    contraception 69
    seizures 201
Prinivil
    heart failure 142
    hypertension 134
Prinzide
    hypertension 135
Prinzmetal angina
    coronary artery disease 139

Pro-Banthine
  medication use, elderly 360
Probenecid
  gouty arthritis 245
  PID 96
Procainamide
  ACLS 399, 403, 404, 405
  atrial fibrillation 146
  drug interactions 268
  emergency drug dosage 407
  emergency drugs, infusion 408
  medication use, elderly 359
Procaine Penicillin
  pharyngitis 26
Procardia
  coronary artery disease 138
  hypertension 134
Progesterone
  amenorrhea 83
  contraception 73
  menopause & HRT 86
  uterine bleeding 81
Progestin
  contraception 71
Prolactin
  amenorrhea 82
Proloprim
  UTI 250
Prometrium
  abnormal uterine bleeding 81
  amenorrhea 83
  menopause & HRT 84, 85, 86
Pronestyl
  drug interactions 268
Propafenone
  atrial fibrillation 146
  drug interactions 266
Propantheline
  medication use, elderly 360
Proparacaine
  ocular disorders 226
Propecia
  hair loss 315
Propionibacterium
  contact dermatitis 305
Propoxyphene
  medication use, elderly 361
  pain management 329
Propranolol
  anxiety 341
  atrial fibrillation 146
  coronary artery disease 138
  drug interactions 266
  heart failure 144
  hypertension 133, 135
  medication use, elderly 360
  pregnancy 58
  thyroid disease 185, 186
Propylthiouracil
  pregnancy 56, 57, 58
  thyroid disease 186
Proscar
  BPH 259
  sexual dysfunction 348
Prostate specific antigen
  BPH 258

  health screening, elderly 357
Prostatectomy
  BPH 259
Prostatitis
  UTI 252
PROTEINURIA 255–257
Prothrombin time
  hepatitis B 210
  liver function tests 207
Protime
  liver function tests 205, 207
Proton pump inhibitors
  GERD 213
  rheumatoid arthritis 241
Protonix
  GERD 213
Protriptyline
  medication use, elderly 361
Proventil
  COPD 167
Provera
  menopause & HRT 84, 85, 86
  uterine bleeding 80, 81
  vaginitis/STDs 94
Prozac
  anxiety 341
  depression & dysthymia 345
  drug interactions 269
  medication use, elderly 361
  PMS 89
  postpartum 66
Pruritis
  contact dermatitis 303
  vaginitis/STDs 94
Pseudoephedrine 396, 397
  allergic rhinitis 231
  urinary incontinence, elderly 367
Pseudogout
  arthritis 235, 236
  knee injuries 281
Pseudohypoparathyroidism
  calcium disorders 262
Pseudomenses
  newborn exam 3
Pseudomonas
  sinusitis 234
Psorcon
  steroids 312
Psychoactive medications
  pregnancy 57
  sexual dysfunction 347, 350
Psychotherapy
  anxiety 341
Psyllium
  constipation in adults 220
  diverticula 324
  pregnancy 63
PTU
  thyroid disease 186, 188
Pulmicort Turbuhaler
  COPD 167
Pulmonary angiography
  shortness of breath 157
Pulmonary complications
  HIV/AIDS 387

Pulmonary embolism
    ECG 121
    shortness of breath 156
Pulmonary function test
    asthma in children 18
    preoperative evaluation 336
Purpura
    dermatologic lesions 301
Pustule
    dermatologic lesions 301
Pyelonephritis
    urinary tract infections 250
Pyridium
    UTI 250, 254
Pyridoxine
    tuberculosis screening 109, 110

Q

QUESTIONS EXPECTING PARENTS COMMONLY
    ASK/RADIATION 61–64
Quetiapine
    mental status changes 371
Quinapril
    heart failure 142
    hypertension 134, 135
Quinidex
    drug interactions 268
Quinidine
    atrial fibrillation 146
    drug interactions 267, 268
    ECG 121
    medication use, elderly 359, 360
Quinolones
    diarrhea in adults 218
    diverticulitis 324
    drug interactions 267
    ocular disorders 226

R

R wave progression
    ECG 121
Rabeprazole
    GERD 213
Racemic Epinephrine
    croup 28
Radiculopathy
    back pain 294
Radioactive iodine
    thyroid disease 186
Radiograph
    abdominal pain 320
    wounds 325
Radiographic contrast dye
    drug interactions 269
Raloxifene
    osteoporosis 248
Ramipril
    heart failure 142
    hypertension 134
Ranitidine
    GERD 213
    medication use, elderly 360
    pregnancy 56

Rapid strep test
    pharyngitis 25
RASHES IN CHILDREN 42–45
Red reflex
    newborn exam 4
Reglan
    GERD 213
Relaxation exercises
    headache 191
Remeron
    depression & dysthymia 346
Reminyl
    mental status changes 371
Renal insufficiency
    calcium disorders 261
Renal toxicity
    drug interactions 269
Renese
    hypertension 133
Repaglinide
    diabetes 180
Replens
    sexual dysfunction 351
Repolarization/normal variant
    ECG 122
Rescriptor
    HIV/AIDS 382
Reserpine
    hypertension 135
    sexual dysfunction 347
Restoril
    medication use, elderly 360
    mental status changes 371
Retin-A
    acne 307
    warts 313
Retinoic acid
    acne 307
Retinoids
    warts 313
Retinopathy
    diabetes 178
Retropharyngeal abscess
    pharyngitis 27
    shortness of breath 154, 157
Retrovir
    HIV/AIDS 381
ReVia
    alcohol & drug abuse 353, 354
RHEUMATOID ARTHRITIS 239–255
    anxiety 339
    back pain 295
    depression & dysthymia 344
    diagnosis 236
    knee injuries 281
Rheumatoid factor
    rheumatoid arthritis 239
Rheumatrex
    osteoporosis 246
RHINITIS, ALLERGIC 229–232
Rhinocort
    allergic rhinitis 230
RhoGAM
    prenatal care 53
Rhus dermatitis
    contact dermatitis 303, 304

Rifabutin
  HIV/AIDS 377
Rifampin
  contraception 69
Ringer's Lactate
  diarrhea in children 32
Risedronate
  osteoporosis 247
Risperdal
  drug interactions 268
  mental status changes 371
Risperidone
  drug interactions 268
  mental status changes 371
RIT
  HIV/AIDS 382
Ritalin
  ADHD 47
Ritonavir
  drug interactions 267
  HIV/AIDS 380, 382
Rivastigmine
  mental status changes 371
Rizatriptan
  headache 191
Robaxin
  medication use, elderly 360
Robitussin 396, 397
  COPD 168
Rocaltrol
  calcium disorders 262
Rocephin
  vaginitis/STDs 93
Rocky Mountain Spotted Fever
  rashes in children 44
Rofecoxib
  pain management 330
Rogaine
  hair loss 315
Rolando's fracture 277
Rondec 396, 397
ROSACEA 305–309
Roseola
  rashes in children 42
Rosiglitazone
  diabetes 180
Rotator cuff
  shoulder injuries 285, 286, 287
Rotavirus
  diarrhea in adults 216
  diarrhea in children 31, 34
Rotor's syndrome
  liver function tests 206
  neonatal jaundice 13
Round ligament pain
  pregnancy 63
Roxanol
  pain management 329
Rubella
  neonatal jaundice 13
  rashes in children 42
Rubeola
  rashes in children 42
Ruptured TM
  otitis media 23

S

Sacral dimple
  newborn exam 4
Salicylates
  pregnancy 57
Salicylic Acid
  acne 306
  warts 313
Saline X
  allergic rhinitis 231
Salmeterol
  asthma 164
  asthma in children 20
  COPD 167
Salmonella
  diarrhea in adults 216, 218
  diarrhea in children 31
  HIV/AIDS 383
Salter classification
  fractures 276
Sandimmune
  osteoporosis 246
Saquinavir
  drug interactions 267
  HIV/AIDS 380, 382
Sarcoidosis
  calcium disorders 260, 261
  heart failure 140
Scabene
  scabies 313
SCABIES 313
Scale
  dermatologic lesions 301
Scarlet fever
  rashes in children 42
Sciatica
  back pain 295
Seborrhea
  acne 306
Secobarbital
  medication use, elderly 360
Sectral
  hypertension 133
SEIZURE DISORDERS 199–202
Selenium Sulfide
  tinea versicolor 314
Senna
  constipation in children 37
  pregnancy 63
Sensorcaine
  joint injections 297
Separation anxiety 342
Septic arthritis 236
Septra
  otitis media 23
  UTI 250
Sequestrants
  hyperlipidemia 126
Serax
  medication use, elderly 360
  mental status changes 371
Serentil
  drug interactions 268
Serevent
  COPD 167

Seroquel
  mental status changes 371
Serotonin selective reuptake inhibitors (SSRIs)
  anxiety 341
  headache 191
  postpartum 66
Serous OM
  otitis media 23
Sertraline
  anxiety 341
  depression & dysthymia 344, 345, 346
  drug interactions 269
  medication use, elderly 361
  pregnancy 58
Serum albumin concentration
  medication use, elderly 359
Serum creatinine
  BPH 258
Serum osmolality
  formulas 395
Serum protein immunoelectrophoresis
  proteinuria 256
Serzone
  anxiety 341
  depression & dysthymia 346
Sestamibi
  cardiac stress testing 153
SEXUAL DYSFUNCTION 347–352
SEXUALLY TRANSMITTED DISEASES &
    VAGINITIS 92–95
Shigella
  diarrhea in adults 216, 218
  diarrhea in children 31
SHORTNESS OF BREATH 154–158
  asthma 162
SHOULDER INJURIES 285–288
Sick sinus syndrome
  ECG 122
Sickle cell anemia
  hematuria 253
Sideroblastic anemia
  anemia 223
Sigmoidoscopy
  constipation in adults 219
Sildenafil
  drug interactions 267
  sexual dysfunction 349
Silver Nitrate
  skin biopsies 311
Simvastatin
  hyperlipidemia 126
Sinequan
  depression & dysthymia 345
  medication use, elderly 361
SINUSITIS 232–235
  asthma 162
  chronic sinusitis 234
  medications 396–397
  pharyngitis 27
Sjogren's syndrome
  GERD 211
Skelaxin
  medication use, elderly 360
SKIN BIOPSIES 309–312
SL NTG
  coronary artery disease 139

Slow-K
  potassium metabolism 265
Smith's fracture 276
Smoking
  anxiety 340
  asthma 162
  bronchitis 169
  COPD 167
  diabetes 177
  GERD 213
  hyperlipidemia 124
  pneumonia 159
  post-MI 150
  preoperative evaluation 332, 336
  PUD 214
  sexual dysfunction 349
  shortness of breath 155
SMOKING CESSATION 102–104
SMX
  sinusitis 234
Sodium Bicarbonate
  emergency drug dosage 407
  potassium disorders 264
Sodium Sulfacetamide
  rosacea 308
Soma
  medication use, elderly 360
Sorbitol
  constipation in adults 220
  constipation in children 37
  pregnancy 56
Sotalol
  ACLS, tachycardia 404, 405
  atrial fibrillation 146
  breast-feeding 60
  drug interactions 268
Soy formulas
  infant formulas 12
Soy supplementation
  menopause & HRT 86
Sparfloxacin
  drug interactions 267, 269
SPECT perfusion imaging
  cardiac stress testing 153
Spermicides
  contraception 74
  pregnancy 57
Spherocytosis
  neonatal jaundice 13
Spinal stenosis
  back pain 294, 295
Spironolactone
  heart failure 143
  hypertension 133, 135
  PMS 89
  sexual dysfunction 347
Spondylolisthesis
  back pain 294, 295
  fractures 276
Spondylolysis
  fractures 276
Sporanox
  tinea unguium 314
SSRIs. *See* Serotonin selective reuptake inhibitors
St. John's Wort
  contraception 69

INDEX

Staphylococcus aureus
  diarrhea in adults 216
Staples
  wounds 326
Starlix
  diabetes 180
Statins
  hyperlipidemia 126, 127
  post-MI 151
Stavudine
  HIV/AIDS 380, 381
Steeple sign
  croup 28
Stenosis, pyloric
  neonatal jaundice 13
Stepping reflex
  newborn exam 4
Sterilization
  contraception 74
Steroids
  acne 307
  asthma 165
  elbow injuries 288
  joint injections 296
  shortness of breath 157
  shoulder injuries 287
STEROIDS, TOPICAL 312
Strabismus
  ocular disorders 226, 228
Straight leg raise test
  back pain 293
Strattera
  ADHD 48
Strep test, rapid
  pharyngitis 25
Streptococcal pharyngitis 25
Streptokinase
  pregnancy 56
Stress ECHO
  cardiac stress testing 152
Stress testing 152-154
  post-MI 150
  preoperative evaluation 333
Stroke 195–199
  atrial fibrillation 146, 147, 148
Subacute thyroiditis 186
Subarachnoid hemorrhage
  anxiety 339
Subcutaneous Epinephrine
  shortness of breath 157
Subdural hemorrhage
  concussion 204
Subglottic stenosis
  croup 28
Subluxation
  fractures 276
Subutex
  alcohol & drug abuse 354
Sucking & rooting reflex
  newborn exam 4
Sucralfate
  pregnancy 56
  PUD 214
Sudafed 397
  allergic rhinitis 231
  urinary incontinence, elderly 367

Sugar
  ADHD 48
Suicide
  depression & dysthymia 344
Sular
  hypertension 134
Sulfasalazine
  rheumatoid arthritis 242
Sulfisoxazole
  UTIs in children 39
Sulfonamides
  neonatal jaundice 13
  thyroid disease 188
Sulfonylureas
  diabetes 178, 179, 180
  drug interactions 266
  liver function tests 207
  medication use, elderly 361
Sumac
  contact dermatitis 303, 304
Sumatriptan
  headache 191
  pregnancy 58
Suppurative (bacterial) thyroiditis 186
Suprax
  otitis media 23
  UTIs in children 39
  vaginitis/STDs 93
Sustiva
  HIV/AIDS 382
Sutures
  wounds 325, 326
Synalar
  steroids 312
Syncope
  dizziness 192
Syndesmosis squeeze
  ankle injuries 278
Synthroid
  thyroid disease 187
Syphilis
  anxiety 339
  depression & dysthymia 343
Systemic lupus erythematosus
  arthritis 236

T

3TC
  HIV/AIDS 391
Tachycardia
  anxiety 341
  ECG 117, 121, 122
  heart failure 141
  shortness of breath 155
Tachypnea
  asthma 162
  bronchiolitis 29, 30
  croup 28
  fever in children 16
  shortness of breath 155, 157
Tagamet
  COPD 167
  GERD 213
Talar tilt
  ankle injuries 278

Talofibular ligament
    ankle injuries 277
Talwin
    medication use, elderly 361
Tambocor
    drug interactions 268
Tamsulosin
    BPH 259
Tapazole
    thyroid disease 186
Tarka
    hypertension 135
Tazarotene
    acne 307
Tazorac
    acne 307
Tegretol
    contraception 69
    mental status changes 371
    pain 331
    seizures 200, 201
Telangiectasia
    dermatologic lesions 301
Telmisartan
    heart failure 142
    hypertension 134, 135
Temazepam
    medication use, elderly 360
    mental status changes 371
Temovate
    steroids 312
Temporal arteritis
    anxiety 339
Tendonitis
    elbow injuries 289
    knee injuries 284
Tennis elbow 288
Tenofovir
    HIV/AIDS 380, 381
Tenoretic
    hypertension 135
Tenormin
    atrial fibrillation 146
    coronary artery disease 138
    heart failure 144
    hypertension 133
Tequin
    drug interactions 267, 269
    pneumonia 160
Terazol
    vaginitis/STDs 93
Terazosin
    BPH 259
    hypertension 135
    medication use, elderly 359
    urinary incontinence, elderly 366
Terbinafine
    rosacea 308
    tinea pedis 313
    tinea unguium 314
Terbutaline
    COPD 167
    shortness of breath 157
Terconazole
    vaginitis/STDs 93

Terfenadine
    medication use, elderly 360
Teriparatide
    osteoporosis 248
Tessalon 396
Testoderm
    sexual dysfunction 349
Testosterone
    sexual dysfunction 349
Tetanus prophylaxis
    wounds 328
Tetracaine
    ocular disorders 226
    wounds 325
Tetracycline
    acne 307
    breast-feeding 59
    diarrhea in adults 218
    pregnancy 57
    PUD 215
Teveten
    hypertension 134, 135
Thalassemia
    anemia 223
Thalidomide
    pregnancy 57
Thallium
    cardiac stress testing 153
Theophylline
    ADHD 46
    asthma 164
    asthma in children 20
    COPD 167
    drug interactions 267, 270
    medication use, elderly 360, 361
Thiazides
    hypertension 129, 130, 133
    medication use, elderly 361
    sexual dysfunction 347
Thiazolidinediones
    diabetes 179, 180
Thioridazine
    drug interactions 268
    medication use, elderly 360
Thompson test
    ankle injuries 278
Thorazine
    drug interactions 268
Thrombophlebitis
    menopause & HRT 85
Thumb sign
    croup 28
Thyroid cancer
    thyroid disease 187
THYROID DISEASE 182–189
    thyroid nodules 186
    thyrotoxicosis factitia 183, 186
Thyroid hormone 183, 186
    osteoporosis 246
TIA
    CVAs 195
Tiagabine
    seizures 201
Tiazac
    hypertension 134

Tibial sag test
  knee injuries 282
Ticarcillin
  medication use, elderly 360
Ticlid
  CVAs 197
Ticlopidine
  CVAs 197
Tigan
  medication use, elderly 361
Tikosyn
  drug interactions 266, 268
Timolide
  hypertension 135
Timolol
  coronary artery disease 138
  drug interactions 266
  heart failure 144
  hypertension 133, 135
Timoptic
  medication use, elderly 360
Tinactin
  tinea pedis 313
TINEA INFECTION MANAGEMENT 313–315
  tinea capitis 314
  tinea corporis 313
  tinea cruris 313
  tinea pedis 313
  tinea unguium 314
  tinea versicolor 314
Tinel's sign
  carpal tunnel syndrome 291
Tissue adhesive
  wounds 326
TMP. *See* Trimethoprim-Sulfamethoxazole
  sinusitis 234
TMP/SMX
  diverticulitis 324
  HIV/AIDS 376, 377
  medication use, elderly 360
  otitis media 23
  UTI 250, 251
  UTIs in children 39
Tobramycin
  ocular disorders 226
Tofranil
  anxiety 341
  depression & dysthymia 345
  drug interactions 269
  medication use, elderly 361
  pain 331
  urinary incontinence, elderly 367
Tolnaftate
  tinea pedis 313
Tolterodine
  urinary incontinence, elderly 367
Tonometry
  ocular disorders 226
Topamax
  seizures 201
Topicort
  steroids 312
Topiramate
  seizures 201
Toprol XL
  hypertension 133

Toradol
  pain management 330
Torsemide
  hypertension 133
Toxoplasmosis
  HIV/AIDS 383, 385
  neonatal jaundice 13
Tramadol
  ankle injuries 279
  drug interactions 267
  pain management 330
Trandate
  hypertension 133
Trandolapril
  heart failure 142
  hypertension 134, 135
Trans-Ver-Sal
  warts 313
Transdermal NTG
  coronary artery disease 139
Transdermal patches
  sexual dysfunction 349
Trazodone
  anxiety 341
  depression & dysthymia 346
  mental status changes 371
Tretinoin
  acne 307
  pregnancy 56
Tri-Levlen
  contraception 72
Tri-Norinyl
  contraception 72
Triamcinolone
  allergic rhinitis 230
  asthma 164
  asthma in children 20
  COPD 167
  gouty arthritis 245
  steroids 312
Triaminic 396
Triamterene
  hypertension 133, 135
Triazolam
  drug interactions 266
  medication use, elderly 360
  mental status changes 371
Triceps tendonitis
  elbow injuries 289
Trichloroacetic Acid
  vaginitis/STDs 94
  warts 313
Trichomonas
  vaginitis/STDs 92, 93
TriCor
  hyperlipidemia 125
Tricyclic antidepressants
  ADHD 48
  drug interactions 267
  medication use, elderly 361
  postpartum 66
  pregnancy 56, 58
  urinary incontinence, elderly 366
Trigger points
  back pain 293

Triiodothyronine
    thyroid disease 183
Trileptal
    seizures 200, 201
Trimethadione
    pregnancy 57
Trimethobenzamide
    medication use, elderly 361
Trimethoprim. *See also* TMP
    UTI 250
Trimethoprim-Sulfamethoxazole. *See also* TMP/
        SMX
    acne 307
    diarrhea in adults 218
    HIV/AIDS 376, 377
    otitis media 23
    sinusitis 234
Trimpex
    UTI 250
Tripelennamine
    pregnancy 56
Triphasil
    contraception 72
Triprolidine 396, 397
Triptans
    headache 191
Trivora
    contraception 72
Trizivir
    HIV/AIDS 381
Trousseau's sign
    calcium disorders 262
TSH
    thyroid disease 184
Tuberculosis
    depression & dysthymia 343
TUBERCULOSIS SCREENING 108–110
Tubo-ovarian abscess
    PID 96
Tums
    calcium disorders 262
Tussi-Organidin 396
Tylenol
    bronchiolitis 30
    fever in children 16
    pain management 329, 330
    postpartum 65
    pregnancy 63
Tympanic membrane
    otitis media 22

U

Ulcer 214–216
    dermatologic lesions 301
Ultracet
    ankle injuries 279
    pain management 330
Ultralente
    diabetes 181
Ultram
    drug interactions 267
Ultrasound
    abdominal pain 321
    hematuria 254
    prenatal care 52, 53, 64

Ultravate
    steroids 312
Undecylenic Acid
    tinea pedis 313
Uniretic
    hypertension 135
Univasc
    hypertension 134
Urethral suppository
    sexual dysfunction 349
Urethritis
    UTI 252
Uric Acid
    gout 245
    gouty arthritis 243, 244, 245
Urinalysis
    BPH 258
    fever in children 16
    hematuria 254
    UTI 249
URINARY INCONTINENCE IN THE ELDERLY
        365–368
URINARY TRACT INFECTIONS 249–252
URINARY TRACT INFECTIONS IN CHILDREN 38–40
Urine culture
    UTI 249
URIs
    asthma 162
Urised
    UTI 250
Urispas
    urinary incontinence, elderly 367
Urticaria
    contact dermatitis 303
UTERINE BLEEDING, ABNORMAL 79
UTI 249–252

V

Vaccinations
    COPD 168
Vaginal atrophy/dyspareunia
    menopause & HRT 86
Vaginal bleeding
    postpartum 65
Vaginal ultrasound
    menopause & HRT 87
VAGINITIS & SEXUALLY TRANSMITTED
        DISEASES 92–95
    atrophic 92, 93
    Gardnerella 93
    trichomonas 93
Valacyclovir
    pregnancy 62
    vaginitis/STDs 94
Valium
    alcohol & drug abuse 353
    dizziness 194
    medication use, elderly 360
Valproic Acid
    breast-feeding 59
    pregnancy 56, 57, 58
    seizures 201

INDEX

Valsartan
   heart failure 142
   hypertension 134, 135
Valtrex
   vaginitis/STDs 94
Vancenase/Beconase
   allergic rhinitis 230
Vanceril
   COPD 167
Vancomycin
   medication use, elderly 360
Vantin
   UTIs in children 39
Vaporizer
   croup 28
Varicella zoster immune globulin
   HIV/AIDS 376
   rashes in children 43
Varicella zoster virus
   HIV/AIDS 376
   prenatal care 52
Varivax
   prenatal care 52
Varus-valgus stress test
   knee injuries 282
Vascor
   drug interactions 269
Vaseline
   lice 313
Vaseretic
   hypertension 135
Vasocon–A
   ocular disorders 226
Vasopressin
   ACLS 398, 399
   emergency drug dosage 407
Vasotec
   heart failure 142
   hypertension 134
Venlafaxine
   anxiety 341
   depression & dysthymia 344, 345, 346
   drug interactions 269
   menopause & HRT 86
Ventolin
   COPD 167
Ventricular aneurysm
   ECG 122
Ventricular Fibrillation/Pulseless Ventricular
   Tachycardia
   ACLS protocols 399
Verapamil
   atrial fibrillation 146
   coronary artery disease 139
   emergency drug dosage 407
   headache 191
   heart failure 144
   hypertension 134
Verelan
   heart failure 144
   hypertension 134
Vertigo
   dizziness 192, 194
Vesicular exanthem
   rashes in children 43

Vessicle
   dermatologic lesions 301
Viagra
   drug interactions 267
   sexual dysfunction 349
Vibramycin
   sinusitis 234
   vaginitis/STDs 93
Vibrio cholerae
   diarrhea in adults 216
   diarrhea in children 31
Vibrio parahaemolyticus
   diarrhea in adults 216
Vicodin 396
   ankle injuries 279
   pain management 329
Vicoprofen
   pain management 329
Videx
   HIV/AIDS 381
Vioxx
   pain management 330
   rheumatoid arthritis 241
Viracept
   drug interactions 267
   HIV/AIDS 382
Viral load
   HIV/AIDS 378
Viramune
   HIV/AIDS 382
Virchow's triad
   shortness of breath 157
Viread
   HIV/AIDS 381
Vistaril
   allergic rhinitis 231
Vitamin A
   drug interactions 270
Vitamin B6
   morning sickness 61
   PMS 89
Vitamin B12
   anemia 224
Vitamin D
   breast-feeding 11
   calcium disorders 260, 261
   compression fractures 364
   health screening, elderly 358
   osteoporosis 247, 248
Vitamin D3
   menopause & HRT 86
Vitamin deficiencies
   depression & dysthymia 344
Vitamin E
   breast disorders 91
   PMS 89
Vitamin K
   hematuria 253
   liver function tests 207
Vivactil
   medication use, elderly 361
Vivelle
   menopause & HRT 86
Vomiting
   abdominal pain 319
   chest pain 114

concussion 202
diverticulitis 323
dysmenorrhea 89
headache 190
hepatitis B 209
HIV/AIDS 375
liver function tests 205
neonatal jaundice 13
PID 95
potassium disorders 264
PUD 214
UTI 250
Von Willebrand's disease
hematuria 253
Vulvovaginal candidiasis
vaginitis/STDs 93
Vytone
steroids 312
VZIG. *See also* Varicella zoster immune globulin
HIV/AIDS 376

W

Waddell signs
back pain 293
Warfarin
atrial fibrillation 148, 149
breast-feeding 59
CVAs 197
drug interactions 267, 270
hematuria 253
medication use, elderly 360, 361
pregnancy 56, 57, 58
WARTS 313
Wasting syndrome
HIV/AIDS 383
Water-soluble drugs
medication use, elderly 359
Wegener's disease
hematuria 254
Weight loss
diabetes 173
Wellbutrin
ADHD 48
depression & dysthymia 344, 346
Westcort
steroids 312
Wheal
dermatologic lesions 301
Wheezing
asthma 162, 165
bronchitis 169
WHO-ORS
diarrhea in children 32
Wilms' tumor 3
hematuria 252
Wilson's disease
anxiety 339
liver function tests 205
Wolff-Parkinson-White syndrome
ECG 122
WOUND MANAGEMENT 325–329
Wytensin
medication use, elderly 359

X

Xanax
drug interactions 266
medication use, elderly 360
Xopenex
COPD 167
Xylocaine
joint injection 297
skin biopsies 309
Xylometazoline
pregnancy 56

Y

Yasmin
contraception 70
Yersinia
diarrhea in adults 216, 218
Yohimbine
sexual dysfunction 349

Z

Zaditor
ocular disorders 226
Zafirlukast
asthma 164
asthma in children 20
Zagam
drug interactions 267, 269
Zalcitabine
HIV/AIDS 380, 381
Zantac
GERD 213
medication use, elderly 360
Zarontin
seizures 200, 201
Zaroxolyn
hypertension 133
Zebeta
hypertension 133
Zerit
HIV/AIDS 381
Zestril
heart failure 142
hypertension 134
Ziac
hypertension 135
Ziagen
HIV/AIDS 381
Zidovudine
HIV/AIDS 380, 381
Zileuton
asthma 164
Zinc Oxide
pregnancy 56
Ziprasidone
drug interactions 267, 268
Zithromax
HIV/AIDS 377
otitis media 23
pharyngitis 26
pneumonia 160
vaginitis/STDs 93

INDEX

Zofran
  drug interactions 268
Zollinger Ellison syndrome
  GERD 211
  PUD 214
Zolmitriptan
  headache 191
Zoloft
  anxiety 341
  depression & dysthymia 344, 345
  drug interactions 269
  medication use, elderly 361
Zolpidem
  mental status changes 371
Zomig
  headache 191
Zonegran
  seizures 201
Zonisamide
  seizures 201
Zostrix
  pain 331
Zovia
  contraception 72
Zovirax
  rashes in children 43
  vaginitis/STDs 94
Zyban
  smoking cessation 102
Zyprexa
  mental status changes 371
Zyrtec 397
  allergic rhinitis 231

Frequently Called Consultants

Allergy　Name _____

Office _____

Beeper/Cell _____

Cardiology　Name _____

Office _____

Beeper/Cell _____

Dentistry　Name _____

Office _____

Beeper/Cell _____

Dermatology　Name _____

Office _____

Beeper/Cell _____

Endocrinology　Name _____

Office _____

Beeper/Cell _____

Family Medicine　Name _____

Office _____

Beeper/Cell _____

GI　Name _____

Office _____

Beeper/Cell _____

Heme/Onc　Name _____

Office _____

Beeper/Cell _____

Infectious Disease　Name _____

Office _____

Beeper/Cell _____

Nephrology　Name _____

Office _____

Beeper/Cell _____

Neurology　Name _____

Office _____

Beeper/Cell _____

OB/GYN Name _____

Office _____

Beeper/Cell _____

Ophthalmology Name _____

Office _____

Beeper/Cell _____

Podiatry Name _____

Office _____

Beeper/Cell _____

Psychiatry Name _____

Office _____

Beeper/Cell _____

Rheumatology Name _____

Office _____

Beeper/Cell _____

SURGERY

General Name _____

Office _____

Beeper/Cell _____

Neurologic Name _____

Office _____

Beeper/Cell _____

Orthopedic Name _____

Office _____

Beeper/Cell _____

Plastic Name _____

Office _____

Beeper/Cell _____

Urologic Name _____

Office _____

Beeper/Cell _____

Vascular/Thoracic Name _____

Office _____

Beeper/Cell _____

Frequently Used Phone Numbers

Admitting .... _____

CT Scan .... _____

Diabetes Education .... _____

ECG .... _____

EEG .... _____

Emergency Room .... _____

Lab .... _____

Labor & Delivery .... _____

MRI .... _____

Medical Records .... _____

Newborn Nursery .... _____

Pathology .... _____

Peripheral Vascular Lab .... _____

PFT Lab .... _____

Pharmacy .... _____

Physical Therapy .... _____

Protective Services .... _____

X-ray .... _____

_____ .... _____

_____ .... _____

_____ .... _____

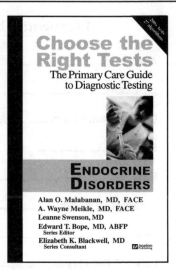